ORGANIZATIONAL BEHAVIOUR

DANIEL KING | SCOTT LAWLEY

THIRD EDITION

OXFORD

UNIVERSITY PRESS

OXFORD

UNIVERSITY PRESS

Great Clarendon Street, Oxford, OX2 6DP,
United Kingdom

Oxford University Press is a department of the University of Oxford.
It furthers the University's objective of excellence in research, scholarship,
and education by publishing worldwide. Oxford is a registered trade mark of
Oxford University Press in the UK and in certain other countries

Published in the United States of America by Oxford University Press
198 Madison Avenue, New York, NY 10016, United States of America

British Library Cataloguing in Publication Data
Data available

Library of Congress Control Number: 2018962525

ISBN 978–0–19–880778–0

Printed in Italy by L.E.G.O. S.p.A.

Links to third party websites are provided by Oxford in good faith and
for information only. Oxford disclaims any responsibility for the materials
contained in any third party website referenced in this work.

PREFACE

Are robots going to steal our jobs? Certainly, if some newspaper headlines are to be believed. Dramatic changes are predicted around how automation, artificial intelligence, big data, increased globalization, and the gig economy will change the way we live and work.

Some theorists like Frey and Osborne (2017) predict huge job cuts, claiming automation and artificial intelligence will take not only manual jobs, but machines will replace many professional jobs in areas such as accountancy and law. Others, like Thompson (2018), are more cynical, arguing that similar claims have been made before, referencing assertions from the 1970s and 80s that the micro-computer (what we call today the PC) would take away jobs – something that clearly did not happen the way it was predicted. Regardless of the view of the impact these changes will have on the number of jobs, it is clear that the traditional idea of the organization, based on concepts from the early Twentieth century, is beginning to recede and new ways of working are emerging.

This new edition of *Organizational Behaviour* reflects on the impact the Fourth Industrial Revolution is having on our understanding of how work is organized and managed. This does not mean we have side-lined theories previously included. Indeed, many of the changes from the Fourth Industrial Revolution extend these existing trends. For instance, in the early 1900s during the Second Industrial Revolution, engineer Fredrick Taylor aimed to automate much of the factory, and the sociologist Max Weber critiqued the way bureaucracy changed our lives, themes echoed in the automation of middle-class jobs and the rise of 'big data'. Therefore, we have revisited existing theories with new questions, such as: how do you create a company culture when many employees work virtually, or as gig economy workers, potentially for more than one company at a time? A distinctive feature of this third edition is our introduction of themes from the Fourth Industrial Revolution as ways of thinking through our existing understandings of the organization of work, and exploring how it both extends, yet differs from, developments in previous industrial revolutions.

Throughout this book, we will refer to the industrial revolutions that have shaped the way business organizations work. These are further discussed in Chapter 4, but we have summarised them here:

- The **First Industrial Revolution**, beginning in the late 1700s, saw the introduction of mechanization and large factories, with labour moving in huge numbers from agriculture to factory work.

- In the **Second Industrial Revolution**, from the early 1900s, management innovators such as Henri Fayol, Frederick Taylor and Henry Ford developed formal bureaucratic structures (discussed in chapter 2) and efficient work designs (discussed in chapter 4) with the aim of rationalizing business organization and production, designing the organization as if it were a machine.

- In the latter half of the twentieth century, the rise of digital technology and automation marked the **Third Industrial Revolution**.

- The **Fourth Industrial Revolution** is unfolding before us, with the internet, big data, automation, and artificial intelligence transforming every arena of life including the world of business.

So how do you protect yourself from robots stealing your job? The jobs currently thought at lower risk from the changes brought about by the Fourth Industrial Revolution are ones that rely on soft skills of communication, teamwork and critical thinking (Schwab, 2016), as they are harder to automate. Critical thinking will be the number one skill needed by 2020, according to the World Economic Forum (Schwab 2016a). Another distinctive feature of this book, therefore, is the focus on this essential skill. This book encourages you to develop your critical thinking skills through the wide range of pedagogical feature boxes including: theory in context, research insights, and new and updated real life cases, all of which are designed to help you question the theory presented and understand it from different perspectives.

One of the most effective ways to think critically and examine a theory is to apply it. Our flagship feature, the running case study based on the fictional Junction Hotel, offers the opportunity to do just that. Conventional textbooks often have a tendency to present organizational life as a logical and rational experience. Yet this image does not really reflect organizational life, which, because it is full of people, is often messy, confusing, and beset with power and politics. The running case helps you to understand that organizational life is not as straightforward as the models may suggest, but open to different interpretations.

Applying theory to real situations is suggested by learning theorists, such as Kolb (1984), to be far more effective than simply examining theory alone. It helps us understand real dilemmas and challenges that managers, workers, or society face. Just think of it this way: a manager does not try to motivate their staff because a textbook says that they should do it; rather, they look at ideas surrounding motivation because they are facing a problem that they need to solve. The theories covered in this book were largely produced in response to challenges in real life. Our aim throughout this book is to use the Junction Hotel case study as a way of viewing organizations as alive, full of paradox, emotions and contradictions, much like any real-life organization is.

As you read the theories in this book try to place yourself in the position of the characters, of the managers and workers, at the Junction Hotel. What would you do if you were in their shoes? How would you feel if you were trying to bring about one of the changes or had that change imposed upon you? What other actions do you think are available to them? We also hope that reading the case might trigger you to reflect on your own experiences.

Each chapter opens with a dilemma or issue that a member of staff at Junction Hotel is facing. We then explore this issue through the theory covered in the chapter, and view the dilemma through the eyes of different members of Junction Hotel's staff. Our new feature at the end of each chapter, 'Connecting case and theory', makes explicit connections between theory and practice in a manner that can help you develop your analytical capacities.

Finally, having the case study does not mean that you must read the book from cover to cover or in the order that it is presented. Different lecturers will have their own order that they like to teach organizational behaviour, and the book and the case study is written deliberately in a way that allows you to read it in any order that you like. Each chapter is self-contained and it might be helpful to think about the case study as mini-episodes, rather than as a linear narrative.

We hope that you enjoy the book, the debates that are in here, and find that it offers you new ways to think about work and society.

Daniel and Scott

References

Frey, C. B., & Osborne, M. A. (2017). The future of employment: how susceptible are jobs to computerisation?, *Technological forecasting and social change*, 114, 254-280.

Kolb, D.A. 1984. Experiential learning: Experience as the source of learning and development. Prentice Hall: Englewood Cliffs, NJ.

Schwab, K (2016) The Global Competitiveness Report 2016–2017, *World Economic forum*, Geneva

Schwab., K. 2016b. The fourth industrial revolution: What it means, how to respond. World Economic Forum. 14 January. Available at https://www.weforum.org/agenda/2016/01/the-fourth-industrial-revolution-what-it-means-and-how-to-respond/

Thompson, P (2018) The Refusal of Work: Past, Present and Future, Futures of Work, Bristol University Press, available at https://futuresofwork.co.uk/2018/09/05/the-refusal-of-work-past-present-and-future/ accessed 1st November 2018

ACKNOWLEDGEMENTS

A textbook like this is not just the work of the two individuals on the front cover but a network of people who have offered support, ideas and practical work to bring it to production. We are grateful to the thousands of students that we have taught at Nottingham Trent University over the last eleven years on the module Foundations of Managing and Organising, and the countless colleagues who we have shared our teaching with. Teaching you all and exploring our understanding of work today continues to be a source of inspiration for this textbook.

We are very grateful for the input of our Commissioning Editor Nicola Hartley throughout the whole process of the new edition. She has been a fantastic editor, inspiring us with new ideas, giving guidance and support, helping us think about the book in new ways and giving constructive feedback. Many of the new developments for this edition have come out of our numerous conversations and her input in thinking through new ways of presenting the material. We are thankful to Sarah Smith for working with us to develop the online resources, to our copyeditor Lucy Hyde, and to Joe Matthews for bringing the book to print. We are also extremely grateful for the reviewers of this edition who have helped us to develop this book, and the many adopters throughout the world who have taken on the previous editions and used them in their teaching.

We would like to thank all the interviewees from business, the public sector and charities who have given up their time to be filmed for this new edition. Your insights into the everyday workings of organizations and how they connect with the theory in this book has helped to ground the book in the practical realities of organizational practice.

Daniel would like to thank Steph for her continued support in giving up so much time whilst he was finishing off the book, and Saffron, Ellerby and Josh for their understanding. He is also grateful for his family and friends' ideas and support throughout the time of writing the book.

Scott would like to thank colleagues past and present for their ideas and inspiration over the years, and all friends and family for their support during the writing of this book.

EDITORIAL ADVISORY PANEL

How to use this book

 Running case: a tour of Junction Hotel

Sue Marshall arrives at Junction Hotel for her first day
Armfield, a receptionist, greets her with a smile and tak
'This, obviously, is the front of house. You'll get a chan
friendly bunch.' Sue notices a computer, which must be
room number, and a list. 'Oh, that,' Mandy says, noticing
maintenance team'.

'It's all very organized in here,' Sue comments.

Running case:

The flagship feature of this text is the fictional
running case, which is set in Junction Hotel, and
presents organizational problems and theories
in a familiar context. The case will help you
explore issues from multiple perspectives and
discover that there is often no 'one best way' to
do things. The running case is closely integrated with the theories discussed in each chapter,
and a new end-of-chapter 'Connecting case and
theory' feature blends the two seamlessly.

Real life case boxes:

Organizational behaviour theories are
played out in the real world every day. The
real life case boxes illustrate the concepts
discussed using contemporary and varied
examples from the business world (including
recognizable organizations such as Uber, as
well as social movements and smaller not-
for-profit organizations) to help you make
the link between theory and practice.

 Real life case: Uber

Uber was in crisis, having hit the headlines when forme
her blog accusing the company of a culture of sexism (Fo
and CEO Travis Kalanick took a leave of absence, saying h
mother and 'work on himself'. Uber had arranged for fori
to investigate claims of sexism and to offer recommen

 Theory in context: the nature vs nurt

A frequent discussion point related to personality is whe
natural and pre-determined part of who we are, or whethe
being nurtured as a result of our surroundings. A couple o

• Undoubtedly the actions of tyrannical dictators su
a question often asked is whether Hitler was born
part of who he was—or whether influences in his li
have turned him that way (e.g. Stein, 2000).

Theory in context boxes:

Where do theories about organizational
behaviour come from? What influenced the
theorists' thoughts and the resulting theories? The wider contexts of society, technology, politics, and economics are considered,
and you are encouraged to critically analyse
theories to deepen your understanding.

Research insight boxes:

The body of academic literature on the subject of organizational behaviour is vast. This
feature highlights seminal research articles
that made a significant contribution to the
topic. The full reference is provided so you
can follow up your textbook reading with
further research.

 Research insight: is culture really th

Lorsch, J.W., and McTague, E. 2016. Culture is not the culpri
When organizations get into trouble we often see the
of the 2008 banking crisis, the sexual harassment cases
corporate wrongdoing such as the Volkswagen vehicle er
ture is often seen as the culprit. The remedy to the prob
stop problems happening again. Even in situations that d
that an organization's culture needs to be changed, fo

Stop and think questions:

These short, reflective questions appear throughout the chapters, either as part of a boxed feature or within the main body of the text itself, and encourage you to consider the topics in light of your own experience.

 Have you ever fallen out with someone durin happen? How much of it was because of pers

 Employability skills: critical thinking 2020

What do you think will be the most important skill for er to the World Economic Forum, the answer is critical th a body that brings together leading politicians, busine

Study and employability skills boxes:

Skills tips to help boost your grades and your employability. These are linked to topics being discussed in the book, and further reinforce the relevance of organizational behaviour to real life.

Review questions:

At the end of every chapter section, review questions help you assess your understanding of the central themes and your readiness to progress to the next part of the topic.

 Review questions

Describe	What are the main features of the assembly
Explain	How does the assembly line draw upon, but Taylorism?

 Connecting case and theory

This chapter has examined the nature of **personality** a **recruitment** and **selection** process. At the start of the c by Junction Hotel that they had thought about some centre manager, such as qualifications and experience,

Connecting case and theory:

This new end-of-chapter resource blends themes from the running case study with the theories discussed in the chapter to further strengthen the link between theory and practice.

Further reading:

To take your learning further, reading lists have been provided as guides to finding out more about the issues raised within each chapter and to help you locate the useful academic literature in the field.

 Further reading

Brewer, E., and Westerman, J. 2017. *Organizational communic text*. Oxford University Press: Oxford.

A more in-depth introduction to organizational communication.

Rice, R.E. 1992. Task analyzability, use of new media, and e

How to use the online resources

www.oup.com/uk/king-lawley3e

The online resources that accompany this book provide students and registered adopters with ready-to-use teaching and learning materials.

FOR STUDENTS

Videos:

The world of work can sometimes seem far removed from the theories being discussed in the textbook. A range of business professionals (some new to this edition) are interviewed about their experiences helping to emphasise the link between theory, practice, and employability.

Study skills and personal development PDFs

New for this edition, the authors have drafted a set of downloadable PDFs covering key study and personal development skills including: how to develop critical thinking skills, how to write an essay, how to study independently, how to read effectively, and how to study and prepare for an OB exam. It is hoped these will support you in developing key skills throughout your course.

PERSONAL DEVELOPMENT

Developing time management skills

Do you ever feel overwhelmed, thinking there is too much do to and yourself procrastinating or feeling stressed, not knowing what you sh management is a core skill for university and working life. You proba you use your time than you have ever had. So how do you use time v stressed?

Fortunately there are many good books, websites and apps that can effectively manage your time. Using these systems can help you achi

Guided reading

Reading journal articles can be quite difficult as the writing style and conceptual knowledge assumed can make them seem inaccessible. To bridge this gap this new guided reading feature will seek to introduce you to one article per chapter and support your reading of it through author commentary, analysis and key questions to demystify the key arguments made.

1. Bureaucracy in Morgan (2006)

This first set of questions focuses on how bureaucracy is examined in Morgan's chapter

a. According to Morgan what is a bureaucracy?

A brief definition, from Weber's perspective is towards the foot of p17. More detail is 22, although some of these more specific elements feature in the questions below. Ho students will pick out the table with Fayol's principles of classical management theory this was outlined very briefly in the lecture on bureaucracy, this puts more flesh onto t factors.

Extension material:

Additional explanation and analysis of key theories which go beyond what is covered in the textbook are available to help you to take your learning a step further.

King and Lawley: Organizational Behaviour 3rd edition: Extension mate

OXFORD
UNIVERSITY PRESS

Table of Contents

A. Introduction
B. Chapter 1: Introducing Organizational Behaviour
  1. Applied Psychology
  2. Approaches
  3. Behaviourism
  4. Durkheim
  5. Marx
  6. Phenomenological
  7. Psychoanalytical
  8. Social cognitive
  9. Trait theory
  10. Weber
  11. Pay inequality

Behaviourism

See pages 10-12, 300-6, and 333 of book.

The behaviourist perspective does not look at how people think or how their its attention only on their behaviour. Behaviourists criticize other psychologic inner workings of people's minds or categorize them according to certain abst really know these invisible phenomena - all we can ever see with any certain

The most prominent behaviourist was B. F. Skinner, who argued that how we the environment. He believed that this was the result of our upbringing. For i attention when they are bad are more likely to behave badly because this beha that our behaviour can be changed through rewards and punishments in beha form of *conditioning* trains people to act in appropriate ways that are in line w

Ivan Pavlov suggests that this conditioning can be used on people and create particular stimulus. For instance in his famous experiments with dogs he star and then giving them food. The dog learnt to associate the bell (the stimulus)

Multiple-choice questions:

A bank of self-marking, multiple-choice questions has been provided for each chapter of the text and includes instant feedback on your answers, cross-referencing the textbook to assist with independent self-study.

What does OB stand for?
- Organizational Business
- Organizational Behaviour
- Organizing Behaviour
- Organizing Business

Which of these is a core underlying discipline that informs organizational behaviour?
- Motivation
- Sociology
- Teamwork
- Leadership

Study guide material

Critical thinking

These pages contain some interesting information about critical thinking and can be used to help you develop this important skill. When looking at this material it should not be thought of as a one-off but something you return to and build on throughout your time at university:

https://www.plymouth.ac.uk/uploads/production/document/path/1/1710/Critical_Thinking.pdf

http://www.uefap.com/reading/readfram.htm

Academic reading

Reading academic material, such as journal articles and textbooks, can be difficult as they sometimes use concepts that we do not understand. These resources provide material to help you overcome some of these challenges with really useful tips and strategies as well as some thought-provoking questions about how you read and use material. Well worth looking at and considering at

Web links:

A series of annotated web links, organized by chapter, has been provided to point you in the direction of important material on organizational behaviour.

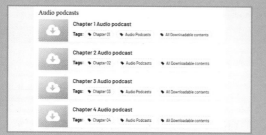

Podcast re-cap:
New for this edition are short audio summaries of each chapter from the authors, to listen to on the go and help you revise.

FOR INSTRUCTORS

Guide for lecturers:
For this edition we have created a new guide for lecturers which outlines how to get the most out of the online resources (and quickly!).

Junction Hotel: Initial Fact-finding Report

Giving Junction Hotel the Second-Chance Treatment

Hotel in decline
Junction Hotel was once a luxury hotel with a strong business and tourist following. However, years of under-investment and poor management have left it with a sense of *faded glory*. It is the Second-Chance Consortium's goal to turn this into a profitable enterprise once again.

Considerable potential
Whilst the hotel has been struggling for a number of years it shows signs of considerable potential. These include:

- Restaurant
  - An award-winning chef who is ambitious
  - Currently only doing 50 covers a night – has potential for 140
  - Room occupancy

Seminar resources:
A suite of fully developed seminar activities, updated for this edition, and tutor notes has been prepared for use in class. Activities are based around extension material from the running case and additional real-life case studies, articles, and video clips.

Test bank:
A fully customizable resource containing interactive multiple-choice questions accompanied by answers and feedback with which to test your students.

PowerPoint® slides:
Customizable PowerPoint® slides have been included for use in lecture presentations. Arranged by chapter theme, the slides may also be used as hand-outs in class.

GUIDED TOUR OF THE DASHBOARD

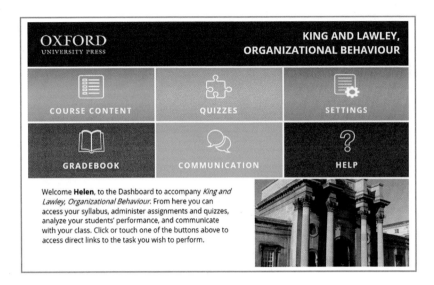

Simple. Informative. Mobile.

Dashboard is a cloud-based online assessment and revision tool. It comes pre-loaded with test questions for students, a homework course if your module leader has adopted Dashboard, and additional resources as listed below. If your lecturer has adopted Dashboard and you have purchased the Dashboard Edition of the book, your standalone access code should be included and will provide instructions on how to sign up for the platform. If you have not purchased the Dashboard Edition or if you have purchased a second-hand copy, you can purchase standalone access online—visit www.oxfordtextbooks.co.uk/dashboard for more information.

SIMPLE: With a highly intuitive design, it will take you less than fifteen minutes to learn and master the system.

MOBILE: You can access Dashboard from every major platform and device connected to the Internet, whether that's a computer, tablet, or smartphone.

INFORMATIVE: Your assignment and assessment results are automatically graded, giving your instructor a clear view of the class's understanding of the course content.

Student resources

Dashboard offers all the online resource features but comes with additional questions to take your learning further.

Lecturer resources

Preloaded homework assignments and test bank

A preloaded homework course structured around the book is available, supported by a test bank containing a additional multiple-choice questions. Your students can follow the pre-loaded course, or you can customize it, allowing you to add questions from the test bank or from your existing materials to meet your specific teaching needs.

Gradebook

Dashboard will automatically grade the homework assignments that you set for your students. The Gradebook also provides heat maps for you to view your students' progress which helps you to quickly identify areas of the course where your students may need more practice, as well as the areas they are most confident in. This feature helps you focus your teaching time on the areas that matter.

The Gradebook also allows you to administer grading schemes, manage checklists, and administer learning objectives and competencies.

ORGANIZATION CHART FOR JUNCTION HOTEL STAFF

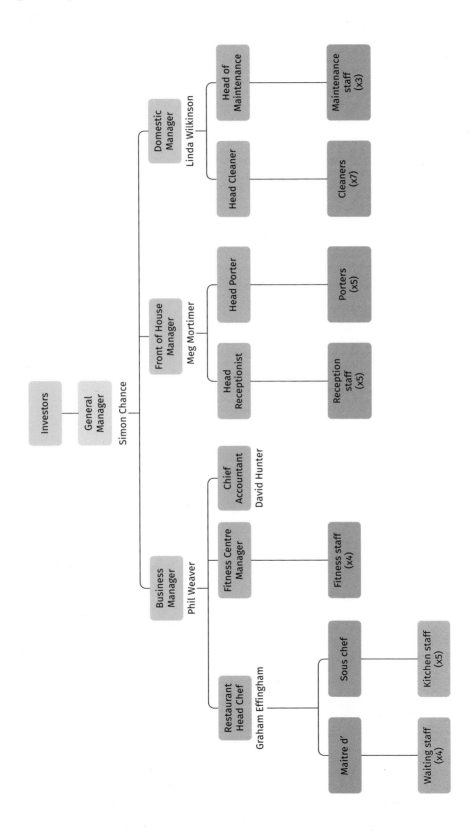

CONTENTS

DETAILED CONTENTS

Part 3

xxiii

CHAPTER 1
Introducing organizational behaviour
New beginnings

What is organizational behaviour?

🔍 Running case: Simon Chance begins work at Junction Hotel

It is 7.45 am and Simon Chance, the president of Second-Chance Consortium, sits at his desk reflecting on his group's latest acquisition, Junction Hotel. It is an upmarket, city-centre hotel with a proud heritage of strong customer service and a traditional approach. In its heyday, people would flock to the hotel for its high-class service, great food, and friendly but formal style. But those days are long gone, and the hotel has undergone numerous changes of ownership and attempts to revive it. With paint peeling off the walls, worn carpets, and an antiquated computer system, Junction Hotel needs some real investment.

Chance's office is a bit like Junction Hotel: faded glory. A dark green leather chair from the 1940s sits in the corner—stylish but uncomfortable. Instead, Chance uses an IKEA chair. Hardly elegant, but far more practical. The room is oak-clad, but some of the wooden panels are loose and a couple now have gaps between them. 'I must fix that,' Chance muses. 'This place is a mess. Nothing works properly. Yet I'm sure we can turn it around.'

The Second-Chance Consortium is a venture capitalist company specializing in turning failed businesses into profitable enterprises. Simon Chance, a former footballer who retired early because of injury, has reinvented himself as a business entrepreneur. Teaming up with his former agent and self-styled business guru Phil Weaver, Chance has led the consortium for six years, starting with the local football team and gradually building up a portfolio of successfully transformed firms. Chance feels confident that he can make the hotel a success. 'They just need strong leadership and a good strategy,' he thinks. 'I'm sure that we can succeed here.'

Why do people act as they do at work? What factors affect whether people are productive, committed, and motivated? Whether people work together well as teams? Whether they are good at being innovative and creative? What factors prevent people from really achieving their best? This book, and the area of organizational behaviour more broadly, is about people. It is about human behaviour in a work environment: how human behaviour is impacted by leadership, culture, group norms, organizational structure, and power and politics. It is about how we learn, communicate, are motivated, and interact. It is about how we work in teams, how we can bring about change, and how we can make sure people are acting in ethically sound ways. It is about the psychology and behaviour of individuals, understanding how our personalities and perceptions shape how we work; and it is also about sociology, how the wider social environment shapes the way we think and behave.

We study organizational behaviour because we want to learn about the way that people act in organizations—what makes people tick, how they are shaped by the organizational culture that surrounds them, how to get people to collaborate, and how to make organizations run better. The topics we cover in the book apply anywhere from work organizations through to sports teams and even your flatmates at university. Ultimately this is a book about understanding people at work. It is about getting inside organizations to really understand what is going on, and how individual behaviour is shaped by the processes, practices, and cultures that surround us.

Managing organizations can be difficult, because they involve people. People can be unpredictable and complex. To manage or work alongside people, you need to understand how they think, how they are motivated, what increases their commitment, how to organize them, and how to ensure they act ethically. Working with and managing people, therefore, is likely to be one of the most difficult and challenging things you do.

The study of organizational behaviour (OB) is also about how organizations are structured and run through systems and procedures, as well as how they relate to the wider, globalized world. Furthermore it is about society—or, more precisely, the impact that organizations have on the people that work for them, the communities around them, and society as a whole. To study OB, therefore, is to begin to really understand how and why things happen in workplaces and organizations.

Introducing Junction Hotel

Running case: understanding the complexity

From:	Phil Weaver
Sent:	2 September
To:	Simon Chance
Subject:	Junction Hotel Report

Hi Simon,

I have done a full survey of the hotel, looking back at its accounts for the last five years and surveying the building, kitchen, and staff. Having stayed in the hotel overnight as part of the mystery shopper exercise, I found the staff courteous and friendly, but the systems slow and cumbersome. Checking in took 20 minutes as they had lost my registration details, and we had to walk to the restaurant in order to pay my bill as the 'machine was not working'. The rooms were comfortable and fairly clean, but did seem to be of an inconsistent standard. I must say that the food at the restaurant was excellent and shows real class, but service was slow.

Overall, this hotel shows potential but there is much to improve. They are quite disorganized, some staff seem unmotivated and unclear in their tasks, and the service, while polite and professional, is not what you would expect.

Speak soon

Phil

Chance turns to the main report. The Second-Chance Consortium always create a comprehensive report when they take over a failing venture and collect good management data so that they can work out what to improve. Chance reads about the hotel's history and is interested to learn that back in its heyday, Junction Hotel hosted some stars from the stage and screen, its restaurant won awards, and it had successful conference facilities. As he reads more of the report, however, his mood changes. 'This won't be a quick fix,' he thinks, looking in detail at the problems that Weaver identified: poor systems, unmotivated staff, erratic schedules, no clear identity or purpose to the hotel, and running at a loss for the last five years. 'We need to sort this place out,' Chance thinks, staring out of the window. 'I'll get Weaver on the phone and work out our plan.'

What do you think are the key challenges that Simon Chance faces in transforming Junction Hotel?

Many of the theories we will cover in this book were developed as a response to real life problems that practitioners face in their everyday lives. These theories were attempts by practitioners, consultants, and academics to find ways of doing such things as motivating workers, increasing productivity, or understanding power. These theories, therefore, are not dry, abstract views separated from the world, but responses to real world problems that people face in practice.

One of the best ways to understand organizational behaviour is to explore it in the context of organizational practice. This book does this through our innovative and unique fictional running case study, Junction Hotel. This case study is based in a hotel which has recently been bought by a consortium led by Simon Chance. Through this case study we will learn about the hotel's characters, their personalities, backgrounds, and experiences, and the dilemmas they face. We will see their emotions, reactions, and different interpretations of the same event. We use the running case to make sense of the challenges the characters face and how they seek to overcome them, from the workers through to the managers. In this way, we give a more rounded picture of organizational life rather than just looking at organizational behaviour from the manager's viewpoint (for more details on how to use the running case, see the Preface of this book).

The structure of this book

This book is divided into five parts corresponding to five themes, each with its own focus and issues:

1. The rational organization
2. The social organization
3. Managing the individual
4. Managing the organization
5. The organization and its environment

As we will see, these themes offer us different perspectives on what goes on within organizations and different ideas about how to manage them (Figure 1.1).

Figure 1.1 Key themes in organizational behaviour.

Theme 1: The rational organization

Chapter 2: Organizational structure, design, and bureaucracy: From rationality to flexibility
Chapter 3: Rational work design: The simplification and automation of work
Chapter 4: Developments in rational organization: Towards the Fourth Industrial Revolution

---

🔍 Running case: 8.15 am, Phil Weaver discusses his report with Simon Chance

'We need systems and procedures,' Weaver states boldly to Chance, 'like we had at the football club, to make this place run like clockwork.' Weaver animatedly discusses his plans with Chance. 'I've been looking at the booking-in procedure. I'm sure we could make it run quicker by streamlining it. Also, the cleaners seem to be getting away with murder—working slowly without set targets or procedures,' he continues, hardly taking a breath.

Getting out a grid drawn on a sheet of A3 paper, Weaver lays out targets for every individual and department, with measurements for every aspect of the hotel—from customer satisfaction through to room cleanliness. 'It's another Weaver masterplan,' Chance declares excitedly. Impressed, Chance picks up a document entitled 'Streamlining food production,' which has detailed step-by-step guides for tasks from peeling carrots through to cooking chicken. 'I've only just started,' Weaver states. 'I think we should work on the cleaners first. I'm sure that we could come up with detailed ways of doing everything in this hotel to make it run more efficiently.'

What makes Uber, Amazon, and Deliveroo so financially successful? One thing that unites them is the drive for efficiency. While recent developments in automation, artificial intelligence, big data, and the gig economy are all transforming the way that we work, the impetus that is driving them is hardly new. For well over 100 years, managers have dreamed of creating rational, logical, and efficient organizations. This first theme looks at these modern issues in the light of their historical developments.

While big data is transforming the way we live and work, it is part of a wider bureaucratic society. As we will examine in Chapter 2, by creating bureaucratic procedures, policies, and practices, organizations aim to create standardized, predictable, and efficient working models so that management gain maximum control over, and efficiency from, workers (see Chapter 3). This control is enhanced by the use of data and computer technology.

This ambition for control was exemplified by the work of Frederick Taylor. As we will see in Chapter 3, Taylor (1911) believed that through scientific analysis he could discover the one best way of performing every task and through this approach create a more efficient, productive, and rational way of working. For Taylor, and other industrialists such as Henry Ford, the ideal worker was like a machine, an attitude that would not look out of place in the modern highly automated factory. These approaches can be seen today in other types of workplace: for example, in warehouses that deliver goods to us that we order online, workers' movements are controlled precisely by wearable technology and computer tracking systems.

As we will examine in Chapter 4, such an approach continues to underpin much of what we do today: for example in fast-food chains such as McDonald's, and in hotel chains such as Travelodge. This rational approach has come to dominate the thinking of much of Western capitalism. Indeed, sociologist George Ritzer (2019) has described our society as McDonaldized, where the principles of the fast-food restaurant, and therefore rational production, have come to dominate more and more parts of society. We will see how rationalization has been further developed in many of the ways in which work is organized as we enter a Fourth Industrial Revolution, in which automation and the gig economy represent profound, ongoing changes to the nature of work.

The rationalization approach has brought with it many positive features. The vast improvements in productivity it created have enabled mass production, and this has dramatically cut the cost of most consumer goods, making cars, televisions, clothes, and furniture affordable to many people. Yet these rationalized practices come with human costs—they can be boring, predictable, and routinized, and an imbalance of power between management and workers is created. This approach also transfers knowledge and power from the workers to the managers, creating systems that reduce the worker to a small cog in a very large machine. As Marxist theorist Harry Braverman (1974) argued, this rational approach deskills the workers and leaves them dehumanized in the process. We will see how workers have resisted the negative impacts of such practices throughout history, from strikes and riots in Ford's early car factories, to modern-day protests and legal action to gain employment rights for gig economy workers.

Theme 2: The social organization

Chapter 5: Discovering the social organization: The Hawthorne studies and the human side of the organization
Chapter 6: Managing groups and teams: From managing the individual to managing the collective
Chapter 7: Organizational culture: The hidden side of the organization

Running case: 8.20 am, Meg Mortimer prepares herself for the board meeting

Meg Mortimer sits at her desk in the little cubbyhole-cum-office behind the reception desk busying herself in readiness for the new day. 'I've seen it all before,' she thinks, as she prepares herself for the staff-wide meeting that morning. 'These new owners will come in with their grand plans and new procedures and try to lay their mark on the hotel, but they are not going to take us away from what we really are,' she thinks to herself, 'a caring and considerate hotel based on traditional quality service.'

Mortimer, the second-longest-serving member of the Junction Hotel team, started life as a cleaner and has worked through every position in the hotel to eventually become one of the senior managers. 'Owners come and go,' she thinks, 'but the Junction Hotel way will outlive any of them.'

One of the fundamental problems with the rationalization approach is that it ignores people. Not only can this create dehumanizing jobs, but also there is a danger that the creativity and imagination that people bring can be sucked out of them by a focus on the formal, rational organization and not paying attention to how people are shaped by the groups around them. The social side of the organization, the way that groups, teams, and wider culture shape how we think and act, provides an alternative way to think about how we manage people.

Chapter 5 focuses on the Hawthorne studies, among the most detailed and influential studies of people at work. The researchers studied workers at the Hawthorne plant of the Western Electric Company in Illinois, USA, in the 1920s and 30s. They claimed to have 'discovered' that people are social beings who are influenced by the social norms of their peer group. One of the researchers, Elton Mayo (1949), proposed that organizations should be seen as social spaces, full of people with feelings and desires, rather than as machines. We will also see in this chapter that their claims are not all that they seem. Taking a **critical** perspective, as we will do in Chapter 5, another way of seeing Mayo's interpretation of the Hawthorne studies is as a more powerful and subtle way of controlling people. This more humanistic approach may be, in its ultimate ambition of seeking to get the maximum productivity out of workers, not too dissimilar to that of Frederick Taylor.

Chapter 6 will develop the analysis of group norms, illustrating how groups and teams have become increasingly important ways of managing people and increasing productivity. However, teamwork can be challenging, as it often fails to work as effectively as it might. Models such as Belbin's theory of group membership (2010) present techniques which claim to make teams more effective.

Finally, in Chapter 7 we look at the social phenomenon of organizational culture—the behaviours, language, stories, and symbols of an organization that are enacted through the groups and teams within the organization. Again, we will see that culture is something that organizations seek to manage, but some argue that it is to a large degree beyond their control. Moreover, recent changes in how we work, particularly with the advent of remote working and the gig economy, are challenging the idea of stable organizational cultures.

Theme 3: Managing the individual

Chapter 8: Personality and individual differences: Can personality be measured?
Chapter 9: Motivation and the meaning of work: Is it all about the money?
Chapter 10: Knowledge and learning: Developing the individual: developing the organization
Chapter 11: Perception and communication: Is communication ever perfect?

Running case: 8.30 am, Linda Wilkinson, domestic manager, arrives at work

Linda Wilkinson makes her way hurriedly across the car park of Junction Hotel, clutching her briefcase. 'Flipping traffic,' she mutters under her breath, 'the school run will be the death of me.' As she rushes past the boardroom window, she notices a man in his mid-50s staring into the distance. 'Is that Simon Chance,' she wonders to herself, 'the new owner of Junction Hotel? And who's he with?' as she spots a smaller, earnest man pointing aggressively at some charts. As she does so, she catches a glimpse of herself in the window. Tall, blonde, and still quite elegant—or so her friends tell her—the forty-something mother of two notices the vomit stain left on her jacket's left shoulder by Sam, her youngest, as she dropped him off at nursery this morning. 'Grrrrh,' she declares, slightly louder than she had intended. 'This is the last thing I need today,' she mutters. Her slight outburst alerts the man, who looks up at her. Trying to subtly hide her shoulder, Wilkinson smiles positively at him even though today she feels anything but positive. 'This is a big day,' she thinks to herself, 'I need to make a good impression and present myself as the manager-in-waiting.'

In the third theme we focus our attention on individuals within the organization and how they are managed. Chapter 8 examines the theories of personality—what are the traits that make us all different, and can they be measured? We see how managers use such theories to create 'personality tests' that are used in procedures such as recruitment and appraisal, and how these tests have recently become part of the 'big data' that is being used to automate more and more parts of the recruitment and selection process.

Seeing people as having differences is also important when examining what motivates people to work harder; the motivation of workers is the subject of Chapter 9. Maslow's hierarchy of needs (1943) is a familiar tool for analysing human motivation, but we discover that motivation is, in fact, a much more complex phenomenon—individual differences can relate not only to factors of personality, but also to the social factors that people bring in from their life outside the workplace.

We then turn our attention to knowledge and learning in Chapter 10. We will see that in the knowledge-intensive economy, the way that knowledge is developed, captured, and distributed is an increasingly vital aspect that differentiates successful firms from those that fail. What, though, do we mean by knowledge? Is it a set of facts that can be learned, or is it something that we acquire through experience? And does the rise of artificial intelligence mean that human knowledge is no longer needed, or are there aspects of human intelligence, such as empathy and emotion, that machines cannot yet replace?

Chapter 11 focuses on perception and communication. Once again we see that individuals can perceive the same things in different ways. This has implications for communication in organizations, which we will see is fraught with difficulty and open to miscommunication. We will also discover that technologies such as mobile phones and the internet can increase our abilities to communicate, but also provide further possibilities for misperception and miscommunication.

Theme 4: Managing the organization

Chapter 12: Changing the organization: Planning and emergence
Chapter 13: Leadership: Leading the way
Chapter 14: Power and politics: The murky world of organizational life

> ### 🔍 Running case: 10.00 am, Simon Chance meets all the staff
>
> Chance, followed closely by Weaver, walks purposefully into the conference room, reaches the podium, and surveys his expectant audience. All the staff of Junction Hotel are gathered, somewhat nervously, to hear from the hotel's new owner and chief executive officer.
>
> Chance starts by introducing himself and his consortium and explaining why they bought the hotel. He says that it has a proud tradition of quality customer service, but the world is changing and the hotel needs to change with it. He, with all their help, is going to transform this place, to bring it back to its former glory.
>
> 'Junction Hotel is going to feel like a new place,' he goes on to say, 'a new culture where hard work gets rewarded and the best people succeed. This is a clean slate for everyone and I am going to set the hotel on a new course.'
>
> 'This is an exciting time for all of us,' Chance continues, warming to his theme, 'but let's be under no illusions, it is going to be challenging. Some of you are going to find the changes that we put in place difficult. Some of you might not even want to come with us in this new direction. I respect that. But we have a direction,' he warned, 'and we will not be blown off course.'
>
> 'Over the next few months we will all need to pull together. Working together, I'm sure we can make Junction Hotel great again.'
>
> Weaver then gets up, unravels his A3 sheets, and starts laying out the new direction for Junction Hotel.

Our fourth theme focuses on how the organization as a whole is managed. In a sense, the whole book is about organizational change, but we particularly focus on this topic in Chapter 12. We will see through that chapter that there are two major models of change: the emergent approach and the planned approach. While the discussion focuses predominantly on the role of the senior managers in organizations, we will see that how the rest of the staff respond to that change is critical in the organization's success. We also look at how theories of individual learning and development contribute to successful change and development on an organizational scale.

This brings us on to the issue of leadership and followership in Chapter 13. What makes a leader great? Are leaders born or made? Is there one best leadership style, or does this depend on the situation? And are leaders as important as we think (and indeed as the amount they are paid implies)? This chapter looks at the topic of leadership: the many models of leadership that have been presented and the debates that surround them. We will see that while there is still fascination with great leaders, more attention now is on the way leaders shape followers, whether leaders have to be authentic to be believed, and whether there are alternative ways of organizing that de-emphasize leadership.

Far from the rational organization that we begin the book with, our final chapter in this theme will examine the more messy realities of organizational life, where organizational decisions are products of power games and politics between competing people (e.g. senior managers) or interest groups (e.g. workers and managers).

Theme 5: The organization and its environment

Chapter 15: Work, emotion, and aesthetics: Organizations as an experience, work as a performance
Chapter 16: Globalization: Managing between the global and the local
Chapter 17: Corporate social responsibility, sustainability, and business ethics: Can businesses act sustainably, ethically, and responsibly?

Chapter 1: Introducing organizational behaviour

Running case: 10.48 am, the meeting ends and all the staff leave the conference room

As they file out of the meeting, Graham Effingham, Junction Hotel's award-winning chef, goes on his phone and writes a quick blog post. His blog is where he goes undercover and says what is really going on in the hotel, but without ever saying exactly where it is.

> Just come out the staff meeting with our new owners—arrrgh what a load of old clap-trap. I won't say the name of the new owners but all I can say is I think they have no chance.
>
> They gave us all this talk about transforming the business, making it a place that people will be proud to come to and we would all feel excited by working for it. How it would be a hard journey, but if we all stick together (which I read as following what they say) then we will all be a success.
>
> Nonsense—we've all been through this before with the last owners. It won't last. This lot, though, say they have a plan. The owner's side-kick had all these charts and tables about how we compare to other hotels—the man has an obsession with graphs and stuff, I can tell you. He kept on comparing us to more 'efficient' hotels, like Travelodge, saying that we can learn from them, or this European one Etap. It seems like a race to the bottom, I can tell you. Sounds like they are trying to turn us into a sweatshop!
>
> Then, as we all left, we were given our department's A3—a set of targets that we are meant to achieve over the year. Mine is to cut the cost of the food by 30% and make it 23% quicker. 23% quicker, what on earth does that mean? I have to come back in a few weeks with a plan as to how we will do this and keep the costs 'reasonable,' otherwise they are going to look into getting our food from one of these catering suppliers. They only do processed food, not the direction we want to go!

9

In the book's final theme we turn our attention to how organizations are shaped by their environment. One of the challenges that the Fourth Industrial Revolution has created is that the internet has moved things like shopping increasingly online, meaning that traditional ways of working have had to adapt. One effect, which we explore in Chapter 15, is that organizations increasingly have to pay attention to the experience that they create in order to compete with online offerings. This means that the ways in which workers control their behaviours and appearance become increasingly important as part of the customer experience. We therefore look at emotional and aesthetic labour as the ways in which people are expected to put on a type of performance when they are at work. We will also see how this performance is increasingly monitored through online customer ratings and feedback, another key trend within the Fourth Industrial Revolution.

In Chapter 16, we examine globalization. As demonstrated by the global recession following the financial crisis of 2008, we live, perhaps more than ever, in a highly interconnected and integrated world. Large multinationals have grown to become hugely powerful—in some cases more so than many countries. However, the globalized economy brings with it its own challenges for management. As Hofstede (1980) noted, national cultures still have their own unique differences, and this presents multinational companies with significant challenges in managing the differences between cultures.

Rarely a day goes by, it seems, when a scandal about a large corporation is not in the news, raising questions about ethical conduct and the responsibility of businesses to the world around them. These scandals have put the spotlight on our final theoretical chapter, which discusses corporate social responsibility (CSR). We will examine some of the key ethical challenges that organizations face, how they respond to them, and the criticisms that campaigners and activists have about these responses.

Organizational behaviour—an interconnected discipline

> **Q Running case:** 11.15 am, Weaver and Chance meet again in the boardroom
>
> 'Well, that went well,' says Weaver in a confident way, 'I think we really hammered home our message. This place needs a good shake-up and we're the people to do it. With our new targets and management practices, Junction Hotel is going to be a very different place in a year's time.'
>
> Meanwhile, Linda Wilkinson is less jubilant as she talks to Meg by reception. 'They talk very positively,' Linda says with an air of despondency, 'but they cannot just come here and impose their views on us like that.'

In our final chapter we draw all the issues together and look forward to the future challenges that face organizations. We will see that, while we have discussed all these topics as discrete entities, in practice they are highly interconnected and rely on each other.

It is, therefore, important to be aware of the connections between the themes as you read the chapters and prepare to write your essay or answer your exam questions.

Key underlying disciplines

What we are interested in within organizational behaviour is people: how they are managed, motivated, and shaped by the world around them, and how they behave. To examine these issues we draw on a number of underlying disciplines (Figure 1.2), which think about the world in different ways. We rely primarily on five disciplines.

- Sociology explores how society shapes people. It helps us understand that no action takes place in a social vacuum and helps us appreciate how individual experiences are part of broader society.
- Psychology seeks to measure, explain, and occasionally change human behaviour. It is often considered the science of the mind.
- Social psychology bridges sociology and psychology, and tries to understand the impact the group has on the outlook of the individual.
- Anthropology examines rites and rituals that shape how groups and cultures work.
- Political science, as applied to organizational behaviour, examines the role of power within organizations.

Figure 1.2 The disciplines that underlie the study of organizational behaviour.
Source: Robbins, Stephen P.; Judge, Timothy A., Essentials of Organizational Behaviour, 10th Edition © 2010, p. 5. Reprinted by permission of Pearson Education, Inc., Upper Saddle River, NJ.

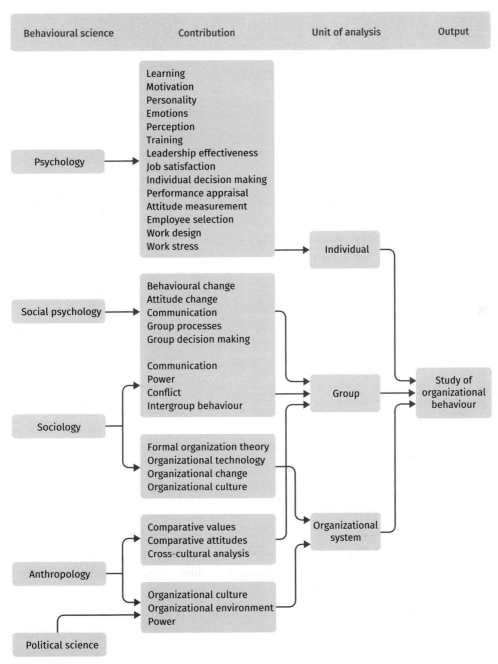

11

OB is an applied discipline (in that it is interested in what goes on in real organizations). It draws on and uses these underlying disciplines to inform its thinking. For instance, a researcher drawing on a sociological perspective will look to how society shapes the individual, whereas a theorist drawing on a psychological perspective will look primarily at the individual. It is important, as you read through the book, to be aware of the significance of these underlying theories and how they shape OB theories.

Visit the online resources and take a look at the extension material for Chapter 1 for a deeper analysis of the theories underlying OB.

Critical thinking and multiple perspectives: why there are no right answers in organizational behaviour

 Real life case: Dan Price, the CEO who raised his firms' minimum wage to £50,000 by cutting his own salary, was then sued by his brother

How would you like to work for a company where the minimum wage is $70,000 (around £50,000)? In April 2015 Dan Price, the CEO of the Seattle-based payment processing company Gravity Payments, took a very controversial decision. He raised the minimum wage of all his employees to $70,000 (£50,000) within three years (Cohen, 2015a) and also gave unlimited paid time off (Gravity Payments, 2018). This resulted in 70 out of the 120 employees getting pay rises, with 30 having their salaries almost doubled (Torabi, 2015).

Price, the co-founder of Gravity, told the *New York Times* (Cohen, 2015a) that he decided to do it after reading an article on happiness. The article was on the links between well-being and pay, which argued that emotional well-being rose progressively until it reached $75,000. While above $75,000 a year brings pleasure, it does not increase happiness (Kahneman and Deaton, 2010).

The article made a deep impression on Price. He had heard many stories from his employees about how difficult it was to live off $40,000 a year, and he wanted to make a difference. Price stated he felt there was a 'moral imperative to actually do it … I want everybody that I'm partnered with at Gravity to really live the fullest, best life that they can' (cited in Torabi, 2015). To achieve this he decided to cut his own salary from just under $1 million to $70,000 (Torabi, 2015), stating that the 'market rate for me as a CEO compared to a regular person is ridiculous, it's absurd' (cited in Cohen, 2015a). He also felt it made business sense. 'I honestly believe that removing that distraction [of living from pay cheque to pay cheque] will significantly increase our ability to take care of our clients' (cited in Torabi, 2015). This has been reflected by some of the employees, who say that they are now working harder. For instance, one employee stated that they are willing to put in more hours. '"I never thought I would go to a job where I would want to work extra hours, but this is something that I, and everyone else, want to do," said Ortiz, one of the employees. "It's really inspirational to see so many people dedicating most of their day to this job"' (cited in Elkins, 2015). Some also felt it was the start of a movement that aimed to reduce the differences between high and low earners. As Dan Price states, 'Income inequality has been racing in the wrong direction … I want to fight for the idea that if someone is intelligent, hard-working and does a good job, then they are entitled to live a middle-class lifestyle' (cited in Cohen, 2015b).

Yet a couple of months later, Dan Price was sued by his brother because as a minority shareholder he believed the increased wages of the staff were reducing the firm's profits. Dan Price was also struggling financially: he had to cut his own salary and rent out his house. He also faced criticism on Facebook, in letters, and in phone calls (Cohen, 2015b). Some customers left, feeling it was a political statement. Some employees also left. For instance, a former financial manager told the *New York Times*: 'He gave raises to people who have the least skills and are the least

→

equipped to do the job, and the ones who were taking on the most didn't get much of a bump' (Cohen, 2015b). Others did not like the fact that the gap between the higher- and lower-paid was reduced, and some even questioned if they were really worth the increased salary.

So how has it worked out? Reflecting on the decision, Dan Price states 'employees whose salaries rose under the new policy have experienced a noticeable improvement in their quality of life and have been able to do the things they'd previously had to put off for financial reasons' (Price, 2017), such as having children, buying a house, or saving for a pension. It also worked very well for the company. Gravity became known for its higher pay, attracted high-quality candidates for jobs, and itself saw 'a leap in productivity of 30–40%' (Georgescu, 2018). One downside is that Gravity became known as 'the $70K company' (Price, 2017), which impacted the image that people had of the company. As for the legal case of Lucas Price suing his brother, Dan Price won the court battle and says he still has unconditional love for his brother (Keegan, 2016).

The business case: motivation

Dan Price makes an interesting claim that having a minimum wage of around £50,000 will increase motivation and customer service. The business case for imposing this minimum wage is based on the assumption that the increased wages will lead to higher productivity. As we have seen, this did occur, with Gravity seeing 'a leap in productivity of 30–40%' (Georgescu, 2018). One factor in this change may be that high-quality staff have applied for jobs at Gravity; another may be that higher pay increased motivation.

One argument drawn from psychology and behavioural economics, particularly the work of Daniel Kahneman, is that feelings of well-being increase up until a salary of around £48,000, but do not with higher increases. Therefore a salary of this level will produce the maximum well-being for everyone. By setting pay at around £48,000 according to Kahneman's theory, Price has maximized the staff's feelings of well-being and through this has increased their motivation.

However, as we will see in Chapter 9, the question of whether higher pay increases motivation is a complex one. Adams's equity theory (Adams, 1963), argues that individuals will calculate the ratio of their inputs (time, effort, and skill) against the outputs (e.g. pay, job security) and against those of others. If they feel someone is receiving greater levels of output in relation to their input, then this will cause dissatisfaction. Therefore, highly skilled Gravity employees might experience the change as unfair because even though they received an increase in their wages, it was a smaller increase than the less skilled workers were receiving in proportion to their skill level.

The ethics case: the gap between highest- and lowest-paid

Another way of looking at this is the ethical case. As co-founder and CEO of Gravity, Dan Price was earning around $1m a year, about 25 times more than the lowest-paid employee (who earned $36,000). Not only did Price say that it was difficult for the lowest-paid to live on $36,000 (approximately £23,275), but the gap between rich and poor was too high. As we will see in Chapter 17, this interest in inequality has been reflected more broadly, with critical theorists arguing that the importance of chief executive officers is overestimated and their pay is disproportionate for what they do.

A sociological perspective might point to how the question of pay can be seen as part of issues within wider society. A 2018 report by US politician Keith Ellison stated that within Fortune 500 companies (the biggest 500 companies listed on the US stock exchange), the average CEO received 339 times the pay of the average employee (Ellison, 2018). Sociologists Richard Wilkinson and Kate Pickett argue that this gap is important not only from a business point of view but because the gap between rich and poor creates higher levels of crime and even health problems (Wilkinson and Pickett, 2010) for the rest of society. From this perspective, businesses should not be seen as isolated from the rest of society but as producing and reflecting wider inequalities within society.

Yet while Dan Price's position might be seen as a noble gesture, some argue it is not a sustainable one. For instance, getting high-quality senior managers is a significant challenge and, as we will see in Chapter 13, many leadership theories see the CEO as vital to increasing the long-term profits of the company. It is often argued there is a 'war for talent' (Peacock, 2010), with top people able to travel anywhere in the world; therefore, firms have to pay competitive salaries and bonus packages in order to attract and retain the best people. Furthermore, in a related argument, supporters of shareholder capitalism would argue that Dan Price did not have the right as CEO to make this decision alone because effectively he was spending shareholders' money (through the increase in wages), which was not (solely) his choice to make. Theorists such as Milton Friedman (see Chapter 17) argue that it is immoral to spend shareholders' money on something just because you as a manager believe it is ethical.

The importance of analysis

Our brief discussion of the pay at Gravity has shown that there are many different perspectives, drawn from sociology and psychology, from **mainstream** pro-business and critical perspectives, that provide different interpretations of Dan Price's decision. There is not one right answer: whether you think Dan Price did the right thing will be dependent on the assumptions that you have about what is more important, i.e. the business case or the ethical one, or if you are looking at this from the point of view of society (sociological perspective) or that of the individual (psychology).

It would be easy to read the preceding section and think 'Well, anything goes in this subject. If there are no right answers, then it is just about opinion. All I need to do is put forward my opinion, as it is as valid as anyone else's.' While tempting, we believe such a perspective is dangerous for a number of reasons. First, the ideas developed in this book are based upon years of research built up through numerous investigations, theoretical reflections, and analysis, and argued through many lectures, articles, and books. They are, therefore, more than simply opinions: they are built on reasoned arguments and investigations into actual practice. Second, they draw on (as we have seen in the preceding section) a variety of different underlying perspectives that are built on deep theoretical foundations. These are more than simply personal opinions or gut reactions, but reasoned arguments based on fundamentally different ways of thinking about and discussing the world. Finally, as we will explore in more detail in the following sections, these perspectives are built on wider theoretical reflections about the nature of societies and the roles that organizations should play in them.

 Study skills: the difference between personal opinion and an academically-informed perspective

My opinion

- uses my own taken-for-granted assumptions;
- is based on gut reaction and personal opinion;
- is likely to contain sentences beginning e.g. 'I think that ... '.

→

→

An academically-informed perspective

- challenges received opinion and taken-for-granted assumptions;
- is based on theoretical reasoning, evidence, academic literature, and evaluation of competing perspectives;
- is based on evidence;
- is likely to contain sentences beginning e.g. 'Research shows that ... '.

Therefore, while at first glance informed **critical analysis** might seem to resemble simply stating your own opinion, in practice developing an academically-informed perspective is more rigorous, thoughtful, and evidence-based. While your personal opinion might, therefore, be a starting point, bear in mind that your opinion begins with common-sense or taken-for-granted assumptions that you may not have questioned, rather than being based on evidence and theory. Indeed, often the best assessments are completed by students who have changed their view on a subject, having read and really engaged with the academic arguments.

Because there are no set answers, we sometimes call this approach a 'contested' view. There are multiple perspectives because the issues that we are interested in cannot be 'solved' in any straightforward way and, consequently, it is an area of constant debate. The skill of a good analyst is to uncover these underlying assumptions and to see how they inform the research and how one perspective differs from alternatives. One of the central study skills that you will need throughout your time studying OB (and at university as a whole) is to be able to uncover the key underlying assumptions that inform the theories.

The need to develop critical thinking

Developing your critical thinking skills is a long-term process of acquiring skills and also a mindset of approaching the world in a different way. As we can see from the real life case in this section, such an approach can be highly beneficial as it helps you to think more deeply and to be more innovative—something that employers throughout the world are increasingly looking for.

Real life case: innovative thinking in Singapore

The Singaporean education system has been widely praised for heading up the international league tables, coming top of the 2016 rankings in maths announced by the Programme for International Student Assessment (PISA) run by the Organisation for Economic Co-operation and Development (OECD) (Ward, 2017). This success is attributed to a highly scripted teaching style and high levels of discipline and commitment from the students.

On the other hand, the focus on always being right and finding the right answers is increasingly criticized. While their approach has been hugely successful in attracting multinational firms and making the country prosperous, as the economy has developed questions are increasingly being raised about Singaporeans' ability to undertake more creative and innovative jobs. Being innovative and being able to solve complex problems requires the ability to be prepared to think differently, to question one's assumptions, and to cope with uncertainty

→

→ and doubt. To tackle this the Singaporean government are integrating critical thinking as part of an overall goal with programmes such as the 'Thinking Programme' (Tan, 2017).

One of us (Daniel) discovered this when teaching in Singapore. At the end of a week of intensive teaching of OB to a group of Singaporean undergraduates, one of them came over to say that they both loved and hated the course. It made them think differently and question what they knew, and at the same time made them feel uncertainty and doubt. Studying OB can get us all to feel this way.

So how do I develop critical thinking skills?

Teaching yourself to question things and also to learn in a different way can be a difficult, but exciting, process. At university your lecturers will want you to demonstrate a higher level of critical analysis than you may have encountered before and also a different approach to thinking. Rather than simply recounting the strengths and weaknesses of particular theories, they will be expecting you to look at the wider implications for our understanding of broader issues in society. This requires deeper thinking and engagement, opening yourself up to competing perspectives and interpretations of the world, and a readiness to engage in complex ideas. This can be particularly challenging given that, on the surface, OB seems little more than 'common sense'.

One example of the value of critical and analytical thinking is that it encourages us to go beyond these general assumptions to really examine the implications of these theories, not just for management practice but for society as well. This moves us to ask not only pragmatic questions, such as how things are done, but also wider ones, such as in whose interest things are done. This requires alternative ways of thinking.

This can be challenging. One of our students describes how she has struggled with wanting to find the *right* answer:

I am a bit of a perfectionist really and I want to know the answers. At A-level I studied History—where there were a lot of dates and facts, Law—where there were many cases, and Business (where there was a lot of accounting)—where there were right answers. At university, studying organizational behaviour, I have realized that there are no right answers and I need to think outside the box.

You might find studying OB difficult and challenging, particularly if you come from a scientific or mathematics background, which tend to have 'correct' and 'true' answers. For many students, this desire for the right answers and anxiety about getting the wrong answer leads them to want to memorize and learn facts about theories, as these seem more certain and understandable. For instance, we have seen countless students put in details about when key theorists were born and when they died, or long descriptions of a theory, presumably believing this is the 'correct information'. However, it demonstrates very little understanding and often has a negative impact on their grade.

To really develop critical thinking requires asking different types of questions and focusing on different levels of thought (Figure 1.3).

At the surface level is **description**. At this level you simply describe the theory, giving details of what it is, how it works, and its basic concepts. You will discuss the basic facts, models, or theories, and you will need to show familiarity with the theories, but little more. However, this level largely involves repeating back the theory. You do not need to do much thinking, as you are merely reproducing what you have been told in lectures or in this book. You need this level as it is the foundation for the subject, but you need to remember that it is not enough at degree level.

Figure 1.3 Levels of critical thinking.

Description	Recalling and describing the theory: multiple choice questions, facts, recall, definitions, and models
Explanation	Applying to real life and own experience, and what the theory means for organizations in practice
Analysis	Considering strengths and weaknesses, exploring alternative viewpoints and the underlying assumptions
Critical analysis	How the theory challenges our fundamental understanding of OB: in whose interest is the theory?

The next level down is **explanation**, **comprehension**, and **evidence**. At this level you show that you really understand the theory and its relevance to the question and to real life practice. To do this you can apply the theory to an organization and show the implications for organizational practice. You can also identify the relevant points of the theory to the actual question asked. This shows a far deeper level of understanding, as it takes a stronger appreciation of what the theory entails in order to apply it to practice.

Within this level is also the application of theory. This is where you link what you have learned to actual organizational examples. In this book, this might be either from real life examples or from examples from the Junction Hotel running case. The idea here is to show that theories are not simply words on a page. They are tools that can both explain what happens in real life organizations and, furthermore, make recommendations for how organizations might solve particular management issues.

Application is based on what you know about the theories, including their strengths and weaknesses. For example, in Chapter 3 we introduce Taylorism, which outlines a way of designing work to make it more efficient. We sometimes ask our students to apply this to our running case. A very simplistic answer that we often hear is that 'Junction Hotel should introduce Taylorism because it would increase efficiency.' This is too simplistic and vague—it isn't good enough as an answer. Imagine if you presented something like this to a board of a company. They would rightly ask questions such as 'How would it increase efficiency in our organization specifically?' 'What problems might its implementation cause for us?' or 'Can you show evidence that it has worked in similar organizations?' Applying a theory thus moves from talking about general theoretical ideas to presenting them in the context of a specific organizational setting.

While this level shows a greater level of insight, it does little to question the assumptions that underpin the theories. It simply takes things for granted and does not show the deeper level of thinking that is necessary to make judgements about a theory.

Progressing further down the diagram is where we begin to **analyse** the theory. This level looks at the theory's strengths and weaknesses, identifying the advantages and disadvantages of the theory or the benefits and drawbacks that the theory offers. This form of analysis is common at post-16 qualifications (e.g. A-level) and demonstrates a stronger appreciation of the theory itself and how it works in practice.

The deepest level of critical analysis includes synthesis, comparison, evaluation, and creativity. It requires a much higher level of thinking because it does not merely assume that the theory is correct but looks as much at what the author does not say and who it impacts. Because of its greater complexity and more advanced level of understanding, this approach often gets higher marks. To achieve this you need to really understand the theory and its implications, read between the lines, and not accept things at face value but question everything. This also involves judgement, weighing-up of the relative merits of the theory, and then drawing conclusions to see if the perspective offered is fair and valid.

Table 1.1 The structure of the review questions

Describe	These are the most basic questions. They invite you to recall and describe theory, providing basic facts, definitions, and models.
Explain	These go beyond basic definitions, explaining what theories actually mean, or why they are important for the study of organizations and management.
Analyse	Here you are invited to go much deeper, considering the strengths and weaknesses of theories, exploring alternative viewpoints and underlying assumptions, and showing how theories may have challenged existing and widely accepted viewpoints.
Apply	Here you are comparing theory with organizational examples, from both real life cases and the Junction Hotel running case. You may be asked to find evidence of theories in these examples, or even act as a consultant and make recommendations to organizations based on the theory that you have learned.

To develop your critical thinking, the following questions are useful when reading academic theory:

- What are its strengths and weaknesses?
- How does it compare with other theories?
- What evidence is it based on and is it reliable?
- What are the implications of the theory for practice?
- What are the underlying assumptions?
- Whose interest does it serve?
- What is its implication for answering the question?

As we can see, to really get to the heart of the issue and understand its significance we need to go beyond merely describing a theory and seek to understand its underlying assumptions.

Throughout this book are questions to get you thinking. 'Stop and think' questions appear throughout the chapters. They invite you to reflect on what you have just read and to put it in the context of your own thoughts and experiences. There are also review questions within the chapters. These have been structured to take your thoughts from simple description (at the top of the critical thinking iceberg) towards much deeper levels of critical analysis, which will be useful in your essays and exams. These review questions have been labelled 'describe', 'explain', 'analyse', and 'apply', as outlined in Table 1.1.

Degree-level analysis

Throughout this discussion you may have thought that much of this talk of analysis is familiar to you, as you have heard the terms 'analysis', 'evaluation', and 'application'. While post-16 education uses these terms, we require deeper and more engaged thinking to do well at degree level.

For instance, at post-16 analysis often consists of describing the strengths and weaknesses of a particular theory, and may compare it to other theories; at university, we are after a deeper examination of the implications of the theory to the fundamental assumptions of the discipline. Table 1.2 summarizes these differences.

Table 1.2 The differences between post-16 and degree-level thinking

	Post-16	Degree level
Ability you should show	Ability to reproduce material taught and show you understand which theorists are relevant	Ability to digest the material and demonstrate understanding of its implications
What markers are looking for	Correct answers to match the mark scheme	A critical response to the literature
How you use the theory	Show understanding of the theory and both sides of the argument	Make an argument by writing within a school of thought, using accepted concepts and theoretical tools
Analysis is ...	Stating the strengths and weaknesses of a theory	Questioning the underlying assumptions of the theory and their implications for the question
Evaluation is ...	Demonstrating understanding of both sides of the argument, comparing and weighing them up	Providing your own response to the question based on the theories in question
Material used	Specific texts you are given to investigate	Materials chosen by you in undertaking your own research
Paragraph structure	Key points, quote to back up, followed by evaluation	Linked together to make an overall argument that fully answers the question

Ultimately, at degree level, the emphasis for answers in essays and exams is on making an argument, based on theory, which responds directly to the question asked.

Critical thinking: mainstream and critical views

🔍 **Running case:** the day draws to a close

Simon Chance's office (5.50 pm)
As evening approaches, Simon Chance opens his diary and starts making a few notes to himself about his reflections on his first full day at Junction Hotel.

> The staff seemed friendly and generally professional, and seemed to take the meeting well. That chef, though (Effingham, I think he's called), looked a bit of a livewire and will need keeping an eye on. Everything here feels slightly chaotic, unmanageable even. Everyone goes about their jobs OK, but from where I'm sitting they are not working effectively. It will take some doing to kick this lot into shape.

The bar (10.00 pm)
As the kitchen staff's shift ends, Effingham, Josh, and Toby are sitting round the bar enjoying their evening 'nightcap'. 'What do you think about this new owner?' Josh asks Effingham.

→

Effingham snorts, 'Same old management clap-trap, if you ask me. They come out with all these phrases and buzz words, "blue sky thinking, A3s, gold standard customer service", but they don't have a clue what it's really like.' Toby butts in, 'Yeah, I'd love to see him prepping for evening service or doing the breakfast run, then tell me all that management speak really means anything.' 'Yes,' Josh smiles, 'it's us who run the show really.'

Critical thinking can also mean a political view that asks you to question the underlying assumptions and values of theories for the purposes of understanding and challenging their impact on society—e.g. workers, the environment—and that is seen in opposition to mainstream theory. (Used in this sense, this is often called the 'critical management studies perspective'.)

The mainstream or dominant view represents the general established thinking about management. This includes assumptions: for example, the view that managers have the right to manage, or that the central objective of a business is to make profits for its shareholders. This perspective is primarily concerned with creating theory that helps to understand management practice better and generally to improve it. The goal of management theory, within this perspective, is to achieve performance, efficiency, productivity, order, and control.

The critical view argues that these mainstream views systematically favour elite interests at the expense of disadvantaged groups, for instance managers over workers; men over women; profit over society; and economic growth over the environment—arguing that this limits freedom of all (Grey and Willmott, 2005). The critical perspective suggests that there is a 'dark side' to organizations that these mainstream accounts rarely discuss. A critical perspective, among other things, draws on Marxist theory and seeks to challenge the assumptions of mainstream management theory by stressing the impact that it has on employees and society.

While the critical perspective might seem negative, its proponents would argue that it is aiming at a more positive society. The critical perspective argues that organizations should exist for freedom and fulfilment, creativity and expression, and for the benefit of society, not just for shareholders. Critical perspectives therefore aim for emancipation (freedom from slavery). This form of critical thinking can be hard—it may challenge many of our basic assumptions of the world—but it can also be highly transformative.

 For whose benefit should the theory of OB be written? Management? Shareholders? Employees? Customers/clients? Society?

◎✦ Study skills: questioning taken-for-granted assumptions

Having recently received back comments on her assignment for her OB module, one of our students has come to realize that the type of analysis required at degree level is deeper than she had previously been asked to do before university.

Having read the assignment I thought that I was doing analysis by listing the strengths and weaknesses as we were asked to do in my previous studies. I now see that this was only part of what analysing means and you want us to think a lot deeper at degree level.

→

→

The central intention here is that you will become independent critical thinkers who are able to develop arguments through critical analysis of others' positions.

When reading a theory, instead of taking the ideas for granted, the following questions can give you a more critical perspective.

- What are the underlying perspectives presented in the text?
- What are the taken-for-granted assumptions contained (but not expressed) in the theory?
- Whose interests are being served by this perspective?
- What issues are being glossed over or downplayed?
- What are the implications for power and control?
- What are the effects of the theory on people, society, and the planet?
- What other perspectives have been downplayed or ignored by this theory?

◎ Employability skills: critical thinking—the number one skill for 2020

What do you think will be the most important skill for employees to have in 2020? According to the World Economic Forum, the answer is critical thinking. The World Economic Forum, a body that brings together leading politicians, business leaders, and economists, in 2016 published a report looking at the future of the economy. In particular it was concerned with the way that jobs were going to change due to the Fourth Industrial Revolution, a dramatic change in the economy brought about by automation, artificial intelligence, and such developments as the gig economy (see the Preface and Chapter 4 for more details). They argued that the Fourth Industrial Revolution was attacking routinized and repetitive work, which is better done by machines. The jobs more likely to be safer from automation were ones that use such core skills as cognitive flexibility, logical reasoning, active learning, active listening, negotiation complex problem solving, and in particular critical thinking (Schwab, 2016: 21). The report argued that fact-based learning, such as that which focuses on description (as shown in Figure 1.3), was increasingly less important as such facts quickly go out of date, 'with nearly 50% of subject knowledge acquired during the first year of a four-year technical degree outdated by the time students graduate, according to one popular estimate' (Schwab, 2016: 20). Instead, the higher-level thought processes of creativity, enhanced decision-making, and critical thinking, the type of thinking exemplified by analysis and application, are the skills needed for the future.

The links between study skills and employability skills

While we often think that the skills we need to study are different from those that we will use in a work situation, the links between the two are surprisingly similar, as we can see in Table 1.3.

Therefore, as you go through your university career it is valuable to develop these study skills as they are often transferable to a work situation.

Table 1.3 The similarities between study skills and employability skills

	Study skill	Employability skill
Time management	Many assignments due at the same time A lot of study time and therefore personal responsibility Juggling paid employment, studying, clubs and societies, and personal responsibilities	Working on numerous projects in which you have to manage your own time and that of others
Synthesis of a lot of complex information	Reading dozens of academic articles and pulling out the key themes, arguments, and positions of the authors	Reading numerous reports, background briefings, and market research, and being asked to make sense of them
Working with ambiguous briefs	Getting an assignment brief and needing to work out what you need to do to get a good grade	Being given a loosely-defined task and being told to 'get on with it'
Writing for different audiences	Studying different modules with their various approaches to academic work such as referencing, analysis, and styles	Writing for different managers, for your staff, and to clients—all of which have different requirements

 Visit the online resources and take a look at the extension material for Chapter 1 for more information on transferable skills.

Employability and study skills: keeping a journal of skills and a diary for reflection

To prepare for your entry into the world of work after you graduate, we recommend that you keep a journal in which you collect evidence and examples of the skills you have developed at university and outside, and a diary to reflect on what you are learning.

When you apply for most graduate jobs you will need to fill in an application form which will ask you for *evidence* that you have hit a number of requirements, such as teamwork, taking initiative, or project management. One way that you can significantly improve your chances is to keep a record of *actual examples* of your meeting any of these criteria. This could be through assignments at university—teamwork, working with different nationalities; or external activities, such as being involved in the football club (planning and organizing as you arrange matches and transport).

Studying OB is particularly useful in this regard, as the subject matter deals with many of the key skill areas that you will need at work. Therefore, as you read about topics such as motivation, leadership, and teamwork, consider your own experiences and how you can demonstrate examples of actual practice.

Throughout this book we will also offer study skills that give you opportunities to develop your abilities as a student. As you go through your course, it is really helpful to keep a diary in which you can honestly and openly reflect on what you would like to achieve in your working life and how you would like to get there.

Connecting case and theory

Simon Chance has just started his tenure at Junction Hotel as the CEO of the Second Chance Consortium. In his first day at the hotel he has, like us, begun to get to know some of the employees of the hotel and a bit about them. While Chance is seeing many of the hotel's problems as being to do with **structure**, and hoping to solve them by bringing in forms of **monitoring** and **control** (for instance the A3s), the problems are also about people. As we have seen, organizations are fundamentally about people, and people can be complex and make organizational life messy. Rather than being rational and logical places, as we often like to believe, organizations can be full of emotion—pain, joy, excitement, disappointment, hope, fear, and anxiety—**power** and **politics**, struggles over **leadership**, changes in culture, clashes of **personality**, challenges of **teamwork**, and different perspectives. We can see this through Linda Wilkinson's nervous arrival at work and Effingham's dismissal of plans by the new owners to bring about **change**. Our fictional running case, Junction Hotel, therefore, instead of presenting the theories as abstract and separate from real life, gives an insight into how theories can play out in practice.

To sum up, there are no right answers within OB as it is a subjective discipline, born out of various theoretical disciplines and subject to different social and political perspectives. We can see this in the different reactions that the characters have to the changes that are going on around them. Simon Chance and Phil Weaver see the hotel through the lens of strategy, rationalization, and trying to bring in new 'improvements'. Meg Mortimer, the most experienced of Junction Hotel's staff, thinks she has seen it all before, and Effingham and his team are sceptical of anything that the management say. To study OB effectively requires critical thinking and questioning: the ability to understand different perspectives and to seek to challenge your own assumptions.

The study of OB is also heavily linked to real practice. The employability and study skills presented in this book can bring some of these issues to life as you develop your abilities for your university and employment career. Keeping a diary and working through the exercises in the book and the online resources will help you to maximize your experience and gain a fuller understanding of the subject.

Further reading

Cottrell, S. 2017. *Critical thinking skills: Developing effective analysis and argument.* Palgrave Macmillan: Basingstoke.

This popular study skills book provides some really useful material on the importance of critical thinking and offers practical, as well as theoretical, ideas on how to improve in this area. Reading this will be helpful, not only in studying this subject but also for other subjects on your degree course.

Bowell, T., and Kemp, G. 2015. *Critical thinking: A concise guide.* Routledge: London.

Another popular study skills book that stresses how to develop and build arguments. It looks at how to assess the strengths of an argument and how to develop your own.

Gallagher, K. 2016. *Essential study and employment skills for business and management students.* Oxford University Press: Oxford.

This study skills guide provides useful ideas on how to develop your all-round skills as a business and management student, including teamwork, presentation, and reading skills.

References

Adams, J.S. 1963. Towards an understanding of inequity. *Journal of Abnormal and Social Psychology* 67 (5): 422.

Belbin, R.M. 2010. *Team roles at work.* Butterworth-Heinemann: Oxford.

Braverman, H. 1974. *Labor and monopoly capital: The degradation of work in the twentieth century.* Monthly Review Press: New York.

Cohen, P. 2015a. One company's new minimum wage: $70,000 a year. *New York Times*, 13 April.

Cohen, P. 2015b. A company copes with backlash against the raise that roared. *New York Times*, 31 July.

Elkins, K. 2015. How one employee felt when the CEO announced her salary would double to $70,000 a year. *Business Insider*, 30 April.

Georgescu, P. 2018. What are we waiting for? Forbes. Available at: https://www.forbes.com/sites/petergeorgescu/2018/01/24/what-are-we-waiting-for/#33c9a6ed56e3 (last accessed 17 June 2018).

Gravity Payments. 2018. Work with U. Available at: http://gravitypayments.com/about (last accessed 17 June 2018).

Grey, C., and Willmott, H. 2005. *Critical management studies.* Oxford University Press: Oxford.

Hofstede, G.H. 1980. *Culture's consequences: International differences in work-related values.* Sage Publications: Beverly Hills, CA.

Kahneman, D., and Deaton, A. 2010. High income improves evaluation of life but not emotional well-being. *Proceedings of the National Academy of Sciences* 107 (38): 16489–93.

Keegan, P. 2016. Gravity Payments' Dan Price wins court battle with his brother. *Inc.* Available at: https://www.inc.com/paul-keegan/dan-price-gravity-lawsuit-win.html (last accessed 17 June 2018).

Maslow, A.H. 1943. A theory of human motivation. *Psychological Review* 50 (4): 370.

Mayo, E. 1949. *The social problems of an industrial civilisation.* Routledge: London.

Peacock, L. 2010. War for talent resumes as salaries climb. *Daily Telegraph*, 5 August.

Price, D. 2017. The $70k minimum wage: Where it went wrong and where it went right. *Inc.* Available at: https://www.inc.com/dan-price/70-thousand-dollar-minimum-wage-where-it-went-wrong-right.html (last accessed 17 June 2018).

Ritzer, G. 2018. *The McDonaldization of society: Into the digital age.* Sage: Thousand Oaks, CA.

Schwab, K. (2016). The Global Competitiveness Report 2016–2017, *World Economic forum*, Geneva

Tan, C. 2017. Teaching critical thinking: Cultural challenges and strategies in Singapore. *British Educational Research Journal* 43 (5): 988–1002.

Taylor, F.W. 1911. *The principles of scientific management.* Harper: New York.

Torabi, F. 2015. Why this CEO pays every employee $70,000 a year. *Time Magazine*, 23 April.

Ward, H. 2017. Pisa: UK does better than expected in collaborative problem-solving—rankings at a glance. *Times Education Supplement*, 21 November. Available at: https://www.tes.com/news/pisa-uk-does-better-expected-collaborative-problem-solving-rankings-glance (last accessed 17 June 2018).

Wilkinson, R., and Pickett, K. 2010. *The spirit level: Why equality is better for everyone.* Penguin Books: London.

PART 1

The rational organization

CHAPTER 2
Organizational structure, design, and bureaucracy
From rationality to flexibility

Chapter overview and learning outcomes

By the end of this chapter you should be able to:

- describe the main features of bureaucratic organization

- explain how bureaucracy is a form of rational organizational design that helps managers to control organizations as they grow in size

- analyse the negative effects of bureaucracy that Weber described as an 'iron cage'

- describe dysfunctions of bureaucracy, such as red tape and the bureaucratic personality

- explain how bureaucracy has developed through the use of digital technology, including the management and control of workers in the gig economy

Key theorists	
Max Weber	A sociologist who observed the increasing dominance of bureaucracy within society, noting its technical achievements but also its negative impacts on people
Henri Fayol	An industrialist known for outlining a rational, structured approach to bureaucratic organizational design and administration
Shoshana Zuboff	Wrote about the 'informated' organization, which generates a large amount of computerized data around its own activities
Frank Blackler	Noted the simultaneous nature of organizations 'imploding' into computer code and 'exploding' into computer networks
Gilles Deleuze and Félix Guattari	Philosophers who devised the concept of the rhizome, which has been used to describe organizations which operate through computer networks

CHAPTER 2

Key terms	
Bureaucracy	Official aspects of an organization, such as the hierarchical structure, rules, procedures, and paperwork which allow control to be exerted over the whole organization
Rational organizational design	As championed by Fayol, the design of bureaucratic features in the most technically efficient way so as to achieve the organization's goals
Iron cage of bureaucracy	A phrase which summarizes Weber's critique of bureaucracy and rationality, suggesting that it is inescapable and leads to monotonous, dull routines
Informating	Where a large amount of an organization's activity and knowledge is stored as computer code in a database
Network	Where organizations are linked by sharing data through computer networks or through the internet

Introduction

🔍 Running case: 'a disorganized mess'

Simon Chance likes order and being in charge, but after a week with the management team he has inherited at Junction Hotel, he feels frustrated. 'This place is a disorganized mess,' he thinks to himself. 'No one seems to know what they are doing—it's unmanageable.'

The lack of formal organization is highlighted when Chance asks Meg Mortimer, the general manager, for an organization chart. 'Organization chart?' she says with a surprised tone. 'No, we don't have one of those. I know everyone personally and we work together as a friendly little group.'

Mortimer has been at the hotel for over twenty-five years, from when it was a small organization. Although the hotel has grown, she still tries to manage with a personal touch, as if it still had a small group of staff.

Chance soon realizes, however, that Mortimer delegates much of the hands-on management to her deputy, Linda Wilkinson. Wilkinson's role has grown over the years to include responsibility for the reception area, the cleaners, the waiting staff the maintenance staff, and the fitness centre employees. Wilkinson also processes stock orders and similar paperwork—something she generally does in a rush whenever she finds time.

While concerned about Wilkinson's workload, Chance also notes that Mortimer can't resist interfering in these everyday decisions, particularly with the cleaners and the reception staff. 'I know their jobs inside out,' Mortimer explains. 'I used to be a cleaner and I was the main receptionist here for years!'

Chance speaks to Linda Wilkinson, who seems stressed. 'I feel like I run the place on my own—it's a lot for one person.' Chance asks about Mortimer's interference: 'Meg feels that she

→

→

needs to be involved in everything,' Wilkinson continues. 'I value her occasional input, but sometimes I would like to be left to get on with it.'

Chance notes that Wilkinson becomes more stressed when the conversation turns to restaurant staff. 'The waiting staff are supposed to be managed by me. But Graham Effingham … well, he thinks they work for him.'

Head chef Graham Effingham confirms this confusion.

I have official control over the chefs, but not the waiting staff. That's stupid, especially when Linda is so overworked already. So, I tell the waiting staff what to do anyway—it gets the job done. Sometimes they go moaning to Linda when I shout at them, but needs must. They're probably confused about who exactly is their boss, though. I wish I could just run the whole restaurant without any interference.

Chance feels that things don't run as smoothly as Mortimer has suggested, sensing further problems with David Hunter, an old friend of Mortimer who works part-time maintaining the accounts. Mortimer often confides in Hunter and trusts his advice—he often chips in with his thoughts on running the reception area and procedures for stock ordering. 'To be honest,' chortles Hunter, 'who gets bonuses and pay rises is pretty much on my say-so.' Again, Wilkinson resents this interference.

While Mortimer's presence seems to hold the hotel together, Chance can't help thinking that there are simmering tensions, many caused by a lack of a clear structure, with blurred roles and responsibilities. Furthermore, there is a lack of clear rules and procedures, and paperwork in the files is far from ordered. While Mortimer gives the hotel a veneer of being well-organized and managed, underneath the surface it is ad hoc and dysfunctional.

A meeting with his team of investors is imminent, and they have given him a clear instruction to get a grip on the hotel and make it profitable. Chance realizes that he needs to bring coherent management and organization to the hotel.

29

Have you ever used an app such as Deliveroo to order food or Uber to hire a cab? Have you thought about what happens between you sending the order from your phone and the food arriving at your door, or the taxi coming to pick you up? With Deliveroo, there are customers in their various homes, numerous restaurants producing the food, and bicycle couriers dispersed across a number of locations waiting to receive their next job. It is the software and algorithms behind the app which take the order, instruct the restaurant to make the food, and find the nearest free cyclist to deliver. The app's role is to control and coordinate the various people involved, all without a single human being telling another what to do. Instructions are delivered at a distance to the phones of the cyclists, or of the cab drivers in the case of Uber.

Companies like Uber and Deliveroo are examples of the **gig economy**—a modern day form of organization typical of the Fourth Industrial Revolution (which we will examine later in this chapter and throughout the book). However, while the gig economy is often presented as a new development in our modern-day world, this chapter will show how it has its origins in, and can be seen as a development of, early **bureaucracy**. Bureaucracy covers aspects of an organization such as structure, hierarchy, rules, policies, procedures, and paperwork, which together form a rational set of techniques designed to control and coordinate an organization—to keep it in order rather than being disorganized. The chapter is structured as follows.

- First, we see how the classic form of bureaucracy developed during the Second Industrial Revolution as a rational and efficient way of controlling an organization. Using the work of industrialist Henri Fayol, we introduce three features of bureaucracy—structure, rules, and paperwork. These features help to control and coordinate an organization as it grows in size, with management moving from direct, face-to-face control to impersonal control at a distance.

- Second, bureaucracy is evaluated. Its advantages in controlling organizations on a large, even global, scale are contrasted with the negative impact that sociologist Max Weber suggested bureaucracy had on people. We also see how bureaucracy can be **dysfunctional**—it does not always create the rational, efficient control that it has been designed for.

- Finally, we see how bureaucracy has recently evolved. An unpredictable **environment** has seen organizations adopt more flexible, **post-bureaucratic** organizational structures in place of classical bureaucracy. At the same time, computer technology has increased bureaucratic power, with data used increasingly to control aspects of organizational activity. It is somewhere between these two seemingly contradictory trends that we find the computer-driven yet flexible control found in today's gig economy.

The development of bureaucracy in the Second Industrial Revolution

 Real life case: from small beginnings

Many of today's large-scale companies began as small enterprises with a handful of employees. These humble origins are often presented as part of the history and folklore of these organizations. Greggs the Bakers, which now has 1,700 stores in the UK, began as a single store bakery in north-east England in the 1950s (Greggs the Bakers, 2018). The UK-wide department store John Lewis, which currently has 90,000 employees (John Lewis, 2018), started out as a single drapery shop on London's Oxford Street in the 1860s (Butler, 2014). Aldi, the German multinational budget supermarket chain, is a family-owned business which started with a single store run by the Albrecht family in Essen, Germany, in 1940 (Ruddick, 2013).

 How do you think these well-known large-scale organizations have had to change and adapt their management styles as they have grown over the years from small-scale, single-branch companies?

 Visit the online resources and take a look at the web links for Chapter 2 for more information about the growth of these companies.

Bureaucracy has existed for centuries: for example, in the ranks and strict rules and regulations of armies (Morgan, 2006: 21) or in the hierarchical nature of religious organizations.

However, in the early 1900s, the Second Industrial Revolution saw the widespread emergence of large-scale industrial organizations, such as factories, in the Western world (Thompson and McHugh, 2009: 19–27). This linked with bureaucracy to create a particularly efficient form of rationalization (Ritzer, 2019).

These larger organizations needed a different way to manage and control people. In a small-scale organization, such as a hairdressing salon, a café, or a car repair workshop, management can be done on a direct, personal, face-to-face basis. The owner knows all employees by name. Rotas, holidays, and similar tasks can be arranged through conversation between the owner and the team. The owner knows the personalities and characteristics of their staff, including who to reward as a good worker and, likewise, who might occasionally need a quiet telling-off.

This personal style of management might work for a small enterprise with a handful of workers, but what if it grew to 100 employees, or 1,000, or even became a multinational with tens of thousands of people across different continents? The larger an organization becomes, the more difficult it is to manage and organize in a personal, informal style. **Direct control** by one individual owner/manager at the top of the organization is no longer possible. This section examines how, as an organization grows in size, managers adopt more indirect, **impersonal control**, using, in particular, the bureaucratic structures and procedures of **rational organizational design**. **Rationality** suggests that the structures and procedures of the organization are designed logically and systematically to achieve the organization's aims in a technically efficient manner. These impersonal, rational forms of organizational design and control are termed **bureaucracy**, from the French word *bureau*, meaning 'office.' Bureaucracy relates to the 'official' or formal side of the organization, particularly the organizational **structure** and **hierarchy**; **rules**, **policies** and **procedures**; and official **records** and paperwork.

Henri Fayol and the development of bureaucracy

 Theory in context: Henri Fayol and the profession of management

Henri Fayol (1841–1925) was a French mining engineer who became a manager. He suggested that, regardless of the person holding the office, good and efficient management was achieved by following a set of general principles, which he set out in his 1916 work, *Administration industrielle et générale* (English translation, Fayol, 1949).

Management became a profession in itself (Pryor and Taneja, 2010), with the training of managers becoming as important as training for production skills or other functions in the organization, such as finance. In Chapter 3 we will encounter Taylor, a fellow management pioneer. Unlike Taylor, who concentrated on making individual work tasks more efficient, Fayol was interested in efficiency *at the level of the organization overall*.

Fayol's and Taylor's work was the basis for what became known in the UK as the Classical Management School (see Smith and Boyns, 2005)—a form of management developed around the early 1900s that emphasizes rationality and searches for the 'one best way' to manage an organization. This is in contrast to the disordered, ad hoc, and chaotic form of organization that might exist were it not for bureaucracy.

Fayol (1949) was one of the people who laid the foundations for our view of what orderly managing and organizing entails, providing a useful initial definition of the five main functions that managers perform (see Table 2.1).

We can see how these five functions could be achieved easily on a face-to-face basis within a small-scale organization, but become more difficult as an organization grows in size. Fayol, who was writing and managing around the time of the Second Industrial Revolution, saw bureaucracy as the solution to this problem of *how to manage an organization as it grows in size*. Furthermore, he saw bureaucracy as an issue of rational, technical design—achieving the optimum combination of bureaucratic elements. Rational organizational design is about finding the most direct and efficient means—the 'one best way'—to achieve organizational ends. From this, Fayol created fourteen general principles of management. While space prevents us from examining these principles in detail, they encompass three aspects of bureaucracy that we will discuss in in the sections that follow: structure and hierarchy; rules, policies, and procedures; and records and paperwork.

Visit the online resources and take a look at the extension material for Chapter 2 for a full list of Fayol's fourteen principles.

Table 2.1 Fayol's five functions of management (1949)

Planning/ forecasting	Looking to the future, trying to calculate and predict future circumstances (such as demand, competitors, etc.), and acting so as to be prepared to respond to these
Organizing	Building up the necessary structures, resources, and people to best meet the needs and goals of the organization
Coordinating	Bringing together the structural, human, and resource elements of the organization to act in harmony in working towards the goals of the organization
Commanding	Giving orders and directions to people within the organization to maintain activity aimed at achieving the organization's goals
Controlling	Checking and inspecting work—monitoring and surveillance of work done, rather than direct command

Bureaucratic structure and hierarchy

Q Running case: mapping the structure at Junction Hotel

Chance phones Phil Weaver, a friend and trusted colleague from the football club he runs. Weaver has a reputation as a fixer—his hard-headed, no-nonsense attitude is needed to bring order and organization to the hotel. Weaver is seconded to work two days a week at the hotel to 'shake things up a bit'. With a roving 'trouble-shooter' role, he will take a particular interest in the restaurant and the fitness centre, two areas that Chance wants to develop and make more profitable.

With Mortimer unable to provide an organization chart for the hotel, Chance and Weaver begin their work by sketching out the current organizational structure. As best they can, they try to show where each person fits into the structure—who reports to whom, and what authority each person has. Their first attempt is shown in Figure 2.1.

Some problems are apparent immediately.

- Too many people at the top—there are too many levels of hierarchy with just one person occupying each level. Mortimer and Chance both seem to be running the hotel, and bringing in Weaver results in another level of senior management.

- Hunter assists Mortimer, but his role in the hierarchy is ill-defined—he seems to 'float around' at the side. The same can be said of newly-introduced Weaver, who is assisting Chance.

- Wilkinson seems to be overburdened with supervisory responsibility (34 people) in addition to other tasks she performs.

While this chart outlines the official structure and associated roles and responsibilities, it doesn't tell the full story. People are acting in unofficial capacities not shown by the chart. Chance takes the original diagram and adds a series of dotted lines to show areas of control and supervision that are not officially defined, but which happen in practice (see Figure 2.2).

Mortimer intervenes regularly in the supervision of reception and cleaning staff. Hunter also tries to influence reception procedures, while Weaver now has responsibility for the development of the fitness centre. It is unsurprising that Wilkinson is confused as to her exact power and authority within the hotel: for example, with the waiting staff, lines of authority are confused between Wilkinson and Effingham. Effingham himself now seems to report to Weaver, even though the official organization structure suggests the restaurant is under Effingham's control.

Figure 2.1 The current structure at Junction Hotel.

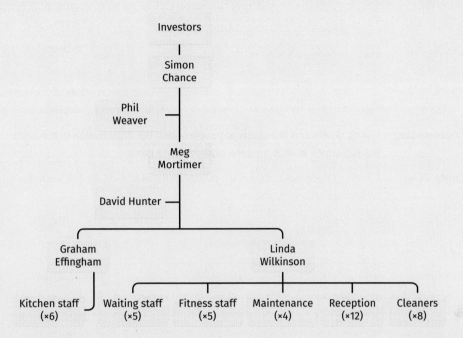

Overall, there is a picture of confusion, with ill-defined, blurred roles and responsibilities coupled with an unevenly distributed hierarchy that is too narrow at the top and too wide at the bottom.

Chance and Weaver begin to think about restructuring the hierarchy.

Figure 2.2 The unofficial structure in practice at Junction Hotel.

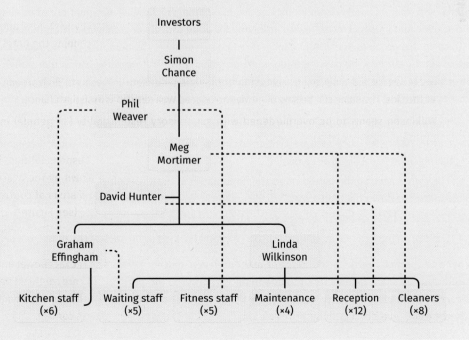

Figure 2.3 Structure and hierarchy develop as an organization grows in size.

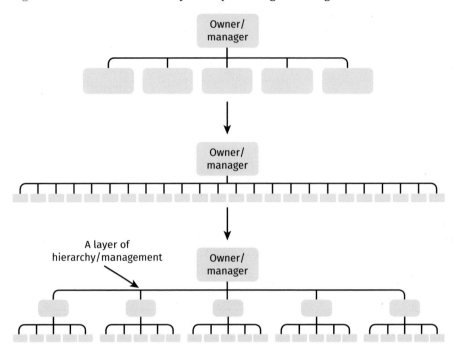

An organizational structure, or hierarchy, develops as a response to the problem of controlling people as an organization grows in size. Figure 2.3 illustrates such a situation. At the start there are a handful of employees managed directly on a face-to-face basis. As more employees are taken on, the organization moves to the middle position where the **span of control**—the number of employees that a manager supervises directly—has increased. While a span of control of five was manageable, a much larger span of control stretches the capabilities of any one individual. Indiscipline and disorganization within the workforce may arise from this lack of control. Furthermore, managing with such a large span of control is an inefficient use of a manager's time. Time spent mired in matters of discipline and personal issues leaves little time for other aspects of managing the organization.

To solve this problem of control, managers relinquish some of the personal, face-to-face control and instead **delegate**, by passing a job, task, or order down to lower levels of a hierarchy. The lower part of Figure 2.3 shows the development of **organizational structure**—the roles and positions in an organization, often presented in an organization chart diagram—and hierarchy.

- There is a level of management between the owner and the other workers.
- Day-to-day tasks, such as supervision, discipline, and calculating pay, are now delegated to managers at a level below the owner.
- The owner neeed only issue commands to managers at the level below, who will then pass the commands down the hierarchy.
- The owner no longer needs to even see, or have any contact with, the workers at the lower level.
- The owner returns to a manageable span of control of five, as do each of the managers below.

When the span of control is too much at any one level, another level of hierarchy can be introduced. From a small factory to a multinational corporation, the principle of control through the hierarchical structure remains the same; only the number of levels differs. The larger the organization, the more levels of hierarchy will exist.

The structure of the organization allows the owner, or a delegated management representative such as a chief executive officer (CEO), control of the organization which passes down through the levels of the hierarchy. Between each of the levels in the hierarchy there is still personal, direct, face-to-face control. But, as orders and commands pass down the hierarchy, a form of control emerges which is impersonal, indirect, and at a distance. It is also an efficient form of control because the owner needs to deal only with the level of management below, freeing time to perform other management tasks.

Vertical and horizontal differentiation

The development of hierarchy creates **vertical differentiation**, where employees are separated vertically from one level of the hierarchy to the next. Managers are also further differentiated by their specific responsibilities. **Horizontal differentiation** (or functional differentiation) describes the different 'branches' of the structure, which might be grouped together in the ways shown in Table 2.2.

In practice, most organizational structures use a mix of these. Figure 2.4 shows a typical factory organization with higher levels of the organization organized by function (sales and marketing,

Table 2.2 Horizontal differentiation

Type of horizontal differentiation	Examples	Example job titles
Product, service, or area of activity	Factories divided by product lines; schools divided into subject areas; local authorities structured into service areas (e.g. housing, social services, etc.)	Head of maths department
Specific function performed	Manufacturing companies divided into departments for sales, marketing, production, human resources, etc.	Director of human resources
Geographical area	Multinationals divided along continental lines; sales departments divided into territories	European sales manager

Figure 2.4 A typical factory organization.

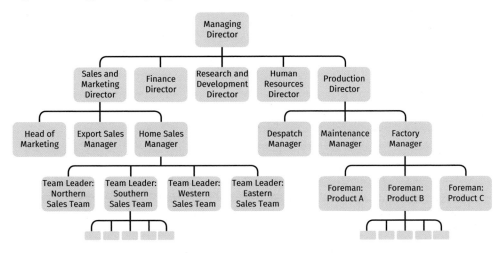

finance, etc.), home sales organized geographically (northern, southern, etc.), and the factory floor organized by product (product A, B, C, etc.). There is no one correct way for how organizations should be differentiated either horizontally or vertically—different structures will be more appropriate in different circumstances.

Roles and relationships

 Real life case: Telefónica's organizational structure

Telefónica is a multinational telecommunications group based in Spain. As with many multinationals, it has a group holding company that owns and manages various national subsidiaries and divisions. The group organizational structure shows that, beneath the CEO, the board level is organized both by function (e.g. finance, marketing, and human resources) and by geographical areas, such as Brazil, Spain, and Germany.

The structure gives a clear line of command and control that can go from the CEO at the top down to an assistant in a mobile phone store in Germany or any of the other countries in which the company operates. While the CEO may never meet most of the workers in the global organization, the structure still allows for command and control over the whole workforce.

Sources: Telefónica (2018); The Official Board (2018); Telefónica Deutschland (2018).

 Visit the online resources and take a look at the web links for Chapter 2 for more information about Telefónica's organization chart and examples of different organizational structures. Compare the structures shown: can you describe the structures using such terminology as 'span of control', 'hierarchy', 'horizontal differentiation', etc?

Running case: the new structure

At a management team meeting, Chance hands out an outline of the new structure (see Figure 2.5).

Explaining his rationale for the new design, Chance makes the following points.

- Previously, people have taken on tasks because of who they were or who they knew, or had simply fallen into doing different jobs over time. Now, people have defined roles with written job descriptions to show the precise tasks to be performed.

- Chance will assume a more hands-on role as general manager. Beneath him, the managerial workload will be split more evenly, with new positions and levels of hierarchy being created.

- Meg Mortimer will become front-of-house manager with responsibility for the reception staff and porters. There will be a promotion within each team to the positions of head receptionist and head porter, each reporting directly to Mortimer.

- The cleaning and maintenance teams will be the responsibility of the role of domestic manager, filled by Linda Wilkinson. Promotions within the cleaning and maintenance teams will create another layer of hierarchy, giving Wilkinson a manageable workload. The lines of authority also mean that Mortimer no longer has a legitimate reason to interfere in the work of the cleaners.

→

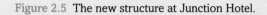

Figure 2.5 The new structure at Junction Hotel.

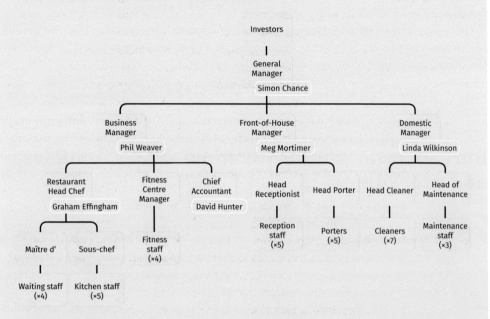

37

- Phil Weaver will fill a new role of business manager, with responsibility for finance, marketing, and business development. The restaurant and fitness centre will fall under this part of the structure. Graham Effingham will remain head chef of the restaurant, with a sous-chef and maître d' forming a further level of hierarchy over the kitchen and waiting teams respectively. This clears up the confusion over who manages the waiting staff, placing them under Effingham's control. One of the fitness centre staff will be promoted to fitness centre manager. Finally, David Hunter will report to Phil Weaver as chief accountant; his 'cosy' relationship with Mortimer will be broken up. Both Weaver's and Hunter's uncertain roles within the organization are now clear.

 How do you think the changes made to the Junction Hotel structure improve the running of the hotel? Who do you think might be happy or unhappy with the changes made, and why?

Each position on an organization chart represents an **office**—a role to be carried out by a person acting on behalf of the organization in an **official** capacity. The bureaucratic structure maps out the relationships between people acting in different official roles within the organization. Lines of authority demonstrate who a worker is controlled by and, likewise, who a worker has control over. It also shows the limits of such authority, namely who a worker has no legitimate authority over and to whom a worker is not answerable. Horizontal differentiation specifies each role even further.

Positions within a bureaucratic structure often have a **job description** outlining the level within the hierarchy, and the specific tasks and duties that the office holder is expected to perform—this is usually sent to you when you apply for a job. The job description and the tight definition of roles highlight the power of bureaucratic structure. Such a structure maps out and controls both the large-scale general nature of the organization and the small-scale specifics of job roles and relationships, all on a single diagram.

The requirement for job descriptions indicates that bureaucracy needs more than just structure to operate. Written rules, procedures, and paperwork are just as important a part of bureaucratic functioning and control, as we shall discuss in the next section.

 Visit the online resources and take a look at the web links for Chapter 2 to see some examples of job descriptions.

Bureaucratic standardization—rules, policies, and procedures

 Q Running case: implementing procedures

The new structure makes running the organization much more straightforward. However, while Chance has delegated authority, managers are implementing that authority in different ways—some staff are complaining that this is unfair.

- Mortimer is authoritative, but she has her favourites when it comes to taking breaks or being able to leave early to deal with family issues. Her favourites also seem to be first in line when any opportunities for extra shifts or overtime arise.

- Wilkinson is seen as a soft touch—cleaners and maintenance workers take extended breaks and are allowed to leave early for spurious reasons. If workers are off sick, Wilkinson takes their word for it, not insisting on a medical note, which leaves others to suspect that people are getting away with taking 'sickies'.

- Effingham rules the restaurant with an iron rod, bawling out waiting staff and kitchen staff directly, without going through the managers below him. He is unsympathetic to people who are ill and insists people work through breaks during a busy shift. If a shift extends beyond the set hours, Effingham sees this as a part of the job and does not pay any overtime. He is even known to dock pay if he feels that work is poor.

Chance decides to create rules and procedures to even out conditions across the workforce. Two policy documents are sent to the three managers below Chance, who are asked to implement them immediately.

The Pay and Working Hours Policy specifies a standard working day with defined hours and break times. Employees sign in and out at the start and end of the day, and for all breaks. Managers send this data weekly to David Hunter, who calculates pay and prepares pay packets. Absence is reported directly to Hunter, who asks employees to provide appropriate evidence of the reason for absence.

The Disciplinary Policy specifies expectations of staff behaviour, creating a series of set offences with related punishments. Chance wants to take discipline out of individual managers' hands. They seem to make up their own rules, leading to a lot of the unfairness felt by workers. Any disciplining of staff will, therefore, be referred to Chance directly.

How might managers react to having to follow the rules and procedures outlined in the Junction Hotel case?

Table 2.3 Examples of rules, policies, and procedures in organizations

Grievance	Policies which outline how workers themselves may pursue grievances if they are unhappy with how they are being managed
Finance	Procedures relating to expense claims, outlining what workers might legitimately claim (e.g. car mileage or transport costs) and how much
Equal opportunities	Policies that ensure equality of treatment and prohibit discrimination on grounds such as gender, race, age, sexual orientation, and disability
Appraisal and promotion	Procedures for monitoring the standard of work that employees do, often done in a standardized appraisal procedure which feeds into decisions on promotion or pay increases
Recruitment and selection	Policies that cover such decisions as where a job is advertised, criteria for selecting candidates, and types of evidence required to demonstrate that candidates meet different selection criteria (see Chapter 8 for more on recruitment and selection techniques to match personalities to job descriptions)

While bureaucratic hierarchy allows senior management to control the organization in an indirect and more efficient manner, there is a risk that at each level of the hierarchy control is lost because of the way in which it is *implemented* at these levels. Are individual managers following orders to the letter or are they acting as they please? If workers find that they are being treated unfavourably compared with other workers, it can cause unrest and disruption. **Rules, policies, and procedures**, the formal instructions within the organization, exist to standardize behaviours and activities throughout the organization, with control implemented in a standardized way throughout the hierarchy. They aim to ensure a form of **impersonal fairness** whereby all workers are treated equally with reference to the rules and procedures in place (see du Gay, 2000).

Pay rates and scales are an example of a procedure which may standardize remuneration across a whole organization or even across a whole industry sector (e.g. in the UK's education system, local government, and health service). They also include other terms and conditions, such as working hours, holidays, sick pay, pension entitlements, etc. In doing so they remove **discretion**, the ability for an individual manager to make their own autonomous judgements, from individual managers' hands, giving senior management increased control over the organization. Managers are controlled by adherence to the written rules and procedures, with behaviour standardized across the organization.

There are many other areas within modern-day organizations where activities are controlled by rules, or a policy or procedure. See Table 2.3 for some examples.

In some cases, requirements for bureaucratic rules and procedures come not just from a desire for management control, but also from a legal imperative, such as equal opportunities, health and safety, and disciplinary aspects (e.g. unfair dismissal and workplace bullying). Many bureaucratic procedures in workplaces are thus as much about ensuring compliance with such laws as they are about enforcing management control.

Visit the online resources and take a look at the extension material for Chapter 2 for further examples of rules, policies, and procedures.

Bureaucratic records and paperwork

Running case: for the record

David Hunter is finding the paperwork associated with running the new payroll and absence procedure burdensome. With clocking-on records and absence reports coming in daily, and pay cheques to prepare weekly, he is overwhelmed.

Some managers scribble their daily records on to a scrap of paper; others create a well-ordered spreadsheet. Storing the scraps of paper in his notebook makes it difficult for Hunter to access and process payroll and absence information as more and more of it comes in. When asked for details of any specific employee, he spends most of his time wading through a mass of paper.

Hunter decides that a standard system of record-keeping is needed. Opening a filing cabinet, he allocates a folder to each employee. On the front of each he creates a standard template to record details of the employee—name, address, date of birth, tax code, and other relevant information. Each employee is allocated an employee number.

A set of forms is created—one where managers can record clocking-on and clocking-off details for each employee, one for reporting absences, and one to record any disciplinary incidents. For each of these, the first box to be filled in is the employee number. Hunter can then file the forms immediately when received and access them rapidly when required.

The forms help Hunter to manage the payroll process much more efficiently; however, Simon Chance spots a further benefit. Every so often he asks Hunter to send up the file of a particular employee. Even if Chance doesn't know the employee personally, he can read the file and get a good picture of their working history, e.g. their absences, time taken on breaks, and disciplinary issues.

Even though the employees may be distant and unknown to Chance within the structure, their employee records make them instantly visible.

 What control over individual workers does the record-keeping at Junction Hotel give to the managers?

While rules and procedures standardize aspects of workplace control, such procedures both necessitate, and are facilitated by, the keeping of records and **paperwork**, the official documentation within an organization. This is the final aspect of bureaucracy that we examine in this chapter.

Bureaucratic paperwork is typified by the **pro-forma**. Sometimes call a form, it is a blank template with standard fields for different types of relevant information, for example about employees. It is filled in as a means of capturing information for the records of an organization. Such record-keeping serves two purposes for management in controlling the organization.

- In order to implement rules and procedures, information about the organization and its workers is required. A payroll policy needs information about the hours worked by each employee, an absence policy needs to record reasons for absence, etc. If this information were unstructured (e.g. scribbled on scraps of paper) it would be difficult to manage. A pro-forma standardizes the information and thus makes it easy to access, retrieve, and use in implementing the policies that it supports.

- A by-product of this paperwork is that a record is kept of an employee's activities that can be accessed at any time. Such records allow added control through surveillance and monitoring of employees. While an employee might be invisible within a large organizational structure, their records allow management to still cast an eye over their activity and exert control—for example, if there is a problematic absence record. (See Chapter 4 for a discussion of control through surveillance.)

Computers and bureaucratic record-keeping

Bureaucratic records are now usually stored as computer data rather than as paperwork in filing cabinets. Indeed, the words used to describe how computer data is stored—'files' and 'folders'— come from bureaucratic terminology. As with pre-defined fields on a pro-forma, computers use pre-defined information fields within a database. The implications of databases for organizations are examined later in this chapter.

Traditional filing system.
Source: © Elena Elisseeva/123RF.

The bureaucratic power of organizations is enhanced by the information processing power and speed of computers. Computers also aid the monitoring and control function of bureaucracy, with computer databases able to store more information than could be realistically held as paper records, and allowing information to be accessed within seconds. In this respect, databases can control not only organizations but entire populations. Government bodies and organizations exist as massive bureaucracies, processing information and paperwork about their populations, with the intent of ordering and controlling that population in one way or another. The ability of such systems to pinpoint an individual amongst millions and make them instantly visible and controllable, and to do the same to each and every one of those millions, highlights the power of bureaucracy.

Real life case: bureaucracies which control populations

In the UK, the Driver and Vehicle Licensing Agency (DVLA) maintains records for all licensed drivers and their vehicles. Such records control who can and cannot drive, and even manage the exclusion of individuals from driving based on penalty points accrued or failure to pay car tax. Similar giant national bureaucracies keep records of tax details and health records. Privately-owned, commercial record-keeping organizations, such as Experian in the UK, keep similar records, for example about the financial history of an individual for use in credit checks.

Visit the online resources and take a look at the extension material for Chapter 2 to see more examples of bureaucracies that maintain records about the population, including a description of how bureaucracy helps the UK university admissions system to operate.

The power of bureaucracy: large-scale control and rational design

> Phil—what you've done is great. Such simple ideas, but they give me so much control!

The various functions of bureaucracy allow an organization, as it grows in size, to remain ordered and controlled rather than descending into chaos. With face-to-face control becoming more difficult, if not impossible, control is implemented through impersonal elements, such as the structure, rules, and paperwork. In that bureaucracy can achieve this control across large-scale organizations, even national populations, it creates tremendous organizational power.

The ordering and controlling power of bureaucracy makes possible many achievements of organizations that we take for granted, but which, without bureaucracy, would be beyond human capability. Quite simply, the organizations that we know today would be incapable of operating without bureaucracy—it is 'ubiquitous and inevitable' (Watson, 2002: 239). Think of something like a railway timetable, for example—one simple sheet of paper, as Chia (1995) notes, can order trains, passengers, and workers across a whole rail network. In a similar manner, a university timetable exerts power over a vast number of students and staff, allocating them to set rooms and times throughout the week. Without the timetable it would be impossible to run a university—it would be a disorganized mass of people milling around without direction.

To conclude this section we return to Fayol's five functions of management. The techniques of bureaucracy that we have encountered in this chapter follow Fayol's bureaucratic principles for managing and organizing. In Table 2.4 we show how these techniques help to achieve Fayol's five functions of management in large-scale organizations, thus answering our initial question: how do you control an organization as it grows in size and scale?

❓ Review questions

Describe	What are the main features of bureaucracy?
Explain	How does bureaucracy allow Fayol's five functions of management to be implemented over large-scale organizations?
Analyse	What is meant when bureaucracy is described as exerting 'power' over large numbers of people?
Apply	Think of an organization that you engage with regularly. What kinds of structure, rules and procedures, and record-keeping do they use? How does this help them to maintain order and control?

Chapter 2: Organizational structure, design, and bureaucracy

Table 2.4 Bureaucratic techniques and Fayol's five principles of management (1949) in large-scale organizations

Planning/ forecasting	Standard rules and procedures make behaviour and actions more predictable across the organization and thus easier to plan for. Paperwork and computer records give data which can be used for forecasting, e.g. planning staffing requirements.
Organizing	A structure is created to encompass the vertical and horizontal levels of hierarchy needed to achieve the organization's aims. Tightly defined job roles and recruitment procedures allow the development of an appropriately qualified workforce.
Coordinating	Standard procedures (e.g. for pay) make it easier to coordinate activities across the organization (e.g. through a payroll department). The bureaucratic structure and rules make clear what each person does and how they relate and report to each other across the organization.
Commanding	Command is delegated through the hierarchical levels of bureaucratic structure. Rules and procedures tell people what to do without a human presence being necessary.
Controlling	Paper records and computer data can be used to monitor work performance and associated issues, such as absence.

43

Weber and the critique of bureaucracy

🔍 **Running case:** what happened to the magic?

Chance feels that the new procedures enhance his power over the organization; however, reactions from the staff seem hostile. What seemed rational to Chance as a means of running the organization efficiently is not perceived in the same way by others.

Meg Mortimer feels that she has been demoted to a place in the hierarchy alongside Linda Wilkinson. The job description limits her sphere of influence and she is unhappy that she will no longer be working closely with her friend David Hunter.

Linda Wilkinson feels disappointed. Although her workload is reduced, she is insulted that many areas she had managed are being taken away from her.

Graham Effingham is enraged to find himself a level below Wilkinson. Chance reassures him that the restaurant will be run as a separate unit, and that the appointment of a maître d' and sous-chef means that he has as many levels of hierarchy beneath him as Wilkinson and Mortimer. Effingham is still not happy, however, muttering about his reduced status.

Overall, a general lack of morale is developing, especially as more and more policies and procedures are introduced to the hotel. Chance takes Meg Mortimer to one side to ask what the problem is. Mortimer replies:

It's all paperwork and not enough working with people. I spend most of my time in the office but I need to be around people—that's the part of the job I really love. It's the same with the receptionists. We're meant to go out there, be cheerful and welcoming to customers, but how can we show enthusiasm when we don't feel any?

→

> Last week you gave us another form that we have to fill in every day, something about staff rotas. It just adds to the drudgery. We are expected to go out there and create magic—really create the atmosphere for the customers. But how can we when the magic has gone?

While bureaucracy may increase the power and control of organizations and managers, and their ability to operate on a large scale, Max Weber saw it as something of a double-edged sword. In particular he was wary about its increasing dominance within society and its negative effects upon society and people.

 Theory in context: Weber and the study of organizations

Max Weber's name is synonymous with bureaucracy. However, while he wrote in the early 1900s (at the same time as Fayol) it should be noted that *Weber was not a manager like Fayol* and thus had no interest in implementing bureaucracy within organizations so as to increase efficiency and control within them, *nor was he a management theorist*.

As a *sociologist*, Weber was interested in a wide range of aspects of society (MacRae, 1974)—economy, religion, and music being examples. One interest (Weber, 1958) was in forms of authority and control within society, which led him to analyse bureaucracy in terms of its characteristics, its power, and its effects on people and society.

When Weber (1968) speaks of an 'ideal type' of bureaucracy, it is seen by some people as some form of blueprint for the design of organizations in a similar, technically-efficient sense to that suggested earlier by Fayol. The value of Weber's contribution, however, is that as a sociologist he took a more critical view of bureaucracy, its dominance in society, and the effects that it has upon society.

Weber (1958) concluded that power and authority in society during his lifetime were moving from a grounding in tradition and religion towards bureaucratic forms of authority such as rules and hierarchical structures, which he described as **rational–legal authority**. Rational–legal authority is where authority comes neither from tradition nor from the charisma of an individual, but from the office they hold and the bureaucratic rules and procedures associated with that position.

Noting the increasing dominance of rational, bureaucratic organizational forms within society, Weber (1968) outlined features of an 'ideal type' of rational, technically-efficient bureaucracy, including:

- functional division of labour (horizontal differentiation);
- hierarchical structure (vertical differentiation);
- rules and regulations;
- impersonality—the separation of working lives from personal lives;
- unbiased decision making, including recruitment, selection, and promotion.

The ideal type contains some now familiar aspects of bureaucracy and, indeed, has some aspects in common with Fayol. However, while noting it as a technically efficient 'ideal type', Weber did not suggest that this was necessarily the right way to manage and organize. In particular, while bureaucracy might be a rational way to manage efficiently, he noted that rationality might mean different things to different people.

Formal and substantive rationality

For Weber, the **formal rationality** of the ideal type is but one type of rationality. It is a technical form of rationality which finds the most efficient means to achieving ends. *But this does not mean that pursuing those ends is rational in human terms.* Weber proposed another form of rationality—**substantive rationality**—to take account of the effects of actions in human and ethical terms.

👁 Research insight: Modernity and the Holocaust

Bauman, Z. 1989. *Modernity and the Holocaust.* Polity Press: Cambridge.

In a compelling account of the Nazi Holocaust, Zygmunt Bauman (1989) asks how individuals working in death camps, where prisoners were killed in mass extermination chambers, could bring themselves to commit such horrific acts. His answer lies in the nature of bureaucracy.

Giving individuals just a small, tightly-defined role in the overall organization shielded them from the end result. In an organization with many levels of hierarchy, orders given from the top can seem very distant and impersonal from the bottom—and their consequences come without a human face.

Thus, workers in death camps saw only their one small part in the process (it might be recording a name in a log book) rather than the overall end result.

Bauman's work on the Holocaust reflects some of the dehumanizing aspects of observed by Weber. It also highlights different forms of rationality. In terms of *formal rationality* the Nazi death camps were perfectly rational—with a task set of killing many prisoners en masse, it achieved the most technically rational way of achieving this. But in terms of *substantive rationality*, how can it be rational in human terms for an organization to exist to pursue such an ethically abhorrent act in such a ruthless and efficient manner?

The Holocaust is an extreme example of the abuse of bureaucracy, but we can think of examples in organizations today. In Chapter 17 we examine contemporary organizational arrangements that can be seen as ethically dubious, for instance in creating pollution or using sweatshop labour in the developing world. These may be formally rational in that they are the most efficient ways for an organization to operate, but are they substantively rational in terms of their effects upon humans or upon the environment?

Such issues also highlight Bauman's idea of individuals within an organization being distanced from the end result of that organization's activities. Does a sales assistant in a UK clothes shop feel personally responsible for the sweatshop conditions in which the clothes they sell were produced? Does a forecourt cashier in Sweden feel responsibility for pollution caused by oil spills on the other side of the planet?

Disenchantment—the loss of magical elements

Weber (1958) noted that as society moved from religious and traditional views of the world towards more formal, bureaucratic procedures—both in religion and in society generally—there was loss of the 'magical', enchanted elements in life. This removal of 'magical' elements in life, replaced with procedure, formality, and rationality, was termed **disenchantment** by Weber. While his term originally described the loss of magical elements in society generally, 'disenchantment' also highlights the dehumanizing and stifling effect of bureaucracy. It brings with it monotonous, repetitive routines, with people unable to act spontaneously and independently but instead bound by rules and procedures, becoming unthinking and detached from their work. In other words, bureaucracy has negative, dehumanizing effects on people and society—life becomes predictable and dull.

The iron cage of rationality

The phrase most associated with Weber (1958) is the **iron cage of rationality**. This stems from Weber's caution about the prevalence of bureaucracy within society and its potentially negative effects.

For Weber, bureaucracy, even when he was writing in 1922, was increasingly coming to dominate people's lives and society in general. Thus, the 'iron cage' gives a sense of people being trapped—small, insignificant elements in large-scale organizations. This view of bureaucracy is far from the positive view championed by Fayol, and instead sees bureaucracy as sinister and inhuman—an 'invisible enemy' (Bell, 2008: 65) through unquestioning, faceless rules and procedures, leaving people with very small, meaningless jobs and routines to pursue.

 Have you ever tried to get an error corrected by a large-scale organization, such as an error with your phone contract or car insurance? How easy did you find it? Could the person you first spoke to deal with it by themselves?

? Review questions

Describe	What is meant by rational–legal authority?
Explain	What were the main problems that Weber found with bureaucracy?
Analyse	What is the difference between formal and substantive rationality? How can the Holocaust be discussed in terms of these two forms of rationality?
Apply	Which of Weber's critiques of bureaucracy applies most to the 'drudgery' encountered at Junction Hotel, and why?

Dysfunctions of bureaucracy

Q Running case: unintended consequences

Chance had thought that his rules, procedures, and paperwork would standardize behaviour among the Junction Hotel workforce. However, in practice, he finds a number of unintended consequences.

- The fitness centre manager meticulously completes the paperwork related to attendance. His preoccupation with paperwork leads, on occasions, to the fitness centre opening late.

- Effingham is upset at not being able to shout at staff. In protest, he follows the disciplinary procedures to the letter, sending staff to Chance for the most minor infringements. At one point, all of the kitchen staff are waiting outside Chance's office to be disciplined while the kitchen lies empty with a restaurant full of unhappy customers waiting for food.

→

- It is rumoured that Wilkinson has told staff not to bother clocking in and that she will cover up any absences when she fills out the paperwork. She feels that this creates good staff relations, but also makes her own life easier—she doesn't have to spend time calculating absence rates and can get on with other management tasks.

- Check-in times at reception have increased. The receptionists are so frightened that Mortimer will pick up on any deviation from procedures that they're following them to the letter, even when common sense suggests otherwise. On one occasion, a couple who, to all eyes, appeared to be over 80 years old were asked for proof of their year of birth to qualify for a pensioners' discount. As the woman reached for her documentation, she strained her back and was taken to hospital, vowing loudly never to return as she was stretchered out past the, by then, massive queue in the foyer.

Chance wonders whether he is achieving efficient control over the organization after all—it seems like a return to the ad hoc dysfunctionality that he has tried to avoid.

While Weber presented a number of critiques of the social consequences of bureaucracy, he still noted its technical efficiency. However, a number of studies found that bureaucracy may not even be particularly efficient *in practice*. Rules in bureaucracies either had unintended, inefficient consequences or were ignored in the name of the smooth running of the organization. Many of these **dysfunctions of bureaucracy**, where bureaucracy does not function as efficiently as intended, are still encountered today.

Red tape

'Red tape' describes situations where rules and regulations get in the way of an organization achieving its goals. It is typically characterized as paperwork, form-filling, 'box-ticking', and rules and procedures which create extra work rather than helping with the work that people have to do. This is a typical source of discontent in many professions such as teaching, social work, and policing—the feeling that paperwork and form-filling prevent people from doing their actual jobs (Berry, 2010; Munro, 2010). If a police officer is in an office filling out forms, they are unable to get out and prevent crimes, for example.

Visit the online resources and take a look at the extension material for Chapter 2 to discover more about how red tape affects organizations.

The bureaucratic personality

Many of us may have encountered a 'jobsworth': an official who follows rules to the letter rather than thinking of the bigger picture or more reasonable outcomes. They follow rules rigidly and inflexibly—to do otherwise is 'more than my job's worth'. A familiar example can be found on the BBC comedy *Little Britain*, where an office worker types requests from customers and clients into a computer, responding 'Computer says no.' Rather than using her own initiative and discretion, she simply enforces the rules and procedures as dictated by the computer.

An unquestioning adherence to rules is an example of what Merton (1940) termed the **bureaucratic personality**. The rules are seen as important above all else, to the extent that 'conformity with the rules interferes with the achievement of the purposes of the organization' (Merton, 1940:

563). Rather than using common sense about what would be of benefit to the organization overall, or to a particular client or customer of the organization, a bureaucratic personality follows the rules.

A similar unflinching adherence to rules and procedures is encapsulated by the phrase **trained incapacity**, which describes people so reliant on rules and procedures that they become inflexible and unable to act in any other way. If something new or different happens, they are so set in their ways that they are unable to adapt and deal with the change.

 Visit the online resources and take a look at the web links for Chapter 2 to see other examples of dysfunctions of bureaucracy.

As with red tape, the notion of a bureaucratic personality suggests that, rather than being technically efficient, bureaucracy can have the opposite effect and hinder an organization in achieving its aims. Indeed, a common form of industrial action is the **work to rule**. Through strictly following rules and procedures to the letter, workers actually slow down dramatically—bureaucracy is used against the organization.

Real life case: bureaucracy and visas

Anybody who has applied for a visa to travel overseas will know that it can often feel like a bureaucratic headache. This real life case explores two examples from two different countries and time periods which highlight some of the dysfunctions of bureaucracy that we have explored.

The story of Anne Frank, whose family hid from the Nazi regime in a room in Amsterdam during World War II, is familiar to many of us. It is commonly assumed that the Frank family were in hiding because they were refused visas to escape to the US. However, recent evidence suggests that they were never denied a visa and that it was bureaucracy and red tape in the visa application process that hampered their efforts.

To apply for the visa, Otto Frank, Anne's father, had to gather evidence such as birth certificates, military records, and proof of a paid ticket to the US. Once submitted to the US consulate in Rotterdam in 1938, the application languished alongside many other applications—stuck in a system where a mass of paperwork had to be assessed by complex rules. In 1940, the consulate was bombed and the paperwork necessary for the application was destroyed. For Erbelding and Broek (2018), the application was thwarted by 'bureaucracy, war and time'.

More recently in India, bureaucracy in the civil service has been described as 'labyrinthine' (Sircar, 2017), an 'Achilles heel' of the nation (Shankaran, 2017), and 'the worst in Asia' (BBC News, 2012). It is characterized by strict hierarchies and subjugation to rank, files taking circuitous routes among various officials before decisions are made, and strict adherence to petty rules which blinds officials to wider instances of corruption.

An example of this unquestioning bureaucracy is described by Stacey (2018), who as an overseas worker in India had to apply for a visa for his recently born son. He describes his encounter in the Foreign Regional Registration Office, where the costs seemed to be high. The civil servant explained that there was a fine for not applying for the visa within 14 days of the son's arrival in India. This, however, would be impossible to do given that the son's 'arrival' was his birth, and that to get a visa needs a passport, which takes months to process, much longer than the 14 days for the visa. The response from the civil servant is reminiscent of the jobsworth or bureaucratic personality: 'But these are the rules—what can I do?' As Stacey (2018) states, workers are 'simply not empowered to question or adapt the rules they enforce'—even when common sense would suggest otherwise.

Sources: BBC News (2012); Shankaran (2017); Sircar (2017); Erbelding and Broek (2018); Helmore (2018); Zaveri (2018); Stacey (2018).

Bending the rules and exercising discretion

You may have heard the phrase 'rules are meant to be broken'. Many bureaucracies operate *despite* their rules—if people followed them to the letter the rules would get in the way of the organization running smoothly, creating too much red tape or inflexibility. In this respect, people are seen to operate not with a bureaucratic personality, but by interpreting and bending the rules where necessary. For example, Blau (1963) studied workers in a US business law enforcement agency and found that workers who bent rules actually got jobs done more efficiently and achieved organizational goals better than those who followed rules to the letter.

Lipsky (1980) noted that discretion is required by social work professionals, who deploy a form of 'street-level bureaucracy', judging each case in its own context rather than applying rules to the letter—a more flexible application of rules than that exercised by the rigid bureaucratic personality. Barton (2003) notes a similar exercise of discretion in police work. While the purpose of police work is to enforce rules (or in this case laws), at street level officers use their own judgement and discretion as to which laws to apply and when. The best end result might come from a 'quiet word' rather than applying a particular law to the letter, which could inflame a sensitive situation.

The ultimate in bending rules is where they are ignored. Gouldner (1954) suggested that where rules are imposed and seen as unnecessary there might exist a **mock bureaucracy**—the rules exist on paper but are ignored in practice. Sometimes the phrase 'we have a policy' suggests that the policy exists but is not necessarily followed.

 Review questions

Describe	What are the different dysfunctions of bureaucracy?
Explain	What is meant when bureaucracy is described as being inflexible?
Analyse	How might red tape prevent people from doing the work that they are employed to do?
Apply	In the Junction Hotel case, what type of bureaucratic dysfunctions can you see in the different actions of staff at the hotel?

From bureaucracy to post-bureaucracy

Real life case: Accenture ditches annual performance reviews

Accenture is a global management consultancy and professional services company headquartered in Ireland. In 2015 it announced that it would no longer subject employees to the bureaucratic demands of annual performance reviews (Cunningham, 2015a). These reviews are a form of appraisal, where employees fill in forms and paperwork to demonstrate how they have met a set of performance targets. Data about employee performance are also fed into the process so that employees can be ranked against each other.

While performance review is a means of managing a large number of globally-dispersed employees, for Vara (2015), it is an example of the 'bureaucratic corporate cultures' of the twentieth century. The CEO of Accenture, Pierre Nanterme, saw problems with what he de-scribed as this 'maximum bureaucracy'. He suggested that rather than motivating people to perform better it 'blocked' people, stifling them beneath a mass of metrics and objectives (Cunningham, 2015b). Even for workers with good performance reviews, there is evidence that the process can trigger disengagement and constrict openness to creativity and growth (Cunningham, 2015c). As Bright (2015) notes, performance review leads to people directing their work effort towards meeting the objectives being measured—why put effort into the informal work and goodwill that organizations often rely on if those results are not measured officially as part of your performance review?

For Accenture, bureaucracy failed to achieve its goal of improving performance, and was wasteful in terms of the time and expense spent on filling out forms and carrying out evaluations. The new system gave more regular individual feedback to employees on specific projects undertaken, with the aim of being more relevant and effective and also taking away 90 per cent of the bureaucratic burden associated with performance review for over 300,000 employees (Cunningham, 2015c).

The Accenture case demonstrates many of problems of bureaucracy. We see the disengagement and lack of creativity of staff reflected in Weber's ideas of disenchantment and being trapped in the 'iron cage' as they are stifled by the bureaucratic demands of the performance review. We also see dysfunctions of the bureaucracy—the red tape of form-filling distracting workers from their proper jobs. Accenture's response was to move away from bureaucracy, removing bureaucratic procedures such as the performance review.

Dysfunctions of bureaucracy, alongside the negative consequences observed by Weber, have led to a backlash against classical bureaucracy, with Accenture being one example. In particular, classical bureaucracy is viewed as being inflexible. Its rigid structures and fixed rules and procedures might provide certainty and predictability, but when orders have to be passed through several levels of hierarchy and urgently-needed changes run up against inflexible rules, bureaucracies are seen as unable to react quickly.

As far back as 1966 people were predicting the 'coming death of bureaucracy' (Bennis, 1966). Organizations were seen as being too inflexible to cope with a more changeable and unpredictable **environment**. In this section we begin by examining the nature of this changeable environment, before examining how organizational structure and design has evolved from bureaucratic to **post-bureaucratic** forms as a way of dealing with this environment more flexibly.

The organization and its environment

Organizations are not hermetically sealed; they interact with, and are affected by, things going on around them—their environment. The **PEST model** (Figure 2.6) splits this environment into four sectors:

- political—government policies and laws
- economic—e.g. the state of the economy, demand, exchange rates, etc.
- social—consumer tastes, fashions, and opinions
- technological—current technology and innovation

Figure 2.6 The PEST model.

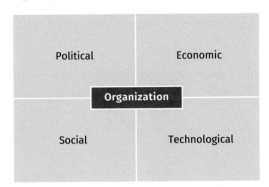

The environment impacts organizations, which might have to react and make changes. For example, Brexit can be seen as a part of the political environment which has caused uncertainty for many companies, even causing some to relocate to countries that will remain in the European Union. Within the social environment, recent television images of plastic on the ocean floors has led to pressure on companies to minimize their use of disposable plastics.

Visit the online resources and take a look at the extension material for Chapter 2 for more examples of environmental factors which impact organizations.

Contingency theory

An initial retreat from the 'one best way' approach of classical bureaucracy was **contingency theory**, a set of theories developed in the 1970s (e.g. Woodward, 1958; Thompson, 1967). Rather than one ideal type, there were a number of different ideal types of bureaucratic structure and functioning, depending on the environment facing the organization. Environmental variables, such as uncertainty, the technology used by an organization, and the size of the organization, demanded different types of bureaucratic organization—organizational design was about making the best 'fit' between the organization and its environment. While contingency theory moves away from one ideal type of bureaucracy, it is still quite rational in focus, matching the ideal organizational structure to a set of environmental variables.

Liquid modernity

In more recent years, the environment facing organizations has become more unstable and changeable then when Fayol's and Weber's theories of bureaucracy were first formulated. Clegg and Baumeler (2010) describe a shift from the static, unchanging nature of 'iron cages' of bureaucracy to a world that is fast-moving, changeable, and in constant flow. Rather than static and stable, Bauman (2000) describes this as a dynamic, changeable world of **liquid modernity**, where organizations, workers, and consumers experience a more uncertain and precarious side to life (Kociatkiewicz, 2014). The widely unexpected votes for Brexit in the UK and for Donald Trump in the USA can be viewed as part of this volatility and unpredictability. With such a turbulent, dynamic, changeable, and uncertain environment, 'one best way' approaches begin to creak at the seams and are seen as inflexible and slow to react. In contrast, more flexible, nimble organizations cope better, resulting in a move from classical bureaucracy to post-bureaucratic forms of organization.

Visit the online resources and take a look at the web links for Chapter 2 for more analysis of the contemporary organizational environment.

Post-bureaucratic structures

Post-bureaucratic structures are more flexible and less hierarchical, and they remove rules and regulations. They are designed to overcome dysfunctions of bureaucracy, such as red tape and trained incapacity where people do not think for themselves and where organizations are unable to change and adapt to new situations. In doing so, they attempt to free workers from the constraints of bureaucracy, promoting their own creativity.

Matrix structures

An example of a move away from the traditional bureaucratic hierarchy is the **matrix structure**. This combines a traditional functional hierarchy with separately-managed project teams that draw people from across different functional departments. In Figure 2.7, project A might be the development of a new product, for example. While there are heads of different departments, there is also a head of the project who coordinates staff from across the production, finance, and sales departments to bring their particular knowledge and expertise to that project.

People move between different teams rather than being in one fixed position or workgroup within the hierarchy. More knowledge and information can be shared across the organization (see the section on 'Organizational learning' in Chapter 10) and specialists with particular knowledge can be brought into particular project groups where they are needed. While this moves away from the rigidity of bureaucracy, it also brings the danger of confusion as to who is in charge of any one individual, that individual having divided loyalties between their different 'bosses'.

 Visit the online resources and take a look at the web links for Chapter 2 to see how the global technology firm Cisco has used and adapted matrix structures.

The post-bureaucratic 'structureless' organization

Post-bureaucratic organizations go further than matrix organizations in minimizing bureaucratic structures and rules and regulations. They aim to promote creativity, innovation, and rapid

Figure 2.7 A typical matrix structure.

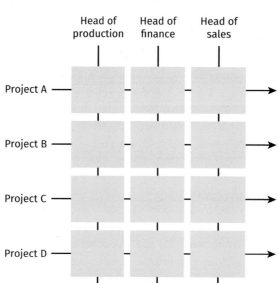

response among their workers by focusing on how to use their workers' competencies for particular tasks, rather than workers having to do just what their official positions or roles say they should do. The post-bureaucratic organization tries to foster dialogue and discussion among its workers in order to share ideas and innovations (see Chapter 10 for a discussion of 'collisionable hours').

Post-bureaucratic organizations are so radically different from traditional bureaucratic structures, rules, and procedures that they are sometimes described as **structureless**. While they do have some structure and rules, they operate in many different, flexible ways. Some examples follow.

- The Danish hearing technology firm Oticon removed traditional hierarchy and even job titles and roles. Workers are free to cluster in projects that interest them. Paperwork is scanned electronically and symbolically shredded in full view of the staff canteen (Larsen, 2002).

- The Googleplex is the famous headquarters of Google and, similar to Oticon, has few fixed spaces, with workers encourages to move freely. At times it resembles a playground, with workers playing pool or gathering to eat free food in the cafés. While the company insists on work being done, it does not encumber workers with some of the more traditional bureaucratic rules, with workers even free to attend work late if they wish to sleep in.

- At the headquarters of Virgin UK, Richard Branson has gone further, allowing workers unlimited holidays (Branson, 2014).

Visit the online resources and take a look at the extension material for Chapter 2 for more discussion about structureless organizations.

Are post-bureaucratic organizations proof, then, of the 'coming death' of bureaucracy—is bureaucracy too rigid and inflexible for our fast-moving, contemporary world? In the following section we see how information technology has been used to process bureaucracy, and how this provides a mixed response to this question.

53

? Review questions

Describe	What is meant by post-bureaucracy?
Explain	How do post-bureaucratic forms increase flexibility?
Analyse	Do you think that post-bureaucratic organizations can completely remove structure, rules, and procedures?
Apply	Many 'structureless' organizations, such as Google and Oticon, are in the technology sector of industry. Is there anything about this sector that makes organizations more likely to abandon traditional bureaucratic forms?

Bureaucracy and information technology: from the informated organization to rhizomes

It is difficult to think of bureaucracy, made up of structures, rules, and records, as a form of technology. However, Cooper (1993) suggests that this is exactly what it is—it standardizes information about people and organizational processes and as such becomes a form of tool, or technology, which is used as a means of controlling, managing, and ordering people and even whole populations.

As we saw earlier, computers can increase the processing power of bureaucracy. Given the processing power of information technology and computers, a greater amount of information can be stored and processed. In this section we examine two implications of this. On the one hand, we examine the informated organization—as organizations are increasingly computerized, *their ability to exert bureaucratic control increases*. On the other hand, we see that when organizations start to share data through computer networks they become like rhizomes—decentralized structures with random connections—*the opposite of the bureaucratic, hierarchical structure* and more like the structureless organizations that we examined at the start of the chapter.

The informated organization and big data

Shoshana Zuboff's (1988) concept of the informated organization suggests that more and more of what an organization actually does—its processes and the information that it holds—is stored as computerized information. Think about how your bank knows you—it is a 'highly caricatured' (Poster, 1995: 91) version of you that boils you down to a few database fields, such as name, address, account number, etc. Add to this database the records of other customers and all of the financial transactions that they do, and the main activity of the bank seems to become the processing of computer data.

For Zuboff (1985: 10), it is not that banks simply use databases as a kind of tool: banks are 'becoming more like databases'. So much of their activity is done through the computer data that they hold, it is as if the database is the equivalent of the bank itself. Zuboff outlined a fundamental change in the nature of what the organization actually is—it becomes almost purely computer data, or in Blackler's terms (1995: 1032) it has 'imploded' into code.

In the Fourth Industrial Revolution, this process of implosion into code has grown and intensified. The term big data is used to describe organizations that store vast amounts of data about their processes, their customers and their employees (big data will be explored more in Chapter 4).

 Real life case: big data at Amazon

Kantor and Streitfeld (2015) explain how, by its very nature as an online retailer, Amazon holds vast amounts of data about customers: not just what they buy, but how long they stay on particular web pages, what they look at but don't buy, etc. This data-driven analysis extends to Amazon's employees: they are measured with a vast array of metrics and data in what an ex-employee describes as a 'continual performance improvement algorithm' (Kantor and Streitfeld, 2015). Much of Amazon's activity, decision-making, and performance review is done in this way, reflecting the philosophy of founder Jeff Bezos that all problems can be analysed clearly using data. In the words of another former employee, 'Amazon is driven by data' (Kantor and Streitfeld, 2015).

The performance management system at Amazon could not be more different from that at Accenture—rather than rejecting the evaluation of staff using metrics, they draw upon a vast array of data to intensify this process (Kantor and Streitfeld, 2015). While this is a particularly contemporary phenomenon, it can be linked to the original purpose of bureaucracy—to control a large number of employees in an efficient manner. Records are kept about employees, in the form of data, and rules and procedures are applied to this data, for example for performance management and appraisal. As with bureaucracy, the control is impersonal and at a distance—with data-driven performance management, it is a computer algorithm which encodes the performance management procedures and then applies them to the data about each employee, so that face-to-face human control is not needed.

The use of algorithms to apply rules and procedures to data is linked to the use of artificial intelligence in organizations, with procedures and decisions carried out by software rather than human judgement. This is examined further in Chapter 10. Certainly one consequence of information technology is to intensify bureaucratic control, but in the next section we see how it has, conversely, disrupted traditional bureaucratic structures.

The 'implosion' and 'explosion' of organizations

In the previous section we saw how organizations have imploded into code, becoming like a database, a mass of computer code. However Frank Blackler (1995: 1032) notes that this *implosion* has been accompanied by a simultaneous *explosion* out into computer networks. As more of what an organization does is imploded into code, at the same time that code can be shared, for example through the internet or computer networks.

The implosion and explosion of contemporary organizations.
Source: bellenixe/Shutterstock

The example of Lloyds Bank highlights how, when exploded into computer networks, organizations can 'operate relatively independently from geographical location' (Blackler, 1995: 1033). This makes us think again about the structure of organizations—it becomes difficult to draw the boundary around where an organization begins and ends. This blurs the boundaries of organizations in a number of ways.

Real life case: the 'digitization' of Lloyds Bank

In October 2014, the UK-based Lloyds Banking Group announced plans to close 200 branches, with 9,000 job losses, as part of a process of 'digitizing' the business (Treanor, 2014). The move was a response to a trend for customers to use online and mobile technology to make banking transactions rather than going into physical branches (Arnold, 2014; Ahmed, 2014). One banking executive reflected this by stating that their busiest branch was the '7.20 commuter service to Waterloo' (Arnold, 2014): people are doing transactions on their mobile phones on the way in to work.

Visit the online resources and take a look at the extension material for Chapter 2 for more discussion about the transformation of bank branches.

How could you view the case above in terms of Zuboff's and Blackler's theories?

- *Boundaries between organizations and their customers/clients.* As with the Lloyds Bank case, customers can be dispersed geographically yet still interact with the organization. Think about where you interact with your university—submitting an essay, renewing a library book, emailing a tutor, etc.? Are you on the premises or elsewhere, through a computer network?

- *Boundaries between work and home.* **Teleworking** or **telecommuting** (Nilles, 1975) is where computer networks allow a worker to do work remotely—for example, at home—that they would in the past have done at the workplace (Castells, 1996: 394), accessing organizational files, databases, and communications online. As such, the worker's home becomes a part of the organization's computer network and the distinction between home and work life becomes blurred—we are simultaneously at home and at work.

- *Boundaries between different organizations.* While informated organizations hold data about their own operations, this is shared with other organizations through networks. When you book a hotel, it is often done online through booking sites which link with the computer networks of hotel chains in response to a customer enquiry, and make bookings on behalf of the customer. When you pay for goods at a supermarket, you may ask for 'cashback'—the networks of the supermarket and your bank link together to process the payment. When the cashier hands you the cash, it is difficult to say whether they are acting as a supermarket cashier or a bank teller—the boundaries between the supermarket and the bank have become blurred (based on Lawley, 2006: 105–6).

Organizations as rhizomes

Computer networks challenge our traditional views of organizational structure, both removing the geographical boundaries of organizations and blurring the distinctions between organizations. It is as if an organization can pop up anywhere and at any time within a computer network. Such organizations can be understood as rhizomes, a mass of random, tangled connections which some people suggest is similar to the nature of the internet and cyberspace.

The root-tree and the rhizome.
Sources: Shutterstock

Deleuze and Guattari's (1987) concepts of the 'rhizome' and the 'root-tree' are a useful means of contrasting this view of the organization with the traditional bureaucratic structure. These botanical metaphors illustrate contrasting types of structure—as Jackson and Carter (2007: 306) suggest, they explore different ways that we might be 'rooted to the spot'.

- A tree always grows in relation to a central structure—its roots and trunk—from which other outgrowths 'branch out'. In this respect, it is similar to the hierarchical bureaucratic structure, as represented by the organization chart (as was illustrated in Figures 2.3 and 2.4), where different parts of the organization 'branch out' from the level above.

- The rhizome, however, is an underground root system typified by the random growth movement of grass. It develops randomly and is not constrained by any central structure or root system; it is 'a tangled mass of randomly developing connections following no logical pattern. It is always connecting points to other points' (Jackson and Carter, 2007: 306).

Cubitt (2001: 129) suggests that the nature of organizations is rhizomatic: a shifting random set of data connections. In the previous section we saw data as helping to intensify bureaucratic instruments such as performance review. Now we see the opposite—computer data leads to rhizomatic structures more reminiscent of post-bureaucratic structureless organizations than the rigid, root-and-branch classical bureaucratic structure. This seeming contradiction can be seen by returning to the case of the gig economy.

The gig economy, bureaucracy, and technology

At the start of the chapter we looked at the gig economy organizations Uber and Deliveroo. These can be seen as contemporary examples of the problem of how to control an organization as it grows in size—cars, bicycles, workers, customers, restaurants are all dispersed geographically, and yet are coordinated into a smoothly running service. And this control is done at a distance—no human contact takes place between the customer ordering food from their home, and instructions to collect that food appearing on the phone of a delivery cyclist.

These examples highlight how the two seemingly contradictory elements of bureaucracy and information technology—the intensified control of big data against the structureless nature of the rhizome—can actually coexist. On the one hand, the dispersal of people, customers, etc. makes these organizations like rhizomes, with multiple and random connections made between them on an ongoing basis. On the other hand, it is big data which manages these connections. Similar to the Amazon example, algorithms manage the process from an order being placed, to locating the nearest free cyclist or taxi, and then instructing the driver to take the job. And the algorithms can also carry out functions such as performance management—in Chapter 15 we will see how ratings given to Uber cab drivers can determine whether they will be allocated jobs in the future by the algorithm.

While the gig economy may be a contemporary form of organization, we can see its roots in early bureaucratic control. To conclude, in Table 2.5 we return to Fayol's five functions of management, this time matching them with how gig economy companies such as Uber and Deliveroo use bureaucratic techniques to achieve these functions.

? Review questions

Describe	How is information technology used to carry out bureaucratic functions?
Explain	What does Zuboff mean when she says that banks are becoming more like databases?
Analyse	Does information technology help to overcome some of the dysfunctions of bureaucracy?
Apply	Can you think of any other industries that have been transformed by information technology in a manner similar to what has happened in the banking industry?

Table 2.5 Fayol's five functions of management (1949) and the gig economy

Planning/ forecasting	Big data is able to make plans and forecasts and adapt these on an ongoing basis such that staff are only used as and when needed—the zero-hours model of employment.
Organizing	A database of workers and customers, and related information such as location maps, is set up. On the one hand, this 'big data' acts as a central-ized structure to manage the organization, and on the other hand it is able to apply this across rhizomatically dispersed elements of the company.
Coordinating	Algorithms coordinate the activities of people, such as customers and workers, and resources, such as food, cars, and bicycles, in a similar manner to bureaucratic rules and procedures.
Commanding	The algorithm delivers commands directly to workers, e.g. to an app on the phones of drivers or cyclists, resembling the impersonal at-a-distance control of classical bureaucracy.
Controlling	Algorithms are used for the monitoring and surveillance of work done, rather than direct command.

 Connecting case and theory

In this chapter we saw bureaucracy as an answer to the question 'how do you control an organization as it grows in size?' As the chapter began, Junction Hotel was an organization that had grown in size but in which direct, face-to-face control was becoming difficult to maintain. Roles and responsibilities had grown in a random and ad hoc way, and the organization was finding it difficult to maintain control overall.

Structure, rules and procedures, and paperwork and record-keeping were seen as three aspects of bureaucracy which allow Fayol's five functions of planning, organizing, coordinating, commanding, and control to take place in an impersonal and indirect manner. As the chapter progressed, we saw how Junction Hotel used bureaucracy to bring back some control and order, but also how this brought about some problems and unintended consequences of its own.

The initial problems were highlighted when the initial **organization charts** were drawn up, showing an uneven spread of managerial responsibility, with some managers having little responsibility and others, such as Wilkinson, having an unmanageable **span of control**. Furthermore, many of the roles and responsibilities of individual managers seemed to be unclear. The new structure was an attempt to address some of these issues, creating clearer and more structured control at a distance from Simon Chance at the top, **delegated** down the hierarchy and throughout the whole organization. Spans of control were evened out, with managers given more equal managerial workloads and new levels of hierarchy created. Alongside this **vertical differentiation**, the structure was also differentiated horizontally, with different branches of the structure representing different functions such as front-of-house, domestic and business.

While this new structure was more evenly designed and provides clear roles and responsibilities, as the case continued it became obvious that the **structure** alone was not enough to keep control over the behaviour of individual managers, who were still acting of their own accord in terms of how lenient they were with staff, how they calculated the pay of their staff, and other working conditions. Other aspects of bureaucracy became necessary, and **rules, policies, and procedures** were bought in to reduce the **discretion** of managers to act of their own accord and to standardize the ways in which they implement key aspects of the working relationship such as pay and discipline. In order to run these rules and procedures, it became necessary to set up bureaucratic systems, such as a payroll system, which use standardized **records** and **paperwork** to keep track of the information needed to calculate pay in accordance with the new rules and procedures.

Bureaucracy can be seen as a technically efficient means of managing large-scale, even global organizations. The vast majority of the organizations that exist today would not be possible without bureaucracy. However, while the implementation of bureaucratic structures, rules, and record-keeping helped Simon Chance to regain control over Junction Hotel, the consequences of implementing these bureaucratic measures also reflect criticisms of them.

Managers felt that their autonomy and independence were taken away from them, they were reduced to performing strictly defined roles in accordance with the rules, and alongside that they had increased paperwork to fill in, as if they were becoming trapped by what Max Weber termed the **iron cage of bureaucracy**. The comments from staff seemed to suggest that when the hotel was more disorganized, workers at least had more freedom and more personal connection with the job. Complaints about 'where has the magic gone?' are in line with Weber's observation that bureaucracy causes **disenchantment**: the spark and variability of working life is replaced by adherence to predictable and standardized rules and structures.

In addition to the negative effects felt by the staff, the consequences of introducing bureaucracy also mirrored some of the **dysfunctions of bureaucracy** described in the chapter. When the fitness centre manager opened up the centre late because he was too busy filling in paperwork, this is an example of **red tape**, where the bureaucracy that is meant to make the organization run more smoothly actually gets in the way of people doing their jobs. Graham Effingham and Meg Mortimer are both examples of the **bureaucratic personality**, where rules are followed to the letter regardless of any negative consequences for the hotel. Linda Wilkinson, on the other hand, bends the rules and exercises her own **discretion** to keep her staff happier and keep things running smoothly: in other words, she ignores and bypasses the bureaucracy that has been put in place in order to get her job done.

The case thus shows bureaucracy to be a **double-edged sword**. While it allows efficient control to be exerted over the hotel, and saves it from being disorganized and disorderly, it comes at a price. The price is the dehumanization of workers, whose work becomes more boring and meaningless, and who even stop thinking for themselves as they become too used to following rules and procedures.

This lack of thinking can feed into a lack of flexibility. In response, post-bureaucratic forms have evolved to be more flexible and agile in our turbulent and unpredictable contemporary environment. However, while Bennis predicted 'the coming death of bureaucracy' and while the classical bureaucracy of Fayol's and Weber's time may now seem outdated, the chapter concluded by showing that information technology has helped to adapt bureaucratic techniques to allow control and management of large-scale organizations in the present day.

Further reading

Hatchuel, A., and Segrestin, B. 2018. A century old and still visionary: Fayol's innovative theory of management. *European Management Review*, https://doi.org/10.1111/emre.12292

An in-depth introduction to, and reappraisal of, Fayol's work.

Clegg, S., Pina e Cunha, M., Munro, I., Rego, A., and Oom de Sousa, M. 2016. Kafkaesque power and bureaucracy. *Journal of Political Power* 9 (2): 157–81.

A study of some of the dysfunctions of bureaucracy.

Dischner, S. 2015. Organizational structure, organizational form, and counterproductive work behavior: A competitive test of the bureaucratic and post-bureaucratic views. *Scandinavian Journal of Management* 31 (4): 501–14.

A detailed investigation of the effects of bureaucracy and post-bureaucracy on negative workplace behaviours.

Zuboff, S. 1985. Automate/informate: The two faces of intelligent technology. *Organizational Dynamics* 14 (2): 5–18.

An older reading, but a good introduction to the informated organization and Zuboff's idea of banks becoming like databases.

References

Ahmed, K. 2014. High street branches are still important for Lloyds. *BBC News Online*, 28 October.

Arnold, M. 2014. Banks must cut costs but remember what their customers want. *Financial Times*, 20 October.

Barton, H. 2003. Understanding occupational (sub) culture—a precursor for reform: The case of the police service in England and Wales. *International Journal of Public Sector Management* 16 (5): 346–58.

Bauman, Z. 1989. *Modernity and the holocaust*. Polity Press: Cambridge.

Bauman, Z. 2000. *Liquid modernity*. Polity Press, Blackwell: Cambridge, UK, and Malden, MA.

BBC News, 2012. India's bureaucracy is 'worst in Asia'. 12 January. Available at: https://www.bbc.co.uk/news/world-asia-india-16523672

Bell, E. 2008. *Reading management and organization in film*. Palgrave Macmillan: Basingstoke.

Bennis, W. 1966. The coming death of bureaucracy. *Think Magazine*, November–December: 30–5.

Berry, J. 2010. *Reducing bureaucracy in policing*. Home Office: London.

Blackler, F. 1995. Knowledge, knowledge work and organizations: An overview and interpretation. *Organization Studies* 16 (6): 1021–46.

Blau, P.M. 1963. *The dynamics of bureaucracy: A study of interpersonal relations in two government agencies*. University of Chicago Press: Chicago.

Branson, R. 2014. *The Virgin Way*. Random House: London.

Bright, J. 2015. Accenture dumps annual performance reviews and emphasises freedom and trust. *Sydney Morning Herald*, 1 August.

Butler, S. 2014. John Lewis in party mood as 150th anniversary nears. *The Guardian*, 19 April.

Castells, M. 1996. *The rise of the network society*. Blackwell: Malden, MA.

Chia, R. 1995. From modern to postmodern organizational analysis. *Organization Studies* 16 (4): 579–604.

Clegg, S., and Baumeler, C. 2010. Essai: From iron cages to liquid modernity in organization analysis. *Organization Studies* 31 (12): 1713–33.

Cooper, R. 1993. Technologies of representation. In: Ahonen, P. (ed.) *Tracing the *semiotic boundaries of politics.* Mouton de Gruyter: Berlin, pp. 279–312.

Cubitt, S. 2001. *Simulation and social theory.* Sage: London and Thousand Oaks, CA.

Cunningham, L. 2015a. In big move, Accenture will get rid of annual performance reviews and rankings. *Washington Post*, 21 July.

Cunningham, L. 2015b. Accenture CEO explains why he's overhauling performance reviews. *Washington Post*, 23 July.

Cunningham, L. 2015c. Accenture: One of world's biggest companies to scrap annual performance reviews. *The Independent*, 28 July.

Deleuze, G., and Guattari, F. 1987. *A thousand plateaus: Capitalism and schizophrenia.* University of Minnesota Press: Minneapolis.

du Gay, P. 2000. *In praise of bureaucracy: Weber, organization, ethics.* Sage: London.

Erbelding, R., and Broek, G. 2018. German bombs and US bureaucrats: How escape lines from Europe were cut off. Anne Frank House, July. Available at: https://www.annefrank.org/en/about-us/news-and-press/news/2018/7/6/research-otto-franks-attempts-emigrate-united-stat/

Fayol, H. 1949. *General and industrial management.* Pitman: London.

Gouldner, A.W. 1954. *Patterns of industrial bureaucracy.* Free Press: Glencoe, IL.

Greggs the Bakers. 2018. About Greggs. Available at: https://www.greggs.co.uk/about (last accessed 10 May 2018).

Helmore, E. 2018. Anne Frank's family tried escaping to US but thwarted by 'bureaucracy'—report. *The Guardian*, 8 July: Available at: https://www.theguardian.com/books/2018/jul/08/anne-frank-family-escape-us-visa-thwarted

Jackson, N., and Carter, P. 2007. *Rethinking organisational behaviour.* Financial Times/Prentice Hall: Harlow.

John Lewis Partnership. 2018. Our Founder. Available at: http://www.johnlewispartnership.co.uk/about/our-founder.html (last accessed 10 May 2018).

Kantor, J., and Streitfeld, D. 2015. Inside Amazon: Wrestling big ideas in a bruising workplace. *New York Times*, 15 August. Available at: https://www.nytimes.com/2015/08/16/technology/inside-amazon-wrestling-big-ideas-in-a-bruising-workplace.html

Kociatkiewicz, J. 2014. Life in the liquid organization: Control and ambiguity in organizational experience. In: Kociatkiewicz, J., and Kostera, M. (eds) *Liquid organization: Zygmunt Bauman and organization theory.* Routledge: London, pp. 58–70.

Larsen, H.H. 2002. Oticon: Unorthodox project-based management and careers in a 'spaghetti organization'. *Human Resource Planning* 25: 30–7.

Lawley, S. 2006. Accelerating organisations through representational infrastructures: The possibilities for power and resistance. *Advances in Organization Studies* 19: 91–118.

Lipsky, M. 1980. *Street-level bureaucracy: Dilemmas of the individual and public services.* Russell Sage Foundation: New York.

MacRae, D.G. 1974. *Weber.* Fontana: Glasgow.

Merton, R.K. 1940. Bureaucratic structure and personality. *Social Forces* 18 (4): 560–8.

Morgan, G. 2006. *Images of organization.* Sage Publications: Thousand Oaks, CA.

Munro, E. 2010. *The Munro review of child protection.* Department for Education: London.

Nilles, J.M. 1975. Telecommunications and organizational decentralization. *IEEE Transactions on Communications* 23: 1142–7.

Poster, M. 1995. *The second media age.* Polity Press: Cambridge.

Pryor, M.G., and Taneja, S. 2010. Henri Fayol, practitioner and theoretician—revered and reviled. *Journal of Management History* 16 (4): 489–503.

Ritzer, G. 2019. *The McDonaldization of society*, 9th edn. Sage Publications: Thousand Oaks, CA.

Ruddick, G. 2013. Aldi: A history of the low-cost supermarket. *Daily Telegraph*, 30 September.

Shankaran, S. 2017. India's Achilles heel: Bureaucracy—2G judgment indicates the nation's civil servants are the real weak link in its governance. *The Times of India*, 22 December. Available at: https://blogs.timesofindia.indiatimes.com/cash-flow/indias-achilles-heel-bureaucracy-2g-judgment-indicates-the-nations-civil-servants-are-the-real-weak-link-in-its-governance/

Sircar, J. 2017. The bureaucracy is ailing. *The Telegraph India*, 14 September. Available at: https://www.telegraphindia.com/1170914/jsp/opinion/story_172999.jsp

Smith, I., and Boyns, T. 2005. British management theory and practice: The impact of Fayol. *Management Decision* 43 (10): 1317–34.

Stacey, K. 2018. Battling India's bureaucracy for babies and businesses. *Financial Times*, 9 January. Available at: https://www.ft.com/content/73dfb5ae-f532-11e7-8715-e94187b3017e

Telefónica. 2018. Executive team, January 2018. Available at: https://www.telefonica.com/en/web/about_telefonica/organisation/executive-team (last accessed 10 May 2018).

Telefónica Deutschland. 2018. Management board of Telefónica Deutschland Holding AG. Available at: https://www.telefonica.de/company/management.html (last accessed 10 May 2018).

The Official Board. 2018. Telefónica. Available at: http://www.theofficialboard.com/org-chart/telefonica (last accessed 10 May 2018).

Thompson, J.D. 1967. *Organizations in action*. McGraw Hill: New York.

Thompson, P., and McHugh, D. 2009. *Work organisations: A critical approach*. Palgrave Macmillan: Basingstoke.

Treanor, J. 2014. Lloyds Banking Group to axe 9,000 jobs and 200 branches. *The Guardian*, 28 October.

Vara, V. 2015. The push against performance reviews. *New Yorker*, 24 July.

Watson, T.J. 2002. *Organising and managing work: Organisational, managerial, and strategic behaviour in theory and practice*. Financial Times/Prentice Hall: Harlow.

Weber, M. 1958. *The Protestant ethic and the spirit of capitalism*. Scribner: New York.

Weber, M. 1968. *Economy and society: An outline of interpretive sociology*. Bedminster Press: New York.

Woodward, J. 1958. *Management and technology*. HMSO: London.

Zaveri, M. 2018. Anne Frank's family was thwarted by U.S. immigration rules, research shows. *New York Times*, 6 July. Available at: https://www.nytimes.com/2018/07/06/us/anne-frank-family-escape-usa.html

Zuboff, S. 1985. Automate/informate: The two faces of intelligent technology. *Organizational Dynamics* 14 (2): 5–18.

Zuboff, S. 1988. *In the age of the smart machine: The future of work and power*. Heinemann Professional: Oxford.

CHAPTER 3

Rational work design
The simplification and automation of work

Chapter overview and learning outcomes

By the end of this chapter you should be able to:

- describe the principles behind Taylorist and Fordist rational work design

- explain how Taylorism and Fordism contributed to control over the workforce and the creation of more efficient forms of working

- analyse the effects that Taylorism and Fordism are said to have upon workers

by reducing them to 'cogs in a machine', including the critiques by Marx and Braverman

- explain the legacy of Taylorism and the developments of Fordism and their prevalence in working methods today, such that they have been described as 'the most enduring social change of the 20th century' (Donkin, 2001: 159)

Key theorists	
Frederick Winslow Taylor	An industrialist and one of the prominent pioneers of efficient, rational work design, Taylor developed the system of 'scientific management'
Henry Ford	An industrialist and pioneer of rational management techniques, Ford created systems of mass automobile production with his innovation of the moving assembly line
Lillian and Frank Gilbreth	Contemporaries and associates of Taylor, known particularly for developing the time and motion study and ergonomic work design
Karl Marx	A political philosopher who commented on the inequalities of power between capital and workers and the negative, alienating effects of capitalist work upon workers
Harry Braverman	From a Marxist perspective, developed the deskilling thesis that criticized the loss of craft skills under rational production methods

CHAPTER 3

Introduction

🔍 Running case: the bottom line

Simon Chance is worried. Junction Hotel is not breaking even, and a budget hotel is opening nearby. He is presented with a report by his investors, which makes for grim reading:

- having weathered a recession, the hotel industry is suffering—corporate customers are reducing spend on hotels;
- prices need to come down in order for Junction Hotel to remain competitive and stay in business—*to afford that price reduction, Junction Hotel needs to reduce its costs*;
- budget hotels are aggressively cutting costs, for example by removing free toiletries.

Chance has a dilemma. Junction is a luxury hotel—if they cut corners, then customers will complain and the hotel will lose its reputation. At the same time, low-cost competitors are taking their business.

Chance calls in business manager Phil Weaver, who has overseen many efficiency drives in his career. Weaver looks over the accounts and declares: 'You know, your biggest cost isn't

→

→

shampoo or wallpaper or anything like that—it's your wage bill. That's the bottom line—it's losing you money and making you uncompetitive. *There's a lot of waste and inefficiency.*

'There are many opportunities to reduce your wage bill and still get the job done. I've stayed here before and seen your cleaners stood around gossiping. Tell you what: let me have a closer look at what they do—I bet I can make them much more productive and bring down the wage bill.'

Chance replies apprehensively: 'I don't know ... they do a good job—I wouldn't want to rock the boat. I don't think they would like you interfering in what they do.'

'The problem is you haven't got a clue what they do!' retorts Weaver. 'If you want this hotel to survive then you need to take *control*. Your cleaners are taking you to the cleaners! Let me try to get them to work for their money.'

Most of you have ordered goods from online stores and waited for the items to arrive. But have you ever thought about what happens behind the scenes between you clicking the button to send a payment and the goods arriving at your front door? Behind most online operations are massive warehouses underpinned by a logistics operation which allows individual orders to be picked out and delivered, often on the next working day. For example, the Amazon warehouse in Swansea, Wales, is the size of eleven football pitches, and on its busiest days at Christmas can despatch up to 450,000 items (Cadwalladr, 2013).

Within the online distribution industry there are ongoing attempts to decrease the delivery times of goods. It is a process which strives for increasing levels of *efficiency*, but at the same time, given that there are so many items in a warehouse, workers need to be *controlled* so that they pick out precisely the correct items for each of the thousands of individual orders that they send out.

While online retailing and distribution is a feature of our modern economy and, as we will see in Chapter 4, uses cyber-physical systems typical of the Fourth Industrial Revolution, the techniques used to ensure efficiency and control over large-scale organizations can be traced back to the Second Industrial Revolution and the beginnings of the factory system. In particular, there was a desire to cut costs by making workers work more efficiently for the wages that they were paid. In this chapter, we examine how rational work design is applied to the labour process (the way in which work is designed and controlled) in order to make workers more cost-effective. Through the design of work itself, workers become more efficient and productive, doing more for the wages they are paid.

Industrialists such as Frederick Taylor and Henry Ford are most closely associated with rational work design (the terms Taylorism and Fordism being used, respectively, to describe their scientific management and assembly line innovations); however, they share the key features of rational work design with many other innovators of their time, which we summarize as:

- work is seen as a means of achieving a clearly defined goal;

- work is designed to achieve this goal in the optimum, most efficient possible manner, in terms of both time and cost;

- work is designed scientifically, using measurement and calculation, as if designing a machine;

- work is broken down into simple, repetitive tasks which take little or no skill to perform—a division of labour;

- waste is designed out of the work process.

We will see how rational work design makes workers more efficient, but also how this comes at a cost. Workers are subject to increased managerial control and given monotonous, simple work, leaving their skills surplus to requirements. The chapter will look at critiques of rational work design from Karl Marx and Harry Braverman, examining the considerable resistance encountered when implementing such techniques.

Furthermore, we will see how Taylorism and Fordism have been adapted to be relevant to the contemporary environment, which is more uncertain and requires more flexibility than the days of the early factory systems (as discussed in Chapter 2). Post-Fordism and neo-Fordism allow organizations to be more flexible, but we will see that neo-Fordism in particular still retains a focus on efficiency and control of the workplace.

We will return to our contemporary example of online retailing later in the chapter. We begin at the start of the Second Industrial Revolution.

The capitalist wage–labour relationship: cost and control

🔍 Running case: Amy Turtle

Amy Turtle is in her mid-50s and has always worked as a cleaner. She has been with Junction Hotel for ten years, and before was self-employed for twenty years. She had enjoyed the independence of working for herself, but joined the hotel at a time when her client list was dwindling, opting for a regular salary rather than the risk and hassle of managing her own business.

Her relationship with Linda Wilkinson is good—they are both old-timers at the hotel. With Wilkinson being busy enough with other tasks, she happily leaves the cleaning side to run itself. It's as if Turtle is still managing herself and, indeed, she resents any attempt by management to interfere in her cleaning work.

During her time at Junction Hotel, Turtle has developed a reputation as being a knowledgeable cleaner and a formidable character. She brings experience and knowledge into the workplace. Sometimes, she even brings in her own cleaning products to try out—she likes nothing more than the challenge of a new or mysterious stain to tackle.

Turtle socializes with the older cleaners and is a respected presence with the younger ones. In the reorganization she is promoted to Head Cleaner. This very much reflects the role she held informally for many years as part supervisor—instilling fear in the younger cleaners who might stray—and part champion, sticking up for her 'gang' when necessary and taking their concerns to the management.

We all like our money to stretch as far as possible, especially when on a tight budget. Think about how you minimize your own personal **costs**—shopping around, using comparison websites, and taking advantage of 'happy hours' and 'two-for-one'-type offers which allow us to get more for our money.

Saving money is also a concern in organizations. The ongoing economic difficulties that high-street firms have faced show that organizations always need to think about costs. Reduced costs can mean lower prices, giving a competitive advantage, or increased profits, leading to increased shareholder dividends.

💡 Theory in context: Wedgwood and costs

Cost control is not just a recent issue. In the eighteenth century, the pottery industrialist Josiah Wedgwood identified costs as a major area of measurement and control in setting market prices for his goods. Beforehand, pricing had been a result of educated guesswork, leading to Wedgwood making a loss. While Wedgwood was a one-off pioneer in his own day, costs are now a major area of control for companies and organizations (McKendrick, 1970; Hoskin and Macve, 1986: 124; Morgan, 1990: 103–6).

For most organizations, the largest cost is labour—money spent on wages (Simpson, 1999: 52)—and it follows that just as we like to get the most out of our money, so organizations are interested in getting as much work as possible out of their employees for the wages that they pay. However, getting this optimum performance may not be so easy: indeed, workers may be entitled to be treated in a way that does not mean they are constantly working at the optimum level in return for their wages. In this section we introduce the capitalist working relationship as a means of understanding the relationship between the cost of wages and control over the labour process.

The capitalist wage–labour relationship

Rational work design needs to be understood in the context of changes that the early factory system brought about in the early 1900s. Prior to the Second Industrial Revolution, manufacturing work was often based around the household—the backyard workshop or furnace was commonplace (see Thompson and McHugh, 2009: 20). The work had many features which may seem unusual today other than for people who are self-employed:

- workers owned their own means of production—tools, equipment, etc. to manufacture goods;

- workers were independent and autonomous, i.e. they were their own boss—they decided their own working time, the amount they would sell goods for, the amount they would take as a wage or reinvest in the business, etc.

While many workers today might crave such independence, it comes with a degree of risk. The individual worker is exposed if, say, equipment breaks down and needs expensive repairs, or if orders drop suddenly (see Chapter 4 for how this risk has returned for workers in the gig economy, such as cycle couriers having to provide and maintain their own bikes). Furthermore, such production is inefficient—it doesn't take advantage of economies of scale, the cost reduction that comes from manufacturing in large amounts.

Visit the online resources and take a look at the extension material for Chapter 3 for a description of how the textile industry in Nottingham, UK, developed from home-based working into industrial, factory-based production.

The factory system took advantage of economies of scale. Rather than having individual workers, each investing in their own small-scale equipment, a factory brought together a group of workers in one space, operating large-scale equipment (see Simpson, 1999: 48). The initial spending on equipment might be more expensive, but it works out as less per worker than each of them buying their own equipment individually.

The factory system brought about a new working relationship.

- Workers no longer owned the means of production. Factories required massive capital outlay, which only wealthy individuals or groups of shareholders could afford. It was now the capitalists who provided the initial outlay and who owned the means of production.

- Capitalists paid a wage to workers who would work in their factory. Workers lost their previous independence and autonomy—their working hours would be dictated and their tasks set, and they would have no control over the price of goods or investment decisions, etc. Their role was simply to turn up and do a day's work.

The capitalist wage–labour relationship is an exchange between capitalists, who pay wages, and labour, who work in return for those wages (Figure 3.1). The capitalist who owns and invests capital in a company pays a wage to workers. In return for this wage, workers supply their labour.

Figure 3.1 The capitalist wage–labour relationship.

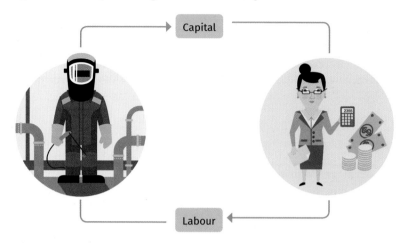

The capitalist wage–labour relationship creates a need for management. Workers are told what to do, when to arrive, when to leave work, etc. This all needs to be implemented by management. But where would management appear in Figure 3.1? On one hand, management are agents of capital, doing their bidding in directing workers. On the other hand, managers are not owners: they too are providing work in return for a wage.

Tensions in the capitalist wage–labour relationship

This relationship between capital and labour might seem like a simple exchange, but a fundamental tension lies at its heart: capital and labour want different things and have different priorities.

Capital wants to get the most work done for the wages they pay, i.e. maximum efficiency. This means employees working to their maximum possible output. However, as we saw in Chapter 2, what might be rational from one perspective may not be from another. Rather than working to the optimum, workers can reasonably expect regular breaks, holidays, paid sick leave, etc. All of these conflict with the capitalist's desire to maximize effort in return for the wage (Figure 3.2).

As we will see, from a Marxist perspective the capitalist wage–labour relationship becomes a battle for control between two conflicting sets of interests, which can result in conflict and resistance.

Figure 3.2 Conflict in the capitalist wage–labour relationship.

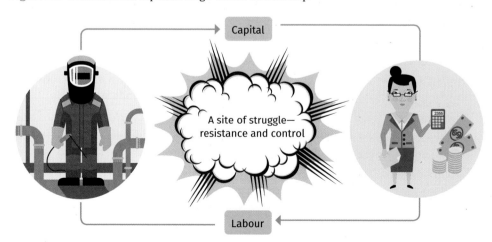

Industrial action, such as strikes, is often a result of disagreements over aspects of the capitalist working relationship, such as pay, working conditions, etc.

In the following sections we see how rational work design was used by Taylor, Ford, and their contemporaries not just as a means of gaining efficiency, which minimizes the costs for less input of time and money for the wages paid, but also as a means of asserting control over the wage–labour relationship. The Marxist critique, examined later in the chapter, recognizes how conflict might be an inevitable outcome of such control given the tensions within the relationship.

? Review questions

Describe	What are the main features of the capitalist wage–labour relationship?
Explain	Why was the factory 'a revolutionary organizational form' (Simpson, 1999: 48)?
Analyse	Why might workers not want the same things as capitalists in the wage–labour relationship?
Apply	How can the employment of Amy Turtle (a) before and (b) after she joined Junction Hotel be explained in terms of the capitalist wage–labour relationship? Do you think that the hotel is getting the most from her for the wages that they pay her?

Frederick W. Taylor: efficiency and control

🔍 Running case: initial observations

Phil Weaver has made his initial notes on his observations of the cleaning process, which he shows to Linda Wilkinson.

> *Amazing—no method or routine. Cleaners in pairs, given list of rooms then left to get on with it—all approach the task in different ways and have had different training. Lots of gossiping—with each other and with guests. Turtle might tell the younger ones off but she covers up for them in front of management—she looks after her own first. They deliberately speed up the morning shift to get an extra 30 mins gossiping time over lunch. If they can work that quickly they should be doing more. Problem is, there's no control over them: they are a law unto themselves.*

Wilkinson gives him a knowing smile and replies, 'Phil, don't you think I realize that? Thing is—they're happy, the job gets done, and I get an easy life'. Weaver, however, is getting more and more frustrated: 'That's 30 minutes when they could be doing something else—30 minutes you are paying them for.' 'Look,' says Wilkinson more seriously, 'I learned my lesson a few years back. I did ask Amy whether they would be able to squeeze a few more rooms in before lunch but she blinded me with science—told me how long different processes would take. She outlined different cleaning methods, all built up from her years of experience, and

→

talked about the dangers from different bacteria if she didn't clean thoroughly. In the end, I gave up.'

'This is nonsense!' yells Weaver. 'You have no control over them. If anything, they control you and, as a result, you are getting far less out of them than is possible for the wages you pay.'

'Let me have a look at this more closely,' says Wilkinson.

Taylor's rational work design transformed how organizations operated, and, as we will see in Chapter 4, they still have a major impact on how we live and work today in organizations such as Amazon and McDonald's. Taylor's book *The principles of scientific management* (1911), based on theories Taylor developed in the early 1900s whilst working in the Philadelphia steel industry, identified a set of techniques that came to be known simply as 'Taylorism'.

As suggested by the term scientific management, there was a *science* of management and the organization was to be managed as efficiently as possible, as if it were a machine. An industrial engineer by training, Taylor approached management problems just like mechanical and engineering problems. In the words of his biographer, Taylor viewed the world through the eyes of both an economist and an engineer (Copley, 1923a: xviii).

Taylorism is often seen as being simply about efficiency, minimizing waste, and increasing output. However, such attempts at efficiency are directed within the capitalist wage–labour relationship at people rather than machines. And, while Taylor wanted to design organizations like machines, people do not necessarily behave in the same precisely controllable manner.

💡 **Theory in context:** Taylor's obsessions

Bahnisch (2000) notes that a number of commentators have written about the 'obsessional' and 'neurotic' nature of Taylor's personality and his desire for control. His meticulous attention to detail crossed over into aspects of his private life, such as positions for sleeping and steps to be taken when dancing. His hobby of golf was also addressed with a similar attention to detail, he devoted time to designing golf clubs and even analysing different types of grass which would provide the optimum performance on the putting green (Copley, 1923b). It is this obsession and attention to detail that he took into his workplace experiments, and which feeds into many rational management techniques that exist today.

Taylor's 'problems' of control over labour

When Taylor first began working in factories, he viewed the approach to work as rather amateurish, governed by traditions and habits—all of which were controlled by the workers. The management, Taylor thought, had little control over what was happening and did little to influence the work process, in particular this got in the way of the efficiency that Taylor craved.

 Visit the online resources and take a look at the extension material for Chapter 3 for more information on early factory systems.

Non-standard and unpredictable labour

In the Philadelphia steel industry, where Taylor worked, there was a mix of workers within his factory. They came from different craft traditions, each with their own ways of performing jobs; and they had a variety of cultural backgrounds, languages, and, indeed, attitudes to work (Jaffee, 2001:

51; Thompson and McHugh, 2009: 29). Workers could not be seen as standard units that would behave and be controlled in the same way as components in a machine.

Craft knowledge and power

Craft knowledge is where workers have specialist expertise in the work that they do, which often comes from a long period of training. This was a problem for Taylor, because it meant that the workers held power over him as a manager. He did not know the work as intimately as his workers and, thus, when he asked a question about how long a process would take or how much it would cost, he relied to a large extent on the workers being truthful about their expert knowledge.

Workers would use their craft knowledge to create a rule of thumb (Taylor, 1911: 16)—the estimate, based on the workers' knowledge, that the workers would give for the time a job would take. This was the workers controlling the work process—they could blind management with science, take longer to do tasks, and even demand higher wages because their skills were not easily replaceable.

 Have you ever had to take your phone or car to be repaired? When you are given a quote for the amount that the repairs will cost and the time that it will take, do you feel you are in a position to argue back and negotiate? If not, why not?

Soldiering

Taylor believed that workers were naturally lazy, with no motivation to work other than the wages: 'this man plans to do as little as he safely can … to do not more than one-third to one-half of a proper day's work' (Taylor, 1911: 13). Because of this Taylor thought people engaged in soldiering, creating time for themselves during the working day and not working as efficiently as possible. This soldiering became worse as tightly-knit gangs of workers put pressure on co-workers to 'underperform'. Using their expert knowledge and the 'rule of thumb', they could cover for each other, overestimating to management the time that it would take to complete a job and thus improving their own conditions of work by making more time available, leaving room for breaks, and thus not working to the optimum.

From Taylor's perspective, the drive to control workers for greater efficiency and his frustration with workers' own control over the work process was understandable. However, it is also understandable why workers wanted to maintain and exert that control—they maintained autonomy over the pace and nature of their work, earned extra time in the form of breaks, and generally helped to maintain some balance in their side of the capitalist working relationship. Taylor's innovations in scientific management tipped this balance more firmly in favour of management.

Scientific management: finding the 'one best way'

Q Running case: the one best way

Weaver observes the cleaners, making notes with a clipboard, timing workers with a stopwatch, and measuring the distances they walk from room to room. He even sets up a video camera to record cleaners as they go around a room. When he plays it back, he can make further detailed measurements, analysing the pictures with specialist computer software.

He starts practising different movements with the cleaners, demonstrating a series of basic moves to perform every time they clean a toilet, constantly measuring and refining the moves to make them more and more efficient and reduce the cleaning time.

→

→

Similar routines are devised for such tasks as making beds, replacing towels, and cleaning all parts of the room. In each case, the task is broken down into a set of pre-defined movements which Weaver then refines to make more efficient. In all cases, wasted movements are to be eliminated—including stopping and gossiping mid-way through a shift. Everything has its right place in the room—the TV remote, the kettle, sachets of tea and coffee, writing paper, etc., with the aim of standardizing the process and removing any variability in the job.

Weaver also suggests that equipment and fittings could be designed to make the process even more efficient. Items would be laid out on the trolley in the order in which they would be placed in the room, for example toiletries first, and tea and coffee second. Trolleys should be big enough to accommodate all the linen and equipment needed so as to avoid wasteful trips down to the laundry or the store cupboard to reload.

Eventually, Weaver presents the 'one best way' to clean a room, proudly written down in a training manual given to all cleaners. Whereas a room previously took an average of 30 minutes to clean, Weaver sets a target of 15 minutes per room.

Taylor firmly believed there was one best way to perform any job. Using the four principles of scientific management (Taylor, 1911) he used scientific measurement to discover the most efficient way of doing a job. In doing so he put power in the hands of management by letting managers understand exactly what work people did to make a product and creating the standard method for workers to then perform that task.

Principle 1: Division of labour and scientific design of work

Scientific management begins by breaking a job down into a series of simple repetitive tasks—a division of labour. A worker no longer manufactures a product from start to finish, for example making a whole wheel. Instead, the worker is one of many who each perform one repetitive and simple task in a chain, for example inserting a spoke in a wheel.

 Have you ever assembled a piece of flat-pack furniture? Even though you may have no previous experience or skill in furniture-making, the way in which the job is broken down into small, manageable tasks with a set of basic instructions means that you are able to assemble your new bookcase. Now imagine that you and a group of friends had 100 flat-pack bookcases to assemble. What would be the most efficient way to do this? Would you each sit and make bookcases individually from start to finish, or would you use a form of division of labour, where each of you specializes in just one task, performing that one task on each of the bookcases?

Taylor was not the first nor only person to use the division of labour, but the degree to which he then scientifically analysed the work process marks him out.

 Visit the online resources and take a look at the extension material for Chapter 3 for a description of the economist Adam Smith's earlier observations of the division of labour.

Taylor was interested in designing work that eliminated waste movements and created the most efficient way to perform a task. This might be through instructing workers on what moves to make, or designing machinery and the physical layout of the factory to minimize waste movement. Work was designed like a machine, with workers managed as if they were a part of that machine, using precise, scientific measurement and calculation.

Taylor was a pioneer of the time and motion study, a technique still used in modern-day organizations. This involved closely observing and measuring every movement made by a worker using a stopwatch and measuring tape, and redesigning how the work was performed to maximize efficiency.

The most famous example of this given by Taylor (1911: 43ff) was his story of a Dutch labourer, Schmidt, in *The principles of scientific management*. He speaks (in mostly disparaging terms) of how he observed this labourer's shovelling pig-iron—a very basic task—and redesigned the movements to be performed at the optimum efficiency. At the Bethlehem Steel Works, where these observations took place, the number of pig-iron handlers required for the same task was reduced from 600 to 140 (ibid.: 71)—a massive reduction in labour costs. In return for this punishing and monotonous work, Taylor increased pay, but by a level more than offset by the efficiency gains.

The Gilbreths: time and motion study

Schmidt's work was very basic, unskilled labouring; however, Taylor argued that the same principles of scientific management could be applied to any task. Taylor approvingly cites the work of his contemporaries Lillian and Frank Gilbreth, who studied the work of bricklayers. They looked not just at the motion of bricklaying, but also the position of the bricks and tools next to the bricklayer, and proposed changes so as to further decrease waste motion. They redesigned the process of laying one brick from an initial 18 individual moves down to just 5, with a resulting efficiency gain from 120 bricks laid per hour to 350 (Taylor, 1911: 81).

The Gilbreths were, arguably, the top experts at time and motion study, extending it into a number of different areas—not just factory work but also retail work and office work, such as typing. In their quest for measurement and efficiency, and using a grid and stopwatch, they filmed people performing their work and then analysed and redesigned their movements to enable them to perform their tasks more efficiently (Price, 1992: 61). They even applied these principles in their own family household, as recounted by their children in the reminiscence *Cheaper by the dozen* (Gilbreth and Carey, 1949).

After the death of Frank, Lillian performed similar work in department stores, introducing time and motion studies to work that requires a greater variety of movement than a simple, repetitive task (Graham, 2000).

The time and motion study will be familiar to many workers today, sometimes with such names as 'Organization and methods'. The same ideas apply—work is observed, measured, and timed with the aim of eliminating waste movements. Either the job itself is redesigned, or the equipment and layout are redesigned so as to eliminate such movement. The redesign can be quite practical: for example, a bank worker who has to constantly walk to a safe at the back of the office could have the safe moved closer to save time and effort (and thus increase their efficiency). A whole science of ergonomics designs the working environment to make it as efficient and convenient as possible while providing the best fit to the movements of the human body.

Visit the online resources and take a look at the extension material for Chapter 3 for more background material about the Gilbreths, including archive videos of the Gilbreths and examples of how the Gilbreths' work has been used in highly skilled jobs where precision is important, such as surgery, and in improving performance at the most highly skilled levels in sport.

Principle 2: Scientific selection of employees

Taylor's design of work went beyond work and equipment to fitting people themselves to different jobs. With work designed like a machine, certain people made better 'components' for different types of work. It is obvious from Taylor's own work that Schmidt, a hefty individual, was better suited for the work he did than others might be. For Taylor, a scientific selection, defining the precise characteristics of the ideal candidate for a job and training individuals for particular jobs, was just as important as the work design itself.

While the scientific selection of workers might make workers seem like components in a machine, the Gilbreths provided a more positive interpretation of this principle. They used their scientific analysis of tasks to highlight those which could be performed by people with different physical impairments and disabilities. Because of the Gilbreth's work, people with disabilities, including injured veterans from World War I, were able to participate in paid work where previously this had not been considered possible (Gotcher, 1992).

Principle 3: Workers work, managers manage

While there was a *horizontal* division of labour on the shop floor (i.e. a division of work tasks) there was also a *vertical* division of labour between management and workers (see Figure 3.3). This builds on the bureaucratic organization structure discussed in Chapter 2 and shows where knowledge of the production process resides within that structure.

Management do all the planning—the work measurement, work design, and so on—and the workers then do simply as they are told. There is a separation between the mental work—the thinking—and the physical work on the shop floor: a separation of planning and doing, where tasks are designed by management, with workers having no input other than to perform those tasks. Taylorism began to introduce levels of management based around the work design—functional foremanship meant that supervisors were assigned to specific tasks, rather than the more informal and ad hoc arrangements under the internal contracting system.

Figure 3.3 The horizontal and vertical division of labour.

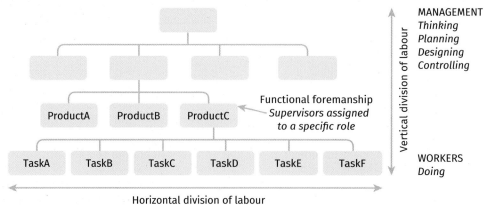

Principle 4: Workers and managers cooperate

A final aspect of scientific management, as described by Taylor, is that it requires the cooperation of workers and management. However, as we see in the next section, such cooperation is more a relationship of control and, furthermore, one where Taylor encountered resistance rather than cooperation.

? Review questions

Describe	What are the four principles of scientific management?
Explain	How do time and motion studies increase efficiency?
Analyse	What is meant by a 'separation of planning and doing?' What does this imply for the roles of managers and workers?
Apply	Think of an organization that you know. Are there any areas where scientific management principles are applied or are there any areas where scientific management principles might improve efficiency?

Control through Taylorism

It was not just efficiency that was increased by scientific management. The rational work design that Taylor pioneered also gave a solution to the problems of control over labour that he had earlier encountered.

1. *Standardization.* By designing the precise nature of work, down to basic movements, Taylor was able to increase uniformity and predictability. Work was standardized, minimizing the variable nature of human labour that Taylor feared. It no longer mattered that people came from different craft traditions; with a tightly-defined and prescribed task, much of this variability in the labour force could be overcome.

2. *Individualization.* Rather than work being organized in gangs, workers were individualized. They had one task to perform, having been selected and trained for that task. Again, this regained control for Taylor as he was able to bypass the soldiering and control from labour gangs.

3. *Surveillance.* Individualization brought about a further type of control through surveillance. If a worker is assigned to one small element of the work process and that element is defective or not being produced to speed, the culprit is easy to single out (see the section on 'Panopticism, surveillance, and control' in Chapter 4).

4. *Knowledge.* The power that workers had from their craft knowledge was made redundant. Atomizing the work process means that workers only have knowledge of their one small task. The separation of planning and doing means that knowledge of the overall process resides with the management who plan the work process. The control that workers had over the pacing and other aspects of their work is now gone and is held by management.

5. *Skill.* As with knowledge, the skill required to perform a job is diminished greatly by scientific management. When managers relied on craft skills, workers were valuable and often irreplaceable. With skill replaced by a simple, repetitive task, workers become more expendable—they can be replaced easily by other unskilled labour. Again, this gives greater bargaining power to management.

Resisting Taylorism

Dear Linda,

With great regret, I offer my resignation from my job at Junction Hotel.

I used to have great pride in my work. I felt part of a family and felt valued, both for my knowledge and for my experience.

Now I feel completely demoralized, and would rather take early retirement than continue to work here.

I feel so sorry for the rest of the gang—they are not happy. They have no control over what they do. Everything is dictated to us, there's no room to breathe. And as for all of that checking up—it feels like we're in the army on parade. I used to love this job—now every task is simply given to us step by step.

Best wishes
Amy

As we will see in Chapter 4, there are few workplaces today that do not employ Taylorist techniques to some extent. However, it was not an instant success, and there was a lot of initial resistance to Taylorism from workers, factory owners, and even governments and his own contemporaries. The adoption of Taylorism was thus piecemeal rather than rapid and comprehensive (Clegg et al., 2005: 21).

Phil Weaver is summoned to Simon Chance's office, where Chance stands with Linda Wilkinson. Chance is enraged: 'What have you started here? We've got our best cleaner resigning, the rest of them are unhappy. We all used to get on so well. Now it feels like civil war.'

'But I've done what you asked,' replies Weaver. 'They are working more efficiently and with such simplified jobs they are easy to control'.

Wilkinson feels uncomfortable—she can see much more trouble ahead.

The monotonous nature of the work, along with a desire to defend their craft traditions, meant that workers were unhappy with Taylorism. Often, as we will also see with Fordism, this led to industrial unrest, such as strikes. For many factory owners, the hassle caused by this unrest simply wasn't worth the efficiency gains; indeed Taylor was eventually sacked from his position at Midvale for this reason. In the UK, factory owners also preferred to maintain stability and avoid upheaval, rather than going for wholesale change and adopting Taylor's more 'modern' techniques (Whitston, 1997: 2). The dissatisfaction with Taylorism went as far as governmental levels. In 1912, the US congress launched an inquiry following a strike at the Watertown Arsenal, a munitions factory where Taylorism was being used (see Kanigel, 1997: 459–84). The report from the inquiry declared Taylorism a failure, with time and motion studies being banned in all US defence plants.

Even Taylor's contemporaries, the Gilbreths, turned against his work. While they still advocated a scientific analysis of work, they did so with the aim of making work movements easier and more straightforward to perform and reducing fatigue amongst workers, and they condemned Taylor for simply using the stopwatch as a means of turning workers into machines to be as efficient as possible (Lawley and Caven, 2019). They became part of a revisionist, social form of Taylorism which aimed to humanize the work rather than treating people simply as components in a machine.

Taylor spent the rest of his working life as a consultant, taking his scientific management ideas into other workplaces and industries.

The rise of Taylorism

🔍 Running case: all hands on deck

Most of the cleaners have walked out in support of Amy Turtle, leaving Simon Chance and Linda Wilkinson with rooms that need cleaning and no cleaners to do the work. 'You've got a lot to answer for, Weaver,' snarls Linda Wilkinson.

'Right,' says Weaver. 'You two get a couple more of the management team, roll your sleeves up and we'll show the cleaners a thing or two.'

Despite not being an experienced cleaner, Weaver is able to demonstrate the routines from the cleaning manual. 'All of the knowledge of cleaning is in here,' he states, 'no more relying on Amy and her experience.'

They quickly pick up the simple tasks and set to work cleaning the rooms and, to their surprise, they learn the tasks fairly easily, getting the job done in not much more time than the usual cleaning team.

A potential crisis is averted. Chance knows that the management can't do this every day—he needs to patch things up with the cleaners—but, at the same time, he sees the value in Weaver's techniques—anyone can now do this work.

From such an initial slow take-up, with outright resistance and controversy, the techniques of Taylorism gained ground in the USA so as to become 'conventional wisdom' (Whitston, 1997: 2) by the end of World War I.

Wartime was when the benefits of Taylorism could be demonstrated. As the (in those days male) factory workers were away fighting, women were the people who replaced them in factories which produced guns, tanks, and other machinery needed for the war effort. They were unskilled but, given the deskilled nature of Taylorist work, were able to be productive with little training. Taylorism could now claim to have been used for patriotic purposes (Kanigel, 1997: 487). Despite the considerable criticism faced by Taylorism, Grey (2005: 41) points out that it also created the tanks which defeated Nazi Germany.

Different countries embraced Taylorism in different ways. Often it had to blend in with their own national culture. Thus, within the USA, the UK, France, Germany, and even Russia and Japan, Taylorist techniques came to dominate the factory floor, albeit taking different routes and time spans to be implemented (Copley, 1923a: xx–xxii; Nelson, 1992: 16ff).

Visit the online resources and take a look at the extension material for Chapter 3 for more detail on the effects of national cultures on Taylorism, and how Taylorism was adopted in different countries.

❓ Review questions

Describe	How did Taylorism allow management to exert control over workers?
Explain	Why was Taylorism not taken up instantly by all organizations?
Analyse	If Taylorism helps managers to increase efficiency and control, why may management be reluctant to implement Taylorist techniques?
Apply	Do you think Taylorist techniques are beneficial to the cleaning department at Junction Hotel, or do they cause more disruption than good?

Henry Ford and the assembly line

🔍 Running case: the laundry factory

Weaver looks for further areas of the cleaning work process that he can redesign, including automating the laundry room, where towels and bed linen are laundered daily. However, he realizes that operations at Junction Hotel are too small-scale to justify such an outlay on equipment. He is beginning to think that he has done all that he can to make the cleaning side of the hotel as cost-effective as possible, when an email from an old golfing partner arrives.

To:	phil_weaver@junctionhotel.com
From:	bob.smith@laundromation.co.uk
Subject:	Of interest???

Phil—long time, no speak. I hear you are in the hotel business—my new venture might interest you, especially as far as your laundry costs go. How about a round of golf next week and then I'll show you around?

Bob

Weaver visits his friend's business, Laundromation, which is effectively a factory for processing laundry on a large scale. Clients, such as local hotels, leisure centres, and restaurants, have their dirty linen picked up by Laundromation and, in return, a fresh batch of clean linen is delivered. The task is *outsourced* to Laundromation.

Weaver looks around the factory in admiration. At one end, vans dump dirty laundry into a chute where it goes on to a conveyor belt. Workers place the laundry into giant washing machines and then into driers. As dry, clean laundry emerges from the driers, workers remove and sort it—there is an individual conveyor for each type and size of laundry, along which workers stand and fold each item as it passes. Workers are trained, in a Taylorist fashion, how to fold an item in the speediest fashion possible and they become expert at this. A worker can spend the entire day standing in one position folding the same types of towel.

→

→

At the end of each conveyor belt the products are stacked so that van drivers can pick up individual orders easily, load them on to a trolley, and pack them into the van for delivery.

'By creating a laundry factory on this scale I can do the job a lot more efficiently,' declares Smith. 'Think what you spend on wages, laundry equipment, etc., and all the hassle of supervising your cleaners. On this scale I can do the job far more cheaply per towel than you could ever do in-house'.

From a manager's perspective Taylorism made great gains, increasing efficiency and shifting control firmly in favour of management. These changes in control and efficiency were taken even further by Henry Ford's development of the moving **assembly line**, an automated conveyor belt that moves a product in front of workers who perform a small, repetitive task on each product that passes before them.

While there is no evidence that Ford and Taylor ever met, these two industrialists were both working in the USA in the early part of the twentieth century and were aware of each others' work. Ford faced the same issue of variability in the workforce as Taylor; indeed, much of Ford's workforce was made up of immigrant labour from Europe, many of whom did not speak English but could be trained easily to perform very basic and standardized work (Beynon, 1984: 36).

While there are similarities between Ford's and Taylor's work, in particular splitting the work process into its component parts, Ford's development of Taylorism was to place these tasks in the order they needed to be completed, creating the *moving* assembly line for his Highland Park car plant in Detroit.

Visit the online resources and take a look at the web links for Chapter 3 for free downloadable original texts from Ford, Taylor, and the Gilbreths.

79

 Theory in context: development of the assembly line

Ford's inspiration for the moving assembly line came from butchery, after an aide had witnessed the way in which carcasses were dismembered in sequence in an abattoir. With the carcass hanging from a pulley, it was moved along a line of various butchers who each took their own particular cut of meat in turn—not so much an assembly line as a disassembly line.

Ford realized that this allowed each butcher to become specialized in one particular task, with the pulley making the process quicker and more efficient. Ford wondered whether the process could be reversed and applied to making products. Placing his workers in two lines in the order of which component they added to the car, Ford had a chassis mounted on a trolley which was wheeled slowly in front of the workers who, in turn, did their small part in putting the car together—the prototype for the automated moving assembly line (Donkin, 2001: 147–8).

Ford broke tasks down into small components, to an even greater extent than Taylor. For instance, even the job of inserting a nut and bolt could be broken down (one man inserts a bolt, one man places a nut on to the bolt, and one man tightens the bolt). Components were designed so as to facilitate easy and speedy assembly in this manner.

A modern assembly line system.
Source: Andrei Kholmov/Shutterstock.com

The moving aspect of the assembly line increased efficiency. Workers did not have to move from the spot to perform their tasks—the work simply passed by in front of them. The assembly line system is also sometimes termed a 'flow-line' system. Work flows along the line and at each point the worker performs a highly specialized task, often with machinery specially designed for that one specific task (e.g. tightening a nut on a wheel) (Figure 3.4).

 Think back to the earlier flat-pack example. How could you organize mass production of such furniture using assembly-line techniques? How much more efficient would this make the process?

The Fordist assembly line increased production efficiency of the Model T Ford automobile. The first Model T cars—made by stationary assembly in 1909—were produced at a rate of approximately 14,000 a year at a cost of $950 per car. By 1916, with the move to a fully automated assembly line, over half a million cars were being made per year, with cost being reduced to $360 per car (Donkin, 2001: 148).

Ford's system worked because his main product, the Model T car, was highly standardized. Ford is famously reported to have said of the Model T: 'Any customer can have a car painted any colour that he wants so long as it is black' (Ford and Crowther, 1922: 71). The standardized nature of the product is vital to the efficiency gains made by the assembly line—too many variations and the line

Figure 3.4 Efficiency on the assembly line.

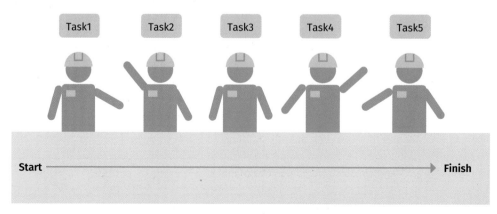

has to be stopped and started again, e.g. to set up a different colour of paint. The fewer variations there are in the product, the more costs are kept down.

The Model T Ford.
Source: David Chapman/imageBROKER/age fotostock

Fordism and mass production

The Fordist system can only operate under large economies of scale, known as mass production. Think of the costs involved in setting up the car factory and all of its specialized equipment—the assembly line is a large-scale, capital-intensive undertaking. Such an initial capital outlay requires massive costs per unit if only a few cars are produced. This is a problem that the electric car company Tesla is encountering today as it tries to increase production of its cars within the confines of existing equipment—it is a big expense and risk to invest in the equipment needed to increase to a mass production scale (Banker, 2018).

Mass production also needs people to buy the cars. Part of Ford's revolution was to create a change in society, as well as the workplace, towards mass consumption, where more people in society can afford to buy items like cars. Beforehand, car ownership was out of the financial reach of many. Now, with cars retailing for below $600 (Raff and Summers, 1987: 64), and with Ford encouraging a savings scheme among his workers, car ownership by the masses was possible.

Mass-produced objects nowadays constitute so much of our daily lives that Donkin describes Taylorism and Fordism as 'the most enduring social change of the 20th century' (Donkin, 2001: 159). It is not just cars, but most electrical items, computers, and clothing that are produced and consumed en masse using the assembly line system or some derivative thereof.

C Real life case: the 'Henry Ford' of heart surgery

'We want everyone in the world to afford heart surgery and healthcare,' states Dr Devi Shetty, also known as the 'Henry Ford of heart surgery.' At his hospital in Bangalore, India, Shetty has devised a method to improve the efficiency of open-heart surgery, inspired by the work of Ford, of whom he is a fan.

Shetty describes his operating theatre with 26 operating blocks which operate for 10 hours a day, with up to 5 operations in progress at any one time. While colleagues perform the tasks of anaesthetizing and opening up the patients and inserting tubes in preparation, Shetty is left to visit each patient in turn and perform the skilled procedures needed. An anaesthetist is able to watch over four patients at any one time.

The procedure is very different to the type of surgery we are used to, where one operation takes place at a time with all staff attending to that one patient. Shetty claims that this has brought about efficiency gains, with 32 operations performed in a day, compared to 2 or 3 in other hospitals. The system works only by having a much larger hospital to make the large volume of operations financially viable, in a similar way to Ford's mass production and consumption.

In a part of the world where few people can afford healthcare, Shetty claims that he can perform an operation for EUR2,000, 15 times cheaper than in Western Europe.

Shetty has opened a further hospital in the Cayman Islands, and his techniques have been considered as a means of cutting healthcare costs in both the UK and the US.

Sources: Morris (2010); Donnelly (2013); Rai (2015); France 24 (2016); Govindarajan and Ramamurti (2018).

 Dr Shetty's techniques do not use a moving assembly line, but what features does his work process have in common with Fordism?

 Visit the online resources and take a look at the web links for Chapter 3 for video news reports about production line heart surgery in India and further links to reports about assembly line surgery.

While its origins are in heavy industry, the assembly line has been applied to many other tasks which have repetitive, standardized elements. Food production often follows an assembly line pattern: for example, the supermarket sandwich originates from a standardized component—the triangular piece of bread (*The food programme*, 2010). In white-collar work, the idea of a 'paper factory' has also emerged, where administrative tasks, such as processing forms, move along a series of stages where simple operations are performed at each (Baldry et al., 1998). With the heart surgery example, we see how assembly line techniques can also be applied to the organization of skilled as well as unskilled work.

 Visit the online resources and take a look at the web links for Chapter 3 to find a link to the podcast of a BBC radio broadcast about sandwich production lines.

 Just how much of an impact does the assembly line have on your everyday life? What items that you are wearing or using in your home, workplace, or place of study have been mass-produced on an assembly line?

? Review questions

Describe	What are the main features of the assembly line?
Explain	How does the assembly line draw upon, but also intensify, the techniques of Taylorism?
Analyse	Why does Fordism need mass production and consumption to realize its efficiency gains?
Apply	What modern-day industries can you think of which use assembly line techniques?

Rational production: the Marxist critique

🔍 Running case: cogs in a machine

Babs Davies is off to clean again, but is looking to work elsewhere.

Babs Davies:	I used to love working at Junction. Now I don't even feel like a human being there.

Debbie Smith:	Feel the same. Since they let that consultant in there's no room to breathe—everything is watched and we're ordered about. Feels like I'm under a microscope all the time. And the work is just boring now. I feel like my soul has been taken away from me.

Andy James:	You've got it lucky. Try coming to work at Laundromation—hot, steamy, folding the same towels day in day out: that's soulless for you.

Babs Davies:	Well, if the rumours are true I might be looking for a job there. Weaver wants to outsource our work to you—there's going to be job cuts if that's the case.

Debbie Smith:	Tell me about it, love. Feel like we're just cogs in a machine these days.

Fordism offers the control of Taylorism in a more intensified form. The speed of work on the assembly line was controlled simply by the *speed of the line itself*; workers would have to perform their individual tasks as and when each car appeared in front of them. The system makes workers more than ever a part of the machine. They have to remain at the line and perform their task, not pausing or taking unauthorized breaks for fear of their one unperformed task being detected later down the line.

The intensification of work by Ford was not without problems. Ford also recognized that work in his factories was monotonous and dehumanizing. He had to pay a decent wage to get people to work in his factories, with the $5 day far exceeding the $2.34 that unskilled workers could previously hope to earn (Raff and Summers, 1987: 69). These problems were not isolated within the factory gates. They had a resonance in wider society, as reflected in various artistic media of the time.

Theory in context: cultural critiques of Ford

Charlie Chaplin's (1936) silent film *Modern times* is a satire on the human effects of assembly line work. In a memorable scene, Chaplin's worker performs a repetitive task as the speed of the line is increased. Hypnotized by the repetitive task and unable to keep up with the speed of the line, Chaplin is carried along into the heart of the machinery. The imagery is deliberate—Chaplin's character has been reduced, literally and figuratively, to being a 'cog in the machine'.

A similar negative view of the factory system and its effects upon individuals was presented by the Mexican artist Diego Rivera. Commissioned by Henry Ford to produce a set of murals for the Ford headquarters, Rivera produced a set of paintings where the imagery of the machine was dominant, the people reduced to small, sullen, expressionless beings. Ford was so incensed by this portrayal of his factory system that the murals were destroyed, never to be exhibited.

In the novel *Brave new world*, Aldous Huxley (1932) presents a world where people are in danger of losing their own identity—a world where people worship a god named Henry Ford. In this novel it is not cars that are mass-produced, but humans themselves. At the lowest levels of society are 'epsilons'—humans produced as workers in mass bundles.

Visit the online resources and take a look at the web links for Chapter 3 for more information on cultural critiques of Fordism.

Common to all three of the works described here are critiques of Ford and Taylor suggesting that humans lose their individuality, their humanity even, in the face of organizations which are run like massive machines. What is rational in terms of organizational efficiency is not necessarily rational in terms of the effects upon humans themselves. The observations of the likes of Chaplin, Rivera, and Huxley suggest a mode of organization that is inherently dehumanizing—workers become components in a larger industrial machine, their human attributes ignored. Beynon's (1984) study of work on the Ford production line has many quotes from workers talking not just about the boredom of the work, but its complete lack of interest and meaning.

Real life case: slaughterhouse injuries

A further example of how seemingly rational production can be seen as irrational when the human costs are taken into account can be found in the present day in slaughterhouse and abattoir settings.

As we saw earlier in the chapter, Ford's inspiration for the assembly line came from the way in which animal carcasses were butchered piece by piece along a line and pulley system. This system, albeit with more modern technology, still exists today in slaughterhouses, and as with the assembly line there are pressures to get the work done as quickly as possible. As Genoways (2014) suggests: 'In modern meat-packing plants, the rate of production is set by a chain conveyor system. The chain determines everything about how a day in the plant goes, and workers often talk about it as if it were a living thing, something to be feared.' This necessity to work at speed can lead to injuries and illness amongst the workforce.

An investigation into the UK meat processing industry (Milmo, Heal, and Wasley, 2018) described dangerous working conditions where employees used 'razor-sharp knives' on 'fast-moving factory lines'. The result is a higher proportion of injuries than in other sectors,

→

with 100 major injuries per year amongst the largely migrant workforce, including eye damage and amputations.

Similar concerns about the health and safety of workers have been raised in the US in response to plans to allow unlimited increases to slaughter line speeds in the pork processing industry. Berkowitz and McMillan (2018) suggest that serious injury rates among these workers are three times higher than the US national average and illness rates are 17 times higher: 'The pork processing industry is one of the most dangerous for workers. The already breakneck line speeds, coupled with the forceful and repetitive nature of the jobs in meat-packing plants, lead to high rates of devastating injuries and illnesses.'

It is not just the production line workers who face dangerous and very unpleasant working conditions. Once the slaughter lines stop, sanitation workers clean up the lines overnight, working amongst the stench of animal waste, and with injuries caused by pressures to clean up amongst moving, heavy machinery (Waldman and Mehrotra, 2017).

It is clear that efficient, rational assembly line production in the slaughter industry might make profit for a firm, but the human costs to workers can be life-changing and even life-threatening.

Sources: Genoways (2014); Waldman and Mehrotra (2017); Berkowitz and McMillan (2018); Milmo, Heal and Wasley (2018).

Visit the online resources and take a look at the web links for Chapter 3 for more background on the dangers of assembly line work in the meat slaughter industry.

Marx's critique of capitalist production

🔍 Running case: on strike

Midshires Gazette

Fresh walkout leaves laundry factory in a spin

Laundry services company Laundromation Ltd has experienced the latest in a series of walkouts over working conditions. Problems began on last night's shift when workers downed tools, bringing all activity in the plant to a halt.

Laundromation provides contract laundry services to a number of local organizations, including hospitals, sports centres, and hotels. Simon Chance, the owner of Junction Hotel, said: 'This is the third time this month. We're left with no towels, no clean linen, no tablecloths—how are we supposed to run a hotel? It feels like we're hostage to the poor industrial relations at Laundromation.'

Andrew Rook, head of the Collectivity union, outlined the reasons for the actions: 'Work has been increasingly intensified. The conveyors which carry the laundry to workers are being speeded up week by week as the company takes on more contracts. Workers are expected—forced—to work harder for no extra money.'

Bob Smith, Managing Director of Laundromation, said, 'We are sorry for the disruption this is causing to our valued customers. At Laundromation we pay highly competitive wages. I would have expected that workers would be grateful for a full order book in such difficult economic times and would work to make sure that we retain our current customer base.'

Karl Marx (1964) saw the desire for efficiency as an inevitable part of the capitalist working relationship. In competitive markets, with capitalists and shareholders demanding high returns on investment, the pressure is on managers to reduce costs, including labour. He suggested that the capitalist working relationship produced surplus value, where the growth in the capital arises from the work done by the workers. By working more efficiently workers help to increase profits, but this profit is enjoyed by capitalists rather than as increased pay by the workers themselves. Conversely, workers experience, through the pursuit of efficiency, a deterioration in their own conditions of work and see their craft skills depleted and replaced with monotonous, repetitive, and dehumanizing tasks.

For Marx, this relationship is fundamentally unequal. Whereas workers previously owned their own means of production, determined their own pace of work, and decided how much they took from the business for their efforts, these terms—wages, hours, and working conditions—are now set by management. Management have the power to do this because they are acting on behalf of capital—the power of the money, property, and equipment tied up in the business. Each individual worker relies on this for their wage—effectively their ability to live, eat, and be housed. However, should they object to the working conditions and wages set they are effectively powerless—management have the ability to hire and fire.

 Have you ever worked in a job where you have felt unhappy with something, such as pay, working hours, the type of work you have to do, or your relationship with your boss? How much power have you felt (or not felt) to do something about it? What might have given you more power in the situation?

Marx and alienation

Karl Marx (1894/1981) took a different view of the nature of workers than Taylor and Ford. Rather than being naturally lazy, workers were naturally creative—they had a desire to transform the world around them. Furthermore, work was, for Marx, fundamentally a social rather than an economic activity. Factory working systems, however, laid to waste a lot of this human potential, trapping workers in dull, monotonous working routines, often in isolation from other workers. Consequently, for Marx (1894/1981), there are a number of negative effects upon workers, which he terms alienation, where workers feel alien from what they produce, from their work, and from the world around them.

1. Workers are alienated from the product. Rather than having a defining role in planning and creating the product, they only play one small part in the production process, with planning done by the capitalists. The worker may not even see the end product, and may not have a role in selling and realizing the profits.

2. Workers are alienated from the production process. Work becomes a series of dull, repetitive, meaningless tasks performed solely for money. There are no intrinsic rewards (see Chapter 9) in the job. Craft skills become redundant as work is deskilled.

3. Workers are alienated from the human species or their 'human essence'. Work is dehumanizing in that the natural human desire for creativity is taken away and workers become 'cogs in a machine'.

4. Workers are alienated from other humans. Work becomes an economic transaction in return for a wage rather than a social activity. Workers are individualized in the production process and also separated from management.

 Visit the online resources and take a look at the web links for Chapter 3 to view a short animation that introduces Marx's concept of alienation.

Braverman and deskilling

Such a waste of human potential is echoed in Braverman's (1974) deskilling thesis. At a basic level this means a degradation in the nature of work, from workers having highly valuable craft skills to workers performing monotonous tasks requiring no skill whatsoever. Deskilling is something that Braverman witnessed first-hand as a worker in the print industry, seeing his own skills replaced by new technology.

Braverman (1974) suggested two particular areas of deskilling.

- Organizational deskilling represents the overall knowledge of the production process being held by management and taken away from the brains of the workers.

- Technological deskilling represents the means by which the design of tasks removes the need for workers' skills; indeed, it can even replace workers with technology and thus lead to job losses, an issue that we will examine in Chapters 4 and 10 and that is at the heart of the current debate around automation and artificial intelligence.

As with Marx, for Braverman the pursuit of efficiency inevitably led to deskilling and the degradation of work. For both theorists, this creates a conflict of interest between workers and capital—a fundamental tension at the heart of the capitalist working relationship.

 How much knowledge and skill do you need to perform a task on a production line? How much would you know about other tasks which go into making the overall product? How would you feel working on a production line and being told what to do all day?

Conflict in the capitalist wage–labour relationship

Marx's conclusion is that alienation and the inequality of the capitalist working relationship leads, inevitably, to conflict between capital and labour. The formation of trade unions, which are able to take collective action, such as strikes, can be seen as an attempt to reintroduce collective power to the workforce—power which was lost through the control mechanisms of Taylor and Ford.

Visit the online resources and take a look at the extension material for Chapter 3 for more detail on attempts to reintroduce collective power.

Ford's factories were certainly plagued by industrial unrest, and unionization was heavy in his factories (see Beynon, 1984). Even with the $5-a-day wage, the boring, monotonous work was resisted fiercely. The nature of his production system left it vulnerable to a 'spanner in the works': with all parts of the work process interdependent in a line, it only took a problem in one small area to bring production to a halt.

Strikes, sabotage, and even riots were commonplace. Ford himself had an abrasive approach to industrial relations. Beynon (1984: 49) describes how, in one period of industrial unrest and rioting, Ford considered arming non-striking workers with the intention of them turning on the strikers.

Resistance doesn't necessarily take the form of organized action, such as strikes. If people opt out of the job—resigning, looking for work elsewhere, etc.—this too is a sign of resistance against the organization. Ford's plants had, on average, a labour turnover rate of 370 per cent—almost four people a year for each position (Raff and Summers, 1987: 63). In other words, each job changed hands every ten weeks.

In this section we have seen that the introduction of rational production techniques came at the cost of a great amount of conflict. In the next section we see how Fordism in particular has been developed in more recent years.

? Review questions

Describe	What is meant by alienation?
Explain	Why might work in Ford's factories be described as 'dehumanizing?'
Analyse	What does Marx mean when he says that the capitalist working relationship favours the side of capital?
Apply	What examples of strikes and industrial action have you seen recently in the news? What are the reasons for such action taking place?

Evaluating rational work design

🔍 Running case: denouement

Simon Chance sits down a few months after the walkout and analyses the situation.

The cleaning department will never be the same again. Where once it had larger-than-life characters who had Junction Hotel running through their veins, now it has part-timers and students walking around like robots. Yes, they are more compliant, easy to control, and easy to replace if they become uncontrollable, but a little something has been lost.

At the same time, Chance realizes that his wage bill is considerably reduced. Rooms are being cleaned much more quickly. There is the odd short-cut being taken and there are a few more complaints from guests, but, overall, the job is being done.

Chance feels there are lessons to be learned for the rest of the hotel. Efficiencies need to be spread, but Chance decides to minimize the overall influence of Weaver as his methods are too extreme and the consequences on the workforce too great. But, at the same time, there are areas throughout the organization where rational work design can be used to some extent to make things more efficient.

The question for Chance is: where would rationalization be appropriate? The check-in desk at reception seems like a good place to start—checking guests in is a fairly simple and standard task, and a bit of efficiency would be useful when queues are long. But at the same time, different guests have different requirements and at a luxury hotel they want to be treated individually—not like cars coming off an assembly line. Chance then thinks about the restaurant—certainly some processes like setting tables could be rationalized, but the head chef considers himself to be a highly skilled artist—he would surely resist any attempts to standardize his work.

While rational work design techniques have encountered considerable resistance and critique, in many ways they mirror how we often routinize tasks in our own lives (Morgan, 2006: 26). Maybe you take part in sports—how do you learn to perform a sport better? Are there advantages to be gained from breaking down movements into smaller parts and analysing them so as to be able to perform them more effectively? Perhaps you have a job around the house, such as making the beds—do you devise a standard routine, with each stage of the process performed in a particular order, that helps you to perform it more efficiently?

Furthermore, not all workers react negatively to rational work designs, such as Taylorism and Fordism. Some people prefer a straightforward task, whereby they can come into work, do a clear and simple job without having to put in too much thought, and collect their wage at the end of the day (see Chapter 9 for this 'instrumental orientation' to work). It can also be argued that rational working methods bring in an element of fairness. Where previously the conditions of work, pace and standard of work expected, payment, and even being hired or not were open to the whims of individual managers, now they are standardized and formalized, and can be applied equally across the workforce. In this respect, there is a link between rational work design and the bureaucratic rules and procedures examined in Chapter 2.

In more practical, operational terms, Gareth Morgan (2006: 26) provides a useful analysis for where Taylorist and Fordist techniques are appropriate and where they would not be successful. They are a strength when there is a straightforward task performed in a stable, unchanging context, and where precision is important. In other words, rational work design is ideal when there is a very machine-like environment in which the tasks are performed. This includes having people within the work process prepared and happy to work as if a part of a machine.

While Morgan saw rational work design as being fine for stable working environments, equally its rigidity makes it difficult for coping with changing circumstances or where a large variety of different products rather than one standard product are produced.

The overall advantages and disadvantages of rational work design are summarized in Table 3.1.

Table 3.1 Advantages and disadvantages of rational production techniques

Advantages	Disadvantages
Increase in production efficiency when there is a simple, standardized product to be produced	Inefficient and inflexible for product ranges with plentiful variation or where market conditions require rapid changes
Increase in control over a large number of factory workers	Workers lose autonomy and control over their day-to-day activities
Tasks and expectations for workers are clear, simple, and unambiguous	Workers lose craft skills and expertise
Workers can participate in the labour market regardless of skill, experience, language and, in some cases, disability	Work is dull, monotonous, and unfulfilling
Fair treatment/equality of opportunity—workers are hired and paid according to pre-existing standards; minimizes potential for favouritism that existed with previous factory systems	Can be inefficient if the alienating and intensive nature of work causes widespread resistance
Provides efficient goods or services in times of need (e.g. war, poverty)	Interdependence of work tasks leaves the assembly line vulnerable to a 'spanner in the works'
Allows goods to be mass-produced at a price that would otherwise be unaffordable to the public	Humans are reduced to being 'cogs in a machine'
Works well with simple, predictable tasks in a stable environment	Not good for complex tasks where there is an uncertain environment and flexibility is required

Post-Fordism and neo-Fordism

As we saw in Chapter 2, the contemporary environment facing organizations is unstable and unpredictable—very much like the environment that Morgan (2006) suggests is not ideal for rational work design, with greater flexibility demanded of organizations that had originally been set up for producing standardized products. This was the case in the 1980s, when many Western economies were in recession. Manufacturing was in decline and the service sector became more dominant. Furthermore, new computer technologies were able to produce goods in a more customized way than the mass-produced assembly line, and tastes in consumption were also becoming more fragmented towards niche and specialist markets, rather than standardized, mass-produced goods.

At the same time, the economy of Japan was becoming more successful. Western organizations, including the Ford company, began to look at Japanese forms of organization, which were much more successful in comparison. In this section we examine two ways in which Fordism has evolved in order to be more flexible for the contemporary environment.

- Post-Fordism is a 'retreat from rationalization' and a movement towards more flexible forms of organization, with skill and autonomy returned to the workers.

- Neo-Fordism achieves flexibility through technology, but this technology is used to make work processes efficient and to exert precise control over the tasks that workers perform.

Post-Fordism—a return to skill and autonomy

Post-Fordism moves away from the traditional Fordist assembly line, where work is highly controlled and jobs are fragmented into small low skilled tasks. Instead, it values the skills and knowledge of workers, allowing them autonomy in how they organize their work emphasizing communication and competencies, rather than command and control. Managers at Ford themselves introduced elements of work organization that can be described as post-Fordist. Japanese firms welcome suggestions and input from shop-floor workers, whereas the traditional Fordist model is one where workers are at the bottom of a hierarchy and do as they are told. In the 1980s, Ford instigated an 'After Japan' programme, to move away from top-down management and engage workers in participative management, whereby they had a say in decisions, and in team working, with cross-functional teams as would be found in a matrix structure like the one we saw in Chapter 2. The intention was to generate trust and cooperation, moving away from the Fordist 'management by fear' (Starkey and McKinlay, 1994).

Visit the online resources and take a look at the extension material for Chapter 3 for more analysis of post-Fordist organizations.

Neo-Fordism—added flexibility

While trends away from the rationalization of Fordism have been observed with post-Fordism, **neo-Fordism** sees Fordism being developed in ways which combine Japanese techniques and culture, but which retain the drive for efficiency of traditional Taylorism and Fordism. Typical of this is the Toyota Production System (TPS, also known as Toyotism) used by Japanese car manufacturers Toyota. Work tasks are designed to be efficient and to minimize waste with the same degree of calculation and precision as Taylor's scientific management. Added to this are techniques that further minimize waste, but in more flexible ways than Taylorism. For example, with the Japanese **just-in-time** system, components are delivered as and when necessary, rather than wasting space in storerooms (Jaffee, 2001: 135ff; Towill, 2010). See Chapter 7 for more about the culture of Japanese management.

The car industry has changed a lot in the hundred or so years since Henry Ford. For instance, rather than the grubby conditions of Ford's factories, Volkswagen's Phaeton factory in Dresden, Germany, is called Gläserne Manufaktur—the factory made of glass. This transparent factory has glass walls so that the whole production process can be seen. The process is so clean that the floors are made of Canadian maple and the workers even wear white overalls (see AutoMotoTV, 2010).

All the parts come in on a tram and are then delivered to the appropriate locations by robots guided by magnets. The entire floor is a giant conveyor belt moving very slowly. Each workstation is powered via the floor. The whole process is also computerized so that the system monitors everything that goes into the vehicle and will even know if a single screw is missing and when the car is ready to go to the next stage. The car is even moved round by a machine to suit the technician's body as they put in the parts.

Visit the online resources and take a look at the web links for Chapter 3 for more information about Toyotism and how it both compares with and differs from traditional Fordist production, and to view videos of modern car factories.

In neo-Fordist organizations, computer technology helps to control large volumes of production, but rather than making Fordist, standardized products, the technology allows for changes to the set-up to be made quickly. When you by a new car today, no longer are you restricted to Henry Ford's restriction that it is only available in black. In fact, there are a whole range of options—paint colour, wheel types, upholstery, sound system, etc. And yet all of these different specifications can be accommodated on one assembly line—rather than producing a set of standard cars, the assembly line today is a standard process which creates a set of individually customized products. Thus, neo-Fordist organizations combine mass production and economies of scale with greater flexibility than a Fordist assembly line.

With neo-Fordist organization comes a ruthless desire for efficiency and the minimization of waste, typified by contemporary techniques such as **lean management** which have developed from Toyotism. Lean management seeks not only to eliminate waste from the production process, but also to evaluate all processes and activities for the value that they add, and to eliminate all activities that fail to add value to the organization.

Under neo-Fordism, workers generally have a better working environment than the traditional noisy, dirty factory. Furthermore, they often have a wider variety of tasks than the one repetitive task of the traditional assembly line. Instead, they engage in job rotation or job enlargement (see Chapter 9), and such worker flexibility is a key feature of the Toyota Production System (Dohse et al., 1985). However, in a manner similar to their counterparts from the traditional Fordist assembly line, they often perform repetitive and tightly-controlled tasks, with little autonomy over their own work.

Bringing the Fordisms together

So far we have seen two ways in which Fordism has evolved and become more flexible in the face of the contemporary environment. Post-Fordism and neo-Fordism are very different developments, but are not necessarily mutually exclusive. They coexist—different organizations use rational work design in different ways, and indeed there are also contemporary organizations which still use traditional Fordist assembly lines or pre-Fordist craft manufacture. Rather than a 'one best way' approach to rationalization, following Morgan (2006) rationalization may be used in the most appropriate way for any one particular organization.

Figure 3.5 brings together in one framework different categories of work, and the degree to which that work is rationalized. The diagram locates type of work according to two qualities:

- *variety of work*—does a worker do a wide variety of tasks, or just a small number of repetitive tasks—or even just one?

- *discretion in work*—the degree of control that a worker has over their own work. Do they have high discretion, with a large amount of autonomy and independence, or low discretion, where their work is very tightly controlled?

The diagram shows how different types of work coexist, displaying different degrees of rationalization. For example, we could relate the framework to the food industry, showing how different types of work in that industry relate to the types of work in the four quadrants.

1. Pre-Fordism is craft or artisan work, where a worker exercises a skill or craft on a small scale. They work independently and so have high discretion, and they work on a small variety of tasks. An example might be a dairy farmhouse kitchen, where one person makes a small amount of speciality cheese.

Figure 3.5 Work categorization framework.
Source: © John Bratton, Peter Sawchuk, Carolyn Forshaw, Militza Callinan and Martin Corbett, Work and organizational behaviour, published 2010. Reproduced with the permission of Palgrave Macmillan.

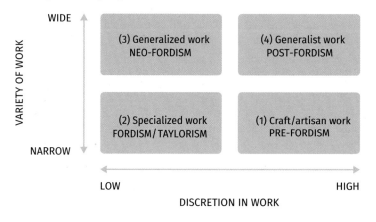

2. Fordist production is specialized work. A single task is performed, and workers are highly controlled and so have low discretion. Some food factories mass-produce food on assembly lines. A worker on such a line may have just one repetitive job, for example sprinkling icing sugar on to cakes as they go past on the line.

3. Neo-Fordist production is generalized work, where a worker performs a wide variety of general tasks, but the tasks are simple and highly controlled and so the worker has low discretion. A fast-food restaurant would be an example of this: a worker rotates between jobs such as serving customers, cleaning tables, and making burgers, but, as we will see in Chapter 4, each of these jobs is designed to be simple and highly controlled.

4. Post-Fordism is generalist work. A person with expert knowledge performs a wide variety of tasks and does so relatively autonomously, i.e. with high discretion. The head chef of a restaurant is an example of this, using their knowledge and expertise to produce any of a wide variety of dishes, creating the menu themselves each day.

? Review questions

Describe	What have been the main changes in the environment that organizations have faced since the time of Taylor and Ford?
Explain	What is meant by post-Fordism and post-bureaucracy?
Analyse	What are the differences between post-Fordism and neo-Fordism in the way that they have each developed from Fordism in the contemporary era?
Apply	How do you think computer technology makes neo-Fordist work design possible? Give some examples of this in practice.

93

Fordism and Taylorism in contemporary warehouse management

The example of online retailing and distribution logistics which began this chapter shares many characteristics with rational work design. While modern warehouses are engaged in a different form of work from that of the early factory system, many of the underlying principles of work design are the same. There is, as outlined in the Introduction to this chapter, a need both for efficiency, to despatch the order as quickly as possible, and control, to make sure the order is picked out accurately. This is all done on a large scale, with the warehouses benefiting from economies of scale.

○ Real life case: Ebuyer

Ebuyer, a UK-based electronics retailer, demonstrates how it can deliver orders the following day if they are ordered up until 11 pm. At the heart of this efficient process is its partly-automated warehouse, where goods can be picked out within 15 minutes, travelling along conveyor belts, with the barcode being scanned at all stages as a means of tracking the product.

Visit the online resources and take a look at the web links for Chapter 3 to view a video of the Ebuyer warehouse in action.

→

> If you look at the video of the Ebuyer warehouse it looks a lot like a Fordist assembly line, with identical crates carrying orders along a long conveyor belt, ready to be packed and despatched. However, although the crates are identical, the contents of each is completely different—each one carries a separate, individual order. The computer software running the system, along with the barcode scanning, allows this coordination to take place. The system is neo-Fordist in that there is a standard, repetitive process (the crates running along the conveyor), but within that is the flexibility to make each order completely different.
>
> Source: Ebuyer (2008).

Warehouse software can also be used to control workers. O'Connor (2015) notes how software can calculate the most efficient route through a warehouse to collect all items in an order, and then use a GPS device to direct the worker where to go. As with Taylorism, the worker does no thinking, but now an algorithm—not a manager—is doing all of the planning. In some warehouses, these devices are strapped straight onto workers' arms, directing them to the next product to pick up (Hencke, 2005). In a Taylorist sense, wasted movement can be minimized—the computer system can identify the nearest worker to the product so that it can be retrieved in the quickest time possible, to the extent that Spicer and Cederström (2015) suggest such technology provides a 'time-and-motion utopia' where employees can be tracked on a second-by-second basis.

While these devices provide Taylorist levels of control over the minutest movements made by workers, they also lead to an intensification of work similar to that of the assembly line. On Ford's assembly line, it was the speed of the line that controlled work; now it is wearable technology that allows the movements of workers not only to be directed, but also to be tracked. As with Taylorism, the work design allows surveillance over the workers: where they have been, how quickly they have been working, etc. (Rawlinson, 2013).

A more recent development in warehouse technology can be seen in two patents filed by Amazon (Boyle, 2018; Solon, 2018) for wireless wristbands which track the hand positions of warehouse workers. They allow haptic feedback, a vibration of the bracelet, to guide a worker's hand to exactly where it needs to be—an instant control over the movement of workers.

 What do you think Taylor would have thought of the wristband patent?

At the time of writing, the wristbands were just a patent and had not been put into operation. However, they demonstrate the capabilities of cyber-physical systems, where software, people, and objects are linked together in one control mechanism. Such systems are a part of the Fourth Industrial Revolution. In the next chapter we find out more about the Fourth Industrial Revolution, but also how these contemporary developments can be traced back to early rationalization.

The levels of control in some warehouses have been viewed as excessive, recalling the concerns with the degree of control of Ford's assembly line examined earlier in the chapter. Where Ford used the speed of the assembly line as a means of control, workers in Amazon warehouses have targets per day to meet. As with Taylorism, idle time is discouraged, such that workers have reported using bottles rather than taking toilet breaks (Sainato, 2018; Frith, 2018). And, as with Ford, there have been calls for unionization and examples of strikes in response to these levels of control (Sainato, 2018; Griffin, 2018).

Connecting case and theory

Rational work design encompasses techniques from, among others, Taylor and Ford. Taylor's scientific management approach addressed issues of organizational control and efficiency by meticulously breaking down the work process into small, discrete tasks. These tasks were then analysed scientifically—through measurement and calculation—and redesigned to be as efficient as possible. This made the process more efficient and gave management much more control over workers—a process intensified by the moving assembly line of Henry Ford.

At the start of the chapter Junction Hotel was facing financial pressures, and Simon Chance realized that it needed to reduce costs in order to stay in business. This is difficult to do in a luxury hotel, but Phil Weaver's identification of labour as the biggest cost—the wage bill—suggested that by getting people to work more efficiently, the wage bill could be decreased with the same amount of work being done. Weaver had identified the cleaning staff as an area where efficiency could be found—as with rational work design, the aim was to remove all waste and inefficiency from their work process.

The situation facing Junction Hotel was similar to the tensions in the capitalist wage–labour relationship. On the one hand, Chance and Weaver wanted to get as much work as possible from the cleaners for the wages that they pay to them. However, to do this they needed to exert control over the cleaners.

Amy Turtle was typical of the kind of worker that Frederick Taylor found problematic. Her long years of experience gave her a form of craft knowledge over the cleaning process, which she used to confuse Linda Wilkinson. The cleaners all tended to group together and had strength from being a gang, with Turtle as their head. When Weaver observed the cleaners, he notes how they engaged in a form of soldiering—speeding up in the morning to get an extra 30 minutes' break over lunch. All of these factors together meant that Wilkinson has little control over the cleaners, just as Taylor felt a lack of control over his factory workers.

Weaver's observation of the workers was very much like that of Taylor, or the time and motion study of the Gilbreths. Movements were measured and calculated scientifically, and Weaver redesigned the work into simple movements. Waste is reduced—for example, unnecessary journeys with the trolley are designed out of the process. The tools and layout of the job are designed to make the work as simple and straightforward as possible, with the cleaner then trained to perform the tasks as specified—the whole cleaning process has been designed according to the principles of scientific management.

The task is undoubtedly made more efficient, with the time taken to clean a room halved, but as with Taylorism and Fordism it creates a lot of unhappiness among the workforce, making their work boring and monotonous.

Weaver's interventions also loaded the working relationship in favour of management. Skills gained through craft knowledge, apprenticeships, and experience became worthless and degraded as deskilling took place, with the knowledge of the overall production process moving from individual workers to levels of management. Turtle's resignation letter suggests that she experienced this deskilling—her craft knowledge was no longer of any value, and she and the rest of the cleaners felt that they had lost their sense of control over their work. The problems were not just felt by the workers; the management were also wary of the unhappiness and disruption that Weaver's ideas were causing within the workforce—as with the managers where Taylor worked, it seems that they would have been happy with some inefficiency if it meant a happy and settled workforce.

Nevertheless, when Weaver got the management to do the cleaning themselves, it showed them just how much power they now had over their workforce. The tasks could be learned in minutes—which makes the workforce easy to replace. The design of the work has given management the control over the workforce that they need in order to make them work more efficiently.

The case shows the application of Taylorist techniques to the cleaning labour process in the hotel. Junction Hotel is too small to apply an assembly line form of work design to the cleaning—assembly lines need a lot of capital investment and so are only cost-efficient for much larger-scale organizations. The Laundromation factory is an example of such a large-scale organization. In the hotel industry, it is common that laundry will not be done in the hotel but subcontracted (along with many other hotels in the area) to an industrial-scale laundry that can benefit from economies of scale—the cost becomes less by processing so much laundry in one place. While the assembly line was developed for manufacturing cars, the Laundromation factory shows how the process can be adapted for other types of task, and not just manufacturing. However, as with the critiques of Ford's factories from the likes of Charlie Chaplin, the messages from the workers showed that they felt they had been dehumanized, reduced to cogs in a machine. As would be predicted by Karl Marx, the workers felt so controlled and alienated that their only option was to strike.

At the end of this chapter's episode of the case, we find Chance reflecting on the advantages and disadvantages of rational work design—it has reduced the wage bill and increased control over the cleaners, but at the expense of their morale and sense of commitment to the work. As he thinks about how rational work design could be used elsewhere in the hotel, he could draw on some of the ways in which Fordism has evolved. The check-in process consists of standard, repetitive tasks, but there needs to be flexibility to adapt this for the individual requests and needs of each guest—a task which might benefit from a neo-Fordist approach. The restaurant tables have a standard layout which does not vary—setting them might be an area where a traditional Taylorist approach could be used. However, the head chef draws on their skill; flexibility here might come from drawing on their experience to know just how to adapt a menu to take account of the seasonal availability of ingredients—suggesting more of a post-Fordist approach. Junction Hotel is an example where all of the types of work shown in Figure 3.5 can coexist within one organization—the skill of the manager in designing work is to work out which types of work design are most appropriate for which task.

Further reading

Taylor, F.W. 1911. *The principles of scientific management*. Harper: New York.

Taylor's original text can be freely downloaded from many sources, and outlines his seminal ideas on scientific management.

Lancaster, J. 2015. *Making time: Lillian Moller Gilbreth—a life beyond 'Cheaper by the dozen'*. Northeastern University Press: Boston, MA.

A biography of Lillian Gilbreth which explores her contribution to scientific management beyond the work of Taylor.

Wood, S. 1993. The Japanization of Fordism. *Economic and Industrial Democracy* 14 (4): 535–55.

An in-depth exploration of how Fordism, under influence from Japan, evolved into post-Fordism and neo-Fordism.

Mousa, F., and Lemak, D. 2009. The Gilbreths' quality system stands the test of time. *Journal of Management History* 15 (2): 198–215.

Introduces the work of the Gilbreths and discusses how its influence is still found in contemporary workplaces.

 ## References

AutoMotoTV. 2010. Volkswagen Phaeton: Die gläserne Manufaktur Dresden. Available at: https://www.youtube.com/watch?v=sFV5EnsRgvw (last accessed 16 July 2018).

Bahnisch, M. 2000. Embodied work, divided labour: Subjectivity and the scientific management of the body in Frederick W. Taylor's 1907 'Lecture on Management'. *Body and Society* 6 (1): 51–68.

Baldry, C., Bain, P., and Taylor, P. 1998. Bright satanic offices: Intensification, control and team Taylorism. In: Thompson, P., and Warhurst, C. (eds) *Workplaces of the future*. Macmillan: Basingstoke, pp. 163–83.

Banker, S. 2018. Tesla's disappointing earnings highlight problems in scaling production. *Forbes*, 3 May. Available at: https://www.forbes.com/sites/steve-banker/2018/05/03/teslas-disappointing-quarter-earnings-highlight-problems-in-scaling-production/#5cf624222e8f

Berkowitz, D., and McMillan, S. 2018. High-speed pig slaughter will be disastrous for everyone involved. *The Guardian*, 17 April. Available at: https://www.theguardian.com/commentisfree/2018/apr/17/trump-administration-usda-swine-slaughter-rule-pigs-pork

Beynon, H. 1984. *Working for Ford*. Penguin: Harmondsworth.

Boyle, A. 2018. Amazon wins a pair of patents for wireless wristbands that track warehouse workers. *Geekwire*, 30 January. Available at: https://www.geekwire.com/2018/amazon-wins-patents-wireless-wristbands-track-warehouse-workers/

Braverman, H. 1974. *Labor and monopoly capital: The degradation of work in the twentieth century.* Monthly Review Press: New York.

Cadwalladr, C. 2013. My week as an Amazon insider. *The Observer*, 1 December. Available at: https://www.theguardian.com/technology/2013/dec/01/week-amazon-insider-feature-treatment-employees-work

Chaplin, C. (dir.) 1936. *Modern times* [film]. United Artists: New York.

Clegg, S., Kornberger, M., and Pitsis, T. 2005. *Managing and organizations: An introduction to theory and practice.* Sage: London.

Copley, F.B. 1923a. *Frederick W. Taylor, father of scientific management*, vol. 1. Harper and Bros: New York.

Copley, F.B. 1923b. *Frederick W. Taylor, father of scientific management*, vol. 2. Routledge/Thoemmes Press: London.

Dohse, K., Jurgens, U., and Malsch, T. 1985. From 'Fordism' to 'Toyotism': The social organization of the labour process in the Japanese automobile industry. *Politics and Society* 14 (2): 115–46.

Donkin, R. 2001. *Blood, sweat and tears: The evolution of work.* Texere: New York.

Donnelly, L. 2013. 'Production line' surgery used in India will 'cut NHS costs'. *Daily Telegraph*, 10 October. Available at: https://www.telegraph.co.uk/news/health/news/10368149/Production-line-surgery-used-in-India-will-cut-NHS-costs.html

Ebuyer. 2008. Ebuyer order process. Available at: https://www.youtube.com/watch?v=PbaVy02u_9s (last accessed 16 July 2018).

Ford, H., and Crowther, S. 1922. *My life and work*. Garden City Publishing Co.: Garden City, NY.

France 24. 2016. Production-line heart surgery in India. March 15. Available at: http://www.france24.com/en/20160314-asia-india-heart-surgery-afghan-refugee-china-flowers-koran-pakistan

Frith, B. 2018. Amazon workers too scared to use the loo due to sacking fears. *HR Grapevine*, 17 April. Available at: https://www.hrgrapevine.com/content/article/news-2018-04-17-amazon-workers-too-scared-to-use-loo-in-case-they-are-sacked

Genoways, T. 2014. 'I felt like a piece of trash'—life inside America's food processing plants. *The Observer*, 21 December. Available at: https://www.theguardian.com/world/2014/dec/21/life-inside-america-food-processing-plants-cheap-meat

Gilbreth, F.B., Jr, and Carey, E.G. 1949. *Cheaper by the dozen*. William Heinemann: London.

Gotcher, J.M. 1992. Assisting the handicapped: The pioneering efforts of Frank and Lillian Gilbreth. *Journal of Management* 18 (1): 5–13.

Govindarajan, V., and Ramamurti, R. 2018. Is this the hospital that will finally push the expensive U.S. health care system to innovate? *Harvard Business Review*, 22 June. Available at: https://hbr.org/2018/06/is-this-the-hospital-that-will-finally-push-the-expensive-u-s-health-care-system-to-innovate

Graham, L. 2000. Lillian Gilbreth and the mental revolution at Macy's, 1925–1928. *Journal of Management History (Archive)* 6 (7): 285–305.

Grey, C. 2005. *A very short, fairly interesting and reasonably cheap book about studying organizations*. Sage: London.

Griffin, A. 2018. Amazon Prime day hit by huge strike as customers asked not to take part in deals. *The Independent*, 13 July. Available at: https://www.independent.co.uk/life-style/gadgets-and-tech/news/amazon-prime-day-2018-strike-deals-uk-sales-latest-a8441726.html

Hencke, D. 2005. AA to log call centre staff's trips to the loo in pay deal. *The Guardian*, 31 October.

Hoskin, K.W., and Macve, R.H. 1986. Accounting and the examination: A genealogy of disciplinary power. *Accounting, Organizations and Society* 11 (2): 105–36.

Huxley, A. 1932. *Brave new world: A novel*. Chatto & Windus: London.

Jaffee, D. 2001. *Organization theory: Tension and change*. McGraw Hill: Singapore.

Kanigel, R. 1997. *The one best way: Frederick Winslow Taylor and the enigma of efficiency*. Little, Brown and Company: London.

Lawley, S. and Caven, V. 2019. Lillian Moller Gilbreth. In: McMurray, R., and Pullen, A. (eds) *Routledge focus on women writers in organization studies: Beyond rationality in organization & management*, vol. 1. Routledge: London.

Marx, K. 1894/1981. *Capital: A critique of political economy*, vol. 3 (transl. Fernbach, D.). Penguin: London.

Marx, K. 1964. *Economic and philosophic manuscripts of 1844*. International Publishers: New York.

McKendrick, N. 1970. Josiah Wedgwood and cost accounting in the Industrial Revolution. *Economic History Review* 23 (1): 45–67.

Milmo, C., Heal, A., and Wasley, A. 2018. Revealed: Heavy toll of injury suffered by slaughter workers in Britain's £8bn meat industry. *I Newspaper*, 29 July. Available at: https://inews.co.uk/news/uk/revealed-heavy-toll-of-injury-and-amputations-suffered-by-slaughter-workers-serving-britains-8bn-meat-industry/

Morgan, G. 1990. *Organizations in society*. Macmillan: Basingstoke.

Morgan, G. 2006. *Images of organization*. Sage Publications: Thousand Oaks, CA.

Morris, C. 2010. 'Production line' heart surgery. BBC News, 2 August. Available at: http://www.bbc.co.uk/news/health-10837726 (last accessed 20 August 2015).

Nelson, D. 1992. Scientific management in retrospect. In: Nelson, D. (ed.) *A mental revolution: Scientific management since Taylor*. Ohio State University Press: Columbus, pp. 5–L 39.

O'Connor, S. 2015. The human cloud: A new world of work. *Financial Times*, 8 October. Available at: https://www.ft.com/content/a4b6e13e-675e-11e5-97d0-1456a776a4f5

Price, B. 1992. Frank and Lillian Gilbreth and the motion study controversy 1907–1930. In: Nelson, D. (ed.) *A mental* revolution: Scientific management since Taylor. Ohio State University Press: Columbus, pp. 58–76.

Raff, D., and Summers, L. 1987. Did Henry Ford pay efficiency wages? *Journal of Labour Economics* 5 (4): 557–86.

Rai, S. 2015. Devi Shetty, who put heart surgeries within reach of India's Poor, is taking Narayana chain public. *Forbes*, 16 December. Available at: https://www.forbes.com/sites/saritharai/2015/12/16/devi-shetty-who-put-heart-surgeries-within-reach-of-indias-poor-is-taking-narayana-chain-public/

Rawlinson, K. 2013. Tesco accused of using electronic armbands to monitor its staff. *The Independent*, 13 February. Available at: https://www.independent.co.uk/news/business/news/tesco-accused-of-using-electronic-armbands-to-monitor-its-staff-8493952.html

Sainato, M. 2018. Exploited Amazon workers need a union. When will they get one? *The Guardian*, 8 July. Available at: https://www.theguardian.com/commentisfree/2018/jul/08/amazon-jeff-bezos-unionize-working-conditions

Simpson, I.H. 1999. Historical patterns of workplace organization: From mechanical to electronic control and beyond. *Current Sociology* 47 (2): 47–75.

Solon, O. 2018. Amazon patents wristband that tracks warehouse workers' movements. *The Guardian*, 1 February. Available at: https://www.theguardian.com/technology/2018/jan/31/amazon-warehouse-wristband-tracking

Spicer, A., and Cederström, C. 2015. What companies should ask before embracing wearables. *Harvard Business Review*, 20 May.

Starkey, K., and McKinlay, A. 1994. Managing for Ford. *Sociology* 28 (4): 975–90.

Taylor, F.W. 1911. *The principles of scientific management*. Harper: New York.

The food programme. 2010. The sandwich. BBC Radio 4, 17 October [radio programme]. Available at: http://www.bbc.co.uk/programmes/b00vc508 (last accessed 20 August 2015).

Thompson, P., and McHugh, D. 2009. *Work organisations: A critical approach*, 4th edn. Palgrave Macmillan: Basingstoke.

Towill, D. 2010. Industrial engineering the Toyota Production System. *Journal of Management History* 16 (3): 327–45.

Waldman, P., and Mehrotra, K. 2017. America's worst graveyard shift is grinding up workers. *Bloomberg*, 29 December. Available at: https://www.bloomberg.com/news/features/2017-12-29/america-s-worst-graveyard-shift-is-grinding-up-workers

Whitston, K. 1997. Worker resistance and Taylorism in Britain. *International Review of Social History* 42: 1–24.

CHAPTER 4

Developments in rational organization
Towards the Fourth Industrial Revolution

Chapter overview and learning outcomes

By the end of this chapter you should be able to:

- describe Ritzer's McDonaldization and other forms of rationalization that emerged in the Third Industrial Revolution

- explain how computer technology allows rational techniques to exert increased control and surveillance in organizations, for example in call centres

- analyse the features of the Fourth Industrial Revolution, including automation and the gig economy, and explain how these features extend ideas that were developed in the second and third industrial revolutions

Key theorists

George Ritzer	American sociologist who examined the hyper-rationalized techniques of the fast-food restaurant, using the term 'McDonaldization' to describe their use in many contemporary organizations
Michel Foucault	French philosopher who used the prison metaphor of the Panopticon to examine how power is exerted through the surveillance methods that rational management techniques produce in organizations
Charles Schwab	Founder of the World Economic Forum who has commented extensively on the implications of the Fourth Industrial Revolution
Phoebe Moore	Has applied the idea of the 'quantified self' to the ways in which people are tracked through data in contemporary organizations

CHAPTER 4

Key terms	
Rationalization	Methods for increasing the efficiency of work, drawing on techniques of bureaucracy (see Chapter 2) and of rational work design, such as Taylorism and Fordism (see Chapter 3)
McDonaldization (of society)	A perspective (Ritzer, 2019) which recognizes the continued use of rationalization in contemporary organizations, as typified by the work design of the fast-food restaurant
Panopticon	Based on a prison design, a metaphor for the levels of control and surveillance in contemporary rationalized organizations
Automation	The process whereby more and more human work is carried out by machines or by computer algorithms
Gig economy	Work arrangements whereby workers undertake short-term jobs as directed by digital platforms

Introduction

Q Running case: the business trip

Heading to London for a business trip, Simon Chance thinks about how much he can introduce rationalization at Junction Hotel. Do nothing, and the hotel becomes disorganized and wasteful—and ultimately may not survive if costs are not kept under control. Go too far, and workers become like robots, demotivated by boring and repetitive work. In a business where guests and workers are constantly in contact, this would not give the best impression. 'Rationalization has efficiency benefits,' thinks Chance, 'but at the end of the day we're not a factory, we're a hotel—and a luxury hotel at that.'

Chance decides to make his trip a fact-finding mission about rationalization in other hotels and organizations. Arriving at his first hotel, a luxury hotel, he writes some notes.

> Hit the jackpot, this hotel is top-end luxury, a massive room with two balconies overlooking a park.
>
> Service at reception is polite and attentive, although all done through a standard computerized procedure, with a key card being issued. At least the staff aren't identikit—they are always happy to pass the time of day, no matter how trivial the request.
>
> I am sat on the balcony. Interesting that, though well-turned out, the rooms use identical furnishings. Indeed, they are identical across the chain—I've stayed in another of these elsewhere. It doesn't detract though, it's good quality stuff. The cleaning seems to be pretty much as we designed it back at Junction, all quite efficient. But they do take time to put a lovely little tuck into the end of the toilet roll . . . .

→

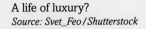

→ A life of luxury?
Source: Svet_Feo / Shutterstock

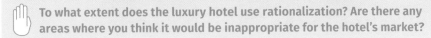

🤚 To what extent does the luxury hotel use rationalization? Are there any areas where you think it would be inappropriate for the hotel's market?

The previous two chapters described management techniques which emerged during the Second Industrial Revolution, characterized by classical bureaucracy (Chapter 2), and rational production, Taylorism, and Fordism (Chapter 3). In this chapter we examine how, rather than being relics of history, these techniques of bureaucracy and rational work design have developed and can be seen today in modern phenomena such as the fast-food restaurant, the gig economy, and the automation of work. While this chapter describes many established and emerging organizational forms that are familiar to us today, the techniques by which they are managed can be traced back to those which emerged in the Second Industrial Revolution.

First we examine how **rationalization** developed in the **Third Industrial Revolution**, drawing upon computerization. Neo-Fordist techniques which, as we saw in Chapter 3, have been applied to manufacturing have also spread to service work, in particular.

- George Ritzer (2019) has suggested that today's society is 'McDonaldized' with hyper-efficient rationalized techniques, which have their roots in bureaucracy and scientific management, found in fast-food restaurants but spreading to more and more organizations.

- Many organizations employ their own particular models of cost-cutting and minimization. We look at examples of contemporary efficient organization such as the 'no-frills' model and 'value engineering'.

- As much as rationalization is about *efficiency*, it allows management to exert *control* over the workforce; computerization allows organizations to do this more intensively. We use Michel Foucault's (1977) metaphor of the Panopticon to examine how rational organization is used to control and exert surveillance over contemporary organizations, which we apply to the example of call centres.

More recently, commentators (e.g. Schwab, 2016a) have suggested that we are entering a **Fourth Industrial Revolution**. While this brings new forms of organization, it is also an evolution and development of the computerization of the Third Industrial Revolution, and the Taylorist and bureaucratic systems of the Second Industrial Revolution. The technologies have developed into **cyber-physical systems**, which link together computer control, people, and physical objects such that they become meshed and blurred together. We examine two current and ongoing examples of the trends of the Fourth Industrial Revolution.

- First, automation and artificial intelligence are natural extensions of the desire in both the second and Third Industrial Revolutions to replace human with machine labour. We examine which jobs are in danger of being automated in the near future.

- Second, we examine the recent rise of the gig economy, as typified by Uber taxis or Deliveroo food delivery, where workers take on one short-term job after another, the whole process managed by computer algorithms. Again, this is viewed as a natural progression of bureaucratic control, Taylorist work design, and the desire for control and efficiency that characterizes the capitalist working relationship.

Rationalization in the Third Industrial Revolution

From around the 1980s onwards, computerization took rationalization from the second towards the Third Industrial Revolution. Computer power increased the control and efficiency of Taylorist and bureaucratic techniques, while simultaneously bringing flexibility to the work process. These ideas spread from their origins in neo-Fordist manufacturing techniques (see Chapter 3) to service industries, particularly through fast-food restaurants, which can be seen as a prototype for hyper-rational control and efficiency systems in other contemporary organizations.

Ritzer's McDonaldization of society

🔍 Running case: the fast-food restaurant

Simon Chance continues making notes while on his trip away.

I'm in a fast-food restaurant. It wasn't planned but I was running late, so I stopped to grab a quick lunch. The contrast between this and the hotel couldn't be more pronounced.

Went to order my food—it felt like I was talking to a machine and the till was giving them lines to say. At one point I ordered a black coffee and was asked 'Do you want milk with that?'

My order was put together. With burgers deposited down chutes and fries scooped into cartons, my meal was eventually presented on a tray—it felt like I was the last station on an assembly line.

It's not the most comfortable dining experience. I am sitting on a hard plastic chair, having to share a table with other (not well-behaved I hasten to add) diners. A cleaner is going around and actually mopped under my chair as I was sitting on it! I can't believe I am expected to even deposit my rubbish in the bin myself. Do they not have waiters here?

Still, it got me fed quickly, and the cost is a fraction of the hotel restaurant. I can only imagine what would happen though if I tried to go back to our place and suggest Effingham run his restaurant like this—he would erupt!

For George Ritzer (2019), rationalization is alive and well today and exemplified through the McDonald's fast-food restaurant chain. If you have ever worked in, eaten at, or managed a branch of a fast-food restaurant chain, you will know that there are few places in the organization that escape its intensive cocktail of rationalization. Ritzer suggests that elements of both bureaucracy and rational work design, such as Taylorism and Fordism, are combined and extended in fast-food restaurant organization. Here are a few examples.

- Making a burger is broken into small, repetitive tasks that can be easily learned by untrained staff, in a similar manner to Taylorism. The burger is 'assembled' from simple components with tasks arranged in a sequence or line, as in a Fordist factory (Ritzer, 2019: 41). However, the fact that each order produced is different suggests that fast-food restaurants have the flexibility to be an example of **neo-Fordism** (see Chapter 3).

- The service encounter, where orders are taken, is a pre-planned set of steps, with the till giving operators lines to say or prompts for what to ask the customers (ibid.: 145–46). Customer interaction is broken down into simplistic Taylorist steps just like making the burgers.

- Manuals outline procedures for almost all aspects of work within the organization (ibid.: 146); for example, there are step-by-step instructions on how to perform a mundane task, such as cleaning a toilet.

- Much of the work of management involves implementing bureaucratic **rules and procedures** that come centrally from the organization (some of which are identical in all restaurants worldwide) or filling out pre-designed forms for such things as pay and stock ordering (Butler and Hammer, 2018).

Characteristics of McDonaldization

Ritzer (2019) outlines four principles of McDonaldization—efficiency, calculability, predictability, and control—through which fast-food restaurants are managed and organized (see Table 4.1). These principles have their origins in bureaucracy and scientific management. In this section we examine these four principles as Ritzer applies them to the fast-food restaurant.

Table 4.1 Principles characterizing the organization of fast-food restaurants

Efficiency	Getting something done in the optimum manner, with as little waste as possible, in the shortest amount of time, and with the least cost input in terms of wages and resources, as was the basis for Taylorism and Fordism
Calculability	Emphasizing what can be measured and calculated so as to achieve that efficiency, as with Taylor's time and motion studies
Predictability	Eliminating variability and unpredictability through standardized products and work processes, as with Taylorism and Fordism, or through standardized bureaucratic rules and procedures
Control	Commanding workers through bureaucratic rules and hierarchy, but also by making work as simple as possible and, where possible, replacing humans with technology

Source: Based on Ritzer (2019: 2–4).

Efficiency

Fast-food restaurants have efficiency inscribed in their DNA—it is even a part of the language of the restaurant (*fast*-food, *express* tills, etc.). Every task is designed to be efficient and to create as little waste as possible. Think about putting together a burger and, in particular, the role of the folding burger box (based on Ritzer, 2019: 10–11):

- one (pre-sliced) half of the roll is placed in each half of the box;
- the meat, sauces, (pre-shredded) lettuce, and other items are placed on the bottom half;
- in a final flourish of efficient work design, the box is closed—with no need to place the bread on top of the burger, the act of closing the box simultaneously, with no extra time or effort, also puts the bread in place.

While this saves just fractions of a second, the aim of a fast-food restaurant is to serve people quickly and in volume. These fractions of a second add up to big efficiency savings if they are repeated at all stages of making a burger and across the hundreds of thousands of burgers made every day.

 Visit the online resources and take a look at the extension material for Chapter 4 to see a video of making a burger and a comparison between fractional time savings in making burgers and designing racing cars.

Efficiency also comes from simplifying the product range in a similar way to Henry Ford's Model T (see Chapter 3). Unlike a luxury restaurant, where a meal is chosen and cooked individually and the menu may change from one day to the next, a fast-food restaurant has a limited number of products and options.

 Real life case: working for free

When you go to a fast-food restaurant, think about how you actually do some of the work for free.

You do the job of waiting staff, taking your own tray of food to the table, and as a cleaner, emptying your tray into a bin. This is all work which would otherwise take up the paid time of members of staff. In some fast-food restaurants, there are 'express' tills where the customer keys in the order, pays by card, and then collects their food. Yet another job—that of the till operator—is now performed for free by the customer (Ritzer, 2019: 74–5).

Craig Lambert (2015) describes this as 'shadow work'—a series of unpaid, unseen jobs that we perform daily. Whether using self-service checkouts, printing out boarding passes for a flight, or booking a hotel through an online booking service, we are doing a job where previously someone else was paid a wage (Bennett, 2015). This all helps businesses such as fast-food restaurants to run more efficiently. Indeed, getting work done for free rather than paying a wage is, perhaps, the ultimate in efficiency and cost-saving.

Source: based on Ritzer (2019: 74–5).

 How do you feel about performing work for free at a fast-food restaurant?
Is it worth it if the cost savings lead to a reduction in price? Can you think of any other organizations where you similarly work for free?

Calculability

Is a fast-food restaurant somewhere you would go to impress a business client or, perhaps, for a romantic date? It would be difficult to overemphasize the difference in quality of a fast-food restaurant compared with, say, a Michelin-starred restaurant. Not only is the food in a completely different league, there is also a difference in the quality of the experience. You would not be expected to clear up in a Michelin-starred restaurant, nor would there be someone cleaning the floor underneath your table as you eat!

For Ritzer (2019: 81), if quality cannot be marketed, then fast-food restaurants emphasize quantity—the amount you get for your money. This can be seen in the names of products—the Big Mac, the Whopper, the Supersize menu.

Calculability also extends to rational work design in fast-food restaurants—hardly surprising given their origin in Taylorist techniques, based around measurement and calculation. While much of the work process is based around calculating the optimum efficiency with which to perform a task, the emphasis on what can be measured can also be seen with 'live' orders on a screen behind the service area, with a clock ticking to show how long has elapsed since the order was taken.

Predictability

Many of you may have travelled abroad and found yourself in an unfamiliar environment where you don't know the language, local customs, or local foods. The sight of the McDonald's golden arches can be a welcome, familiar sign, where the nature of the food is known instantly. Even ordering is simple, as a phrase such as 'Big Mac' is universal.

Ritzer (2019: 99) suggests that McDonald's exhibits predictability—much of what they do is identical on a global scale, whether the restaurant be in Birmingham, Beijing, or Berlin. Such predictability is achieved by using the standardized routines and work patterns of bureaucracy.

- The interiors of fast-food chains look very similar—what Ritzer describes as 'predictable settings'. There are efficiencies from buying fixtures and fittings in bulk, and from having a standard design for a restaurant rather than employing individual designers each time (ibid.: 96) (see also Chapter 16 for discussion on the global standardization of organizational environments).

- As we have seen, fast-food restaurants have a standard range of products and use standardized procedures for making these products. Furthermore, conditions are placed on suppliers for the potatoes, meat, etc. that they provide. This allows a predictable and familiar range of products which look and taste identical wherever they are consumed (ibid.: 3–4).

- The behaviour of employees, who are all trained using the same manuals and procedures, is also predictable from one restaurant to another (ibid.: 145–47).

Control

McDonaldization exhibits Taylorist (see Chapter 3) and bureaucratic (Chapter 2) control through its meticulous use of manuals and procedures for tasks throughout the organization.

Control in a fast-food restaurant.
Source: Kondor83/Shutterstock.com

A major aspect of control is exerted by replacing 'human with non-human labour' (Ritzer, 2019: 154ff)—getting a machine to perform the task where possible. For example, the judgement on the length of time to cook fries is not left to humans as it may be with a trained chef; instead, a timer beeps to tell the operator when to remove the fries. The express till replaces operators completely with a machine. In this respect, this replacement of human with machine technology links with the **automation** of work, which we examine later in this chapter.

The 'McDonaldization' of society

The four aspects of McDonaldization connect to produce a contemporary rationalized organization that is efficient on a global scale. Even small elements of the work process that might go unnoticed can contribute to this process. Think of the scoop that is used to place fries in a carton—it contributes to all four aspects of McDonaldization:

- it is an *efficient* way of transferring fries to the carton;
- it *calculates* the portion size that goes into the carton;
- it allows *predictability* in that the same portion size is served every time;
- it *controls* the worker, preventing them from producing variable portion sizes each time.

When Ritzer refers to the 'McDonaldization of society' he does not mean that society is becoming overrun with fast-food restaurants, but that the rationalized organization and management techniques found in fast-food restaurants are found in *many other* types of contemporary organizations worldwide. McDonaldization, for Ritzer, is thus defined as 'The process by which the principles of the fast-food restaurant are coming to dominate more and more sectors of American society as well as the rest of the world' (Ritzer, 2019: 2).

Examples of McDonaldized organizations

Many other types of organization can be described as McDonaldized—displaying similar characteristics of efficiency, calculability, predictability, and control to those found in fast-food restaurants.

- Banks employ standardized procedures and have similar, predictable branch settings. Efficiency is gained from getting customers to do work for free through online banking and cashpoints. Technology controls and performs many tasks, such as balance transfers or paying bills, which used to be done by cashiers in handwritten ledgers (see also Ritzer, 2019: 77–78).
- Multiplex cinemas have a standard, predictable appearance across a chain, and are made more efficient by maximizing the number of screens within the building. Again, the customer does some work, and technology takes control through online and automated ticket booking.
- Parker and Jary (1995) describe McDonaldization in universities, where courses are divided into standardized modules and assessment may be done using formats such as multiple choice questions, which are designed for speed and efficiency in marking, often using technology such as a scanner to mark the assessment (see also Ritzer, 2019: 84–5).

 What other examples of McDonaldized organizations can you think of? How do they display characteristics of efficiency, calculability, predictability, and control?

Visit the online resources and take a look at the web links for Chapter 4 for more examples of McDonaldized organizations and a discussion about work in the fast-food industry.

The 'iron cage' of McDonaldization

Ritzer echoes Weber's concerns with the **iron cage** of rationality (see Chapter 2) to suggest that there now exists an 'iron cage' of ever-present McDonaldization. Following Weber, Ritzer (2019:

167ff) cautions against the 'irrational' aspects of rationality—the difference between what might be formally rational for an organization in terms of efficiency and what is substantively rational: the effects in human terms.

Ritzer (2019: 174–5) uses Weber's concept of **disenchantment**—a loss of the 'magical aspects' of life (see Chapter 2) as more and more organizations and aspects of life become standardized and routinized. An example this today can be found in campaigns against 'identikit' high streets, where independent retailers are replaced by standardized chains and towns lose something of their individual character (Cornish and Smith, 2018).

Deskilling and McJobs

Restaurant work is often linked with high levels of skill and even artistry. Top chefs train for years to get to their level and have a great deal of personal pride and identity linked to their work. A further critique of McDonaldization parallels Braverman's (1974) **deskilling** thesis, which critiqued the loss of workers' skills under Taylorism (see Chapter 3). Fast-food restaurants deskill food production. No longer is it a highly trained art form; instead, it involves performing a repetitive task which can be learned in a couple of hours. As with Taylorism, individual workers are left with a very limited knowledge of one very simple task. Their autonomy is reduced, as is the amount of control that they can exert—a troublesome worker is easily replaced, and their replacement can be trained and put in place within the day.

The phrase **McJobs** (Etzioni, 1986) has entered common parlance to describe simple, repetitive jobs with little job satisfaction, often performed by younger workers in the service sector (although see Gould, 2010, who suggests that there are some benefits for workers of 'McJobs', including the ability to work flexible hours around an individual lifestyle).

? Review questions

Describe	What are the four main features of McDonaldization?
Explain	How does McDonaldization originate within and further develop more traditional forms of rationalization, such as bureaucracy and scientific management?
Analyse	How could McDonaldization be described as a trade-off between quantity and quality?
Apply	What aspects of McDonaldization can you see in organizations with which you are familiar?

Contemporary models of rationalization

Q Running case: the budget hotel

I'm now in a budget hotel and, after the luxury of the previous hotel, this is a bit of a shock.

The check-in queue extended to the front door. Customer service was perfunctory and efficient—there was a job to do in processing the queue as quickly as possible. Despite the long queue, I soon had my key card, which gave me access to the lift and my room.

→

> The room was identical to other rooms that I've experienced in this chain. There was no door on the wardrobe—it certainly cuts costs: fewer raw materials to make the things in the first place, no moving parts to require repair should they go wrong, and no door for the cleaners to have to open and reach inside.
>
> A small kettle was hard-wired into the wall, next to receptacles for the tea/coffee sachets—almost to a preset size so that the cleaners can just drop in the required amount very quickly. There were no toiletries—I had to purchase those for myself from reception.
>
> Check-out required no human interaction; the key card was simply dropped into a slot on the reception desk.
>
> This place reduces its costs well, but we couldn't go this far with Junction Hotel—service and luxury is what our customers want.

Many organizations that we use regularly run on a rationalized business model of saving costs and increasing efficiency—in some cases it is their main business strategy in order to compete on price. All of the models we will now look at in this section could be described as 'McDonaldized' in Ritzer's terms and do exhibit some of the characteristics of McDonaldization. However, each also has their own particular ways of implementing rationalized techniques, which are worthy of examination in their own right.

'No-frills' rationalization and value engineering

Air travel was once considered glamorous—the province of celebrities and the well-off. Now it can be relatively cheap, thanks to the development of budget airlines such as Ryanair, EasyJet, and German Wings.

These **no-frills** airlines cut costs in the labour process, but their main cost-cutting strategy is to simply eliminate costs that are not essential to providing the basic service of a seat on a plane. If a customer incurs any further optional costs, such as a meal or a baggage allowance, they pay extra for them. Budget airlines strip the offering down to the most basic necessities at the lowest price possible.

A similar pricing and cost minimization model is found in the budget hotel industry. Davis (2007) notes how a budget hotel company, such as Travelodge, engages in value engineering—a meticulous analysis of where costs are incurred and whether they can be pared down. The company has made a value engineering judgement—people will forego luxuries such as trouser presses and chocolates on pillows if their priority is to get a room at a low price (Travelodge Ireland, 2015).

 Visit the online resources and take a look at the extension material for Chapter 4 to see a variety of ways in which hotels use 'no-frills' offerings, and how other industries use value engineering.

 Are there any other industries or organizations where you have seen a 'no-frills' model in operation?

Flat-pack rationalization

 Real life case: 'we hate air at IKEA'

Swedish global retailer IKEA has standardized stores which offer the same range globally. Key to their offering is flat-pack furniture, which saves storage space and space on delivery vehicles, thus saving costs (IKEA, 2003). Chaudhuri (2015) suggests that IKEA obsesses about packaging, working to shave fractions of a millimetre off the size of packaged goods to maximize the number that can go into a delivery vehicle. In this way, the transportation cost per unit drop.

Chaudhuri (2015) outlines how a redesign of the packaging of the IKEA Ektorp sofa reduced the packaging size by 50 per cent, resulting in over 7,000 fewer truck journeys annually. In addition to the environmental benefits of fewer journeys, the costs savings were passed on as a price reduction of 14 per cent on that item. Stefansson (2008) similarly packaging tea-light candles tightly rather than loosely removed wasted air in the packaging, allowing 30 per cent more packages to be placed on a pallet, and reducing transportation by 18,000 pallets per annum. Peter Agnefjäll, CEO of IKEA, said that 'We hate air at IKEA' (Chaudhuri, 2015).

IKEA has similarities to McDonaldized efficiency: whereas McDonald's strives to save fractions of a second, IKEA strives to reduce fractions of a millimetre. In both cases these factor up in huge cost savings. Removing excess air from packaging also links with value engineering, as IKEA's CEO Peter Agnefjäll states: costs that add no value to the end product are designed, or engineered, out of the process (Chaudhuri, 2015).

Other than efficiencies in packaging, there are rationalized aspects of flat-pack furniture which allow costs to be minimized and the product to be sold much more cheaply (see also Ritzer, 2019: 17–18).

- As we noted in Chapter 3, flat-pack furniture is designed as component parts which can be assembled easily, just as Taylor designed work tasks. The customer does the assembly work themselves, saving the manufacturer the costs of assembly, and there is no need for the expensive skills of trained furniture-makers.

- Tasks are so simplified that the instruction sheet can be provided as a set of diagrams rather than words. This helps to standardize packaging, as there is no need to translate and print different instruction booklets for each country. Economies of scale are global.

- It is not just products that are standardized. Standard components, such as shelves and screws, can be used across a number of products.

Barcode technology and rationalization

At the supermarket, you may see the barcode on products as a type of electronic price tag. While it does have that function, the barcode allows a supermarket to do far more than calculate prices at the till. Much rationalization in supermarkets is a result of barcode computer technology, allowing the supermarket to make efficiencies and reduce costs in a number of ways (see also Ritzer, 2019: 76–7).

The ubiquitous barcode.
Source: MicroOne / Shutterstock.com

- The barcode is printed on each individual product, so individual items do not need to be priced up in the supermarket. When a price changes, it can be altered on the computer system for all stores across the country—a massive time saving compared to applying labels to all the individual products.

- Rather than keying in prices for items, the supermarket cashier simply waves the goods in front of a barcode reader. The checkout often has a conveyor belt—the cashier is simply one part of an assembly line with the customer placing goods at one end and packaging them at the other.

- Scanning the barcode updates the total bill, and simultaneously reduces the store's inventory for that product. There is less need for stocktaking to be done by staff, and stock ordering can be done automatically by the computer system. Passing a product in front of a till feeds into a national distribution and supply system similar to the neo-Fordist just-in-time inventory system (see Chapter 3).

- Self-service tills have become commonplace, with the customer doing the work of a cashier and scanning the items themselves.

While barcodes and associated computer technology help supermarkets to get a large volume of customers through the store efficiently, it also leaves it vulnerable. If one area of the system is disrupted then it can stop the system overall from functioning. Many of us will be familiar with waiting in line at a supermarket while there is a delay because the barcode is missing from one item: the system breaks down.

When working well, the barcode produces an efficient system, but the demands of the system are such that, when it breaks down, it can suffer from similar issues of 'red tape' as seen in Chapter 2, where the system and its rules and procedures actually get in the way of work being done efficiently.

 This example draws from large-scale supermarket chains. Which of the techniques and characteristics mentioned have you experienced in smaller stores?

Barcodes, information, and tracking

The tracking capabilities of barcodes can also be used on products or people. In Chapter 3 we saw how the electronics firm Ebuyer runs an efficient, neo-Fordist warehouse system, part of which involves tracking products through the system by scanning barcodes, with the final scan being done when the parcel is delivered to your house. You can follow the progress of the parcel for yourself through a website or app.

While this allows for an efficient handling of products, the workers can also be tracked to see how efficiently they are handling those products. Rather than just accessing existing information on a database, barcodes and computer systems allow for information to be generated about a worker's performance, and allow for control to be exerted over that worker. It is to these issues of surveillance and control in the contemporary rational organization that we turn in the next section.

Review questions

Describe	How do the organizations discussed in this section cut costs and create efficiencies?
Explain	How do barcodes facilitate both efficiency and control?
Analyse	How do you think Frederick Taylor (see Chapter 2) might have been able to use barcode technology in his factories had it been available to him?
Apply	While value engineering is often associated with budget hotels, how might it still be applied in a luxury hotel such as Junction Hotel?

Panopticism, surveillance, and control

Running case: the credit card statement

Midtown Bank

Credit card statement	S. CHANCE (Business a/c)	Card No. 4567 887 999988
Date	Vendor	Amount
1/2/2019	Budgetshack Hotels	34.00
5/2/2019	Magasin Department (Oxford Street)	120.00
5/2/2019	City Casino, Leicester Square	100.00
5/2/2019	The Late Venue, Soho	120.00
5/2/2019	Luxhotel restaurant	180.00
6/2/2019	Fastburgers, Euston Road	4.00
6/2/2019	Budgetshack Hotels	20.99
7/2/2019	Mr Florist	23.00

How much of Chance's business trip can we retrace from this credit card statement? Is there anything on here that he may wish to hide (and does this explain the final entry on the list for when he got home)?

The philosopher Michel Foucault (1977: 228) is renowned for his statement that '[P]risons resemble factories, schools, barracks, hospitals, which all resemble prisons'. Foucault doesn't mean that people are kept under lock and key at school or in hospital; he means that all of these organizations exert power and control through the use of **surveillance**: observation, either overt or covert, of people to gain information about them or to control them.

Foucault's work parallels the way in which control is exerted in the rational organization, whose design facilitates surveillance over workers. This surveillance is intensified by computer and database technology.

Foucault and the Panopticon

Foucault was not interested specifically in organizational issues, but in how control and order were maintained historically in society overall.

Foucault begins with a gruesome description from 1757 of Damiens, the murderer of the king, being hung, drawn, and quartered in Paris. Today, says Foucault, control and punishment in society are not so torturous and direct; instead, power operates by more subtle means within individual organizations and institutions.

The exemplar of this is the **Panopticon**, a prison design which exerts power through indirect means of surveillance. Its design, according to Foucault, is a blueprint for power and surveillance in many organizations that are a part of our daily lives.

The Panopticon was built so that cells were arranged in a circle around a central watch tower. Every prisoner is instantly *visible* and open to surveillance (the word surveillance links with the idea of visibility—*surveiller* being the French word for 'watching over'). Its design means that a prisoner can be selected and observed from the central tower. The prisoner does not know at any one moment whether they are being observed, but the fact that they *might* be observed makes them behave as the guards wish—control is internalized within the prisoner.

The design of the Panopticon allows for a massive efficiency gain in terms of staffing the prison. One guard can maintain order over hundreds of prisoners from the central watch tower, rather than many guards needing to exert direct control. Thus the Panopticon encompasses two aspects of rational organization—efficiency and control.

The modern-day Panopticon

The same type of surveillance operates in CCTV systems. When we are in a store or town centre covered by CCTV cameras, we do not know if the pictures are being observed, but it is the fact that they *might be* which makes a potential miscreant behave. Again, we internalize control and power rather than having it exerted upon us face to face.

Modern-day surveillance.
Source: Andrey_Popov/Shutterstock.com

The image of a security guard sitting in front of a bank of CCTV screens that show different areas of the store or town centre is not too different to the guard in the Panopticon looking at a grid of individual cells. In both cases, an efficient system to exert power and control is in place. The advantage that CCTV has over the Panopticon is that even if the security guard misses something, it is preserved on video to be looked at later. Technology thus enhances the power and surveillance abilities of the Panopticon.

 Think about how you are controlled when driving. A speed camera may not be switched on, but you are not to know this as you approach it. Does the speed camera make you internalize power and control? Are speed cameras a form of modern-day Panopticon?

Organizational Panopticons

The structure of the Panopticon allows surveillance, which brings about two benefits that, no doubt, would interest managers in other types of organization.

- It allows control to be exerted over the organization where otherwise chaos and unpredictability might ensue.
- It allows for this to be done efficiently.

Maybe it is no surprise that the original Panopticon design was based on a factory design (Hume, 2004: 270). Just as control over a large number of prisoners presents an organizational problem, so might control over a large number of workers in a factory.

Production systems based around Taylorism, such as the assembly line or the McDonald's restaurant, also display panoptic principles. Workers are given individual, simple tasks. This improves the efficiency of the production process, but also helps to increase surveillance over each individual worker. If a product is being made with component number 49 incorrectly attached, it is easy to locate the cause of the problem—the worker whose job is to attach component 49.

The call centre as an organizational Panopticon

The **call centre** is a rationalized, efficient form of contemporary organization that has been described as similar to a Panopticon (Fernie and Metcalf, 1998). Whenever we interact with large-scale organizations by telephone (our bank or insurance company, for example) this is often handled by a call centre. Calls are automatically directed to operators—the operator does not pace their own work. The pacing is similar to that of an assembly line—the pace of work is dictated by the line or, in this case, the computer system. Work is passed before the worker and has to be attended to there and then—there is no room to take a rest.

The intensive work is controlled by surveillance within the call centre, which exhibits many similarities to the Panopticon.

- The physical layout of a call centre—workers in their own individual booths—is visually similar to the Panopticon. Workers can be watched, as with the guard in the Panopticon, so anyone leaving their booth for an unauthorized break can be spotted instantly.

- While an operator might be tempted to deal with a rude customer by telling them in no uncertain terms where to go, they are prevented by the possibility that a supervisor may be listening in. As with the Panopticon, this is not constant, direct, face-to-face control—it is the possibility that the supervisor might be listening which makes the operator internalize power and control and behave accordingly.

- Call data is recorded electronically—targets for the number of calls handled per hour can be set and reviewed on a computer by a supervisor. To increase efficiency, the target number of calls per hour can be increased—similar to increasing the speed of the assembly line. Computer data can also be used to review and monitor performance. For example, data can indicate the time spent away from the telephones. There are instances where a maximum toilet time is given and the computer data can monitor if people take longer (Woodcock, 2017; Hencke, 2005).

While not all call centres control and monitor workers to such an extent, and there are examples of how such a system can be resisted (see Bain and Taylor, 2000; and Woodcock, 2017), the potential for electronic monitoring and surveillance leads Fernie and Metcalf (1998) to describe the call centre as an 'electronic panopticon', where supervisory power has been 'rendered perfect'.

In what ways in your life in general, beyond the workplace, are you under surveillance? How can your behaviour be observed even after it has taken place?

The electronic Panopticon and 'dataveillance'

The final aspect of control created within the call centre—the use of electronic data—links back to bureaucratic control (the keeping of records) and rational work design (the calculation of standards and workplace targets). Panoptic power becomes not just about physical observation but also how information is generated and recorded about workers and used to judge their performance, especially when stored electronically (Simpson, 1999: 69).

 Visit the online resources and take a look at the extension material for Chapter 4 to read more on how data can be used as a means of control.

> **Real life case:** credit ratings
>
> We are used to having our credit rating checked when we apply for a loan, for example, or sign up to a mobile phone contract, but do you know how this is calculated?
>
> Credit rating agencies hold masses of data about all individuals—especially their financial history. They have records of credit cards held, loans taken out, and other financial products held. Furthermore, they have records of how well people have kept up with their payments—do they have an unblemished record or have they missed several months of payments in a row? (Lewis, 2018).
>
> From all of this data, the credit rating agency is able to exercise surveillance in that they can see your entire financial history and from that make decisions about whether or not you are a worthy credit risk.

In the contemporary world we are used to a lot of information being generated and held about us. As discussed in Chapter 2, vast amounts of data are held in computer networks and shared between organizations. Terms such as **dataveillance**, which combines surveillance with the electronic data held on individuals, and the **electronic Panopticon** describe the ways in which data can be used by organizations to exert control and surveillance over individuals in a manner similar to the original Panopticon. Such control and surveillance have two important aspects.

- Anything we do that is recorded on a computer system—websites visited, tweets posted, etc.—is potentially discoverable later on. Politicians have found this to their cost when emails that they thought were private are uncovered months later and leaked to the press (e.g. Stewart and Elgot, 2017). It also means that anything which links to a computer system is recorded—bank withdrawals, credit card payments, cards swiped through door entry systems, etc. A lot of electronic data held about us could potentially come back to haunt us.

- Such data can be used not only for surveillance—to find out what we have been doing—but also to make decisions about us. While credit-rating agencies assess our credit-worthiness, insurance companies use data to assess the degree of risk that we pose as drivers, for example, comparing our data with data held on other individuals (Poster, 1995).

The Panopticon thus shows how surveillance and control not only affect us in the workplace, but also are used to exert power and surveillance over us by organizations in society generally. While the Panopticon was first conceived of as a rationalized prison design centuries ago, Foucault shows how its surveillance and ordering mechanisms are just as relevant to rationalized organizations today.

The use of dataveillance, i.e computerization, brings the Panopticon from the Second Industrial Revolution to the third. In the next section we advance the ideas that we have encountered so far in Chapters 2, 3, and 4 to see how they can be found in the Fourth Industrial Revolution.

❓ Review questions

Describe	How did the Panopticon exert control over prisoners?
Explain	How is surveillance used as a means of power and control in contemporary organizations and society?
Analyse	What did Foucault mean when he said that prisons are a blueprint for power and control in many other organizations?
Apply	What examples of surveillance in your own workplace or university can you identify? How do you feel about being watched like this?

The Fourth Industrial Revolution

🔍 Running case: the Grand Hotel Gig

Now I have seen it all. My final hotel was the Grand Hotel Gig, a brand new hotel which claims to use the latest technology to make the whole stay smooth and seamless. There was a lot of technology here, and very few staff.

There was no check-in desk, just a computer terminal where I put in my credit card. Instantly it called up my booking. I was expecting a room key. Instead, the screen asked me to look at a camera. A scan of my iris was taken, and a message informed me that, by looking at a camera, I could open my room door. If I stay at the hotel again, I won't need the credit card, I will be emailed my room number and I can go straight there and gain instant access, no need to even visit reception. I was then asked if I needed assistance with luggage. A motorized trolley next to the terminal suddenly whirred into action. A human-like voice asked me to place the luggage on the trolley, then cheerily it said 'Follow me,' leading me to my room.

Once in my room, the television switched on automatically, and a similar voice greeted me: 'Good afternoon, Mr Chance. I see that this is your first visit to Grand Hotel Gig. Please watch a video about our services.' The video explained that the iris scan would be used to allow me into areas of the hotel such as the restaurant, and the camera and sensor technology would bill me automatically for extras such as the minibar or food.

I decided to put this to the test in the restaurant. '*Bon appétit*, Mr Chance,' said another voice as I walked through the barriers at the entrance. At one end of the restaurant was a set of shelves—one warm with various meals ready to take, another with drinks. I simply took my selection, then sat down and ate. Returning to my room, I asked the TV to show my hotel account—the amounts for the food had already been added.

→

→

As much as I was enjoying the voice within the television, I decided to relax for the night and switched to one of the channels that was showing a wonderful Mozart concert.

The next morning was slightly disconcerting. Clearly the sensors could detect that I was awake and walking around, and so the TV sprang into action again: 'Good morning Mr Chance. There is a classical concert in town tonight, would you like me to book tickets for you?' The computer system had registered what I watched last night and calculated that I might be interested in that concert. Just a bit creepy . . . .

I left my room and saw a cleaner in the corridor. I realized this was the first human member of staff I had seen since I checked in. Clearly some tasks such as making the bed can't quite be handled by robots just yet. 'Another human, can I talk to you?' I said. 'Yes, but keep walking,' said the cleaner. 'I am tracked just like you are, so I can't stand still. I will be assessed on how quickly I have cleaned the rooms. If I am too slow they might not call me in tomorrow.' I asked what was meant by being called in—surely the cleaners have set hours? 'Not at all, I don't even work here officially. I mean, I have the hotel uniform and all that, which I had to buy myself, but I am signed up through an app on my phone. Every morning, I open the app to see if I am needed on that day or not—and if I was slow yesterday then they are less likely to call me in. What is ridiculous is, by working faster the rooms get done more quickly—and if there are no rooms left to do then they send us home early—and we only get paid for the hours we are actually here. On any day I never know how many hours I will actually work, if any at all.'

This hotel saves a lot on labour costs. But would the guests at Junction Hotel really get a luxury experience when there is so little human contact? Even the humans here, like the cleaner, seem to have been reduced to being just like the robots that seem to run the hotel.

 How many features of the Grand Hotel Gig have you seen in hotels, or in other organizations?

Uber, the world's largest taxi company, owns no vehicles. Facebook, the world's most popular media owner, creates no content. Alibaba, the most valuable retailer, has no inventory. And Airbnb, the world's largest accommodation provider, owns no real estate. Something interesting is happening.

(Goodwin, 2015)

Many of us have used some or all of the companies named above. They are huge global companies and household names, used daily by millions. So what is it that Goodwin suggests is 'interesting' about the trend that these companies represent? A common factor between these companies is that they do not provide goods and services directly; instead, they use digital technology to make connections between the producers and consumers of these goods and services (Wilkesmann and Wilkesmann, 2018). You do not, for example, rent an apartment from Airbnb—Airbnb connects you with someone who wishes to rent out their apartment. The platform provided by these companies, through a web browser or a smartphone, is the main focus of business operations.

This, among many other contemporary business and organizational models, represents such a profound change that Klaus Schwab (2016a, 2016b) suggests we have entered a **Fourth Industrial Revolution**. The key feature of this is the emergence of **cyber-physical systems**, which the US National Science Foundation (2016) describes as 'engineered systems that are built from, and depend upon, the seamless integration of computational algorithms and physical components'. While technology has always been with us, it is now 'fusing with people' and 'blurring … into every part of our lives' (Morgan, 2016). For Schwab (2016a) there is a 'fusion of technologies across the physical, digital and biological worlds.'

Real life case: Amazon Go

Amazon is best known for pioneering online retailing, so it is ironic that they have returned to high-street shopping, albeit with a difference. At Amazon Go, which has opened its prototype store in Seattle, shoppers put their items into a bag and walk straight out of the store with no queues, no checkouts, and no payment—at least not in the sense of handing over payment to a cashier.

The whole store is underpinned by technology. Customers scan an app to enter the store. Within the store they are tracked by hundreds of cameras which, together with weight sensors on the shelves, links with the computer system to work out exactly what items each customer has placed in their bag and adds it to their bill. If an item is replaced, it is taken off the bill.

When the shopper leaves the store, the total of the bill is automatically taken from their bank account, and the customer is emailed a digital receipt for the purchases.

Sources: Amazon (2016); Harris (2018); *The Guardian* (2018); Coldewey (2018).

Visit the online resources and take a look at the web links for Chapter 4 for a video of Amazon Go in operation.

Amazon Go is an example of a cyber-physical system. Algorithms direct digital technology which, following Schwab, becomes blurred in a system which enmeshes people (the customers) and physical objects (the goods and the physical layout of the store). While this is heralded as a new form of managing and organizing, in this section we show that it links with and has developed from previous forms of rationalization. The whole system shares with early rationalization (see Chapters 2 and 3) the goals of efficiency (no checkouts to delay the process) and control (customers cannot walk out of the store without paying for goods). The precise tracking of movements has links with time and motion studies first pioneered by Taylor and the Gilbreths (see Chapter 3). Elements of McDonaldization can also be seen in Amazon Go—for example the replacement of the human work of cashiers with technology. Furthermore, Amazon Go extends some of the features of supermarket work examined earlier in this chapter—instead of barcodes we now have the cyber-physical tracking of goods, and instead of the self-checkout we now have the automatic reckoning of the bill and money taken from the customer's bank account. The whole system provides a form of surveillance and tracking which extends the panoptic capabilities of dataveillance.

Table 4.2 shows the four industrial revolutions, leading up to the fourth which we examine in this section. These are not discrete, unconnected stages: they link together, and many elements of today's Fourth Industrial Revolution have their origins in techniques pioneered by Taylor, Ford, and Fayol during the Second Industrial Revolution (see Chapters 2 and 3). We saw in Chapter 2 that classical bureaucracy was a forerunner of the control needed to run the gig economy, and in Chapter 3 that Taylorist work design was a forerunner of modern-day warehouse and distribution logistics.

The remainder of this section examines two aspects of the Fourth Industrial Revolution: the extension of automation into more and more areas of work, especially through artificial intelligence; and the transformation of some areas of work into a flexible and precarious 'gig economy'.

Table 4.2 The four industrial revolutions

Industrial revolution	Approximate dates	Key technologies	Examples
First	1760–1840	Steam power, railroads	Mechanization of production
Second	Early 1900s	Electricity, bureaucratic structure	Division of labour (Taylorism), assembly line, mass production (Fordism)
Third	1980s onwards	Digital technology, electronics, IT	Automation, flexible mass production (neo-Fordism)
Fourth	Present day	Cyber-physical systems	Further automation, artificial intelligence, gig economy

Source: Based on Schwab (2016a, 2016b).

As a current and developing phenomenon of work and organization, these are areas that are subject to ongoing change, however both have origins in techniques developed in the second and third industrial revolutions. There are four particular features which cut across all of the examples in the remainder of this section: big data, algorithms, the quantified self, and flexibility.

Big data. Data has been central to all phases of rationalization. In the Second Industrial Revolution, paperwork and record-keeping were used to maintain information about workers and organizational processes. In the Third Industrial Revolution, computer databases digitized this information, allowing the 'informated organization' to store more data and process it more quickly (see Chapter 2) and allowing this data to be shared through computer networks. In the Fourth Industrial Revolution, this data storage and processing capability has increased. Every use of an app on a smartphone, every click of a product on an online store, every computer key pressed or swipe card used to access a door by a worker—these are just a few of the examples of data that is being constantly generated. 'Big data' refers to this mass of data that is held by organizations.

Algorithms. Linked with big data, algorithms are computer software routines which apply some form of calculation or procedure to that data. An algorithm might apply performance management measures to the data of a worker (see Chapter 2), or apply calculations to work out whether or not an applicant has the required credit rating for a loan. Algorithms can be linked with classical bureaucracy in that they take particular organizational rules and procedures (see Chapter 2) and apply them to people or processes within the organization. In the Fourth Industrial Revolution, algorithms have been linked with artificial intelligence because they can learn to do more and more activities that previously would have been left to human skills or judgement. Furthermore, as data is continually produced from organizational activities, algorithms are able to learn from this new data and adapt what they do with no need for any human input.

Quantified self. Earlier in the chapter we saw how the Panopticon, along with computer data, allows control and surveillance in organizations such as call centres. David Beer (2016: 5) suggests that this control and surveillance has been 'ramped up' in recent years. Big data and algorithms allow more and more data about contemporary life and work to be stored and analysed. Phoebe Moore (2018) describes the application of this to us as workers as the 'quantified self: … the individual worker … whose activities are tracked, monitored, surveilled' (Moore, 2018: 3). We are used to athletes having their performance monitored and subject to computer analysis to improve performance (Moore and Robinson, 2016). Such monitoring and analysis are now applied to many areas of often mundane work. As Moore (2018: 10) states, 'Management can know more than ever before about workers as technology constantly tracks second by second information of their movements and internal functioning.' We have already seen this tracking of the quantified self, for example through the use of big data for performance management (Chapter 2) and the tracking and control of workers in warehouses (Chapter 3). This ability to track and direct the minutest movements of workers, using various sensors, trackers, and algorithms, is compared by Moore and Robinson (2016: 2781) to an intensified form of Taylorism, 'an updated form of time and motion studies originally endorsed by Taylor with enhanced recognition of the corporeal dimension'. In other words, human bodies, physical objects, and digital technology become merged together.

Visit the online resources and take a look at the extension material for Chapter 4 for further comparisons between the quantified self and sports performance, including how we do this voluntarily through the wearing of fitness trackers and similar technology.

Flexibility. A key feature of the Third Industrial Revolution was that it took place in a more uncertain environment and thus developed more flexible systems such as post-bureaucratic form (see Chapter 2) and neo-Fordist flexible production methods (see Chapter 3 and earlier discussion in this chapter). As we will see, the Fourth Industrial Revolution has allowed this flexibility in terms of goods and service provision to be increased while at the same time intensifying control over workers. Furthermore, increasing demands are made upon workers to be flexible, which is one of the controversies that lies at the heart of current debates around the gig economy.

Common to both aspects of the Fourth Industrial Revolution discussed in the following sections—first automation and artificial intelligence, and next the gig economy—are changes to the nature of work experienced by workers. Starting with automation we ask if much of the work that we know today will even exist in the future.

From automation to artificial intelligence

Which jobs that are common today will exist in 20 years' time? Or even within a decade? This is a common question asked in press articles which examine which jobs are at risk of being automated, that is to say which jobs currently performed by humans will be taken over by robots, computers, or some other form of technology.

Visit the online resources and take a look at the extension material for Chapter 4 to see lists of jobs at risk of automation—and those which are considered to be safe.

Automation is not new in the workplace. Robots have been doing assembly line work for decades, and since the Third Industrial Revolution computer technology, such as spreadsheets, has been able to automate areas of office work as well as manufacturing. An element of McDonaldization that we saw earlier was replacing human with non-human technology—when you order from a self-service screen rather than a cashier at a till, this is another example of automation. The foundations for automation were laid in the Second Industrial Revolution: for example when Taylor divided work into simplistic, repetitive tasks (see Chapter 3), this simplicity made the work easier to automate. And when Ford created assembly line work that reduced workers to standing in front of a conveyor belt and doing one task such as fitting a wing mirror, he effectively reduced people to robots or 'cogs in a machine'—and once the technology was available, these human robots were replaced by actual robots. In the Fourth Industrial Revolution, automation has continued, with the technology of cyber-physical systems allowing more tasks to be automated, putting more jobs at risk.

Real life case: Adidas Speedfactory

In 2016, German sportswear company Adidas set up its Speedfactory in Ansbach, Bavaria, manufacturing trainers, with robots to automate most of the production process. This contrasts with other factories where the work of assembling, sewing, bonding, and shaping the trainers is done by people, often subcontracted to the developing world.

Herbert Hainer, CEO of the Adidas Group, described the process as 'automated, decentralized and flexible'. Flexibility is particularly important in reducing the time it takes to develop new designs and get them into stores. Fashions change quickly, but a traditional factory can take up to 18 months to get a new design to market, including making prototypes, ordering new components, and changing the set-up of the factory. In the Speedfactory, this process can be reduced to less than a week. The software takes a new design and instantly coordinates the actions of robots, knitting machines, and 3D printers. New components are made within the factory from raw materials.

Small batches of niche designs can be made, and it is envisaged that eventually people will be able to order their own individually customized trainers, based around scans of their walking or running motion.

There are some jobs where robots are not yet as good as humans, for example with the final shaping of a shoe, and so the factory will still employ around 160 staff, but this is a big reduction on the traditional factories with over a thousand employees. A second Speedfactory has recently been opened in Atlanta, USA, and the company plans to open more worldwide.

Sources: Adidas (2015); *The Economist* (2017); Green (2018).

 Visit the online resources and take a look at the web links for Chapter 4 to see a video of the Adidas Speedfactory.

The Speedfactory exhibits the four characteristics of the Fourth Industrial Revolution. It runs on *big data*, drawing upon a store of coded information about manufacturing processes. It brings in data from computer scans of individuals, suggesting an element of the *quantified self*. It applies *algorithms* to this data to run the production process, instructing the machinery exactly what to do in response to a different design being input in to the system, with no human instruction or decision-making needed. This ability to respond quickly to changes in shoe design gives the factory the ability to operate with *flexibility*.

There are commonalities and differences between the Speedfactory and factories from previous industrial eras. It shares the Second Industrial Revolution's desire for efficiency and control—imagine if Taylor or the Gilbreths were able to use its technology to order movements precisely in their factories. However, the flexibility of the Speedfactory is an advance on the Fordist 'only available in black' model. The ability to mass-produce but to be flexible and constantly change the products suggests a neo-Fordist form of production. However, the fact that some highly skilled human workers are still needed, and that the system is able to do specialized, small-batch production within mass production, also suggests elements of post-Fordism.

There are also elements of the Speedfactory that are unique to the Fourth Industrial Revolution. These **smart factories** (Wilkesmann and Wilkesmann, 2018: 240) are cyber-physical systems which blur together the digital elements (data and algorithms) with physical elements (the robots, the raw materials that make the shoes) and biological elements (data about individual human customers taken from computer analysis of walking and running styles).

The logic of automation goes to the heart of the capitalist working relationship (see Chapter 3). Capitalists want to get as much work as possible for the wages that they pay. If automation can reduce the number of jobs where people need to be employed, then the wage bill drops. At the same time, automation gives control over the work process in ways not possible with human workers. However, this means that people lose their jobs as more and more types of work cease to exist once they are automated: for example, Wong (2016) reports the founder of a fully automated hamburger-making machine as saying, 'Our device isn't meant to make employees more efficient . . . It's meant to completely obviate them.'

 In Chapter 17 we examine some of the problems with sweatshop labour in clothing factories in the developing world. If this work can be automated, then it means that workers are no longer subjected to difficult and dangerous work. At the same time, however, it means that their jobs are taken away from them. How would you solve this dilemma?

Which jobs are at risk of automation?

 Real life case: Singapore—the automated airport

Terminal 4 at Singapore's Changi Airport, which opened in 2017, offers a fully-automated departure process. From self check-in and bag-drop machines to passport control and boarding, no humans are involved. Facial recognition, fingerprint technology, and advance passenger information all play a part in the smooth transition throughout the various stages of departure.

Similar technologies are being developed throughout the airline industry, for example:

- E-passports use biometric data and facial scanning technology to enable automated passport gates;

- British Airways is trialling automated departure gates for flights, with the technology recognizing facial images captured earlier at the security check;

- British Airways is also trialling electronic luggage tags, which would replace paper tags and would be activated for each journey by the passenger using their smartphone.

Sources: Robbins (2017); Lim and Mei (2017); Murgia (2017); Powley (2017).

123

An airport is a prime candidate for the rationalization and automation of work—it has a standard check-in and departure processes which need to be applied to a mass of people to get them through the airport as efficiently as possible. The Second Industrial Revolution applied bureaucracy—creating rules, procedures, and paperwork in order to process passengers. The computerization of the Third Industrial Revolution made this process more efficient, and allowed some of the work to be automated—e.g. online check-in. The case of Singapore's Changi Airport demonstrates airports entering the Fourth Industrial Revolution—the terminal at Singapore is a cyber-physical system, with computer algorithms and biometric data combining to move people and physical objects such as baggage through the system—the passenger becomes a 'quantified self' that is tracked around this system.

The airport also demonstrates how the automation of work is moving beyond robotics in manufacturing to many more areas of work. The tasks in the airport go beyond manual tasks to cognitive tasks such as decision-making—it is now an algorithm, rather than a human, that decides whether a passenger will be allowed to go through passport control. The automation of human thought processes through big data and algorithms is a particular form of automation known as **artificial intelligence.** Chapter 10 examines how more and more areas of human intelligence and skill are being automated by computer systems.

Two UK studies (Roberts et al., 2017; Frey and Osborne, 2017) have estimated that approximately one-third of jobs are at risk of automation in the next two decades, representing 10 million jobs in the UK. This threatens many lower-paid jobs in poorer areas of the UK, for example in the sectors of hospitality, retail, and transport (Elliot, 2017). White-collar and middle-class jobs are also under threat of automation (Wong, 2016), especially those which at some level are 'routine, repetitive and predictable' (Mahdawi, 2017). With the increased use of artificial intelligence, some professional jobs such as accountancy and legal research are also at risk of automation (see Chapter 10 for more discussion of this).

There are still jobs which cannot be automated: for example, at the Adidas Speedfactory some jobs finishing the shoes still require human skill and touch. In Chapter 10 we will see how jobs requiring creativity, social interaction, dealing with uncertainty, manual dexterity, and discretion (see also Chapter 3) are those which still require human input and, for now, are safest from being automated (see also Schwab, 2016a). Frey and Osbourne (2017) carried out an analysis of 702 distinct occupations to work out which were at most risk from computerization within the next 20 years. Table 4.3 shows a small selection of these results.

 Visit the online resources and take a look at the web links for Chapter 4 to see the results for all 702 occupations.

While not all jobs can currently be automated, this does not mean that Fourth Industrial Revolution principles have not also been applied to the work that humans still do. The next section demonstrates this with the gig economy.

Table 4.3 Probablilities of jobs being computerized by 2040

Probability	Example jobs (1 = certain probability; 0 = no probability)
Jobs with an almost 100% probability of being computerized	Telemarketers (0.99) Insurance underwriters (0.99) Umpires, referees, and other sports officials (0.98) Cashiers (0.97) Cooks, restaurant (0.96)
Jobs with a 50/50 probability of being computerized	Teacher assistants (0.56) Commercial pilots (0.55) Court reporters (0.5) Fire inspectors and investigators (0.48) Economists (0.43)
Jobs with an almost 0% probability of being computerized	Chief executives (0.015) Training and development managers (0.0063) Choreographers (0.004) Dieticians and nutritionists (0.0039) Emergency management directors (0.003)

Source: Adapted from Frey and Osbourne (2017).

If a job has a high probability of being automated, does this mean that automation will happen? For example, do you think that technology will eventually replace all football referees, or is there still a need for a human presence on the pitch?

The gig economy

We live in a world of drones, driverless cars, and the automation of human thought through artificial intelligence. However, these technologies are not yet sufficiently developed to replace human labour in many areas of work. Technology has not yet replaced taxi drivers, cycle couriers, and many creative jobs, for example. Nevertheless, digital technology can still control work in the Fourth Industrial Revolution. In particular, the **gig economy** (sometimes also called the platform economy) has received much attention in recent years. Lepanjuuri et al. (2018: 8) define the gig economy as '[T]he exchange of labour for money between individuals or companies via digital platforms that actively facilitate matching between providers and customers, on a short-term and payment by task basis.'

The digital platforms are websites or smartphone apps, such as Uber and Deliveroo, where customers order services, and through which the algorithms allocate the task to a particular worker. The term 'gig' economy is used because, as Balaram et al. (2017: 10) explain, workers use platforms to source individual jobs which are usually completed on demand, like a musician going from one gig to another. These gigs are often small jobs: for example, an Uber driver carrying out a taxi journey is a single 'gig'.

Examples of gig economy work

The gig economy is often associated in the media with low-skilled, simple tasks, but it spans a whole range of work. In fact, Balaram et al. (2017: 14) suggest that 58 per cent of gig work is professional and creative work, with 33 per cent skilled manual work and just 16 per cent driving and delivery services. Lepanjuuri et al. (2018) estimate that around 1.1 million people, generally young people, work in the gig economy, around 4.4 per cent of the UK workforce.

One key distinction in gig economy work is made by Schmidt (2017) between 'cloud work' which is usually web-based and done by a worker sitting at a computer, and 'location based', such as delivery services, which have to be done in a specific geographical location away from a computer. Table 4.4 draws on various classifications to suggest four main categories of gig economy work.

The gig economy brings together the four main characteristics of the Fourth Industrial Revolution. First, the platforms of the gig economy bring together *big data* about customers, workers, and the work which is often codified itself as computer data. Second, this data is managed by *algorithms*. When a customer orders a cab from Uber, the algorithm will identify the closest cab and alert that driver through a smartphone. Third, workers in the gig economy are examples of the *quantified self*. We will see how the algorithms that manage the system also draw on data such as worker performance and customer ratings, which can influence how work is allocated and rewarded. Finally, the gig economy allows for *flexibility*. For workers, the ability to opt into specific 'gigs' gives them more independence over when and where they work: for example, students can work around academic commitments (Balaram et al., 2017: 26).

However, what might be attractive to students or people looking to supplement income in their spare time is not necessarily attractive to people relying on a full-time income. The flexibility of

Table 4.4 Categories of gig economy work

Category	Cloud/ location based	Description	Examples
Creative, IT, and professional	Cloud	Online marketplaces for skilled work such as web development, legal assignments, accounting services, creative tasks such as writing and graphic design. Tasks are posted to a website with freelancers applying for the work, with the customers usually being companies with specific work requirements.	Upwork, Freelancer
Household, personal, and skilled manual	Location	Online marketplaces for work where the customer is usually an individual requiring work done in their own home, such as cleaning, plumbing, DIY tasks. A typical task might be assembling flatpack furniture, which may explain why Taskrabbit has been purchased by IKEA.	Hassle, Taskrabbit, Rated People
Microtasking and click-work	Cloud	Workers accept small and fairly simple tasks, for which they receive small payments, even 1 cent per task. The work is often described as 'clickwork' because it can involve simple tasks such as tagging photographs, or transcribing items from scanned store receipts. The customers are usually companies who divide tasks into small elements (such as one photograph or one receipt) which are performed by many of the workers in the 'cloud'.	Amazon Mechanical Turk (MTurk), Clickworker
Driving and delivery	Location	Workers use their own means of transportation as a taxi service, e.g. Uber, or to deliver food on demand, e.g. Deliveroo. The category also includes courier services where mail-order good are delivered to homes. The customers are usually individuals ordering food or taxi services, or sometimes companies hiring couriers as part of their distribution services.	Uber, Deliveroo, Uber Eats, Just Eat, City Sprint

Sources: Based on O'Connor (2015); Balaram et al. (2017); Schmidt (2017); Lepanjuuri et al. (2018).

the gig economy is also a benefit for employers, with much gig economy work being based on **zero-hours contracts**, which have no set contractual hours—work is only available when the algorithm allocates it. Employers can offer (and pay for) only the amount of work that needs to be done at any particular time, with workers having no guarantee of work or income.

The gig economy can be viewed as a cyber-physical system typical of the Fourth Industrial Revolution. Following Schwab, it meshes together digital aspects (data and algorithms) with physical objects and humans spread across a geographical area and computer networks. It has been described as a 'human cloud' (O'Connor, 2015; Schwab, 2016a) where digital technology coordinates the dispersed activities of workers. However, as with other aspects of the Fourth Industrial Revolution, it originates from and develops previous ideas. In Chapter 2 we saw how companies such as Uber and Deliveroo carry out tasks of coordination and control at a distance, reminiscent of the early aims of bureaucracy in the Second Industrial Revolution. This control can still be exerted even if the workers and customers in such organizations are dispersed like a structureless rhizome, typical of the computer networks of the Third Industrial Revolution. Schmidt (2017: 13) suggests that the breakdown of gig work into small microtasks, as found with clickwork, is reminiscent of Taylorism (see Chapter 3). He notes that this breakdown facilitates the flexibility of this work. In this respect the work can be seen to be neo-Fordist in that it is very simple and standardized work, but also each task (e.g. each food delivery) is different.

Theory in context: forerunners of the gig economy

While the gig economy is very much a phenomenon of our times, many aspects of this work are not necessarily new. The OECD (2017) point out that gigs in themselves are nothing new: for example, they have long existed in the entertainment industry. However, this has now spread to a 'larger and more diverse' range of work. Paul (2017) draws on archive evidence to show that in the early eighteenth century it was common for people to do many different jobs to piece together an income, as is the case for many gig economy workers today.

Atkinson's (1984) flexible-firm model highlights a forerunner of the flexibility that is present within the gig economy. He identified that certain firms had a permanent, core workforce and a **peripheral** workforce of temporary workers who could be hired on a temporary basis, perhaps to meet increased demand, and then let go once they were no longer required. The gig economy seems to shift to an almost entirely peripheral workforce, available on demand, but without work when no gigs are available, a condition which leaves workers with precarious employment prospects.

The gig economy as precarious work

Work in the gig economy is often described as being precarious work (Balaram et al., 2017; Schmidt, 2017), meaning that workers are in a weak position regarding their employment contract and guarantees of both the availability and the quality of work in future. With zero-hours contracts, workers are not guaranteed work, and the digital control of the platforms makes this work even more precarious, with workers constantly rated and assessed.

Visit the online resources and take a look at the web links for Chapter 4 to see a game that examines the precariousness of gig economy work, and more discussion of such work.

The employment status of gig economy workers is a key factor in the precarious nature of the work, and at the time of writing was the subject of media attention, government reports, and discussions about changing employment legislation. When you cycle for a delivery firm, drive a taxi

Table 4.5 Self-employment vs. capitalist wage–labour

	Advantages	Disadvantages
Self-employment	Independence, autonomy, owning the means of production	Risk Need for investment
Capitalist wage–labour	Risk minimized Investment from capitalists Stable, predictable wage income	Loss of autonomy Loss of ownership of the means of production

for Uber, or log on to a clickwork site, you are considered to be self-employed, choosing this work among many other 'gigs' for different companies that you could perform. However, in practice, many people work for the same platform day in, day out, wearing the uniform of that company and taking orders from that company (O'Connor, 2015; Field and Forsey, 2017), as though they were employees—yet without employee benefits.

In Chapter 3 we saw how the Second Industrial Revolution was marked by people moving from independent, small-scale self-employment and into the capitalist wage–labour relationship, where they lost independence and worked under the control of a capitalist in return for a wage. Table 4.5 shows the advantages and disadvantages of each of these. In the gig economy, workers seem to get only the disadvantages of each—*precarious work means getting the worst of both worlds*.

A self-employed worker is independent, free from the control of a boss, and owns their own premises, tools, and means of production. However, this comes at a cost—the self-employed worker has to provide their own investment to set up the business and carries all of the risks of the business—for example if demand in the economy falls, the premises burn down or they fall sick.

By working for an employer, the worker no longer has to find the investment and they gain a relatively risk-free regular wage. However, this is the expense of the control and autonomy that they previously had—they now work under the control of the capitalist who own the means of production.

With the gig economy, workers carry all of the risks associated with self-employment.

- They have to invest in the means to do the work—be this a bicycle, uniform, car, or computer—and bear the expenses of maintaining it (Fleming, 2016; Jones, 2018).
- There is no sick pay if they are ill, or fall off a bike and injure themselves. Indeed, there is a dilemma of whether to spend time maintaining a bike to be road-safe if this means missing time that could be earning money from doing actual gigs (Khaleeli, 2016; Neate, 2017; Parkinson, 2017).
- Basic employment rights and protections are missing—minimum wages, sick pay, holidays, and pensions are not part of self-employment (Field and Forsey, 2017; Parkinson, 2017; Jones, 2018).
- The risks of demand fluctuations are also borne by these self-employed workers. They are paid per gig, but not for time spent waiting for work to appear on the app (Osbourne, 2016; Jones, 2018).

Despite bearing these risks, gig economy workers do not enjoy the advantages traditionally associated with self-employment. Rather than having autonomy, they are very tightly controlled by the platforms they work for. It is the algorithms which run these platforms which control workers through computer screens or their smartphone apps: *your phone becomes your boss*.

- Pay is set by the platform: for example, Uber dictates the fare that a driver will receive (and takes a commission), and companies posting to clickwork sites set the fee. Many disputes have been around platforms taking greater commission, or increasing sector areas and thus making journeys longer, or flooding areas with operators, all of which serve to bring down the amount that an individual can expect to earn (Parkinson, 2017; Semuels, 2018; Jones, 2018; Field and Forsey, 2018).

- Algorithms control the work people do, providing delivery routes for example. This is common with delivery drivers, who follow a set route which is calculated to take a working day. These algorithms do not take account of traffic jams, time to park, and similar delays—meaning that the working day can extend into the night. Drivers have reported urinating in vans to save time, and in one case the death of a delivery driver was blamed on not attending medical appointments that would take him away from the deliveries (BBC News, 2016a; England, 2016; Jones, 2018; Field and Forsey, 2018).

- Algorithms bring in a further element of control and monitoring through customer ratings (see Chapter 15) and analysis of the time taken by workers. This tracking and rating can affect the types of work they are given in future, whether these are lucrative shifts, or whether any further work is given at all (Schmidt, 2017; Parkinson, 2017; Semuels, 2018; Jones, 2018).

Control and resistance in the gig economy

So, gig workers bear all the risks of self-employment while having to surrender to the control of wage labour—*they get the worst of both worlds*. It could be argued that at least they control the means of production—the bicycles, cars, etc.; however, in this case the means of production becomes the platform through which the work is managed—the computer system, algorithms etc. The power of these platforms can be analysed from the point of view of the tensions in the capitalist wage–labour relationship, as introduced in Chapter 3.

First, this type of work is only possible through capitalists having the money to invest in the computer systems which run the gig economy. Schmidt (2017) points out that gig economy platforms tend to gain economies of scale by buying up competitors. They are natural monopolies—one platform tends to dominate for particular areas of gig work such as taxis, food deliveries, etc. For Schmidt, further power derives from the platform having asymmetric access to the big data that it manages. The platform has access to all of the data, whereas customers and workers only see the data on their screens—they have far less knowledge of the market than the platform and therefore less power.

The actions of the platforms follow the logic of the capitalist working relationship, as introduced in Chapter 3. The power in the relationship, as observed by Marx, lies with capital—in this case the platforms. The owners of the platforms have an interest in making as much money as possible; hence they offload as much risk as possible onto workers through keeping them as self-employed contractors rather than taking on the financial obligations associated with them being full-time employees (Fleming, 2016), and they then develop the algorithms to make the payment regimes less favourable to the workers. In this respect, the platforms have continued to make greater financial returns, while gig economy workers face increasingly precarious work for seemingly less reward (Field and Forsey, 2018).

In the Second Industrial Revolution, Marx suggested that the way for workers to gain back power within the capitalist working relationship was to organize collectively and take industrial action, as happened at Ford's factories. Collective action is harder for gig economy workers to organize because they tend to be distributed geographically rather than together in one factory. Nevertheless, resistance and collective action has taken place in many countries, including strikes and class actions, leading to government reviews of the legislation surrounding gig economy work (Neate, 2017; Fleming, 2016; Khaleeli, 2016). For example, Uber drivers in the US took a class action to gain improved conditions of employment (Wong, 2016) and Deliveroo cyclists have taken strike action in the UK, Belgium and the Netherlands (Crisp, 2018).

 Real life case: Rebel Roo and collectivization at Deliveroo

Collective action has taken place amongst Deliveroo cyclists in the UK in protest at new payment terms and plans to employ more riders, which would limit the amount of work available to existing workers.

The cyclists managed to overcome the problems of being isolated and dispersed geographically. First, they were able to speak to each other when gathered in town centres waiting for jobs. Second, they used WhatsApp groups to communicate without being monitored by the algorithms of the platform. Third, a bulletin called Rebel Roo was produced by workers to spread information about strikes and actions being taken, and distributed by the cyclists. Finally, the riders linked up with the Independent Workers Union of Great Britain, who represented them in negotiations.

Actions included public meetings and a mass bike ride in London, with a protest outside the Deliveroo headquarters. This brought about a hiring freeze, but with the riders promising further actions if other demands were not met.

Sources: Osbourne (2016); BBC News (2016b); Rebel Roo (2017); Cant (2017); Woodcock (2018).

? **Review questions**

Describe	What are the main features of the Fourth Industrial Revolution?
Explain	How does big data help to carry out management functions in Fourth Industrial Revolution organizations?
Analyse	How do control and resistance in the gig economy show similarities with the capitalist working relationship in the Second Industrial Revolution?
Apply	What examples of surveillance can you identify in your own workplace or university? How do you feel about being watched like this?

These current developments represent a fundamental shift in the nature of work which, for all of us, will affect the way that we work and even what work is available for us to do. At the same time, they also bear the traces of both the Second Industrial Revolution, as examined in Chapters 2 and 3, and the Third Industrial Revolution, as examined earlier in this chapter. What seems to be contemporary and of our age can be traced back to developments made at the start of the twentieth century.

 Connecting case and theory

This chapter has examined some developments of **rationalization** which are found in modern-day organizations. The roots of these can be seen in the Second Industrial Revolution. Subsequent developments have not turned away from Taylorism, Fordism, and bureaucracy, but have in many cases developed and extended them.

At the start of the chapter, Simon Chance was on a a fact-finding mission to see how other hotels and service industries use these contemporary versions of **rationalization** and assess if they would be appropriate for his hotel.

The first hotel was familiar ground, but even though it was a luxury hotel, it still used rationalization where possible: for example, the room settings were **standardized** across the hotel chain, and staff had a set procedure for managing the check-in and cleaning processes. Here, luxury was not the consideration in a way it would be with fixtures and fittings, for example. The whole process was designed for **efficiency** and speed of service, with the staff programmed into routines so much that they were acting almost like robots.

The **Third Industrial Revolution** saw computerization intensify processes of rationalization and take them into service-sector organizations such as fast-food restaurants, hotels and supermarkets. The **McDonaldization** of society is an intensification of Taylorism and bureaucracy within these organizations, but one which also has the flexibility of **neo-Fordism**.

This could be seen at the budget hotel that Chance visited, a **no-frills** offering where just the basics were provided in the room. McDonaldization could be evidenced in the standardized room layout, and **Taylorist** efficiencies could be seen in the design—the absence of a wardrobe door, for example, meant that cleaners did not have to open the door to clean inside, saving fractions of a second. As in McDonald's, customers did much of the work for themselves, for example by checking out themselves. Chance recognized the efficiency of this model, but realized that while it worked for a budget hotel, he could not offer something so basic in a luxury hotel.

The technology of the Third Industrial Revolution also demonstrated how surveillance becomes a key aspect of managerial control. Chance's credit card bill illustrates how the **Panopticon** exerts **surveillance** over us in many everyday situations. The transactions are not one-off events; they leave data traces which allow us to retrace Chance's steps during the business trip, described in the chapter as **dataveillance**. Chance's partner may well ask questions about the trip to a Soho Late venue and the Casino, and just what did cost £120 at a high-end department store?

The **Fourth Industrial Revolution** sees the Tayloristic and bureaucratic functions of control and efficiency now being intensified **by cyber-physical systems**. This part of the chapter dealt with developments that are current and ongoing—automation and the gig economy are discussed a lot in the media and at government levels.

The final hotel that Chance visited, the Grand Hotel Gig, seemed to take us into the realms of science fiction, with all of the automation, robotics, and tracking. However, the features found within the hotel are all found today in some way or another in organizations as a result of the **Fourth Industrial Revolution**. Some features can be found in hotels today: for example, the interactive television in Chance's hotel recalls Marriot hotels installing Amazon's Alexa digital assistant in their rooms to control room functions and order room service (Bond, 2018). In Japan, a hotel staffed almost entirely by robots already exists (Maceacheran, 2017).

In the hotel Chance stayed in, many tasks such as check-in and luggage carrying had been **automated**, and the computer system which learned from Chance's TV-watching habits and then made recommendations for activities was using artificial intelligence. The whole of the hotel was a **cyber-physical system**, using data and **algorithms** to co-ordinate the physical movement of guests while also using biological data such as iris scans. In this respect, the tracking of people throughout the hotel was similar to the systems in place in the Amazon Go and Singapore airport cases.

The interaction with the cleaner shows how, despite extensive automation, some work still needs to be carried out by humans. Nevertheless, the fact that cleaners only found out each day whether they were working, and that tracking of their performance influenced whether they would be selected, resemble the **control** and precarity experienced by **gig economy** workers. While gig economy work tends to be in a '**human cloud**' rather than one organization, unions involved in **resistance** against the gig economy have questioned how long it is before workers in organizations such as stores and hotels will be on **zero-hours contracts**, logging into an app to see if they were required to work on that day (Jones, 2018).

A question asked during the chapter is whether or not the fact that a job can be automated means that it should be automated. This is the question facing Chance at the end of the chapter, as he questions the degree to which the various forms of rationalization that he has encountered throughout his business trip could be applied to a luxury hotel such as Junction Hotel, or is a **human touch** still required to provide this luxury experience? As with the luxury hotel at the start of the case, there are some areas where rationalization can improve the running of Junction Hotel—the task for Chance is to work out exactly where it would and would not be appropriate.

Further reading

Schwab, K. 2016. *The Fourth Industrial Revolution*. World Economic Forum: Geneva.

An introduction to and overview of the main features of the Fourth Industrial Revolution. Chapter 6 is a good overview of Fordism, post-Fordism, and neo-Fordism.

Ritzer, G. 2019. *The McDonaldization of society*, 9th edn. Sage Publications: Thousand Oaks, CA.

The classic, and accessible, overview of the McDonaldization thesis.

Frey, C.B., and Osborne, M.A. 2017. The future of employment: How susceptible are jobs to computerisation? *Technological Forecasting and Social Change* 114: 254–80.

A study that looks into jobs at risk of computerization, including a table of 702 professions and their chances of being computerized.

Balaram, B., Warden, J., and Wallace-Stephens, F. 2017. Good gigs: A fairer future for the gig economy. Royal Society of Arts. Available at: https://www.thersa.org/globalassets/pdfs/reports/rsa_good-gigs-fairer-gig-economy-report.pdf

A detailed report into the gig economy in the UK.

References

Adidas. 2015. Adidas first Speedfactory lands in Germany. 9 December. Available at: https://www.adidas-group.com/en/media/news-archive/press-releases/2015/adidas-first-speedfactory-lands-germany/ (last accessed 18 July 2018).

Amazon. 2016. Introducing Amazon Go the future grocery store. Available at: https://www.youtube.com/watch?v=B10Edqo-gLU (last accessed 18 July 2018).

Atkinson, J. 1984. Manpower strategies for flexible organisations. *Personnel Management* 16 (8): 28–31.

Bain, P., and Taylor, P., 2000. Entrapped by the 'electronic panopticon'? Worker resistance in the call centre. *New Technology, Work and Employment* 15 (1): 2–18.

Balaram, B., Warden, J., and Wallace-Stephens, F. 2017. Good gigs: A fairer future for the gig economy. Royal Society of Arts, April. Available at: https://www.thersa.org/globalassets/pdfs/reports/rsa_good-gigs-fairer-gig-economy-report.pdf

BBC News. 2016a. A day in the life of an Amazon delivery driver, 11 November. Available at: https://www.bbc.co.uk/news/uk-england-37912858

BBC News. 2016b. Deliveroo offers concessions in pay row, 14 August. Available at: https://www.bbc.co.uk/news/business-37076706

Beer, D. 2016. *Metric power.* London: Palgrave Macmillan.

Bennett, O. 2015. Rage against the machine. *Management Today*, July/August. Available at: https://www.managementtoday.co.uk/rage-against-machine-trouble-self-service/article/1353549

Bond. 2018. Amazon teams with Marriott to put Alexa in hotels *Financial Times* 19 June. Available at https://www.ft.com/content/84e8f960-736c-11e8-aa31-31da4279a601

Braverman, H. 1974. *Labor and monopoly capital: The degradation of work in the twentieth century.* Monthly Review: New York.

Butler, P., and Hammer, A. 2018. 'A minute's a life-time in fast-food!' Managerial job quality in the quick service restaurant sector. *Work, Employment and Society*, https://doi.org/10.1177/0950017018777710

Cant, C. 2017. I'm a Deliveroo rider. Collective action is the only way we'll get a fair deal. *The Guardian,* 31 March. Available at: https://www.theguardian.com/commentisfree/2017/mar/31/deliveroo-organising-wages-conditions-gig-economy

Chaudhuri, S. 2015. IKEA can't stop obsessing about its packaging. *Wall Street Journal*, 17 June.

Coldewey, D. 2018. Inside Amazon's surveillance-powered, no-checkout convenience store. *Techcrunch*, 21 January. Available at: https://techcrunch.com/2018/01/21/inside-amazons-surveillance-powered-no-checkout-convenience-store/

Cornish, C., and Smith, R. 2018. UK's high-yield high street struggles under hefty debt load. *Financial Times*, 17 March. Available at: https://www.ft.com/content/a275f242-2904-11e8-b27e-cc62a39d57a0

Crisp, J. 2018. Deliveroo riders go on strike in Belgium and Netherlands. *Daily Telegraph*, 20 January. Available at: https://www.telegraph.co.uk/news/2018/01/20/deliveroo-riders-go-strike-belgium-netherlands/

Davis, E. 2007. Value engineering. BBC News, 21 May. Available at: http://www.bbc.co.uk/blogs/thereporters/evandavis/2007/05/value_engineering.html (last accessed 13 August 2015).

England, C. 2016. Amazon delivery drivers 'feel compelled to defecate in vans' to save time. *The Independent*, 12 November. Available at: https://www.independent.co.uk/news/uk/home-news/amazon-minimum-wage-delivery-drivers-illegal-hours-have-to-defecate-urinate-in-vans-a7411001.html

Elliott, L. 2017. Robots to replace 1 in 3 UK jobs over next 20 years, warns IPPR. *The Guardian*, 15 April. Available at: https://www.theguardian.com/technology/2017/apr/15/uk-government-urged-help-low-skilled-workers-replaced-robots

Etzioni, A. 1986. The fast-food factories: McJobs are bad for kids. *Washington Post*, 24 August.

Fernie, S., and Metcalf, D. 1998. *(Not) hanging on the telephone: Payment systems in the new sweatshops.* Centre for Economic Performance, London School of Economics and Political Science: London.

Field, F., and Forsey, A. 2017. Inside the gig economy: the 'vulnerable human underbelly' of UK's labour market. *The Guardian*, 24 August. Available at: https://www.theguardian.com/inequality/2017/aug/24/inside-gig-economy-vulnerable-human-underbelly-of-uk-labour-market

Field, F., and Forsey, A. 2018. Don Lane's death must be the impetus to clean up the toxic gig economy. *The Guardian*, 6 February. Available at: https://www.theguardian.com/commentisfree/2018/feb/06/don-lane-death-impetus-gig-economy

133

134

Fleming, P. 2016. Self-employment used to be the dream. Now it's a nightmare. *The Guardian*, 19 October. Available at: https://www.theguardian.com/commentisfree/2016/oct/19/self-employment-dream-governments-gig-economy

Foucault, M. 1977. *Discipline and punish: The birth of the prison*. Pantheon Books: New York.

Frey, C.B., and Osborne, M.A. 2017. The future of employment: How susceptible are jobs to computerisation? *Technological Forecasting and Social Change* 114: 254–80.

Goodwin, T. 2015. The battle is for the customer interface. *Techcrunch*, 3 March. Available at: https://techcrunch.com/2015/03/03/in-the-age-of-disintermediation-the-battle-is-all-for-the-customer-interface/?guccounter=1

Gould, A.M. 2010. Working at McDonald's: Some redeeming features of McJobs. *Work, Employment and Society* 24 (4): 780–802.

Green, D. 2018. Adidas just opened a futuristic new factory—and it will dramatically change how shoes are sold. *Business Insider*, 26 April. Available at: http://uk.businessinsider.com/adidas-high-tech-speedfactory-begins-production-2018-4

Harris, M. 2018. Amazon Go: convenience and concern at new checkout-free corner shop. *The Guardian*, 22 January. Available at: https://www.theguardian.com/us-news/2018/jan/22/amazon-go-convenience-store-corner-shop

Hencke, D. 2005. AA to log call centre staff's trips to the loo in pay deal. *The Guardian*, 31 October.

Hume, L.J. 2004. *Bentham and bureaucracy*. Cambridge University Press: Cambridge.

IKEA. 2003. From supplier to store. Available at: http://www.ikea.com/ms/en_GB/about_ikea/press_room/distribution.pdf (last accessed 13 August 2015).

Jones, O. 2018. Talk to Deliveroo couriers. See a dystopia that could be your future. *The Guardian*, 24 May. Available at: https://www.theguardian.com/commentisfree/2018/may/24/deliveroo-couriers-dystopia-union

Khaleeli, H. 2016. The truth about working for Deliveroo, Uber and the on-demand economy. *The Guardian*, 15 June. Available at: https://www.theguardian.com/money/2016/jun/15/he-truth-about-working-for-deliveroo-uber-and-the-on-demand-economy

Lambert, C. 2015. *Shadow work: The unpaid, unseen jobs that fill your day*. Counterpoint: Berkeley, CA.

Lepanjuuri, K., Wishart, R., and Cornick, P. 2018. The characteristics of those in the gig economy. Department for Business, Energy and Industrial Strategy: Final report. Available at: www.natcen.ac.uk/media/1543748/The-characteristics-of-those-in-the-gig-economy.pdf

Lewis, M. 2018. Credit scores. MoneySavingExpert.com. Available at: http://www.moneysavingexpert.com/loans/credit-rating-credit-score (last accessed 18 July 2018).

Lim, A., and Mei, T.T. 2017. Changi Airport's Terminal 4 opens: It's all automated from check-in to boarding. *The Straits Times*, 1 November. Available at: https://www.straitstimes.com/singapore/transport/its-all-automated-from-check-in-to-boarding

Maceacheran, M. 2017. Henn-na Hotel: What it's like to stay in a Japanese hotel staffed by robots, *The Independent*. 18 December. Available at: https://www.independent.co.uk/travel/asia/japan-robot-hotel-booking-location-hennna-sasebo-tokyo-what-is-it-like-a8103766.html

Mahdawi, A. 2017. What jobs will still be around in 20 years? Read this to prepare your future. *The Guardian*, 26 June. Available at: https://www.theguardian.com/us-news/2017/jun/26/jobs-future-automation-robots-skills-creative-health

Moore, P. 2018. *The quantified self in precarity: Work, technology and what counts*. Routledge: Abingdon, Oxon.

Moore, P., and Robinson, A. 2016. The quantified self: What counts in the neoliberal workplace. *New Media and Society* 18 (11): 2774–92.

Morgan, J. 2016. What is the Fourth Industrial Revolution? *Forbes*, 19 February.

Available at: https://www.forbes.com/sites/jacobmorgan/2016/02/19/what-is-the-4th-industrial-revolution

Murgia, M. 2017. Biometrics take off for BA passengers on boarding. *Financial Times*, 25 March. Available at: https://www.ft.com/content/da415b5a-10b7-11e7-b030-768954394623

National Science Foundation. 2016. Cyber Physical Systems. Available at: https://www.nsf.gov/pubs/2017/nsf17529/nsf17529.htm (last accessed 16 July 2018).

Neate, R. 2017. My week as an Uber courier: my bike got stolen, but I kept my five-star rating. *The Guardian*, 7 April. Available at: https://www.theguardian.com/business/2017/apr/07/uber-cycle-courier-new-york-city

O'Connor, S. 2015. The human cloud: A new world of work. *Financial Times*, 8 October. Available at: https://www.ft.com/content/a4b6e13e-675e-11e5-97d0-1456a776a4f5

OECD. 2017. Entrepreneurship at a Glance 2017. OECD Publishing: Paris.

Osbourne, H. 2016. Deliveroo pay scheme a return to Victorian Britain, says Labour. *The Guardian*, 12 August. Available at: https://www.theguardian.com/money/2016/aug/12/deliveroo-pay-scheme-a-return-to-victorian-britain-says-labour

Parker, M., and Jary, D. 1995. The McUniversity: Organization, management and academic subjectivity. *Organization* 2 (2): 319.

Parkinson, H.J. 2017. 'Sometimes you don't feel human'—how the gig economy chews up and spits out millennials. *The Guardian*, 17 October. Available at: https://www.theguardian.com/business/2017/oct/17/sometimes-you-dont-feel-human-how-the-gig-economy-chews-up-and-spits-out-millennials

Paul, T. 2017. The gig economy is nothing new—it was standard practice in the 18th century. *The Conversation*, 18 July. Available at: https://theconversation.com/the-gig-economy-is-nothing-new-it-was-standard-practice-in-the-18th-century-81057

Poster, M. 1995. *The second media age*. Polity Press: Cambridge.

Powley, T. 2017. Airlines invest in DIY to improve passenger services. *Financial Times*, 30 August. Available at: https://www.ft.com/content/a0250032-45b8-11e5-b3b2-1672f710807b

Rebel Roo. 2017. Rebel Roo #8. 13 November. Available at: https://www.weareplanc.org/blog/rebel-roo-8/

Ritzer, G. 2019. *The McDonaldization of society*, 9th edn. Sage Publications: Thousand Oaks, CA.

Robbins, T. 2017. Travel updates: Monaco, Singapore, France. *Financial Times*, 8 September. Available at: https://www.ft.com/content/c3106a88-93bc-11e7-a9e6-11d2f0ebb7f0

Roberts, C., Lawrence, M., and King, L. 2017. Managing automation: Employment, inequality and ethics in the digital age [discussion paper]. IPPR Commission on Economic Justice. Available at: https://www.ippr.org/publications/managing-automation

Schmidt, F. 2017. Digital labour markets in the platform economy: Mapping the political challenges of crowd work and gig work. Friedrich-Ebert-Stiftung. Available at: http://library.fes.de/pdf-files/wiso/13164.pdf

Schwab, K. 2016a. *The Fourth Industrial Revolution*. World Economic Forum: Geneva.

Schwab, K. 2016b. The Fourth Industrial Revolution: What it means, how to respond. World Economic Forum. 14 January. Available at: https://www.weforum.org/agenda/2016/01/the-fourth-industrial-revolution-what-it-means-and-how-to-respond/

Semuels, A. 2018. The internet is enabling a new kind of poorly paid hell. *The Atlantic*, 23 January. Available at: https://www.theatlantic.com/business/archive/2018/01/amazon-mechanical-turk/551192/

Simpson, I.H. 1999. Historical patterns of workplace organization: From mechanical to electronic control and beyond. *Current Sociology* 47 (2): 47–75.

Stefansson, G. 2008. Case study: IKEA—Increased transport efficiency by product and packaging design. European Commission Bestlog Project.

Stewart, H., and Elgot, J. 2017. Labour suspends Jared O'Mara over offensive online comments. *The Guardian*, 25 October. Available at: https://www.theguardian.com/politics/2017/oct/25/jared-o-mara-labour-suspends-jared-omara-over-offensive-online-comments

The Economist. 2017. Adidas's high-tech factory brings production back to Germany, 14 January. Available at: https://www.economist.com/business/2017/01/14/adidass-high-tech-factory-brings-production-back-to-germany

The Guardian. 2018. Amazon's first checkout-free grocery store opens on Monday, 22 January. Available at: https://www.theguardian.com/business/2018/jan/21/amazons-first-automated-store-opens-to-public-on-monday

Travelodge Ireland. 2015. Everyday low prices—how we do it. Available at: https://www.travelodge.ie/everyday_low_prices/ (last accessed 13 August 2015).

Woodcock, J. 2017. *Working the phones: Control and resistance in call centres*. Pluto Press: London.

Woodcock, J. 2018. Lessons on resistance from Deliveroo and UberEATS. Pluto Books. Available at: https://www.plutobooks.com/blog/lessons-on-resistance-from-deliveroo-and-ubereats/ (last accessed 18 July 2018).

Wilkesmann, M., and Wilkesmann, U. 2018. Industry 4.0—organizing routines or innovations? *VINE Journal of Information and Knowledge Management Systems*, 48 (2): 238–54.

Wong, J.C. 2016. Welcome to the robot-based workforce: will your job become automated too? *The Guardian*, 19 March. Available at: https://www.theguardian.com/technology/2016/mar/19/robot-based-economy-san-francisco

PART 2

The social organization

CHAPTER 5
Discovering the social organization
The Hawthorne studies and the human side of the organization

Chapter overview and learning outcomes

By the end of this chapter you should be able to:

- describe the basic features of the Hawthorne studies

- explain how the Hawthorne studies challenged many of Taylor's assumptions

- explain how the Hawthorne studies led to the foundations of organizational behaviour (OB), challenging the rational perspective and introducing the idea of the social organization

- describe the power of the informal organization

- analyse whether the results of the Hawthorne studies increase worker *freedom* or increase *control* over workers

- analyse the assumptions that Mayo's interpretation of the Hawthorne studies were based on, and explore other perspectives

Key theorists	
Elton Mayo	Seen as the founder of human relations, a key figure in the Hawthorne studies and one of the founders of OB
Fritz Roethlisberger and William Dickson	The writers of the largest account of the Hawthorne studies, which comprises over 600 pages of highly detailed description of the research
Mary Parker Follett	Alongside Lillian Gilbreth, a key female early-management theorist; she was a political scientist, social work pioneer, speaker, and advisor to leaders concerning the relations between workers and management
Daniel Bell	A key social theorist after World War II, who wrote extensively about post-industrialization and its impact on society; provided a key critique of Mayo

CHAPTER 5

Introducing the social side of the organization

🔍 Running case: too much to do and not enough time

Nina Biagini, Junction Hotel's maître d', looks at the pile of napkins piled in front of her: 250 to fold before the restaurant opens at 5.00 pm; 400 glasses also need to be cleaned; and then all the silver cutlery needs to be polished. 'We are never going to be ready for tonight's Rotary International meal, and we need to be on the top of our game with all these business leaders coming,' she thinks. 'This is just the start of it,' she says to herself, 'with our busy season coming up, this place is going to be carnage if we don't get it sorted. We need help.'

Feeling anxious that the restaurant will not be ready in time, Nina Biagini phones Phil Weaver to get an extra pair of hands. 'What?' Phil Weaver blasts down the phone. 'We can't afford more people.' He continues, in a calmer manner: 'Look, I'll get you help today, but I can't keep bailing you out like this. I tell you what, I'll come down and work out how to make this process more efficient so this doesn't happen again.'

Phil Weaver feels confident he can achieve the same efficiencies for the restaurant as he did for the cleaners. So, sitting in his office, he devises detailed napkin-folding instructions, including starching the cloths before they are used, how to sit them in the right way to minimize movement, and how to fold them in the exact order. 'One hundred and twenty napkins folded per hour, per person … easy!' he concludes.

Excited with his new procedure, Phil Weaver is confident this will increase efficiency, thereby making prep-time stress-free. However, when he shows it to the restaurant team the reaction is not as he hoped. 'We're not robots,' complain Naomi and Saffron, two of the servers. 'Weaver should try doing this job day in, day out and see if he can do it. We get tired and it's cold in here—not like in *his* office, which is comfortable with the radiator on.'

Think about a recent experience you have had at work. While your workplace's structures, bureaucracy, and work design are important, they probably do not immediately come to your mind when you think about your recent experience of work: it is more likely the people that you have worked with that you are thinking about. It might be a supervisor that annoyed you, a colleague that you joked around with, or the whole atmosphere of the company that you were working within. Organizations are, after all, made up of people, and people matter.

This chapter is about the importance of the human side of the organization. It tells the story of a fundamental transformation in management theory and practice: from a Taylorist view (see Chapter 3), which saw organizations as purely mechanical, formal, measurable, and rational machines, to one that revealed the significance of informal relations between people. This view, which we will call the social side of the organization, has led to an interest in the importance of teamwork, organizational culture, motivation, and leadership—all of which feature heavily throughout the rest of the book. In other words, this chapter is about the introduction of a new way of thinking about organizations that stresses the importance of the informal, human side of the organization.

The Hawthorne studies' findings have been credited with humanizing management practice. Rather than seeing people as nameless cogs in the machine, following rules and procedures in mechanical, predictable, and routine ways in order to work effectively, management should help people to feel wanted and treat them as human beings. According to this view, the informal group, rather than being a problem as Taylor assumed, becomes a resource, used by management to increase productivity. Consequently, to be productive it is possible—indeed, essential—to treat people as human beings. Management can, therefore, be humanized.

This chapter is about the Hawthorne studies, one of the most important pieces of research to introduce this way of thinking. The name 'Hawthorne studies' is taken from the Hawthorne works, the large US factory where the studies were conducted. These studies, particularly in the way they were popularized by one of the researchers, Elton Mayo, are widely credited as revolutionizing management thinking, appearing to offer a magic cure—an end to conflict between the worker and the manager, producing harmony and progress.

To twenty-first century eyes, the findings (that the social or informal organization shapes how people experience work and in turn affects levels of productivity) might seem obvious. Yet in their time, these ideas sent shockwaves across business circles, fundamentally challenging both management practitioners and the early teachings of the emerging university business schools. They introduced researchers and practitioners to the ideas that teamwork is important and that employees respond better when managers pay attention to them. These ideas have since become an accepted part of management thinking and practice. This chapter is about the emergence of this new way of thinking and its continued importance for management today.

The chapter starts by describing the key studies as most accounts of organizational behaviour describe them. As you will read, these accounts start with Taylorist assumptions—in the case of the Hawthorne studies, the assumption that the levels of lighting and worker fatigue impact employee output. However, as the studies progressed, the researchers, so we are generally told, began to realize the importance of the informal behaviour of the group. These findings lead to a change in the researchers' assumptions about how to manage people.

However, this *typical* account of the Hawthorne studies is not all it appears. While Mayo and his colleagues stated that they 'discovered' the social side of the organization and that workers are naturally cooperative, a number of critics have argued the way Mayo interpreted his data was highly ideological. These critics of Mayo claim that the research methodology and interpretation of findings were flawed. Furthermore, they argue that the results of the Hawthorne studies have been used by management as a better way of controlling workers, rather than empowering the workers as Mayo and his colleagues claimed they were doing. Therefore the second half of this chapter examines these criticisms, drawing attention to the political and social consequences of the Hawthorne studies. The chapter not only looks at the studies but also demonstrates the importance of understanding the historical context of research, and using critical analysis to see other perspectives on well-known research.

The strength of the criticisms of the Hawthorne studies, however, should not detract from the positive contribution that the studies offer to management theory and practice. In comparison with the dehumanizing impacts of Taylorism, an awareness of the significance of the human side of the organization is an important development. However, from the workers' viewpoint, as we will argue in this chapter, it still offers a way that management can control workers—potentially in ways that we do not even see.

Background to the Hawthorne studies: from the mechanical to the social

The Hawthorne studies were a series of six experiments carried out between 1924 and 1932 at the Western Electric Company in Cicero, on the periphery of Chicago, Illinois, USA. It has been considered one of the most significant pieces of research in the history of OB, not only because of the large scale of the research, but also because of the implications for how we understand management theory and practice today. The key findings of the Hawthorne studies were a challenge to the Taylorist view that saw people as little more than machines; rather, the Hawthorne studies revealed the human dimension, the importance of group norms, the relations (or dynamics) between people, and the impact that these factors have on productivity. In doing so, this research introduced a new way of viewing organizations: human relations theory.

The Hawthorne works was a large factory, which has been described as being like a small city with over 29,000 employees (over 40,000 at its peak). At the time it was 'America's largest manufacturer of electrical products', in particular making telephones for Alexander Graham Bell (Hassard, 2012: 1438). These telephones required highly skilled workers to put together the fiddly systems. The studies were conducted from 1924 through to the early 1930s. The main experiments and their findings are shown in Table 5.1.

While the Hawthorne studies are closely associated with Elton Mayo, the fullest account is provided by Fritz Roethlisberger, a professor at Harvard, and William Dickson, the Chief of Employee Relations at the Hawthorne Works. Their book *Management and the worker* (1939), which is over 600 pages, provides a highly detailed and often fascinating account of every experiment, including the methods used, the sometimes surprising reactions of the staff, the questions that the perplexing results raised for the researchers, and how the research led to alternative interpretations of management problems and potential solutions. We will concentrate on the key events, interpretations, and debates.

 Visit the online resources and take a look at the extension material for Chapter 5 for a full account of the research. It is worth reading about this research in some depth, as much of its significance lies in the detail.

The experiments

Experiment 1: testing the link between lighting levels and output—the illumination experiments

🔍 **Running case:** Phil Weaver explores the impact of heating

Looking at the results, Phil Weaver is concerned that the restaurant team are not as effective as he thought they could be. On paper, they should fold at least 120 napkins an hour, but they are still only folding 80. Weaver feels confused and decides to investigate further.

Visiting the restaurant, Weaver starts to watch how the team work, noting their body movements, the way they arrange the napkins and glasses, and the way they perform their tasks. 'It is a little cold in here,' he thinks. 'I wonder if they can't move their fingers properly.' Asking Nina Biagini why this is, she states that when there are no customers they do not heat the room. Weaver thinks this might be the cause of their slow work. Inspired by his time and motion studies, he starts recording the output and heating on a graph, asking them how they feel about the temperature as he does it. 'If we can find the right temperature,' he thinks to himself, 'then we can maximize the output.'

Table 5.1 The experiments in the Hawthorne studies

No.	Name	Dates	Description	Findings
1	*Illumination*	1924–April 1927	Tested how different levels of light impacted productivity	No clear correlation between lighting levels and output
2	*Relay I*	April 1927–June 1929	Assessed impact of rest periods on productivity	No clear correlation between rest periods and output
			Tested fatigue and monotony thesis	No clear correlation between fatigue and output
3	*Relay II*	August 1928–January 1929	Tested effects of wage incentive on output	Some increase in output from wage incentive but not sustained
4	*Mica splitting test room*	October 1928–September 1930	Duplicated relay assembly room experiment, but without wage incentive	Same pattern for first year then declined; output more to do with **psychological** issues than wage incentives
5	*Interview programme*	September 1928–February 1929, extended into 1931	Assessed links between morale and supervision, improvements in employee–supervisor relations, and the attitude of staff	Workers often have obsessive and irrational views; social groups have powerful influence over the actions of individuals
6	*Bank wiring observation*	November 1931–May 1932	The role of the group in determining output	The informal group is key to impacting behaviour

In 1924, a small group of researchers aimed to uncover the links between lighting levels and employee output. By trying to create a 'science of seeing' they thought they would discover the optimum levels of lighting needed to maximize productivity and, given that their research was funded by General Electric—one of the world's largest manufacturers of light bulbs—the research would also lead to increased sales of light bulbs to industry (Donkin, 2001: 165).

This research, begun just over a decade after Taylor had published *The principles of scientific management*, was set firmly within the scientific management tradition. Indeed, Alexander Church, a 'Taylorist' and a supporter of scientific management, had already stated his belief that poor lighting caused a strain on workers and that high-intensity lighting lifted workers' spirits. Frank Gilbreth (see Chapter 3) was also worried that the reflection on surfaces caused tiredness among workers (Donkin, 2001: 165). Thus, the first research shared Taylorist assumptions that physical conditions are an important area for *scientific* research.

Aiming to improve efficiency, the researchers believed that creating the right inputs (in this case physical conditions) would increase output (the workers' productivity). Armed with measurement devices to assess the strength of lighting and record sheets to measure output, the researchers set about monitoring and adjusting the levels of lighting and assessing the effect on output.

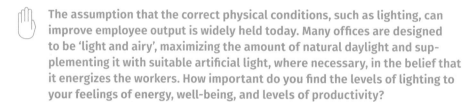

The assumption that the correct physical conditions, such as lighting, can improve employee output is widely held today. Many offices are designed to be 'light and airy', maximizing the amount of natural daylight and supplementing it with suitable artificial light, where necessary, in the belief that it energizes the workers. How important do you find the levels of lighting to your feelings of energy, well-being, and levels of productivity?

The researchers fully expected to find a pattern between the lighting levels and output; however, the results shocked them. Instead of showing a direct correspondence between light levels and employee output as they expected, the 'output [levels] bobbed up and down' in rather confusing ways.

A modern office designed to maximize daylight.
Source: Zastolskiy Victor/Shutterstock.com

Unable to find a link between lighting and output, they made the research more scientific. They set up a control group, for which they kept lighting levels the same, and an experiment group, for which they adjusted the lighting. (In scientific research, a control group does not receive any intervention and therefore is seen as representing the population as a whole. The control group is used as a standard of comparison to the research group, who do receive intervention.) However, again, to their bafflement both groups' productivity went up in 'almost identical magnitude' (Roethlisberger and Dickson, 1939: 16). Lighting, it seemed, did not matter. Still trying to establish a link, they set up a third experiment in which they reduced the lighting to levels where the workers 'were hardly able to see what they were doing' (ibid.: 17). Even at this level, efficiency remained high. At one point they even told workers that they had changed the light bulbs for brighter ones when they had not, and productivity went up.

The researchers, according to Roethlisberger and Dickson (1939: 17), therefore began to question their original assumption that lighting was an important component to productivity, concluding it was 'more "psychological" than real'. They needed to look for other factors involved in increasing productivity.

? Review questions

Describe   What happened in the illumination study?

Explain   Why did the researchers conclude that productivity was 'more "psychological" than real'?

Analyse   Why did a focus on lighting levels reflect Taylorist assumptions? What were the underlying assumptions the researchers held, which led them to expect that lighting was a key factor?

Experiment 2: testing the link between fatigue and output—the Relay I assembly test room

Q Running case: if it's not heating then what is it?

Phil Weaver meets Nina Biagini to discuss the preparations for the busy Christmas period. 'We are making some improvement, but the level of heating doesn't seem to make any difference,' Biagini states. 'Yes, it is odd,' replies Weaver. 'You would have thought that when we dropped the heating back to the original level, their performance would have dipped again. There must be more we can do. In a couple of weeks' time we are going to have three sittings a day, so we are going to have to work extra hard to keep up.'

'But we will never be able to achieve that,' Biagini responds. 'They barely keep going for two hours, let alone for four. They get exhausted doing the same thing over and over again.'

Suddenly, Weaver has a brainwave. 'Exhaustion, you say. I think you might be on to something.'

As the initial experiment suggested, lighting was only a minor factor in employee output. The researchers, continuing in a scientific mindset, believed there must be other physical factors impacting productivity. Their next assumption was that fatigue was the problem: that tired workers would produce less. They therefore aimed to scientifically discover the ideal balance between work and rest.

The role of fatigue was already a subject of much research: the munitions workers of World War I, working seven days a week with only one day off per month, were often so tired they were found asleep at their lathes (Gale, 2004).

The researchers took a group of six women, who were making telephone circuits, from the large factory and put them in a special unit to study them. Trying to control the experiment scientifically, they decided that the women needed to be highly experienced so that productivity increases could not be attributed to improvements in skill, but could be confirmed as a result of what they were testing—the balance between work and rest. Crucially, for their later findings, they also decided to make the research environment as friendly, cooperative, and natural as possible so that they could get closer feedback on the results. We will return to why this was significant later in this chapter, in the section on 'The importance of group norms'.

Theory in context: gender in the Hawthorne studies

One of the fascinating aspects of the Hawthorne studies is the role that gender played. Throughout Roethlisberger and Dickson's (1939: 182) account, the six women in the relay assembly room were referred to as 'girls'. The language that they used indicates it was not a relationship of equals.

As with many aspects of working life at the time, men decided levels of pay, hours, or even if women could have a job at all. In this experiment it was men who decided that the women should work in a separate special room away from the large factory; it was men who decided that the women were talking too much; it was men who decided when it was acceptable for the women to talk; it was men who carried out physical examinations and asked questions as to the women's eating habits, bedtimes, and activities outside of work; and it was men who decided the meaning of the discussions that the women had. Indeed, as Marks argues, when the research was intrusive, it was the women who were investigated, whereas when they were making observations that avoided manipulation the researchers decided to select men as their subject matter (Marks, 1999).

This gendered relationship even extends to the language that the researchers and commentators used. For instance, Elton Mayo (1933) argued that it revealed the existence of 'Social man', which replaced the previous assumption of 'Economic man'. While you may dismiss the use of *man* in this context as semantics, as simply a difference in the meaning of the word, the choice of words reflects the assumptions that were prevalent at that time—that the world of work revolved around male assumptions of the world. Some of the quotations in this chapter use *man* in this way, but in our own text we will be using the more gender-neutral 'social person', as it represents a more inclusive perspective.

The work the women did was mind-numbingly boring. For instance, to put one of the relays together, the worker had to perform thirty-two separate operations with each hand and to make one relay every minute for nine hours a day, five-and-a-half days a week. They had little hope of promotion or even variation in the job (Gillespie, 1991).

Gender in the Hawthorne studies.

Table 5.2 Rest patterns

I	Standard	VIII	As VII, stop 4.30
II	Standard	IX	As VII, stop 4.00
III	Standard	X	As VII
IV	Breaks: 2 × 5 minutes	XI	As VII, Sat. am off
V	Breaks: 2 × 10 minutes	XII	Standard
VI	Breaks: 6 × 5 minutes	XIII	As VII
VII	Breaks: 1 × 15 and 1 × 10 minutes		

The primary objective of the research was to discover the ideal pattern of work and rest. To test this, the researchers started by keeping everything constant for a few weeks and then experimenting with different lengths of break. Table 5.2 shows that by the eighth period of study they had started shortening the working day and then, by the eleventh period, even removing the Saturday morning shift.

To their surprise, the researchers discovered that regardless of how long the rest periods were, or when they were taken, output constantly rose. Even when the employers were returned to the original work patterns output was higher than ever. The researchers concluded that, contrary to their initial assumptions, there was no simple correlation between output and rest patterns.

So why did the output levels not correspond to the rest periods? To find the answer, the researchers devised a number of hypotheses, such as better lighting and ventilation, reduction in overall fatigue, reduction in monotony of work, and increased pay.

Centring on their hypothesis that fatigue was the most important factor, the researchers went to some lengths to test the physical condition of the workers. This included regular physical examinations of the workers' blood pressures and vascular skin reaction to test their level of fatigue (a vascular skin reaction is a white line on the wrist created by a blunt instrument which disappears more quickly when the person is fatigued). They even compared the results with marathon runners, believing that stamina was vital for work.

While they still assumed that physical conditions were important, they also began to notice—which became important for later studies—that the atmosphere and mental attitude in the group improved. At first, they had prevented the women from talking, but as the study continued they allowed them to talk to each other more. Indeed, the researchers felt they needed to create a more harmonious atmosphere in order to undertake the tests they wanted. They came to realize that the workers enjoyed the less formal test room with no formal bosses present and increased freedom. Over the course of the study they noticed that antagonism between the group members was replaced by banter and joking. Attendance improved and they worked well together. The women, by being allowed to talk, managed to overcome some of the monotony of the job and found a way of working that best suited them.

Real life case: fatigue at work today

At the conclusion of the medical assessment of US president Donald Trump, US Navy Rear Admiral Ronny Jackson stated that Donald Trump 'is just one of those people, I think, that just does not require a lot of sleep. He's probably been that way his whole life,' adding, 'That's why he's been successful' (Brantley, 2018). Trump is said to sleep only four hours a night and is part of a long list of successful people, including former Yahoo boss Marissa Mayer, Apple CEO Tim Cook, and film director Tom Ford, who have very little sleep (Cassidy, 2017). India's prime minister Narendra Modi is even said to work around 20 hours a day, needing only three to three-and-a-half hours of sleep a night (*The Telegraph*, 2017).

147

Recently, though, there has been a backlash against this image of endurance, with warnings of the health risks. Arianna Huffington (the founder of the Huffington Post), collapsed, broke her cheekbone and woke up in a pool of blood, having been working 18 hours a day. She puts this down to exhaustion from the intensity of her work, often staying up until 3 am to respond to 'urgent' work emails. Huffington has since become an ambassador for sleep (Huffington, 2017).

There is increasing interest in the links between fatigue and workplace productivity. Fatigue is said to cause 'irritability, bad judgment and long-term health issues and can even impair you worse than alcohol' (Brantley, 2018). Workers who sleep less than 7–8 hours a night experience significant loss of productivity (Katz et al., 2014). This is not only a problem during the working day. A recent survey found that more than half of British workers check their emails while on holiday (O'Conor and Cahillane, 2015).

The cost of insomnia in the US is estimated to be over $100bn when you add in reduced productivity, absenteeism, and presenteeism (Epstein, cited in Munshi, 2017). Research on fatigue argues for regular breaks from work (Fritz et al., 2013), sleep and energy management strategies, such as frequent exercise (Fritz et al., 2011), and micro-breaks to drink water or have a snack (Zacher et al., 2014). To overcome these problems Google have introduced sleeping pods (Moran, 2014), while NASA, Samsung, Zappos, and the Japanese firm Okuta allow workers a 20-minute power nap at their desk (Munshi, 2017). 'Inemuri—or "sleeping while present"—is considered the preserve of employees exhausted by their commitment to hard work, rather than a sign of indolence' (McCurry, 2014).

The King Eye Mask sleeping pillow—one of the many products on sale as a reaction to 'Inemuri' in Japan. Source: *http://www.japantrendshop.com/*

It is also important to get physical and mental breaks from work. These may include several factors:

> *psychological detachment*, not thinking about work during non-work time; *relaxation* having a low activation level; *mastery*, facing a positive challenge to learn something new; and *control*, having a feeling of control over nonwork time.
>
> (Bennett et al., 2018: 1)

Multi-tasking is also said to increase fatigue and reduce productivity because more energy is consumed in switching tasks (Newport, 2016).

 How do you cope with fatigue at university? Do you need to have energy drinks in the morning to get yourself going? Do you come into lectures or seminars tired, and does that affect your performance?

Review questions

Describe	What happened in the Hawthorne fatigue experiments?
Explain	Did the fatigue experiments prove any link between the amount of rest time and productivity?
Analyse	Why do you think it is significant that the research was largely carried out by men on women? Why might the gendered nature of words matter?
Apply	Which of the strategies described in the real life case on fatigue at work today would be desirable or practical for Junction Hotel?

Experiments 3 and 4: testing the link between pay and output—Relay II and the mica-splitting test room

The second relay experiment and the mica splitting test room shifted the focus of the Hawthorne studies dramatically. For the first time the researchers began examining the *psychological* and *social* factors that influenced how people behaved, rather than just the *physical* ones. They therefore became interested in the relationships between group members, shifting their focus from the individual to the group.

Workers in the relay assembly department.
Source: © Baker Library Historical Collections, Harvard Business School.

This change in focus laid the foundations for an area of research known as 'Human Relations', an academic school of thought which examines the *social relations* between people, the *motivation* of workers, and the impact that *employee satisfaction* has on output and productivity. Rather than seeing workers as 'cogs in the machine', this approach saw workers as social beings, with a need for belonging within the group. This approach acted as a precursor to modern-day human resource management which can be defined as a movement emerging out of Organizational Development that studies the behaviour of people in groups.

However, these two experiments did not begin by examining the social relations between group members; rather, they held another Taylorist assumption: that increased pay levels would increase output—an attempt to establish a link between another set of inputs (bonuses) and output.

Initially it seemed that their assumptions were correct. After giving the workers a bonus, output rose sharply. However, to their puzzlement, this rise did not continue. The results, though, proved to be inconclusive, as the experiment had to be cut short. Other groups in the factory discovered the scheme and felt it was unfair that this 'social group' were getting preferential treatment and they 'wanted similar consideration' (Roethlisberger and Dickson, 1939: 133). Fearing upset, the rest of the factory managers demanded that the experiment was ended.

The researchers continued their investigations into whether increased output could be attributed to a wage increase, applying the same principle of modifying the amount of break time to workers who split, measured, and trimmed mica chips used for insulation. In Experiment 4—the mica splitting test room—the researchers tried replicating the relay II experiment, but without the bonus scheme. To their surprise, the first year's results mirrored relay II, with a sharp increase in productivity, even without the bonus. However, in the second year output declined. The researchers believed this was because rumours were spreading that jobs were to be transferred to another city, concluding that the employees' 'fears and anxieties … completely overshadowed the experimentally introduced changes' (ibid.: 153). This suggested to the researchers that it was not wage incentives that impacted performance, but the employees' attitudes (e.g. fear of job loss), introducing the importance of social factors.

As pay did not seem a significant factor, the researchers began to consider other explanations. They discovered that what mattered more than pay was employees' morale, their relationships with their supervisors and each other, and their personal backgrounds. Most importantly, they concluded that the relay assembly test room was a '"group" story' where the members acted as a team: they did not have bosses but cooperated and worked together. By contrast, they thought that the mica splitting test room 'was a story of "individuals" who were self-sufficient and did not feel the need to work together' (ibid.: 156). They thought that individual behaviour was 'rooted in [shaped by] their personal and social background' (ibid.: 171). In other words, the relay experiment was successful because the members cooperated and saw themselves as part of a team, whereas the less successful mica splitting test room subjects were individuals who did not bond.

 Why do you think the researchers at the Hawthorne studies began to see the importance of the relationship between group members to their overall levels of productivity?

Experiment 5: interview programme—discovering the importance of a personal life

Q Running case: listening to the staff

Faced with the confusing results from Weaver's experiments, Nina Biagini is asked to interview the restaurant staff and find out how her team feel about working in the restaurant.

'Right, Isabella, I have been asked by the senior management team to find out the level of staff satisfaction at Junction Hotel. We want to have a happy team, as well as a productive one, so today I want to know your views of working at Junction Hotel. Don't worry, your views will be kept anonymous—we just want to know what you think.'

A little taken aback, Isabella smiles at Biagini. 'Oh, me, well,' pausing before laughing nervously, 'how long have you got!' Isabella begins by cautiously saying that she really enjoys working for Junction Hotel: 'they are all good fun' and 'supportive when you're having a bad day, although I didn't like Weaver watching us like that'. She then goes on to say that she is finding life at home a little hard at the moment: 'there's always so much to do and I feel a little stressed,' she confesses to Biagini. She's just fallen out with her son and isn't talking to her husband—'he's just so distant,' she says with a faraway look in her eye. Listening to all this Biagini starts to feel a little uncomfortable—'I feel more like a counsellor than a manager,' she thinks. Rounding off the discussion, Isabella turns to Biagini—'oh, sorry, I hope I didn't go on to much. Thanks so much for listening'.

Having established the importance of the social side of the organization, the next set of experiments began exploring employees' attitudes to work. Undertaking a large interview programme, the researchers thought that gaining an insight into how employees viewed work and their relationship with their supervisors would unlock ways of increasing productivity. What they found, however, was that it was being listened to in the interview that the employees really responded to.

The researcher team conducted one of the largest investigations of employee attitudes ever undertaken, with an enormous 10,300 interviews lasting between 30 minutes and 1.5 hours, all of which were fully transcribed. This was a time-consuming task as, on average, an hour-long interview can take at least five hours to transcribe. This produced thousands of pages of detailed personal information, providing an amazing insight into the mindset of these ordinary American workers during the Great Depression. Even today, the size and level of detail of this study is hard to match, and it gave a comprehensive insight into the lives of ordinary workers.

The researchers took the thousands of comments and sorted them into categories, such as work conditions, attitudes to supervisors, and the nature of their jobs, and divided them into favourable and unfavourable groups. They discovered the workers disliked certain working conditions, such as the washrooms and the smoke and fumes, but strongly approved of the benefit plan and vacations. Men seemed more interested in economic security, whereas the women were more focused on working conditions. This information, they thought, would help the management understand how workers felt and therefore how to manage them (Roethlisberger and Dickson, 1939).

However, the researchers were surprised (and often frustrated) that the interviewees would become fixated on what they considered irrelevant issues in their personal lives. Employees would recall personal events, sometimes from years before, with full emotion as though it was yesterday. The researchers surmised that doing repetitive factory work gave 'a great deal of time for preoccupation' (Roethlisberger and Dickson, 1939: 133), resulting in the workers being 'obsessive' and 'irrational'. This brooding on their personal lives, they considered, made the workers less productive.

Eventually, though, rather than dismissing their home lives, the researchers began to see that what was happening at home shaped employees' experiences at work. For instance, being treated unfairly by a supervisor at work at the same time as feeling unfairly treated at home (e.g. by a husband) made the employee over-react to the criticism (ibid.: 310–11). The researchers concluded that supervisors need to understand people's home situations to manage them better. Furthermore, being part of a group with 'human comradeship and social conversations' (ibid.: 324) helped employees manage their emotions. These interviews revealed that workers' personal backgrounds and experiences shaped their work performance. Countering the views of Taylorism—where the worker was seen as little more than a cog in a machine—the Hawthorne studies demonstrate the importance of understanding employees' personalities and, as we will see in the next section, how their attitudes were shaped by the group.

Real life case: listening to your staff can reduce their stress

A recent study shows that 45 per cent of sickness absence is caused by stress, costing the UK economy an estimated £5.2 billion per year (HSE, 2016). Digital forms of work, in particular with email via smartphones and global IT networks, mean that employees are constantly accessible, even when not at work, resulting in many employees feeling constantly stressed without psychological downtime vital for recovery. The significance of stress is echoed in a survey about absence management conducted by the Chartered Institute of Personnel and Development, which placed stress as the number one cause of workplace absenteeism (CIPD, 2016). Jill Miller, in the foreword to the report, argues that ongoing support for line managers is essential as a way of seeking to combat this stress. Using emotional intelligence (the ability to recognize your own and others' emotions) is seen as a way of teaching employees to manage their stress, resulting in happier employees (Treanor, 2015).

Attentive managers can help reduce stress.
Source: baranq/Shutterstock.com

Is it realistic to expect that employees will always separate their personal life and working life? Do you think managers manage better when they understand their staff's personal lives?

Sources: Peacock (2011); Treanor (2015); CIPD (2016); HSE (2016).

Experiment 6: bank wiring observation room—the power of the group

Q Running case: slow down, you'll put us out of a job

'Hey Speedy, what are you trying to do—put us all out of a job?' Isabella jokes to Naomi as she sees Naomi's napkin-folding rate on the whiteboard in the staff room. 'One hundred and twenty-five an hour ... you'll kill yourself working as hard as that.'

The final set of experiments produced some of the most startling results, in the perceptions of academics and managers at the time. It revealed that the informal group, by producing group norms (the unwritten rules that shape people's behaviour within a group) and informal rules, controlled behaviour and output more powerfully than rewards (e.g. bonuses) or supervisory influence. In other words, this was the discovery of the power of the informal, social organization.

The researchers' interest was sparked in this area because, during the interview programme, employees that were seen as working too hard were called 'dumb', picked on, given nicknames, and excluded from social activities by their fellow employees. In one particular case the supervisor, rather than praising and trying to protect the productive worker (as rationally he should), feeling powerless and believing the productive worker caused disharmony, gave him extra jobs to reduce his output.

The idea that workers were systematically restricting output was hardly a shock. Fredrick Taylor called this phenomenon 'soldiering' (Chapter 3), arguing that workers systematically tried to restrict their output. However, the investigators decided that rather than trying to get rid of these informal behaviours, they would investigate them.

The researchers decided to watch closely the behaviours of one particular group. This time the group was all male: nine wiremen who placed wires in the correct location (a skilled job); three soldermen who soldered the wires (a less skilled job); and three well-educated inspectors who tested the units to make sure there were no errors. The researchers wanted to investigate these two themes:

- Does the group restrict output and, if so, how?
- What is the relationship between the supervisors and the group?

The role of the group in restricting output

Officially, each worker was supposed to make 7,200 units per day, which if they achieved it would earn them a bonus. However, surprisingly from the researcher's viewpoint, they seemed to *restrict* their efforts.

Investigating further, the researchers discovered informally that the workers believed that making between 6,000 and 6,600 units a day represented 'a day's work' (Figure 5.1). While those that did not produce enough were 'bawled' at by the supervisors, if they made above the (unofficial) average group members excluded them, calling them 'Shrimp', 'Runt', 'Slave', and 'Speed King'. They were even physically harassed by being flicked on the ear or the arm, known as a 'bing', to indicate they were breaking group norms. As one worker put it, those that 'loaf along are liked better than anybody else' (Roethlisberger and Dickson, 1939: 418). The workers' personal relationships were highly complex, full of tension, animosity, teasing, and, at times, physical violence.

From this observation, the researchers stated that the group had the following informal rules.

1. You should not turn out too much work. If you do, you are a 'rate-buster'.
2. You should not turn out too little work. If you do, you are a 'chiseller'.
3. You should not tell a supervisor anything that will react to the detriment of an associate. If you do, you are a 'squealer'.
4. You should not attempt to maintain social distance or act officious. If you are an inspector, for example, you should not act like one (ibid.: 522).

153

Figure 5.1 Pressure on an employee to perform at a certain level.

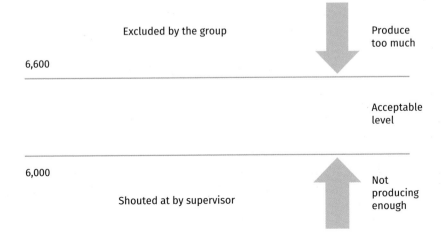

Table 5.3 Behaviour of the two cliques

Clique	1	2
Output	High	Low
Personal behaviour	Sensible	Messing around

The researchers saw that the group was, in fact, two cliques (exclusive groups), each with different ways of behaving and different output levels. In order to fit in with one group, workers had to behave in a particular way (see Table 5.3).

They concluded that the group internally controlled members' behaviour but, at the same time, protected them from external management interference. The workers, they thought, were more motivated by their need to belong to the group than by the management pressure or financial incentives. In short, the group controlled its member's behaviour through *group norms*.

The importance of group norms

One of the central findings of the Hawthorne studies, particularly through Elton Mayo's interpretation, was the power of *group norms*. Group norms provide the rules or standards of conduct that group members have to follow in order to fit in. Unwritten rules guide behaviour and help members gain a sense of belonging, providing group members a framework for how to behave and react to a given situation. These rules are rarely overtly dictated; we pick them up through subtle cues, such as jokes at our expense or being excluded from conversations. They can be seen as a form of peer pressure, causing us to do things in order to fit in. In particular, we often learn these rules when we break them.

Group norms are powerful because if we want to belong to the group and, in particular, gain high social status within it, we have to stick to them. Very few people violate them, as this ultimately means being excluded, isolated, and without social and emotional support. Group norms provide stability to the group by providing an accepted way of behaving. However, they can also be controlling, as there is pressure to go along with the views of the group, even when they might be at odds with your personal views. This can be particularly difficult when working in, say, a sexist or homophobic environment.

Difficult position of the supervisor

🔍 Running case: Nina Biagini goes to Phil Weaver's office

'You are still not hitting the targets,' Weaver complains. 'They should be able to fold at least 140 napkins an hour if they followed my plan ... look, they are only hitting 80. And look at Naomi, she was folding 125 an hour, and now that the chart has gone up she has fallen down to the same level as the rest of them.' Biagini looks downcast. 'It's not as easy as that,' she states. 'I just feel powerless in front of them. Naomi is a good worker, but the rest just drag her down to their level.'

'Why don't you just tell them what to do?' Weaver asks. 'It's not as easy as that,' Biagini replies again. 'You see, if I start having a go at them it will make our relationship difficult and really tense. Then, if I want them to do anything extra, like stay at the end of the shift to clear up or deal with a difficult customer, they will just say no.'

Table 5.4 The supervisor's dilemma

Supervisor action	Let them get away with it	Middle ground	Report to foreman
Consequence of action	Workers' task not performed effectively	Try to balance group and management needs	Be a 'grass' and lose the sympathy of the group

The wiring bank observation room experiment also demonstrated how weak the supervisor's position was. On the one hand, he relied on the group's goodwill to get the job done, meaning he had to maintain friendly relations with them. On the other hand, as a representative of management, he had to keep costs down and keep production levels high. This conflict was particularly evident in how he recorded individuals' work and workers' bonuses. The wiremen pressurized him to record higher figures, but management wanted to keep the records low. If he followed the groups' interest, he was not doing his job properly, but if he tried to impose the management's priorities he faced losing the sympathy of the group, making the working relationship difficult. He was, therefore, under pressure from two directions, as shown in Table 5.4.

The researchers concluded that the supervisor could not change the group purely by the force of his personality. In fact, he was a victim. Indeed, we could argue, following Karl Marx (see Chapter 3), that the supervisor was exploited as much by capitalism as the workers.

This was demonstrated through the results obtained by the two supervisors during the study. The first supervisor was lax about certain rules and could be considered almost part of the group. His replacement was stricter, more authoritative, and rules- and output-focused. Surprisingly, the group were more productive under the first supervisor.

Roethlisberger and Dickson (1939: 531) believed the workers restricted output for a number of reasons. In part, it was because they did not understand the bonus scheme; they thought the workers also acted 'irrationally', choosing to believe that the management might lay people off as productivity rose, but Roethlisberger and Dickson claimed the workers had no concrete evidence of this. The workers were not lazy (as Taylor assumed) or in conflict with managers (as Marx assumed), and the supervisors were not ineffective. To take such a view 'is to mistake symptoms for causes and to neglect the social factors involved' (ibid.: 548). Their key finding was that the informal group controlled output and behaviour, often in ways that went against the interests of the organization *and* the individual employee.

? Review questions

Describe	What are group norms?
Explain	Why should a manager be aware of group norms in order to be effective?
Analyse	How do Roethlisberger and Dickson claim their work is different from Taylor's views?
Apply	How did group norms serve to reduce productivity among the waiting staff at Junction Hotel?

The implications of the Hawthorne studies

> **🔍 Running case:** team meeting
>
> Nina Biagini gathers all the waiting staff together. 'We are the restaurant team,' she declares. 'If we are going to move forward then we need to work together as a team.' She opens the meeting asking for a 'full and frank' discussion, and airing of views.
>
> The team begin cautiously, with everyone being respectful, but after 15 minutes they begin to share more of their thoughts and feelings. Nina Biagini, alongside Meg Mortimer, listens attentively to what everyone is saying, nodding throughout the discussion. At the end of the discussion Nina Biagini thanks everyone for their involvement. 'We are one big team,' she states, 'and all need to work together'.

The results of the Hawthorne studies are widely credited with transforming management theory and practice. They challenged the dehumanizing Taylorist approach by showing it was possible, and even desirable, to be concerned with the interest of the workers. They showed the significance of the informal organization and the power of the group in controlling individual behaviour. Most importantly, they also claimed to provide a more humane approach to management (see Table 5.5). Particularly in the hands of Elton Mayo, who, as we will see, wrote some of the most influential interpretations of the Hawthorne studies, they shifted attention away from focusing simply on work processes towards trying to understand and satisfy employees' needs. To their supporters they offered a better and more enlightened form of management based around harmony and cooperation, laying the foundation for OB today. Most of all, they provided a shift in perspective from seeing people as simply economic beings, solely interested in their own private benefit, to seeing them as social beings who want to belong to groups. The key implications of this will be discussed in the following sections.

A note on the alternative layout

Observant readers will notice that for the rest of this chapter the layout looks a little different from the rest of the book. In this section, we will examine in turn five of the major assumptions made by Mayo and his colleagues on the basis of their research findings, and for each assumption we will assess the contribution it has made to the field of OB. In the following section we will present critical analysis of these assumptions.

Assumption 1: discovery of the 'social person'

The Hawthorne studies are widely credited with discovering the 'social person'—the underlying belief that people are governed by social needs, such as belonging to a group, rather than economic

Table 5.5 Comparison of Taylorism and the Hawthorne studies

	Taylorism	Hawthorne studies
Focus on ...	Individual	Groups
Labour/capital relations ...	Conflict	Harmony
Management is ...	Dehumanizing	Humane and caring

Figure 5.2 The fuller understanding of the social person.

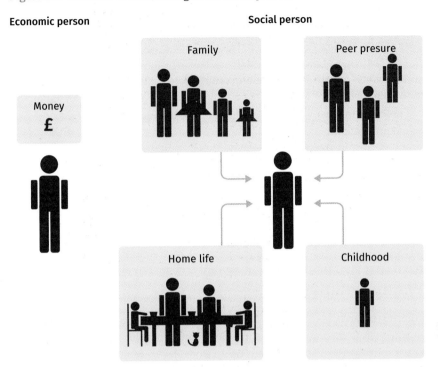

Economic person

Money
£

Social person

Family

Peer presure

Home life

Childhood

needs and self-interest, which Taylorism and other rational theories are based upon. This, they argue, explains why the employees preferred to stick to the norms of the group rather than make the rational, economic decision to work a bit harder and receive more pay.

Elton Mayo, one of the key researchers and popularizers of the Hawthorne studies, argued that the classic 'economic man' thesis provided a negative view of human nature. He called it a 'rabble hypothesis', a view which sees humankind as a horde of unorganized individuals motivated solely by self-interest (Mayo, 1949/1975). The Hawthorne researchers argued for a richer and more rounded view of human nature, which understands the 'relations of mutual interdependence' between people (Roethlisberger and Dickson, 1939: 569). In other words, they argued for a more complex view of workers' lives, concentrating on personal histories, group interactions, and the bonds that develop between people (Figure 5.2).

This, therefore, provided a fundamental reconsideration of human nature and a completely different view on how to manage people.

Contribution to OB

This more complex view of workers opened the door to studying organizational culture (which we will examine in Chapter 7), the importance of personality (Chapter 8), and the issue of motivation (Chapter 9) as a way of understanding why people behave how they do in organizations. It therefore introduced a richer and more complex view of human behaviour.

Assumption 2: management can harness the power of the group

A key implication of the 'social person' thesis was that the group fundamentally influences individual behaviour and restricts output. While Frederick Taylor had already identified the way groups can restrict individual output, his solution was to break the power of the group by individualizing tasks. The Hawthorne researchers acknowledged that Taylor's solution might technically 'make the employees more efficient', but they argued that his approach would 'unwittingly deprive them of those very things which give meaning and significance to their work' (Roethlisberger and Dickson, 1939: 418): the sense of social belonging.

This 'social person' perspective therefore 'reformulated' management's problems (ibid.: 569) by seeing the informal group as 'a necessary prerequisite for effective collaboration' (ibid.: 559) instead of a problem. In other words, rather than being a hindrance to production, the group could be used to aid production.

Contribution to OB

This insight has led to considerable attention being placed on the role of teams and groups (see Chapter 6) and the power of group norms—the informal codes of conduct that shape behaviour. It also has implications for leadership and management (Chapter 13), as it draws attention to how to influence the group rather than focusing on influencing particular individuals.

Assumption 3: there is harmony of interests between workers and managers

The Hawthorne researchers made these bold claims about the power of the group based on their belief that when left to their own devices, groups *naturally* develop spontaneous social organization with their own values and objectivities, which would be 'more likely to be in harmony with the aims of management' (Roethlisberger and Dickson, 1939: 418).

Elton Mayo strongly pushed this view. He argued that people naturally strive for cooperation and harmony. He cited the increased output in the relay assembly room as evidence, claiming it was a result of the behaviour of a 'revolutionized supervisor' who formed a cohesive group of cooperative workers, eager to push production on to a higher level and acting in 'wholehearted cooperation with management' (Mayo, cited in Handel, 2002: 100). This cooperation, Mayo argued, was feasible because all human action comes from a need for social solidarity: in other words, the need to belong to a group. Consequently, when managers act fairly, workers have no need to complain as they are working for collective interests.

This allowed the researchers to make the following bold claim:

> Producing an article at a profit and maintaining good employee relations are frequently regarded as antithetical [opposite] positions. The result of the studies which have been reported indicated, however, that these two sets of problems are interrelated and interdependent.
>
> (Roethlisberger and Dickson, 1939: 552)

They therefore stated that they had solved the problems of Taylorism and Marxism. Management and the workers' interests, they claimed, were no longer in conflict (as assumed by Taylorism or Marxism). Rather, organizations can be more productive only when workers' needs are taken into consideration. Mayo, through the Hawthorne studies, therefore sought to redraw the capitalist working relationship by claiming that workers and management did not need to be in conflict (Figure 5.3).

Contribution to OB

Mayo presents organizations as places of potential harmony and cooperation. However, as we will see in Chapter 14, those on the political left, such as Steven Lukes, disagree by stating that the labour–capital relationship is always fundamentally in conflict—even when it does not appear so at first glance.

Figure 5.3 Mayo's redrawn capitalist working relationship.

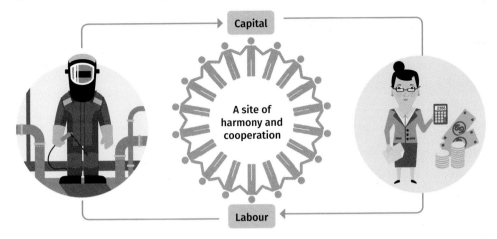

Assumption 4: the nature of leadership needs to change

One of the fundamental shifts in management practice that the findings of the Hawthorne studies produced was to change the way we see management. While Mayo believed harmony and cooperation were possible, this spirit of cooperation is not inevitable. It requires improved communication with leaders listening to their group. Mayo offers us this prescription:

> Before every change of program, the group is consulted. Their comments are listened to and discussed; sometimes their objections are allowed to negative a suggestion. The group undoubtedly develops a sense of participation in the critical determinations and becomes something of a social unit.
>
> (Mayo, 1933: 39)

According to Mayo, managers therefore need to work on transforming the nature of the group, rather than particular individuals, by listening to workers and overcoming any objections.

◎ Employability skills: the importance of soft skills

The Hawthorne studies demonstrated the importance of managers treating their employees as people: listening to them, understanding group norms, and responding to individual and group concerns. To be an effective manager you need to be able to understand and respond to these 'social issues'. Therefore, as well as gaining the technical qualification of your degree, it is important to develop these so-called soft skills. University offers many possibilities for this, such as group work and seminars where you have the chance to work with others and improve your communication skills; joining clubs and societies where you can be on committees, plan events, and learn to work as a team; and volunteering, where you can work with people with different backgrounds in the community. Such experiences are not only great for your CV, but also excellent for self-development.

The World Economic Forum's list of the top ten skills that will be needed by employees in 2020 includes people management, coordinating with others, emotional intelligence, and negotiation, arguing that these skills are essential in the Fourth Industrial Revolution (Schwab, 2016). As jobs change, and automation and artificial intelligence increasingly shape how jobs are designed, communication skills, which often are not able to be automated, become increasingly important.

→

What activities can you do to increase your skills, experience, and confidence in these areas?

Visit the online resources and take a look at the web links for Chapter 5 for links to the World Economic Forum report.

Contribution to OB

The Hawthorne studies showed the importance of *soft skills* in management and leadership, such as listening to staff and understanding their views before making a change. They therefore have implications for our understanding of leadership (Chapter 13) and change management (Chapter 12).

Assumption 5: an alternative view of human nature

The Hawthorne studies thus produced a fundamentally different way of seeing human behaviour and human nature. Table 5.6 compares this with the rational organization approach.

Table 5.6 Difference between the rational approach and the human relations approach

Key theorist	Fredrick Taylor	Elton Mayo
Human nature	Economic person	Social person
Why people act	In rational best interests	Irrationally and governed by sentiment
Employee motivation	Economically motivated	Socially motivated by belonging needs
Mentality of researcher	Engineer	Psychologist
Approach to organization problems	Mechanically fix with technical solutions	Social engineering to get people working together
Reasons workers restrict output	Worker laziness Physical condition, e.g. fatigue Soldiering	Power of informal organization in creating norms that regulate behaviour
Solution to output restrictions	Individualize work by breaking work down into increasingly simple tasks	Collective collaboration
Management control workers by ...	Managing every aspect of the task Time and motion studies	Gaining loyalty of the group, shaping its beliefs to work towards common outcomes
Relation between output and employee satisfaction	Unrelated—employees are just told what to do; they are all replaceable	Inter-related—employees need to be satisfied to be productive

To the supporters of the Hawthorne studies, they are a symbol of a new way to manage, away from a path of conflict and soul-destroying work performed by isolated individuals to new practices based on cooperation, harmony, and understanding of employees' needs while still increasing production.

Contribution to OB

As we stated at the start of this chapter, these studies represent one of the most significant studies in OB and one of the foundations of the discipline.

? Review questions	
Describe	What are the key implications of the Hawthorne studies?
Explain	How did the Hawthorne studies challenge pre-existing assumptions of management theory and practice?
Analyse	How do the Hawthorne studies offer a different view of human nature? How does this affect how they recommend that staff are managed?

Critiques of the Hawthorne studies: understanding critical analysis

Q Running case: leaving the meeting

As they filed out of the meeting Naomi was glowing. 'It is really nice to see management taking an interest in us as people. I mean, we do a good job here and it is good to be noticed.' Saffron looked at her in a surprised manner. 'They just want us to work harder and produce more without being paid more. I'm not falling for that one. Do you think they are really that interested in us?'

As we have seen, the results of the Hawthorne studies have been used to claim that people are naturally cooperative and that harmony between management and workers is not only desirable, but natural. In short, particularly in Mayo's hands, the results provided a fundamentally different way of looking at the world.

The Hawthorne studies have been called part of the 'creation myth' of OB—one of the central studies the field is based on. Yet as scholars of OB it is important that we do not take these findings at face value, but question how the research was constructed and interpreted, its circumstances and background, and what assumptions it was based upon. To do this we need to examine the research methods themselves, the interpretation of the findings, the context of the research, and the background and values of the researchers carrying out the research. The rest of this chapter will aim to carry out this task.

It is important to note that the following types of criticism made of Mayo and the Hawthorne studies could equally be levelled at other theories, such as Taylorism. All academic theories have inbuilt assumptions upon which they are based, and all such theories can be examined from alternative 'critical' perspectives. We need to make clear that the existence of these assumptions does not make the research invalid and does not mean that we should completely discount the researchers' findings. While some of these findings were based on small samples and, arguably, the pre-existing beliefs of the researchers, the social side of the organization is undoubtedly a vital component of organizational life. Moreover, although studying the social side potentially gives managers increased control over the workers, it also offers the potential for a more humane form of management than pure Taylorism.

All research and theory is based on assumptions. The Hawthorne studies were based on assumptions about human nature and the way that society operates or should operate. These assumptions shaped (consciously and unconsciously) the way the research was conducted, which findings were considered important, and how results were interpreted and presented. Uncovering these assumptions helps us better understand the research and judge it for ourselves. We are focusing on the Hawthorne studies in this chapter and highlighting their assumptions as a way of encouraging you to think more critically about *all* research and theory that you read.

For the remainder of the chapter, the headings 'Claim *x*' and 'Critical perspective *x*' will be used to assess the Hawthorne studies' research. We will look at each of the researchers' key claims about the research (Claim *x*) and, for each claim, discuss some of the challenges that later researchers have made to either the research itself or the manner in which it was interpreted (Critical perspective *x*).

 Study skills: the importance of thinking critically—assessing academic theories

Where do your beliefs about management come from? How often do you stop to question them or look for alternatives?

We tend to think that our beliefs about management and organizations are based on common sense. Yet the views we hold today have not always been accepted. Indeed, a quick examination of the history of management theory reveals that people in other times held quite different perspectives to ours. In fact, our common-sense certainties might seem to them to be highly controversial or even wrong. For instance, 50 years ago many thought women incapable of working in the boardroom. Today, such a view would be unacceptable.

So where do our ideas come from and what influences them? One source is academic research. It is not only the research itself that is important, but the way that it has been received, interpreted, and used. Our beliefs are, in part, a product of past debates, where the winning perspective has become accepted as true and is today's common sense.

However, quite often the origins of the research get lost in time and we are only left with the conclusions that become filtered into practice and accepted without question. In the critical analysis we present in this chapter, we argue that it is important that we are aware of this background not only because it gives us a deeper understanding of the theories themselves, but also because it allows us to question their assumptions and challenge the things that we take for granted.

In this section of the chapter we will be assessing the Hawthorne studies *analytically*, taking the arguments apart by seeing the *assumptions* that they are based upon. We will see whether the *research methods* and the *conclusions* they drew were valid, and whether the *evidence* they presented stacks up. We will be exploring this *critically* by examining it from other viewpoints and seeing how these alternative perspectives, based on different *assumptions*, may lead to different conclusions. The chapter will lay the foundations for some *debates* which we will examine in the rest of this book.

→

This chapter aims to encourage you to *think critically*. This means not taking things at face value, being able to weigh up the evidence, and being able to understand the implications of a perspective. By doing so its aim is to help you be a better student and also potentially a better manager. Not taking things for granted will help you learn to think more deeply and not accept things as they are given—to see things from other perspectives and understand the assumptions behind the views people hold.

We have already mentioned the World Economic Forum's list (Schwab, 2016) of skills that will be needed in 2020. The top three on their list are complex problem solving, critical thinking, and creativity. As work becomes more automatic and machines can learn to understand and replicate patterns, they argue, 'process skills (such as active listening and critical thinking) will be a growing part of the core skills requirements for many industries' (Schwab, 2016: 23). Therefore critical thinking is not just a core skill for studying, but also essential in the emerging world of work.

Claim 1: workers are naturally cooperative and harmonious and form groups spontaneously (testing assumptions 1, 2, and 3)

The findings of the Hawthorne studies, and particularly Elton Mayo's interpretation of them, are based on the discovery of the 'social person', who is naturally cooperative and seeks harmony. Mayo based his argument on the experiences witnessed in the first relay assembly room experiment, which he stated saw a smooth and rapid change in the attitude of the staff who became, in his words, a 'team that gave itself wholeheartedly and spontaneously to co-operation in the experiment' (Mayo, 1949: 64).

However, in making this interpretation, Mayo downplayed, and even ignored, key findings that did not fit his perspective. For instance, the departments and participants used for the study were specifically selected to be cooperative, and the supervisors tried to make the relationships as smooth and friendly as possible. It cannot, therefore, be assumed that people naturally want to be cooperative.

This selection for cooperation even went as far replacing two 'uncooperative' workers in the relay assembly room experiment who were 'talking too much' and 'lacked attention to their work'. To his funder, Mayo reported that one worker had '"gone Bolshevik" (an insult indicating that a person is a Russian communist; in other words, that they are troublemakers who want revolution) and had to be dropped' (cited in Bramel and Friend, 1981: 872). Mayo's account, though, ignores these features, simply saying they 'retired' (Mayo, 1949). They were replaced by two new, enthusiastic employees, both of who were immediately more productive than the ones they replaced.

Mayo also downplayed the significance of the arguments between the workers and managers. Roethlisberger and Dickson's research showed the workers often actively resisted management, slowing down output and stating that if they had their rest periods back they would increase productivity. Management responded by threatening to take away perks such as lunch breaks. As Bramel and Friend state:

> The workers were quite consciously adopting a strategy intended to induce the experimenters to return quickly to the preferred conditions. If the workers had in fact had the kind of trust in management's good intentions that Mayo claims, would they have found it necessary to resist the experimenters so actively in this period? The picture we get, instead, is of a group of rather wary workers engaged in a continuing skirmish with management and determined not to be taken advantage of. Rather than become a part of the company 'team', they became a team of

their own, rather coolly looking out for their own economic interests in an adversary relationship with management, regardless of how much they may have personally liked certain members of the research team.

(1981: 874)

The increase in productivity, rather than being assumed to have come about through cooperation, could equally be seen as resulting from stern discipline, e.g. replacing difficult staff (Carey, 1967) and the use of coercion rather than natural cooperation.

Critical perspective 1

The Hawthorne researchers, particularly Elton Mayo, were highly selective in what evidence they reported; findings that did not fit their view were ignored.

 Study skills: implication of this perspective

We need to be careful in assuming that what people report is the only interpretation of the findings. We should not take research at face value. When reading research, try to examine the assumptions of the author.

Claim 2: workers are more motivated by social needs than financial ones (testing assumptions 1 and 2)

Mayo, like Roethlisberger and Dickson, claimed that the group members were more motivated by the need to belong than by financial needs. Workers' concerns that increased production would lead to others losing their jobs were dismissed as 'irrational'.

However, the research took place in the 1930s, a period which saw the deepest and most prolonged depression of the twentieth century, with high levels of unemployment and little social security, producing mass poverty. Clegg and Dunkerley believe of the Hawthorne studies that 'Restriction of output by voluntary norms was a rational response by primarily economically-oriented agents to the increasingly likely prospect of unemployment' (1980: 131). In other words, there were genuine fears that increasing production would mean that other workers would be sacked, as higher production did not necessarily mean higher sales. The workers responded rationally to their economic situation. Carey (1967) also convincingly argues that much of the Hawthorne researchers' own data demonstrates the significance of wage incentives in creating increases in productivity.

Critical perspective 2

The Hawthorne researchers dismissed economic reasons as irrational; however, given the context, the employees' views could be interpreted as quite logical.

 Study skills: implication of this perspective

The ideological position of researchers shapes how they interpret their findings. If you believe that economic reasons motivate action, then you are more likely to see this. If you believe motivation comes from social factors, then this evidence may seem stronger. Understanding the underlying beliefs of the researcher can be a key way of engaging in critical analysis, as it allows you to challenge these views. See Chapter 1 for more details on how to develop critical thinking skills.

Claim 3: the findings of the Hawthorne studies can be replicated in management practice (assumption 5)

The findings of the Hawthorne studies are rightly considered significant because they were one of the first sets of experiments to examine real people in a real factory rather than in a laboratory. Therefore, it is claimed that what the researchers discovered can be applied to management practice. However, the actions of the participants cannot be considered 'natural'. Throughout the study the research subjects were constantly observed, with their level of output recorded every 30 minutes. This form of observation changes behaviour. The implication is that the very act of measuring the output meant that the workers were better able to adjust their output.

This phenomenon was labelled the **Hawthorne effect** by Henry Landsberger. He concluded that the very act of someone observing a person changes their behaviour (Landsberger, 1958). There are two key ways in which this phrase has been used. Firstly, it denotes the increase in productivity that is seen to result from psychological and social factors. Secondly, it points to the impossibility of researching what people *actually* do because the very act of observation (and particularly monitoring performance) changes behaviour. The research findings cannot therefore be assumed to represent what people *naturally* do.

 Imagine yourself at work (or writing a university assignment) on a normal day. Now think how you would act if someone watched everything that you did. Would you act the same? Would you still take sneaky breaks, check Facebook, or talk to your friends at work in the same way?

The research was on a massive scale as a scientific experiment, but it was poorly controlled. One of the key focuses of the research—the changes of human behaviour under supervision—only emerged later in the study, meaning that the researchers had to make assumptions about the workers' early behaviour rather than actively studying it. Equally, in the bank wiring experiment, the researchers did not have a control group and therefore they did not know whether output would have gone up anyway.

The sample sizes were very small (six people for the relay assembly room and thirteen for the Bank Wiring Observation Room). While this gave the researchers unprecedented access and a highly detailed account of workers' daily interactions, it is a mistake to claim that the findings of the research are true for all societies over human history.

Critical perspective 3

The conclusions that may be drawn from the findings are influenced by the researchers being present and the small sample size. Very large claims have been made on what is a small amount of evidence.

Claim 4: the research 'discovered' the social person (assumption 1)

Roethlisberger and Dickson present the Hawthorne studies as a *journey of discovery* where they began their enquiry believing in essentially (although never named) Taylorist assumptions, but, because of the evidence, they came to discover 'social man'. This *'revelatory narrative'* as Hassard calls it, is common in most 'textbooks on organization and management theory' (2012: 1433). However, both Roethlisberger and Mayo had pre-established assumptions which shaped their research findings and which are rarely presented in most textbooks.

Roethlisberger had a strong disliking of Taylorism, calling its effects 'repugnant'. Wickström and Bendix (2000) argue that he used the Hawthorne studies as a platform to provide an alternative scientific basis to management. Equally, Mayo (1949) had a strong preference for cooperation and harmony and a strong dislike of conflict, which he saw as a 'social disease'. Even before the Hawthorne studies, he had already concluded that 'Social and psychological ills could be traced back directly to failure to establish stable systems of cooperation. Individuals must feel that their work is socially necessary and must be able to see beyond their group to the society' (Smith, 1998: 231). Indeed, Mayo's personal beliefs were formed prior to the Hawthorne studies rather than discovered through the research evidence as he claimed (O'Connor, 1999).

Even in the first experiment, the researchers were *already* aware that "human factors could influence production and thereby interfere with the experimental results"' (Gillespie, 1991, cited in Hassard, 2012: 1434). Furthermore, rather than discovering the 'social person' this view was already known within American industry (Nyland and Bruce, 2012). A book by Whiting Williams (1920) had already put forward the discovery that workers form groups to protect themselves from management (Muldoon, 2012).

In exploring the historical archives, John Hassard argues that the organizational culture (see Chapter 7) of the Hawthorne plant was quite unusual. Being a very large factory and the dominant employer in the area, it was like a city in itself. It contained its own hospital, fire brigade, running track, and school; many social events such as dances and concerts were run by the Hawthorne Club. It also operated a form of 'welfare capitalism' where the workers received relatively high pay, pensions, healthcare, and access to sports facilities. The workers mostly lived near each other, making it feel like a 'family culture' (Hassard, 2012). The implication of this, Hassard argues, is that far from being a revelation, or replacing engineering thinking with a psychological perspective, the 'human relations' philosophy was already being promoted by Western Electric.

166

Critical perspective 4

Rather than *discovering* the 'social person', both Roethlisberger and, in particular, Mayo, had long-held views about the importance of cooperation, harmony, and the need for spontaneous forms of organization. Rather than revealing the 'social person', the Hawthorne studies used the 'social person' perspective as the lens through which the research findings were interpreted.

Study skills: implication of this perspective

All theories are based on underlying assumptions. These assumptions shape what the researcher thinks is important and what findings the researcher presents. It is important, therefore, when reading all research findings, to try to understand the assumptions a researcher has and to read alternative interpretations to gain a more rounded picture of a research topic. While the Hawthorne studies did not receive much criticism at the time, they have been subjected to a wide range of critique from many authors (see Muldoon 2012 for a review). It is therefore necessary to understand these critiques, and the assumptions that the researchers bring with them, to be able to make a critical judgement.

Claim 5: the Hawthorne studies represent a progressive alternative to Taylorism (assumption 5)

It is often claimed by supporters that the findings of the Hawthorne studies offer a more humane and holistic approach to managing people. They certainly offer some benefits. Listening and responding to the needs of employees and focusing on teamwork provides a more rounded view of the worker, and a more supportive and person-centred form of management. However, this approach has been widely criticized for also being a stronger form of control.

One of Mayo's earliest critics was the sociologist Daniel Bell, who argued that Mayo did little to challenge the key aims of Taylorism, the focus on increasing productivity. For Bell, all Mayo really did, to quote Bell's title, was 'Adjusting men to machines' (1947).

Mayo's attention to employees' needs, Bell argued, was just another way of controlling them. He did this, Bell stated, by treating anyone who challenged harmony (by which he meant the manager's view) as showing evidence of psychological problems. Bell, like many critical theorists, argued that such harmony was not possible because workers and management have divergent interests. Consequently, the labour–capital conflict cannot simply be solved by improving communication between workers and managers.

Bell went further by stating that people only work in these large organizations because their human spirit has been tamed, and they have been trained to desire consumption rather than meaningful human relations. In an early critique of consumer society he stated that we are obsessed with our next purchase, caught up in material interests and not human ones. 'The belief in man [sic] as an end in himself [sic] has been ground under by the machine, and the social science of the factory researchers is not a science of man but a cow-sociology' (Bell, 1947: 88). In Bell's view, Mayo thus 'fail[ed] to consider whether work offers other possibilities for the expansion of human spontaneity and freedom' (Waters, 1996: 52) and did not offer a true break from Taylorism.

Bell's view is supported by a more recent article by Bruce and Nyland (2011). They argued the Hawthorne studies offered 'a new way to control workers to accept less, while claiming that workers needed psychological counselling about their relations at work that only management could administer' (Bruce and Nyland, 2011: 386).

According to such theorists, the use of psychological counselling offered managers a powerful tool to access the hidden world of employees' unconscious drives and use them for their own purposes. It offered the promise of harmony and cooperation, but only on management's terms and in their interests rather than on the employees' terms. '[C]ooperation in the Mayo perspective', according to Baritz (1974: 113), 'is the relationship involving happily unorganized (nonunionized) workers who unthinkingly and enthusiastically comply with the wishes of management towards the achievement and maintenance of its economic objectives.'

The research was also a way of trying to suppress trade unions at a time where there were company spies to identify labour activists (Hassard, 2012). Indeed, within the 600 pages of Roethlisberger and Dickson's book (1939) there is only one short statement on trade unions. Mayo himself was a known anti-trade-union academic. According to Mayo's research and the tenets of welfare capitalism, giving employees benefits could be interpreted as a way of stopping the workers from trying to overthrow capitalism.

 Theory in context: the philosophical underpinnings of Mayo's theory

Mayo did not restrict his claims on the benefits of the Hawthorne studies to a more considerate form of management—he saw it as a way of saving Western civilization.

Modern society, he argued, was characterized by increasing numbers of unhappy people who are fragmented into groups that are 'not eager to co-operate wholeheartedly with other groups' (1949: 7). The root cause of this, Mayo argued, was the Industrial Revolution. Led by large corporations, it brought rapid changes in technology which, although they produced

→

→ material comfort, did so at the expense of a 'destruction of individual significance' (1949: 7). Through the social ties of what Mayo called *established* society—the structures of families, communities, and traditional authority—were broken, producing a new *adaptive society*, which, Mayo argued, had abandoned its traditional pursuit of cooperation, leading to potential chaos.

Mayo concluded on this basis that worker unhappiness and industrial disputes have a psychological root, rather than an economic one. He argued that an increasing number of unhappy workers had obsessive personalities and did not wish to cooperate. Workers had irrational, or what Mayo called 'non-logical', mindsets. Individual unhappiness was often as a result of their personal lives or childhoods which, when not listened to by managers, reinforced their problems. Mayo saw the interview programme as a therapeutic release of pent-up emotion. It gave workers an opportunity to get rid of useless emotion which enabled them to collaborate better with other workers. An interview 'clears lines of communication of emotional blockage' (1949: 72) to allow the development of cooperation and teamwork.

> Thus, individual happiness and the social 'growth and health' of society are dependent not upon freedom from unreasonable restraint nor upon any rational calculus of pleasure and pain, nor upon the opportunity for self-development, but upon whether or not the individual has a sense of 'social function'.
>
> (Bendix and Fisher, 1949: 313)

Mayo believed that training an administrative elite—which we would now call management—was the solution to this problem: '[C]ollaboration of an industrial society cannot be left to chance' (1949: 8). Current training and research, Mayo argued, had seen considerable advancements in technical expertise (e.g. Taylorism), but social skills had not kept up with this, leading to an imbalance. This administrative elite could be trained in these social skills—the ability to secure cooperation of people—and learn how to manage people. Mayo's assertions were liked by managers as he legitimized their role and their position in society (Child, 1996).

168

? Review questions

Describe	What is the Hawthorne effect?
Explain	Why do some commentators believe Mayo did not 'discover' the social person? What are the implications of this?
Analyse	Why does Mayo's interpretation of the Hawthorne results not necessarily produce a more humane form of management practice?

While Taylorism is often demonized as oppressive to, and controlling of, workers, there were a number of theorists, writing at the same time as Elton Mayo, who were seeking to supplement this with industrial democracy. These progressive Taylorists, such as Mary Parker Follett and Mary van Kleek, wanted workers to choose their own representatives and to be involved in management decisions. Having just endangered their lives in defence of democracy in World War I, as John Dewey argued, it seemed ironic that workers then returned to a system of 'industrial and economic autocracy' (Dewey, 1982: 85). These Taylorist democratists supported the growth and development of unions (Bruce and Nyland, 2011). Mayo, with the support of Rockefeller money, had a strong distrust of such moves.

> There is another difficulty for me in Miss van Kleeck's approach to the investigation—she seems to assume that a 'democratic' method of managing industry is necessarily appropriate ... If it means that industry is to develop a two-party system and to determine any issues that arise by discussion and compromise then it would seem that such a method would revive and accentuate a situation of class conflict. This is indeed exactly what has happened in Australia—the country that has provided a 'shocking example' of how things should not be done in industry.
>
> (Mayo, 1929, cited in Bruce and Nyland, 2011: 397)

 Theory in context: Mary Parker Follett

Mary Parker Follett was one of the earliest management theorists, a writer, speaker, and consultant who, alongside Lillian Gilbreth (see Chapter 3) and Mary van Kleek, was part of a predominantly female group who had an early influence on OB in ways which took a more human and social approach to Taylorism. She had an interest in social work, psychology, administration, learning, teamwork, and, our interest here, democracy. Follett argued not only for local government democracy through things like neighbourhood forums, but also for more industrial democracy.

Follett believed that conflict was inevitable, but rather than imposing power 'it is possible [for management] to develop the conception of power-with, a jointly developed power, a co-active, not a coercive power' (Follett, cited in Fox and Urwick, 1973: 72). The only way, thought Follett, to resolve conflict is not through one side having victory, or through compromise, but as the integration of interests. Like Mayo, she believed that managers should work with a group. However, unlike Mayo, who thought that conflict of any sort was abhorrent (Child, 1996), Follett believed that conflict could be constructive. Consequently she argued that the manager's role should be as a facilitator: 'we are beginning to think of the leader not as the man [sic] who is able to assert his individual will and get others to follow him, but as the one who knows how to relate the different wills in a group so that they will have driving force' (Follett, cited in Fox and Urwick, 1973: 247). She also differed from Mayo, who considered ordinary employees to be governed by 'sentiment'. Instead, Follett believed employees could be rational, and would be able to find mutually acceptable solutions.

Mayo's work, John Child argues, proved more popular because it 'appealed directly to managers' as it 'legitimated their authority' (Child, 1996: 88). Unfortunately this has overshadowed Follett's contribution, which, Child asserts, 'derived from a more profound social, political, and psychological understanding of relationships' (Child, 1996: 89). As Parker and Ritson put it: 'Follett offered an impressive spectrum of contributions to management thought that were well ahead of the practices and theories of her day and which anticipated many subsequently emerging management theories and practices' (Parker and Ritson, 2005: 1342–3).

169

Mayo saw elites, particularly managers, as having the right to manage. Mayo's conclusions about the Hawthorne studies and his 'theory of human relations' were 'based almost entirely on his own political interpretation of worker motivation' (Bruce and Nyland, 2011: 385). Rather than a neutral investigation, critical theorists argue that Mayo's work was a highly political attempt to crush moves towards industrial democracy and give elites more power.

Critical perspective 5

While the Hawthorne studies present a more holistic view of human nature than Taylorist theories, critics say that Mayo and his colleagues did not challenge the fundamental assumptions of the capitalist working relationship; indeed, arguably, they intensified it. The aim of Mayo's work was the psychological control of the workers. In taking this approach, it even diverted attention away from a more democratic form of management.

> Why might Mayo's interpretation of his findings be supported by management? Think about how a critical perspective might challenge this view.

 Study skills: implication of this perspective

It is important to understand the underlying assumptions and politics behind a management theory. Research rarely sits in a vacuum and can be a product of things like funding, the power of journal editors, or what universities want to promote. All researchers on management and organizations have political and social views, but not all research reveals these views explicitly. As you read the research you can begin to understand the authors' views by trying to explore whose perspective they are taking (i.e. the worker or the managers), or what they are trying to support (i.e. increased efficiency or increased autonomy for the workers).

Summing up

While the Hawthorne studies represent a substantial move forward towards a humane form of management practice, we have seen the critics, particularly of Mayo, state that the theories produced are, in fact, a more subtle form of control. Mayo and his colleagues were selective in their evidence, dismissed and psychologized rational alternative perspectives held by the employees, and, rather than changing management control, actually reinforced it. One of the key criticisms is that rather than 'discovering' the social side of the organization through the studies' findings, Mayo already had a long-held belief in this social side which influenced his interpretation of those findings.

Funding the Hawthorne studies

Another underlying influence on the Hawthorne studies was the source of the funding they received, and the social and political circumstances under which they were conducted. A large part of the funding for the research, and particularly for Elton Mayo's role at Harvard Business School, was from the Rockefellers—a highly influential and wealthy family of American businessmen. Bruce and Nyland claim that 'Mayo could conceivably be considered as a mere puppet or servant of far greater power: the Rockefellers' (2011: 388). They argue that 'Mayo simply and shrewdly tuned into what he believed his benefactor wanted to hear' (2011: 391), twisting his personal biases to meet the needs of John Rockefeller.

Because of the Great Depression, many factory owners were scared that workers and trade unions would try to overthrow capitalism and produce a new society. As a consequence, many business leaders were 'seeking to find a way to resolve industrial conflict without jeopardizing their status as the central locus of organizational authority' (O'Connor, 1999: 120).

Bruce and Nyland argue that Mayo used his scientific evidence as a way of justifying the prejudices and interests of his funders (2011), and therefore constructed knowledge that aided managers to the detriment of the workers. Indeed Baritz argues that Mayo believed that 'America's managers were remarkable men without prejudice'—an 'elite which had the ability and therefore the right to rule the rest of the nation' (Baritz, 1974: 200). The findings of the Hawthorne studies, particularly as popularized by Mayo, were appealing to these ruling elites because they explained social problems as the result not of economic inequalities but of irrational thinking on behalf of the worker. Mayo argued that society needed an 'administrative elite' capable of creating cooperation and producing harmony. Consequently, instead of being undermined by these social problems, these powerful people's interests were actually enhanced by them. Mayo's work

> presented business leaders both with an insidious means of monopolizing authority in the workplace and the wider community, as well as a justification for this monopoly founded on the assertion that the minds of workers are not suited to management or political decision making.
>
> (Bruce and Nyland, 2011: 384)

Bruce and Nyland argue that the findings of the Hawthorne studies therefore reinforced the perceived right of managers to manage by demonstrating their need to solve social problems. Mayo's widely criticized pro-management bias was therefore, at least in part, a product of the funding he received.

? Review questions

Describe	Who funded the Hawthorne studies?
Explain	What is the relevance of who funds a piece of research?
Analyse	What is the significance of the historical context (the Great Depression and post–World War I) to the way that the Hawthorne studies' findings have been interpreted?

Connecting case and theory

We opened the chapter with Phil Weaver trying to understand why the workers were only folding 80 napkins per hour, rather than the 120 napkins per hour he predicted. To solve this puzzle, as in the Hawthorne studies, Weaver turned to environmental and physiological explanations. Initially he thought the heating levels, and then fatigue, was causing the output to be lower than expected. As in the conventional narrative of the Hawthorne studies' researchers, Weaver was still stuck in the same assumptions as Fredrick Taylor: that workers are like machines.

Realizing that this mechanical explanation does not really make sense, Nina Biagini decided to interview the staff. To her surprise, like the original Hawthorne researchers she discovered the importance of the employees' home lives and even their experiences of childhood. We saw the beginning of the 'human relations' approach, where it is important to understand the person, informal (group) dynamics, and in particular how peoples' views are shaped by those around them. We could see how these group norms shaped employees' attitudes as Isabella 'joked', at the expense of Naomi, that she was speedy and would put them all out of a job.

Nina Biagini's solution to these issues fit well within Mayo's approach of listening to the staff and seeking to involve them in decisions. Rather than seeing the group as a problem, an attitude that Taylor had, Biagini (and Mayo) saw it as a resource to be used working in harmony. This view offered a more positive view of human nature and of managing people. By introducing the social side of organization, it revealed the importance of the informal organization, demonstrating it was possible—even desirable—for managers to embrace the human side of the organization. This meant that managers no longer had to be restricted to simply looking at processes and managing people through coercive approaches of targets and punishments, but could take a more positive view of getting teams to work together. This approach has laid the foundations for the study of teamwork (which we will look at in Chapter 6), as well as interest in organizational culture (Chapter 7) and reappraising the role of leadership (Chapter 13).

The Hawthorne studies have also been widely criticized for deepening management control over the psychological realm of organizational life, controlling workers' thoughts and feelings—reducing their capacity to resist. By studying people's thoughts and feelings, management is able to turn these insights to their advantage by manipulating them towards management goals. We can see this with Saffron's cynicism about the moves by management to involve them.

The Hawthorne studies therefore remain one of the most significant and powerful influences in management today. In particular, they raise the question: Is informal or social organization an area which creates a more humane form of management, or a stronger and more subtle form of control?

Further reading

Roethlisberger, F., and Dickson, W. 1939. *Management and the worker*. Harvard University Press: Boston.

Provides the most comprehensive and in-depth account of the Hawthorne studies. It gives very detailed descriptions of the Hawthorne studies from the researchers that led the research.

Mayo, E. 1949/1975. *The social problems of an industrial civilisation*. Routledge: London.

Mayo popularized the Hawthorne studies to a wider management audience. This book gives a background to many of his ideas, and his broader thoughts on management and society.

O'Connor, E. 1999. The politics of management thought: A case study of Harvard Business School and the Human Relations School. *Academy of Management Review* 24 (1): 117–31.

This provides a really interesting account of the early development of the human relations movement as led by Elton Mayo. It helps explain the social context in which the Hawthorne studies emerged and the part Mayo played in popularizing it.

Bruce, K., and Nyland, C. 2011. Elton Mayo and the deification of human relations. *Organization Studies* 32 (3): 383–405.

This article shows the importance of the funding that Mayo received in developing the Hawthorne studies and the influence that it had on the findings.

Hassard, J. 2012. Rethinking the Hawthorne studies: The Western Electric research in its social, political and historical context. *Human Relations* 65 (11): 1431–61.

Provides an interesting historical analysis of the context of the Hawthorne studies.

Baritz, L. 1974. *Servants of power: History of the use of social science in American industry.* Greenwood Press: Westport, CT.

Bell, D. 1947. The study of man: Adjusting men to machines. *Commentary* 3: 79–88.

Bendix, R.C., and Fisher, L.H. 1949. The perspectives of Elton Mayo. *Review of Economics and Statistics* 31 (4): 312–19.

Bennett, A.A., Bakker, A.B., and Field, J.G. 2018. Recovery from work-related effort: A meta-analysis. *Journal of Organizational Behaviour* 39 (3): 262–75.

Bramel, D., and Friend, R. 1981. Hawthorne, the myth of the docile worker, and class bias in psychology. *American Psychologist* 36 (8): 867–78.

Brantley, K. 2018. Is sleeplessness REALLY the key to Donald's success? Researchers are baffled after Trump's doctor praised the president's four-hour sleep cycle. *Daily Mail*, 18 January. Available at: http://www.dailymail.co.uk/health/article-5284457/Donald-Trump-sleeps-four-hours-night-wise.html#ixzz55DMd7C4B

Bruce, K., and Nyland, C. 2011. Elton Mayo and the deification of human relations. *Organization Studies* 32 (3): 383–405.

Carey, A. 1967. The Hawthorne studies: A radical criticism. *American Sociological Review* 32 (3): 403–16.

Cassidy, A. 2017. Clocking off: The companies introducing nap time to the workplace. *The Guardian*, 4 December. Available at: https://www.theguardian.com/business-to-business/2017/dec/04/clocking-off-the-companies-introducing-nap-time-to-the-workplace

Child, J. 1996. Commentary Follett: Constructive conflict. In: Graham, P. (ed.) *Mary Parker Follett: Prophet of management*. Harvard Business School Press: Boston, pp. 87–95.

CIPD (Chartered Institute of Personnel and Development). 2016. Absence management survey. Available at: http://www.cipd.co.uk/hr-resources/survey-reports/absence-management-2011.aspx (last accessed 13 June 2012). Update at: https://www.cipd.co.uk/knowledge/fundamentals/relations/absence/absence-management-surveys

Clegg, S., and Dunkerley, D. 1980. *Organization, class and control*. Routledge: London.

Dewey, J. 1982. Internal social reorganization after the war. In: Boydston, J.A. (ed.) *John Dewey: The middle works, 1899–1924*, vol. 11. Southern Illinois University Press: Carbondale, IL, pp. 73–86.

Donkin, R. 2001. *The history of work*. Palgrave Macmillan: London.

Fox, E.M., and Urwick, L. (eds). 1973. *Dynamic administration: The collected papers of Mary Parker Follett*. Pitman: London.

Fritz, C., Ellis, A.M., Demsky, C.A., Lin, B.C., and Guros, F. 2013. Embracing work breaks: Recovering from work stress. *Organizational Dynamics* 42 (4): 274–80.

Fritz, C., Lam, C.F., and Spreitzer, G.M. 2011. It's the little things that matter: An examination of knowledge workers' energy management. *Academy of Management Perspectives* 25 (3): 28–39.

Gale, E.A.M. 2004. The Hawthorne studies—a fable for our times? *QJM: An International Journal of Medicine* 97 (7): 439–49.

Gillespie, R. 1991. *Manufacturing knowledge: A history of the Hawthorne experiments*. Cambridge University Press: Cambridge.

Handel, M. 2002. *The sociology of organizations: Classic, contemporary and critical readings*. Sage: London.

Hassard, J. 2012. Rethinking the Hawthorne studies: The Western Electric research in its social, political and historical context. *Human Relations* 65 (11): 1431–61.

Health and Safety Executive, 2018. Costs to Great Britain of workplace injuries and new cases of work-related Health. Available at: http://www.hse.gov.uk/statistics/cost.htm

Huffington, A. 2017. *The sleep revolution: Transforming your life, one night at a time*. Thorndike Press: Waterville, ME.

Katz, A.S., Pronk, N.P., and Lowry, M. 2014. The association between optimal lifestyle-related health behaviors and employee productivity. *Journal of Occupational and Environmental Medicine*, 56 (7): 708–13.

Landsberger, H.A. 1958. *Hawthorne revisited*. Cornell University Press: Ithaca.

Marks, S.R. 1999. The gendered contexts of inclusive intimacy: The Hawthorne women at work and home. In: Adams, R.G., and Allen, G. (eds) *Placing friendship in context*. Cambridge University Press: Cambridge.

Mayo, E. 1933. *The human problems of an industrial civilization*. Macmillan: New York.

Mayo, E. 1949/1975. *The social problems of an industrial civilisation*. Routledge: London.

McCurry, J. 2014. Japanese firms encourage their dozy workers to sleep on the job. *The Guardian*, 18 August.

Moran, M. 2014. Google has sleep pods, Yelp has beer—why don't we just live at work? *The Guardian*, 11 September. Available at: https://www.theguardian.com/commentisfree/2014/sep/11/google-sleep-pods-yelp-beer-work-leisure-offices

Muldoon, J. 2012. The Hawthorne legacy: A reassessment of the impact of the Hawthorne studies on management scholarship, 1930–1958. *Journal of Management History* 18 (1): 105–19.

Munshi, N. 2017. Sleeping on the job can improve your work. *Financial Times*, 13 September. Available at: https://www.ft.com/content/09067126-3720-11e7-99bd-13beb0903fa3

Newport, C. 2016. *Deep work: Rules for focused success in a distracted world*. Hachette: London.

Nyland, C., and Bruce, K. 2012. Democracy or seduction? The demonization of scientific management and the deification of human relations. In: Lichtenstein, N., and Shermer, E. (eds) *The right and labor in America: Politics, ideology and imagination*. University of Pennsylvania Press: Philadelphia.

O'Connor, E. 1999. The politics of management thought: A case study of Harvard Business School and the Human Relations School. *Academy of Management Review* 24 (1): 117–31.

O'Conor, L., and Cahillane, L. 2015. Are we ever really 'out of the office'? *The Guardian*, 7 July.

Parker, L.D., and Ritson, P. 2005. Fads, stereotypes and management gurus: Fayol and Follett today. *Management Decision* 43 (10): 1335–57.

Peacock, L. 2011. Stress overtakes cancer as main form of sickness absence. *Daily Telegraph*, 5 October.

Roethlisberger, F., and Dickson, W. 1939. *Management and the worker*. Harvard University Press: Boston.

Schwab, K. 2016. The Global Competitiveness Report 2016–2017, *World Economic Forum*, Geneva.

Smith, J.H. 1998. The enduring legacy of Elton Mayo. *Human Relations* 51 (3): 221–49.

The Telegraph. 2017. Donald Trump's four hours a night and the other extreme sleeping habits of our leaders, 9 February. Available at: http://www.telegraph.co.uk/men/the-filter/donald-trumps-four-hours-night-extreme-sleeping-habits-leaders/

Treanor, J. 2015. How to use emotional intelligence to combat stress. *HR Magazine*, 20 July.

Waters, M. 1996. *Daniel Bell*. Routledge: London.

Wickström, G., and Bendix, T. 2000. The 'Hawthorne effect'—what did the original Hawthorne studies actually show? *Scandinavian Journal of Work, Environment and Health* 26 (4): 363–7.

Williams, W. 1920. *What's on the worker's mind*. Scribner's Sons: New York.

Zacher, H., Brailsford, H.A., and Parker, S.L. 2014. Micro-breaks matter: A diary study on the effects of energy management strategies on occupational well-being. *Journal of Vocational Behavior* 85 (3): 287–97.

CHAPTER 6

Managing groups and teams

From managing the individual to managing the collective

Chapter overview and learning outcomes

By the end of this chapter you should be able to:

- explain why teamwork has become a central feature of organizational life

- explain the links between teamwork and productivity

- analyse the factors needed to produce an effective team

- explain how teamwork can lead to greater surveillance and control

- explain how groupthink can have negative implications for teams

Key theorists

Meredith Belbin	British management researcher best known for his classification of team roles
Bruce Tuckman	American psychologist best known for his categorization of stages of group formation
Jon Katzenbach and Douglas Smith	American management consultants and organizational theorists
Irving Janis	American social psychologist who pioneered the groupthink theory
Cristina Gibson	Australian management theorist who explores what makes virtual teams work

Key terms

Group	A collection of people with common bonds but *not* a shared sense of purpose
Team	A group who meet together with a common purpose and mutual interdependence
Groupthink	A psychological phenomenon which limits the range of alternatives being considered because there is an overwhelming desire for consensus
Cohesiveness	Where group members feel bound together, often feeling as though they share a similar fate
Group dynamics	The underlying (and often unconscious) processes which shape the way group members react to each other

Introduction

> ## 🔍 Running case: confusion in the kitchen
>
> Linda Wilkinson walks into the kitchen. 'It's chaos in here,' she thinks. 'Not only are they not getting the food out on time, but they are arguing about it as well.'
>
> Despite the restaurant having Effingham, an award-winning chef, and a great menu, the last few months have seen an increase in customer complaints and negative comments in the local paper. Wilkinson worries that the standard of their day-to-day service is slowly eroding their image.
>
> Looking round the kitchen Wilkinson begins to see why. All the chefs seem to be working very hard, cooking their individual items and putting them on the 'pass' (where the food is checked by the head chef before going out to the customers) when they are done. However, they work in a haphazard order, with some items being completed long before the rest of the table's order is finished, leaving food to go cold.
>
> The orders are also stacking up. Food is going out to different tables at different times, with some customers waiting only ten minutes and others waiting well over an hour.
>
> Effingham, as the head chef, barks orders to the chefs, Josh, Toby, and Ella, who do their best to keep up with the standards he demands. As they cook, they present the food to him— if it is not up to the standard Effingham expects, he sends it back. 'We are trying to win an award here,' he can be heard muttering repeatedly to himself. 'We'll never make it with that standard of food.'
>
> Wilkinson also notices the front-of-house team darting in and out, picking up plates but looking confused as to what to do with them. 'Where is that one for?' she asks Isabella, one of the most experienced waiting staff. 'Umm, Table 17, I think,' and she rushes out, only to come back two minutes later with the same food and looking frantic.
>
> 'What are you doing?' Effingham shouts at her. 'That chicken is for Table 7—come on, you should know that.'
>
> 'But we've served Table 7,' Isabella stammers. 'For goodness' sake,' Effingham shouts, 'look, it's written here, Table 7.'
>
> More worrying still, the waiting staff keep taking orders for items that have sold out and then having to return to the customer to take alternative requests. Getting annoyed with each other, the kitchen and waiting staff can be heard from the restaurant shouting at each other.
>
> 'This is embarrassing,' Wilkinson thinks to herself. 'What should be the flagship part of the hotel is disorganized chaos. I thought we were meant to be a team!'

'Tell me about a time you have worked well in a team.' The next time you apply for a job you will probably be asked a question about your teamwork skills. From being in the 'customer service team' through to being part of the 'senior management team', being a good team member is now seen as a central requirement in modern working life (Dibble and Gibson, 2018). As multinational company Philips state:

> Everything at Philips is a collaborative effort; we are all striving to achieve the same goals, and that can only be accomplished through effective teamwork. (Philips, 2018)

It is not just at work that we are in groups and teams. In our personal lives we might be in sports or pub quiz teams or on a student committee. Even organizing a night out with friends requires teamwork skills including listening, cooperation, and negotiation.

Figure 6.1 Teamworking skills.

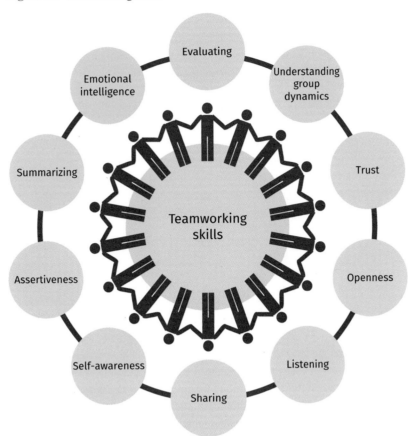

So why do companies value teamwork so highly? Teamwork is linked to increased creativity, problem-solving, and organizational success; it increases employee satisfaction by fulfilling 'social needs' (Mueller, 1994) and providing a sense of belonging and identity (Figure 6.1). Teamwork is often presented as a universal, unquestioned good (Learmonth, 2009).

However, being in a team can be hard. As is often seen on TV show *The Apprentice*, people can fall out, not pull their weight, and have personality clashes, and the team can end up dysfunctional, with no common identity or shared commitment (Maltarich et al., 2018). When these problems reach the boardroom, we see the results of the team breakdown: blame, a lack of trust, infighting, and a lack of common vision.

So what makes teams work well, and why is this so hard to achieve? This chapter looks at what some academic theory says makes 'high performance teams' and some of the barriers that stand in the way of achieving this. It also questions this 'cult' of teamwork (Coutu, 2009), examining the dark side of teamwork.

⊚ Study skills: doing group work at university

Do you like doing group assignments at university? While many people enjoy working in teams, we know from experience that many students say they find it frustrating, particularly when others do not seem to be 'pulling their weight'. To get around this problem, many stu-

→

→ dents simply divide the tasks to do individually before trying to fit them together into a single document. While this might feel quick and easy, it can cause problems because the work is inconsistent in terms of quality and the information presented. Furthermore, many of the benefits of group work, such as creative thinking, alternative perspectives, encouragement, and support, get lost (Dibble and Gibson, 2018).

So how do you create a better group assignment? Having a shared vision of what your group wants to achieve and building trust and communication enables ideas to flow freely, and new insights can be generated. University is a good location in which to develop team skills including listening, facilitation, and understanding of group dynamics. Writing a diary reflecting on how the group has worked together and what you could improve can strengthen your teamwork skills. Joining clubs and societies can also be good ways of demonstrating your teamworking skills and answer that important interview question, 'Are you a good team player?'

Visit the online resources and take a look at the extension material for Chapter 6 for some further practical tips on team working.

The difference between groups and teams

While in everyday terms we tend to use the words 'groups' and 'teams' interchangeably, the academic literature often gives them quite specific meanings (although these are not universally agreed): a **group** exists when there is commonality but *members do not necessarily work together for a common purpose*. Groups include many situations, such as a group of friends. A **team** is seen as having a *more specific purpose* and function. They rely *more on each other*, have a greater sense of *collective vision*, and are *mutually accountable*. A summary of the differences is shown in Table 6.1.

Employability skills: teamwork

Are soft skills like teamwork important? A recent survey by Hay Group found that although 93 per cent of employers think such skills are important, 51 per cent of graduates believe that people skills actually get in the way of getting the job done (Hay Group, 2015). In another recent survey, the British Chambers of Commerce stated that 57 per cent of businesses do not find graduates sufficiently skilled in teamwork. Commenting on these findings, John Longworth, director general of the British Chambers of Commerce, said 'Firms need young people that are resilient, good communicators, and understand how to work as part of a team' (British Chambers of Commerce, 2015). Therefore, while getting a good degree is vital for getting interviews, demonstrating teamwork and interpersonal skills is increasingly essential for getting a job.

So how do you develop your teamwork skills? University is a good time to build your teamwork experience, particularly through outside activities. Spend five minutes thinking about the activities that you regularly engage in and the teamwork skills that you have developed and those you still need to develop. For instance, you might have organized a charity fundraising night or completed a Duke of Edinburgh's award, which requires teamwork. For each area, can you think of one or two good examples of each?

Visit the online resources and take a look at the extension material for Chapter 6 for more details and some related activities.

Table 6.1 Differences between teams and working groups

Team	Working group
Collectively accountable	Individually accountable
Plan together, collaborate, collectively decide future actions	Share information and different perspectives
Focus on team goals and outcomes	Focus on individual goals and outcomes
Work together on collective tasks	Work on individual tasks which sometimes are done in connection with others

What is a team?

The origin of the word 'team' is a set of animals yoked together (pulling a cart), emphasizing the *common purpose* and *mutual interdependence* of the team members.

Within the academic literature there are numerous definitions of teamwork. Two of the popular ones are:

> A team is a collection of individuals who are interdependent in their tasks, who share responsibility for outcomes, who see themselves and who are seen by others as an intact social entity embedded in one or more larger social systems.
>
> (Cohen and Bailey, 1997: 241)

> [S]mall groups of interdependent individuals who share responsibilities for outcomes for their organization.
>
> (Sundstrom et al., 1990: 120)

Most academic definitions stress the importance of mutual reliance, interdependence, and accountability that group members feel when working together.

The origin of the word 'team'.
Source: Margo Harrison / Shutterstock.com

 Real life case: the teamwork behind the ice-bucket challenge

In August 2014 you may have done something very odd: taken out your mobile phone and asked a friend to record you saying you were going to donate to an ALS charity (supporting research into amyotrophic lateral sclerosis and, in the UK, into motor neurone disease) and then saying the names of a few friends you wanted to nominate, only to have a bucket of ice-cold water poured over you (invariably followed by you screaming at the shock of the pain). The 'Ice Bucket Challenge', became viral, with Facebook and Twitter feeds full of videos of people pouring water on their heads and nominating their friends.

For the team behind the challenge, this was a major job. The ALS charity, which normally received around 10 enquiries a day, suddenly received over 200. In an interview for this textbook, Stephanie Dufner, then the ALS communications manager, told us they had to work 14 hours a day, and 6 hours at weekends, answering individual and media enquiries (Dufner, 2015a). The attention the Ice Bucket Challenge received meant they had to constantly update the Frequently Asked Questions, answering questions on the charity's stance on issues such as animal testing and stem cell research, and clarifying miscommunication on social media. Dufner states in an article in *The Guardian* that 'This required me to work with my colleagues in communications and marketing and other departments to formulate consistent messaging that answered these questions in a timely manner' (Dufner, 2015b). They had to constantly keep social media up to date. For a small organization at the centre of a worldwide media spotlight, this required them to work together and support each other at a faster pace than they had ever been used to. 'I recall a sense of camaraderie that occurred during the challenge' Dufner told us (Dufner, 2015a). They also needed excellent communication to keep each other up to date with what was going on.

> What sort of teamwork challenges do you think that the team from ALS faced?

Does teamwork increase productivity?

Running case: Linda Wilkinson meets Graham Effingham

After the service has finished, Linda Wilkinson meets Graham Effingham.

'Look, Graham, we need to get the whole of the restaurant team working together. It is a complete shambles at the moment. You have some skilled individuals but you're not getting the best out of them. We currently have 90 covers a night. We should be doing 130 and have the potential for 180. The food is great, but we are getting a reputation for slow and erratic service, and that isn't going to get any better unless we work together. I want us to run a smooth, slick service and produce food that we are all proud of without you all running around like headless chickens.'

Effingham, taken aback, begins to protest. 'How can you say that? I've won awards for my cooking,' he retorts, pointing to the plaque on the wall.

'I'm not talking about you as a chef, or the food—which is great,' Wilkinson replies calmly. 'It's the way the whole restaurant is functioning. We're just not getting food out quickly enough or in the right order—we're beginning to get a bad reputation.'

'Well, it's not me you should be talking to, is it?' Effingham responds with a menacing stare. 'The problem isn't the kitchen, it's with Nina and her lot. They cause us chaos. They are just completely clueless sometimes. It's like trying to cook blindfolded. Not only do they tell the customers wrong things about the food and put in orders for things that we have sold out of, but they even keep changing the menu, allowing customers to change the food. I had Josh last week pulling mushrooms out of the risotto, that's just crazy. They should try cooking for a week!'

Armed with this information, Wilkinson goes over to speak to Nina Biagini, the maître d', who is sitting with her team in the opposite end of the bar. 'Ha, is that what he said?' Biagini replies indignantly. 'It's his lot that are in chaos. We can only put on the tables what we are given. Effingham just spends his time shouting at everyone—my servers can't stand being in there. We're the ones having to go and see customers and apologize for the slow service— it's painful sometimes. And then whenever the waiting staff go in the kitchen they just get shouted at if they dare say anything about speeding things up. My crew are all good people and we like to put customers first. Effingham and the other chefs never have to face customers. I agree with you it's getting bad, but Effingham is the problem. He's more worried about winning awards and his personal reputation than serving ordinary customers.'

Returning to her office, Wilkinson begins to jot down some notes to herself.

It's the restaurant as a whole. The service is a mess. There is no communication between the front of house and the kitchen: things go in the wrong order and they get in each other's way. They also drink in separate groups at the end of the night.

Since the 1980s there has been an explosion of interest in teamwork, with supporters arguing it offers a more productive, creative, satisfying, and empowering way of working that encourages workers to participate more (Procter and Mueller, 2000).

Teams are vital for sharing and retaining knowledge. They produce more accurate and creative answers because team members bring with them a breadth of knowledge, perspectives, and skills, and challenge each other's views, which leads to better decisions. Also, when one member leaves or is off sick, all of the team's knowledge does not disappear with them.

The benefits of teamwork: more than the sum of its parts

 Research insight: Sony Connect vs the iPod—the problems of solid boundaries

Sony should have been in the prime position to capitalize on the new digital music market. Pioneers of portable music with the innovative Walkman and Diskman, Sony Connect launched a new media player using a hard disk. Sony were the leader in the portable music industry, some ten times larger than Apple. With their skills and experience, they should have been the best company to take advantage of the digital music revolution. Yet they failed, losing out to their smaller rival. The fundamental problem was that 'at Sony, teams worked in isolation from one another, and team boundaries were not crossed' (Dibble and Gibson, 2018: 927): the teams were in 'silos'. Apple, in contrast, had very fluid boundaries. As an Apple leader described it:

> We were all working together late at night, and it was highly energized ... it was just an incredible team project. There were no boundaries. The software guys, the hardware guys, the firmware guys, everybody worked together. It was a pretty amazing experience.

> (Hansen, 2009: 7, cited in Dibble and Gibson, 2018: 927)

The challenge, therefore, is how do you make sure that teams do not get into silos (Figure 6.2)? On the one hand, to get a team to function well they need to have a collective sense of identity and understanding, which requires *strong* boundaries within the team. Yet on the other hand, to achieve creative ideas and take in divergent approaches, it is necessary to get ideas from many

Figure 6.2 The move from silos to cross-functional teams.

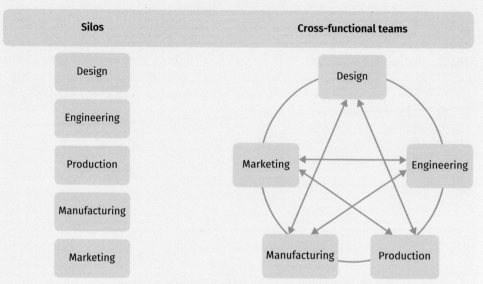

different perspectives, which requires *weak* and *permeable* boundaries so that new approaches can be fed into the team (2018). Dibble and Gibson argue that teams require *both* strong and *weak* boundaries and that different phases of projects often need different forms of team membership. In the ideas phase, it is important to be creative so that divergent, unique, and novel approaches can give new perspectives. Opening up the team to new voices is therefore important. However, when the team focuses on implementation, having a shared history and understanding is really important in order for the team to put the ideas into practice (Dibble and Gibson, 2018).

Being part of a team can create social bonds, giving greater camaraderie (togetherness and bonding), emotional support, and a sense of shared purpose. Team members can learn from each other, gain alternative perspectives on how to tackle problems, and even suffer less stress (West, 2004). Further benefits of teamwork in general are shown in Table 6.2.

The challenges of teamwork

 Theory in context: nearly half of all employees feel their organization does not support their teamwork

Despite the importance and benefits of teamwork, a survey by the consultancy firm Cedar of 2,000 UK employees states that a third of workers dread coming to work because of poor teamwork environment: 47 per cent say that their organization does not support teamwork and 37 per cent prefer to work by themselves. Furthermore, 42 per cent of people aged 18–24 preferred working by themselves. Many businesses, the survey suggests, do not encourage people to work effectively in teams, and employees get frustrated by having to correct the 'sloppy mistakes' of colleagues. Teamwork is certainly difficult.

Sources: HR Grapevine (2013); Onrec (2013); Xenergie Consulting Ltd (2013).

Table 6.2 Benefits of teamwork

Benefits of teamwork to employees	Benefits of teamwork to organizations
• More meaningful work • Sharing of responsibility and of the ups and downs of the challenges that are faced • Learning from others (increasing skills by working alongside others) • Job enrichment and rotation (working as part of a team means that you can do a variety of jobs and therefore not be bored doing just one) • Belonging needs—feeling part of a group • Increased autonomy as team becomes responsible for tasks (do not need to always go to a manager), which can help people feel more involved and interested in their jobs • Motivation—emotional and psychological support	• Better-quality decision making and problem solving by drawing on a wider range of skills • Transfer of skills and technical expertise • Reduced dependency on particular individuals • Task requirements, e.g. designing jobs where it is impossible for one individual to work independently • Increased time utilization—peak/trough jobs • Task responsibility for the whole process rather than an 'it's not my job' attitude • Delegation of authority so people take more responsibility for the outcome • Group becomes responsible for improving their practice • Faster decision making and increased commitment

Teamwork is not always a recipe for success. Poorly performing teams can be highly dysfunctional. They often lack trust, fear conflict, lack commitment, and avoid accountability, and members do not care about results or feel little ability to influence them. Often, instead of expressing ideas openly, members of these teams avoid direct conflict at all costs, either making compromised decisions that nobody is satisfied with and/or having latent conflict which comes out in the form of politics, back-biting, personal resentment, or withdrawal from the group (see Table 6.3).

Why is teamwork difficult?

In the 1970s Bibb Latané and his colleagues (Latané et al., 1979; Harkins et al., 1980) conducted a series of experiments to investigate whether people worked harder in groups or individually. To test this, in a first experiment, they asked people as individuals and then as groups to shout as loud as they could and in a second experiment to clap as loudly as they could.

Table 6.3 The challenges of teamwork

Challenges of teamwork for employees	Challenges of teamwork for organizations
• Personality clashes • Frustration of ideas • Breakdown of trust • Reliance on less conscientious or less skilled members	• Employees becoming unproductive • Personality clashes and dysfunctional activity • Time-consuming practices • Lack of shared identity and purpose

They discovered that people were louder individually than in groups. However, they argued this was not because people decided to put in less effort, they believed they worked as hard in the group. However, unconsciously they tried less hard. The researchers called this phenomenon social loafing (Latané et al., 1979).

This built on earlier research by Max Ringelmann, an agricultural engineer who found that, working alone, an agricultural student could pull a weight of 85 kg but a team of seven could only pull 450 kg instead of the 595 kg they should have been able to pull.

Why did this happen? Latané et al. suggest individuals invest effort into tasks where they can be personally identified. Furthermore, in teams we only work as hard as we need to and therefore reduce effort where we feel tour effort is not require. Therefore, when individuals feel their contribution particularly matters they will try, but when they feel it is less important they try less hard.

However, Norman Triplett (1898) looked at cyclists pedalling around a track. He found that those who pedalled around in groups went faster than those that pedalled alone. Cycling in a group increased performance, which has come to be known as social facilitation theory: the tendency that individuals have to work harder when being watched by others, particularly on simple tasks.

 Reflecting on your own experiences in teams, which do you think captures your experiences better—social loafing or social facilitation theory? Why is this? Do some groups make you want to work harder *for* the team and others to work *only* when you are personally identified?

A related phenomenon is called shirking or free-riding (Schnake, 1991). This occurs when individuals purposely live off the efforts of others, for example a student who does not attend any meetings or put in any work for a group assignment but turns up on the day of the presentation and expects to get the same grade as everyone else. The larger the group, the more opportunity for free-riding exists.

? Review questions

Describe	What is free-riding?
Explain	How can teamwork improve performance?
Analyse	What are the challenges in getting effective teamwork? Does this mean that managers cannot automatically assume people will work well in a team?
Apply	What benefits did increased teamwork at Ford bring to the organization and to individual workers? How had 'working in silos' prevented this team working?

Creating a high performance team

🔍 **Running case:** Wilkinson calls Effingham and Biagini together

'Right, I've called you both together because we need to sort this out. We have got a lot of potential in this restaurant, but we are failing and the customers are beginning to turn against us. We are not serving anywhere near the numbers we should.'

'Well, it is nothing to do with us,' Effingham replies indignantly. 'My team are great, and the food quality is great.'

'Nobody is saying that the food that is produced is not great,' Wilkinson responds a little defensively. 'It's just not getting served quickly enough.'

'Well, that's her lot, then,' Effingham huffs.

Nina Biagini looks shocked at Effingham. 'Us? Come on, get real, we aren't the ones cooking it all so slowly.' 'Exactly,' Effingham huffs back. 'We do our best,' Biagini continues, 'but if it's not cooked quickly enough then there is not much we can do.'

Sensing a row brewing, Wilkinson intervenes. 'Look, this isn't a blame game here. The simple facts are that as a unit we are not getting the food out quick enough. I have spent a lot of time studying what goes on in the restaurant as a whole, and things have to change, starting with you two.' Effingham and Biagini look towards each other in a surprised manner. 'You are both at loggerheads constantly, and it's working its way down through the rest of the restaurant. A restaurant is a team game—we all need each other to perform—and that starts with you two. I want us working as a high performance team, trusting, relying, and working with each other.'

'If you became a team then you could do something really great,' Wilkinson continues evangelically. 'You know, share ideas, learn from each other, work collectively, be committed to each other, and support each other's personal development. Look, you need each other to succeed. You need to start thinking as a team.'

'Umm …,' replies Effingham, softening somewhat. 'I do concede that sometimes things are not that coordinated and we could work better together. Maybe I could go as far as involving the waiting staff a bit more socially, but I'm still in charge round here,' he finishes firmly.

'Well, maybe we could try and understand the chef's position a little more,' Biagini continues in the same spirit. 'We do need each other and we could work better together.'

'This is my baby, my restaurant, my reputation at stake,' Effingham states, trying to retain his authority.

While many of us say that we work in teams, Katzenbach and Smith (1993) argue that, in practice, true teams are rare, as most of us actually are in what they call *working groups*. High performance teams, they state, are special, as everything is focused on the team. Members are highly reliant on each other and focus on team outcome rather than individual outcomes. In contrast, working group members work largely independently and focus on individual performance. Table 6.4 sets out the main differences between working groups and high performance teams.

Becoming a high performance team requires substantial effort; high levels of commitment, trust, and cooperation, with a team focus. This is challenging, requiring a move away from thinking individually to a collective mentality, needing a 'leap of faith' to put one's fate in the hands of others.

Working groups can be effective, as the best ones 'come together to share information, perspectives, and insights, to make decisions that help each person do his or her own job better'

Table 6.4 The differences between working groups and high performance teams (based on Katzenbach and Smith, 1993)

	Working groups	High performance teams
Focus of performance	Individual	Group
Task relationship	Independent	Interdependent
Approach	Takes personal approach	Committed to a common approach
Who takes responsibility	Personal responsibility	Group responsibility and high trust
Outcome	Is the sum of its parts	Magnified—is more than the sum of its parts

(Katzenbach and Smith, 1993: 89). Consequently, Katzenbach and Smith say that where 'there is no performance need for the team approach, efforts spent to improve the effectiveness of the working group make much more sense than floundering around trying to become a team' (1993: 90).

To become a high performance team, Katzenbach and Smith argue that the group will go through four stages (Figure 6.3).

1. The *pseudo-team*. They have the need to be a team (i.e. would benefit from working together), but they have not achieved it as they are not focused on collective performance. Consequently, there is actually a drop in performance as 'their interactions detract from each member's individual performance without delivering any joint benefit' (1993: 91). They are, therefore, less than the sum of their parts.

2. The *potential team*. They try to improve performance, but need greater clarity on purpose, goals, and approach to work, and 'ha[ve] not yet established collective accountability' (1993:

Figure 6.3 Katzenbach and Smith's teamwork performance curve showing the four stages in a team's development.
Source: Katzenbach and Smith (1993). Reproduced by permission of Harvard Business Publishing.

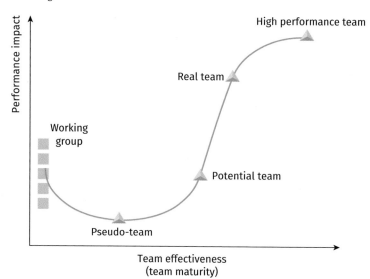

Table 6.5 Comparing high performance and poor performance teams (based on Ket De Vries, 1999)

High performance teams have:	Poorly performing teams have:
<ul><li>members who respect and trust each other</li><li>members who protect and support each other</li><li>members who engage in open dialogue and communication</li><li>members who share a strong common goal</li><li>members who have strong shared values and beliefs</li><li>members who subordinate their own objectives to those of the team</li><li>members who subscribe to 'distributed' leadership</li></ul>	<ul><li>a lack of a clear sense of direction</li><li>insufficient or unequal commitment to the group</li><li>a lack of skills in key areas</li><li>incohesive or outright hostility among group members (Katzenbach and Smith, 1993)</li><li>unresolved goals</li><li>personal conflicts</li><li>poor leadership</li></ul>

91). They are about as effective as a working group, as they gain some benefits of teamwork but have to spend longer communicating.

3. The *real team*. Significant improvement in productivity is made here. They become a small group with complementary skills and a common purpose that members aspire to. Particular goals are an integral part of this purpose—specifics are clearly understood, there is a commonly-agreed working approach, and members are mutually accountable. Katzenbach and Smith believe that the key to achieving a real team is a focus on performance rather than personal chemistry (1993: 61).

4. The *high performance team*. Teams that achieve this level are rare but highly productive. They are like *real teams*, but with greater levels of trust and commitment to each other's personal growth, professional development, and success. They work on the model that 'if one of us fails, we all fail' (1993: 66). They have interchangeable skills, greater flexibility, shared leadership, a deeper sense of purpose, and even greater humour and more fun. High performance teams have 'a deeper sense of purpose, more ambitious performance goals, more complete approaches, fuller mutual accountability, and interchangeable as well as complementary skills' (1993: 79).

A comparison of high performance and poor performance teams is given in Table 6.5.

 Think of teams that you have been involved in—what stage of the team performance curve do you think they are or were at?

⟳ Real life case: Leicester City win the Premier League

Nobody thought it would happen. Indeed some pundits had them down as possible relegation candidates, having narrowly avoided relegation the previous season. Yet Leicester City, a small and unfashionable football club in England, the 5000-1 outsiders, won the 2015-16 Premier League, seeing off far more affluent rivals like Manchester City, Manchester United, Liverpool, Chelsea, Tottenham Hotspur, and Arsenal. Whilst they had some good players,

→

187

Leicester City had few 'stars' bar Kanté who was signed for £5.6m. Their manager, Ranieri, was widely mocked when he took over and was the bookmakers' favourite to be the first to be sacked that season. Leicester winning the Premier League was described as a fairytale, one of the most unexpected and remarkable stories in English football history (James, 2016a). So how did they do it? Even within the football club they 'shake their heads in disbelief' at what happened. Yet the main reason they say is: 'exhilarating mix of team spirit and talent within a group of players who possess a rare commodity in a game awash with money: hunger' (James, 2016b).

Building an effective team

Running case: Linda Wilkinson gathers the entire restaurant staff together

'Welcome to the first restaurant team meeting,' declares Linda Wilkinson, as she paces up and down in front of the front-of-house and kitchen staff. 'You might have wondered why you're here.' 'You're telling me,' Effingham whispers to Toby, who sniggers. 'Well, we felt,' says Linda, continuing to look directly at Effingham as if to keep him in his place, 'that we really want the restaurant to work together—you are one big team. So today we are launching "Team Junction Restaurant".'

'We all need to work together and act as one big unit if we are going to achieve our mission—providing high quality service to the customer.'

'As members of "Team Junction Restaurant" you all need to work together and rely on and trust each other—if we are to succeed, we succeed together; if we are to fail, we fail together.'

'This is a chair from Malawi in eastern Africa,' Wilkinson continues, pointing to a carved wooden chair. 'What I love about it is it shows everyone doing their job but being part of one big community. Everyone is important, from the lowliest basket carrier to the most senior chief. If you remove any one of them the whole thing would come crashing down—this is how I see "Team Junction Restaurant": one big community.'

As we have seen earlier, teamwork is central to most organizations but is difficult to get right. A group of individuals cannot simply be put together and be expected to become a team (Katzenbach and Smith, 1993). So, how do you build a successful team? Unfortunately, despite the numerous attempts by academics, business consultants, and managers to discover a formula to create a well-functioning team, there is no single, quick-fix solution (Katzenbach and Smith, 1993) (Figure 6.4).

To build an effective team requires finding the right people with the right technical and team-working skills, with a sense of commitment to each other, and then setting the right environment for them to succeed. It also requires the team members to cooperate, trust, and be committed to each other, and to take collective ownership of problems. It is to the question of how to develop these aspects that we now turn.

Figure 6.4 What makes an effective team?

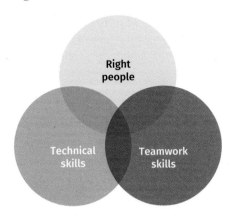

? Review questions

Describe What are the four stages in becoming a high performance team?

Explain What is the difference between the working group and a high performance team?

Analyse Why do Katzenbach and Smith counsel that a working group should not always try to become a high performance team?

Apply What stage of Katzenbach and Smith's teamworking cycle do you think Junction Hotel are at?

Skills balance

Having the right balance of the skills and knowledge is essential for a successful team. This can be having specialists who carry out specific tasks (such as an orchestra where each person carries out one task or skills spread across the team). Some organizations, such as the UK's National Health Service (NHS), conduct a skills audit matrix to decide whether the team is equipped with the necessary skills. While sometimes the team leader will be able to build the team from scratch, often they are required to develop these skills within the existing team; therefore, it is important to identify potential within the current members' skills potential or gaps that need to be filled by new members.

C Real life case: building teams around strength

How do you build a team based around the strengths of those that work in them? One solution is provided by Strengthscope™. This tool allows individuals, teams, and organizations to assess the strengths that each individual team member and map these strengths across the whole team. Rather than examining technical expertise, such as accounting, they look at work-based strengths, such as courage, emotional control, compassion, decisiveness,

→

→

self-improvement, and critical thinking. With a skilled facilitator, the Strengthscope™ producers believe that a team can be made more effective by tapping into the strengths (sometimes hidden in normal working arrangements). They claim that using their system can lead to:

- improved team communication, problem-solving, and focus on results
- heightened appreciation of, and respect for, individual differences
- enhanced accountability for delivering team goals
- higher levels of team morale and enhancement
- increased confidence and resourcefulness to overcome performance blockages
- improved understanding of the team's weaker areas and ways to manage or mitigate these.

Source: www.strengthscope.com

As we will see in Chapter 8, such personality tests should come with a health warning, as some researchers are sceptical of their ability to capture the 'essence' of a personality. Such tests also require considerable levels of trust within the team, as members reveal private information about how they see themselves and how others see them.

Team roles

🔍 **Running case:** teamwork results

Linda Wilkinson stands in front of Team Junction Restaurant. 'Right, each of you has an envelope which contains a report about your teamworking skills. There are no superior roles—everyone is equally important. What we need to do is merge you into a team. Over the next week I will be meeting all of you to discuss your role and how we can all work better together.'

'Plant,' declares Toby in a slightly puzzled way. 'Oh, I get it,' he declares as he reads more. 'I always told you I'm creative! What are you, Josh?' 'Monitor Evaluator,' Josh replies, in a more muted fashion. 'Goody-two-shoes,' Toby mocks. 'Effingham, what are you?' 'Shaper,' Effingham replies, barely able to hide his smirk. 'Told you I'm the one to get things going round here—right, let's get on with some real work and stop this nonsense!'

Team-role theorists argue that a team only reaches its full potential when it has a balance of team roles. They create models of how the ideal team should look, the most popular of these theories is provided by Meredith Belbin (2010), who devised his famous Team Role Inventory (Figure 6.5). These different roles are useful for the group as, for instance, the Resource Investigator in Belbin's model is often good at kick-starting projects, but loses interest after the initial enthusiasm has passed, whereas the Completer Finisher is not as good at these initial phases but can bring a project to completion.

To perform well, a team needs a good balance of all these roles. The theory states that every person has a series of traits that lead them to have a preference for one particular role, but also to be capable of one or two back-up roles should the team's work demand it.

Figure 6.5 Belbin's team role summary descriptions.
Source: Belbin® 2018 www.belbin.com

Belbin® **Team Role Summary Descriptions**

Resource Investigator

Contribution: Outgoing, enthusiastic. Explores opportunities and develops contacts.

Allowable Weaknesses: Might be over-optimistic, and can lose interest once the initial enthusiasm has passed.

Teamworker

Contribution: Co-operative, perceptive and diplomatic. Listens and averts friction.

Allowable Weaknesses: Can be indecisive in crunch situations and tends to avoid confrontation.

Co-ordinator

Contribution: Mature, confident, identifies talent. Clarifies goals. Delegates effectively.

Allowable Weaknesses: Can be seen as manipulative and might offload their own share of the work.

Plant

Contribution: Creative, imaginative, free-thinking. Generates ideas and solves difficult problems.

Allowable Weaknesses: Might ignore incidentals, and may be too pre-occupied to communicate effectively.

Monitor Evaluator

Contribution: Sober, strategic and discerning. Sees all options and judges accurately.

Allowable Weaknesses: Sometimes lacks the drive and ability to inspire others and can be overly critical.

Specialist

Contribution: Single-minded, self-starting and dedicated. They provide specialist knowledge and skills.

Allowable Weaknesses: Can only contribute on a narrow front and tends to dwell on the technicalities.

Shaper

Contribution: Challenging, dynamic, thrives on pressure. Has the drive and courage to overcome obstacles.

Allowable Weaknesses: Can be prone to provocation, and may sometimes offend people's feelings.

Implementer

Contribution: Practical, reliable, efficient. Turns ideas into actions and organises work that needs to be done.

Allowable Weaknesses: Can be a bit inflexible and slow to respond to new possibilities.

Completer Finisher

Contribution: Painstaking, conscientious, anxious. Searches out errors. Polishes and perfects.

Allowable Weaknesses: Can be inclined to worry unduly, and reluctant to delegate.

For more information:
+44 (0)1223 264975 | www.belbin.com

BELBIN®

Each role has strengths and allowable weaknesses, e.g. the price that has to be paid for the strength. For instance, in the Belbin model the Shaper role is dynamic and has a strong drive which can push through ideas; however, this can lead to that person offending people's feelings and being provocative.

Each individual discovers their team roles through completing a self-assessment inventory, which can be supplemented by assessments by managers, colleagues, and those you manage.

This approach has become a mini-industry in itself, with many paid-for online assessment exercises as well as numerous books, games, and group activities based on similar models.

While Belbin's is the most famous, others include the Team Management Systems (TMS Worldwide, 2018) model and Peter Honey's (2001) five team roles.

 Visit the online resources and take a look at the extension material for Chapter 6 to read more about these models.

According to Fisher et al. (2001), the background of Belbin's model is a combination of the need for clearly defined roles that are matched to specific individuals, drawn from bureaucratic theory (see Chapter 2), and the desire to involve team members in decision making, which originates in the human relations approach (Chapter 5).

Despite their popularity, concerns exist over their validity and usefulness. Furnham et al. (1993) argue that Belbin's original research was based on limited evidence, and the questionnaires are vague and do not necessarily relate to how people behave within a team. Negative personality traits like neuroticism are not included in the models, despite the fact that they have significant impact on team performance. Most troubling is that the questionnaires rely on self-reporting, which is not a dependable way to discover how we act. Fisher et al. go as far as to argue that these measures are 'psychometrically unsound' (2001: 142), and Anderson and Sleap (2004) state that they take little account of gender.

 Real life case: hiring for teamwork

Leadership Solutions, Belbin New Zealand, are a licence distributor for the Belbin Team Roles model in the New Zealand and Pacific Islands. They run workshops and sell the licence for the Belbin Team Roles to organizations and individuals who want to understand their team dynamics. They argue that this is the key to high performance and productivity, through getting the right combination of people to produce strong teams. This, they claim, is good for organizations in an increasingly complex world. They also provide booklets teaching people how to make the most of Belbin for their own careers, which they say is particularly useful if you are starting out on your career.

Source: http://www.leadershipsolutions.co.nz/index.cfm

 Have you ever done a team role profile? How helpful do you think it would be?

Personality clashes

 Running case: tensions rise in the kitchen

Despite Linda Wilkinson's best efforts, on Friday night when service resumes, the tensions between the kitchen and the front of house still continue. Orders keep being misplaced, and arguments are breaking out between the kitchen and the waiting staff. Concerned that the heads

of the kitchen and front of house are still at loggerheads, Wilkinson decides she needs to intervene.

'He just thinks he's God's gift,' Biagini complains. 'He is more bothered about winning that
wretched award than serving customers. It is just not right.' Looking away from Wilkinson,
Biagini mutters, 'I just can't really cope with him. He's arrogant and loud-mouthed, just not
the type of person I can work with. I don't want my team being treated like that.'

Concerned, Wilkinson goes to visit Effingham. 'If you can't stand the heat, then you need
to get out of the kitchen,' he replies gruffly as Wilkinson tentatively raises Biagini's concerns.
'Look, the kitchen is a tough environment. We can't be pussyfooting around being bothered
by how the waiting staff feel. They should just concentrate on getting the orders right.'

Wilkinson looks on in despair. Despite her best efforts, things seem more difficult than she
ever thought.

Even when a team has the right balance of skills and roles, some teams fail because of personality differences (see Chapter 8), caused, personality theorist argue, by the imbalance of personality traits within the group. Groups need the correct balance of personality characteristics and make sure that no individual dominates. For instance, extraverts have positive influences, being sociable, enthusiastic, energetic, and optimistic. However, Barry and Steward's findings (1997, cited in Barrick et al., 1998: 381) suggest that 'teams may be more effective when there is greater variance among member levels of extraversion, so that complementary roles of leading and following are carried out'. Similarly, high levels of emotional stability can be important to create a well-functioning team as it promotes a relaxed atmosphere, reduces anxiety, and promotes cooperation. However, as is often documented in the creative industries, sometimes a clash of personalities or having a group with heightened emotional sensibilities can lead to more creative work, even if this is difficult to sustain in the long term.

Some personality researchers see personality traits as relatively fixed and knowable. They devise complex numerical formulas to capture the personalities within a team and work out their ideal balance (see Barrick et al., 1998, as an example). The aim here is for managers to use these tools to set up the ideal balanced team.

However, as we will see in Chapter 8, other personality theorists see personality as changeable over time (see Chapter 8 for an in-depth discussion of personality traits). They question the validity of reducing personalities down to a set of numbers (as these studies tend to) and if people really act as these computer models predict.

 Have you ever fallen out with someone during a team exercise? Why did this happen? How much of it was because of personality clashes?

Social identity theory

Social identity theorists (Abrams and Hogg, 2001) argue that an individual has two identities: (i) personal identity, comprising personal and social beliefs, (ii) group identity, comprising the benefits of belonging to the team. Ideally, these identities will be aligned, but if not, the team membership identity should be stronger.

To make this change, such theorists argue that individuals need to be 'de-individualized' (Abrams and Hogg, 2001), transformed from thinking and feeling like an individual to feeling 'psychologically intertwined with the group's fate' (Mael and Ashforth, 1995: 310). In other words, their primary identity is that of a member of the team rather than as an individual (Tajfel and Turner, 1986). This shifts their outlook from 'my task' to 'our tasks', thus thinking as a team and being committed to the collective output.

Employability skills: forming your team's shared identity

How do you get a group of people who come together to think like a team? Getting them to think as a team, with a shared sense of identity is a central way of getting people to work together. Social identity theorists argue that the way that those in a leadership position speak, talking in terms of a collective team rather than as a bunch of individuals, can produce this collective thinking. Praising the team collectively, using words like 'we' instead of 'I', or always referring to the team as a whole rather than any individual, can shift the group members to thinking of themselves as a team with collective interests.

So next time that you have a collective assignment, be it for university, a sports club or society, or for a work situation, try using more collective language and see if you can develop the team spirit and collective thinking that can build a team.

? Review questions

Describe	What are Belbin's team roles?
Explain	Why is it important according to Belbin to have a balance of team roles within any one team?
Analyse	What are the strengths and weaknesses of Belbin's model? Do you think that people fit into such defined roles within a team?
Apply	In the running case, what effects are personality clashes having upon teamwork?

Tuckman's stages of group formation

Q Running case: the three-legged race

'Why are we like this?' Josh asks quizzically of Saffron, looking down at his leg, which is tied to hers. 'It looks like we are about to do a three-legged race,' she replies, in an equally confused tone.

'I've gathered you all together,' Linda Wilkinson declares, 'to get us all working together'. She looks across at her staff, who are all in a line, in pairs—one from the kitchen, the other front of house—with their legs tied together. 'Over the last few months we have been working against each other. Today, we want to be working as a team. In pairs, you need to complete

→

the obstacle course, carrying your uncooked egg and the balloon to the finish line. We have a trophy for the winner and a booby prize of cleaning out the deep-fat fryer for the loser.' With that, she blows her whistle and begins the contest.

At first, the restaurant staff, all feeling a little silly, go through the obstacle course reluctantly, not wanting to be seen as too enthusiastic for what they all collectively feel is a little embarrassing. However, after the first circuit, Effingham shouts 'blow this' and suddenly makes a dash for the front, dragging Biagini with him. 'Come on, Nina, you're with the kitchen team now,' he shouts as they charge for the front. Sensing the change in attitude, Saffron calls to Josh, 'Come on, we can beat them.' Suddenly, the race gets going.

As they go round for the second time Linda Wilkinson looks on in great delight. For the first time the two departments seem to be genuinely working together. For the open parts of the course the more cavalier attitude of the chefs seem to drive them forward, whereas when they come to the obstacle section the front-of-house workers guide them through better.

They then move on to a blindfolded obstacle course, where one of the pairs has to guide their partner around the field avoiding various items while the other is blindfolded. Finally, they have to build a tower.

'Well, I've not had so much fun in ages,' declares Effingham as they reflect on events in the bar afterwards. 'You know what,' he says, looking directly at Biagini, 'I was impressed with how you guided me around that blindfold course. You really made it clear what to do.' Biagini smiles. 'You weren't so bad yourself. You really had a good eye for that tower.' Effingham picks up the trophy. 'Yep, we won this together.'

To build a sense of identity, organizations often engage in team-building activities, the most famous of which was developed by Bruce Tuckman (Tuckman, 1965; Tuckman and Jensen, 1977).

Tuckman's model lays out the path to high performance. The central concept is that teams have to go through stages in order to become mature and function effectively. A fully mature team, he argued, functions well because they have established norms of behaviour and trust.

Tuckman argued there are two key factors: **interpersonal relationships** and **task orientation**, the latter referring to a focus on tasks rather than on people. These two factors shape the members' behaviours within the team (the group dynamics) and how the team deals with different perspectives, communication, conflict, leadership, and trust (Figure 6.6).

Figure 6.6 Tuckman and Jensen's (1977) team formation.

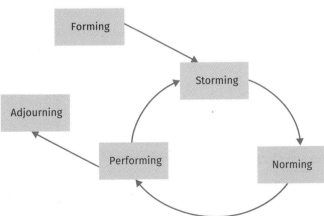

Tuckman's five stages

In Tuckman's model teams go through five stages: forming, storming, norming, performing, and adjourning.

Stage 1: forming

During this initial stage, team members often feel lost, apprehensive, and uncertain how to behave. Tuckman describes this as the orientation stage, as team members are looking to work out how the group functions. To reduce their anxiety they look for ground rules and a leader to tell them what to do. They also seek to reduce anxiety by creating irrelevant discussions on peripheral problems and over-intellectualizing issues to avoiding making decisions. At the formation stage, team members are normally polite and tentative, to avoid saying anything that offends others.

Stage 2: storming

This politeness does not last too long, and eventually the group members become hostile and begin infighting. At this stage, the group lacks unity and often get polarized over key issues. Many resist becoming members of the group, seeking to retain their individuality, and conflict arises as the differences between personal goals and group goals are revealed (see the discussion of social identity theory in the previous section). This often leads members to become defensive, negative, or aggressive, or to withdraw—what Wilfred Bion (1961) calls fight or flight. Members often clash with one another as the 'pecking order' is established. The initial leaders do not always survive this period.

Stage 3: norming

The norming stage occurs when the group begin what Tuckman calls 'a "patching-up" phase' (Tuckman, 1965: 392) where the 'group norms and values emerge' (ibid.). At this stage, group conflicts are being resolved and a sense of togetherness forms, and what Tuckman calls 'we-feelings' emerge. The group becomes a cohesive unit where the members accept the group and 'idiosyncrasies of fellow members' (ibid.: 386). Significantly, the group members want the group to exist and therefore value harmony. Emotions are still high, but are focused on the tasks.

Stage 4: performing

At this stage the group has bonded; interpersonal issues are solved, the group structure is accepted, and the group has matured. The group, therefore, is focused on problem-solving and tasks. Members provide each other with mutual support and have strong interpersonal bonds.

Stage 5: adjourning

This is the stage where the team is dissolved, either because the team members leave or the task is complete. This can be a difficult stage for team members, as they will have felt a personal connection with the team and can feel like mourning the death of it.

 Think of a group that you have been a part of. Can you see the five stages of Tuckman's model in action? How closely does Tuckman's model replicate your experiences?

The changing role of the team leader

Not only does the team change over time, but also, as we will see in Chapter 13, the leader's role changes, from a *telling* approach to the *forming* team to give them certainty, to *selling* and the *storming* to deal with potential infighting. In the *norming* stage the leader needs to encourage more *participatory* decision-making processes to help the team develop its norms. As the team reaches the *performing* stage the leader needs to *delegate* to the team, as members have increased commitment and experience. Overall, the team leader moves from a position of cop (controlling the team) to coach (facilitating their growth and development).

 Real life case: playing games all day for work

How would you like to spend a day at work playing games? While it might sound like just a fun way to spend a day, live-gaming has become one of a range of ways to build teams. Michelle Henry, managing director of HNS Signs, said her business had been struggling with communication, particularly passing on messages from clients. Playing a live-action zombie-killing game meant that they had to devise strategies and communicate better. Henry stated that they 'found that it helped us avoid any unnecessary waffling and get right to the point. We're now always clear, concise and consistent' (*The Telegraph*, 2018).

Live-gaming is far from the only type of teamworking activity. Organizations often invest a lot of time and energy in team-building activities. These can be anything from outdoor activities such as rope-climbing through to cooking, drum circles, or building towers out of spaghetti. Some activities rely on apps: for example, wearewildgoose.com uses GPS to make virtual hotspots, and workers in teams of around 5–6 people are required to follow the map to each of these hotspots. Once they reach a hotspot, they face a series of challenges before moving on to the next hotspot. Completing these challenges requires the teams to work together. For example, their 'Escape' activity pitches teams against the clock and requires them to work through difficult puzzles together in order to finish the game before the time runs out.

Sources: https://www.telegraph.co.uk/connect/small-business/talent-culture-leadership/activities-to-help-build-a-stronger-team/ https://wearewildgoose.com

Developments of Tuckman's model

Rickards and Moger (1999, 2000) developed Tuckman's model by reducing the five stages to three (Figure 6.7). They argue that between each pair of stages there is a barrier, which acts like a glass ceiling and which needs to be broken to progress.

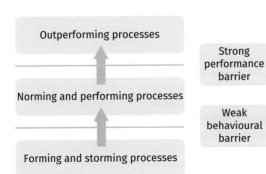

Figure 6.7 Rickards and Moger's team development model.
Source: © Rickards, T. and Moger, S. (2000). Creative leadership processes in project team development: An alternative Tuckman's stage model. British Journal of Management 11: 273–83, Wiley-Blackwell.

The first barrier, behavioural, involves interpersonal forces. The group must work through this in order to develop its norms. This barrier is weak and so is easy to break, resulting in around 85 per cent of teams achieving this. Once they reach the second stage, they establish the group and function quite effectively. They do not become a high performance team or what Rickards and Moger (1999) call the 'dream team' until they smash the second barrier, performance, and break out of conventional expectations. Very few groups go through this barrier.

The implication is that it is relatively easy for a team to reach normal performance levels but difficult to reach high performance ones. Rickards and Moger suggest training to help teams break through these barriers.

Observations of organizational practice, however, state that groups do not necessarily follow these stages. Rickards and Moger's own experiences of teams are that they 'never seemed to achieve a satisfactory level of coherence' (2000: 277). Ed Kur goes further, arguing that the linear direction of Tuckman's model is misplaced. He suggests that 'teams move from moderate to high levels of performance, then into dysfunctional conflicts, through self-assessment and back to high performance' (1996: 32). Rather than stages of development building on each other, the team has 'faces', or personalities, which rotate. Therefore, rather than being static 'even the highest perform-ing, most empowered and most productive teams periodically put on the other faces' (Kur, 1996: 33). A team might have a 'performing face' and then have a negative experience which makes them reassess their mission (the forming face) before returning to the 'performing face' again.

- *Informing face:* shared mindset; debating, exploring, and testing values.
- *Forming face:* clarifying mission; getting to know each other and expectations.
- *Storming face:* confusion and anger with way things are, or misalignment with hopes for the group and what it has become.
- *Norming face:* group rules with a focus on harmony.
- *Performing face:* team with high trust, energy, and innovation (based on Kur, 1996).

One of the great strengths of Tuckman's model is also, arguably, its weakness. It is very straightfor-ward and easy to understand, and this has led it to be applied widely. However, it is too simplistic: it represents group development as clear-cut stages. The stages are idealized and they do not neces-sarily represent what happens in reality.

 Theory in context: the background to Tuckman's model

Although Tuckman's model is very popular, it was not based on direct research or even ac-counts of business practice. Instead, Tuckman's model is a hypothesis (a proposition to be tested), based on synthesizing 50 published studies of group development. The majority of these studies were based on therapy groups (rather than based in businesses), and the main purpose of these therapy groups was to learn from the experience of being in groups, in particular the emotional dynamics between the individuals, rather than get on with a work task. Of the few studies that he reviewed which were conducted in an organizational setting, Tuckman notes, they missed the storming stage, as the work based teams were more focused on completing the tasks than on the social processes involved in becoming a group which the therapy groups focused on. Therefore Tuckman's work, while helpful, can only be read as a hypothesis, and one which was not really focused on team-building in a work setting.

Teams in work organizations, Tuckman argues (1965; Tuckman and Jensen, 1977), therefore develop this pattern.

- *Forming:* as in the earlier description, members are uncertain, but they reduce uncertainty by making judgements about each other based on the roles they occupy outside of the team, e.g. other accountants they have met. This, Tuckman concludes, 'is somewhat suggestive of testing'.
- *Storming:* while in an organization there is still some rebellion, opposition and conflict are not personal as in therapy groups, which most of Tuckman's hypothesis was based on. Therefore, in organizations, teams tend not to go through the storming stage.
- *Norming:* group members discover what they have in common and there is a growth of interlocking friendships, role interdependence, increased harmony, establishment of group norms, and feeling able to exchange ideas, a key task activity.
- *Performing:* there is positive interdependence and emphasis on task achievement; the group develops its own subculture.

Consequently, while there are similarities, groups in organizations act in a more subtle way than Tuckman's hypothesis suggests. Furthermore, in real life, teams generally have more fluid membership that has evolved over many years and therefore do not go through the cycles that Tuckman describes. Groups today are often more diverse, with a wide range of backgrounds, leading Lembke and Wilson to suggest that it is 'difficult to apply traditional group dynamics models' (1998: 927) to modern organizational life.

◎ Study skills: gaining a deeper insight by understanding the background to theories

Although Tuckman's work has been highly influential, the way that it is often used (and is often presented in textbooks) is largely based on a simplified version of his original article. The original article was based on therapy groups, groups that were set up to help people work through their personal problems—for instance if they were suffering from mental health problems—as opposed to groups in work organizations, which are designed to achieve particular tasks. Furthermore, Tuckman only developed a hypothesis and was not saying that his was a proven theory. Therefore we should be more cautious about applying it to work organizations. As a hypothesis Tuckman was suggesting that this is how teams *might* form, rather than being a definitive model of how they *will* form.

Often research in organizational behaviour originates from other fields: for example, Maslow's hierarchy of needs, discussed in Chapter 9, is based in part on primatology, and Lewin's three leadership styles, covered in Chapter 13, originate from researching maskmaking by ten-year-old children. If you are aware of the background of such research, and how it may not always be straightforwardly relevant to work organizations, you can achieve a more subtle understanding of the theory and can clarify the challenges of using it in practice.

 Why do you think that groups in organizations seem to go through the stages a bit differently from therapy groups?

?	Review questions	
Describe	What are the five stages of Tuckman's model?	
Explain	How has group formation in actual organizational practice been said to differ from that suggested in Tuckman's model?	
Analyse	Does researching the group processes in therapy groups necessarily translate to work organizations? What are the implications of Tuckman's model being a hypothesis?	
Apply	Have a quick search online to see what other types of team-building activities there are. What claims do these websites make about their effectiveness, and do you think these claims are justified?	

Group dynamics

Tuckman's work derives from a theory called **group dynamics**, which looks at the processes involved in interaction between group members. This perspective argued that groups have their own dynamic, or we might say personality or patterns that exist independently of a single individual. These patterns are powerful forces, as they shape the way that the group and individuals act.

According to group dynamic theory, groups operate at two levels: the task level, the work tasks a group needs to complete; and the group processes, the underlying way the group behaves. These group processes or dynamics exist outside of the conscious awareness of the group members, but shape the way they interact and behave.

Group dynamics theory was named by Kurt Lewin and developed by, among others, Gustave Le Bon (2009). Wilfred Bion (1961) and Lewin argued that 'the group to which an individual belongs is the ground for his perceptions, his feelings and his actions' (Allport, 1948: vii). In other words, the group you belong to provides the basis for how you see the world, what you judge to be acceptable and unacceptable, what you aspire to, and how you interpret events. The group could thus be thought of as a lens through which we interpret the world.

Furthermore, it is argued that it is 'usually easier to change individuals formed into a group than to change any one of them separately' (Lewin, 1947: 76, cited in Burke et al., 2008). Therefore, he claimed, the leader should focus on changing the team rather than any one individual.

Unconscious group dynamics

Some group dynamics theorists stress the importance of the **unconscious** processes that shape the group behaviour. Within psychology, particularly psychoanalysis, the unconscious is an area of thinking that is not directly available to the conscious mind, and is below the level of personal awareness. Developing this notion from psychoanalytical theory, such as that of Sigmund Freud and Melanie Klein (see Freud and Riviere, 1927; Likierman, 2001), these theorists argue that the group is shaped by unconscious forces that members of the group are largely unaware of.

Wilfred Bion (1961), one of the earliest to put forward this view, argued that group behaviour occupies the three basic assumptions shown in Table 6.6.

These three 'basic assumptions' shape the way that the group acts. They create defensive positions that unconsciously protect group members from harm. Bion states they are primitive in

Table 6.6 Bion's dynamics of group behaviour compared with Tuckman's (1965) stages of group formation

Bion's three basic assumptions		Cf. Tuckman's model
Dependency	Group aims for security by looking for a leader to remove all anxieties and solve their problems. The leader is seen as god-like and can do no wrong. If the leader does not miraculously achieve this then they will look for a new leader.	Forming
Flight/Fight	The group tries to preserve itself at all costs; it either fights or runs away from a common enemy, or directs this energy inwards where the group argues and falls apart. The group ignores all other activities when it is in this phase.	Storming
Pairing	Two people dominate the group. The group hopes that they will produce a new leader to save them.	Norming

origin and provide the emotional energy of the group. They provide an essential conflict within team members between the need to belong and the frustration felt by having to conform. Bion argues that the group needs to mature to become an effective or what he calls a 'sophisticated' group, where it is more cooperative and not controlled by these basic assumptions. Bion's work draws from psychoanalytical theory and can be difficult to grasp. However, it does alert us to the challenges of creating a well-functioning team, as groups are often shaped by unconscious assumptions that members are only dimly aware of.

❓ Review questions

Describe	What is group dynamics theory?
Explain	What is meant by 'unconscious' group dynamics?
Analyse	What are the implications of these unconscious group dynamics for our understanding of how groups and teams form?

Decision making in groups: opportunities and challenges

Decision making in teams and groups can be hard. Sometimes different members have different perspectives which can be in conflict and passions can run high. At other times one person, such as a head of department, can try to dictate what is decided, leaving little room for collective decision making. Helping everyone come to a common understanding and consensus about a decision can be difficult (King and Land, 2018).

Research has shown that groups are better at making decisions than an individual alone because they have a wider variety of perspectives. However, for conjunctive tasks, which are group tasks everyone must contribute to, the group is normally only as effective as the least capable member (Steiner, 1966; Frank and Anderson, 1971). Steiner argued that the success of a group can be a combination of the nature of the task, the resources group members have available, the motivation of the group, and the patterns the group develops (Steiner, 1966).

One long-standing solution is for groups to have a discussion, followed by a decision taken either by the chair of the meeting or by a group vote. While this can lead to quick decisions, often alternative perspectives can be stifled, particularly if there is a domineering chair. The other approach is through consensus decision making. This approach, led by a facilitator, seeks to draw out as wide a range of views as possible, to encourage group members to truly listen to opposing perspectives, and to achieve consensus, where all group members feel happy with the decision taken (Hartnett, 2010). While this approach might be slower to achieve, its proponents argue that it creates a shared sense of ownership and more creative solutions than traditional group decision making.

Sociocracy, which is a form of collaborative governance, offers a highly structured way of making decision. It works on the basis of consent (rather than consensus) where decisions are made so long as nobody has any objections to a decision that is proposed. This is generally quicker than consensus, which can take a long time (Reedy et al., 2016). The sociocracy circle starts with 'picture forming', which is a process of trying to work out in more detail what the issue is and the different features of the issue are. Then proposals are formed, in small pieces, drawing on the wisdom of the group. Finally a full proposal is made and all members of the circle are asked if they have any objections (Rau and Koch-Gonzalez, 2018).

 Visit the online resources and take a look at the web links for Chapter 6 for more information on sociocracy.

◉ Research insight: can groups make better decisions?

Shore, J., Bernstein, E., and Lazer, D. 2015. Facts and figuring: An experimental investigation of network structure and performance in information and solution spaces. *Organization Science* 26 (5): 1432–46.

Does working in large groups improve or hinder problem solving and decision making? One factor that academic research has investigated suggests that it depends on how interconnected and similar group members are (Shore et al., 2015). One key perspective argues that connecting people together improves problem solving by increasing coordination; however, other research argues that it can also encourage unproductive behaviour resulting in exploitation, even for simple tasks (Lazer and Friedman, 2007). Research by Shore et al. argues that large networks of people are better at collecting information but are less effective at making decisions and problem solving (Shore et al., 2015). This is because when members of these networks share information and are aware of each other's theories, they do not search for alternative solutions. The researchers argue that a more effective way is for information to be collected at a large group level and then problems to be solved within small groups or pairs. They also claimed that more diverse groups are better at generating ideas than those with similar views. One of the implications of this is that next time you are working on a collective project, it might be useful to work in large groups to collect information but better to establish small groups to look for solutions. Also look for people to work with who have different skills and interests from yours so that you can generate new, original insights.

Strong bonds: the dangers of a close team

 Running case: Team Junction Restaurant sitting together at the end of the night

'Well, I must say, I'm in shock,' Effingham declares to Biagini. 'I really thought that tonight would work. I just can't see why it didn't.' Biagini smiles at him. 'Nor me. It seemed such a good idea—a toga night with all the customers dressing up for Valentine's night with our Roman menu and a Venus and Mars waiting team! We put so much effort into the layout of the restaurant tonight and the statues. With only ten bookings, including three couples who didn't even dress up, tonight was a disaster. Where did we go wrong? It seemed such a good idea at the team meeting.'

As we have seen, most team theories see a successful team as having strong bonds, where individuals should see their identity primarily as team members and should be loyal, committed to the team's purpose, and sharing similar outlooks. This can be highly beneficial: without competing perspectives, decision making is quicker, as members do not need to explain what they mean each time a decision is made or try to understand each other's perspective. However, such a close relationship can cause problems.

Over-conformity potentially stifles creativity and growth. With everyone sharing the same basic assumptions, alternative viewpoints do not get debated and therefore opportunities, or risks, can be ignored. Strong teams can therefore have collective beliefs or delusions which result in outside evidence either being ignored or being interpreted in such a way as suits the group's mindset.

Amanda Sinclair argues that the emphasis on consensus and the assumptions that mature teams are task-focused narrows the definition of what a team is. In particular, she argues that what appears to be consensus is often a result of downplaying division, as political pressure is placed on non-conforming members. 'Behaviour which recognizes and defers to the dominant power-holders in the group is likely to be labelled constructive or task-orientated, while behaviour which challenges that power is labelled disruptive and counter-productive' (Sinclair, 1992: 621).

Groupthink

Real life case: groupthink—it's just not cricket

In the cold light of day it seemed a foolish thing to do. Cameron Bancroft, a young player in the Australian cricket team, playing only his eighth test match, had brought onto the field a small piece of sandpaper to tamper with the ball and gain his team an advantage. Not only was this cheating, but the chances of getting caught were very high, with around 30 television cameras focused on everything that was going on in the match (de Menezes, 2018). Sure enough, the cameras picked it up, and cricket commentators, ex-players, and even the Australian prime minister jumped in to criticize the players (Malyon, 2018).

Bancroft did not do this alone but 'the leadership group knew about it'. Australia captain Steve Smith said they 'spoke about it at lunch' and 'thought it was a possible way of getting an

→

advantage', but that it was a 'poor choice' and they had 'made a serious error of judgement'. In the dressing room, with their focus on winning the match, using a bit of sandpaper to affect the ball seemed a good idea at the time. In retrospect it was anything but a good idea. It broke the rules, and maybe more importantly the spirit of the game. Smith, Warner (the vice-captain), and Bancroft were all suspended for a year, and Lehmann, the coach, resigned his role. They all lost lucrative contracts and sponsorship.

Writing in the *Financial Times*, Andrew Hill describes this as an example of groupthink.

> One risk is operating a closed 'leadership group'. Senior members of any team accumulate a natural authority. But, in the case of Australia's leadership group, there was little leadership and much groupthink. If you always huddle together with just a few senior colleagues, all of whom think the same way, then some of the unchallenged ideas you hatch are bound to be bad. In the heat of a competitive battle, a few may even be ethically wrong.
>
> (Hill, 2017)

The closed nature of the Australian team's 'leadership group' made them think tampering with the ball was a good idea; other people, outside of the group, might have helped them realize it was a bad idea. Hill also argues that there is a danger of deference. Bancroft stated he was 'was merely "in the vicinity" of the leadership group's discussion, and was not ordered to cheat. But the young player was put in the invidious position of having to countermand the unethical plan of his boss and senior colleagues' (Hill, 2017). Junior colleagues should be encouraged to feel able to speak up against unethical practices. Hill concludes by arguing that companies have much to learn from these occurrences in sport about the need for transparency to overcome groupthink.

 Visit the online resources and take a look at the web links for Chapter 6 to see a video describing groupthink.

Have you ever been part of a group and thought that the group was making a wrong decision but did not speak out? Within academic theory, this is called *groupthink*. Groupthink (Janis, 1971) occurs when powerful social pressures are put upon group members to think in a particular way, or not to voice concerns or alternative viewpoints.

Groups that suffer this problem have a tendency to minimize conflict and therefore do not explore alternative options. They also often stick to agreements that the group has committed to, even if they turn out to be the wrong options. Janis argued that this results in a 'deterioration in mental efficiency, reality testing, and moral judgments as a result of group pressures' (1971: 84).

> The more cohesive the group, the greater the inner compulsion on the part of each member to avoid creating disunity, which inclines him [sic] to believe in the soundness of whatever proposals are promoted by the leader or by a majority of the group's members.
>
> (Janis, 1971: 85)

💡 Theory in context: the background to groupthink theory

Irving Janis devised the concept of groupthink to explain US foreign policy fiascos, such as the 'failure to be prepared for the attack on Pearl Harbor, the Korean War stalemate and the escalation of the Vietnam War' (1971: 84). The most famous example was the botched Bay of Pigs invasion.

The US government was trying to overthrow the Cuban leader, Fidel Castro, but they did not want anyone to know it was them. Therefore, they trained 1,400 Cuban exiles to be ready to invade the Bay of Pigs, as the CIA believed the invasion would cause an uprising in Cuba.

However, the planned uprising did not happen because the invasion was some 80 miles from where people lived. The Cuban exiles were massively outnumbered, without air support, enough ammunition, or even an escape route, leaving most to surrender or be killed. It ended in massive failure.

The Cuban flag.
Source: Gilmanshin/Shutterstock.com

Some could argue that this was a failure of planning, organizing, and thinking. 'How could we have been so stupid?' President Kennedy was heard muttering regularly to himself afterwards, reflecting on the Bay of Pigs fiasco. It was, he said, a 'colossal mistake' which ended in complete failure (Dallek, 2004: 367, 375).

Janis (1971) states that the Bay of Pigs fiasco was a result of groupthink, particularly of overconfidence and not accepting evidence to the contrary of assumptions. According to this theory, the danger is not that the group member will not reveal criticisms, but that they will not even think them, will not carry out careful scrutiny of the ideas, and will reject any misgivings that they might have. Groupthink, Janis argued, has the following characteristics.

1. *Illusion of invulnerability*—the group overestimates its power, is over-optimistic, takes extraordinary risks, and ignores warnings.

2. *Construction of rationales to avoid warnings and negative feedback*—being selective with information and discounting ideas that contradict their perspective.

3. *Belief in the inherent morality of their group*—feeling morally justified in the actions they take.

4. *Stereotyped view of the enemy*—as evil, stupid, or ineffective.

5. *Pressure on opponents*—attacking anyone who puts forward an alternative viewpoint.

6. *Self-censorship*—avoiding deviation from the group consensus and minimizing personal doubts.

7. *Illusion of unanimity (consensus)*—taking the false view that anyone silent is in agreement, which prevents disagreements from arising.

8. *Tendency to become mindguards*—protecting themselves and the leader of the group by stopping the discussion or not passing on information.

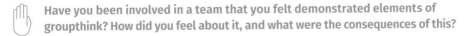

Have you been involved in a team that you felt demonstrated elements of groupthink? How did you feel about it, and what were the consequences of this?

The result of groupthink is that members look at very few options, fail to consider the costs of decisions, do not take into account what outside experts say, or do not consider how opponents might react. Believing in their own righteousness and invulnerability, they can make a decision that might be perceived by an outsider as a bad one (Janis, 1971). For instance, in the Iraq war many members of the Bush administration in the USA were convinced that the Iraqis would be so pleased to see them that they would be welcomed with open arms. They failed to consider that many would not like a foreign occupying force and would resist it; therefore, they did not properly plan for the aftermath of the war, with what some commentators have argued to be disastrous consequences (Fox News, 2004; Badie, 2010).

Groupthink also happens in businesses. In the Volkswagen emissions scandal, where engineers designed diesel cars to cheat emissions tests, a possibility is that the 'wrongdoers were trapped in a micro-bubble and thought that their behaviour was "normal". This might have been because they had witnessed colleagues fit or develop such defeat devices; or perhaps because they believed that rival firms were also at it' (Heath, 2015). Oliver Schmidt, a Volkswagen executive, 'agreed to follow a script, or talking points, agreed by Volkswagen management and a high-ranking lawyer' when talking to regulators (Hill, 2017).

In May 2015 six banks were fined a total of $5.7 billion for manipulating foreign exchange markets. The traders used chatrooms, describing themselves as 'The Cartel', to manipulate the markets (Titcomb, 2015). It appears that although the traders knew they were breaking the rules they reinforced each other's belief that they were not going to get caught, and senior managers at least gave tacit approval for the trading to occur (Enrich, 2018).

This scandal, involving the Libor (London Inter-bank Offered Rate), is by no means the first financial scandal in recent years. The banking crisis of 2008 saw evidence of collective delusion, with traders believing that the stock market would always rise and that complicated financial models would continually produce profit. When Paul Moore, HBOS's head of regulatory risk, challenged their practices, saying they were too risky, he was criticized and then sacked (BBC, 2009; *Daily Telegraph*, 2009). One of the most famous examples of groupthink was Enron, who despite having claimed a profit of over $100 billion the previous year went bankrupt. The senior management group shared a similar background, felt cohesive, had a superstar culture, and believed that they were changing society. These features meant that they did not ask sufficiently probing questions about how the company was operating (O'Connor, 2002; Sims and Brinkman, 2003).

When we are in groups we tend to take more risky decisions than we do when alone. This is called the 'risk-shift phenomenon'. This occurs because when we are in groups we feel more secure and responsibility is spread across the group, and individual members do not want to let others down. By listening to others in the group who are more open to risk, individual members move towards greater risk.

All of the financial scandals mentioned above demonstrate elements of groupthink. Very senior, intelligent, and well-paid people failed to question the practices that they were engaged in. A 2010 parliamentary report (UK Parliament, 2010) argued that 'the lack of diversity on the boards of many, if not most, of our major financial institutions, may have heightened the problems of "groupthink" and made effective challenge and scrutiny of executive decisions less effective'. The chair of the committee, John McFall, argued that a solution would be to introduce more women. 'Diversity at the top is one way to challenge potentially dangerous "group-think"' (UK Parliament, 2010).

◉ Research insight: the Abilene paradox

Harvey, J. B. 1988. *The Abilene paradox and other meditations on management*. Jossey-Bass: New York.

The Abilene paradox states: 'Organizations frequently take actions in contradiction to what they really want to do and therefore defeat the very purposes they are trying to achieve' (Harvey, 1988: 19). This occurs when a group collectively makes a decision that actually goes against the preference of any individual. It is a failure to manage agreement and has six stages:

→

1. Agree privately as individuals the nature of the problem the organization faces.

2. Agree privately as individuals the steps to take.

3. Organization members fail to communicate accurately their desires or beliefs to each other, but do the opposite.

4. With inaccurate information they make contrary decisions to what they want to do.

5. By making counterproductive decisions members become frustrated and angry, form subgroups, and blame each other—particularly blaming leaders.

6. This cycle repeats itself and becomes more intensive.

To check that they are not falling into the trap of 'groupthink', Wilkinson suggests that group members should ask each other 'Are we going to Abilene?' to make sure that the decision is really desired by the group.

To overcome groupthink Janis recommends an approach with nine elements.

1. Encouraging *critical evaluation* in every member.

2. Encouraging an *impartial stance* at the beginning of meetings to create open-mindedness.

3. Setting up *evaluation groups* for decisions.

4. Discussing decisions with *outsiders* and reporting back.

5. Inviting *outside experts to question decisions*.

6. Members playing *devil's advocate* for key decisions.

7. Considering *rivals' reactions* to a decision.

8. Occasionally dividing into two groups and returning to discuss different perspectives.

9. 'Second chance' meetings to express remaining doubts.

The concept of groupthink therefore makes an important challenge to the underlying ideas of teamwork by warning of the dangers which occur when people share perspectives that are too similar and reject dissenting voices. While the examples that Janis gives are quite extreme in their consequences (potentially costing thousands of lives and billions of pounds), groupthink often occurs on a more mundane level when members of a team, despite their personal misgivings, go along with decisions that outsiders would question. All teamwork requires a balance between coherence/conformity and dissent/creativity—the challenge is to get the balance right.

? Review questions

Describe	What is groupthink?
Explain	Why does groupthink happen?
Analyse	What are the implications of groupthink to our understanding of teamwork? Do you think that Janis's advice on overcoming groupthink is helpful?
Apply	What evidence of groupthink can you find in the real life case of the banking crisis?

207

Does teamwork increase freedom?

> **Q Running case:** clearing up
>
> Isabella phones her boyfriend Steve. 'Hi, Steve, it's me. Look, I know its Valentine's night and I promised you a night out, but we're having to clear up after tonight's meal. Oh, it was such a disaster. Nobody came, so we are going to all go out to drown our sorrows. I was involved in the planning for this, so I feel I need to help clear up the pieces. Look, I know I'm letting you down, but I really feel I owe it to this lot to stick together. I've got tomorrow night off—I'll make it up to you, I promise.'

One of the great claims made about teamwork is that it gives the potential for greater freedom and autonomy for the team members. As we can see in Figure 6.8, the greater skill level of the team members, the more freedom (or empowerment) the team can have.

When team members have low skill levels, being part of a team can give greater variety through *job rotation*. In firms such as McDonald's, relatively unskilled workers can change roles, e.g. making

Figure 6.8 Empowerment continuum.
Source: Reproduced from Management, Daft et al. (2001), South Western. Reproduced by permission of Cengage Learning.

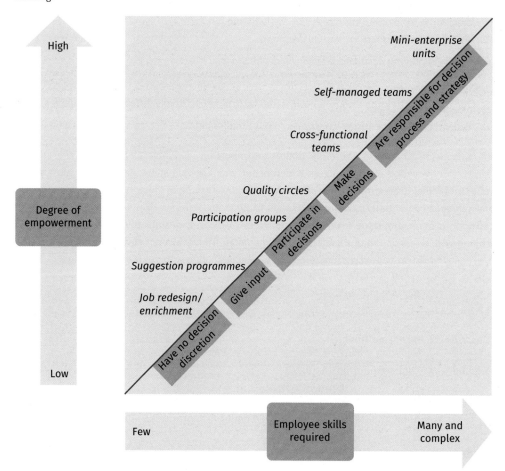

fries, then putting burgers together, etc., which makes the job more interesting. The concept of *job enrichment*, developed by Frederick Herzberg, involves giving individual workers more autonomy (see Chapter 9). Both these approaches give workers more opportunity to use skills and, according to Herzberg, increase motivation (Paul et al., 1969).

Employees can also be involved in recommending changes through suggestion programmes. These schemes, however, give them little opportunity to implement the changes, as a *recommending team* (e.g. a group of managers) makes the final decision.

A strong level of empowerment can be achieved by employees forming **quality circles**, where a group of workers come together, often under the supervision of a leader, to identify, analyse, and solve organizational problems (Marks et al., 1986). Members of these groups are ordinary members of staff (e.g. from production or service delivery) who meet together for a few hours a week or month and discuss solutions to work-related problems and then present them to management. In doing so they aim for continuous improvement, from health and safety through to production processes. Quality circles therefore combine the *recommending team* and the *doing team*. While quality circles have not lived up to their promise since the 1980s (Lawler and Mohrmann, 1985), they can be effective ways of bringing about improvements lead by the employees themselves.

Interdisciplinary teams or **multifunctioning teams**, where the members come from different disciplines, have, in recent years, become increasingly popular and used in areas such as social services, health, and policing (Schofield and Amodeo, 1999). They are often used in skilled professions and have more autonomy as they can make decisions. Interdisciplinary teams can be powerful in that they draw together multiple skills and diverse knowledge to tackle complex problems, but they are also challenging to work in because different professions within the team often hold competing understandings of problems and can, therefore, find it difficult to establish a common language.

Such teams may draw people in from many different professions. For example, doctors, nurses, occupational therapists, mental health nurses, and others may come together to talk about a patient, offender, or drug addict and to make sure that all the different services are sharing information and working together to deliver 'joined up services' rather than piecemeal delivery where the services sometimes work in contradiction to each other (Robinson and Cottrell, 2005). Within businesses, multifunctioning teams might come together to discuss the launch of a new product or service.

C Real life case: making multifunction teams work can save lives

It should just have been a routine ear, nose, and throat (ENT) operation. Yet soon after the anaesthetic drugs were injected, 37-year-old Elaine Bromiley struggled for her life and died (Fong, 2013). One of the causes of the problem is that two nurses involved subsequently reported they 'had known what should have been done but had not asserted themselves because of the hierarchy in the operating theatre. Instead, they had used passive and indirect statements, which had had no effect during the crisis' (Green et al., 2017: 449–50). The ability for all members of the operating team to speak up and work cooperatively is critical.

The operating theatre is a complex location with consultants, anaesthetists, and nursing staff all having to work together to ensure that the patient stays safe throughout the procedure. One of the challenges is that each of these professions has different training and expertise that can sometimes conflict. Intensive care theatres in particular can be stressful places where emotions run high, and conflict can result between these professionals (Coombs,

→

2003). This inter-professional conflict has been claimed to lead to high levels of medical errors, particularly due to communication and teamwork problems (Buttigieg et al., 2011), which potentially put patients' lives at risk (Baldwin and Daugherty, 2008). Indeed, it 'is thought that half of adverse events in surgery are avoidable and "the majority" are due to poor communication, decision making and teamwork' (Smith, 2014). If you are about to go for an operation, one of the last things that you would probably think about is how good the teamwork is among the surgical team. But maybe you should. A hospital on the east coast of the US has sought to tackle this problem by delivering communications training to help the different professionals try to understand each other, using a group dynamics expert to understand the group processes that were occurring and help aid individuals' self-understanding of how their behaviour impacted others. By coaching, modelling positive behaviour, and understanding the group dynamics, the hospital has reported better outcomes for all (Eiser, 2015).

Simon Paterson-Brown, a fellow of the Royal College of Surgeons of Edinburgh, states:

It's all about being aware of what's going on and communicating with the nurses and junior staff, allowing other people to speak up in theatre and say, 'I think you're getting this wrong; this isn't right.' All of these things we didn't really do in surgery. Consultants in the past didn't really like to be questioned by their junior staff.

(cited in Rimmer, 2014)

Time will tell how easy it will be to change the power dynamics in hospitals to enable junior staff to speak up, but achieving this result will be critical to help improve the outcomes for everyone involved.

Empowered or **self-managed teams** have increased autonomy and higher skill levels (Cohen and Ledford, 1994) and collective responsibility for planning and executing tasks (Magpili and Pazos, 2018). The key trait of these teams is that they have the authority to solve their own problems and directly respond to the needs of their customers. This means that they can be much more flexible and responsive, as they do not have managers telling them what to do: the group makes decisions and has collective responsibility for its actions. This can be done by rotating the leader or by using collective decision-making processes. Self-managed teams can often set their own hours, the planning of tasks, and even their own budgets.

Self-managed teams can be more productive because they can make quicker decisions, create stronger bonds between team members as they tackle challenges collectively, and increase commitment as the team members have more freedom to experiment and have an increased say in how things are run. 'In theory, ownership, responsibility and involvement in the strategic direction [by self-managing teams] are likely to lead to more rapid development and implementation of the strategy by workers dealing directly with customers' (Dunphy and Bryant, 1996: 692).

However, such teams can be harder to manage, particularly initially, as their management requires managers to be able to trust the team to work well together, be committed to the aims of the team and customers, and be skilled in the task that they are doing. It can also be challenging for managers schooled in traditional 'command and control' practices, as it requires a different relationship with the team. It has been described as moving from 'cop' to 'coach', or 'controlling' to 'involving' (Lawler, 1986). The senior manager's role is to set the parameters for the group, such as its vision, objectives, and key milestones, whereas the team works out the operational details, such as the most effective way to perform the tasks and meet the objectives.

Thus, teamwork proponents argue that teamwork simultaneously enables increased organizational performance, improves employees' working lives, and even addresses the problem of alienation within society.

Is teamwork a way of enhancing control?

Q Running case: Josh asks Isabella to help out in the kitchen

'Can you give me a hand?' Josh, one of the chefs, calls over to Isabella, one of the waiting staff. 'We really need to get this food prepped before we go home so it is ready for the breakfast team in the morning.' 'It's not my job ...' Isabella stammers, before Josh interrupts. 'Teamwork,' he states knowingly. 'We are all one big team now.' Sensing her reluctance, he carries on. 'Look, if you give me a hand with this then maybe I'll help you lay the tables for the morning when we are done.'

The use of teamwork is claimed to increase autonomy and participatory decision making and to enable staff to form positive social bonds with colleagues (Mueller, 1994). However, more critical voices have questioned if teamwork can be presented as unequivocally positive. Returning to the example of the operating theatre, Rachael Finn challenges the view that teamwork really equalizes the balance between surgeons and other medical staff. Finn argues that while teamwork gives the image of everyone working together equally, in practice the language of teamwork can be used as a resource that reinforces the powerful, privileged position of surgeons (2008; Finn et al., 2010).

Other critical theorists claim that self-managed teams can result in **downsizing** by removing layers of management and making the team take on these responsibilities (Dunphy and Bryant, 1996). This, they argue, increases the burden on ordinary members of staff as they become more responsible for delivering products and services, but without additional pay. They argue that this is an intensification of work as employees come to be seen as more responsible for solving problems—traditionally a manager's domain. Barker (1993) and Sewell (1998) thus argue that it can actually represent a stronger form of control, producing what Sinclair calls the tyranny of teamwork (1992).

Barker argues that, on the surface, *self-managing teams* represent a shift in power from management to workers. 'Instead of being told what to do by a supervisor, self-managing workers must gather and synthesize information, act on it, and take collective responsibility for those actions' (Barker, 1993: 413).

This can result in increasing their commitment, as employees feel responsible for completing a task. As one of the employees in Barker's study states, 'Under the old [bureaucratic and hierarchical] system, who gave a hoot if the boards shipped today or not? We just did our jobs. Now we have more buy-in by the team members. We feel more personal responsibility for the product' (1993: 422).

While at first glance it might appear that management have given up control, Barker argues that, in fact, self-managed teams represent a more subtle and intensive form of control. Team members, he argues, control each other's actions.

> Team members rewarded their teammates who readily conformed to their team's norms by making them feel a part of the team and a participant in the team's success. In turn, they punished teammates who had bad attitudes ... with guilt and peer pressure to conform.
>
> (1993: 425)

211

For instance, the increased levels of responsibility may mean that team members miss their children's school plays, work on weekends, and start work at 5.00 am to meet production schedules, because they feel more responsible. Control is thus intensified because more experienced members of staff watch and discipline the less experienced and reinforce the rules and group norms, and staff self-discipline by taking personal responsibility. This results in the experienced staff feeling like unpaid supervisors and suffering burnout, and the new staff feeling that they were constantly being watched. This creates a stronger 'iron cage', as termed by Weber (see Chapter 2), this time of control not by bureaucracy but by the discipline of the team.

Teamwork, therefore, could be seen as a way of shifting the responsibility from managers on to the shoulders of staff, what Sewell (1998) calls *responsible autonomy*. Workers have freedom so long as they hit the targets set and use their discretion for the good of the organization.

At a deeper level, teamwork changes the outlook of employees: 'management is concerned not only with changing the way in which employees work but also the way they think' (Knights and McCabe, 2000: 1494).

🔍 Running case: Linda Wilkinson, Nina Biagini, and Graham Effingham sit down for an end-of-day drink

'It all is running a lot more smoothly now,' Linda Wilkinson says with satisfaction, watching the waiting staff and chefs working together to clear the last of the tables after another busy day of service. 'It almost runs itself.' Graham Effingham smiles. 'Yes, it's good to see. We now do 150 covers a night. We run well as a team.' 'It wasn't always like that,' Nina Biagini interjects. 'We took a while to gel, didn't we? But I must say I like working here now. It didn't always feel so good.' The three managers look on as their staff, or team members as they now call them, systematically work calmly together, clearing up the tables and laying out for the breakfast sitting. 'Sometimes,' Biagini says wistfully, 'I almost wonder if they need us at all.' Effingham nudges her in the ribs. 'Don't let Weaver hear you say that,' he says half-jokingly, 'or you'll be down the job centre in the morning!'

Connecting case and theory

Linda Wilkinson faced a problem. At the outset of the chapter we saw her concern about the way the restaurant was run. A lot of people seemed busy and were working hard, but the food was not going out on time, or was even going to the wrong people. Despite the hotel having an award-winning chef, customer complaints were on the rise. We saw a classic problem of poor teamwork: poor communication, lack of clarity of roles and responsibilities, and fear of questioning authority. Junction Hotel was also not getting the benefits of teamwork: increases in productivity, creativity, and employee satisfaction (Procter and Mueller, 2000), or the useful combining of skills, experience, and different perspectives.

Seeing these issues, Wilkinson decided that she needed to work on the dynamics of the **team**. At first, Effingham was resistant, feeling that he was being personally accused. We could see some of the power and politics coming into play, where Effingham was putting his personal reputation ahead of the needs of the wider team; yet at the same time he began to realize that he also needed the waiting staff to be able to serve the food, otherwise he would not stand a chance of winning his awards. The difficulty was that the restaurant was in two silos, and they needed to work together.

Wilkinson therefore sought to engage in team-building activities to improve trust, communication, and mutual understanding. We saw her attempts at team-building, using techniques akin to Belbin's team role inventory and then team-building activities to help the team transition through the stages of team formation.

Even though each role was meant to be seen as equal, we could see that Effingham thought that he was superior. These processes are not straightforward, and we get clashes of personality that need to be overcome. **Social identity theory** argues that to be part of a team requires the ability to forgo an individualistic outlook and to see yourself as part of a team. This can be a painful and challenging process, as it can mean giving up personal ideas and putting faith in other people. **Tuckman's stages of group formation** demonstrate the difficult path team members have to take, by going through the forming, storming, and norming stages before they are performing. Using team-building activities can be a way of breaking down barriers and helping individuals begin to gel as a team.

Once the team have been established we see the danger of **groupthink**, where a tightly knit **group** see the world in the same way and are not exposed to alternative perspectives which might lead them to question their views; this can lead them to make mistakes. Despite its positive aspects, teamwork can also be thought of as another form of control, as it hides the more subtle differences in power between team members (Finn, 2008) and, as Barker (1993) argues, is a form of surveillance as team members watch each other, controlling each other's effort and output.

By forming a more cohesive team at Junction Hotel, the restaurant and waiting staff are less likely to resist and more likely to work hard. This is good for the organization, but it does mean that rather than having a manager like Wilkinson watching you, suddenly everyone you work with is like a manager.

||\ Further reading

Tuckman, B., and Jensen, M. 1977. Stages of small-group development revisited. *Group and Organization Management* 2 (4): 419–27.

This classic text describes the key stages of Tuckman's group formation model. It also provides an interesting insight into the background of the theory.

Dibble, R., and Gibson, C.B. 2018. Crossing team boundaries: A theoretical model of team boundary permeability and a discussion of why it matters. *Human Relations* 71 (7): 925–50.

Explores the idea that increasingly the boundaries of teams are fluid and many people work across a number of different teams. The authors assess the implications for this, arguing it might be challenging to coordinate but also produces numerous benefits to the staff and the organization.

Belbin, R.M. 2010. *Team roles at work*. Butterworth-Heinemann: Oxford.

Describes one of the most popular teamwork models and gives some practical insight into how the theory works in practice.

Janis, I.L. 1971. Groupthink. Psychology Today 5 (November): 43–6, 74–6.

A classic description of groupthink with some interesting historical accounts.

Barker, J.R. 1993. Tightening the iron cage: Concertive control in self-managing teams. *Administrative Science Quarterly* 38 (3): 408–37.

Provides an interesting critical perspective on why teamwork can be a strong form of control.

References

Abrams, D., and Hogg, M.A. 2001. Collective identity: Group membership and self-conception. In: Hogg, M.A., and Tindale, S. (eds) *Blackwell handbook of social psychology: Group processes*. Blackwell Publishers: Oxford, pp. 425–61.

Allport, G.W. 1948. Foreword. In: Lewin, G.W. (ed.) *Resolving social conflict*. Harper & Row: London.

Anderson, N., and Sleap, S. 2004. An evaluation of gender differences on the Belbin Team Role Self-Perception Inventory. *Journal of Occupational and Organizational Psychology* 77 (3): 429–37.

Badie, D. 2010. Groupthink, Iraq, and the War on Terror: Explaining US policy shift toward Iraq. *Foreign Policy Analysis* 6 (4): 277–96.

Baldwin, D.C., Jr, and Daugherty, S.R. 2008. Interprofessional conflict and medical errors: Results of a national multi-specialty survey of hospital residents in the US. *Journal of Interprofessional Care*, 22 (6): 573–86.

Barker, J.R. 1993. Tightening the iron cage: Concertive control in self-managing teams. *Administrative Science Quarterly* 38 (3): 408–37.

Barrick, M.R., Stewart, G.L., Neubert, M.J., and Mount, M.K. 1998. Relating member ability and personality to work-team processes and team effectiveness. *Journal of Applied Psychology* 83 (3): 377–91.

BBC. 2009. The choice. BBC Radio 4, 3 November. Available at: http://www.bbc.co.uk/programmes/b00nk2c2

Belbin, R.M. 2010. *Team roles at work*. Butterworth-Heinemann: Oxford.

Bion, W. 1961. *Experiences in groups and other papers*. Tavistock: London.

British Chambers of Commerce. 2015. Young people need more support to make transition from education to work, says BCC. Available at: http://www.britishchambers.org.uk/press-office/press-releases/young-people-need-more-support-to-make-transition-from-education-to-work,-says-bcc.html (last accessed 1 August 2015).

Burke, W., Lake, D.G., and Paine, J.W. (eds). 2008. *Organization change: A comprehensive reader*. Jossey-Bass: San Francisco.

Buttigieg, S.C., West, M., and Dawson, J.F. 2011. Well-structured teams and the buffering of hospital employees from stress. *Health Service Management Research* 24: 203–12.

Cohen, S.G., and Bailey, D.E. 1997. What makes teams work: Group effectiveness research from the shop floor to the executive suite. *Journal of Management* 23 (3): 239–90.

Cohen, S.G., and Ledford, G.E. 1994. The effectiveness of self-managing teams: A quasi-experiment. *Human Relations* 47 (1): 13–43.

Coombs, M. 2003. Power and conflict in intensive care clinical decision making. *Intensive and Critical Care Nursing* 19 (3): 125–35.

Coutu, D. 2009. Why teams don't work. *Harvard Business Review* 86 (9): 64–72.

Daft, R.L. 2001. *Organization Theory and Design*, 7th edn. South-Western Publishing: Cincinnati.

Daily Telegraph. 2009. HBOS whistleblower Paul Moore: Evidence to House of Commons 'Banking Crisis' hearing, 11 February. Available at: http://www.telegraph.co.uk/finance/newsbysector/banksandfinance/4590996/HBOS-whistleblower-Paul-Moore-Evidence-to-House-of-Commons-Banking-Crisis-hearing.html

Dallek, R. 2004. *John F. Kennedy: An unfinished life*. Penguin: London.

de Menezes, J. 2018. Cameron Bancroft 'ball-tampering': Australia batsman seen on camera apparently hiding object in his trousers. *The Independent*, 24 March. Available at: https://www.independent.co.uk/sport/cricket/cameron-bancroft-ball-tampering-video-south-africa-vs-australia-a8272051.html

Dibble, R., and Gibson, C. B. (2018). Crossing team boundaries: A theoretical model of team boundary permeability and a discussion of why it matters. *Human Relations* 71 (7): 925–50.

Dufner, S. 2015a. Working during the Ice Bucket Challenge. Personal communication with Daniel King.

Dufner, S. 2015b. What I learned during the Ice Bucket Challenge: Be ready for anything. *The Guardian*, 1 July.

Dunphy, D., and Bryant, B. 1996. Teams: Panaceas or prescriptions for improved performance? *Human Relations* 49 (5): 677–99.

Eiser, B. 2015. Improving physician–nurse teamwork. *Hospitals and Health Networks*, 12 March.

Enrich, D. 2018. *The spider network: The wild story of a maths genius and one of the greatest scams in financial history*. Penguin Random House: London.

Finn, R. 2008. The language of teamwork: Reproducing professional divisions in the operating theatre. *Human Relations* 61 (1): 103–30.

Finn, R., Learmonth, M., and Reedy, P. 2010. Some unintended effects of teamwork in healthcare. *Social Science and Medicine* 70 (8): 1148–54.

Fisher, S.G., Hunter, T.A., and Macrosson, W.D.K. 2001. A validation study of Belbin's team roles. *European Journal of Work and Organizational Psychology* 10 (2): 121–44.

Fong, K. 2013. What we can learn from fatal mistakes in surgery. BBC. Available at: http://www.bbc.co.uk/news/health-21829540

Fox News. 2004. 'Group think' led to Iraq WMD assessment, 11 July. Available at: http://www.foxnews.com/story/0,2933,125123,00.html

Frank, F., and Anderson, L.R. 1971. Effects of task and group size upon group productivity and member satisfaction. *Sociometry* 34 (1): 135–49.

Freud, S., and Riviere, J.T. 1927. *The ego and the id* (authorized transl. Riviere, J.). Hogarth Press: London.

Furnham, A., Steele, H., and Pendleton, D. 1993. A psychometric assessment of the Belbin Teamrole Self-perception Inventory. *Journal of Occupational and Organizational Psychology* 66 (3): 245–57.

Green, B., Oeppen, R.S., Smith, D.W., and Brennan, P.A. 2017. Challenging hierarchy in healthcare teams—ways to flatten gradients to improve teamwork and patient care. *British Journal of Oral and Maxillofacial Surgery*, 55 (5): 449–53.

Gibson, C.B., and Gibbs, J.L. (2006). Unpacking the concept of virtuality: The effects of geographic dispersion, electronic dependence, dynamic structure, and national diversity on team innovation. *Administrative Science Quarterly*, 51 (3): 451–95

Harkins, S.G., Latané, B., and Williams, K. 1980. Social loafing: Allocating effort or taking it easy. *Journal of Experimental Social Psychology* 16: 457–65.

Hartnett, T. 2010. *Consensus-oriented decision-making*. New Society Publishers: Gabriola Island.

Harvey, J.B. 1988. The Abilene paradox: The management of agreement. *Organizational Dynamics* 17 (1): 17–43.

Hay Group. 2015. The business/graduate divide: Are poor 'people skills' stifling UK graduates' potential? Available at: http://www.haygroup.com/uk/Press/Details.aspx?ID=46164 (last accessed 13 July 2015).

Heath, A. 2015. Group-think and delusion: Why VW lost its bearings. *The Telegraph*, 24 September. Available at: https://www.telegraph.co.uk/finance/newsbysector/industry/11889781/Group-think-and-delusion-why-VW-lost-its-bearings.html

Hill, A. 2017. Employees must call out corporate misuse. *Financial Times*, 7 December. Available at: https://www.ft.com/content/58b8b07e-db37-11e7-a039-c64b-1c09b482

Honey, P. 2001. *Improve your people skills*. Chartered Institute of Personnel and Development: London.

HR Grapevine. 2013. Businesses that fail to support team working risk productivity

216

fall. Available at: http://www.hrgrapevine.com/markets/hr/article/2013-01-30-businesses-that-fail-to-support-team-working-risk-productivity-fall (last accessed 10 July 2015).

James, S. 2016a. Leicester City win the Premier League title after a fairytale season. *The Guardian*, 3 May. Available at: https://www.theguardian.com/football/2016/may/02/leicester-city-win-the-premier-league-title-after-fairytale-season

James, S. 2016b. Leicester City's title triumph: the inside story of an extraordinary season. *The Guardian*, 3 May. Available at: https://www.theguardian.com/football/2016/may/03/leicester-city-title-inside-story-premier-league-champions-claudio-ranieri

Janis, I.L. 1971. Groupthink. *Psychology Today* 5 (November): 43–6, 74–6.

Katzenbach, J.R., and Smith, D.K. 1993. *The wisdom of teams: Creating the high performance organization*. Harvard Business School: Boston.

Ket De Vries, M. 1999. High-performance teams: Lessons for the Pygmies. *Organizational Dynamics* 27 (3): 66–77.

King, D., and Land, C. 2018. The democratic rejection of democracy: Performative failure and the limits of critical performativity in an organizational change project. *Human Relations* 71 (11): 1535–1557. https://doi.org/10.1177/0018726717751841

Knights, D., and McCabe, D. 2000. Bewitched, bothered and bewildered: The meaning and experience of teamworking for employees in an automobile company. *Human Relations* 53 (11): 1481–517.

Kur, E. 1996. The faces model of high performing team development. *Leadership and Organization Development Journal* 17 (1): 32–41.

Latané, B., Williams, K., and Harkins, S. 1979. Many hands make light work: The causes and consequences of social loafing. *Journal of Personality and Social Psychology* 37 (6): 822–32.

Lawler, E.E. 1986. *High-involvement management: Participative strategies for improving organizational performance*. Jossey-Bass: San Francisco.

Lawler, E.E., and Mohrman, S.A. 1985. Quality circles after the fad. *Harvard Business Review* 63 (1): 65.

Lazer, D., and Friedman, A. 2007. The network structure of exploration and exploitation. *Administrative Science Quarterly* 52 (4): 667–94.

Learmonth, M. 2009. 'Girls' working together without 'teams': How to avoid the colonization of management language. *Human Relations* 62 (12): 1887–906.

Le Bon, G. 2009. *The crowd: A study of the popular mind*. Classic Books International: New York.

Lembke, S., and Wilson, M.G. 1998. Putting the 'team' into teamwork: Alternative theoretical contributions for contemporary management practice. *Human Relations* 51 (7): 927–44.

Likierman, M. 2001. *Melanie Klein: Her work in context*. Continuum: London.

Mael, F., and Ashforth, B.E. 1995. Loyal from day one: Biodata, organizational identification, and turnover among newcomers. *Personnel Psychology* 48: 309–33.

Magpili, N., and Pazos, P. 2018. Self-managing team performance: A systematic review of multilevel input factors, *Small Group Research* 49 (1): 3–33.

Maltarich, M.A., Kukenberger, M., Reilly, G., and Mathieu, J. 2018. Conflict in teams: Modeling early and late conflict states and the interactive effects of conflict processes. *Group and Organization Management*, 143 (1): 6–37.

Malyon, E. 2018. Steve Smith: I cried for four days after ball-tampering scandal. *The Independent*, 4 June. Available at: https://www.independent.co.uk/sport/cricket/steve-smith-australia-cricket-balltampering-scandal-south-africa-david-warner-cameron-bancroft-a8382726.html

Marks, M.L., Mirvis, P.H., Hackett, E.J., and Grady, J.F. 1986. Employee participation in a Quality Circle program: Impact on quality of work life, productivity, and absenteeism. *Journal of Applied Psychology* 71 (1): 61–9.

Mueller, F. 1994. Teams between hierarchy and commitment: Change strategies and the 'internal environment'. *Journal of Management Studies* 31 (3): 383–403.

O'Connor, M.A. 2002. The Enron board: The perils of groupthink. *University of Cincinnati Law Review* 71: 1233.

Onrec. 2013. Businesses that fail to support team working risk drop in productivity, 30 January. Available at: http://www.onrec.com/news/news-archive/businesses-that-fail-to-support-team-working-risk-drop-in-productivity (last accessed 20 July 2015).

Paul, J.P., Robertson, K.B., and Herzberg, F. 1969. Job enrichment pays off. *Harvard Business Review* 45 (March–April): 61–78.

Philips. 2018. Coder profile. Available at: https://www.philips.com/a-w/asiapac/careers/healthtech/functional-areas/software-development/articles/article-9.html (last accessed 28 March 2018).

Procter, S.C., and Mueller, F. (eds). 2000. *Teamworking.* Macmillan: Basingstoke.

Rau, T., and Koch-Gonzalez, J. 2018. *Many voices one song: Shared power with sociocracy*, Sociocracy for All: Amherst, MA.

Reedy, P., King, D., and Coupland, C. 2016. Organizing for individuation: Alternative organizing, politics and new identities. *Organization Studies* 37 (11): 1553–73.

Rickards, T., and Moger, S. 1999. *Handbook for creative team leaders*. Gower Press: Farnborough.

Rickards, T., and Moger, S. 2000. Creative leadership processes in project team development: An alternative to Tuckman's stage model. *British Journal of Management* 11 (4): 273–83.

Rimmer, A. 2014. Surgical trainees will be taught about communication and teamwork. *BMJ Careers*, 27 August. Available at: http://careers.bmj.com/careers/advice/view-article.html?id=20019002 (last accessed 15 July 2015).

Robinson, M., and Cottrell, D. 2005. Health professionals in multi-disciplinary and multi-agency teams: Changing professional practice. *Journal of Interprofessional Care* 19 (6): 547–60.

Schnake, M.E. 1991. Organizational citizenship: A review, proposed model, and research agenda. *Human Relations* 44 (7): 735–59.

Schofield, R.F., and Amodeo, M. 1999. Interdisciplinary teams in health care and human services settings: Are they effective? *Health and Social Work* 24 (3): 210–19.

Sewell, G. 1998. The discipline of teams: The control of team-based industrial work through electronic and peer surveillance. *Administrative Science Quarterly* 43 (2): 397–428.

Shore, J., Bernstein, E., and Lazer, D. 2015. Facts and figuring: An experimental investigation of network structure and performance in information and solution spaces. *Organization Science* 26 (5): 1432–46.

Sims, R., and Brinkman, J. 2003. Enron ethics (or: Culture matters more than codes). *Journal of Business Ethics* 45 (3): 243–56.

Sinclair, A. 1992. The tyranny of a team ideology. *Organization Studies* 13 (4): 611–24.

Smith, R. 2014. Surgeons are to be tested on 'people skills'. *The Telegraph*, 23 August.

Steiner, I.D. 1966. Models for inferring relationships between group size and potential group productivity. *Behavioral Science* 11 (4): 273–83.

Sundstrom, E., De Meuse, K.P., and Futrell, D. 1990. Work teams: Applications and effectiveness. *American Psychologist* 45 (2): 120–33.

Tajfel, H., and Turner, J.C. 1986. The social identity theory of intergroup behaviour. In: Worchel, S., and Austin, W.G. (eds) *Psychology of intergroup relations*. Nelson-Hall: Chicago, pp. 7–24.

The Telegraph. 2018. Four activities that will help to build a stronger team, 23 March, https://www.telegraph.co.uk/connect/small-business/talent-culture-leadership/activities-to-help-build-a-stronger-team/

Titcomb, J. 2015. Banks fined £3.7bn for rigging foreign exchange markets. *The Telegraph*, 20 May.

TMS Worldwide. 2018. Team Management Systems website. Available at: http://www.tmsworldwide.com/ (last accessed 29 March 2018).

Triplett, N. 1898. The dynamogenic factors in pacemaking and competition. *American Journal of Psychology* 9: 507–33.

Tuckman, B. 1965. Developmental sequence in small groups. *Psychological Bulletin* 63 (6): 384–99.

Tuckman, B., and Jensen, M. 1977. Stages of small-group development revisited. *Group and Organization Management* 2 (4): 419–27.

UK Parliament. 2010. Report calls for more women in City to challenge group-think. Available at: http://www.parliament.uk/business/news/2010/04/report-calls-for-more-women-in-city-to-challenge-group-think/ (last accessed 25 June 2012).

West, M.A. 2004. *Effective teamwork: Practical lessons from organizational research*. Blackwell: Oxford.

Xenergie Consulting Ltd. 2013. Staff performance hit as leaders fail to develop team working. Available at: http://www.xenergie.com/staff-performance-hit-as-leaders-fail-to-develop-team-working/ (last accessed 20 July 2015).

CHAPTER 7
Organizational culture
The hidden side of the organization

Chapter overview and learning outcomes

By the end of this chapter you should be able to:

- describe what organizational culture is

- describe why 'organizational culture' has become a popular term within management practice and academic theory

- explain how organizational culture shapes the behaviour of organizational members

- explain how managers try to change culture

- analyse the extent to which managers can change culture

- analyse whether managing through culture represents greater freedom or increased control

---

Key theorists

Tom Peters and Robert Waterman	Popular management writers and consultants who spearheaded interest in organizational culture as a management resource. They argued that organizations need a 'strong culture' to be successful
Edgar Schein	Schein provided one of the first real models of organizational culture. His model presents organizational culture at three levels which are progressively harder to access, but are more significant the deeper down they are. He believes organizational culture is significantly influenced by the founder and leadership, and that by following the ten-step programme it is possible to change an organization's culture
Charles Handy	Business guru and writer Handy is well known for developing a typology that proposes four types of culture
Linda Smircich	Smircich sees culture as something that the organization either ● *has*—something that is a possession of the organization that managers (and others) can control, or ● *is*—an integral part of the organization
Hugh Willmott	A critical management theorist who argues that there is a dark side of organizational culture—a form of slavery and control

CHAPTER 7

Key terms	
Organizational culture	The collective behaviour exhibited by members of an organization, often seen as comprising values, beliefs, practices, history, and traditions
Mission statement	The stated aim of the organization—often written with the intention of inspiring the employees and differentiating them from others
Cultural typology	A classification of the types of organizational culture
Cultural change	Often driven by management or consultants with the intention of making the organization more productive, an approach that sees culture as a possession that management can control

Introduction: learning a new culture—new situation, new rules

Running case: first-day nerves

Sue Marshall looks into her mirror, preparing for her first day working at Junction Hotel. 'What will people be like? Friendly, I hope. Am I dressed correctly?' she says, looking down at her new suit. 'Not too formal, I hope, but I need to be taken seriously. This is an important job for me.'

Sue still feels nervous but tries to relax. 'How should I act when I get there? They seemed friendly when I looked round, but you never know. Linda Wilkinson said they are one big happy family.' Sue hopes this is true, but she's heard rumours about the head chef, Effingham. Her friend Isabella said he shouts and swears. 'I do hope that Isabella was just saying that to scare me. I'm not sure if I'll fit in if that's the case. Oh well, only one way to find out.'

Going into any new social situation can be unsettling—think back to your first few days at university. When we enter any new organization we are often trying to understand what the place is like and how to fit in. We largely do this without consciously thinking about it. We look for clues in the appearance of buildings, the organization's reputation, and any other clues we can pick up, such as how people came across in the interview. Sometimes the culture is spelt out in policy documents, mission statements, official histories, induction packs, and dress codes. However, it also comes across in more informal, less visible ways, such as the jokes and stories, the subtle put-downs, or the praise people receive. Through observing these subtle clues we pick up the unwritten rules of behaviour and learn how to fit in.

Employability skills: how to quickly get up to speed in a new culture

Being able to adapt quickly to a new culture is an important skill at work. An organization's culture gives you the clues about the right way to behave: what things you need to do to fit in and succeed at work. Understanding the culture you are in therefore is an important part of being seen as successful.

There are a number of things that you can do to understand the culture.

- Research the culture before you apply to make sure that you can fit in—talk to people who work there or read up about the organization.

- When joining, spend the first few weeks observing the culture to pick up clues on how it works, focusing particularly on:
  - the norms and patterns of behaviour: how other people act within the organization;
  - the formal *and* informal aspects of culture—do not just follow what the official culture the management try to promote, but also be aware of how your colleagues respond to what people say and do.

- Be aware that there is often more going on than first meets the eye, and that there might be more than one culture in different departments within the organization.

- Build and maintain strong relationships with key people within the organization, particularly those that can act as mentors and supporters.

However, it is also important not to become too drawn into the culture or to accept it unquestioningly. A strong organizational culture can shape what you believe, potentially teaching you to think in ways that go against the values you held before joining the organization. Therefore, while it is important to learn the organization's culture it is also vital to gain critical distance from it so that you are not drawn into it. Talking to people from outside of work can be helpful in giving you some perspective on what is going on in your own organization.

Source: https://www.cnbc.com/2018/04/03/how-to-score-a-job-at-netflix.html

221

What is organizational culture? At its most basic level, it is the way things are done, the values the organization holds and the characteristics that make the organization unique. Culture shapes how people think and behave. Culture is a central concept in organizational behaviour. It is essential to understanding the differences between the values and beliefs of different organizations and professions, the way that change occurs in organizations, and what shapes people's behaviour (Giorgi et al., 2015). This has led many managers, consultants, and academics to see organizational culture as a resource that may be used to increase performance and commitment.

However, some critical theorists argue that a strong culture can have a dark side, acting as a trap, with little room for resistance. This can end up producing what critical theorist Hugh Willmott has called a type of slavery, to 'exploit, distort and drain the dwindling cultural resource of caring, democratic values' (1993: 541).

Throughout this chapter we will debate whether managing through culture offers increased freedom or greater (and more insidious) control. Is it a resource that management may use, or is it beyond the scope of any individual or group?

What is organizational culture?

One of the most straightforward definitions of organizational culture is 'the way we do things around here' (Deal and Kennedy, 1982: 4). Organizational culture encompasses the common practices, attitudes, behaviours, beliefs, and values that are shared between organizational members (Schein, 2010). It is like 'glue' that binds people together (Chatman and O'Reilly, 2016).

Some popular definitions of culture include:

- 'Culture is the system of such publicly and collectively accepted meanings operating for a given group at a given time' (Pettigrew, 1979: 574);

- 'the collective programming of the mind which distinguishes the members of one organization from another' (Hofstede, 1991: 262);

- 'the basic assumptions and beliefs which are shared by members of an organization, that operate unconsciously, and that define in a basic "taken-for-granted" fashion an organization's view of itself and its environment' (Schein, 2010). Schein also defines culture as 'a set of basic assumptions [that] defines for us what to pay attention to, what things mean' (2010: 32).

However, as with many of the subjects in this book, there is little consensus on what organizational culture is, how it operates, or its importance to organizations (see Chatman and O'Reilly, 2016, for a review). Giorgi et al. argue that there are five dominant models of culture:

1. values—what we hold dear, the meanings we make;
2. stories—the written or verbal narratives through which ideas and meanings are communicated;
3. frames—that shape what we pay attention to;
4. toolkits—that we use to make meaning or take action;
5. categories—different types of culture that help us understand what makes an organization distinctive.

Despite there being little agreement on what organizational culture is, the 'concept of culture', Giorgi et al. argue, 'is central to organization studies' (2015: 2).

Why study organizational culture? The rise of management interest

In 1982 two management consultants for McKinsey's, Tom Peters and Robert Waterman, published a book that caused a storm within management circles. *In search of excellence* became a global hit, selling over 3 million copies within its first four years, and was commonly seen in boardrooms, airport lounges, and business schools. This phenomenal success led to 'organizational culture' becoming the **buzzword** (a briefly fashionable phrase) for businesses.

At the book's heart was the claim that *excellent* companies had one key thing in common: a strong set of shared values. Successful firms, Peters and Waterman argued, were defined by a strong, unified culture; a bias for action; being close to the customers; innovation; being value driven; and having autonomy in decision making. 'In fact,' Peters and Waterman state, 'we wonder whether it is possible to be an excellent company without clarity on values' (1982: 280).

From the late 1970s academics and consultants such as Deal and Kennedy (1982) and Hofstede (1991) argued that organizational culture is central to business success. For instance, '[t]o be successful,' Tichy argues, 'a company's culture needs to support the kind of business the organization is in and its strategy for handling that business' (1982: 71). Carl-Henrik Svanberg, Ericsson's CEO, stated:

'culture always defeats strategy' (quoted in Alvesson and Sveningsson, 2015: 4). Culture and shared values, therefore, were seen as central for organizational success. As Google executives Eric Schmidt and Jonathan Rosenberg have recently stated, 'culture and success go hand in hand' (2015: 23).

Do strong cultures equal strong performance?

> ## Q Running case: Simon Chance looks at changingculture.info.uk
>
> Simon Chance has been thinking about the culture of Junction Hotel. He recently attended a talk led by an inspirational speaker. The speaker talked passionately about how he turned his food manufacturing business from a small-scale enterprise into a market leader through changing his firm's culture, by focusing on the customer and excellence in everything. Simon has decided to do a little more digging and looks through the changingculture.info.uk website. He reads:
>
>> If your people continue to act and think as they now do, will you be able to achieve the results you need? If your answer is no, then changing your organizational culture is not simply an option—it's essential. Organizational culture can be the difference between success and failure, change or stagnation ... Changing your culture can drive spectacular results by capitalizing on your greatest asset, your people ... You can change the way that people think and act ... become more competitive and focused ... be the best in your field ... To succeed, you must win the hearts and minds of your staff. changingculture.info.uk develop winning corporate cultures with shared beliefs and passion for the organization where all the energy of the company pulls in the same direction.
>
> 'Great stuff,' thinks Chance. 'The staff seem committed, but I'm not sure I have won their "hearts and minds". Maybe I should give culture change a go?'

These management consultants' interest in organizational culture hangs on one central claim: having the right culture increases productivity. This right culture, they argue, is produced by creating a shared sense of purpose. It increases staff motivation (Peters and Waterman, 1982) and commitment (Deal and Kennedy, 1982); reduces conflict; produces higher levels of productivity, quality, efficiency, and morale (Cameron and Quinn, 2011); and can drive innovation (Naranjo-Valencia et al., 2016). Some very bold assertions have been made to support this suggestion. Deal and Kennedy claim 'we estimate that a company can gain as much as one or two hours of productive work per employee per day' (1982: 15). Similarly, Collins and Porras argued that visionary companies outperformed non-visionary companies by about 1,500 per cent over 64 years (1994). With figures like this, it is easy to see why managers and management consultants get excited.

> ## ? Review questions
>
> **Describe** What is organizational culture?
>
> **Explain** What is meant when culture is described as 'the way we do things around here'?
>
> **Analyse** Why do you think managers have taken a great interest in organizational culture? How could changing culture benefit them?
>
> **Apply** Why do you think management consultants see culture as so important? What claims do culture change consultancies make regarding the impact that they can make on organizational performance? Do you think the claims are justified?
>
> Visit the online resources and take a look at the web links for Chapter 7 for further discussion about culture change consultancies.

223

In their article, Boyce et al. (2015) look at the relationship between culture and the performance of 95 car dealership franchises over six years. They conclude that culture 'comes first' and that it is a consistent predictor of customer satisfaction and sales. Similarly, Kotrba et al. (2012) argue that there is a close connection between culture and effectiveness, particularly for organizations that are able to be consistent but adaptable.

Research insight: is culture really the problem?

Lorsch, J.W., and McTague, E. 2016. Culture is not the culprit. *Harvard Business Review*, 94 (4): 21.

When organizations get into trouble we often see the culture being blamed. In discussions of the 2008 banking crisis, the sexual harassment cases raised in the #MeToo campaign, and corporate wrongdoing such as the Volkswagen vehicle emissions scandal, organizational culture is often seen as the culprit. The remedy to the problem is therefore to fix the culture to stop problems happening again. Even in situations that do not involve scandal, it is often said that an organization's culture needs to be changed, for example to improve performance. Based on interviews with top business executives, Lorsch and McTague (2016) argue that rather than being the fix to the problem, culture is the outcome of changes in processes and evolves as you do important work.

This argument runs counter to the assumptions that many academics and in particular consultants have that culture is an entity, a thing that can be changed. Instead, if it is seen as an outcome, business leaders may decide that they need to focus on the processes and practices of their organization.

Real life case: Google

Google have not only transformed the way that we use the internet, they have also been heralded by *Fortune* magazine as the best place to work in the world (2015). Why is that? Google are well known for their trendy, playful, and even weird office designs with slides for staircases, caravans as meeting rooms, and video games and playrooms (Fast Company, 2015; also see Chapter 11 on Googleplex), but the phenomenon goes deeper than that. According to Google's senior vice-president for people operations, Laszlo Bock, Google's culture is based on seeing work as a calling and giving people 'more trust, freedom, and authority than you are comfortable giving them' (2015: 53). This is echoed by Google executives Schmidt and Rosenberg, who say that for Google to be successful the employees 'need to *care* about the place they work' and Google succeeds by 'giving people responsibility and freedom' (Schmidt and Rosenberg, 2015: 29 and 52, italics in original). Part of this freedom comes with the company's tolerance for dissent, encouraging strong opinions and creating 'an environment where all employees feel valued and empowered' (2015: 42). They tell a story of how in 2002 Larry Page, Google's co-founder, was unhappy with the ads that were appearing on the Google searches because they were largely unrelated to what he had searched for. On a Friday afternoon he printed the search results he received, wrote 'THESE ADS SUCK' at the top of the page, pinned it to the noticeboard by the pool table, and left. On Monday at 5:05 am a search engineer sent an email agreeing with Page and offered a diagnosis and solution. The engineer and colleagues had spent the weekend trying to solve the problem, and they were not even in the team responsible for the original problem. This solution was the foundation to Google AdWords, the key money-making tool for Google. Schmidt and Rosenberg state that the fact these engineers 'spent their weekends transforming someone else's problem into a profitable solution speaks to the power of culture' (2015: 29).

Sources: Schmidt and Rosenberg (2015); Bock (2015).

From managing machines to managing dreams: a new way to manage organizations

This focus on organizational culture led to considerable hype predicting that organizations would be transformed. These management gurus presented a tantalizing, almost messianic, vision of businesses changing from the top down, from hierarchical control with all the problems of conflict we saw in Chapters 2, 3, and 4 to a culture of harmony and productivity, where workers and management come together around shared values.

Theory in context: responding to the rise of Japanese manufacturing

The growing interest in organizational culture occurred at a point when the USA's position as the economic superpower was being challenged by the rise of Japanese firms. For example, Harley Davidson was challenged by Honda's smaller, more efficient bikes (Ouchi, 1981).

Japanese culture was seen as key in their success (see Chapter 3 on rational work design for more details). For instance, Peters and Waterman recounted a story of a 'Honda worker who, on his way home each evening, straightens up windshield wiper blades on all the Hondas he passes. He can't stand to see a flaw in a Honda!' (1982: 37). In contrast, some US workers were seen as purposely destructive. For example, one worker described how 'he would go home at night chuckling to himself about the things he had thought up during the day to mess up the system. He'd leave his sandwich behind the door panel of a car, for example ... Or he would put loose screws in the compartment of the frame that was to be welded shut' (Cameron and Quinn, 2011: 15).

Real life case: Netflix

Netflix are famous for such TV shows as *Black Mirror, Stranger Things,* and *Orange is the New Black,* but within business circles they are also becoming known for redefining our view of work culture. One of the main reasons is that Netflix are explicit about their culture, particularly their expectations of employees. In 2009 Netflix produced a 125-page PowerPoint describing their culture. It has been viewed 18 million times; Sheryl Sandberg, Facebook's chief operating officer, says it 'may well be the most important document ever to come out of [Silicon] Valley' (quoted in Ferenstein, 2013).

Netflix state their central premise is 'people over process' to create a more 'flexible, fun, stimulating, creative, and successful organization' (Netflix, 2018a). They have no rules about when and how much people work, you can take holidays when you like, and new parents are encouraged to take the time off that they feel is right. Netflix states five core principles.

1. Encourage independent decision-making by employees
2. Share information openly, broadly and deliberately
3. Are extraordinarily candid with each other
4. Keep only our highly effective people
5. Avoid rules

(Netflix, 2018a)

They aim to 'liberate teams from unnecessary rules and approvals' (McCord, 2018: 10), share documents freely within the company and seek to create a 'dream team ... in which all of your colleagues are extraordinary at what they do and are highly effective collaborators' (Netflix, 2018a). They work on the basis of trust and radical honesty, in which everyone gives direct, honest, and often difficult feedback to their colleagues.

Netflix also have a demanding 'high performance' and results-focused culture. Managers are told to 'put their confidence in people who've proven they can produce' (McCord, 2018: 11) and 'pay top of the market' (2018: 117) and 'don't measure people by how many hours they work' or how much effort they put in. They should focus on results (Netflix, 2018b). One of their core principles is the 'keeper test':

> if one of the members of the team was thinking of leaving for another firm, would the manager try hard to keep them from leaving? Those that do not pass the keeper test (i.e. their manager would not fight to keep them) are promptly and respectfully given a generous severance package so we can find someone for that position that makes us an even better dream team. Getting cut from our team is very disappointing, but there is no shame. Being on a dream team can be the thrill of a professional lifetime.
>
> (Netflix, 2018a)

As Patty McCord, their former chief talent officer, states: 'In product development, if something doesn't work, you get rid of it. I realized we could apply that same principle of managing people' (McCord, 2018: 7).

 How would you feel working at Netflix? Does their culture inspire you or make you feel fearful, worried that you might lose your job? Would having young children and a mortgage make you feel any different?

Sources: McCord (2018); https://jobs.netflix.com/culture https://eatsleepworkrepeat.fm/2017/05/13/4-were-not-a-family/ https://www.slideshare.net/reed2001/culture-1798664

Because of the competitive threat from Japanese firms, US business consultants argued that organizational culture was a way for US firms to reassert their dominance and confidence. As Deal and Kennedy put it: 'a strong culture has almost always been the driving force behind continuing success in American Business' (1982: 5).

This required new roles for managers. They no longer simply controlled 'hard' financial measures, structure, and strategy, but needed to manage 'soft', less measurable aspects of visions and values, mission and purpose, unifying the workplace around core values everyone believed in. Table 7.1 presents a summary of these contrasts.

Managing through culture and values presented a new, more innovative and exciting way of managing. Tom Peters (2001) later called it 'soft stuff that determines what really gets accomplished and how well it gets done. It turned out to be a revolutionary message.'

Table 7.1 Rational and cultural management (based on Peters and Waterman, 1982)

Rational management	Cultural management
• Hard	• Soft
• Rational argument based on facts and figures	• Emotional appeal through shared values
• Managed through budgets, strategy, and targets	• Managed through shared values and purpose
• Management control imposed on workers via rules, procedures, and systems of accountability	• Workers control themselves through shared beliefs and values
• Formal communication through newsletters, emails, etc.	• Informal communication through symbols and stories
• Formal authority structures and hierarchy	• Reliance on informal opinion leaders, traditions, accepted practices, and sense of mission
• Control, monitoring, and evaluation	• Trust, commitment, and autonomy

 Theory in context: culture producing a new form of worker

Peters and Waterman (1982) argued that managing through culture would produce a radical alternative to the standard bureaucratic model that stressed rules and regulations and carrot-and-stick motivation. They thought this would be replaced by organizations where freedom and autonomy ruled, governed through a shared sense of values and purpose. This, they claimed, would produce a different type of workplace and with it a new type of worker.

The idea was simple. If the worker was released from the constraints of bureaucratic standardization and given something to believe in, the organizational members would be committed to the mission of the organization and work harder as a consequence. Peters and Waterman (ibid.) pronounced that 'The individual', so dehumanized by Taylorism, 'still counts'.

Peters and Waterman offered a vision where workers would love their company and believe in its values. Gone was Taylorism with its standardization and uniformity, top-down command-and-control management, and repetitive tasks. In its place was a shared sense of vision and values, mission and purpose.

The workers' personalities and individuality, so disliked by Taylor, would be rediscovered and harnessed for the organization's benefit. Peters and Waterman thought a new society could be created around individual autonomy and freedom, governed by shared values. As Sewell later commented, 'direct control of the labor process is no longer seen as necessarily the most effective way to realize organizational goals' (1998: 401).

Organizational culture therefore promises that the worker can be productive *and* have increased job satisfaction. The conflict between labour and capital, Peters and Waterman argued, is solved because there is no longer a conflict between the workers' interests and that of the organization.

Such a move was needed, its proponents argued, because the nature of society was changing. From the 1960s, respect for authority began to diminish and workers were less accepting of hierarchical relations. Indeed, Deal and Kennedy argued that the loss of faith in large-scale institutions, such as government and church, meant that 'corporations may be the last institutions in America that can effectively take on the role of shaping values' (1982: 16).

Real life case: Zappos—delivering happiness the Zappos way

Zappos, the US online shoe retailer, was founded in 1999 and was sold to Amazon in 2009 for $1.2 billion. It is not just their phenomenal growth that has made the headlines, but their culture.

They call themselves the 'Zappos family' and place an emphasis on fun and 'wow' elements (Zappos, 2015). Their CEO, Tony Hsieh, comes to work in jeans and a t-shirt and earns only $36,000 per year (Wei, 2010). They have a chief happiness officer and a culture evangelist, Donavan Roberson, who states that they invest money in 'building a culture dedicated to the happiness of our people' (cited in Michelli, 2012: 71). Managers are asked to spend 10–20 per cent of their time socializing with employees. They run competitions and games for employees and provide perks such as free food. They conduct regular staff surveys and have unusual practices. For example, when an employee logs in to the computer system, in addition to their password, they are shown a random photo of another employee and are asked to name them. After they answer, a brief profile of that employee is shown 'so that everyone can learn more about each other' (Hsieh, 2010: 173). They also have an online culture book where employees can submit uncensored photos and ideas about Zappos' culture (Zappos Insights, 2015) and write about it in blog posts (blogs.zappos. com). This leads Tony Hsieh to claim that 'everyone at Zappos lives by the 10 Core Values' (Hsieh, 2010: 162). These values include 'Pursue Growth and Learning' and 'Deliver WOW Through Service', as well as more unusual ones like 'Be Passionate' and 'Create Fun and a Little Weirdness'.

Hsieh states, 'Our employees know that our number one priority at Zappos is our company culture' (2010: 171). Employees are recruited not only for the skills they offer but if they fit with Zappos culture. 'I know Zappos has a well-defined technical education curriculum, and if the person fits our values regarding learning and growth, we can teach the technical aspects of the job,' states Markel, director of casual lifestyle at Zappos (cited by Michelli, 2012). All new employees (right up to senior leaders) have to go through a one-month induction process that was originally designed for entry-level jobs, in order to give everyone a common experience. It includes an overview of the ten core values and the history behind each value, presentations from senior managers, and four weeks of customer service training. This training culminates in answering the phone to actual customers for two weeks (Michelli, 2012). There is a further check to see if employees fit; after their induction, newly oriented employees are offered one month's salary to leave if they do not feel they fit with the culture (Taylor, 2014).

 Why do Zappos try to recruit for cultural fit? Would you like to work at Zappos?

 Visit the online resources and take a look at the extension material for Chapter 7 for more information on Zappos, and Chapter 8 for more information around recruiting for cultural fit.

? Review questions

Describe	What are rational management and cultural management?
Explain	What are the key claims about why cultural management increases performance?
Analyse	In what way does managing through culture shift the manager's role?
Apply	Can you describe the key features of the culture at Zappos? How does this culture benefit the organization? Do you think it might have any drawbacks?

How to understand culture

> **Q Running case:** Chance wonders whether cultural change will work at Junction Hotel
>
> Impressed with the claims that changingculture.info.uk make about the importance of organizational culture, Chance decides to delve a little deeper. 'It would be great to get the staff all sharing the same vision of Junction Hotel and all our energy directed towards making the hotel a success,' he muses.
>
> 'The first thing you need to do,' he reads on the website, 'is to diagnose what your existing culture is. Take our free self-diagnostic test,' the website suggests, 'and find out what your culture is.' 'OK,' thinks Chance, 'it can't do any harm.'
>
> Completing the survey, Simon Chance clicks on the result: 'A Role Culture'. 'Umm ...,' thinks Chance. 'I guess so, although I'm not sure it is really like that. Anyway, what can I do with this information?' At the end of the result page, Chance reads: 'If you want more information and to talk through your result, phone this number.' He decides to give them a call.
>
> The consultants explain that the culture survey is only a snapshot of the organization and it is only based on Chance's own perspective. 'To really understand what is going on,' Mark Wickham continues, 'a full survey of the organization is necessary. This will give you a chance to understand how your staff view Junction Hotel.'

A popular way of understanding and trying to change an organization's culture is to use a cultural classification, also known as a typology. A typology is a system of classification of traits that organizations have in common. These **typologies** are useful in that they provide a way of quickly capturing an overall impression of the organization and allowing it to be compared to other organizations. There is no single 'best culture'. Rather, the role of managers is to fit the organizational culture with the external environment.

Deal and Kennedy's typology

One of the first such models was provided by Deal and Kennedy (1982) (see Table 7.2). They argued that an organization's culture is a product of the environment in which it operates—particularly how risky key activities are and how quickly workers receive feedback. For example, a car sales person generally gets quick feedback (someone either buys or does not buy a car), but the risk of a single transaction is fairly small, producing a work hard/play hard culture. If someone works in a government bureaucracy it has low risk and slow feedback, producing a process culture. Each of these cultures has their own strengths and weaknesses. It is important the culture and environment match.

Charles Handy's typology

Another typology is offered by Charles Handy in his book *Gods of management* (2009). Handy argues that organizations should try to match their type of culture to the external needs of the organization. He offered the following four cultural categories based on Greek gods (Table 7.3, adapted from Handy, 2009).

Table 7.2 The link between culture and feedback (Deal and Kennedy, 1982)

	Low	High
Fast	**Work hard/play hard** • Fun-focused • Performance- and action-driven • Strong customer focus • Small risks • High energy level • Example—sales and manufacturing	**Tough-guy macho** • Quick decision making • High risk—all or nothing • Highly driven people • Individualistic • Competitive—low teamwork • Example—stockbrokers, media, sports, and construction
Slow	**Process culture** • Bureaucratic—clear rules that must be followed • Highly regulated • Often need for precision • Status orientated • Takes years to discover if decision was correct • Example—government bureaucracies	**Bet-your-company culture** • Long-term outlook • High-risk and high-cost decisions but years before outcome is known • High planning, technical expertise and diligence throughout • Examples—pharmaceutical firm devising a new drug, oil companies

Speed of feedback

Degree of risk

Based on Deal, T., and Kennedy, A., *Corporate Cultures: The Rites and Rituals of Corporate Life* (1982). Reproduced by permission of Perseus Books.

Table 7.3 Handy's four cultural categories

Power culture—Zeus	Role culture—Apollo
• Power and decision making concentrated on the centre, e.g. founder/manager • Control of centre becomes weaker as firm grows, so normally split into subdivisions • Tough and competitive environment • Few set rules, as is more about power and choosing people who think in similar ways • Examples—family firms, new businesses, and small entrepreneurs	• Bureaucracy in its purest form • Roof—senior management decision making • Pillars—functional units • Staff do their roles • Authority based on position in hierarchy • Predictable • Works well in predictable environments, but is difficult to adapt to change • Examples—civil service and high-street banks
Task culture—Athena	**Personal or cluster culture—Dionysius**
• Focus on getting the job done • Temporary project teams to meet task needed, then disbanded • Expertise is central • Control through allocation of people and resources • Examples—project management, construction, and advertising	• Consensus management; power is shared • Individual freedom is key • Exist for the members • No collective goal • Reject formal hierarchies • Examples—self-help groups and architect partnerships

Quinn and Rohrbaugh's competing values framework

The final framework we present was developed by Quinn and Rohrbaugh (1983; see Cameron and Quinn, 2011) and is used to assess not only organizational culture but leadership, communication, and employee selection. Like the other frameworks, it divides culture into four types (see Table 7.4). The key dimensions on the horizontal axis are if the organization is inward-focused on itself or outward, in favour of customers. The vertical axis shows whether the control is with management (at the bottom) or autonomy is with the staff (at the top). Each of the four therefore represents opposite sets of assumptions.

It is interesting to note that these categories of culture also reflect the organizational structure (see Chapter 2), as they involve how decisions are made and how power operates within the organization. In a study of Spanish firms, Naranjo-Valencia and colleagues found that hierarchical cultures, for instance, are far less innovative than adhocracy cultures, which have 'the highest positive effect on performance' (Naranjo-Valencia et al., 2016: 38).

Cultural typologies assessed

Cultural typologies are popular because they provide a quick way of capturing what an organization is like, its strengths and weaknesses, and comparing it to other organizations. However, they should be treated with caution.

They tend to generalize rather than provide specific descriptions of how a culture operates. Organizations do not necessarily fit neatly in categories, and applying these typologies in a rigid way can mean we lose sight of some of the features that make an organization unique. These

Table 7.4 Competing values framework

	Internally-focused and integrated	Externally-focused and differentiated
Flexibility and discretion	**Clan (late 1960s onwards)** • Like a family organization • Shared values and cohesion • Teamwork and employee empowerment, friendly place to work • Customers are partners • Leaders are mentors/parent figures • Example—PeopleExpress	**Adhocracy (information age)** Ad hoc—temporary and specialized, disbands when the task is complete No centralized power—power flows from individual to individual Emphasis on individuality, risk-taking, and creativity Example—software development, think-tanks
Stability and control	**Hierarchy (from 1900 onwards)** • Bureaucratic culture • Clear lines of decision making • Stable and efficient • Standardized rules and procedures with no discretion • Environment is stable • Leaders are good organizers • Example—McDonald's and Ford	**Market (from 1960s onwards)** • Organization functions as a market with competition • Aims to reduce transaction costs • Profit is key; highly results-orientated • Meeting customers' needs • Customers competitive for best price • Leaders are highly competitive • Example—General Electric

(Adapted from Cameron and Quinn, 2011.)

typologies also focus on the structural elements of the culture and tend to ignore the more mundane, everyday aspects of organizational life. Their accuracy also depends on the ability of the individual to successfully understand the culture and match it to the framework. Finally, they present organizations as having a unified, homogeneous culture and thus miss some of the subtleties between departments or different sites. They therefore provide a useful frame of reference but should only be used as a starting point for analysis.

Visit the online resources and take a look at the web links for Chapter 7 to complete the culture diagnostic test for an organization you know well. How well do you think it represents the organization?

? Review questions

Describe	What are the main features of Schein's cultural iceberg?
Explain	In what way do typologies and management change frameworks see culture as management's property?
Analyse	What are the implications of managers seeing culture as a tool for organizational practice? What are the potential negative repercussions of seeing culture as a property that managers can control?
Apply	Can you apply Schein's model to the real life cases in this chapter? Which parts of the model are easy to describe and which are more difficult?

Edgar Schein's cultural iceberg

One of the most popular and respected models of culture was created by Edgar Schein. Schein sees culture as being like an iceberg, where the important parts of the culture occur below the surface (Figure 7.1 and Table 7.5). The things near the top are the easiest to change, but have the least

Figure 7.1 Schein's cultural iceberg.
Source: Schein, Organizational Culture and Leadership, 2010, John Wiley & Sons Inc.

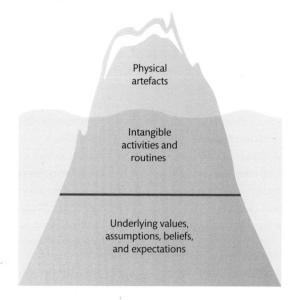

Table 7.5   Levels of Schein's cultural iceberg (based on Schein, 2010)

Level	Description	Examples	Analysis	Ability to change
Artefacts	What one sees and hears	Physical environment Language Technology Clothing Emotional display Myths and stories about the organization	Visible, but hard to decipher Cannot rely on alone, as observer will project their own feelings and reactions	Relatively straightforward but also fairly superficial and therefore not going to change the culture dramatically
Espoused beliefs and values	Beliefs and key practices spoken initially by leader/founder and then validated by the group	What people say in particular situations Mission statements Strategies and goals	Stated assumptions shared by the group Often leave many aspects of behaviour unexplained	The leader can change this level and may be good at training new members how to behave
Basic underlying assumptions	Regular solution to a problem, it becomes taken for granted; preferred solution, any other option inconceivable	Values that guide behaviour Values shared and therefore reinforced Fundamental aspects of life, human nature, nature of truth, importance of family, work, self-development, etc.	Unconscious, taken for granted, not discussable; anything that challenges this produces defence mechanisms	Very difficult to change as often unconscious and completely taken for granted

© Schein, *Organizational Culture and Leadership*, 2010, John Wiley & Sons Inc.

significance. The further one goes down the iceberg, the deeper ingrained the culture is and the less conscious the participants are of it. These levels are harder to change but have greater impact.

At the top are physical artefacts, such as the building or staff uniforms. They express certain aspects of the culture, but they are open to interpretation by the observer. Chan et al. state that where 'artifacts [sic] reinforce centrally directed messages … the subconscious of collective culture, may change' (Chan et al., 2018: 193). The middle layer represents the **intangible** beliefs or values of the organization. Schein suggests that these often start from the founder or leader and are passed on to the organizational members through mission statements or strategy. The deepest level holds strongly held values and assumptions. For Schein, underlying assumptions are the essence of culture. Changing them can result in anxiety and defence mechanisms, but 'unless one digs down to the level of the basic assumptions one cannot really decipher the artefacts, values, and norms' (Schein, 2010: 59).

Changing culture is, therefore, a complex process. Because much of culture is unconscious it can be hard to change; however, this is not to suggest that it is impossible to change. Schein argues that by following a ten-step process, cultures can be understood in a single day (2010: 348) and begin changing after that.

 Can you apply Schein's model to an organization or workplace that you know?

Changing organizational culture

Owing to the importance of culture for organizational performance, many cultural change consultants offer step-by-step guidelines to change culture, involving several stages:

- diagnosing the current culture;
- deciding what needs changing;
- transforming the culture to its new way of operating;
- entrenching the new culture in the way that the organization works.

The underlying assumption within these typologies and management change frameworks is that culture is management's property, something tangible, knowable, and controllable. This perspective assumes that senior managers, with the support of a consultant, can diagnose what the culture is, change it, and control it in the way that they want. In this view, culture is a resource that is used and manipulated by the management to increase commitment and to enhance performance. Culture, therefore, is a tool that can be used to increase profitability.

? Review questions

Describe	What is a cultural typology?
Explain	How might a manager use a cultural typology?
Analyse	What are the strengths and weaknesses of cultural typologies?
Apply	Can you apply the cultural typologies in this section to some of the real life cases throughout this chapter? Can you apply them to Junction Hotel as a whole? Do different cultural types exist in different parts of the hotel?

👁 Research insight: practical guides to changing organizational culture

Cameron, K., and Quinn, R.E. 2011. *Diagnosing and changing organizational culture*. Jossey Bass: London.

Cameron and Quinn offer a popular, and quite practical, guide to changing organizational culture. This guide includes a range of tools, such as questions, surveys, and instruments, for organizational managers to use in diagnosing and changing their organization's culture, and a framework in which managers can understand the basic assumptions and communication styles within the organization.

Their key tips include:

- identifying what can be changed easily
- changing it and then publicizing it—so that everyone knows what has happened
- identifying illustrative stories of the type of culture you want to produce
- measuring change so people know what to focus on
- holding a funeral for the past approach of the organization and celebrating that past—this helps employees gain closure on the old culture
- focusing on process.

This approach is quite simple and, as we will see in Chapter 12, it is questionable whether change can occur through such a linear approach.

Visit the online resources and take a look at the extension material for Chapter 7 for Schein's ten-step approach to changing organizational culture.

While there are many models that claim to be able to change culture, as we will see in the following sections, in practice, culture is often more complicated than these recipe-book approaches suggest.

The manager changing culture: the role of founders and organizational leaders

🔍 **Running case:** cultural change report

To:	s.chance@junctionhotel.net
From:	m.wickham@changingculture.info.uk
Subject:	Culture change at Junction Hotel—Report

Junction Hotel Current Culture Report

Dear Mr Chance

Many thanks for choosing *changingculture.info.uk*. We are delighted to attach your full report for Junction Hotel's corporate culture. We had a good response rate for the survey, with 73% of staff taking part. The full report gives extensive detail about the culture, but the headline issues are:

- only 23% of staff could name Junction Hotel's mission statement and most of them were managers
- 37% of staff felt that they identified with the hotel
- 76% felt that they enjoyed being part of the hotel
- 27% felt that they were listened to.

Getting the right culture can mean long-term success for your firm, a more committed workforce, higher productivity, and increased job satisfaction. I suggest that we arrange a meeting next week to discuss what contribution *changingculture.info.uk* can offer Junction Hotel.

With very best wishes

Mark Wickham PhD

changingculture.info.uk—bringing cultural change to UK business, for profits and people

> →
>
> Chance looks at the email in shock—this was not the result he was expecting. He had always thought that people valued working at Junction Hotel and that they shared the same vision, but the survey results seem to be saying something altogether different. He calls in Linda Wilkinson for a chat, as she has the ear of the staff.
>
> 'What do you think of this? Shocking, isn't it—don't the staff care?' asks Chance.
>
> 'I think ... ,' stammers Wilkinson, 'that they value the organization, but not in the same way that you do.'
>
> 'Oh,' Chance responds indignantly, 'what do you mean?'
>
> Wilkinson looks up at him. 'Well, sometimes,' she responds hesitantly, 'we don't include them in what we do.'
>
> 'So what are you saying?' Chance asks. 'That we need a strong shared culture?'
>
> Linda looks back quizzically. 'Yes, something like that,' she says.
>
> Visit the online resources and take a look at the extension material for Chapter 7 to read the Junction Hotel Culture Report in full.

For many writers, the most significant figures for establishing or changing the culture are the **founders** and leaders of the organization. As Edgar Schein has argued, 'organizations begin to create cultures through the actions of founders who operate as strong leaders' (2010: 242). The personality of the founder sets the environment for the first members of staff. 'Typically, the founders and his or her successor's leadership helps shape a culture of shared values and assumptions guided and restricted by the founders' personal beliefs' (Bass and Avolio, 1993: 114).

As the firm grows, the founder's ability to directly influence the staff might diminish, but their influence is often sustained through stories and myths about their actions. These stories can provide the organization with a sense of history and purpose and a framework within which to operate (see the following sections for more discussion on the power of stories). Founders' stories can provide powerful ways to communicate the values of the organization and give the company a sense of tradition and purpose.

How leaders can change culture

🔍 Running case: Chance looks for solutions

'So what can we do about this?' enquires Chance of Wickham, the culture consultant. 'Our staff do not seem to share the same passion for Junction Hotel as I do. I thought it was obvious what we stand for,' Chance continues.

'We need a few quick hits,' Wickham suggests. 'You need to put across your vision for the hotel, show the staff what is important. You are the most important person in the organization. They will follow you.'

Although the organizational founder certainly has significant influence, as they leave or the organization grows, their influence diminishes and the organization's managers gain more influence. In Edgar Schein's (2010: 257) words, leaders 'create the conditions for culture formation'. Similarly, Bass and Avolio (1993: 113) claim 'The characteristics and qualities of an organization's culture are taught by its leadership and eventually adopted by its followers'. Indeed, as Selznick argues, leaders can be seen as the embodiment of organizational values (cited in Schein, 2010).

Schein argues that, given the influence of the leaders, they have to be consistent in their actions; otherwise their influence on their followers is diminished. He suggests that they have the following tools to change culture.

Primary embedding mechanism

- What leaders pay attention to, measure, and control on a regular basis
- How leaders react to critical incidents and organizational crises
- How leaders allocate resources
- Deliberate role modelling, teaching, and coaching
- How leaders allocate rewards and status
- How leaders recruit, select, promote, and excommunicate

Secondary articulation and reinforcement mechanisms

- Organizational design and structure
- Organizational systems and procedures
- Rites and rituals of the organization
- Design of physical space, façades, and buildings
- Stories about important events and people
- Formal statements of organizational philosophy, creeds, and charters

(Schein, 2010: 246)

Quin (1984) and Cameron and Quinn (2011) argue it is important that the leadership style matches the culture as represented in the competing values framework (see Table 7.6), as otherwise leadership will not be effective.

One of the most powerful ways that leaders can influence their culture is through symbolic acts and strong stories. These stories have powerful effects in that they transmit the values that the leaders hold and communicate to members what they deem important. As Smircich and Morgan argue, 'Through words and images, symbolic actions and gestures, leaders can structure attention and evoke patterns of meaning that give them considerable control over the situation being managed' (1982: 263). 'The reason culture is important is because top management can directly influence culture through activities and symbols' (Daft, 1986: 486). In other words, leaders, through their actions, can shape the culture of the organization.

Table 7.6 Matching leadership style to culture

Hierarchy	• Coordinator
	• Organizer
	• Administrator
Adhocracy	• Entrepreneur
	• Innovator
	• Risk-taker
Market	• Decision maker
	• Producer
	• Achiever
Clan	• Participative mentor
	• Facilitator
	• Parent-figure

(based on Cameron and Quinn, 2011)

It is not just in the academic literature that these views are popular. Management consultant Dan Look argues that instilling a strong sense of culture is a key role for leadership. He claims that 'in the long term, culture is the only strategic differentiator'. Leaders are key to achieving this because 'culture is reinforced by everything a leader does' (cited in Roper, 2015a). Peter Cheese, the chief executive of the CIPD, agrees, stating: 'Where does culture start? At the top' (cited in Roper, 2015b). However, leaders are often not very good at managing culture: 'Managers often don't understand the culture because they are not very good at listening to employees' (Roper, 2015b). While these senior practitioners see the value of culture, they argue that many leaders are not sufficiently skilled at utilizing it.

 Real life case: Lendlease—the importance of the founders' values

Founded in Australia in 1958, Lendlease is an international property and infrastructure group that specializes in world-leading developments, investment management, and construction project management. Its projects include everything from roads and bridges to state-of-the-art buildings and hospitals, including the iconic Sydney Opera House, the 2012 Olympic Games Athletes' Village in London, and the National September 11 Memorial and Museum in New York City. Like many companies, it has core values including respect, collaboration, trust, and integrity (see *Lendlease: Our Values*, http://www.lendlease.com/worldwide/about-us/values).

These beliefs can be traced back to the company's Dutch-born founder Dick Dusseldorp, who recognized the responsibility his company had to society, arguing: 'Companies must start justifying their worth to society, with greater emphasis placed on environmental and social impact rather than straight economics.'

Alex Christie, Lendlease's head of human resources, said:

It was this statement that embedded our governing principles and defined how we do business. For example, there are times when we have decided not to work on projects or with clients because they have not been aligned with our sustainability and ethical standards. We are also encouraging tenants at the International Quarter, our new commercial development on the Olympic Park, to embrace agile and flexible working, with new offices designed to improve productivity and wellbeing.

(Christie, 2015)

The Lendlease Foundation was set up within the company by Dusseldorp in 1983 to specifically nurture and support the development and benefit of all employees—as well as a social responsibility to communities. The Lendlease Foundation continues to gain momentum to this day, with designated employee representatives in each region running new policies, programmes, and community initiatives across the globe.

The company runs a family intern programme, continues to increase the diversity of its employee base, and hosts a yearly personal development programme in Tasmania for employees from across its regions. More recently it introduced Wellbeing Leave, a policy which gives employees the opportunity to take time off work to focus on their own mental and physical health.

Lendlease's company website states:

Dick Dusseldorp dreamt of building an organisation that would be measured not just on its financial returns, but on its positive contribution to the environment and society ... He also believed the wellbeing and best interests of his employees was paramount. More than 50 years later, this is where our focus remains.

(Lendlease: Working at Lendlease, http://www.lendlease.com/worldwide/careers/working-at-lend-lease)

The influence of the founder's values, particularly the importance of stakeholders (rather than just shareholders), is key. Clark, who wrote *Finding a common interest* (Clark, 2002), a book about Dick Dusseldorp, argues that Lendlease's 'entire corporate culture—that has been embedded in the company from the start ... begins with its founder Dick Dusseldorp' (2002: 9). Alex Christie added:

> There is a strong business case for us to take the health and wellbeing of our employees seriously. Recent initiatives such as Wellbeing Leave are good examples of Dick's philosophy. It is a proactive investment in the health and wellbeing of our employees, and acknowledges the importance of a balanced work–family life. A healthier, happier workforce is naturally a more productive and engaged one—and less likely to take regular sick leave.

(Christie, 2015)

Changing layout, changing cultures

🔍 Running case: a tour of Junction Hotel

Sue Marshall arrives at Junction Hotel for her first day, feeling quite nervous, but Mandy Armfield, a receptionist, greets her with a smile and takes Sue on a tour of Junction Hotel. 'This, obviously, is the front of house. You'll get a chance to meet the girls later—we're a friendly bunch.' Sue notices a computer, which must be for booking in, a board with every room number, and a list. 'Oh, that,' Mandy says, noticing Sue's attention on it, 'that's for the maintenance team'.

'It's all very organized in here,' Sue comments.

'Oh yes, we like to keep on top of things. In here, this is our office—we call it our cubby-hole. It's not much, but we like it.' Sue looks in amazement: a tiny room with no natural light, one desk with an old-looking computer, and a couple of mugs of tea. 'We come here for a gossip,' Mandy says with a wink.

Continuing on, Sue is shown some of the plush bedrooms, one with a four-poster bed, the dining room with staff busily preparing for the lunchtime meal, and the kitchen, which is incredibly organized with colour-coordinated chopping boards and lists of the week's meals. They then take a right turn through a door which says 'Staff Only' and go up some stairs. The light flickers on the staircase, the carpet is threadbare, and paint is peeling off the walls. Seeing Sue's face, Mandy moves to reassure her: 'Oh, this is just a short-cut to the meeting rooms. We don't let customers or the board come in this way.'

'What about us?' Sue wonders. They proceed through what Sue imagines is the staff room, which has a few old magazines in the corner next to the coffee machine. Back through another door, they return to the plush carpet and are faced with a large oak door with the label 'Office—Simon Chance' on it.

> In the office, Sue Marshall looks around at the oak-panelled walls and the luxury deep-pile carpet. In the corner Jenny Hyam, Simon Chance's secretary, sits on a small swivel chair in front of a pine veneer desk—'IKEA,' thinks Sue as she assesses the scene. Rows of box files, all neatly ordered, are on shelves behind Jenny's desk, colour-coded and alphabetically arranged. Jenny has a picture of her holding a small child—her daughter, Sue assumes—in a pretty red dress.
>
> Jenny looks over at Sue. 'He won't be long now,' she says calmly. 'Mondays are always a busy day for Mr Chance.'
>
> The oak panelling continues throughout the boardroom, which has a large mahogany table in the centre. Looking down on the room are ten austere-looking men captured in oil paintings with plaques beneath giving their names and dates. The door opens and Simon Chance pops his head round. 'You must be Sue,' he says shaking her hand firmly, 'pleased to meet you. I would love to stay and chat, but we are making a lot of changes at the moment and I am rather busy. Maybe we can catch up at the end of the month—I'd love to hear your views on the place.' And with that, the phone rings and he rushes back into his office.

One of the ways managers try to change organizational culture is to change the physical surroundings. As Turner and Myerson (1998: 1) state, 'workspaces themselves usually reflect the style and personality of the organization'. The design and layout reflect the culture that the organization wants to project to the outside world. They also reflect

> who and what is valued in the organization. For example, arranging offices by rank so that the highest-level executives occupy the top floor(s) and/or the largest and most nicely appointed office space (e.g., corner offices with large windows) and lower-level employees occupy successively lower floors and smaller offices, conveys the message that the organization places a high value on status.
>
> (Ornstein, 1989: 145)

Overall, 'Office design might best be analyzed as symbols produced by organizational cultures' (Hatch, 1992: 143).

For instance, the change to an open-plan arrangement is argued by some to lead to greater bonding, teamwork, and communication (Ornstein, 1989). However, open-plan offices can also lead many staff to feel resentment, as such offices produce increased noise and staff sometimes have concerns about loss of status and privacy (Tierney, 2012; Frontczak et al., 2012).

Corporate status symbols.
Source: S.Borisov/Shutterstock.com.

Merchant banks often favour high-rise office blocks, which may be signs of status—for instance, the Burj Khalifa building is the tallest in the world. These images, it can be argued, express power and authority, with status linked to the highest offices. They present a highly formalized corporate culture stressing trustworthiness, wealth, and power.

🔍 **Running case:** changing the culture at Junction Hotel

It was Mark Wickham from changingculture.info.uk on the phone.

'Do your staff know your values?' asks Wickham.

'No, not really,' reflects Chance. 'We have a mission statement, but never really communicate it.'

'Then I suggest that you teach your staff your mission statement,' Wickham replies. 'This is the best way to get across what your vision of Junction Hotel is. Without a clear vision, many firms fail.'

Thinking through this suggestion, Chance decides to make the mission statement the central focus of the Wednesday morning team meeting. He wants to make the hotel an upbeat, positive place, where people feel good about coming to work, and to provide a really high-quality service.

Wednesday morning team meeting

The restaurant is packed, as every member of Junction Hotel had been called in to listen to Chance on what he has labelled 'mission day'.

'Junction Hotel is a great place to work. It is full of exceptional people with a passion for what they do,' Chance begins almost evangelically. 'We have a top-class chef, excellent front-of-house team, fantastic support staff, and quality cleaners. But we do not always work together and see the big picture. So, today I am unveiling our new mission—Gold Standard Service. This will make Junction Hotel stand out from the competition.' Standing in front of the flip chart, he unveils the mission statement. He stands back to let the staff read it:

> Junction Hotel aims to be the hotel of choice because we completely satisfy our guests.
>
> Through a gold standard service we are committed to making your stay a pleasant experience by making a difference every day.
>
> We aim to continually improve our service and go the extra mile for all our guests.

Covering the tables with big sheets of paper, Chance asks each department's team leader to facilitate a session to think about how they need to change how they work to meet the Gold Standard Service mission. 'It is important,' Chance states, 'that everyone is on board with the mission and knows how they personally, and how Junction Hotel collectively, can meet it. These documents will be fed back to the group via the new monthly newsletter—*Junction News*.'

Chance ends the team meeting with everyone repeating the mission statement. He says that it will be put up on notice boards, and at the start of the next meeting he will pick one member of staff at random to repeat back the mission in front of everyone.

Josh

> Just sat through a ridiculous meeting where Chance made us repeat our mission statement over and over again. I felt like we were braying donkeys.
>
> 2 seconds ago via Android Like Comment

 Do you know the mission statement of your university or the place that you work? Have you ever been told it? How did you react to it?

241

Mission statements

Mission statements are often presented as one of the key tools for senior managers to change the 'espoused beliefs' of organizational members (level 2 on Schein's iceberg). They became popular during the latter half of the 1980s and are now an almost obligatory feature of most organizations.

Mission statements offer senior management an opportunity to define explicitly the purpose of the organization (Drucker, 1974) and create a vision that all stakeholders (shareholders, employees, customers, and the general public) can buy into. This vision should be uplifting and thus, it is claimed, provide an opportunity for the organization to improve its public image and increase the commitment of the employees, and for senior management to assert their authority over the organization. Finally, a mission statement provides a common language for the organization.

Real life case: mission statements

This table outlines the mission statements of some of the world's most recognizable organizations.

Google	'to organize the world's information and make it universally accessible and useful' (Google, 2018).
Amazon	'We're a company of pioneers. It's our job to make bold bets, and we get our energy from inventing on behalf of customers. Success is measured against the possible, not the probable. For today's pioneers, that's exactly why there's no place on Earth they'd rather build than Amazon' (Amazon, 2018).
Starbucks	'to inspire and nurture the human spirit—one person, one cup, and one neighbourhood at a time' (Starbucks, 2018).
Greenpeace	'to ensure the ability of Earth to nurture life in all its diversity' (Greenpeace, 2018).
ASOS	'Our mission is to become the world's number-one online shopping destination for fashion-loving 20-somethings' (ASOS, 2018).

Visit the online resources and take a look at the videos for Chapter 7 to watch an interview with Janet Dalziell, the director of global human resources for Greenpeace, about their organizational culture.

Mission statements provide a way to define the organization's core objectives, requiring senior managers (or in some organizations all staff) to step back from everyday activity and think what the organization exists for. At times, this involves settling differences between competing visions of the organization that the senior managers hold and debating the future direction of the organization. Mission statements often state not only business objectives (such as being number one in the field) but also the ethical stance of the organization, including its contribution to society. This can be useful in attracting high-quality employees, in particular millennials who may tend to be concerned with issues such as the environment and social justice (Deloitte, 2017). Consequently, mission statements are often written in uplifting language aiming to inspire employees and customers.

Real life case: putting values into practice

It is one thing to publish a mission statement in a company brochure or a declaration of corporate social responsibility. It is quite another to practise the values set out in such a statement. Yet increasingly, according to Chatterji and Toffel, organizations, and particularly CEOs, are more inclined to speak out about social and political issues such as race, sexual orientation, gender, immigration, and the environment (Chatterji and Toffel, 2018). In what Chatterji and Toffel call CEO activism, business leaders such as Tim Cook of Apple or Marc Benioff of Salesforce are publicly engaging in political issues. For instance, in the wake of American school shootings, the Dick's Sporting Goods chain of stores announced they were 'going to take a stand' by not selling firearms to those under 21. PayPal stated they would cancel their plans for a new global operations centre in Charlotte, North Carolina, due to the threatened 'bathroom law', which they saw as discriminating against transgendered individuals. CEOs of 14 major food companies, including Mars, Ben & Jerry's, Nestlé, and Coca-Cola, co-signed an open letter calling on world governments to address climate change (Ceres, 2016).

Organizations are increasingly expected to take action. As Marc Benioff of cloud computing company Salesforce states, 'CEOs have to realize that Millennials are coming into the organization and expecting the CEO to represent the values of that organization. That's why every CEO has to be in touch with those values' (quoted in Chatterji and Toffel, 2018). Yet critics argue that such practices are often more public relations stunts than real change. For instance, Nestlé were a cosignatory on the letter about climate change, yet they still use palm oil in many of their products, which leads to the destruction of the rain forest (see Chapter 17 for a discussion).

While mission statements have been highly popular with senior management, they are not always accepted by employees. Sometimes many of the employees simply pay lip service to them or do not treat them seriously (Bart, 1997). While the following mission statements might sound inspiring, when we investigate what happened to the companies, they can sound rather hollow:

Respect, Integrity, Communication and Excellence (Enron—who went bankrupt after committing planned accounting fraud) (Seeger and Ulmer, 2003).

Our mission is to build unrivalled partnerships with and value for our clients, through the knowledge, creativity, and dedication of our people, leading to superior results for our shareholders (Lehman Brothers—who went bankrupt in 2008, sparking the worldwide financial crisis) (cited in Schmidt and Rosenberg, 2015: 31).

True mission statements, therefore, are not what is written down but what people actually do. As Tony Hsieh, CEO of the successful Zappos, says, 'Values are not what we put on paper; they're what people do and how they feel doing it' (quoted in Michelli, 2012: 16).

What makes an organization's culture?

The culture of any organization has many components, some of which can be easily observed and others that the members may be unaware of. These may include rites, rituals, and ceremonies; informal behaviours and exchanges; and various kinds of symbol. There may also be more than one culture present within the organization.

Rites, rituals, and ceremonies

Ending the meeting, Simon Chance looks across at Sue Marshall. 'Thank you everyone. As some of you will be aware, we have a new member of the Junction Hotel family with us today. I am sure you will join me in our customary greeting,' at which point they burst out clapping. 'We also can congratulate Sam, who has been here 25 years as one of our receptionists.'

'You get less for murder!' Effingham shouts out to some laughter. 'It is my pleasure,' continues Chance undeterred, 'to offer her our Junction Hotel commemorative plaque and a special meal for two at our expense.' Again, everyone claps.

Deeper aspects of the culture are expressed through rites, rituals, and ceremonies. These may be formal events, such as the graduation ceremony, or informal activities, such as initiation ceremonies that members of a team do to each other. Rites, rituals, and ceremonies all play an important role in creating and reinforcing an organization's culture.

A **rite**, according to Trice and Beyer, is a 'Relatively elaborate, dramatic, planned set of activities that consolidate various forms of cultural expressions into one event, which is carried out through social interactions, usually for the benefit of an audience' (1984: 655). In other words, rites are events which express important parts of the culture. They include rites of renewal, such as teambuilding; rites of conflict reduction, to restore harmony; and rites of passage, when someone passes from one life or working stage to another. Trice and Beyer give the example of how new army recruits 'receive uniforms and severe haircuts, are taught to make their beds in a ritualized fashion, learn to salute and march, are repeatedly humiliated and told to behave differently than in the past, and are generally stripped of past identities and statuses' (1984: 658). Another type are rites of integration, which make everyone feel part of the group: for example, an office Christmas party where everyone eats and drinks together, symbolizing togetherness. Such parties can also provide both a release from rules and a reinforcement of them:

> Otherwise deviant behaviors, such as the acting out of sexual and other attractions, are sanctioned. Such occasions thus provide a break from the strict codes of behavior normally enforced, and they tend to reassert the importance and rightness of these codes by the clearly temporary and exceptional basis on which the usual prohibitions have been lifted.

(Trice and Beyer, 1984: 663)

However, as Bell and King (2010) point out, some of these rites of integration can equally exclude certain individuals and groups, reinforcing existing power relations and masculine values.

Ceremonies are a formal and symbolic way of celebrating the key organizational values and provide senior management with the opportunity to publicly support actions they think are positive. Universities have many formal ceremonies, like graduation, inaugural lectures for a new professor, and annual dinners at academic conferences at which people give speeches. They are set-piece occasions for the organization to express publicly values they hold.

Unlike planned events, such as ceremonies, **rituals** are more like habits that most members do without thinking. As Ott states, rituals 'are the mundane, systematic, stylized, programmed routines of daily organizational life that tell an alert observer about an organizational culture' (1989: 36). While they often start for particular purposes, '[f]requently, the meanings and purposes of powerful rites and rituals are forgotten and take on lives of their own' (Ott, 1989: 37) and become solely of symbolic importance. They are ways for management to be socialized (i.e. taught to see the world), and for employees to know how to behave and what is seen as important.

While many rites of passage are official, many organizations have informal (but often sanctioned) rites of passage, such as initiation ceremonies. They sometimes involve fairly extreme activities, like drinking a lot of alcohol or doing something humiliating in front of the rest of the group. They are often displays of strength and endurance, but can also be practices to humiliate the new recruit and, through this, stress the importance of belonging to the group. A great example of this is provided by Ackroyd and Crowdy (1990), who provide a fascinating account of a slaughterhouse. They describe practical jokes such as filling the boots of those considered to be working too hard with blood at room temperature, and spraying blood on their clothes, as signs of defiance to produce togetherness and common identity.

Visit the online resources and take a look at the extension material for Chapter 7 for more information on rites of passage and initiation ceremonies.

 Real life case: apple-bobbing for dead rats—student initiation ceremonies

The Rugby Football Union (FRU) are concerned that the extreme initiation ceremonies within many university teams are putting their students off joining the university rugby club. For instance, students at the University of Bath were reported to have been blindfolded, told to put their out hands and then urinated on. Loughborough University students were instructed to drink four litres of cider and then be sick in a bucket. Whoever was last then had the vomit thrown at him. At another unnamed university, players had to 'fish dead rats out of buckets with their mouths' (Lowe, 2017). In Australia, freshers are reported to be forced to drink beer off older male students' genitals (Funnell, 2018). One student complained 'we were expected to drink whatever they asked us to and I'm not talking alcohol and strip naked whilst they dragged our knees across the street' (cited in Myall, 2017).

Have you been involved in an initiation ceremony? If so, did you feel you had to take part? Did you feel more part of the group afterwards?

Informal culture

Only joking: the power of stories and jokes

 Running case: Sue is warned about Effingham

The meeting ends and Sue goes for coffee with the other receptionist. 'Who was the guy who made the joke about getting longer for working here than murder?' she enquires.

'Oh, that will be Effingham,' pipes up Mandy. 'Watch out for him. I don't know if this is true, but he once killed a chicken with his bare hands.'

'Really?' Sue replies in a shocked tone.

'No, not really ... but I wouldn't put it past him,' Mandy says with a smirk.

Have you ever heard someone say 'I'm only joking' when they have just criticized someone? Claiming it to be 'just a joke' allows the speaker to pass off the negative message in the criticism. Such 'jokes' allow us to make criticisms in indirect ways (Pouthier, 2017). Hidden in jokes and stories are messages about how to behave and the values of the organization. Sometimes managers and leaders use them formally, to put images of how a company wants to be seen. They are more commonly informal, such as when colleagues tell new recruits stories about things that have happened in the organization.

Stories communicate many things, such as about people that have done well—organizational heroes—demonstrating values that the employee should follow. They can also be about villains or scapegoats, acting as warnings about what is considered bad behaviour. Stories communicate how the organization sees itself, such as being cautious or brave, steady or dynamic. They are also based on certain metaphors, such as the organization as a family, school, or prison (Morgan, 2006), subtly capturing the underlying assumptions of the members of the organization. They are particularly useful for new members to learn the informal rules and expectations of an organization.

Jokes, like stories, are a powerful way to communicate culture. They can produce a positive, harmonious environment which can aid collaboration (Wang et al., 2016). They can be used to teach employees the right way to behave, e.g. through subtle teasing to indicate when someone acts in the wrong way.

For example, in describing her experience working as a stockbroker, Thompson states:

> Being given a nickname was a rite of passage; whether racist, sexist, homophobic or just insulting, nicknames were willingly accepted by the recipients and thrown around with little thought as to what was actually being said, or whether it was in violation of some code of conduct in the Company handbook.

(2010: 51)

Jokes are, therefore, like stories but with the added advantage that they allow us to say things that we would not otherwise be allowed to, acting as a 'licence' for negative communication (Collinson, 1988). Consequently, through jokes certain home truths can be told or, for staff resistant to management, can weaken management's authority (Taylor and Bain, 2003).

Wang et al. (2016) argue that while laughter enables teams to communicate more, they found that the pattern of laughter impacts the communication within the team. Researching the communication patterns of airline pilots and their crew, they found that where laughter was expressed primarily by one pilot the crew's communication was more open and effective than when both pilots laughed. Shared laughter, they argue, shows signs of agreeableness (where everyone wants to be liked) and therefore such communication is less likely to be honest.

👁 Research insight: joking as communication

Pouthier, V. (2017). Griping and joking as identification rituals and tools for engagement in cross-boundary team meetings. *Organization Studies* 38 (6), 753–74.

Palliative care in hospitals, where dying patients' treatment and conditions are managed, is not a setting in which you would expect much humour. Yet, as Vanessa Pouthier's study of team meetings in a large US hospital shows, not only was joking commonplace, it also helped to bond the people working in the hospital. Pouthier conducted observations and interviews over one year and found two main types of humour: griping (complaining) rituals, in which team members vented about deep issues, and joking rituals, which were more light-hearted and intended to be humorous. In both of these forms of humour, Pouthier states, it was not always obvious to her what was humorous, and it was largely only the laughter after someone spoke that enabled Pouthier to realize that a humorous remark was made.

→

The griping rituals were often about patients, and their families, that the team members found challenging, but also other healthcare provider who made decisions that the multi-functioning team did not agree with. These gripes allowed the members to externalize feelings of frustration (burnout is a particularly common issue in palliative care) but also allowed them to develop a sense of 'we-ness', feeling together as a team and a shared moral identity. It was a way to acknowledge they shared the same struggles and to feel 'closer to one another, despite differences in occupational roles and priorities' (Pouthier, 2017: 762).

Joking rituals were more light-hearted than griping, often mocking the team's own expertise and status. These jokes, which presented certain patients as challenging, allowed the team members to challenge their own and others' expertise and also produced a shared sense of belonging. Joking, Pouthier argued, 'gives team members an outlet for the stress and frustration' that their roles include (2017: 767) but also to make criticisms in a non-threatening way.

Both griping and joking, Pouthier concludes, are ways to help the team feel closer together, more emotionally attuned, and to get rid of negative emotions in an acceptable way.

Breaking taboos—the hidden rules of culture

Q Running case: Sue breaks a cultural taboo

'Do you remember the time he chopped off all those rabbit's heads and put them on the top table?' recounts Mandy.

'Yep, and when he pulled the guts out of that duck and threw them across the room when Chance walked in,' recalls Sam.

'He's a player, isn't he,' Mandy declares.

'He seems that way with the waiting staff as well,' Sue pipes up, trying to join in. 'I saw the way he looked at that blonde.' Suddenly, the room goes quiet and Sue goes red, knowing that she has said something wrong. Mandy quickly changes the subject.

'What did I say wrong?' Sue asks Mandy when everyone leaves.

'Oh, it's nothing, dear,' Mandy answers, clearly uncomfortable. 'Just be careful … the "blonde" is Simon Chance's daughter.'

While stories and jokes can give access to the hidden culture, it is often only by actually breaking the rules that employees discover deeper rules. These rules are not written down and, indeed, many of the organizational members are not aware that they exist.

American sociologist Harold Garfinkel developed a method called 'breaching experiments' to uncover cultural rules that we often do not know about. He asked research participants to breach (step over or break) certain social norms and disrupt shared realities (i.e. the common ways that people think). This is one of Garfinkel's examples:

The victim waved his hand cheerily.

(S) How are you?

(E) How am I in regard to what? My health, my finances, my school work, my peace of mind, my … ?

(S) (Red in the face and suddenly out of control.) Look! I was just trying to be polite. Frankly, I don't give a damn how you are.

(Garfinkel, 1967: 42–4, cited in Feldman, 1995: 10)

Garfinkel's work demonstrates that there are numerous social norms that we often only learn by breaking them. They are important for understanding culture because they reveal the hidden, unspoken side of organizational life and the deep values that are unexpressed. Culture is thus continually created and recreated through conversations, actions, and meanings expressed by all organizational members.

? Review questions

Describe	What is meant by the 'underlying values' within an organizational culture?
Explain	How can underlying values be uncovered?
Explain	What role does humour play in organizational culture?
Analyse	Why are the underlying values within an organization hard to change?

The symbolic side of culture

🔍 Running case: Gold Standard Service

Two weeks later

'Eighty percent of your staff now know your mission statement,' declares Wickham proudly, 'and the Gold Standard Service is ready to be rolled out. How do you feel it is going?'

'Good, I think we've cracked it,' Chance replies.

Most management interventions to change corporate culture focus on the physical surroundings, the espoused (spoken) organizational aims, and stories about the organization's history and actions of the leaders; they rarely go to the deeper parts of the organizational culture (the depths of Edgar Schein's iceberg). To access these deeper parts we need to access the symbolic side of organizations—the language, metaphors, and stories. This deepest layer of the culture could be seen as the organization's subconscious. It shapes how organizational members experience the world, but they are not always aware of its existence. In order to get to this level of culture, stories are interpreted, and techniques from psychology and the therapeutic arts are used.

Mary Jo Hatch (1993) argues that while Schein's model is relevant and useful as it provides a guide for understanding culture, it would be more useful if it also focused on symbols and symbolic behaviour. While Schein (and other cultural typologies) describe culture based on observations of artefacts, beliefs and values, and basic assumptions, Hatch claims her model gives a more sophisticated understanding by presenting the dynamism of organizational culture, linking the values, artefacts, symbols, and assumptions more explicitly together (see Figure 7.2 and Table 7.7). The Hatch cultural dynamics framework demonstrates how cultural assumptions 'reveal themselves in the perceptions, cognitions, and emotions of organizational members' (Hatch, 1993: 662). Culture, in this sense, is continually constructed and reconstructed, where meaning is created and recreated.

Figure 7.2 The cultural dynamics model.
Source: Hatch (2013). Reproduced with permission of The Academy of Management.

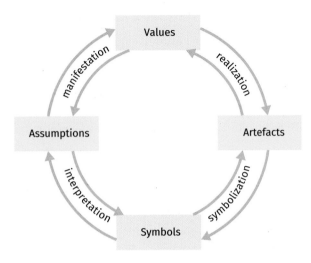

Table 7.7 The cultural dynamics model

Feature	Description	Example	How to study it
Manifestations	The process through which people become aware of their values without necessarily being aware of the underlying assumptions	Assumption is people are hard-working; this manifests itself in empowering practices that make members feel positive about the organization (values)	Explore how expectations 'come to be' within the organization: what emotions and perceptions are encouraged or constrained
Realization	The process of translating values into artefacts (rites, rituals, stories, and humour)	Prize-giving events (artefact) for best employees to celebrate hard work (values)	Observation—to see how artefacts are used in everyday practice and how values change
Symbols	Some artefacts are symbols because they come to mean something extra to organizational members; they represent consciously or unconsciously a more abstract meaning, e.g. a bunch of flowers symbolizing love	Receiving a certificate for employee of the month (artefact) is seen as a sign of promotion potential (symbolic) as extra meaning is placed on the certificate	Observation—a researcher immersing themselves in the field to see how these artefacts are interpreted by the members
Interpretation	How organizational members use their assumptions to experience and give meaning to the symbols	The interpretation, thinking, and feelings that an organizational member goes through when receiving the employee of the month award	How symbols are moulded by organizational members, through observation, interviews, and analysing the words people use (discourse analysis)

Rosen, M. 1985. Breakfast at Spiro's: dramaturgy and dominance. *Journal of Management* 11: 31–48.

In this influential article Michael Rosen (1985) provides an excellent account of how these rites of passage, rituals, and ceremonies are played out in practice. He provides a detailed description of the annual 'agency breakfast' for an advertising agency, Spiro's. It is held in a luxury hotel; all the 'associates' are formally dressed, eating off fine china, being served eggs Benedict by suited servers—demonstrating an elite image. They listen to speeches which highlight successes and explain away failure, and celebrate the awards they have won.

Rosen sees this breakfast not simply as an annual gathering, but as an opportunity for management to present certain messages and use symbols to put across key messages. These include being an elite (eating fine breakfasts at a quality hotel—the 'good life' that members aspire to); presenting members with a gift each time they reach five years' working for the company, symbolizing the importance of loyalty; and explicitly stating their values: 'laid-back people have no place in this agency ... Drive is what it takes to win. Get drive or get out of the kitchen ... I want people who want to win' (1985: 45). Rosen's case demonstrates the importance of being able to read these cultural clues.

250

Subcultures and professional cultures

We tend to think of organizations having one culture, but some, particularly large organizations, may have many subcultures. Subcultures are smaller groups within the organization that have their own distinctive cultural characteristics, including their own rites and rituals, language, norms, etc. They can develop informally (e.g. social networks) and formally (e.g. departments). In large multinational corporations they may be based on national differences (see Chapter 16) or different internal histories. Similarly, in chain stores different branches can develop their own distinct cultures based around regional cultures, branch histories, local practices, or the influence of a strong leader. Different departments can have distinct cultures, often produced because of the professions they represent (e.g. accounting might be more cautious than, say, marketing), as well as developing internal histories.

 Real life case: organizational culture at Royal Bank of Scotland

Over the years prior to its near-collapse in 2008, the Royal Bank of Scotland (RBS) grew considerably through buying up other banks and financial institutions, not only in the UK but internationally. The group spanned different business lines (high-street and investment banking), as well as different continents (such as Europe, North America, and Asia). They also represented different companies with their own backgrounds and histories.

In an exclusive interview for this book, RBS's then CEO Stephen Hester stated: 'the types of people we have serving customers in our branches in the UK might be completely differ-

→

⟶

ent from traders sitting in a trading desk in Tokyo owing to the location, culture, and type of activity'. But, he concluded:

> I do not think it is desirable or possible to have a single culture across such a diverse set of inputs. So in the end what you really find is the majority of the culture is specific to the business unit and the geography and its history. Then you have some things that cross businesses and geographies that would be more shared by the senior management team.

Source: Author interview with Stephen Hester, Royal Bank of Scotland, February 2012.

Visit the online resources and take a look at the extension material for Chapter 7 to read the full interview with Stephen Hester.

One reason organizations can have multiple subcultures is they have different professions with their own values and outlooks. Raelin argues that often professionals are more loyal towards their profession than to the organization they are working for (Raelin, 1986). For instance, engineers might be interested in the advancing science, creating an elegant design, or their own pet project, rather than profit for the company. Similarly, in areas such as the National Health Service, doctors' aims are often in conflict with management targets (Robinson, 2012).

Different subcultures can be a challenge for those managing organizations, as they have to work with a range of professionals with their distinct values and ways of looking at the world. In order to be successful the manager needs to understand these different perspectives and find ways to communicate with various subcultures.

Melting the iceberg: culture and the Fourth Industrial Revolution

Think back to Schein's model of organizational culture. It is often represented as an iceberg: a large, solid, and slow-to-change object. While this metaphor works well for the traditional organization, increasingly this image of stability is less appropriate for contemporary workplace, particularly within the Fourth Industrial Revolution (see Chapter 4). Increasingly, not all workers go in to work every day as permanent employees of an organization. Many are now remote workers. For the traditional worker, who is onsite and paid directly by the company, it is relatively easy to pick up the culture; but the remote worker, who for instance works from home, does not have the opportunity to directly observe the social norms of the organization and can only pick up such information from electronic communication such as websites and emails.

The situation is even more extreme for 'gig economy' workers, such as those that do ad hoc work through apps like TaskRabbit. Gig economy workers often only interact with the organization through an app. Indeed, they might only work for the organization a few hours a week and even go between multiple employers in one day. Work, in this sense, is fluid, ever-changing, and flexible. This gives such workers a different type of relationship to the organization. According to a recent article by Petriglieri and colleagues, gig economy workers experience both loneliness and freedom. Rather than seeing themselves as integral to the organization, they see themselves, particularly those in more high-level professions, e.g. writers, as a brand that can be marketed (Petriglieri et al., 2018). They also struggle to resist management requests and to organize collective action, as they lack physical proximity (although increasingly they are developing their own platforms, including WhatsApp groups, to organize their own resistance).

There is currently little research on organizational culture and the Fourth Industrial Revolution, or consideration of how companies are seeking to install a culture when much of their workforce is fluid, flowing between different organizations and tasks. It may be, as the Fourth Industrial Revolution becomes more prominent, that this becomes an increasingly important question for organizational behaviour theorists and practitioners to grapple with.

Can organizational culture really be managed?

Throughout this chapter we have seen attempts by organizational managers and consultants to categorize, understand, and change culture to improve performance. In the view exemplified by Peters and Waterman, a strong, i.e. unified, culture performs better, gives the employees a sense of purpose, and increases job satisfaction. However, this view has been heavily criticized.

A mere two years after Peters and Waterman (1982) published their *In search of excellence*, the magazine *Business Week* (1984) printed an article arguing that a third of all Peters and Waterman's 'excellent' companies were performing poorly. Similarly, many (e.g. Willmott, 1993) have criticized Peters and Waterman's work, arguing that it lacks conceptual development and did not really investigate the values and beliefs of the staff; rather, the authors took the management rhetoric as true and failed to investigate how it was interpreted by the staff.

Indeed, further questions have been raised recently about the research that underpinned *In search of excellence*. In an article for *Fast Company*, Tom Peters states they 'faked the data'. This is not to say that they made it all up, but that rather than using a 'scientific' approach, the theorizing was developed by gut instinct (Peters, 2001).

Many academics (e.g. Meek, 1988) have argued that the way many of these management gurus have used the idea of culture trivializes it by exploring only the aspects that managers can control. They argue that organizational culture is far more complex and richer than simply a tool for management and, as a result, the research actually reduces our understanding of organizations.

Led by Linda Smircich, these academics state that the underlying assumption of these mainstream management views is that culture is something the organization *has*, i.e. a possession (1983) that can be changed and controlled. This is from the structural-functionist perspective that aims for unity and consensus. Culture is something owned and designed by the top management and available for manipulation (Meek, 1988: 455).

 Visit the online resources and take a look at the extension material for Chapter 7 for more information about the structural-functionist perspective.

Furthermore, Lynn Meek (1988) has argued that this perspective, while borrowing the language of anthropology, has not used this theory appropriately, has drawn from a very limited range of the literature, and has mutated the theory by over-emphasizing the aspects of unity and control.

The alternative view sees culture as something the organization *is* (Smircich, 1983): a root metaphor, a way of looking at the world—everything can be seen as culture. This view does not see organizational culture as something separate from the organization available for one group (management) to control, but as part of the organization. Culture, therefore, is not owned by the management: everyone is involved in creating it and no group has power to define it. Rather, it emerges over time and through negotiation (Table 7.8).

The problem of seeing culture as something the organization *has* is emphasized in an account by the academics and business consultants Deal and Kennedy (1984) (who developed the model we saw earlier in the chapter). They describe how after giving a presentation to the board about culture, the chairman claimed it to be the finest presentation he had heard in ten years and then turned to his chief executive officer.

Table 7.8 Culture as something the organization has or is? (developed from Smircich, 1983)

Organizational culture is something the organization ...	... has	... is
Culture is	a property of management	a social process
Sees culture as	a controllable independent variable	everything that the organization is
Produced by	the leader	negotiation of the group
Culture produces	harmony and consensus	conflict
Researchers look for	a single organizational culture	multiple and contested realities
Culture is useful as	a management tool	a way of making sense of reality
Cultural change is produced	by the management	through interaction and shared meaning

'George,' he said forcefully, 'I want a culture installed here next Monday.'

'With all due respect,' we interrupted, 'we believe you have a culture here now; that's one of our key points.'

'Bulls**t!' said the chairman. 'We don't have one, and as you pointed out, that's the problem. George, I want a culture here and I want it now—by next week. Your butt is on the line.'

We left.

(1984: 21)

This story illustrates the difficulty of the managerialist perspective. The senior managers thought that culture is something they could simply 'have' and that could be ordered in by the following week, like buying a machine. They failed to see that their organization already had a culture and, furthermore, that it is not something that management can simply control, but is integral to the fabric of the organization.

The dark side of culture

Running case: is it really Gold Standard?

'Well, that was a waste of time,' Josh states to Toby on their way out of another Wednesday morning meeting. 'I mean they keep going on about this Gold Standard Service, but I don't see anything different.'

'More than that,' says Toby in agreement, 'they keep cutting back on the things that would make a difference to us, like giving more time before serving to get everything ready, rather than quizzing us on the mission statement.'

Josh smiles at him. 'Well, I pretty much ignore the whole thing anyway. It's just a fad. It will be a new thing in a couple of weeks—mark my words.'

Hugh Willmott argues that organizational culture is a form of control. By getting employees to believe in the values of the organization and winning their 'hearts and minds', corporate culture, he argues, is 'governance of the employee's soul' (Willmott, 1993: 517) and a way of getting employees to discipline themselves. According to Willmott, because they believe in the organization's mission, employees lose their critical faculties and will accept things that are not in their best interests. Willmott argues that corporate culture is therefore a way for management to extend their control. Instead of controlling employees' bodies (as in Taylorism—see Chapter 3), corporate culture controls people's hearts, minds, and souls.

Therefore, while organizational culture is presented by its supporters as progressive and more humane (as previously discussed), from this critical perspective culture is controlling. The unified culture presented by those such as Peters and Waterman 'systematically suppresses ideas and practices that might problematize the authority of core corporate values' (Willmott, 1993: 531). Willmott goes on to compare the practices of these strong cultures to totalitarian regimes where alternative perspectives are not tolerated. 'Those who kick against the monoculture [single standardized culture] are "moved sideways" or they are expelled.' As Peters and Waterman put it bluntly: 'The excellent companies are marked by very strong cultures, so strong that you either buy into their norms or get out. There's no halfway house for most people in the excellent companies' (1982: 77).

Some of the dark side of organizational culture can also be seen in the work of Edger Schein. Schein developed his ideas of organizational culture through his experiences of a prisoner of war camp (Schein, 1961). Schein highlights the importance of peer pressure in shaping the action of an individual. Chan et al. show the similarities between the techniques that Schein observed in the prisoner of war camp and modern organizational techniques (Chan et al., 2018). These include role modelling, peer pressure, performance assessment, and reward systems (see Chan et al., 2018: 195).

A modern example of this is Netflix (see the 'Real life case' earlier in the chapter). Netflix not only have an explicit cultural statement, they also tie it into performance measurement, which means that only the most successful employees stay within the organization. On the one hand, this approach is very honest, as the norms and expectations are explicitly stated by the company. On the other, it gives little room for resistance or opposition. Throughout the document workers are instructed to put Netflix first, even when it goes against their personal interest. This is echoed in a modern Chinese company researched by Gore in which 'Enterprise Party committees are to "encourage workers to work hard and love the enterprises as if their own"' (Gore, 2011: 96). One Chinese company does this by getting workers to recite in unison the company declaration, another through board game nights and a company trivia quiz. It is these everyday practices, Chan and colleagues argue, that 'induce usefulness, concordance, and docility' (2018: 201), teaching the employees to follow orders. Organizational culture, therefore, could be seen as a more subtle form of control.

Read through Netflix's culture statement. How might Hugh Willmott critique it? In what ways might cultural management represent a prisoner of war camp or Big Brother from George Orwell's *Nineteen eighty-four*?

⟳ Real life case: the Presidents Club

The Presidents Club Charity Dinner was a male-only event which was attended by some of the most powerful men in the world: peers, politicians, oligarchs, property tycoons, film producers, and chief executives. Taking place at London's exclusive five-star Dorchester Hotel, it featured auctions with prizes including meeting influential people such as the former UK foreign

→

secretary, Boris Johnson, to raise money for charities such as the British Olympic Association and Great Ormond Street Hospital (Marriage, 2018). It was also a great way for people from high society to network together.

Yet in early 2018 the *Financial Times* published an exposé on the club's secretive annual dinner. Undercover reporter Madison Marriage stated 'All of the women were told to wear skimpy black outfits with matching underwear and high heels. At an after-party many host-esses—some of them students earning extra cash—were groped, sexually harassed and prop-ositioned' (Marriage, 2018). It was a place where sexual harassment was common-place (Lee et al., 2018) including one man exposing his penis (Marriage, 2018). Prizes included 'A boob job for the missus' and after the auction the entertainment featured 'a troupe of exotic dancers' (Thompson, 2018).

The exposé raised questions about the culture of the Presidents Club and the City of London more generally. According to the *Financial Times* finance editor Patrick Jenkins, 'Being un-PC [politically correct] is seen as a badge of honour among swaths of the City, particularly veterans from its middle ranks for whom equal rights for women are inimical and the promotion of diversity is faddish' (Jenkins, 2018). Soon after the scandal broke, many of the attendees distanced themselves from the event and the Presidents Club announced its closure.

The fact that the Presidents Club existed for so long without anyone questioning it shows how its culture, which many rightly considered shocking when it was exposed, was taken for granted as acceptable by many who participated. This type of culture, in which many powerful men networked, not only was degrading for many of the women who participated, but also excluded many women working in business from the potential networking opportunities that events like this afforded. It shows a dark side of culture that often doesn't get reported.

 How would you have felt working in that environment? The Presidents Club ran from 1985 to 2018. How did its culture allow it to continue so long?

255

While Hugh Willmott presents the dark side of organizational culture as leaving little room for escape, other critical theorists stress the opportunities for resistance. For instance, David Collinson (1992) presents a case study of an engineering firm in the north of England, which was originally a family-run business. The American-run company that had taken over the firm wanted to bring about a culture change, from a grimy, complacent, and oppositional culture to one which is more dynamic and based on greater trust and harmony between workers and management. As part of this, they painted the factory walls in a bright white and instituted a newsletter. The first newsletter had the headline 'Call Me Barney'—a reference to the new boss's attempt to engender an informal, first-name culture. However, following its publication, a doctored version of the newsletter appeared on the union notice-board with the headline 'Bulls**t from Barney' (Collinson, 1992: 13).

Other commentators have also questioned the extent to which employees internalize an official culture. They argue that many employees pay lip service to the cultural change programmes but sometimes actively, and often passively, resist the official organizational culture. In other words, these commentators question if employees really believe in these cultural programmes. Professionals, in particular, often believe they have a calling and are thus less likely to tolerate management constraints.

Review questions

Describe	What is a subculture?
Explain	What is the difference between seeing culture as something the organization *is* and seeing culture as something it *has*?
Analyse	Consider the view that culture is something the organization *is*. How does this view challenge mainstream management thinking?
Apply	What do cases such as 'Call me Barney' tell us about how employees can resist cultural control?

Connecting case and theory

Our chapter began with Sue Marshall nervously thinking about her first day at Junction Hotel. Of the many questions and concerns she had, what the hotel will be like and how she will fit in were at the forefront of her mind. What Marshall was really concerned about was the culture of Junction Hotel and if she would quickly be able to understand, learn, and fit in with the formal and informal rules that shape how the hotel (indeed any organization) works.

We then saw Simon Chance going to a business seminar and understanding the value of **organizational culture** from a different point of view: that is, as a source of competitive advantage. This view sees culture as something the organization *has* (Smircich, 1983), a resource that can be used to achieve greater levels of productivity. Indeed, the concept of culture is one that management consultants, from Peters and Waterman (1982) onwards, have presented as something that senior managers can control, an approach that has led to multiple models and toolkits for understanding and changing culture (Giorgi et al., 2015). Culture is seen as a tool that may be used to increase a sense of belonging and commitment to the organization. For proponents such as Peters and Waterman it is an alternative approach to managing organizations because it moves beyond simply controlling people by telling them what to do, and engages their hearts and minds.

Chance therefore took a culture survey to understand what type of culture Junction Hotel has. This typology is one of the tools that consultants, and some academics, use to diagnose culture. Chance hoped, through making these changes, to be able to create top-down change.

However, as we see, **cultural change** is rarely as straightforward as these management consultants promise. Firstly we see that **informal culture**, such as jokes and stories, are not just in the control of management but also the workers as well. Through these symbolic mechanisms workers can, for example, express criticism but pass it off as a joke (Pouthier, 2017). There are often hidden, informal rules of culture that you pick up only when you have been part of the organization for some time.

We see, therefore, a struggle between management trying to impose culture, through **cultural change** programmes and **mission statements**, and workers' attempts at resisting. The managerial perspective, demonstrated by the management consultant Mark Wickham, sees culture as a tool for binding organizational members together for a common purpose. Culture is thus something the organization *has*, and it *can be managed*. The opposite perspective, which can be seen in how some of the employees react to these culture change initiatives, is that culture is shared and negotiated, constantly in flux, and continually interpreted by individual members. Culture is thus something the organization *is*, and it *cannot be managed*.

Finally, critical researchers have questioned the social consequences of **cultural change** programmes on the well-being of employees. Some see culture as something that controls and conditions employees to the extent that any who resist are excluded. Yet as we see in Toby and Josh's reaction to being forced to learn the **mission statement**, employees can resist these cultural programmes, and often take a position of cynical distance from them.

Culture shapes much of what we say and do, often in ways that we are not conscious of, so that there is much going on below the surface that we often do not see.

Further reading

Schein, E. 2010. *Organizational culture and leadership.* Jossey Bass: San Francisco.

A popular management writer and consultant, Schein provides a good overview of organizational culture from a management viewpoint. He offers ways to understand culture and practical tools to change it.

Giorgi, S., Lockwood, C., and Glynn, M.A. 2015. The many faces of culture: Making sense of 30 years of research on culture in organization studies. *Academy of Management Annals* 9 (1): 1–54.

A detailed review of the last 30 years of research on organizational culture, which the authors bring together into a framework. They argue that while there has been some good work in the field recently, it has fragmented and lost focus.

Chatman, J.A., and O'Reilly, C.A. 2016. Paradigm lost: Reinvigorating the study of organizational culture. *Research in Organizational Behavior* 36: 199–224.

Similarly to Giorgi et al., Chatman and O'Reilly argue that the concept of culture needs reinvigorating. This article provides a more accessible overview of the concept of culture and proposes areas for future research.

Smircich, L. 1983. Concepts of culture and organizational analysis. *Administrative Science Quarterly* 28 (3): 339–58.

This highly influential article provides a rigorous critique of the underlying assumptions of the notion that culture is something that managers can control. Smircich introduces notions from anthropology to offer a richer way of understanding culture.

Willmott, H. 1993. Strength is ignorance; slavery is freedom: Managing culture in modern organizations. *Journal of Management Studies* 30 (4): 515–52.

Provides a fascinating critical reading of the corporate culture literature. Willmott argues that there is a dark side of organizational culture, as it results in employees disciplining themselves.

References

Ackroyd, S., and Crowdy, P. 1990. Can culture be managed? Working with raw material: The case of the English slaughtermen. *Personnel Review* 19 (5): 3–13.

Alvesson, M., and Sveningsson, S. 2015. *Changing organizational culture: Cultural change work in progress.* Routledge: Abingdon.

Amazon. 2018. We pioneer. Available at: https://www.amazon.jobs/working/working-amazon

ASOS. 2018. We are authentic, brave and creative to our core. Available at: https://www.asosplc.com/

Bart, C. 1997. Sex, lies and mission statements. *Business Horizons* November–December: 9–18.

Bass, B.M., and Avolio, B.J. 1993. Transformational leadership: A response to critiques. In: Chemers, M.M. (ed.) *Leadership theory and research: Perspectives and directions.* Academic Press: New York.

Bell, E., and King, D. 2010. The elephant in the room: Critical management studies conferences as a site of body pedagogics. *Management Learning* 41 (4): 429–42.

Bock, L. 2015. *Work rules! Insights from inside Google that will transform how you live and lead.* John Murray: London.

Boyce, A.S., Nieminen, L.R., Gillespie, M.A., Ryan, A.M., and Denison, D.R. 2015. Which comes first, organizational culture or performance? A longitudinal study of causal priority with automobile dealerships. *Journal of Organizational Behavior* 36 (3): 339–59.

Business Week. 1984. Oops! Who's excellent now? 2867 (5 November): 76–88.

Cameron, K., and Quinn, R.E. 2011. *Diagnosing and changing organizational culture,* 3rd edn. Jossey Bass: London.

Ceres. 2016. Global food and beverage executives call for action on climate and food security at COP22, 17 November. Available at: https://www.ceres.org/news-center/press-releases/global-food-and-beverage-executives-call-action-climate-and-food

Chan, A., Clegg, S., and Warr, M. 2018. Translating intervention: When corporate culture meets Chinese socialism. *Journal of Management Inquiry* 27 (2): 190–203.

Chatman, J.A., and O'Reilly, C.A. 2016. Paradigm lost: Reinvigorating the study of organizational culture. *Research in Organizational Behavior* 36: 199–224.

Chatterji, A.K., and Toffel, M.W. 2018. The new CEO activists: A playbook for polarized political times. *Harvard Business Review* 96 (1): 78–89.

Christie, A. 2015. Lend lease values. Personal communication with Daniel King.

Clark, L. 2002. *Finding a common interest.* Cambridge University Press: Cambridge.

Collins, J.C., and Porras, J.I. 1994. *Built to last: Successful habits of visionary companies.* Harper Collins: New York.

Collinson, D. 1988. Engineering humour: Masculinity, joking and conflict in shopfloor relations. *Organization Studies* 9 (2): 181–99.

Collinson, D. 1992. *Managing the shopfloor: Subjectivity, masculinity and workplace culture.* De Gruyter: Berlin.

Daft, R.L. 1986. *Organization theory and design,* 2nd edn. West: Eagan, MN.

Deal, T.E., and Kennedy, A.A. 1982. *Corporate cultures: The rites and rituals of corporate life.* Penguin Books: Harmondsworth.

Deal, T.E., and Kennedy, A.A. 1984. Tales for the trails: A journey into the existential underbelly of American business. *Hospital Forum* May–June: 16–26.

Deloitte. 2017. The 2017 Deloitte millennial survey. Available at: https://www2.deloitte.com/content/dam/Deloitte/global/Documents/About-Deloitte/gx-deloitte-millennial-survey-2017-executive-summary.pdf

Drucker, P. 1974. *Management: Tasks, responsibilities and practices.* Harper and Row: New York.

Fast Company. 2015. Google London. Available at: http://www.fastcodesign.com/3028909/8-of-googles-craziest-offices (last accessed 22 June 2015).

Feldman, M. 1995. *Strategies for interpreting qualitative data.* Sage: London.

Ferenstein, G. 2013. Read what Facebook's Sandberg calls maybe 'the most important document ever to come out of the valley'. TechCrunch. Available at: https://techcrunch.com/2013/01/31/read-what-facebooks-sandberg-calls-maybe-the-most-important-document-ever-to-come-out-of-the-valley/

Fortune. 2015. 100 best companies to work for 2015. Available at: http://fortune.com/best-companies/ (last accessed 12 August 2015).

Frontczak, M., Schiavon, S., Goins, J., Arens, E., Zhang, H., and Wargocki, P. 2012. Quantitative relationships between occupant satisfaction and satisfaction aspects of indoor environmental quality and building design. *Indoor Air* 22 (2): 119–31.

Funnell, N. 2018. 'Lads' weekend' shame: Sick 'penis drinking' initiation ritual sweeps Aussie unis as new students are forced to guzzle beer off older lads' todgers. *The Sun*, 19 February. Available at: https://www.thesun.co.uk/news/5612810/penis-drinking-initiation-australian-university-ritual-students/

Giorgi, S., Lockwood, C., and Glynn, M.A. 2015. The many faces of culture: Making sense of 30 years of research on culture in organization studies. *Academy of Management Annals*, 9 (1): 1–54.

Google. 2018. Google's mission is to organize the world's information and make it universally accessible and useful. Available at: http://www.google.com/about/company/ (last accessed 16 April 2018).

Gore, L. 2011. *The Chinese Communist Party and China's capitalist revolution: The politicial impact of market*. Routledge: London.

Greenpeace. 2018. Our values. Available at: https://www.greenpeace.org/international/values/.

Handy, C. 2009. *Gods of management: The changing work of organisations*. Arrow Books: London.

Hatch, M. 1992. The symbolics of office design: An empirical exploration. In: Gagliardi, P. (ed.) *Symbolics of corporate artifacts*. De Gruyter: Berlin, pp. 129–43.

Hatch, M.J. 1993. The dynamics of organizational culture. *Academy of Management Review* 18 (4): 657–93.

Hofstede, G. 1991. *Cultures and organizations: Software of the mind*. McGraw-Hill: New York.

Hsieh, T. 2010. *Delivering happiness: A path to profits, passion, and purpose*. Business Plus: New York.

Jenkins, P. 2018. The Presidents Club exposé hints at the City's seedy side. *Financial Times*, 24 January. Available at: https://www.ft.com/content/406dcb40-00e8-11e8-9650-9c0ad2d7c5b5

Kotrba, L.M., Gillespie, M.A., Schmidt, A.M., Smerek, R.E., Ritchie, S.A., and Denison, D.R. 2012. Do consistent corporate cultures have better business performance? Exploring the interaction effects. *Human Relations* 65 (2): 241–62.

Lee, D., Quinn, B., Wood, Z., and Neate, R. 2018. Sex and the City: Life as a hostess in London's gilded halls. *The Guardian*, 27 January. Available at: https://www.theguardian.com/world/2018/jan/27/other-city-events-tainted-by-presidents-club-style-harassment

Lorsch, J.W., and McTague, E. 2016. Culture is not the culprit. *Harvard Business Review* 94 (4): 21.

Lowe, A. 2017. Student initiations are turning players away from rugby, says RFU. *The Times*, 25 October. Available at: https://www.thetimes.co.uk/article/rugby-in-crisis-over-student-initiations-wp82tvkxl

Marriage, M. 2018. Men only: Inside the charity fundraiser where hostesses are put on show. *Financial Times*, 23 January. Available at: https://www.ft.com/content/075d679e-0033-11e8-9650-9c0ad2d7c5b5

McCord, P. 2018. *Powerful: Building a culture of freedom and responsibility*. Silicon Guild: San Francisco.

Meek, L. 1988. Organizational culture: Origins and weaknesses. *Organization Studies* 9 (4): 453–73.

Michelli, J.A. 2012. *The Zappos experience: 5 Principles to inspire, engage, and WOW*. McGraw Hill: New York.

Morgan, G. 2006. *Images of organization*. Sage Publications: Thousand Oaks, CA.

260

Myall, S. 2017. Sickening initiations for university rugby teams include apple bobbing for dead rats and chilli powder 'punishments'. *The Mirror*, 25 October. Available at: https://www.mirror.co.uk/news/real-life-stories/sickening-initiations-university-rugby-teams-11405187

Naranjo-Valencia, J.C., Jiménez-Jiménez, D., and Sanz-Valle, R. 2016. Studying the links between organizational culture, innovation, and performance in Spanish companies. *Revista Latinoamericana de Psicología* 48 (1): 30–41.

Netflix. 2018a. Netflix culture. Available at: https://jobs.netflix.com/culture

Netflix. 2018b. Netflix culture: Freedom and responsibility. Available at: https://www.slideshare.net/reed2001/culture-1798664/35-Hard_Work_Not_Relevant_

Ornstein, S. 1989. The hidden influences of office design. *Academy of Management Executive* 3 (2): 144–7.

Ott, J. 1989. *The organizational culture perspective*. Brooks/Cole Publishing Company: Pacific Grove, CA.

Ouchi, W. 1981. *Theory Z: How American business can meet the Japanese challenge*. Addison-Wesley: New York.

Peters, T. 2001. Tom Peters's true confessions. Available at: http://www.fastcompany.com/magazine/53/peters.html?page=0%2C3 (last accessed 17 June 2012).

Peters, T.J., and Waterman, R.H., Jr. 1982. *In search of excellence: Lessons from America's best run companies*. Harper Row: London.

Petriglieri, G., Ashford, S.J., and Wrzesniewski, A. 2018. Agony and ecstasy in the gig economy: Cultivating holding environments for precarious and personalized work identities. *Administrative Science Quarterly*, published online: https://doi.org/10.1177/0001839218759646.

Pettigrew, A. 1979. On studying organizational cultures. *Administrative Science Quarterly* 24 (4): 570–81.

Pouthier, V. 2017. Griping and joking as identification rituals and tools for engagement in cross-boundary team meetings. *Organization Studies* 38 (6): 753–74.

Raelin, J. 1986. *Clash of cultures: Managers and professionals*. Harvard Business School Press: Boston.

Robinson, S. 2012. GPC warns of 'target culture' as GP commissioning framework revealed. GP Online. Available at: http://www.gponline.com/News/article/1115181/GPC-warns-target-culture-GP-commissioning-framework-revealed/

Roper, J. 2015a. Company culture should come from leaders. *HR Magazine*, 26 May.

Roper, J. 2015b. Leaders still don't understand culture. *HR Magazine*, 4 June.

Rosen, M. 1985. Breakfast at Spiro's, dramaturgy and dominance. *Journal of Management* 11: 31–48.

Schein, E.H. 1961. *Coercive persuasion: A socio-psychological analysis of the brainwashing of American civilian prisoners by the Chinese Communists*. W.W. Norton: New York.

Schein, E.H. 2010. *Organizational culture and leadership*. Jossey Bass: San Francisco.

Schmidt, E., and Rosenberg, J. 2015. *How Google works*. John Murray: London.

Seeger, M.W., and Ulmer, R.R. 2003. Explaining Enron communication and responsible leadership. *Management Communication Quarterly* 17 (1): 58–84.

Sewell, G. 1998. The discipline of teams: The control of team-based industrial work through electronic and peer surveillance. *Administrative Science Quarterly* 43 (2): 397–428.

Smircich, L. 1983. Concepts of culture and organizational analysis. *Administrative Science Quarterly* 28 (3): 339–58.

Smircich, L., and Morgan, G. 1982. Leadership: The management of meaning. *Journal of Applied Behavioural Studies* 18: 257–73.

Starbucks. 2018. *Starbucks: Our mission statement*. Available at: https://www.starbucks.co.uk/about-us/company-information/mission-statement (last accessed 16 April 2018).

Taylor, B. 2014. Why Amazon is copying Zappos and paying employees to quit. *Harvard Business Review*, 15 April.

Taylor, P., and Bain, P. 2003. Subterranean worksick blues: Humour as subversion in two call centres. *Organization Studies* 24 (9): 1487–509.

Thompson, B. 2018. 'A boob job for the missus'—a night at the Presidents Club. *Financial Times*, 23 January. Available at: https://www.ft.com/content/c6c8d488-0060-11e8-9650-9c0ad2d7c5b5

Thompson, V. 2010. *Gross misconduct: My year of excess in the city*. Pocket Books: London.

Tichy, N.M. 1982. Managing change strategically: The technical, political, and cultural keys. *Organizational Dynamics* 11: 59–80.

Tierney, J. 2012. From cubicles, cry for quiet pierces office buzz. *New York Times*, 20 May.

Trice, H., and Beyer, J. 1984. Studying organizational cultures through rites and ceremonials. *Academy of Management Review* 9 (4): 653–69.

Turner, G., and Myerson, J. 1998. *New workspace, new culture: Office design as a catalyst for change*. Gower Publishing Ltd: Aldershot.

Wang, L., Doucet, L., Waller, M., Sanders, K., and Phillips, S. 2016. A laughing matter: Patterns of laughter and the effectiveness of working dyads. *Organization Science* 27 (5): 1142–60.

Wei, W. 2010. Amazon is paying Zappos CEO Tony Hsieh only $36,000. *Business Insider*, 22 October.

Willmott, H. 1993. Strength is ignorance; slavery is freedom: Managing culture in modern organizations. *Journal of Management Studies* 30 (4): 515–52.

Zappos. 2015. About Zappos culture. Available at: http://www.zappos.com/d/about-zappos-culture (last accessed 23 June 2015).

Zappos Insights. 2015. Zappos culture book. Available at: http://www.zapposinsights.com/culture-book (last accessed 25 June 2015).

PART 3

Managing the individual

CHAPTER 8
Personality and individual differences
Can personality be measured?

Chapter overview and learning outcomes

By the end of this chapter you should be able to:

- describe the main features of the nomothetic, ideographic, and social–radical approaches to personality

- describe a variety of models of personality

- explain how personality is measured in organizational settings

- analyse the effectiveness of different selection methods in assessing the personality of candidates for a job

- explain how characteristics of the Fourth Industrial Revolution, including artificial intelligence and big data, are being used to automate personality measurement in contemporary recruitment and selection

Key theorists	
Carl Gustav Jung	Swiss psychoanalyst who noted the distinction between introverted and extraverted personalities
Katharine Cook Briggs and Isobel Briggs Myers	American psychologists who applied Jung's theory to create the Myers–Briggs Type Indicator personality test
Susan Cain	American writer and lecturer who argued for the advantages of the introvert personality within the workplace
Hans Eysenck	German psychologist who noted the role of emotional stability and instability in personality formation
Sigmund Freud	Austrian psychoanalyst who outlined ways in which personalities change and develop

Key terms	
Nomothetic approach	Views personality as a set of measurable traits or types which can be represented on a static framework or model
Personality testing	The use of questionnaires to measure personality, often used in recruitment and selection in organizations
Ideographic approach	Views personality as complex and unique to each individual, and as something which changes through influences from the world around us
Social–radical approach	Recognizes that rather than just being able to measure personality, organizations have an effect upon the personalities of their members

Introduction

🔍 **Running case:** finding new staff

New Vacancy at Junction Hotel
Fitness Centre Duty Manager
Full-time, fixed-term (12 months initially)
Salary negotiable

We are looking for an individual with a big personality to join the team of duty managers at our fitness centre.

Reporting to the Fitness Centre Manager and, on occasions, deputizing, you will be responsible for the day-to-day line management of a team of five full-time fitness centre staff and the recruitment of new staff when necessary.

Working with customers, including delivering personal training sessions, you will also have management and administration responsibilities, including preparation of staff rotas and associated paperwork.

Holding a degree in sports or leisure management, or a related area, you will have at least five years of experience in the leisure and fitness industry, at least two of which should be at management level.

We need an individual who is self-motivated and dynamic, and who can motivate both staff and customers.

Please send CVs and a covering letter to:

Simon Chance
General Manager
Junction Hotel

To what extent do we go into organizations as individuals with our own distinct personalities? So far in this book, theories of management and organization have paid little attention to the perspective of the individual.

- In the rational organization (Chapters 2, 3, 4), the individual is seen as useful only for the precise part they can play on an assembly line, as if they were a cog in the machine. When dealing with a large bureaucracy, such as our bank or even our university, we may feel aggrieved that the organization sees us as a computer record rather than as an individual: 'I am a name, not a number'.

- With the social organization (Chapters 5, 6, 7), a human aspect of the organization is recognized, but only as a part of a larger group or team. Group dynamics have a powerful influence over individual behaviour and perceptions. Anyone who has played sport may feel that they have to put the team before themselves as an individual: 'There is no *I* in *team*.'

In both of these cases the individual is, in one way or another, reduced within a greater entity. However, as we will see in this and the following three chapters, organizations do have an interest in managing people at the level of the individual. Theories of motivation and learning, for example, use psychological knowledge to try to understand how the individual mind works.

In this chapter, we use psychological insights to examine the characteristics that make us distinct individuals, different from other people. It is common to speak of ourselves and others as having a *personality*, a set of behavioural characteristics that identifies us as an individual. We examine three approaches to the study of personality.

- The *nomothetic approach* sees personality as a set of measurable traits or characteristics, and sorts people into particular **personality types** or scales. Such an approach is most familiar in the workplace in the form of personality tests.

- The *ideographic approach* rejects the idea of personality as a set of traits as too simplistic, instead seeing personality as something much more dynamic which develops as a result of our experiences and interactions. People have rich, complex personalities, rather than fitting into a simple personality type.

- The *social–radical approach* sees personality and its definition entirely as a product of society and its organizational and power structures. For example, rather than the workplace simply measuring an individual's personality, as in the nomothetic approach, the workplace plays a part in shaping their personality.

Personality in the recruitment and selection process

Running case: whittling down the candidates

Chance is met by a deluge of paperwork. Over 200 CVs have been submitted for the duty manager job and just over half of them seem to be suitable candidates.

Looking at the covering letters and CVs, Chance realizes that he can't use these alone to create a shortlist. Many letters simply parrot standard phrases, such as 'I am self-motivated', 'I am dedicated to the task', and 'I work well with other people', but what proof is there to back up these statements?

Chance starts to think about how to whittle down the shortlist and draws up a list of characteristics that a successful candidate will need:

- appropriate qualifications and experience
- good organizational skills to manage rotas and similar paperwork
- calmness in a fast-moving work environment
- good leadership skills—motivating and enthusing the team during the course of a shift
- flexibility—prepared to do different tasks at short notice
- an upbeat, motivating personality—especially when greeting customers at reception or engaging them in a personal training session
- good communication abilities to transmit instructions clearly in a fast-paced atmosphere.

The various qualities are drawn up into a person specification which will be put in an application pack and sent to candidates.

Throughout the chapter we will see how individual personalities are assessed by organizations when filling a vacancy, i.e. finding someone with the personality characteristics that are most suitable for that job. While often used together as a phrase, the term *recruitment and selection* refers to two distinct phases of the process of filling a vacancy (French and Rumbles, 2010).

- **Recruitment** is where the vacancy is publicized in order to generate a pool of applicants, and involves the advertising of jobs and the creation of relevant documentation such as a person specification.
- **Selection** is where the choice is made of who to employ from the field of candidates and, as such, includes such techniques as interviewing, reviewing CVs, personality tests, or assessment centres.

Personality and recruitment

When recruiting for a vacancy, for example in a job advert or on a website, employers will specify the characteristics that they desire in a successful applicant, for example the degree grades required, the amount of experience in a similar job, the skills that they can offer to the organization, etc. This usually also includes explicit reference to particular personality characteristics, such as 'outgoing', 'dynamic', or 'conscientious', or the behaviours that imply particular characteristics: for example, 'good with customers' implies personality characteristics such as patience and friendliness.

Some organizations place considerable emphasis on the types of personality that they wish to recruit. For example, Callaghan and Thompson (2002) studied a call centre which prioritized a positive, energetic, can-do attitude and the ability to use humour, over and above technical skills such as numeracy and computer literacy. This was summed up by one manager who stated: '[W]e recruit attitude' (p. 240). The high-street sandwich chain Pret a Manger also recruits staff for their personalities rather specific skills that they can demonstrate on their CV, with a happy, sociable personality that creases a sense of fun favoured over moody and easily-flustered personalities (Rawlinson, 2013; Myerscough, 2013; Moore, 2015; Jacobs, 2015).

Visit the online resources and take a look at the extension material for Chapter 8 for further analysis of the research on the call centre and Pret a Manger.

In the recruitment process, personality characteristics may also be stated in the documentation sent to or downloaded by interested candidates:

- the **job description** is a description of the tasks and duties to be performed as part of the job;
- the **person specification** is a list of knowledge, skills, experience, qualifications, and competencies—including personality characteristics—that a successful candidate would be expected to have, usually split into 'essential' and 'desirable' characteristics. A person specification will also outline the ways in which different characteristics will be assessed: that is, the selection processes that will be used to match candidates to those characteristics.

Visit the online resources and take a look at the web links for Chapter 8 for examples of job descriptions and person specifications.

Personality and selection

A number of techniques may be used in a selection process. A CV assesses whether the relevant qualifications are held; references are used to check up on relevant experience; and aptitude tests measure specific skills such as numeracy. But how would a recruiter assess the personality characteristics of a candidate to see how they match those which are desired? How, for example, can you measure somebody's 'enthusiasm' or 'friendliness'?

 When you first started at university you will have met many new people and made judgements about their personalities upon first meeting them. But how long, with friends, does it take to really get to know every facet of their personalities?

Getting to know someone's personality is a lengthy process. We get to know a person and their personality over time. Even with our closest friends we sometimes find aspects of their personality that are new or that surprise us.

Assessing large numbers of people can be problematic.
Source: Shutterstock.

With a large field of candidates, there is not enough time available to get to know each of them well enough to know every aspect of their personality in the same way that we might do with friends. Even a face-to-face interview gives only a superficial view of personality. To overcome this, techniques such as personality tests and questionnaires are used as an efficient way to measure the personality of a large number of candidates. However, this comes at the expense of an in-depth understanding of the person, with personality presented, instead, as an abstract set of numbers and measurements.

The measurement of personality in the selection process is therefore a trade-off between the time available and the depth and richness of knowledge about a candidate's personality that can be gained. This trade-off relates to the nomothetic and ideographic approaches to personality introduced previously.

- The nomothetic approach suggests that personalities can be represented as a set of standard characteristics and can thus be measured efficiently using instruments such as personality questionnaires.

- The ideographic approach sees personalities as rich and complex. Representing personalities though efficient means, such as a personality test, comes at the expense of the richness of personality data gained—the complexity and insight into an individual personality is lost.

Taken in isolation, any one technique of recruitment and selection fares badly in its *predictive validity*: that is to say, how well it predicts performance in the job or gets an accurate picture of personality. Yet given the costs and time associated with recruitment and selection, it is important for organizations to get it right, i.e. to fit the right person to the vacancy.

? Review questions

Describe	What is meant by recruitment and selection?
Explain	What are the main differences in the nomothetic and ideographic approaches to personality?
Analyse	Why is the evaluation of the personality characteristics of a candidate a trade-off between efficiency and the richness of personality data gained?
Apply	Have a look at a variety of job advertisements, either in print or online. For each advert, consider what personality characteristics are required of the successful candidate.

Nomothetic approaches to personality

> ### 🔍 Running case: personality test
>
> Having compiled the person specification, Chance realizes that most aspects would be easy to screen—qualifications and experience can be evidenced from a CV, certificates, and references, for example. But what of the personality characteristics?
>
> What Chance needs to know is: Which one of the applicants can really cut the mustard? Who has the personality to manage staff and keep them motivated in a fast-moving environment?
>
> Business manager Phil Weaver advises Chance to get them to undertake a personality test. Using the services of a personality testing firm, a link is sent to the candidates to fill out an online questionnaire. The software then produces personality profiles for all candidates.
>
> 'I've used them before. They save a lot of time and effort,' says Weaver. 'For a start, they screen out anyone unsuitable—any shy, retiring types will be shown up by the test and we can reject them straight away. We don't even need to look at their profiles—the software will just give a list of people with unsuitable personalities. And for those still in the running, we can use their profiles as extra information to draw up the final shortlist.'
>
> Chance likes this idea—it is an efficient way to deal with the 200-odd applications quickly, leaving him just the most suitable personalities to deal with.

Many of us, when younger, read the *Mr. Men* and *Little Miss* books. Each book in this series focuses on a different cartoon character whose characteristics match their name—Mr Grumpy, Little Miss Shy, Mr Happy, etc. The characters' personalities can be summed up by one particular personality characteristic, or as it is also known, a personality **trait**.

> ### 🔄 Real life case: the Mister Men interview technique at Timpson
>
> Sir John Timpson, chairman of UK shoe-repair, key-cutting, and dry-cleaning business Timpson, suggests that 'the only thing that matters is personality' (Bearne, 2018) when recruiting new staff. Skills and qualifications become relevant only for specialist roles such as finance or IT.
>
> To assess personality during the selection process, Timpson devised a test based on the *Mr. Men* and *Little Miss* books. Recruiters form their own impression of a candidate's personality and tick boxes on a form next to characters from the books which best represent that personality. A good candidate might be likened to Ms Happy or Mr Positive, for example, whereas the less desirable candidates might be described as Mr Grumpy or Ms Lazy. Candidates who tick the right boxes are then given a half-day trial working in one of the company's stores.
>
> Sources: Fulham (2017); Bearne (2018); Timpson (2018).

While our personalities are hopefully not so one-dimensional that—like the Mr. Men and Little Misses—they can be summed up in one word, the idea that personality can be described as a set of traits is one with which we are familiar. Often when asked what a person 'is like' we will respond with a set of adjectives which relate to particular personality traits—friendly, sullen, outgoing, shy, etc.

The **nomothetic** approach is based on a view of personality as a measurable set of traits, which are organized into a model or framework. Traits are viewed as characteristics of a person, just like the colour of our eyes or hair, and as remaining relatively stable over time. In this section we examine two particular approaches to nomothetic theories of personality:

- some theories classify people into broad personality *types* which encompass a number of different traits;
- some theories start from the *traits* themselves, plotting personality on scales between two opposite ends of a particular trait (for example, between reserved and outgoing).

In both cases, the nomothetic approach suggests that personality is measurable, using instruments such as personality questionnaires. The personality types and scales are the frameworks on which an individual's personality can be represented and categorized. We will see that such personality tests are used in workplaces for training, for development, and, relevant to this chapter, for selecting candidates for a job.

Theories of personality type

Theories of personality type bring together different traits in broad groupings, seeing the traits as being representative characteristics of the broader personality types. A popular tool today is the **Myers–Briggs Type Indicator** (MBTI); however, the idea of categorizing personalities into different types stretches back into antiquity.

 Theory in context: Hippocrates and the four humours

In Ancient Greece, around 400 BC, Hippocrates drew out four main personality types from his medical theory of the **four humours**. Blood, phlegm, yellow bile, and black bile were four basic substances, or humours, which Hippocrates believed made up the human body and were associated with certain characteristics and personality types (see Table 8.1). An imbalance in the presence of one of the humours would have effects both on physical health and an individual's personality type.

While much of Hippocrates' work has been disproven or superseded, the four personality types that he outlines—melancholic, sanguine, phlegmatic, and choleric—are still used today to describe people's personalities and are also used in more recent personality-type models.

 Can you think of jobs which are particularly suited to the four personality types described? Do you think of personality in such terms today, or are there other words that you might use for such personality types?

Table 8.1 Hippocrates' four humours and associated personality types

Humour	Personality type	Description
Blood	Sanguine	Warm and outgoing, a person who thrives in social environments—lively, with few concerns and cares in the world
Phlegm	Phlegmatic	Cool and rational—a controlled, thoughtful, and calm personality
Yellow bile	Choleric	The most volatile of the four personality types—impulsive, excitable, perhaps touchy and bad-tempered
Black bile	Melancholic	Reserved and withdrawn—quiet and socially the opposite to sanguine; an anxious temperament, governed by worries, concerns, and even despondency

Carl Jung: introverts and extraverts

While Hippocrates introduces the notion of personality types, it is with the work of psychoanalyst Carl Jung that we see the origins of the personality scales and type theories that are more commonly applied in the contemporary workplace. Jung's *Psychological types* (1923) outlines a distinction between **introversion** and **extraversion** (this is the way it is spelled in psychological theory), which is mirrored in many of the personality types and scales that we will see in this chapter. Introversion is often described as a tendency to focus and gain energy from within the self, while extraversion, on the other hand, is a tendency to focus and gain energy externally, rather than from within.

Our common-sense understanding of these terms perhaps differs from the depth of Jung's analysis. We tend to think of an extravert as someone who is sociable and outgoing, able to 'work a room' and start up a conversation with people, engaging in small talk. The introvert is more reserved, possibly uncomfortable in social situations, and might seem unsociable and withdrawn.

Certainly these common-sense understandings ring true, but they need to be understood in the specific context of Jung's original work, which is about how we balance our inner and external worlds, and particularly how we gain energy from each of these.

- An extravert thrives on action and being engaged with people and their external world—if inactive, an extravert can feel restless. *An extravert gets little energy from within, instead getting their energy from others in a social situation.*

- An introvert is capable of, and indeed thrives on, working alone, doing work that needs contemplation and engagement with their inner world rather than needing to be a part of a crowd or a team. *An introvert gets their energy from within—social situations drain them of that energy.*

With the example of a person 'working a room', it's not that an introvert is incapable of this; however, they would find that it drains them of energy, while an extravert would gain energy from such a situation.

👁 Research insight: introverts in the workplace

Cain, S. 2012. *Quiet: The power of introverts in a world that can't stop talking.* Viking: London.

Susan Cain (2012) argues that contemporary workplaces tend to favour the personality characteristics of extraverts, with working environments such as open-plan offices, and job adverts calling for 'team players' and upbeat personalities. This doesn't mean that an extravert personality is better, but simply that working environments suit that side of the scale more.

Indeed, Cain suggests that such environments could miss out on valuable ideas that are generated by more contemplative introverts. Being actively engaged doesn't necessarily mean speaking up all the time as an extravert may do. Smart (2017) suggests that introverts bring qualities of listening, reflection, and critical thinking to the workplace. As Kaufman and Gregoire (2016) suggest, solitude and quiet contemplation can provide the space, away from distraction, that allows for creativity and innovative thinking. And Cain suggests that such considered contributions are where introverts excel, but that these contributions tend to be overlooked alongside the more visible contributions of extraverts.

 Can you think of any jobs which would be more suited to an introvert personality? Are there any where you think an extravert personality would be more suitable?

It is not a simple either/or distinction between an individual being either introverted or extraverted: they are two important and complimentary aspects of personality as opposed to mutually exclusive opposites. However, an individual may lean more towards one end or the other on this scale. Jung's (1923) work suggested a complex relationship between an individual's position on the introversion/extraversion scale on the one hand, and two psychological functions on the other: how we perceive the world (sensing or intuition) and how we make judgements about the world (thinking or feeling). These relationships form the basis for one of the most familiar workplace personality instruments—the Myers–Briggs Type Indicator (MBTI).

Myers–Briggs and the application of Jung

The MBTI is one of the most popular personality profiling instruments in the workplace, with around 2 million people taking the test every year, earning $20 million for the company that produces the test (Hosie, 2017). The origins of the MBTI were an amateur interest in personality types held by Katharine Cook Briggs and her daughter Isabel Briggs Myers. They were heavily influenced by Jung's work on personality types and they used these as a basis for their own classification of personality types, eventually published as the MBTI (Myers, 1962).

The MBTI uses a questionnaire to work out where an individual lies between a set of four personality indices:

- *extraversion/introversion (E/I)*—as outlined by Jung, to which orientation are we more inclined when directing our actions and energies: the world around us or our inner selves?

- *sensing/intuition (S/I)*—how do we perceive and gather information about the world around us?

- *thinking/feeling (T/F)*—once we have information, how do we analyse and act upon it, using it to make judgements and decisions?

- *judgement/perception (J/P)*—how do we deal with, and act upon, the world around us? Do we plan in advance or act in the moment?

Figure 8.1 shows these four indices, with examples of the types of behaviour and personality that might be expected at either end.

 Where do you think you lie on each of the MBTI indices shown in Figure 8.1? Do you think that, following MBTI, you share a personality type with one-sixteenth of the world's population?

While people can lie at points along this scale (e.g. a medium preference for sensing, a strong preference for feeling, etc.) the results tend to be presented as a four-letter personality type according to which end of each index an individual is more inclined towards. A person might be an ENTP (Extravert–Intuition–Thinking–Perceiving) personality type, or an ISTP, or an ESTP—or any of the sixteen possible combinations of the letters.

The strength of the MBTI instrument is not as a recruitment and selection tool, indeed Angelina Bennet (2010) has suggested that whilst it can identify personality types, this does not necessarily equate to actual behaviour in a job. Nevertheless, Bennet still sees the tool as valuable as a means of raising self-awareness and, as such, it tends to be used more as a personal development tool for individuals. For example, in staff development and training it is used to help people understand their own personalities and how they relate to their external world, to their work, and to their colleagues.

Figure 8.1 The Myers–Briggs Type Indicator (MBTI) personality indices.
Source: Reproduced from the MBTI Manual by Isabel Briggs Myers, Mary H. MacCaulley, Naomi L. Quenk & Allen L. Hammer (2012) by permission of CPP, Inc.

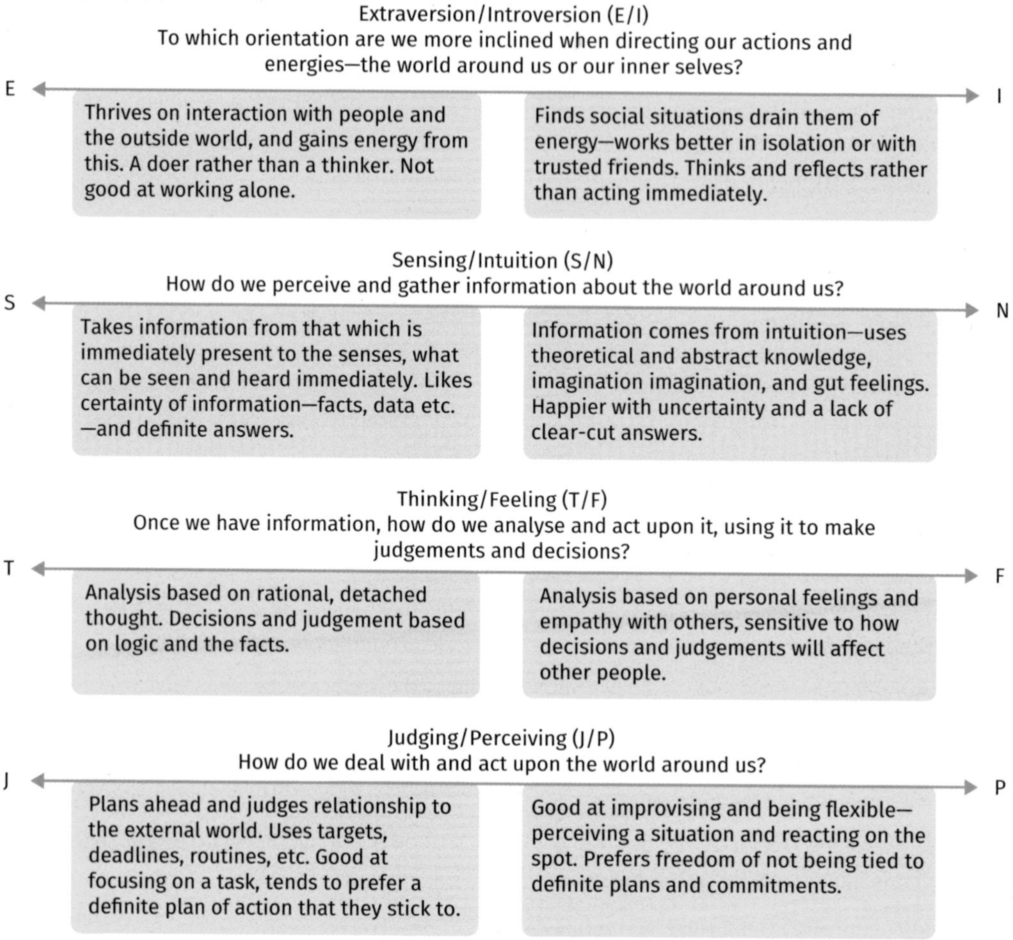

Extraversion/Introversion (E/I)
To which orientation are we more inclined when directing our actions and energies—the world around us or our inner selves?

E ◄───► I

Thrives on interaction with people and the outside world, and gains energy from this. A doer rather than a thinker. Not good at working alone.	Finds social situations drain them of energy—works better in isolation or with trusted friends. Thinks and reflects rather than acting immediately.

Sensing/Intuition (S/N)
How do we perceive and gather information about the world around us?

S ◄───► N

Takes information from that which is immediately present to the senses, what can be seen and heard immediately. Likes certainty of information—facts, data etc. —and definite answers.	Information comes from intuition—uses theoretical and abstract knowledge, imagination imagination, and gut feelings. Happier with uncertainty and a lack of clear-cut answers.

Thinking/Feeling (T/F)
Once we have information, how do we analyse and act upon it, using it to make judgements and decisions?

T ◄───► F

Analysis based on rational, detached thought. Decisions and judgement based on logic and the facts.	Analysis based on personal feelings and empathy with others, sensitive to how decisions and judgements will affect other people.

Judging/Perceiving (J/P)
How do we deal with and act upon the world around us?

J ◄───► P

Plans ahead and judges relationship to the external world. Uses targets, deadlines, routines, etc. Good at focusing on a task, tends to prefer a definite plan of action that they stick to.	Good at improvising and being flexible—perceiving a situation and reacting on the spot. Prefers freedom of not being tied to definite plans and commitments.

The MBTI instrument is also used for career development by matching particular personalities to suitable careers. This was one of the original aims of Myers and Briggs in developing the MBTI test—one of its earliest uses was during World War II in matching women's personalities to wartime jobs that would best suit them (Myers and Myers, 1995: xiii), and following the war it was used to highlight women's suitability for jobs, particularly where they had no prior work experience that they could use to demonstrate this suitability (Cunningham, 2012).

A specific link between personality 'temperaments' and specific occupational areas was made by David Keirsey (1998). Keirsey was influenced by the MBTI instrument, sorting the sixteen MBTI combinations into four groups, which correspond to the original personality types of Hippocrates (see Table 8.2). **Keirsey's temperament sorter** then links each of the sixteen MBTI combinations to a particular type of role or occupation.

For example, ENFJ is characterized by Keirsey as 'the teacher'. We can see how the different characteristics that make up this personality type would contribute to this role:

- (E)xtraversion—the teacher will be working mainly with groups of people rather than in isolation
- I(N)tuition—Chapter 10 discusses the suggestion that learning comes best from going beyond learning simple facts and instead recognizing patterns and associations, as an intuitive person would do

Table 8.2 Keirsey's temperament sorter

Grouping	Artisan	Guardian	Rational	Idealist
Common characteristics from MBTI	SP (Sensing–Perceiving)	SJ (Sensing–Judging)	NT (Intuition–Thinking)	NF (Intuition–Feeling)
Related Hippocratic group	Sanguine	Melancholic	Phlegmatic	Choleric
Personality types and related occupations	Promoter (ESTP) Crafter (ISTP) Performer (ESFP) Composer (ISFP)	Supervisor (ESTJ) Inspector (ISTJ) Provider (ESFJ) Protector (ISFJ)	Fieldmarshal (ENTJ) Mastermind (INTJ) Inventor (ENTP) Architect (INTP)	Teacher (ENFJ) Counsellor (INFJ) Champion (ENFP) Healer (INFP)

Source: Keirsey (1998).

- (F)eeling—the teacher has a degree of empathy with, and can respond to, students
- (J)udgement—the teacher is able to plan lessons methodically rather than making things up on the hoof.

Interestingly, just one change of letter—from Extraversion to Intraversion—gives INFJ, suggested as 'the counsellor'. Similar skills are required, but here it is in a much more private, individual situation than teaching.

As with the MBTI, Keirsey has an associated personality questionnaire which is used to place people in the relevant groupings (www.keirsey.com has more about the groupings and a test questionnaire).

Visit the online resources and take a look at the web links for Chapter 8 for more analysis of occupations within the Keirsey groupings.

Trait theories of personality

While type theories sort people's personalities into broad types from which particular traits emerge, **trait theories** see personality traits as the main building blocks of a personality. Usually, traits are arranged in pairs of opposites (e.g. sociable–unsociable), with people scored at some point in between each pairing so as to build up a personality profile. As with type theories, a questionnaire is used. In this section we examine two of the more popular trait theory testing instruments used in the workplace: the **16 personality factor** and the big five personality scale.

Eysenck: from types to traits

Similarly to Keirsey, Hans Eysenck (in Eysenck and Eysenck, 1985) made groupings of personality types which mapped on to the ancient groupings of Hippocrates and, similarly to all the modern-day theories of personality examined so far, he made a distinction between extraversion and introversion.

However, Eysenk added another dimension between emotional stability and emotional instability (the latter sometimes called **neuroticism**). Eysenck's two scales were plotted on to a matrix giving four personality types, the quadrants of which map on to Hippocrates' original four

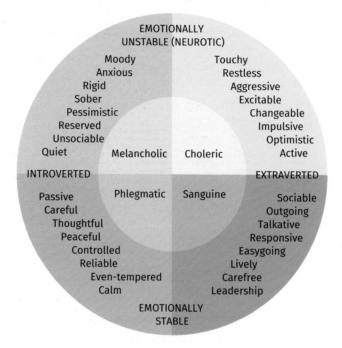

Figure 8.2 Eysenck's model of personality.
Source: Eysenck, H.J. and Eysenck, M.W. (1985). Personality and Individual Differences. Plenum Publishing.

humours (see Figure 8.3). Again, this is a classification of personality types that has an associated questionnaire.

Eysenck's work, while still dividing personalities into types, moves us towards trait theories. First, it outlines a set of specific traits within each quadrant (e.g. a stable extraverted person is sociable, outgoing, talkative, etc., as shown in Figure 8.2). Second, Eysenck's dimension of emotional stability and instability features alongside the extraversion–introversion scale in many trait theories.

Cattell's 16 PF traits

Cattell's (1966) 16 personality factor (16 PF) theory is one of the most popular personality questionnaires used in selection processes (e.g. Dakin et al., 1994; Pietrzak et al., 2015). Cattell analysed questionnaires and the words within them that people used to describe personality (Newell and Rice, 1999: 140), and by grouping similar ideas together, suggested that a personality boils down to sixteen core factors (see Figure 8.3).

These factors are arranged in opposites: for example, the 'Dominance' scale ranges between deferential and avoiding conflict at one end to being dominant and forceful at the other. The scale is normally distributed: that is to say that on any of the scales, approximately one-third of the population should be located in the middle band, with numbers tailing off towards the extremities.

Both Jung's extraversion and introversion aspects can be seen in the scale (e.g. factor H—social boldness), as can Eysenck's emotional stability (factor C).

The big five personality factors

The **big five personality scale** (McCrae and Costa, 1990, 1996), another of the well-known trait theories used in the workplace, suggests that the number of factors whereby a personality can be

Figure 8.3 Cattell's 16 personality factors.
Source: Reproduced by permission of the Institute for Personality and Ability Testing, Inc. (IPAT), Champaign, Illinois, USA.

16PF5

INSTRUCTIONS FOR PLOTTING SCORES

1. Write the raw score for each factor in the column labelled 'Raw' to the right of this page.
2. Refer to *The UK Standardization of the 16PF5: A Supplement of Norms and Technical Data* in the *User's Manual*. Choose the appropriate table following the guidelines given and convert raw scores to sten scores for each Factor.
3. Plot the sten scores for each Primary Factor on the graph below.

Surname: _____
Forename: _____
Date: ____ ____ ____
Age: _____
Sex: M/F
Norm Group: _____

RESPONSE STYLE
Impression Management _____

Primary Factors

Factor		Standard Ten Score (STEN)										
		1	2	3	4	5	6	7	8	9	10	
A: Warmth	Emotionally distant from people	+	+	+	+	+	+	+	+	+	+	Attentive and warm towards others
B: Reasoning	Fewer reasoning items correct	+	+	+	+	+	+	+	+	+	+	More reasoning items correct
C: Emotional Stability	Reactive, Emotionally changeable	+	+	+	+	+	+	+	+	+	+	Emotionally stable, Adaptive
E: Dominance	Deferential, Cooperative, Avoids conflict	+	+	+	+	+	+	+	+	+	+	Dominant, Forceful
F: Liveliness	Serious, Cautious, Careful	+	+	+	+	+	+	+	+	+	+	Lively, Animated, Spontaneous
G: Rule-Consciousness	Expedient, Non-Conforming	+	+	+	+	+	+	+	+	+	+	Rule-Conscious, Dutiful
H: Social Boldness	Shy, Threat-Sensitive, Timid	+	+	+	+	+	+	+	+	+	+	Socially bold, Adventurous, Thick-Skinned
I: Sensitivity	Objective, Unsentimental	+	+	+	+	+	+	+	+	+	+	Subjective, Sentimental
L: Vigilance	Trusting, Unsuspecting, Accepting	+	+	+	+	+	+	+	+	+	+	Vigilant, Suspicious, Sceptical, Wary
M: Abstractedness	Grounded, Practical, Solution-Oriented	+	+	+	+	+	+	+	+	+	+	Abstracted, Theoretical, Idea-Oriented
N: Privateness	Forthright, Straightforward	+	+	+	+	+	+	+	+	+	+	Private, Discreet, Non-Disclosing
O: Apprehension	Self-Assured, Unworried	+	+	+	+	+	+	+	+	+	+	Apprehensive, Self-Doubting, Worried
Q1: Openness to Change	Traditional, Values the familiar	+	+	+	+	+	+	+	+	+	+	Open to change, Experimenting
Q2: Self-Reliance	Group-Oriented, Affiliative	+	+	+	+	+	+	+	+	+	+	Self-Reliant, Individualistic
Q3: Perfectionism	Tolerates disorder, Unexacting, Flexible	+	+	+	+	+	+	+	+	+	+	Perfectionist, Organised, Self-Disciplined
Q4: Tension	Relaxed, Placid, Patient	+	+	+	+	+	+	+	+	+	+	Tense, High energy, Impatient, Driven

Global Factors

EX: Extraversion	Introverted, Socially inhibited	+	+	+	+	+	+	+	+	+	+	Extraverted, Socially participating
IN: Independence	Accommodating, Agreeable, Selfless	+	+	+	+	+	+	+	+	+	+	Independent, Persuasive, Wilful
TM: Tough-Mindedness	Receptive, Open-Minded	+	+	+	+	+	+	+	+	+	+	Tough-Minded, Resolute
SC: Self-Control	Unrestrained, Follows urges	+	+	+	+	+	+	+	+	+	+	Self-Controlled, Inhibits urges
AX: Anxiety	Relaxed, Unperturbed	+	+	+	+	+	+	+	+	+	+	Anxious, Perturbable

adequately represented boils down to five. The big five is also known as the OCEAN scale, OCEAN being an acronym for its five personality dimensions:

- *openness to experience*—the degree to which people are open to new ideas, questioning and imaginative, or prefer existing ways of doing things
- *conscientiousness*—the degree to which people are good, orderly, diligent workers
- *extraversion/introversion*—as with the MBTI, the degree to which a person is outgoing and gregarious, their energies directed externally rather than internally
- *agreeableness*—the degree to which someone is a 'good person', trustworthy and cooperative, and will get along with others in the organization
- *neuroticism (emotional stability)*—as with Eysenck, the degree to which somebody is calm and emotionally stable, or more prone to anxiety and anger.

The main questionnaire for the big five personality test (Costa and McCrae, 1992) runs to 240 questions and takes approximately 45 minutes to complete; however, Gosling et al. (2003) note that a number of shorter questionnaires have been based around the framework, some as short as ten, or even five, questions. The results of 'big five' tests can thus be presented with a range of precision, from detailed percentages which break each factor down into sub-elements, to broad results such as 'mid-agreeableness', 'high conscientiousness', etc.

 Visit the online resources and take a look at the web links for Chapter 8 for information about a UK-wide experiment to test personality against the big five scale.

Nomothetic approaches in recruitment and selection

🔍 Running case: the personality test

Chance chooses a personality test based on the 'big five' characteristics. He is asked to think about the ideal candidate for the job, and, in consultation with the testing company that he had employed, an ideal range in each scale is drawn up:

Openness to experience—Mid

Some flexibility needed, but in many respects this is a routine job. Someone too creative might be too disruptive, but someone completely reliant on routine would not be flexible enough when the need arises.

Conscientiousness—High

Needs to be well-organized, for example in putting together rotas and managing the paperwork, and being able to take charge of a shift from start to finish with no one else above them to refer to.

Extraversion—High

Needs to have a very outgoing personality, both in leadership of the team and being able to motivate them for a shift, and in dealing with, and motivating, customers in the gym.

Agreeableness—High

Needs to be warm and friendly in dealing with customers—most of the time will be spent on the gym floor.

→

→

Neuroticism—Mid-to-Low

A bit of nervous energy would be good, but, overall, the gym is a fast-paced atmosphere and the person in charge needs to maintain a sense of calm. This is especially the case as injuries and medical emergencies sometimes need to be dealt with.

The tests are administered. Candidates who are nowhere near the ideal profile are rejected instantly. A list of 20 candidates who match the desired profile, or are fairly close to it, is sent to Chance. Chance looks at the list alongside the original application forms and CVs, and draws up a shortlist of five candidates.

 How would you feel if you had been rejected from the shortlist by the method just outlined?

Nomothetic approaches to personality suggest that personality is an objective entity which can be measured and either categorized or plotted out on some form of personality scale as a combination of different strengths of different traits. In the process of recruitment and selection, this suggests that, if a desired personality profile can be outlined for a particular role, in a person specification for example, then personality tests can be used as an instrument to find the most appropriate candidate to match that personality profile.

The **personality test** is usually a questionnaire where a candidate selects one of a number of different options for a set of different questions. Some questionnaires will ask candidates to locate themselves on a scale, as in Table 8.3.

Such a question would be part of the calculation of a candidate's position on the extra version/introversion scale—the more strongly a candidate agrees with this proposition, the more likely they are to be extravert in nature. The scale allows neutral responses, and there might be some subjectivity in answering: for example, how easy is it to tell the difference between agreeing and agreeing strongly?

Other questionnaires might try to force an opinion one way or another, and thus the question might be a simpler one:

I enjoy parties and social gatherings: YES/NO

or:

Do you tend to prefer:

A quiet night in, or
Parties and social gatherings

This means that neutral answers are avoided, leading to a more definite position on a personality scale. However, this does not allow for subtleties in a personality to be expressed—a person might enjoy parties occasionally, for example, but be equally happy with quiet nights in.

Table 8.3 A typical personality test scale question

	Strongly agree	Agree	Neutral	Disagree	Strongly disagree
I enjoy parties and social gatherings					

The questionnaires are usually trademarked commercial products for which a company wishing to recruit will pay for the right to use.

 Real life case: McDonald's Australia's personality test

A personality test given to would-be workers at McDonald's Australia attracted attention for the variety of questions that it asked. Some of these relate to the job, for example asking candidates about their interest in food, or what they would do if a teammate asks for help while they were also busy. However, other questions seem irrelevant to the job, described as 'unexpected' (Smith, 2015) and even 'intrusive' (Jefferson, 2015).

One question asks what you would do if approached by a group of kids to play soccer in a park. Possible answers include: 'Apologize and explain that you really don't have time to play with them'; 'Join in for a couple of minutes just to make them happy'; 'Join in with them as you really enjoy playing with kids'; or 'Ignore them or tell them to go away'.

Another question asks what you would do with 15 minutes to spare in an exam. Answers include reviewing your answers to be sure they are correct; thinking about what you will do with friends later that day; or looking over at someone else's paper to see if they have the same answers.

Further questions ask what you would do if someone dropped their supermarket shopping in front of you; how you would deal with an elderly lady worried about a late bus; how you would deal with a noisy neighbour; and how you behave at parties.

McDonald's Australia say that the personality test helps them to understand which position within a team best suits the candidate.

 Visit the online resources and take a look at the web links for Chapter 8 for links to some personality tests that you can try for free, and links to more questions from the McDonald's Australia personality test.

✋ **What information about candidates' personalities do you think McDonald's Australia is trying to get from these questions? Can you relate this information to any of the scales on the 'big five' personality test?**

Sources: Jefferson (2015); Radulova (2015); Smith (2015).

Personality testing assessed

Personality tests provide an efficient means of screening candidates and are thus often used for pre-screening, especially when there is a large volume of applications for a job which needs to be whittled down quickly. Thus a personality test is sometimes administered at the same time as the application, especially in online applications. In other instances a personality test may be used further down the selection process, possibly alongside other selection tools such as the interview or references.

However, the efficacy of personality tests is a matter of great debate, particularly around their **predictive validity**—the degree to which the result of a personality test accurately predicts the performance of a candidate in the job itself. The results for personality tests suggest that their predictive validity is low, at the most 40 per cent (Pilbeam and Corbridge, 2010: 189), and as low as 15 per cent for some self-administered tests (Reilly and Chao, 1982: 32). More positive results emerged from the 1990s onwards, leading to renewed interest in personality testing; however, Morgeson et al. (2007) suggest that the better results come from tests which are customized and specific to a particular job, and that generic, off-the-shelf personality tests remain poor in their predictive validity. Judge et al. (2015) and Faragher (2014) further note that while such tests can produce a personality profile, they need to be interpreted within the specific context of the organization, the nature of the work, and the person to which they are being applied—the danger comes from relying solely upon the test result.

> ## ⟳ Real life case: Flowers and the dirt
>
> In March 2018, the UK Financial Conduct Authority (FCA) banned Paul Flowers, former chair of the Co-operative Bank, from working in the financial services industry stating that his 'conduct demonstrated a lack of fitness and propriety required to work in financial services'. In 2013, Flowers had presided over the bank when it came close to collapse, requiring a bailout due to a £1.5 billion black hole in the finances. However, it was Flowers' personal conduct which captured the public attention. After the collapse, revelations emerged of Flowers, a former Methodist minister, purchasing Class A drugs and procuring the services of sex workers. The FCA investigation further found that he used his work mobile to call premium rate sex-lines, and work emails to send sexually explicit messages.
>
> Questions were asked about why this candidate with no previous experience in the finance industry, and who turned out to be wholly unsuitable for the role, had been given the job ahead of other more experienced candidates. It emerged that he had aced the psychometric tests that candidates had to complete, finishing well ahead of the rest of the field. Clearly the results of the tests were not an accurate prediction of his future behaviour.
>
> Sources: Boffey and Treanor (2013); Treanor (2014); Moore (2014); Financial Conduct Authority (2018); Jacobs (2018); Goodley (2018); Clark (2018).

While we do not know the circumstances that caused such a difference between the results of the tests undertaken by Paul Flowers and his job performance (as explored in the real life case), there are a number of issues which potentially diminish the predictive validity and usefulness of personality tests.

- Candidates may consciously fake the answers to a test, giving answers that they think will improve their scores, rather than giving an honest answer (Furnham, 1997; Morgeson et al., 2007); or, more subconsciously, their stated preferences on a test may not reflect their actual behaviour (Pilbeam and Corbridge, 2010: 202).

- The language and assumptions of tests may lead them to have a particular bias; for example, Thompson and McHugh (2009: 283) suggest that personality tests are good at finding managers who are '"male, middle-class and middle-aged," and in the West, white'.

- Passer et al. (2003) question the extent to which the different traits are independent variables that can be measured, or whether they have an effect upon each other?

This final point invites us to question just how realistic personality profiles are as a representation of personalities. They can be seen as reductionist: they reduce a complex, human phenomenon such as a personality down to a few figures on a set of scales. For example, we saw earlier that the different letters on the MBTI instrument are the extreme ends of a scale—a person could be almost mid-way between, for example, extraversion or introversion, but their representation in the final four-letter score would be a simplistic, binary 'E' or 'I'.

Do you feel that human characteristics and emotions can be represented on a numerical scale? How would you feel if you received a Valentine's card stating 'On a scale between love and hate, my feelings for you measure 78.3%'?

This is part of the trade-off in recruitment and selection that we encountered earlier (see Figure 8.1). Personality tests give a snapshot of a personality, but they don't give the full picture of its richness. In this respect, personality tests are often not relied on by themselves, but are used alongside other selection techniques that will give further information (Jacobs, 2018), especially, as we shall see, in an assessment-centre approach.

? Review questions

Describe	What is meant by a nomothetic approach to personality?
Explain	How are personality tests used to measure personality in type and trait theories?
Analyse	Why do personality tests have a low predictive validity?
Apply	What type of personality do you think would work well in a fast-food restaurant? Use scales such as MBTI, OCEAN, Eysenck, or Cattell to formulate your recommendations, and refer back to the McDonald's Australia case earlier in this chapter.

The ideographic approach to personality

Q Running case: the whites of their eyes

The five candidates had been called in for interview. The panel, made up of Simon Chance, Meg Mortimer, Linda Wilkinson, and the current fitness centre manager, Carl Jones, have a discussion beforehand to work out their lines of questioning. They have the candidates' CVs, application forms, and personality test results before them. Chance suggests that the interview would be an opportunity to get a more accurate view of the candidates' personalities, i.e. to see whether they matched with the results of the personality tests.

'These personality tests are just figures on a piece of paper,' says Chance. 'They may give us an overview of what they are like, but we need to confirm that they are accurate. Not only that, there's much more to what people are—what makes them tick—than a few points plotted out on a scale. We need to dig behind that to get a much more rounded picture of what these people are like.

'A piece of paper isn't enough. We need to see the whites of their eyes.'

Whatever your views are of President Donald Trump, there has never been a personality like his in the White House. The foibles of his personality get as much media attention as do his actions in office. To consider the uniqueness of a personality like Trump's brings to the fore some of the failings of the nomothetic approach.

- Firstly, could any personality test and its associated personality scale really put across the true complexity of Trump's personality? Do the results on paper get anywhere close to the reality of the person in the flesh? For example, we could describe his impetuous outbursts on Twitter as an example of a choleric personality, but does this really tell the full story?

- Secondly, with methods such as MBTI, there are only sixteen possible combinations of personality type (ENTJ, ISFP, etc.), so on this reading one-sixteenth of the world's population would share a personality type with Donald Trump. The Keirsey website (https://keirsey.com/temperament/artisan-promoter/) assesses Trump to be an ESTP on the MBTI scale, yet he shares this rating with Madonna, Winston Churchill, and Mohammed Ali—surely their personalities are all very different even though they are all lumped together within this rating?

Donald Trump
Source: Jstone/Shutterstock.com

While Donald Trump might be a particularly far-fetched yardstick by which to measure our own personalities, the argument of the **ideographic approach** is that, while our own personalities might be a little more mundane, they are nevertheless equally unique. It argues that we are all far richer and more complex as individuals than nomothetic trait theories would suggest.

In the previous section, we encountered a number of nomothetic theories that saw personalities in static, fixed terms: that is to say they could be plotted out on a set of scales or a framework. The ideographic approach suggests that our personality is not so static: that, instead, it is developed and moulded through social interaction. Our personality is adaptable and open to being changed by new experiences.

 Theory in context: the nature vs nurture debate

A frequent discussion point related to personality is whether our personalities are genetic, a natural and pre-determined part of who we are, or whether our personalities develop over time, being nurtured as a result of our surroundings. A couple of examples illustrate this debate.

- Undoubtedly the actions of tyrannical dictators such as Adolf Hitler are evil. However, a question often asked is whether Hitler was born evil—it was just a pre-determined part of who he was—or whether influences in his life, for example in childhood, might have turned him that way (e.g. Stein, 2000).

- Following widespread rioting in London in 2011, two explanations emerged for the behaviour of the rioters, many of whom seemed to be engaging in the action for enjoyment rather than protest. On the one hand were suggestions that the rioters were simply innately criminal—this was a part of their nature—while others suggested that this was the result of external influences such as social deprivation and the impact of gangs (e.g. *The Guardian*, 2011).

The **nature versus nurture** debate parallels the distinction between nomothetic and ideographic approaches. Are our personalities a fixed and measurable phenomenon, as the nomothetic approach suggests, or are they in a continual process of being changed and influenced, as the ideographic approach suggests?

Sigmund Freud: the personality as dynamic

The ideographic approach has its roots in the **psychodynamic** approach of Sigmund Freud (1927). This suggests that personality is dynamic—constantly changing—rather than static. Personalities are not reducible to broad types or measurements; instead, each personality is unique and is the result of the influences and experiences that we are exposed to during our lives from childhood onwards.

- A key focus in Freud's work is the effects that our *family and upbringing* have on our early personality development. This is where we learn rules, values, etc. from birth onwards and is therefore an important formative stage in our personalities.

- *School* brings in more influences: rules, teachers, things learned, alongside peer pressure and group dynamics (see Chapter 6) involving other pupils.

- For many readers of this book, *university* is a major influence on personality right now. Some of you will be starting your very first term at university. It's common when returning home after the first few weeks to hear people say 'you've changed'. The implication is that the new influences and experiences at university have, in some way, changed your personality and behaviour.

- In our careers we are likely to work in several *organizations and workplaces*. Like schools and universities, these are social institutions where we interact with people and have new experiences, and so our personality encounters more influences (we examine this later in the chapter, in the section covering the social–radical approach).

- *Social categories* give us a sense of self—possibly with pressures to conform to certain types of behaviour—while at the same time acting as markers of our identity within society. For example, gender not only marks our identity in society but also produces pressures for certain types of behaviour (e.g. 'boys don't cry'), which carries over into expected workplace behaviours (see, for example, the discussion of women and emotional labour in Chapter 15). Other social categories, such as ethnicity, religion, and social class, also have an impact on identity and personality in terms of how we develop as individuals, but also how others see us.

 Visit the online resources and take a look at the extension material for Chapter 8 for more analysis of social categories and the individual and more background to Freud's work.

If our personality develops from our experiences and interactions, then any aspect of society can have an influence on us: the list is potentially infinite. Given that we all have unique histories of social interaction and influence (we all come from different families, schools, etc.), the ideographic approach sees every personality as unique, rather than conforming to a standard set of measurements.

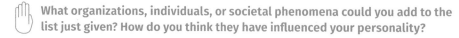 What organizations, individuals, or societal phenomena could you add to the list just given? How do you think they have influenced your personality?

Problems with the ideographic approach

While the ideographic approach recognizes the individuality of personalities over and above broad personality types or scales, this approach does bring some drawbacks.

- Freud's work has not been used in mainstream management theory to the same extent as we saw with Jung. Its origins are in a clinical setting—the therapist's couch—and it is more concerned with identifying personality problems rather than measuring personality types.

- The ideographic approach doesn't solve the problem of the time needed to become familiar with a personality. Understanding comes from lengthy therapy sessions, which is impractical and inappropriate for a workplace recruitment setting. It brings us back to the problem that personality tests were meant to solve—the need for efficiency.

- While the nomothetic approach reduces personality to calculated measurement, the ideographic approach has no form of standardized description of personalities. Given that personalities are unique and open-ended, different people may interpret the same personality differently and, as we will see in the next section on interviewing, there are many factors that can alter and cause bias in that interpretation.

In many respects, the ideographic approach raises questions, albeit valid questions, about the measurement of personality, rather than offering solutions. It recognizes that nomothetic approaches do not give a measurement of the entirety of an individual's personality, but rather than offering an alternative way of measuring personality it highlights the difficulties in getting such a full measurement. The ideographic approach lays out the complexity of personality rather than offering any hope of measuring that full complexity.

Nevertheless, the ideographic approach does allow us to appreciate the limited nature of information gained about personality in different selection processes. Furthermore, as we will see, it allows us to view the ideal selection process as one of building up information about personality from different sources rather than relying on any single, limited source.

🔍 Running case: interview thoughts

As the interviews progress at Junction Hotel, different panel members react differently to the candidates. Although they don't record it officially in their notes, each has their own reasons for liking or disliking particular candidates.

- Meg Mortimer dislikes one candidate who she thought was 'too common' for the hotel.
- Linda Wilkinson looks favourably upon a candidate who comes from her home town.
- Simon Chance takes a dislike to the accent of one of the candidates, which he feels sounds arrogant.
- Carl Jones dislikes a candidate who works at a chain of gyms that he has had a major dispute with.
- Linda Wilkinson is not keen on a candidate who mistakenly calls her 'Leslie' when they are introduced.
- Simon Chance is drawn to a candidate who supports the football club of which he is chair.
- Carl Jones thinks that a young mother will be unable to juggle parenting responsibilities with commitment to the fitness centre.

The ideographic approach and selection

The job interview seems to be a way to make up for the deficiencies of nomothetic approaches, such as a personality test. If a personality test gives just a snapshot of a personality, presented as a few numbers and percentages, then the interview at least allows the selection panel the chance to get a better understanding of personality by seeing people in the flesh.

 Think of a time when you have had a job interview—how well did you think the panel were able to judge your personality?

The bad news is that the predictive validity of interviews is even worse than that of personality tests (Reilly and Chao, 1982: 15; Pilbeam and Corbridge, 2010: 189). Dana et al. (2013) demonstrated that, in unstructured interviews, the interviewers have a false confidence in their ability to judge the interviewee. For them, the interview is not only useless but it can also be damaging to the overall selection process by bringing in misjudgements and unsound information. Why should it be that being able to meet and speak to the candidate in person produces even worse results?

Newell and Rice (1999: 159) suggest that many of the problems are due to **interpersonal perception** (the way in which one individual perceives the personality of another) in the interview process (see also Chapter 11 for more on perception). That is to say, the interpretation of the personality of a candidate can be biased by certain factors. Dana et al. (2013) further suggest that interview panels tend to make any evidence from an interview fit into their own preconceived narratives about the person.

- The **halo/horns effect** suggests that a positive or negative trait that is picked up early in an interview can then bias the way in which an interviewer perceives an interviewee from then onwards. So, a good initial impression can lead to a **confirmation bias**—other perceptions confirming that initial impression, and vice versa for a bad first impression (CIPD, 2015).

- Similarly, interviewers can be drawn to candidates with characteristics similar to themselves—a sort of halo effect generated by seeing aspects of themselves in the candidate (CIPD, 2015).

- The interview can also be subject to **stereotypes** and **discrimination** (see Chapter 11). In the previous section it was suggested that ethnicity, gender, class, and religion are all aspects of society that feed into the development of our personality and social identity. They can also be factors which bias people's interpretation in an interview. For example, Reilly and Chao (1982) suggest that both ethnicity and gender are aspects where stereotypes and discriminatory views can affect women and black candidates negatively.

In the latter case such discrimination would not only be unfair, but also illegal if discovered to be the basis for making appointing or rejecting a job candidate. For example, in the United Kingdom, the Equality Act (2010) names nine 'protected characteristics' for individuals (see Table 8.4). The law protects people against discrimination on the basis of these categories in many areas of life, including workplace recruitment and selection. The UK government's Department for Business and Industry provides guidance on avoiding the perceptual biases which might lead to discrimination on these grounds.

Table 8.4 The UK's nine protected characteristics

age	marriage and civil partnership	religion or belief
disability	pregnancy and maternity	sex
gender reassignment	race	sexual orientation

Source: Equality Act (2010).

Visit the online resources and take a look at the extension material for Chapter 8 for more discussion on avoiding these biases.

 Real life case: name-blind recruitment at Deloitte

It is not only in the interview process that unconscious bias can lead to discrimination. Studies in many different countries have shown that names on application forms and CVs can also lead to discrimination because they give away the gender, nationality, or ethnic origin of the candidate (Parkinson and Smith-Walters, 2015). A UK government-funded study found that CVs that were identical apart from the name were more likely to get a favourable response if the name of the applicant sounded 'white' (Syal, 2009). To eliminate this bias, many recruiters have adopted 'name-blind' recruitment where the name of the candidate is replaced by a code so as to reduce the possibility of unconscious, discriminatory judgements being made on the basis of the name (O'Connor, 2016). The extract below is from the recruitment website of the multinational financial and management consulting company Deloitte. Not only do they remove names from the application form, which hides the gender and ethnic origin of the applicant, they also remove information such as educational background to try to avoid any class-based inferences being made.

Your unique candidate ID

We've introduced 'name blind' recruitment, to help stop any unconscious bias against our potential recruits. It means your name, email address, and the schools and university you went to can't be seen by our recruitment team when they screen your application. You still need to complete these details on your application form, but we'll give you a candidate ID number when you submit the form, which you'll use throughout the selection process.

(Deloitte, 2018)

A selection interview may have no formal structure: an **unstructured interview**. Much greater predictive validity comes from **structured interviews**, which have a set format and standardized, often job-specific, questions (Pilbeam and Corbridge, 2010: 189). Structured interviews focus on behaviours relevant to the actual job. Interviewers might ask hypothetical questions, such as 'What would you do in this particular situation?', or questions which draw upon actual working experience, such as 'Describe what you did in a particular situation when ... '.

This structure, formality, and focus minimize the opportunities for perceptual biases to creep in on the part of interviewers; however, it also minimizes the extent to which interviewers are able to get a picture of the personality of the candidate. Newell and Rice (1999: 160) suggest that, while the structured interview is more valid, the unstructured interview still remains the most popular form of interview in practice.

? Review questions

Describe	What social factors may have an effect on our personality?
Explain	What is meant when the ideographic approach describes personalities as 'dynamic'?
Analyse	What differences are there between the assumptions about the nature of personality made by the ideographic and the nomothetic approaches?
Apply	How does 'name-blind' recruitment help to remove unconscious bias from the recruitment and selection process?

Contemporary recruitment: further sources of information

🔍 Running case: informal measures

During a break in proceedings, Chance peruses his list of five candidates and decides to undertake a bit of his own detective work.

First, he tries to find them on social networking sites. Many of the candidates have, sensibly, set their privacy settings high. However, one candidate has left all of their information visible. This was unfortunate, as their most recent status update reads: 'Pulled a sickie today—good times, afternoon in pub for me. Hope I can get out of this job soon, interview tomorrow, fingers crossed!' Chance finds this bizarre as the candidate had scored well on the 'conscientiousness' aspect of the scale and seemed very sincere in the interview.

Chance also realizes that one of the candidates had previously worked in a gym owned by a former colleague. Chance gives his friend a call and asks about the candidate. 'I was glad to be rid of him,' says the friend. 'He had no warmth with customers—he was cold and aloof. I wouldn't employ him if I were you—you'll have the customers leaving in droves.'

Again, Chance finds this strange, as the personality test had scored the candidate high on 'agreeableness' and he had presented himself well in the interview.

Chance feels that his informal enquiries have provided some useful information to add to the selection process, but is left unable to ask the candidates about what he had found out—it wouldn't look good to tell them he'd been snooping around their social media and talking to their ex-bosses.

Given the low predictive validity of selection techniques such as interviews and personality tests, it is no surprise that recruiters look to many other selection techniques to try to get more information about the personality of candidates. In this section we examine techniques which range from the legally dubious, such as the use of social media profiles, to those such as assessment centres which try to use as many methods as possible to increase the amount of data about a candidate's personality.

Informal measures

 Real life case: social media as a selection tool

Around 70 per cent of recruiters use social media profiles (e.g. Instagram, Twitter, Facebook) as a means of screening candidates, with social media becoming widely understood as one of the hurdles in a job application process. A survey by US online recruitment consultants Jobvite (2017) found that postings that refer to marijuana and alcohol, that engage in political rants, or that contain errors in spelling and grammar give a negative impression to recruiters. Conversely, examples of the candidate's work, engagement in volunteering, and mutual connections can cast the candidate in a more favourable light.

While this might make candidates abandon their social media profiles, or hide behind increased privacy settings, it is worth considering that 12 per cent of recruiters also see a limited social media presence as detrimental.

 What information about you is freely available online and potentially available for current and potential employers to see?

It would be a naïve job applicant who thought that informal selection measures were not used. Phone calls to previous employers and checks of social networking sites are commonplace even if on dubious legal and ethical grounds. From an ideographic perspective, we can see how social networks and online information provide an insight into personalities that is not given by formal methods. All aspects of a person's life are laid bare—their interests, the comments they have made, and the photographs that they are tagged in. A candidate who says they are 'serious and hardworking' on an application form might find this undermined by numerous social media photographs of them falling out of nightclubs, for example.

Kluemper and Rosen (2009) discovered that, compared to an instrument such as a personality test, social media give a rich and wide-ranging insight into a person's lifestyle, giving a good estimation of a personality on the big five scale. However, they caution about the nature of information available through social media. Recruiters are able to discover aspects of a person's life which relate to protected characteristics—marital status, sexual orientation, religion, etc.—and which might feed into discrimination and stereotyping. This raises legal issues—employers have access, through social networking sites, to information that cannot be used legally as the basis for selection decisions.

Many career and professional development courses now encourage you to manage your 'digital presence'—the information that is available about you to potential employers online and through social media. However, while increased privacy settings can hide much of this content from public view, there have been cases where employers have asked for passwords to be handed over so that they can view the entirety of their content (*Time Magazine*, 2012). Facebook (2012) has described this as 'distressing', stating that passwords should not be handed over because it compromises the privacy of the information of the candidate's linked friends on Facebook. More recently, the European Union has decreed that recruiters need sufficient legal grounds to consult social media profiles.

Visit the online resources and take a look at the extension material for Chapter 8 for more information about your digital presence and the use of social media in selection and personality assessment.

289

Automation and artificial intelligence: the big data approach

Whilst recruiters might use social media profiles to make informal decisions, these profiles also create a lot of data. Furthermore, there are recruitment agencies which store CVs and other data of potential recruits which they use when their clients present them with vacancies that need to be filled (Wall, 2014). Computer systems and algorithms are used to analyse this data, thus automating the recruitment process (see Chapter 4), using artificial intelligence (AI; see Chapter 10) to make recruitment and selection decisions. People can be rejected and, in some cases, hired without any human judgement being made (Buranyi, 2018; Finley, 2018).

Simple applications of AI to the recruitment process can include screening CVs for keywords, or psychometric tests which candidates undertake as part of an online recruitment process. Suitable candidates can be singled out from a large number of CVs, or rejected automatically based on the scores of a personality test. The recruitment company Hays has even developed an analysis of changes made to LinkedIn profiles which predicts when users are about to start looking for jobs and targets them for vacancies (Murphy, 2018).

This type of data analysis automates parts of the recruitment and selection process associated with the nomothetic approach—simple, measurable characteristics. However, such automation has also been applied to parts of the process associated more with the ideographic approach—the interview. Online video interviews are analysed using artificial intelligence algorithms, with speech, tone, and facial expressions compared against those of top-performing employees to make judgements about the personality and future behaviours of the candidate. Again, a rejection can be made automatically with no human judgement (Buranyi, 2018; Finley, 2018).

Using data in this way has potential advantages for both recruiters and candidates.

- It helps recruiters to deal efficiently with a large number of applications, adding more ways by which unsuitable candidates can be screened out of the process. This is especially important for recruitment agencies which hold data on hundreds of thousands of clients, but may need to pinpoint specific candidates quickly for a vacancy.

- It promotes fairness by increasing the parts of the process which are 'name blind,' reducing the possibility for unconscious bias even in the interview process. The analysis of data can eliminate misconceptions that are held about candidates (Faragher, 2014). For example, Wall (2014) suggests that data has shown that, contrary to widely held opinion, long-term unemployed candidates are as effective in work as those with more recent work experience.

However, there are also disadvantages to the big data approach.

- For candidates the approach can be impersonal, with no human contact, and automated rejection letters offer no opportunity for personal feedback on the application process (Buranyi, 2018; Finley, 2018).

- The online aspect can be a disadvantage to older applicants or those not familiar with or without access to such technology (Buranyi, 2018).

- Artificial intelligence can learn biases already existing within organizations—for example, if an organization learns behaviours from an overwhelmingly white workforce then these are the personality characteristics that it will learn and then favour within its systems (Boyde, 2017).

- As explored earlier with personality tests, people can be trained to present themselves in the best way in video interviews, or can cheat the system: for example, by putting hidden text in their CVs containing keywords that the system will interpret favourably (Buranyi, 2018).

Although such systems can draw on more data points, they are still prone to the criticisms of the nomothetic approach in that they create an abstract version of the personality. A 'human touch' is still needed within the process, such as face-to-face interviews (Wall, 2014) or using references to verify the data on CVs (Finley, 2018).

Getting an overall picture: assessment centres and triangulation

🔍 Running case: the new duty manager

The interviews prove inconclusive, with different members of the panel having wildly differing perceptions of the candidates. It becomes apparent that few of the opinions have anything to do with people's aptitudes for the job and, in some cases, the grounds that panel members have for rejecting a candidate would be illegal and discriminatory.

'Only one way to settle this,' says Chance. 'Let's get them down on the gym floor and see them actually doing the job'.

Each of the candidates is asked to meet with an actual gym member, speak to them, and devise and deliver a workout plan.

Following this the candidates are given an 'in-tray' exercise. Each is placed in front of a computer and given a number of tasks to address: timetabling classes, staff rotas, etc.

Finally, a second interview is offered to the candidates. In this instance, questions are worked out in advance, with each being of relevance to the job or reflecting on the exercise that had taken place.

One candidate above all others shines through. Although his personality test wasn't the best fit, he has done well on the extraversion and agreeableness aspects. The interview and his work with the customers brings this out, and the in-tray exercise shows that he can also apply himself to individual administrative tasks.

The job of duty manager is offered to David Smith, who accepts.

Pilbeam and Corbridge (2010) summarize research into different methods and their predictive validities (Table 8.5). Taken by themselves, any of the formal assessment methods that we have so far encountered in this chapter score woefully low in predictive validity.

An **assessment centre**, however, blends a variety of assessment tools, such as observation, interviews, and tests, which can provide a more complete a picture of the candidate and can also add the human element missing from purely data-driven selection methods. This approach creates greater predictive validity by using more methods, therefore overcoming the weaknesses of single assessment tools.

While methods such as personality testing and interviews may still be used, methods that have found to be effective include those that are related to the work itself, for example so-called 'in-tray exercises', where a candidate actually works through some of the tasks that might be expected of them. In the earlier examples of Timpson and Pret a Manger, one of the techniques used to assess whether or not an applicant possesses the desired personality characteristics is to get them to actually work a shift in one of their stores.

While an assessment centre approach doesn't give an understanding of personality in its full ideographic form, it does draw upon more sources of information than a personality test or an interview alone. Furthermore, its formal nature can avoid the assessors being party to some of the legally problematic information that more informal methods, while giving a fuller picture of personality, might provide.

Table 8.5 Predictive validities of different selection methods

1.0	Certain prediction
0.9	
0.8	
0.7	Assessment centres for development
0.6	Skilful and structured interviews Ability tests, including numerical and verbal reasoning
0.5	Work sampling
0.4	Assessment centres for job performance Biographical data Personality assessment
0.3	Unstructured interviews
0.2	
0.1	References Interests Years of job experience
0.0	Graphology Astrology Age

© People Resourcing and Talent Planning: Contemporary HRM in Practice, Pilbeam, S., and Corbridge, M., Pearson Education Limited, 2010 (p. 189).

⟳ Real life case: multiple selection methods at Nissan

The car manufacturer Nissan outline the various stages of the selection process for their graduate and placement recruitment scheme in the UK. At each stage, candidates can be rejected or move on to the next stage. The earlier stages are online, and more in line with 'big data' approaches, with face-to-face contact happening later in the assessment centre and interview stages. The stages for the application are shown in Table 8.6.

Table 8.6 Stages in Nissan's selection process

Online stages	Online application form, including uploading a CV and covering letter Online assessment—a type of personality test to ensure that 'our values are aligned with each other' Video interview—pre-recorded interview questions which are uploaded to a cloud server
Face-to-face stages	Assessment centre stage, with various group and individual activities including a structured, competency-based interview and a presentation Individual interview, with a possible final, informal interview to discuss the candidate's 'specific organizational fit'

Source: Nissan (2018).

❓ Review questions

Describe	What is an assessment centre approach?
Explain	How can social media lead to discriminatory judgements being made in the recruitment and selection process?
Analyse	Do you think that the automation of recruitment and selection through big data makes the process fairer?
Apply	Look again at the stages of the selection process at Nissan. What information about a candidate do you think each stage adds to the selection process? Can you relate each stage to nomothetic or ideographic approaches?

Towards a social–radical approach

🔍 Running case: the spark is extinguished

Six months after his appointment, David Smith is seeing out the last of the evening's guests and is about to lock up. Simon Chance catches a glimpse of him looking sullen, barely raising his voice to say goodbye to the remaining guests, then slamming the door shut and lamely throwing the keys on to his desk.

This confirms what Chance had been hearing—the bubbly, outgoing, motivated personality that Chance had recruited six months ago has become withdrawn, barely raising a smile during the day. It isn't the best image to project to customers.

Chance is puzzled as to what has happened. All of the recruitment stages—the personality test, the interviews, the situational assessments—had marked Smith out as having the exact personality that they had wanted. And to begin with, he had been just that—it was as if his personality had changed.

Chance calls Smith over to find out what has happened.

'It's the work here,' replies Smith. 'I have to fill in so many forms—rotas, pay sheets, class timetables, and accident reports. I feel like I'm suffocating in paperwork. It's all just me and a computer. I need to be around people, that's how I get my buzz. I have to just pass on orders to the other guys in the team—they see me as someone who gives them work, not works with them. And it's rubbing off on them, too. We have to go out there and motivate customers, but with this kind of work the spark is just extinguished.'

The nomothetic approach saw personality as something which can be measured and sorted into particular types and categories. The ideographic approach saw personalities as more unique and complex, developing as a result of social interaction and experiences. In both cases, however, they see personality as a something independent of the organization or workplace, which the organization, in some way, observes and tries to understand.

However, we saw with the ideographic approach that organizations themselves are one of the many societal influences on the self which change and develop our personalities. The workplace thus has a direct effect on the very thing it is trying to measure—personality.

The social–radical view that we introduce in this final section brings about a shift in perception of the relationship between organizations and personality. It suggests that rather than personality being an objective 'thing,' independent of the organization, the organization plays a part in creating and shaping personalities.

- Firstly, we see personality categorizations as a tool of organizations which come to take on lives of their own and actually have an effect on personalities, rather than simply measuring them. This is symptomatic of how Michel Foucault (1977) saw power operating in society, and so we term this the social part of the social–radical approach.
- Secondly, organizations directly affect personalities and this can be in a negative, as much as positive, way. This negative effect was observed by radical psychiatrist Félix Guattari (e.g. Guattari and Negri, 1990). We see this as the radical aspect of the social–radical approach.

Foucault's critique of categorization

In Chapters 4 and 14 we encounter Michel Foucault, who examined ways in which power operates throughout society. One of Foucault's (1977) interests, examined in Chapter 4, is how power is exercised by the categorizing, calculating, and ordering of the world around us. We are categorized and labelled as a means of convenience, i.e. it is a simple way of understanding and managing the world. What is important for Foucault is that although such categorizations are shortcuts, they come to take on lives of their own and people identify themselves by these labels.

Think of the results of personality tests. Such categories as INTJ, ENFP, etc. are frameworks that have been created as a simple way to categorize personalities and make measuring them more efficient. But once such tests are administered, people often wear the results as labels that they identify with—people say 'I am an ENTP', etc. The label starts to define not only how the person identifies themselves, but how they actually act. Rather than simply reflecting a personality, the test and its label starts to affect and change that personality.

Deleuze and Guattari (1983) build on Foucault's work to examine how psychoanalytical traditions place labels upon people in both nomothetic and ideographic approaches. Jung orders the personality into certain types; they also criticize Freud for his 'ordering role' (Deleuze and Parnet, 2002: 14) in interpreting people's unique personalities.

Félix Guattari worked as a radical psychiatrist in France. He was interested in trying new and different means of treating patients rather than traditional methods. Guattari treated patients not by labelling them as a particular personality type, as Jung would, nor by labelling them as having some sort of abnormality, as Freud would. Instead, Guattari saw people as having the potential to become something else, striving for new experiences and interactions so that their personality can constantly develop.

The radical critique of the effects of organization on personality

The problem for Deleuze and Guattari, particularly Guattari, is that the potential of people to strive for new experiences and interactions is often stifled—no more so than by the effects of what organizations actually do and the way in which people are organized.

This is something that we saw in Chapters 2 and 3, with Weber noting how bureaucracy, with its repetitive routines, led to disenchantment and Chaplin's film *Modern times* showing people as dehumanized, their personalities deadened by monotonous factory work.

Rational modes of organization are thus seen as having a stifling effect upon the personalities of workers. For Guattari, however, there is an alternative, and organizations could operate in such a way as to allow individual potential to be realized. Guattari describes work that is focused on promoting individual potential and creativity:

> [A]ctivities in which people can develop themselves as they produce, organizations in which the individual is valuable rather than functional ... And redefining work as creative activity can only happen as individuals emerge from stifled, emotionally blocked rhythms of constraint.
>
> (Guattari and Negri, 1990: 15)

The social–radical view is a complex and critical view of personality which shifts the attention from most of what we have examined in the chapter, i.e. rather than organizations measuring personalities we now see organizations having a direct effect upon people's personalities, more often than not constraining what those personalities could have the potential to be.

The suggestion of the social–radical approach—that organizations should operate in a way that frees individual personalities to reach their potential—may sound idealistic. However, in the following chapters, where we see motivation theories that suggest people should 'self-actualize' and maximize their potential (Chapter 9), and where we see theories of learning that promote the reflective self-development of individuals (Chapter 10), we see people working towards achieving their potential rather than being stifled by the organization.

? Review questions

Describe	What is meant by a 'social–radical' approach to personality?
Explain	How can personality types be viewed as putting 'labels' upon us?
Analyse	How can organizations stifle the potential for personalities to develop? What could they do to prevent this?
Apply	In the running case, what has been the main influence in changing Smith's personality? Is this a fault of the selection process assessing his personality incorrectly or of Junction Hotel in changing his personality?

▌ Connecting case and theory

This chapter has examined the nature of **personality** and how it is assessed as part of the **recruitment** and **selection** process. At the start of the chapter we saw in the advert placed by Junction Hotel that they had thought about some characteristics of the ideal fitness centre manager, such as qualifications and experience, but had given little thought to the ideal personality type for the role, other than a few vague words such as 'self-motivated' and 'dynamic'. It is only when 200 applications were received—too many for Chance to process—that he started to think in more detail about the types of personality characteristics that the ideal candidate would demonstrate.

Chance began to realize that measuring personality is a lengthy process. Personality characteristics are not easy to tell from a CV, but there was not enough time to get to know candidates well enough to really know their personalities. Chance was facing the personality measurement trade-off that was introduced in the chapter: where time is limited, recruiters may have to use efficient techniques which give a less rich picture of a candidate's personality. This is reflected in two approaches to personality introduced in the chapter.

The **nomothetic** approach sees personality as something which is measurable and which can be outlined in terms of models of personality types and/or traits. Such models are the basis for **personality testing** in organizations, and some of these models are used in the recruitment and selection process. Chance and Weaver used a personality test to get an instant snapshot of the personalities of 200 candidates. Using the OCEAN **big five scale**, they were able to eliminate any candidates who were not close to their desired personality profile without even having to look at their application forms or speak to them personally—part of the screening process was **automated**, as with the use of **data** and **artificial intelligence** to make selection decisions a lot more efficient. However, the simplistic numerical results of the personality tests showed the other side of the trade-off—the nomothetic approach reduces personalities to simplistic numbers and scores which have a low **predictive validity**.

A contrasting view of personality is the **ideographic** approach, which sees personality as complex and unique to each individual, and as something which is changed constantly by our interactions with society. It criticizes the nomothetic approach for giving too simplistic a view of personality. Chance did not feel that he had enough of a picture of the remaining candidates, and so he called them in for face-to-face interviews. However, while the interviews were intended to give much more deep and rounded information about the candidates' personalities—as would be suggested by the ideographic approach—the process itself seemed to reflect the low predictive validity which we saw with unstructured interviews. Each of the interviewers demonstrated examples of **perceptual bias** which causes them to make incorrect judgements about the candidates. The **halo/horns** effect came into play when Linda's negative first impression of a candidate getting her name wrong clouded her judgement for the rest of the interview. Simon and Linda showed how people are drawn to people similar to themselves when they look favourably upon candidates who support their football team or come from their home town. Many of the interview panel were guilty of **stereotyping** or **discrimination**, making incorrect judgements based upon the class, accent, or parental status of the candidates—something which could be judged to be illegal if it were to be proven in an industrial tribunal.

The lack of consistent and meaningful information and low predictive validity from the formal selection procedures led Simon to look at the candidates' social media profiles and to ring his contacts. This suggested very different personality traits from those suggested by the personality tests and interviews, showing how such means can give much more accurate personality information. While the use of social networks and other informal methods can provide more insight into personality, the practice is ethically dubious. Simon at least realized that he could not, for legal reasons, use this information in the formal process and so finally decided upon a multi-method approach to select the best candidate.

The chapter introduced an **assessment centre** approach, which blends selection methods in a more formal setting and can provide more accurate and valid results in the selection process. In this case, Junction Hotel eventually used a similar blend of techniques. The work simulation, where candidates worked in the gym work with an actual client, is similar to the approach used at Pret a Manger and Timpson, where candidates work a trial shift. Further techniques for the duty manager role included an **in-tray exercise** and then a second, **structured interview** which related to work-based competencies, both of which are often found within an assessment centre approach.

However, while the assessment centre approach delivered a clear winning candidate in David Smith, he turned out to perform much differently than was predicted by the various selection methods. The change—from a predicted energetic personality to one that is demotivated and sullen in reality—could suggest that the selection methods got his personality wrong, as is often the case, or could be an example of the **social-radical approach**. Here, personality is not just an independent variable that the organization tries to measure—it is something that the organization affects directly. And the bureaucracy and paperwork that is a constant feature of David Smith's work has clearly had an impact in shaping his personality at work from one that is lively and motivated to one where the 'spark' has been extinguished.

Further reading

Chartered Institute of Personnel and Development. 2015. A head for hiring: the behavioural science of recruitment and selection. Available at: http://www.cipd.co.uk/binaries/a-head-for-hiring_2015-behavioural-science-of-recruitment-and-selection.pdf

This research report gives an overview of recruitment and selection techniques, how they link to psychological perspectives on personality, and how bias is found in the process and can be minimized.

Cain, S. 2012. *Quiet: The power of introverts in a world that can't stop talking.* Viking: London.

An overview of Jung's introversion and extraversion from the perspective of the introvert.

Jobvite. 2017. Recruiter nation report. Available at: https://www.jobvite.com/wp-content/uploads/2017/09/Jobvite_2017_Recruiter_Nation_Report.pdf

An overview of US recruitment and selection practices, including the use of social media and the biases that affect both recruiters and candidates.

Roth, Philip L., Bobko, P., Van Iddekinge, C.H., and Thatcher, J.B. 2016. Social media in employee-selection-related decisions: A research agenda for uncharted territory. *Journal of Management* 42 (1): 269–98.

An overview of recent thinking on the use of social media in recruitment and selection.

References

BBC News. 2017. EU clamps down on social media job snoops, 13 July. Available at: https://www.bbc.co.uk/news/technology-40592516

Bearne, S. 2018. Virtual reality and Mr Men books: Companies reveal their unusual recruitment tools. *The Guardian*, 22 January. Available at: https://www.theguardian.com/small-business-network/2018/jan/22/virtual-reality-and-mr-men-books-companies-reveal-their-unusual-recruitment-tools

Bennet, A. 2010. *The shadows of type: Psychological type through seven levels of development.* Lulu: London.

Boffey, D., and Treanor, J. 2013. The Co-op scandal: Drugs, sex, religion ... and the humiliation of a movement. *The Observer*, 23 November. Available at: https://www.theguardian.com/business/2013/nov/23/coop-scandal-paul-flowers-mutual-societies

Boyde, E. 2017. Robo-recruiters are quick to replicate human bias. *Financial Times*, 7 December. Available at: https://www.ft.com/content/1300a86e-c57c-11e7-b30e-a7c1c7c13aab

Buranyi, S. 2018. How to persuade a robot that you should get the job. *The Observer*, 4 March. Available at: https://www.theguardian.com/technology/2018/mar/04/robots-screen-candidates-for-jobs-artificial-intelligence

Cain, S. 2012. *Quiet: The power of introverts in a world that can't stop talking.* Viking: London.

Callaghan, G., and Thompson, P. 2002. 'We recruit attitude': The selection and shaping of routine call centre labour. *Journal of Management Studies* 39 (2): 233–54.

Cattell, R.B. 1966. *The scientific analysis of personality.* Aldine: Chicago.

CIPD (Chartered Institute of Personnel and Development). 2015. A head for hiring: The behavioural science of recruitment and selection. Available at: http://www.cipd.co.uk/binaries/a-head-for-hiring_2015-behavioural-science-of-recruitment-and-selection.pdf

Clark, P. 2018. Our faith in psychometric testing is flawed. *Financial Times*, 28 January. Available at: https://www.ft.com/content/8680e8e6-01e3-11e8-9650-9c0ad2d7c5b5

Costa, P.T. Jr, and McCrae, R.R. 1992. *Revised NEO Personality Inventory (NEO-PI-R) and NEO Five-Factor Inventory (NEO-FFI) manual.* Psychological Assessment Resources: Odessa, FL.

Cunningham, L. 2012. Myers-Briggs: Does it pay to know your type? *Washington Post*, 14 December. Available at: https://www.washingtonpost.com/national/on-leadership/myers-briggs-does-it-pay-to-know-your-type/2012/12/14/eaed51ae-3fcc-11e2-bca3-aadc9b7e29c5_story.html?noredirect=on&utm_term=.1172310d0d27

Dakin, S., Nilakant, V., and Jensen, R. 1994. The role of personality testing in managerial selection. *Journal of Managerial Psychology* 9 (5): 3–11.

Deleuze, G., and Guattari, F. 1983. *Anti-Oedipus: Capitalism and schizophrenia*. University of Minnesota Press: Minneapolis.

Deleuze, G., and Parnet, C. 2002. *Dialogues II*. Continuum: New York.

Deloitte. 2018. Our selection process. Available at: https://www2.deloitte.com/uk/en/pages/careers/articles/selection-process.html (last accessed 30 April 2018).

Dana, J., Dawes, R., and Peterson, N. 2013. Belief in the unstructured interview: The persistence of an illusion. *Judgment and Decision Making* 8 (5): 512–20.

Eysenck, H.J., and Eysenck, M.W. 1985. *Personality and individual differences: A natural science approach*. Plenum Publishing Corporation: New York.

Facebook. 2012. Protecting your passwords and your privacy, 23 March. Available at: https://www.facebook.com/notes/facebookand-privacy/protecting-your-passwords-and-your-privacy/326598317390057C (last accessed 20 August 2015).

Faragher, J. 2014. Psychometric testing: The stark truth. *People Management*, June.

Financial Conduct Authority. 2018. FCA bans former Co-operative Bank Chair, Paul Flowers, from the financial services industry. 6 March. Available at: https://www.fca.org.uk/news/press-releases/fca-bans-former-co-operative-bank-chair-paul-flowers-financial-services-industry (last accessed 30 April 2018).

Finley, S. 2018. 'I didn't even meet my potential employers'. *BBC News*, 6 February.

Available at: http://www.bbc.co.uk/news/business-42905515

Foucault, M. 1977. *Discipline and punish: The birth of the prison*. Pantheon Books: New York.

French, R., and Rumbles, S. 2010. Recruitment and selection. In: Rees, G., and French, R. (eds) *Leading, managing and developing people*, 3rd edn. Chartered Institute of Personnel and Development: London, pp. 169–90.

Freud, S. 1927. *The ego and the id* (authorized transl. Riviere, J.). Hogarth Press: London.

Fulham, R. 2017. Why Timpson uses Mr Men characters to recruit staff. *HR Grapevine*, 24 April. Available at: https://www.hrgrapevine.com/content/article/news-2017-04-24-why-timpson-uses-mr-men-characters-to-recruit-staff (last accessed 16 July 2018).

Furnham, A.F. 1997. Knowing and faking one's five-factor personality score. *Journal of Personality Assessment* 69 (1): 229–43.

Godley. 2018. City watchdog bans ex-Co-op bank boss for sending emails about sex and drugs *The Guardian* 6 March. Available at: https://www.theguardian.com/business/2018/mar/06/disgraced-ex-co-op-bank-boss-paul-flowers-crystal-methodist-banned-from-financial-services

Gosling, S.D., Rentfrow, P.J., and Swann, W.B. Jr 2003. A very brief measure of the big-five personality domains. *Journal of Research in Personality* 37: 504–28.

Guattari, F., and Negri, A. 1990. *Communists like us: New spaces of liberty, new lines of alliance*. Semiotext(e): New York.

Hosie, R. 2017. Why the Myers-Briggs test should never be used in recruitment. *The Independent*, 11 August. Available at: https://www.independent.co.uk/life-style/myers-briggs-test-recruitment-why-never-use-occupation-psychologists-a7888076.html?cmpid=facebook-post

Jacobs, K. 2015. Pret's people management secrets. *HR Magazine*, 23 January.

Jacobs, K. 2018. Psychometric testing no longer meets my business needs. *People Management*, March.

Jefferson, E. 2015. Could you pass this ridiculously intrusive personality test to get a job at McDonald's? *Mirror Online*, 15 April. Available at: https://www.mirror.co.uk/usvsth3m/could-you-pass-ridiculously-intrusive-5524546

Jobvite. 2017. Recruiter nation report. Available at: https://www.jobvite.com/wp-content/uploads/2017/09/Jobvite_2017_Recruiter_Nation_Report.pdf

Judge, T.A., and Zapata, C.P. 2015. 'The person–situation debate revisited: Effect of situation strength and trait activation on the validity of the big five personality traits in predicting job performance.' *Academy of Management Journal* 58 (4): 1149–79.

Jung, C.G. 1923. *Psychological types: or, The psychology of individuation* (transl H. Godwyn Baynes). Harcourt Brace: New York.

Kaufman, S.B., and Gregoire, C. 2016. Wired to create: Unravelling the mysteries of the creative mind. Ebury Digital: London.

Keirsey, D. 1998. *Please understand me II: Temperament, character, intelligence.* Prometheus Nemesis: Del Mar, CA.

Keogh, O. 2018. Should you erase your digital footprint to progress your career? *Irish Times*, 23 March. Available at: https://www.irishtimes.com/business/work/should-you-erase-your-digital-footprint-to-progress-your-career-1.3434973

Kluemper, D.H., and Rosen, P.A. 2009. Future employment selection methods: Evaluating social networking web sites. *Journal of Managerial Psychology* 24 (6): 567–80.

McCrae, R.R., and Costa, P.T. Jr. 1990. *Personality in adulthood.* Guilford Press: New York.

McCrae, R.R., and Costa, P.T. Jr. 1996. Toward a new generation of personality theories: Theoretical contexts for the five-factor model. In: Wiggins, J.S. (ed.) *The five-factor model of personality: Theoretical perspectives.* Guilford Press: New York, pp. 51–87.

Moore, J. 2014. Disgraced Paul Flowers won Co-op job thanks to 'psychometric tests' results. *The Independent*, 28 January. Available at: https://www.independent. co.uk/news/business/news/disgraced-paul-flowers-won-co-op-job-thanks-to-psychometric-tests-results-9090641.html

Moore, P. 2015. Pret a Manger—behind the scenes at the 'Happy Factory'. *The Guardian*, 14 April.

Morgeson, F.P., Campion, M.A., Dipboye, R.L., Hollenbeck, J.R., Murphy, K., and Schmitt, N. 2007. Reconsidering the use of personality tests in personnel selection contexts. *Personnel Psychology* 60 (3): 683–729.

Murphy, H. 2018. UK recruiters use technology to offer 'pre-emptive' jobs. *Financial Times*, 6 April. Available at: https://www.ft.com/content/46346c46-2e79-11e8-9b4b-bc4b9f08f381

Myers, I.B. 1962. *Manual: The Myers-Briggs type indicator.* Consulting Psychologist Press: Palo Alto, CA.

Myers, I.B., and Myers, P.B. 1995. *Gifts differing: Understanding personality type.* Davies-Black: Palo Alto, CA.

Myerscough, P. 2013. Short cuts. *London Review of Books*, 3 January.

Newell, S., and Rice, C. 1999. Assessment, selection and evaluation: Problems and pitfalls. In: Leopold, J., Harris, L., and Watson, T. (eds) *Strategic human resourcing: Principles, perspectives and practices.* Financial Times/Pitman: London, pp. 129–65.

Nissan. 2018. What to expect at application and interview: Nissan Sunderland graduates and placements. Available at: https://careersatnissan.co.uk/nissan-graduate-scheme-placements/graduate-schemes/ (last accessed 30 April 2018).

O'Connor, S. 2016. Q&A: Does 'name-blind' recruitment combat bias? *Finacial Times*, 17 October. Available at: https://www.ft.com/content/3d7b6590-9443-11e6-a80e-bcd69f323a8b

Passer, M.W., Smith, R., Atkinson, M., Mitchell, J., and Muir, D. 2003. *Psychology: Frontiers and applications.* McGraw-Hill Ryerson: Toronto.

Parkinson, J., and Smith-Walters, M. 2015. Who, What, Why: What is name-blind recruitment? *BBC News*, 26 October.

Available at: http://www.bbc.co.uk/news/magazine-34636464

Pietrzak, D., Page, B., Korcuska, J.S., and Bach Gorman, A. 2015. An examination of the relationship of the 16PF fifth edition to a multidimensional model of self-esteem. SAGE Open 5 (4), https://doi.org/10.1177/2158244015611453.

Pilbeam, S., and Corbridge, M. 2010. *People resourcing and talent management: HRM in practice*, 4th edn. Financial Times/Prentice Hall: Harlow.

Radulova, L. 2015. So could YOU pass the McDonald's job quiz? Fast food restaurant uses 'personality' test to find out whether potential employees are suitable (and it's not as straightforward as you think!) *Mail Online*, 15 April. Available at: http://www.dailymail.co.uk/news/article-3039260/So-pass-McDonald-s-job-quiz-Fast-food-restaurant-uses-personality-test-potential-employees-suitable-s-not-easy-think.html

Rawlinson, K. 2013. Pret workers want more for their smile: Enough pay and hours to live on. *The Independent*, 4 January.

Reilly, R.R., and Chao, G.T. 1982. Validity and fairness of some alternative employee selection procedures 1. *Personnel Psychology* 35 (1): 1–62.

Roth, P.L., Bobko, P., Van Iddekinge, C.H., and Thatcher, J.B. 2016. Social media in employee-selection-related decisions: A research agenda for uncharted territory. *Journal of Management* 42 (1): 269–98.

Smith, R. 2015. McDonald's serves up the unexpected with personality test for candidates. *HR Grapevine*, 16 April. Available at: https://www.hrgrapevine.com/content/article/2015-04-16-mcdonalds-serves-up-the-unexpected-with-personality-test-for-candidates

Smart, V. 2017. The power of introverts. *People Management*, 25 January. Available at: https://www.peoplemanagement.co.uk/long-reads/articles/power-introverts

Stein, D. 2000. The neurobiology of evil: Psychiatric perspectives on perpetrators, *Ethnicity and Health*, 5 (3–4): 303–15.

Syal, R. 2009. Undercover job hunters reveal huge race bias in Britain's workplaces. *The Observer*, 18 October. Available at: https://www.theguardian.com/money/2009/oct/18/racism-discrimination-employment-undercover

The Guardian. 2011. Reading the riots: Investigating England's summer of disorder [series]. Available at: http://www.guardian.co.uk/uk/series/reading-the-riots

Thompson, P., and McHugh, D. 2009. *Work organisations: A critical approach*. Palgrave Macmillan: Basingstoke.

Time Magazine. 2012. Job seekers getting asked for Facebook passwords, 20 March.

Timpson, J. 2018. How to uncover an interview candidate's personality. *Daily Telegraph*, 3 April. Available at: https://www.telegraph.co.uk/connect/small-business/how-to-uncover-an-interview-candidates-personality/

Treanor, J. 2014. Ex-Co-op Bank chairman Paul Flowers aced psychometric tests—deputy. *The Guardian*, 28 January. Available at: https://www.theguardian.com/business/2014/jan/28/coop-bank-deputy-chairman-quit-project-verde

Wall, M. 2014. Does job success depend on data rather than your CV? *BBC News*, 2 October. Available at: http://www.bbc.co.uk/news/business-29343425

CHAPTER 9

Motivation and the meaning of work

Is it all about the money?

Chapter overview and learning outcomes

By the end of this chapter you should be able to:

- describe the differences between extrinsic, intrinsic, and social factors of motivation

- explain the role of pay and the extent to which it motivates workers

- analyse the role of psychology in understanding motivation, explaining the main contributions of behaviourist, content, and process approaches

- analyse why organizations are increasingly looking to gamification and needs-based theories of motivation as a new ways of motivating employees

- explain how social factors, such as identity and orientations to work, contribute to our understanding of what motivates people to work

Key theorists	
Burrhus Frederic (B.F.) Skinner	Pioneered operant conditioning, which is used in workplace behavioural modification techniques
Abraham Maslow	Developed the hierarchy of needs, which was then used as a theory of workplace motivation
Frederick Herzberg	Suggested that only some job characteristics motivate people in the workplace, while other hygiene factors can only cause dissatisfaction
John Stacey Adams	Developed equity theory, which suggests that people are motivated by comparing their workplace rewards with others
Victor Vroom	Developed expectancy theory, which suggests that people are motivated by actions which help them achieve their desired goals
Carol Dweck	Argued that individuals should move from a fixed mindset, where people are thought to have innate talent and skills, to adopting a growth mindset, a belief that abilities can be developed through dedication and hard work

Key terms

Extrinsic motivators	Motivating factors that come from rewards factors external to an activity, e.g. pay, praise, or prestige
Intrinsic motivators	Motivating factors that come from the activity itself: personal or internal rewards, e.g. curiosity or pleasure deriving from the experience
Behavioural theories of motivation	A use of stimulus and response techniques whereby behaviour is altered by a planned provision of rewards and punishments
Content theories of motivation	Theories of motivation which suggest that the content of work be designed so as best to meet the needs which motivate workers; examples include Maslow's hierarchy of needs and Herzberg's motivators and hygiene theory
Process theories of motivation	Theories of motivation which suggest that motivation is a result of individual processes of perception, comparison, and calculation; examples include equity theory and expectancy theory
Social theories of motivation	Theories of motivation which see motivation as part of the role of work in creating meaning and identity for people within society

Introduction

🔍 Running case: a sense of lethargy

Something is wrong in reception; Meg Mortimer looks at her team. 'They look sluggish,' she thinks to herself. 'They are all doing their jobs, but their efforts seem half-hearted, and they're not going the extra mile. There is no enthusiasm,' she thinks. 'What can I do to get it going again? I need to find an incentive.'

But Mortimer knows her team are not usually like this. She makes some notes:

* David Morrison—a young porter who, in his spare time, is training to do a triathlon;
* Jane Foster—a receptionist who is also undertaking a hospitality course and is tipped for great things within the hotel;
* Sue Ridgewell—another receptionist who Mortimer considers to be good, but not as ambitious as Jane;
* Steve Long and John McAuley—two students who work part time either as porters or sometimes behind reception; and
* Ellerby Peters, a student on work experience.

The reception area is quiet and all that Mortimer sees are the sullen faces of the reception team. What can she possibly do to make these people more motivated towards their work?

Why are you reading this chapter? Would you not rather be playing computer games, or hanging out with friends? Is it because you have a test, essay, or seminar to prepare for, or are you genuinely interested in motivation and want to know more? Without some motivation you will quickly stop reading and put the book away. We all need motivation in order to do work.

Yet despite its importance, motivation and engagement are widely reported as key problems that businesses face. According to a Gallup survey in 2017, only 15 per cent of full-time adult employees worldwide (and in East Asia only 6 per cent) felt highly involved and enthusiastic about their work (Gallup, 2017). Another survey by management consultants Full Potential stated that 51-year-olds said they were 77 per cent motivated whereas 20-year-olds said they were only 59 per cent motivated. For millennials, a lack of work-life balance and not being able to work remotely were reported as two key demotivating factors (Haslett, 2017). Furthermore, a 2018 Gallup survey revealed that only 20 per cent of employees strongly agree that their performance is managed in a way that motivates them to do outstanding work (McDonald, 2018).

Low motivation matters. It can lead to poor performance, dissatisfaction spreading to other workers, poor customer service, and regular mistakes. So how do you motivate employees? For Ford and Taylor, the answer was simple. Work is not interesting, and often workers are lazy, so the only way to motivate them is by rewards and punishments. This approach sees all motivation as external, with motivating factors being extrinsic to the individual. Yet for Maslow, Herzberg, and many others these external motivators are not enough. They argue that we can redesign jobs to be more meaningful and interesting and to give room for autonomy and self-expression. They see motivation as also internal to the task itself.

At the heart of this debate are fundamental questions about human nature: what makes us tick, and how can we get the best out of people? One solution is to redesign work in a way that can motivate workers. These content theory approaches redesign work to motivate staff, and look at what goes on around the individual. In contrast, process theories see motivation as more individual and changeable, focusing on how motivation changes over time.

Psychological theories focus on the individual and what motivates them. They have dominated motivation theory as they provide insights into how people think and the secrets of motivation. While they offer interesting insights they do not fully explain workplace motivation. Sociological perspectives offer an alternative view of motivation, which we consider at the end of the chapter. Sociological perspectives examine the meanings people attach to work and how this feeds into their identity in society.

How do you motivate people? Extrinsic and intrinsic motivation

Running case: triathlon man

David Morrison sprints to the finish and quickly reaches for his phone to press 'Finish' on his Strava app as he completes his latest 10K run. '50:23, not too bad,' he thinks to himself, 'but I really want to get under 50 minutes.' As sweat pours off his brow the young porter at Junction Hotel feels a sense of elation and joy at his latest run. Despite having to drag himself out of his warm bed at 6 am to do his run in these freezing conditions, Morrison feels a sense of meaning and purpose. Morrison is obviously not getting paid for any of this. Indeed, he had to spend quite a lot of his own money for equipment, entry fees, and sports club memberships. And the sponsorship money for the triathlon will all be going to his charity—again, a feeling which makes him proud.

'Oh, no,' he thinks to himself, as he contemplates the day ahead, 'a day of standing around reception, being told what to do, just opening doors and taking bags up to rooms.' He has to do what he is told, when he is told, and he rarely feels challenged at work. As he gets into his porter's outfit, David walks towards reception to perform the one element of the day for which he will actually be rewarded with a wage. His response to starting this part of the day is negative: he lets out a sigh, feeling all of his enthusiasm drain away. He looks up at the clock, 'I can't wait for lunchtime, to go in the pool,' he thinks.

If we think work is something dull, repetitive, and often unchallenging, we may try to avoid working hard wherever possible. If you have ever had a part-time job to get through university, such as stacking shelves in a supermarket, you probably don't work for the fun of it. So how can we motivate people? Frederick Taylor and Henry Ford (see Chapter 3) said the answer was pay:

- Taylor believed that workers had a 'natural laziness' (1911: 20)—they were inherently de-motivated. He used piece rates (payment for the actual amount of work done) to motivate people.

- Ford similarly believed that pay motivated people, but rather than piece rates, he introduced the $5 day. This was a massive increase from the previous $2.40 per day (Raff and Summers, 1987: 69). However, the Fordist factory was rationalization and highly mechanized, producing highly controlled and quite dull working conditions (Beynon, 1984: 34). Workers disliked the conditions intensely, but the high wage motivated many job-seekers to want to work in Ford's factories (see Chapter 3).

Both Taylor and Ford had a simple, coercive view of motivation based on the assumption of *homo economicus*—that people are motivated by pay and economic reasons alone (see Chapter 5). They saw motivation as extrinsic, external to the individual. The most popular incentive is pay, but things such as grade, praise, or recognition could also incentivize workers (Cerasoli et al., 2014). Because work is dull, you have to force people to do it. People do not *want* to work, so to get them to take action they need a prod, and to keep them working they need direction and control (Pink, 2018). The assumption about human nature here is that people are passive but motivated to avoid pain and seek pleasure, so managers need to create external motivations through punishment and rewards. Rewards and punishments are conditional, working on an 'if–then' approach—i.e. *if* you hit a sales target, *then* you receive a bonus. To enforce this, all workers need monitoring to make sure they do their job.

Whereas Taylor used time and motion studies and supervisors to measure and monitor staff, modern workplaces, such as Amazon's warehouses, can provide even closer scrutiny. Amazon's patented wristband (see Chapter 3) will monitor where workers are, their movements, how many items they pick, and will vibrate to guide individual actions (*The Economist*, 2018). Rather than having a supervisor telling you what to do, it is the bracelet, responding to real-time body movements, controlling the worker. This form of control is based on extrinsic motivation, as it works on the basis of reward and punishment. It also borders on coercion, as staff are highly controlled with punishments, such as being sacked, if they fail to meet their targets.

 How would you feel being monitored constantly by a wristband? Would you act differently if you were always watched?

Do rewards increase or decrease motivation?

 Real life case: how to get your employees to work for free

Pandora was one of the trailblazers of digital music and is a rival to Spotify and iTunes. It works by analysing music and connecting it together through a 'music genome', to enable users to discover new music.

It was founded in 2000 with $2 million start-up money, but just one year later, amid the bursting of the dot-com bubble, it went bankrupt. To get round this, CEO Tim Westergren convinced the employees to work for an ever smaller share of their salary, and by the end of 2001 they were not getting paid at all, getting stock options (on a company that was losing money) rather than salaries. Ultimately 50 employees worked for two years for free, Pandora owed $2m in back salaries (which they since have learnt is illegal), and Tim Westergren had personal debts of $500,000. Eventually they held out long enough for an investor, which meant that everyone could be paid.

How did he motivate these 50 employees to work for free? Westergren, a former musician, led by example, being the first to take a salary deferral. But it was more than money. He said he had a clear sense of purpose that everyone believed in. Everyone involved was passionate about music and believed the site would help artists. Westergren gave great speeches, stressing how unique, important, and life-changing the product they were making was. He stressed that what they were doing was magical. Westergren said that Pandora was changing culture, and he asked his employees 'How many times in your life do you have a chance to do that?' (Executive Grapevine, 2015a).

Yet was it a risk that paid off? Pandora have continued to struggle, and in 2016 and 2017 have continued to lay off staff (Nicolaou, 2018) with Tim Westergren himself departing as part of a $480m investment from satellite radio company SiriusXM (Dye, 2017).

Pandora logo.

Visit the online resources and take a look at the extension material for Chapter 9 to view Tim Westergren's full speech.

 Why do you think Westergren's speeches convinced people to work for free? Would you work for free for two years for a company in the hope of getting paid if they became successful? How would you feel if you had worked for free for two years because you believed in the mission of Pandora, only for them to be invested in by a bigger company?

Sources: Executive Grapevine (2015a); Harrison (2015); Dye (2017); Nicolaou (2018).

Tim Westergren's ability to get his employees working for free for over two years might be an extreme example, but it does show that pay is not the only factor affecting motivation. For employees of Pandora, the belief that they were doing a once-in-a-lifetime piece of work was also exciting.

Studies into the relationship between motivation, pay, and other types of reward have shown a similar mixed picture.

- The 2014 Global Workforce Study of 32,000 employees worldwide stated that the number one top attraction to an employee was the basic pay, with the number two factor being job security (Towers Watson, 2014).

- In an analysis of 45 studies, Condly et al. (2003) found that money produced higher performance gains than other incentives such as gifts. However, Kuvaas et al. (2017) found that extrinsic incentives (i.e. pay) decreased motivation whereas intrinsic factors, such as staff involvement in decision-making, increased motivation.

- In a global survey of executives, managers, and employees (Dewhurst et al., 2009), financial rewards, such as bonuses and an increase in base pay, played an important part in motivating workers; however, non-financial incentives, such as praise from a manager, attention from managers, and being given responsibility, were shown as being slightly more effective motivating factors.

Pay, it seems, has an important role in motivation. However, praise from the boss can motivate employees just as much. Rewards such as praise or interesting work are not as tangible as pay, but they are still extrinsic motivators and management have a role in providing these motivating factors within the workplace. However, such rewards may also contribute to workers gaining intrinsic rewards, through feeling more involved in their jobs (Kuvaas et al., 2017).

Intrinsic motivation

 Real life case: lottery millionaires

How much money would it take for you to give up work and retire immediately? This is sometimes known as the lottery question, because many people enjoy speculating on what they would do if they won the lottery. According to an opinion poll conducted in 2017, 45 per cent of British workers would immediately retire if they were given £1m, 53 per cent would retire for £2m, and 66 per cent would retire for £10m. However, 12 per cent of workers said that no money would persuade them to give up working (Fishwick, 2017).

In November 2014 a syndicate of five paper-mill workers shared a £2.9 million lottery jackpot, giving them around £600,000 each. Yet rather than instantly quitting their jobs, they were straight back to work 'due to the workload'. Gary, one of the winners, said the company were 'quite short staffed' so they didn't want to walk away because of their win. As it was a family business, they felt a loyalty to the company (Flanagan, 2014). Even when lottery winners do give up paid work, this does not necessarily stop them from taking on unpaid work. Canadian Rachel Lapierre won a guaranteed $1,000 per week for the rest of her life, and although she quit her job, instead of spoiling herself the former nurse set up a charity helping people in such places as Haiti, Senegal, and India (Coleman, 2018).

Would you keep on working even if you had enough money to live off? Many lottery winners, football managers, and business executives continue to work despite having more money than they need to live off. Most people want to be involved in some form of work. Whereas extrinsic views of motivation are based on the assumption that we need to be forced (through reward or punishment) to work, intrinsic motivation theory suggests that we are more motivated to do work for its own sake. Indeed, there are lots of examples where people work for free, such as the web-browser Firefox, Linux operating system, or Wikipedia (most entries on the online encyclopaedia Wikipedia are written by people for free). The work is done out of interest, curiosity, or pleasure, or for the satisfaction that comes from the experience. This might be because we love the work or because we believe in it, for example in caring and public-service occupations such as nursing and teaching (de Gieter et al., 2006). The work itself is inherently satisfying and motivating because workers enjoy doing it (Ward and King, 2017). Daniel Pink argues that 'Intrinsically motivated people usually achieve more than their reward-seeking counterparts' (Pink, 2018: 79) and that intrinsic motivation is a renewable resource, whereas extrinsic motivation often needs to increase in order to remain effective. Deci argues that 'we [should] concentrate on structuring situations and jobs to arouse intrinsic motivation' (Deci, 1972: 227).

Extrinsic vs intrinsic motivation

 Real life case: Gamification

Do you spend hours online playing games, or do you know someone who does? Think about what a person is like when they are playing. Gamers often stay focused on a problem, overcome obstacles, work together with others, and take on difficult and challenging tasks. This leaves Jane McGonigal to argue that when playing games we are the best version of ourselves (McGonigal, 2011). Now imagine that you could translate that focus, dedication, teamwork, and desire for challenge into your studies or work. Some, like McGonigal, want to 'incorporate game mechanics into working processes with the attempt to increase employee motivation' (Dymek and Zackariasson, 2016: 21). As Richter et al. argue, 'Gamification attempts to harness the motivational power of games in order to promote participation, persistence and achievements' (2015: 23). Examples include EpicWin, which turns to-do lists into games where you collect points and move up levels to incentivize things that you would not want to do; Stack Overflow, a website for programmers which gives badges for participation in answering questions; and FoldIT, in which users work for free to solve scientific puzzles. Gamification seeks to turn work into a game, using extrinsic motivations (points, levels, etc.) to create intrinsic motivations.

While extrinsic motivations have been demonstrated to produce good short-term boosts in output, the long-term impacts are far more contested. In a famous experiment, psychologists Lepper, Green, and Nisbett examined the impact that extrinsic rewards had on intrinsic motivation. Most 3 to 5-year-olds intrinsically enjoy drawing. Lepper, Green, and Nisbett wanted to find out if giving the child a reward impacted this intrinsic motivation. They placed them into three groups:

1) **expected reward**—where they were told they would receive a gold star or red ribbon if they took part;

2) **unexpected reward**—where they were told about the reward only after doing the drawing;

3) **no reward**—where the child received no reward at all.

Over the next few days the children were observed. Those that had the unexpected reward produced the most drawings, closely followed by those who did not receive a reward. However, the group who had expected a reward produced significantly less drawings over the next few days, leading the researchers to conclude that expecting a reward significantly reduces intrinsic motivation (Lepper et al., 1973). Their 'overjustification effect' hypothesis stated that extrinsic rewards will probably decrease intrinsic motivation. This 'undermining effect' mean that the 'presentation of incentives on an initially enjoyable task reduces subsequent intrinsic motivation for the task' (Cerasoli et al., 2014: 981).

Which is better, intrinsic or extrinsic motivation? Do extrinsic incentives undermine intrinsic motivation, or can you have both? This is a hotly contested topic. Carasoli and colleagues, having surveyed 40 years of literature, argue that it is not conclusive but on balance extrinsic incentives can coexist with intrinsic motivation. Highly repetitive tasks that are not inherently enjoyable do benefit from extrinsic incentives. However, tasks that require more absorption and personal investment and are more complex should not be linked to performance incentives: for example, teachers should not be paid based on their students' performance (Cerasoli et al., 2014: 999). Could work be redesigned to allow greater freedom and autonomy, room for self-expression?

? Review questions

Describe	What is meant by extrinsic motivation and intrinsic motivation?
Explain	How can extrinsic forms of motivation be used at work?
Analyse	What is the role of pay in motivating people to work?
Apply	In the running case, what extrinsic and intrinsic rewards motivate David Morrison?

Behavioural theories and motivation

🔍 Running case: the smile card

Concerned that the reception staff do not seem motivated, Meg Mortimer asks business manager Phil Weaver to help her increase morale. 'Easy,' he responds confidently, 'just reward them for smiling at customers, and punish them if they don't. That'll get the grins back on their faces. All you have to do is measure it, then you can manage them. How about a smile card?' Weaver suggests.

Weaver takes out a pen and quickly starts drawing out a card (Figure 9.1). 'All staff will carry the card with them and get ticks for desirable behaviours—like smiling at a customer, or offering information about the local area. They will get a black mark for those things that we don't want them to do, like being unpleasant to a customer or not offering to help with baggage,' Weaver tells Mortimer.

'Once a month we will gather in the cards. Black marks will be subtracted from ticks, and the winning total will get a pay bonus for that month.'

✋ How well do you think the smile card will tackle issues of morale and motivation among the reception staff?

→

→ Figure 9.1 Junction Hotel's smile card.

Name: John McAuley   Month: May

Desirable behaviours: Black marks:

Date	Behaviour observed	Manager initials	Tick	Date	Behaviour observed	Manager initials	Cross
1/5	Helpful to customer with heavy suitcases	MM	✓	2/5	Passed through reception—ignored guest waiting at desk	SC	x
3/5	Helped guest with airport taxi	MM	✓				
4/5	Very cheerful with group of tourists	SC	✓				

If someone were pointing a gun at you, would you do what they said? Probably yes, for fear of being shot. But, deep down, would you be genuinely *motivated*? What if, instead, they offered you money? Would this motivate you to do anything at any time?

In this section we examine approaches to motivation derived from behaviourism. Behaviourism is an area of psychology which suggests that behaviour can be changed through the planned use of rewards and punishments, sometimes referred to as the 'carrot and stick' approach.

Do you ever use rewards to motivate yourself? For example, if you have an essay to complete you might give yourself a reward, like a night out or a shopping trip, when you have completed it.

An effective motivator?

Source: Daniel Jedzura / Shutterstock.com

Behaviourism is also known as stimulus–response psychology. A stimulus, be it a punishment or a reward, is provided as a means to encourage some form of behaviour or response. In the workplace such stimuli includes extrinsic motivators, such as pay for turning up to work, no matter how monotonous or dehumanizing that work may be, or bonuses to encourage behaviours such as upselling. Pay can also be the basis of punishment, for example withholding bonuses or, ultimately, firing a worker. While we may not work at gunpoint, many people may feel a metaphorical gun is pointed at their head as they need to work to pay bills and survive.

 Real life case: a McDonald's for every win—reward and punishment in football

The secret for Accrington Stanley's success in winning the 2017/18 football League Two title might, at least in part, be down to an unusual bonus. The club Accrington Stanley, once maligned as a joke due to a 1980s advert for milk, has more recently been made famous for another food product, McDonald's. Every time they win, Accrington Stanley owner Andy Holt gives his players £200 to spend on 'McDonald's or the like' as a reward for their victory (Searles, 2018). This bonus pales into insignificance in relation to the reported £4 million each that Manchester United could have earned (although they didn't win) (Perrin, 2017) or the £1 million each that Manchester City players could have got if they had won the Premier League and Champions League (they won only the Premier League) (McGrath, 2018).

In this section we examine how pay and other extrinsic motivators are used as stimuli in behavioural motivation techniques, and to what extent such techniques genuinely motivate workers rather than simply coercing them into performing particular behaviours.

Pavlov and classical conditioning

Running case: grinning like an idiot

From: John McAuley

Been grinning like an idiot all day—not a manager here to see me. Then, one frown and Chance suddenly appears putting a black cross on the card.

From: Steve Long

Haha, bad luck mate.

From: John McAuley

I mean, what an idiot Chance is. Feels like he's writing my school report or something.

Have you ever tried to stop biting your nails? One method you may have used is a foul-tasting nail varnish. Because it tastes so bad, the motivation to stop biting your nails comes from the negative association you develop between the behaviour, nail-biting, and the immediate punishment for that behaviour, the unpleasant taste. This association, and the subsequent modification of behaviour, is termed classical conditioning and was discovered by Russian psychologist Ivan Pavlov (Pavlov and Anrep, 1927).

Pavlov, while investigating the digestive systems of dogs, noticed that a dog's natural response is to salivate when faced with the stimulus of a bowl of food. Pavlov began to ring a bell whenever the food was presented. When this was repeated often enough, Pavlov could ring the bell with no food present and the dogs would still salivate. To maintain the conditioned response and stop it becoming extinct, continuous reinforcement—ringing the bell whenever food was present—was required to maintain the conditioned response.

While classical conditioning might be applicable to humans in clinical settings, such as aversion therapies, its workplace use is limited.

- Punishment needs to be immediate and happen every time a behaviour occurs. In a workplace setting, punishments can have the by-product of causing anxiety and resentment towards managers and lowering morale (Villere and Hartman, 1991: 28).

- To motivate workers, management need to supply rewards continually to avoid extinction of that behaviour. Villere and Hartman (1991: 29) suggest that even something as simple as a boss smiling at an employee every morning needs to be maintained—a morning where the smile doesn't occur stands out and can be demotivating.

Skinner and operant conditioning

Running case: automatically, all the time

From:	meg_mortimer@junctionhotel.co.uk
To:	phil_weaver@junctionhotel.co.uk
Subject:	Smile cards

Phil,

Not sure about these smile cards—I feel like I have to be in reception all the time to be able to give out ticks on the card. They'll only smile when I'm around.

From:	phil_weaver@junctionhotel.co.uk
To:	meg_mortimer@junctionhotel.co.uk
Subject:	RE: Smile cards

Meg,

No—don't worry about being there 100% of the time. Just make sure you pass through there a few times a day. Reward them every so often and they'll smile automatically all the time.

When we are at work, we don't expect that after every customer served, call answered from a customer, or pint pulled, the boss will hand us a part of our wages. Rather than the reward being instant and occurring after every desirable action, as is the case with classical conditioning, we know that a wage comes along at regular intervals—weekly or monthly, for example.

311

American psychologist B.F. Skinner (1969) developed the ideas of classical conditioning into operant conditioning. While Pavlov experimented with dogs, Skinner experimented with animals in an observation box. In one such experiment, if a rat pressed a lever in the box it received a reward in the form of a piece of food. Skinner discovered that the rewards even worked when they were intermittent, and the effect was stronger when the awards (also called reinforcements) were variable rather than fixed.

Variable rewards are stronger because they come with surprise and unpredictability, which is why gambling can become so addictive: 'The potential of winning on the next race keeps gamblers coming back again and again' (Villere and Hartman, 1991: 29). Indeed, fixed-odds betting terminals (slot machines) have been described as the 'crack cocaine' of gambling (Shipman, 2018). In the UK the government have been so concerned about the power of these machines that they have limited the maximum stake to £2.

Variable rewards.
Source: antoniodiaz/Shutterstock.com

However, if you won every time it would become less addictive: it would feel more like a job than a pleasurable activity. Variable incentives mean that you never know when you might win, which makes the potential for a random and variable payout more exciting. The interval (time between when you put in the money and potentially receive a payout) is very short, making it still more exciting. Professor Mark Griffith argues that this 'process (operant conditioning) conditions habits by rewarding behaviour, such as through presentation of a reward (e.g., money), reinforcement occurs. To produce high rates of response, those schedules which present rewards intermittently (random and variable ratio schedules) have shown to be most effective (Skinner, 1933)' (Griffith, 1999: 269). This is why Twitter, Instagram, Pinterest, and email are so addictive, not because we know we will be rewarded each time we use them, but because we believe we might be. As Oliver Burkeman states, 'If slot machines delivered £1 every time you inserted 50p, you might use them, but you'd never get addicted' (Burkeman, 2011).

Skinner's work has been applied in the workplace by Luthans and Kreitner (1985) as organizational behaviour modification. They suggest that fixed and variable schedules of reinforcement have different effects in terms of motivating employees into particular types of desired behaviours. Villere and Hartman (1991: 29) give examples.

- A regular salary, paid weekly or monthly, is an example of a fixed-interval reward—it is provided regularly at a set time. While this might motivate us to turn up and work, it doesn't necessarily motivate us into putting in any extra effort.

- Variable rewards—such as a bonus, an award, a promotion, or even a pat on the back from the boss—tend to have a higher success rate in motivating workers into specific behaviours that managers wish to encourage, over and above what is done simply in order to collect the monthly pay cheque.

Operant conditioning thus demonstrates the motivational value of blending different types of reward and reinforcement. For most people, a regular salary is important; however, variable rewards such as bonuses have a greater effect in motivating specific day-to-day behaviours.

 How could you apply Skinner's concepts to your own studies?

Visit the online resources and take a look at the extension material for Chapter 9 for more on variable and fixed schedules of reinforcement in the workplace.

 Real life case: *Nudge*

How do you get men to pee into the toilet rather than miss? You put an image of a fly on the toilet bowl. Men, it seems, 'cannot help but take aim, saving on clean-up costs as well as alleviating unpleasantness' (Hooker, 2017). The 'house fly target' was trialled at Schiphol airport, Amsterdam, and it reduced the spillage rate by around 80 per cent.

The fly in the toilet is an example of a new form of behavioural economics called *Nudge* (Thaler and Sunstein, 2008). Nudge works by altering the environment in which we make choices in order to produce better outcomes. It uses 'choice architecture', the way choices are designed, to alter the decisions that we make. It does not remove choices but makes more preferable choices, so that we use our heuristics (shortcuts in thinking) to make the choice that we see as more beneficial to us.

Fly in the toilet, an example of nudge theory.
Source: P.Fabian / Shutterstock.com

313

Behaviourism: advantages and disadvantages

 Running case: target behaviours

Steve Long is on portering duty, delivering room service to an elderly guest. While engaging her in pleasant chat, he notices through the window that Chance is walking into the crowded reception area.

Steve instantly cuts off the guest mid-sentence and runs out of the room, slamming the door behind him. Leaving the customer upset and bemused in his wake, he rushes down to reception and starts engaging a group of waiting guests in conversation, showing them some tourist information leaflets, even though they have shown little interest in visiting the local attractions.

As reception empties, Chance walks over with his pen. 'Well done, young man,' says Chance, placing a tick on Steve's smile card.

Organizational behaviour modification works on a seemingly common-sense principle that 'if a particular pattern of behaviour is rewarded, it will occur more often' (Makin and Sutherland, 1994: 6). However, behind this seemingly simple idea lies a pitfall—exactly what behaviour is being rewarded?

For example, in order to get trains to run on time, train operators are given targets for how many are allowed to be late before they get fined by the government. Yet some train operators have been accused of cancelling services, as this is cheaper than the fine they could receive (BBC News, 2018b). This demonstrates that people can often find creative ways to meet targets that don't necessarily correspond to the initial behaviours desired by management.

Makin and Sutherland (1994) suggested that a way to promote safety-conscious behaviour in organizations could be to reward a lack of accidents. However, rather than motivating people into more safety-conscious behaviours, for example wearing safety goggles, a response can be simply not to report any accidents, so as to meet the target. The underlying behaviour change—being more safety-conscious—is not addressed; people just engage in behaviours that they think will help them meet the target and get the reward.

At the start of this section, we asked if coercive behaviour, through punishment, genuinely motivates people within or simply alters their behaviour in response to a threat, such as a gun. A critique of behavioural techniques is that it sees people in simplistic, mechanistic terms (Martinko and Fadil, 1994: 16), like robots, unquestioningly responding to stimuli or rewards. Behavioural techniques therefore can change the surface level, the behaviour an individual shows, rather than making any change in an individual's thinking. Also, behaviour theories are often applied in a simple way whereas the original concepts are often more subtle, recognizing the internal cognition (thinking) of the individual (McGee and Johnson, 2015).

Overall, behavioural theories provide a 'one size fits all' approach to motivation, assuming everyone will respond to the same stimulus, without taking into account individual motivation. In the next section we see motivation theory taking account of individual differences in what motivates people.

? Review questions

Describe	What are the main features of classical and operant conditioning?
Explain	How can variable reinforcement have a strong motivational effect on people?
Analyse	Why might Skinner's work be seen as controlling?
Apply	How is the smile card at Junction Hotel an example of organizational behaviour modification? How well do you think it motivates the staff into appearing more lively and engaged with guests in the reception area?

Content theories of motivation

Q Running case: differences in motivation

Jane Foster has been working at Junction Hotel as a receptionist for five years. She and her partner have not yet had children, and they are easily covering their mortgage payments and other outgoings.

Foster receives constant praise for the quality of her work from her boss, Meg Mortimer, and when Mortimer is away, Foster is the first choice to deputize as the front-of-house manager.

→

She has been singled out as potential managerial material and, because of this, Junction Hotel are sponsoring her to do a part-time degree in hospitality management at the local university.

Mortimer is surprised that Foster has barely participated in the smile card scheme, even not handing in her card on occasions. 'I know when I'm working well, and that gives me pride,' says Foster. 'I don't need ticks in a box to tell me that.'

Student Steve Long is working next to Foster today. His circumstances, however, are different. He is studying full-time for a degree in accountancy and works part-time in the reception area to supplement his income—he needs the money to pay his rent. Mortimer thinks his work is also good, but is surprised that he refuses when she asks him if he would like managerial responsibility. Nevertheless, he has thrown himself head-first into the smile card scheme and has twice been the winner, pocketing the bonus cheque.

Would it be right to assume that a university student working part-time on a short-term contract would have the same motivation as a permanent employee? Whereas behavioural theories used extrinsic motivators to design motivation techniques that were applied equally to all workers in one organization, content theories recognize that a range of different motivators—extrinsic, intrinsic, and social—may exert a different level of motivation on different people.

Content theories assume that individuals have a set of needs and that the content of work can be designed to meet those needs and thus motivate the individual. In this section we examine two widely used content theories—Maslow's hierarchy of needs, and Herzberg's motivators and hygiene theory.

Maslow's hierarchy of needs

For many management students and practitioners, Maslow's hierarchy of needs is overwhelmingly the most familiar model of motivation; indeed, some former business students say that it is one of the few theories that they remember from the entirety of their studies. The ubiquitous triangle (see Figure 9.2) pops up in lectures, training courses, and textbooks such as this—although Bridgman

Figure 9.2 Maslow's hierarchy of needs, represented as a triangle.

- Self-actualization
- Esteem
- Social/belongingness
- Safety
- Physiological needs

et al. (2018) argue that the triangle image significantly alters and simplifies Maslow's original ideas, an argument that we will turn to at the end of this section (see Research insight: what's in a shape?). We will introduce Maslow's work here before looking at the critiques of it.

Maslow (1943) suggested that people have five basic needs:

- physiological needs—basic physical needs for survival, such as food and water;
- safety needs—a need for safety, physical health, and security;
- love and belongingness—social needs, such as being part of a group, interacting with others, and a need for affection;
- esteem needs—a need for status, recognition, and self-respect;
- self-actualization—a form of ultimate self-fulfilment, the achievement of our ultimate potential and creativity and what we, according to Maslow, are 'fitted for'.

Maslow offers a needs-based view of motivation. Needs are 'internal forces that are essential for supporting life and growth. Unmet needs create states of physical and psychological tension that energize action' (Kanfer et al., 2017: 340). For Maslow, these needs are arranged in a hierarchy of **prepotency** (power or influence), with those at the bottom the most powerful (see Figure 9.2). Once these lower psychological and safety needs are satisfied, they become less strong, and less prepotent needs, i.e. belongingness, become more powerful. So, if an individual is starving (rather than simply having an appetite), they will be motivated by the most basic need for food. When this need is satisfied they will be motivated by safety needs, and so on, moving up the hierarchy. The needs do not have to be 100 per cent satisfied before the next level emerges. Indeed, for Maslow 'most members of our society, who are normal, are partially satisfied in all their basic needs and partially unsatisfied in all their basic needs at the same time' (1987: 69–70). Needs are also not permanently satisfied and can re-emerge, creating tensions and therefore calls to action.

 Theory in context: Abraham Maslow

An aspect of Maslow's work that is often missing from management accounts is that his research interests began far away from workplace motivation. Maslow made a significant contribution to primatology (the scientific study of primates) and much of his research was about patterns of dominance within monkey populations (Cullen, 1997; Dye et al., 2005).

These interests then transferred into an interest in dominance in sexual behaviour in humans. His particular focus was based on interviewing women in their twenties about their sexual desires (Cullen and Gotell, 2002). It is from these streams of research that he developed his hierarchy of needs. In its original form it was not a theory of workplace motivation, but a theory of needs that humans had to fulfil in order to attain psychological health and well-being.

His interest in dominance both in primates and in sexual behaviour is important here—the hierarchy of needs is essentially a theory of how any one unsatisfied need dominates over others in its motivational effects at any one time.

The hierarchy of needs was not first applied to workplace settings by Maslow, but by Davis (1957), drawing upon Maslow's work. In this reading, different workers will be motivated by different factors depending on their position in the hierarchy of needs. For example:

- a worker with not enough money to feed themselves will probably take on any work—they will be motivated by the immediate need to eat (physiological needs);

- a worker who has money for food but is only just about managing to cover bills and rent might be motivated by job security to meet these safety needs (shelter, warmth, etc.);

- a worker who is meeting their bills easily will be motivated more by the social/belongingness aspects of the organization—group and team dynamics, and the culture of the organization become important;

- as people fulfil their social needs, workers are motivated by esteem needs, such as a desire for promotion within an organization, or recognition of their work, for example by an appreciative word from a manager;

- the final aspect of motivation is self-actualization—fulfilment of potential and achievement within the workplace.

Insights from Maslow

Maslow's hierarchy provides valuable insights into human motivation which have relevance to the workplace. In particular, he goes beyond behavioural psychology, which he viewed as too simplistic, deterministic, and having 'no earthly use in any complex human situation' (Maslow, 2000: 7), towards a more multifaceted view of what motivates behaviour.

- The hierarchy shows that individuals are motivated differently—what motivates one worker may not motivate another. This provides an important counter-argument to the likes of Taylor, who saw pay as a universal motivator. In Maslow's hierarchy, pay is one of a number of motivators—it may work at certain lower levels of the hierarchy, but other motivating forces take over as an individual moves upwards. People are often motivated by a number of the basic needs at any one time.

- The hierarchy integrates different types of motivating factors within its framework. Extrinsic rewards, such as pay, are important, particularly at lower levels; social rewards are important motivators at the belongingness level; and at higher levels, intrinsic rewards such as achievement and self-respect become important.

- The hierarchy shows that an individual's motivation is not fixed—it is dynamic and people can progress over time. Thus a student might be motivated by pay in order to meet safety needs of paying rent and bills, but later in life, a professional might be motivated by esteem needs such as promotion.

- A person's background and previous experiences might shape what needs are dominant for them. For instance, Maslow argues that a person who had an unstable childhood might be dominated by 'belonging needs'. For other people, self-esteem needs might be more important than love (Maslow, 1943).

- People do not necessarily start from the bottom of the hierarchy and work their way up. For the average American, Maslow considered, they do not experience hunger (which for Maslow was more akin to starvation) and therefore might strive for higher needs (self-esteem or self-actualization) and in doing so risk their lower needs not being fulfilled. For instance, someone might give up their job rather than lose self-respect, even if they might be in danger of going hungry over a six-month period (Maslow, 1943).

- Some people, particularly with strong characters, might even give everything up for the sake of their values.

Maslow provides a much more positive view of motivation than the simple coercive carrot-and-stick approaches. Indeed, in his original work, Maslow placed a strong emphasis on human values, showing that people might be motivated by factors beyond pay and promotion, such as growth and creativity. For Maslow, preconditions for these higher levels include autonomy, freedom of inquiry and expression, and freedom to defend yourself and seek justice (Maslow, 1987). Indeed, the aspect of his hierarchy that Maslow emphasized most was self-actualization. His views on human nature are similar to the social–radical approach covered in Chapter 8, namely that people have unrealized potential and that it is the role of society, and organizations within society, to help them to achieve this potential (Dye et al., 2005: 1383). Therefore Maslow was interested in 'what the human being should grow *toward*' (Maslow, 1964: 7), the type of people we may become. Maslow argues that to make 'growth [a] choice, rather than the fear choice a dozen times a day is to move a dozen times a day to self-actualization' (Maslow, 1971: 44). This humanistic view looks at motivation from the viewpoint of the individual and stresses the uniqueness of each individual. Self-actualization is a concept of people developing their creativity and reaching a sense of self-fulfilment and achievement, in the same way as an artist or musician might do. This is not an endpoint, which you complete, but an 'on-going process that involves dozens of little growth choices that entail risk and require courage' (O'Connor and Yballe, 2007: 742).

Critique of Maslow and the use of Maslow

While Maslow offers some fascinating insights, unfortunately they are frequently misapplied in the study of management and organizations (O'Connor and Yballe, 2007). The triangle offers a promise of a simple framework to understand what motivates people at work. Unfortunately this simplification often means Maslow's original insights either misrepresented or simply removed. Indeed, Maslow did not see his work as a theory of workplace motivation and suggested that he had not seen any empirical proof that it worked in a workplace context (Dye et al., 2005: 1380). An example of how it can be badly applied is explored through the Real life case: Maslow at Tesco.

 Real life case: Maslow at Tesco

A case study presented by a leading UK newspaper, along with classroom teaching materials, maps the work practices of UK supermarket Tesco on to Maslow's hierarchy.
Examples provided are:

- physiological needs are met by providing regular monthly pay, a restaurant, and lockers for belongings;
- formal contracts of employment and health and safety procedures meet security needs;
- social needs are met by team and group working;
- esteem comes from praise for hard work, ensured through the appraisal system;
- self-actualization (here renamed self-fulfilment) comes from promotion opportunities, a personal development plan, and fast-track management schemes.

At first sight, this case seems to apply Maslow to Tesco's work practices well—a restaurant surely meets the physiological need for food, for example. But it is a very simplistic application, categorizing a number of practices under Maslow's headings without understanding how people are really motivated by these drives in Maslow's work.

- It ignores the dynamic nature of Maslow's model—it would seem that all motivating forces are acting at once and Tesco is seen to provide for those needs, whereas in Maslow's model it is only the most immediate unsatisfied need that motivates individuals.

→

→

- A physiological need for food comes from being deprived of food—a very basic urge. It does not describe people popping casually into the staff canteen for lunch. We assume that Tesco already pay enough for workers to afford food, so this more basic need would not be acting as a motivator—it is one which is already satisfied and so the model has been misapplied.
- This application of Maslow underplays the role of self-actualization, even renaming it as self-fulfilment. In Maslow's original work, self-actualization is an ultimate realization of creativity and potential as a human being, not simply being on a fast-track promotion scheme.

Source: http://businesscasestudies.co.uk/tesco/motivational-theory-in-practice-at-tesco/

 Why, at first glance, might the Tesco motivation study seem appealing? What features of Maslow's work, particularly ideas about self-actualization, does it ignore? Why might these ideas of self-actualization be important to really understand Maslow's work?

The problem with the use of Maslow's theory in the Tesco case is that it has been applied too simplistically. This is symptomatic of many of the uses of Maslow's work in management theory. It is not that Maslow's work itself is simplistic—indeed, it offers some far-reaching perspectives for the understanding of human nature—but rather it is the way that it is often applied that is problematic (Bridgman et al., 2018).

For instance, in Maslow's work, self-actualization is a healthy state—being at any level below shows that not all basic human needs are met and thus a person is psychologically unhealthy. Often self-actualization is presented as career progression. In any of these instances, according to Maslow, the individual would be unhealthy (Dye et al., 2005). A further problem with the use of Maslow's theory is that, while it is often presented in management theory as an exact depiction of human motivation or a guideline on how to motivate, in fact it is not supported by empirical evidence. That is to say, the applicability of the theory in workplace reality has not been proven.

There are concerns with seeking to apply Maslow's ideas directly to the workplace. Wahba and Bridwell (1976) reviewed a number of studies into Maslow's hierarchy, showing that not even the existence of the five levels of the hierarchy as distinct and separate categories have been proven empirically in the workplace, let alone the idea that people move up from one level to the next. As we saw earlier, Maslow himself stated that he had not seen proof of his theory working in organizational settings. Rather 'Maslow understood that there is a very fluid emergence and combination of needs and activity in the rhythm of day-to-day life' (O'Connor and Yballe, 2007: 740).

Furthermore, while there are problems with the application of Maslow's hierarchy in workplace settings, it is also often applied without any consideration of critiques of Maslow's original theory itself.

For example, looking back to Maslow's original studies on domination, Cullen and Gotell (2002: 538) argue that his work is highly gendered in nature. 'Implicit in Maslow's portrayal is an assertion of the naturalness of female submission and the eroticization of male dominance and this assertion, in turn, forms the gendered foundation of the needs hierarchy' (2002: 538). Dye et al. (2005: 1389) note that Maslow is also dismissive of gay men and of black people.

The concept of self-actualization, in Maslow's terms, is thus founded on particular assumptions which privilege white, male, heterosexual ways of being. Furthermore, the concept of self-actualization can be seen as elitist. Maslow suggests throughout his work that not everyone is capable of self-actualization or seems to want to be able to self-actualize (see the collected works in Maslow, 2000). Dye et al. (2005) suggest that maybe this is why the model is so popular in the management context—it suggests that management is an elite capable of self-actualization and, at the same time, dismisses other workers as being motivated by basic, ultimately unhealthy needs.

These critiques both of the misapplication of Maslow and of Maslow's original theory show that while his theory may have widespread and popular use in management theory, it should be *handled with care*. Certainly, it should not be seen as the one and only model of motivation in itself—many other theories of motivation are discussed in this chapter.

👁 **Research insight:** what's in a shape? The representation of Maslow's work as a triangle

Bridgman, T., Cummings, S., and Ballard, J. 2018. Who built Maslow's pyramid? A history of the creation of management studies' most famous symbol and its implications for management education. *Academy of Management Learning and Education*, published online: https://doi.org/10.5465/amle.2017.0351

If you mention the name Maslow to anyone with even a passing interest in the ideas of organizational behaviour or motivation theory, the word that generally springs to mind is *triangle*. Maslow's triangle, as his theory of motivation is generally depicted, provides a nice, neat,

Figure 9.3 Keith Davis's representation of Maslow's hierarchy of needs.
Source: Davis (1957: 41).

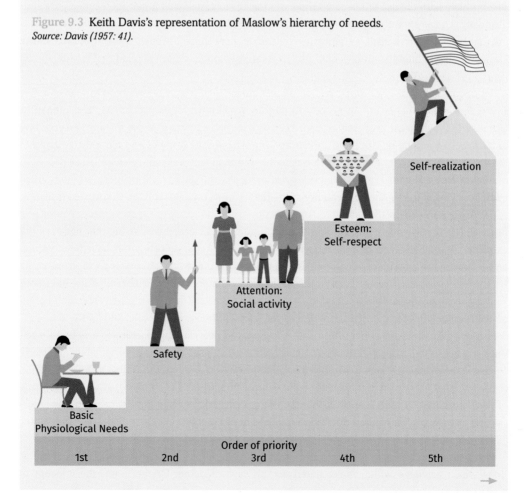

and elegant summary of one of the most famous concepts in management studies. You would think, therefore, that Maslow invented the triangle to present his work, but as Bridgman, Cummings, and Ballard argue, not only did Maslow not invent the triangle, it is a poor representation of his theory.

One of the first visual representations of Maslow's work as applied to management theory was made by Keith Davis (Figure 9.3), a management theorist who was seeking to elevate management theory's status within the university. Davis represented Maslow's work as a series of steps, from basic physiological needs to self-realization. This image, Bridgman et al. argue, 'was clearly pitched for the American market too: the flag-raising reminiscent of the famous image of the flag-raising on Iwo Jima' (2018: 13).

The triangle itself was first introduced some three years later by Charles McDermid, a consulting psychologist (1960). McDermid saw it as a tool for managers to evaluate the needs of their employees and adjust pay accordingly. So it was not Maslow that invented the triangle, but a consultant trying to achieve the 'maximum motivation at lowest cost' (McDermid, 1960: 98, cited in Bridgman et al., 2018: 13).

Why does this matter? Understanding these origins, Bridgman and colleagues argue, helps us think more about the origins of management theory and how ideas are presented in lectures and textbooks like this. First, the simplicity of the triangle goes quite a long way to explain the longevity and prominence of Maslow's work in the field of organizational behaviour. While the applicability of Maslow's work to our understanding of management theory has been widely criticized (see our discussion above), because it can be easily presented into a diagram Maslow's theory really took off. Indeed, Bridgman et al. argue that it was the early versions of organizational behaviour textbooks in the 1970s and 80s that really fuelled growth in its interest when serious research was questioning it.

Second, the presentation of the triangle was a powerful image presenting a certain view of society. A triangle or pyramid, of which Maslow's is the most famous example, was a highly popular image among management consultants who 'were in the business of building and selling pyramids' (Bridgman et al., 2018: 17), including the hierarchical image of the organization itself. In putting forward an image of the triangle they also presented the idea of hierarchical societies where certain groups of people, such as 'upper levels of management, … researchers and some engineers' have opportunities for self-actualization (Argyris, 1964: 255, cited in Bridgman et al., 2018: 16).

Third, the image of the triangle presents an overly simplistic image of Maslow's work. It implies that you can only be at one level at a time, that you just move up the hierarchy, that self-actualization is the top and also that those at the top of the organization are more likely to be self-actualized. The triangle therefore obscures many of the key features of Maslow's ideas.

Bridgman et al. suggest that a ladder might be a more appropriate image (see Figure 9.4): you can be on more than one level and can move up and down the hierarchy, and might even go beyond self-actualization. More widely they argue that management textbooks should present theories in a more contextualized manner, understanding their historical context and the original aims of the research and providing a more nuanced understanding. Also, they argue that we should read the original work. If we did, we would see that 'Maslow was about individual growth and fulfillment, knowing yourself, reaching your potential' (Bridgman et al., 2018: 25) and therefore get a wider and deeper understanding of this much misunderstood concept.

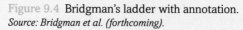

Figure 9.4 Bridgman's ladder with annotation.
Source: Bridgman et al. (forthcoming).

Self-actualization

Esteem

Social/belonging

Safety

Physiological

Why is the image of the triangle so popular in management courses? Do you prefer a simplified image, such as a triangle, when you are learning about a subject such as motivation? What might you gain by reading Maslow's original work? Should we follow the advice of Bridgman et al. and get rid of the triangle altogether in teaching and textbooks?

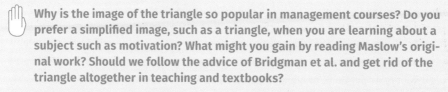

Study skills: models and heuristics

The simple nature of models such as Maslow's hierarchy gives them an appeal to students and managers alike—it is a nice idea to think that motivation can be plotted out in such a simple framework. Indeed, some students write very poor essays on motivation which see motivation as nothing more than Maslow's hierarchy, ignoring all other theories on the subject.

Models exist as simple ways to present complex ideas. A model is what is known as a heuristic—a way of presenting information or theories in an accessible, easily understandable manner.

The danger is that people rely on these simplified versions rather than looking at the topic in depth. A model is also just one viewpoint on a topic—there may be other models which present the same area of study in a different way and from a different viewpoint.

If using a model such as the Maslow triangle in an essay, don't simply repeat it. Think about approaching it in more depth.

- What is the model actually trying to say about the nature of motivation? Don't just draw the triangle—say what each level means and what it implies about how people are motivated.

→

- What assumptions underpin the model? For example, we have seen how Maslow's hierarchy derives from his earlier research about domination and we have noted the importance he places on self-actualization.

- What alternative views are there? What other models exist, and what do they say that is different or that challenges Maslow's model?

- Does it hold up to empirical scrutiny? We have seen how Maslow's hierarchy has not been proven in a workplace setting. Have other models been applied successfully or unsuccessfully in the workplace?

See Chapter 1 for more discussion on critical thinking.

Herzberg: motivators and hygiene factors

🔍 Running case: a sense of responsibility

For three months in a row Steve Long has won the smile card challenge and each time has received a bonus. He is starting to see the bonus as a part of the regular pay he expects to receive. He has already allocated this month's bonus towards a trip to London to see his friends. He is, therefore, shocked when his friend John McAuley is announced as this month's winner. Having to cancel his trip, Long is unhappy, feeling like he's had a pay cut.

The contrast with Jane Foster can't be greater. With her degree studies progressing, she is now being given the responsibility of managing shifts in the reception from start to finish, even if Mortimer is around. And where usually she leaves paperwork in Mortimer's pigeon hole to be signed off, Mortimer has said 'sign it yourself—if you're in charge you have the responsibility'. Foster does all of this, willingly and happily, for the same level of pay as Long.

While Maslow's hierarchy is based in the needs of individuals and other theorists have then looked at how they might be satisfied in the workplace, Herzberg's motivators and hygiene framework starts with the actual characteristics of the job itself. For Herzberg (1966, 2003), these characteristics of the job can be divided into two distinct groups.

- Motivating factors are factors that have the potential to increase the satisfaction of a worker. They include achievement, recognition for that achievement, the work itself, having responsibility, and the potential for personal growth (Herzberg, 1987: 9). These are largely intrinsic factors and are factors that are likely to satisfy the higher levels of Maslow's hierarchy.

- Hygiene factors cannot, in themselves, do anything to increase satisfaction; however, this does not mean that they can be ignored. If they are not provided or addressed sufficiently, this has the potential to cause dissatisfaction. Such factors are extrinsic factors, such as company policy, supervision, interpersonal relationships, working conditions, job status, job security, and pay (Herzberg, 1987: 9), and are more likely to satisfy lower level needs on Maslow's hierarchy.

Herzberg's research was carried out originally with engineers and accountants, and consisted of asking them to name an event at work that had caused them extreme satisfaction or extreme dissatisfaction. The results, shown in Figure 9.5, show the motivating factors at the top of the diagram, providing more instances of satisfaction than dissatisfaction, and hygiene factors at the bottom, showing greater instances of dissatisfaction.

Figure 9.5 Herzberg's motivators and hygiene model.
Source: based on Herzberg (2003: 87–96). Reproduced by permission of Harvard Business Publishing.

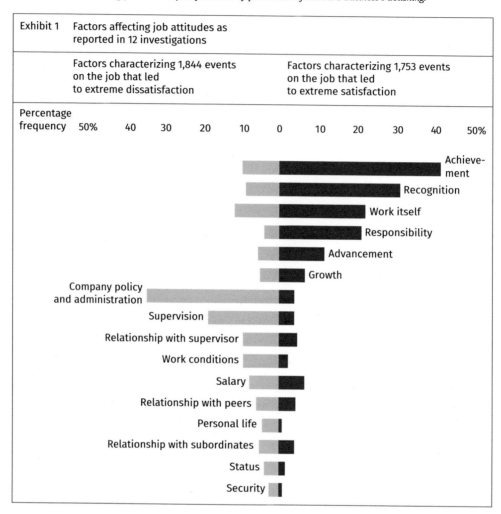

Herzberg's view of pay as a hygiene factor seems to go against our common-sense view of pay—surely a pay rise motivates people? Herzberg (1987: 6) suggests, however, that while a pay rise might motivate in the short term, it only motivates people as far as seeking the next rise. In other words, a pay rise soon comes to be seen as a 'normal' level of pay, which doesn't motivate in its own right. While it provides no extra motivation, if the pay were to be reduced back to its old level it would then demotivate. All that happens, for Herzberg, is that pay levels spiral while adding no additional motivation to workers.

Herzberg and job enrichment

For Herzberg, increased satisfaction comes from the design of work itself in a way that minimizes hygiene factors and maximizes motivators. This suggests a move away from job simplification, as seen with rational work design (see Chapter 3) where work is broken down into simple tasks, and towards increasing the intrinsic motivation that workers derive from jobs.

Herzberg (1987) first discusses two forms of job redesign which emphasize the horizontal loading of the task. Rather than performing one repetitive task, the worker is given an expanded variety of tasks.

- Job rotation is where a worker moves between different tasks in the work process rather than sticking to one repetitive task. For example, a worker in a fast-food restaurant does not generally spend the whole of their working life at one task; instead, they will rotate between working on the till, making burgers, cleaning tables, etc.
- Job enlargement is where a worker is given several tasks at the same level of difficulty: for example, a fast-food worker assembles all elements of the burger rather than just adding the relish.

For Herzberg (1987: 10), such forms of work do not increase motivation. If two forms of work have zero motivation, then adding them together still makes zero. Instead, he suggests that intrinsic motivators, and thus job satisfaction, will be increased through job enrichment. Enrichment comes from vertical loading, where more authority and autonomy over tasks are given to workers, for example through increasing individual responsibility or the complexity of tasks, and allowing self-directed teams rather than tightly-controlled individuals. This gives the individual increased responsibility, autonomy, and variety of tasks.

The aim of job enrichment is to increase not just the number and variety of tasks, but also their quality and ability to provide intrinsic forms of motivation. Vertical loading suggests that workers have a part in much more of the work process from start to finish, rather than being just one small 'cog in a machine'.

Herzberg's model can be seen to bring about motivation at the equivalent of higher levels of Maslow's hierarchy, designing work to bring about intrinsic rewards. A bias towards these factors could come about owing to his original research featuring white-collar workers. The insight from Goldthorpe later in this chapter shows that some people will work for instrumental reasons—the pay—rather than for any sense of growth or intrinsic reward.

In such an instance, job enrichment (or rotation or enlargement) could, potentially, be seen as a form of intensification of work. For example, workers may not want extra responsibility, especially if there is no extra pay attached to this. Workers would be having to learn and perform extra tasks as part of their work for potentially the same wage.

Again, Herzberg (1987: 13) noted that not all people want job enrichment, nor can all jobs be enriched. We get an idea of how motivation can be increased in some instances by job enrichment, but not a recommendation that this should be applied in all cases.

? Review questions

Describe	What are the main features of Maslow's and Herzberg's models?
Explain	What is the role of intrinsic motivators in both of the models?
Analyse	What are the problems in the way Maslow's original theory has been used as a theory of workplace motivation?
Apply	Can you use Maslow and Herzberg's models to explain the differences in motivation between Long and Foster in the running case?

Process theories of motivation

We all enter the workplace with different prior life experiences, different feelings, and different interpretations of the world. As we saw in Chapter 8, we are all individuals. Process theories focus on motivation as a function of individual thought processes, moving from the content of work and static frameworks, as seen in the previous section, to motivation as a far more individual, fluid, and subjective process.

Motivation is based on people's past experiences and the meanings that people attach to those experiences. While content theories might try to explain *how* people act in relation to different motivating factors, with process theories the unique and individual ways in which people *feel and interpret* these factors are also considered.

In this section we examine two examples of process theories—equity theory, where people compare their rewards to those of others, and expectancy theory, where people evaluate different actions to judge how they will achieve their desired goals.

Running case: it's not fair

Sue Ridgewell, working on reception, has long suspected that her co-receptionist, Jane Foster, gets favourable treatment from Meg Mortimer. It was the little snide comments and criticisms from Mortimer that did it—nothing serious, but Foster, the blue-eyed girl who was taking the hospitality course, seems to get far more positive comments.

At first, Ridgewell tries to do better, thinking she must be in the wrong and that maybe if she tries harder she, too, will get praise from the boss. But after a while, she realizes that whatever she does there is no praise or reward, and she seems to get fewer ticks on her smile card, even though she feels she is putting in much more effort with the customers.

Ridgewell stops trying as she sees little point, and feels further demotivated by the overall sense of unfairness of the treatment that she receives relative to Foster. Her feeling is compounded when she accidentally overhears a conversation behind the reception between Mortimer and Foster. It seems Foster will get more paid time off to do the coursework for her course and other staff will be asked to cover.

Adams—equity theory

Imagine that you have just received feedback for an essay that you worked really hard for and you got a low 2:1. You then discover that someone in your class, who you know wrote it the night before (and hardly ever turns up to class) got exactly the same grade as you. Would this feel fair? We like to think that the treatment we receive is always fair. Adams (1963) argues that when we see something as unequal or unfair, we are likely to be less motivated. Adam's concept of equity theory is based on our perceptions of fairness and justice—do we feel that we are getting what we deserve based on the efforts we put in (inputs) and the rewards that we get compared with others (outcomes)? It is very much an individual, subjective level of motivation compared with content theories, for two reasons:

- it is motivation that comes not from the total amount of a reward (e.g. the amount of a pay rise) but from how fairly individuals feel that reward has been distributed;

- it is based on individual perceptions of fairness—what one person feels to be fair may be perceived as unfair by another.

Adams (1963) suggests different reactions that individuals might have if they perceive an inequity between inputs and rewards.

- If people feel they are being under-rewarded compared with others, they will feel anger and try to redress the balance, either by negotiating a pay rise, decreasing their level of effort, or engaging in some form of workplace resistance.

- If people feel over-rewarded compared with others, they will feel guilt and work harder and, although Adams realizes this is unlikely, may take a pay cut.

In both cases, individuals attempt to change either inputs or outcomes to redress the inequity. Adams suggest that other actions may be taken, such as changing the point of comparison (comparing with different people); trying to find reasons and explanations for the inequity; or, ultimately, leaving the job. Yet does this occur in practice? There is little evidence, for example, in support of the idea that guilt for over-reward will make people work harder. Huseman et al. (1987) suggest that not all people fit into the equity theory model of comparative behaviour. However, equity theory does indicate that when organizations are designing pay and reward systems they need to be seen to be fair. People are thus judging the fairness of the system and how they are treated as much as what they personally will get out of it. If they believe they are treated unfairly, then this can have a negative effect on their motivation.

It is very difficult for managers to control something as subjective as individual perceptions of fairness. Tyler and Bies (1990) suggest that such perceptions can, to some degree, be managed through discussion and explanation by management of changes to pay systems, and by making certain that reward criteria are applied consistently and without personal bias.

For example, Greenberg (1990a) studied levels of theft in a US manufacturing plant following a 15 per cent pay cut due to a drop in orders. The theft can be seen as resistance due to a perceived inequity following the pay cut. However, Greenberg found that theft levels were much lower among workers who had been given a detailed explanation for the cut from management than those who had been given a short, inadequate explanation. The discussion and explanation had helped lower the amount of perceived inequity.

 Real life case: the battle for equal pay

In early January 2018, instead of reporting on the news, Carrie Gracie became the headlines herself. The BBC's China editor resigned from her £135,000-a-year post citing pay inequality after discovering that the male international editors were earning substantially more than her. Furthermore, she had refused a £45,000 pay rise, saying it 'still left a "big gap" between her and her male counterparts when all she wanted was to be "made equal"' (BBC News, 2018a). Speaking on BBC Radio 4's *Woman's Hour*, Gracie stated: 'I didn't want more money—do you understand—I wanted equality' (Martinson, 2018). The controversy over pay inequality grew as the *Today* programme presenter John Humphrys, who earns £600,000 per year, was caught on an off-air microphone joking about the gender pay gap (Martinson, 2018). In the light of this scandal Humphrys agreed to cut his salary by about £150,000 (Singh, 2018).

Imagine you were Carrie Gracie and heard your male colleagues were getting paid significantly more than you for the same job. How would you feel? Recently, research attention has moved from equity theory to the concept of organizational justice, which states that not only does the outcome matter but, building on equity theory, the *processes* through which a decision is reached needs to be seen as fair as well (Colquitt et al., 2001). Organizational justice separates the final decision, what researchers call distributive justice (as in equity theory), from how it is implemented, what researchers call procedural justice (Greenberg, 1990b). Poor procedural justice can have significant health implications including loss of sleep and even musculoskeletal disorders (Manville et al., 2016). What is interesting from the research is that the negative effects of receiving a negative outcome can be mitigated when the process is seen to be fair (Skarlicki and Folger, 1997). In recent research, who makes the decision is also seen as important. Kouchaki et al. argue that if a decision is made by a group it is seen as less fair than if it is made by an individual (Kouchaki et al., 2015).

Vroom—expectancy theory

While equity theory is based on individual perceptions of fairness, Vroom's (1964) expectancy theory examines the ways that individuals link specific actions to how they perceive they will help them achieve specific goals. People will seek out positive rewards or outcomes for themselves and will pursue behaviours that they *expect* will lead them to that reward.

Expectancy theory suggests three elements which form the calculation of what will motivate people towards a particular behaviour and away from other potential behaviours.

- (E)xpectancy is the belief that a particular effort or action will lead to a particular outcome.
- (I)nstrumentality is the belief that that outcome will attract a particular reward.
- (V)alence is the value that an individual attaches to that reward.

For Vroom, the motivational force (MF) of a particular action boils down to a calculation, MF = V × I × E. Expectancy theory suggests that people will be motivated to perform actions that they believe will be instrumental in them achieving goals and rewards that they value. Similarly, if an effort cannot be linked to a goal that they value, or if it is linked to a goal that they do not value highly, the motivation to perform that effort will diminish.

Say a person highly desires a pay rise (V). They believe that increased sales figures will be instrumental in them getting that pay rise (I). From experience, they have found that doorstep selling generates most sales (E), so the effort to which they are motivated is to go out selling from door to door. Likewise, an effort which doesn't contribute to increased sales, for example helping a colleague to write a report, is something they will not be motivated to perform.

However, a colleague who values good working relationships (V) may find that the respect of colleagues is instrumental in achieving this (I) and would thus be more motivated to the effort of helping a colleague with a report if they believed it would gain them respect from that colleague (E).

Q Running case: where do I start?

Ellerby Peters has his head in his hands. He was excited to get the work experience placement at Junction Hotel and wanted to do well so that he could get a reference for his CV, but now only one day into his placement he felt despondent—'I don't know what to do', he thinks to himself. In his briefing meeting with Meg Mortimer he was told his job was to sort out the back office behind the reception desk. 'Just do your best,' Mortimer told him as she headed off for a meeting. But what did that mean? It felt just so overwhelming. 'Where do I start?' he thought, 'Why did I ever take this placement?'

As he sat there Jane Foster walked in and spied the upset-looking student. 'Are you alright, Ellerby?' she enquired attentively. 'I just don't know what to do,' Peters replied honestly. 'I was told to sort this room out, and all Mrs Mortimer said was "good luck". I've no idea how to do this'. Jane Foster smiled sympathetically. 'Don't worry, let's start. What is it we want to achieve?'

Goal setting theory

Goal setting theory is one of the most widely researched and supported process models of work motivation. It underpins many work practices, from appraisal systems to funding in the voluntary sector. It works on the principle that we respond much better to specific, clear, stretching goals with good feedback rather than vague phrases such as 'do your best' (Locke and Latham, 1990a). Goal setting theory argues that motivation is influenced by the difficulty, specificity, and feedback of reaching your goals. Goals need to be measurable and are often captured in the acronym SMART (specific, measurable, achievable, realistic, and time-related). Providing the person is committed to the goals, does not have other conflicting goals, and has the skills to achieve the goals, then this approach has a positive impact on performance (Locke and Latham, 1990b). The person puts their energy into achieving their goals.

The concept is based on the principles that hard goals are more satisfying when they are achieved and therefore can make work feel more meaningful (Locke and Latham, 2006), having clear outcomes helps give focus, and getting feedback means people can judge their progress. Often this approach works best with short- and medium-term goals, because they are easier to set clearly and have feedback; long-term goals, while useful, are often less specific and harder to measure.

One of the dangers of the goal setting approach is that it results in 'tunnel vision', where employees only focus on their goals and lose sight of wider objectives. This can be seen in many areas including the National Health Service, which has been criticized for being too focused on hitting targets and not enough on caring for patients. Similarly, charities are criticized for focusing on narrow business-like goals, to the exclusion of their original missions (King, 2017). Goal setting can also be seen as encouraging unethical behaviour, such as at Enron, where employees received large bonuses for posting large revenues. The appeal of the bonuses, Ordóñez et al. argue (2009), meant Enron employees focused on increasing revenues even at the expense of making real profits (ultimately leading to the company going bankrupt). Goal setting can also mean that employees focus only on things that are measurable and ignore less tangible parts of the job which might be important (Welsh and Ordóñez, 2014). They might even demotivate, because motivation becomes extrinsic (a focus on the goals) rather than being the intrinsic satisfaction with the task itself. Therefore, having goals can be useful but they should be used carefully.

◎ Study skills: setting your own goals

One of the challenges of being a student is that many of the goals that you might set yourself (getting a good degree and a good job) are often quite distant, a long time in the future, and therefore not good to motivate yourself consistently. Similarly, they are not that specific and therefore may actually lose you motivation. Using goal setting theory, you can break these goals down into more concrete and immediate goals. Some systems, such as that described in David Allen's book *Getting things done*, offer practical ways of managing yourself and motivating yourself for short-term goals (Allen, 2015). To gain a broader perspective on what is useful in your life, Steven Covey's *The seven habits of highly effective people* encourages you to reflect on the wider goals that you want in your life and how to get there (Covey, 1989). Covey encourages a 'character ethic' rather than narrow goal setting (see Chapter 17 for a wider discussion). Understanding what your goals are can give you a greater sense of focus, so long as you do not lose sight of the possibilities of learning new things that you had not planned to.

These process theories of motivation certainly offer some common-sense insights such as the idea that we manage our behaviours to concentrate on those which bring us a reward. They offer organizations guidelines on designing pay and reward systems (to make sure that they not only are fair but also appear to be fair to everyone) and also some practical suggestions for individual motivation (such as goal setting theory). However, questions remain as to whether they bear up to empirical scrutiny—do they really match up to the reality of how people are motivated? In particular, do we calculate our inputs and outputs in quite the precise, mathematical way suggested by expectancy theory?

Contemporary needs-based theory

One of the most popular contemporary theories of motivation is growth-mindset (see below). This perspective is based on self-determination theory (SDT), developed by Deci and Ryan (1985), who argue that we have three basic needs:

1) for autonomy (being able to initiate and regulate your own actions),

2) for competence (being able to control the outcome of an experience), and

3) for relatedness (being able to connect to others).

If these needs are met, SDT argues, then we can become self-determined and are able to be intrinsically motivated. The assumption that these authors make is that as human beings we want to be intrinsically motivated, and in doing so live better lives. Indeed, a study of university graduates a few years into their working lives found that those who had achieved intrinsic aspirations had positive psychological health whereas those who had achieved extrinsic aspirations (i.e. lots of money and 'career' goals) actually had indicators of poor psychological health (Niemiec et al., 2009).

Carole Dweck's goal orientation theory examines how the beliefs that individuals have about their abilities influence how individuals understand a task. She argues that there are two types of mindset: a fixed mindset, referring to people who believe that their basic qualities such as intelligence or talent are fixed, and a growth mindset, referring to people who believe that even their most basic qualities such as intelligence can be changed through hard work and dedication (Dweck, 1986/2017). Dweck argues that the view that you have about yourself has profound implications for how you live your life. Faced with something hard, those with a growth mindset take a learning or mastery frame, enjoy the challenge, and see failure as an opportunity to grow. Those with a fixed mindset always want to show to others that they are intelligent and avoid doing things that might demonstrate incompetence. It is not enough just to look smart, you have to be flawless—to be perfect right now. This can serve them well for a while. They like to be right and do well. But when things get hard, their identity as successful and flawless can quickly crumble and with it their motivation.

Dweck argues that it is possible to create the conditions that encourage a growth mindset. Instead of praising intelligence (in an attempt to boost self-esteem), managers, or parents and teachers, should praise effort and process, to stress how the individual is developing. Having a growth mindset helps you be able to cope with challenges and change.

 Imagine that you are a successful student who needs to earn high grades to get into a top university. You submit your first essay but rather than a top grade as you expected, your lecturer has given you a lot of criticism and a mid or low grade. How would you respond to this situation differently if you had a growth mindset rather than a fixed mindset? Which mindset do you think you have?

❓ Review questions

Describe	What are the main features of equity theory and expectancy theory?
Explain	How do process theories see motivation from the point of view of the individual?
Analyse	Why might goal setting theory produce unintended consequences that might lead to ethically questionable outcomes?
Apply	What examples can you see of expectancy theory, where people match actions to expected rewards, throughout the running case in the chapter?

Social approaches to motivation: the meaning of work

🔍 Running case: the meaning of work

Meg is confused by how differently everyone in the reception area seems to be motivated. Some workers respond well to the smile card scheme; others ignore it, but still seem to work hard. She can't put her finger on exactly what she needs to do to motivate her staff. She decides to find out what the employees feel and hands out an anonymous questionnaire to all employees. One of the questions, 'What does your work mean to you?', brings some differing yet revealing answers.

- Work is a means to an end—I come in, do my shift, take the cheque. It has no other meaning.

- I get a lot out of work and it is really helping me get on in life. I'm really proud to tell people about what I do and the responsibility I have here.

- My work is nothing but constant drudgery. I only express myself and get any meaning in life through my sports.

- I'm here because my parents told me they were ashamed of me being on the dole—they have been constantly nagging me to get a job.

Watch any quiz or game show on television—when a contestant is introduced to the audience, more often than not their occupation will be stated alongside their name, age, and where they live. As one of just four facts given in a brief introduction, their work is presented as a key aspect of that person's identity.

This is not just on television—think about when you are introduced to people, at a party for example. One of the first questions asked is about work. Indeed—the centrality of work to life is perhaps encapsulated in the question 'what do you do for a living?'

Visit the online resources and take a look at the extension material for Chapter 9 to read more about the effects of class and gender on personal identity.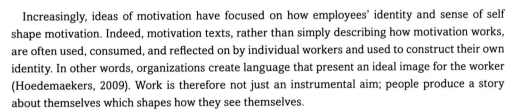

Increasingly, ideas of motivation have focused on how employees' identity and sense of self shape motivation. Indeed, motivation texts, rather than simply describing how motivation works, are often used, consumed, and reflected on by individual workers and used to construct their own identity. In other words, organizations create language that present an ideal image for the worker (Hoedemaekers, 2009). Work is therefore not just an instrumental aim; people produce a story about themselves which shapes how they see themselves.

The approaches to motivation that we have discussed so far have taken a psychological approach—motivation is determined by a number of stimuli, needs, perceptions, etc. It sees motivation as a series of levers to be pulled (Driver, 2017). These concepts suggest that if management understand all these factors then they can design work which will increase workers' motivation. Taken overall, we suggest that these psychological approaches have a number of problems.

- It is difficult to find empirical evidence for many of these theories—they may appear plausible, but do they reflect the reality of workplace motivation?

- Can broad frameworks of motivation, such as Maslow's hierarchy, ever appreciate the complex, individual nature of personalities, as discussed with the ideographic approach in Chapter 8?

- Often when applied to work, these complex theories of motivation are boiled down to a simplistic and narrow framework (e.g. Maslow) or even an equation (expectancy theory).
- Motivation theories tends to focus on just one aspect of the job—reward, satisfaction, etc.—rather than having an overall view of both the job and how it links to the outside world.

In this final section we suggest that the motivation also comes from work being an indicator of our identity within the rest of society. Motivation, and the meanings we attach to work, are as much a social phenomenon as they are a psychological one. What, for example, does it mean to be a doctor within society? Or a cleaner? Or to be without work?

Why do we work?

Why do we work at all? Is it out of economic necessity or to gain a sense of identity within society? Part of the reason is the imperative from society to work—it is something that we are expected to do; furthermore, not working is almost seen as a form of deviant behaviour, against the norms of society. One of the current debates about the Fourth Industrial Revolution is that with artificial intelligence and automation potentially replacing millions of jobs, it might be that we do not need as many people to work. Will this be freeing people from the drudgery of work or create meaninglessness, depression and a loss of purpose?

 Theory in context: the parable of the talents

The English word 'talent', meaning aptitude or skill, originates in the name of an ancient biblical currency—i.e. money. It is referred to in the 'parable of the talents' in the Gospel of St Matthew. A master entrusts his servants with a number of talents. On his return, two of the servants have put their talents to work, doubling their value, for which they are rewarded. The third has buried his talents in a hole in the ground, gaining nothing, and is punished for laziness. The parable of the talents, from the Christian bible, is about money, but the use of the word 'talent' in English to mean aptitudes suggests an obligation to work and be productive—not to let our abilities and skills go to waste. Max Weber (1930) is noted for the notion of the Protestant work ethic, whereby religious salvation comes about as a result of hard work throughout life. Noon and Blyton (2007) note similar work ethics in Islamic, Buddhist, and Catholic faiths. A similar message is given by each—work is good and a religious duty, while not working is seen as lazy and contrary to religious teachings.

Although the influence of religious teaching may have diminished in the UK in recent years, beliefs in the work ethic remains. This is seen in the tabloid media, with screaming headlines about 'Dole scroungers' and 'Benefit cheats', or in television programmes such as *Benefits street*—it is as if one were not playing a rightful role in society unless economically productive.

Furthermore, for those excluded from work, especially at a time of recession, stories in the papers are of pity and of their own frustration, again as if they are barred from a fundamental aspect of existence and expression within society—the right to work. For example, Kingsley et al. (2011) interviewed young, long-term unemployed people in the UK. While they spoke about the financial problems of being unemployed, they also explained how a lack of work hits at their sense of self-identity within society, giving them less self-belief.

 Visit the online resources and take a look at the extension material for Chapter 9 for more insights about the effects of unemployment on self-identity.

For Michel Foucault, who believed that power shapes our view of the world (see Chapter 14), society overall creates the idea that our bodies are working bodies and that it is abnormal if one's inclination is not to work: 'the body becomes a useful force only if it is a productive body' (Foucault and Rabinow, 1984: 173).

It is not just in religion and the media that a normal working life is presented. In school and university we are taught and guided towards our ultimate goal of work—even this textbook includes 'employability skills'. From many social and institutional angles, work becomes an obligation or duty. Rather than something for which we are motivated by some form of reward, work has a much more central part in our sense of self and identity, fuelled by a societal sense of obligation.

We are also socialized from a young age that work will be a central part of our identity. Young children are often asked 'What will you be when you grow up?', shaping their sense of the importance of work. Research shows that from an early age our expectations are shaped not only by what we aspire to but also by what we think we can achieve. Due to their background and previous experiences, many people 'simply eliminate from consideration occupations they believe to be beyond their capabilities, however attractive the occupations may be' (Bandura et al., 2001: 188). Many factors—socioeconomic, family, academic, and self-perception—may shape people's career choices and what they consider valuable and important in life. These can be considered vital, deep-seated sources of motivation.

Research insight: learning about work through Disney

Griffin, M., Learmonth, M., and Piper, N. 2018. Organizational readiness: Culturally mediated learning through Disney animation. *Academy of Management Learning & Education* 17 (1): 4–23.

Griffin, M., Harding, N., and Learmonth, M. 2017. Whistle while you work? Disney animation, organizational readiness and gendered subjugation. *Organization Studies* 38 (7): 869–94.

Where do you get your ideas of work from? One source, Martyn Griffin and his colleagues argue, is Disney films.

They develop the concept of 'organizational readiness' which they describe as the 'socio-cultural expectations about working selves that prepare young people ... for their future life in organizations' (Griffin et al., 2017: 869). It is a state of mind, which includes expectations about work, which they argue we gradually develop over our childhood and internalize from the culture that surrounds us (Griffin et al., 2018). These include schools, government bodies, teachers and parents, and cultural sources including films. One such source for many children are Disney films. Disney films present particular images of work, from it being dangerous or unfulfilling (think of Cinderella cleaning for the ugly sisters) to being driven by manipulative bosses (for instance in *Mulan*, where the young woman pretending to be a man is picked on repeatedly by the army captain). Yet despite these problems, characters often learn to accentuate the positives (Pinocchio singing 'I've got no strings to tie me down, to make me fret or make me frown'). They either are rescued from meaningless work (to marry a prince) or find a new role (such as Moana learning how to master the sea). Griffin et al. conclude that the message here is 'We can be happy and fulfilled in our work, but we will need support along the way from our friends' (2018: 14). Furthermore, while older films tended to portray work as no place for women, more recent films offer a more positive image, such as Elsa in *Frozen* or the central character in *Moana*, who embrace more positive images of work.

Orientations to work

The extent to which our working life links with our life in general and gives us a sense of identity within society was investigated by Goldthorpe (1968). In his study of workers in a Luton car factory, he noted a particular paradox. On one hand, workers did not seem to be deriving an intrinsic or social satisfaction from their work. On the other hand, workers were not expressing any dissatisfaction with their work, even though they disliked some aspects of it.

Goldthorpe (1968) concluded that such workers had an 'instrumental orientation to work'. They saw their work merely as a means to an end. They had no desire for intrinsic satisfaction from the work—they would simply keep their head down, do their shift, and then pick up the pay packet at the end of the week.

Goldthorpe brings a different perspective to motivation. It is not simply a workplace phenomenon with managers manipulating certain rewards; instead, orientations to work have more of a link with our working identity in society. Goldthorpe (1968) suggests three orientations to work.

- The instrumental orientation to work suggests a strong separation between working life and non-working life. The only aspect of working life that is carried into the outside world is the pay packet. It is this which—following an instrumental calculation—allows the worker to enjoy the life that they do in the outside world, and they desire nothing more from work.

- A bureaucratic orientation to work suggests more of a loyalty to the organization—service in return for progress. Meaning and social identity are carried into the outside world—a promotion within the organization is seen as a marker of status and identity in the outside world.

- A solidaristic orientation to work is one where meaning, again, is carried outwards into society, but it is a meaning that derives from membership of a group rather than individual status. There is, thus, solidarity between the workers. While there are economic benefits which derive from the organization, loyalty and moral leaning is to the group rather than the organization itself.

Goldthorpe's work shows that professional status contributes to our working identity in the outside world, but that elements in society, such as class, also contribute to that identity. Many accounts of solidaristic group loyalty, for example, link group loyalty in industrial environments to an element of working-class identity (see, for example, Collinson, 1988; Ackroyd and Crowdy, 1990).

A more recent workplace issue is that of work–life balance, a desire to achieve a sensible balance between work commitments and private life. The degree to which people achieve this has also been analysed in terms of professional identity (Caven, 2004) and the links with social factors, such as class and gender (Hakim, 2000; Özbilgin et al., 2011).

 Theory in context: the value of deep work

Throughout this chapter we have concentrated on the idea of motivation, thinking about getting people to work—but it might be more beneficial to rephrase the aim as getting people to do the right *type* of work. As we have highlighted throughout this chapter, we often have a tendency to avoid pain and seek pleasure. When it comes to work this means that we may seek work that is less challenging (painful) in favour of work that might give us short-term satisfaction. This does not mean that we are not working; we might be very *busy*, but the work we are doing is of less importance. This easier work is what Cal Newport calls shallow work. This might include things like emails, meetings, or phone calls, all of which are work, but they

→

→

are shallow and not cognitively demanding, and they add little value to the organization. In contrast, Newport asks us to focus on what he calls *deep work*, professional activities that demand concentration, 'push your cognitive capabilities to their limits', and create significant value for the organization and you (Newport, 2016: 3). Newport argues that the current office environment and wider culture (think about the ubiquity of smartphones, social media, open-plan offices, etc.) reduce our possibilities of deep work, yet these difficult, demanding types of work (particularly as the Fourth Industrial Revolution takes hold with computers increasingly able to do more shallow work effectively and quickly) are more important. Therefore while we might be motivated to work hard, we might put our energies into the wrong things. This does not mean having to work longer hours, but rather with greater intensity and real focus.

 Do you really engage with deep work or do you allow distractions (email, Twitter, WhatsApp) to interrupt your thinking? Why do you think we find deep work so much more difficult?

Work and innate creativity

For a final word on motivation and society, we turn to Karl Marx (1867/1990) who, as we saw in Chapter 3, suggested that people are inherently creative—they have a desire to transform the world around them. In a Marxist sense, motivation is thus innate—a very different view of motivation from that of Taylor and Ford seen earlier in this chapter, who saw people as innately lazy.

A similar view of natural human creativity was seen in Chapter 8 with the social–radical approach. People have unlimited potential; it is the nature of work which demotivates them from achieving this rather than workers being disinclined to work.

Ironically, this is the view of people that Maslow held with his self-actualization concept, but it has been written out of the interpretation of Maslow used in management theory. Perhaps if management were able to tap into this aspect of human motivation or design work to enable people to fulfil it, then the whole area of motivation theory, with its associated models and theories, would be rendered obsolete—an important part of management (motivating people to work) would be covered by the innate motivation of people themselves.

? Review questions

Describe	What are the three orientations to work suggested by Goldthorpe?
Explain	How does work provide us with an identity and meaning within society?
Analyse	Are motivational techniques just another way of getting staff to do things that they would otherwise not do? What would work be like if it were designed to produce the maximum level of self-actualization rather than productivity?
Apply	What orientations to work do you see in the Junction Hotel staff?

335

Connecting case and theory

Meg Mortimer faced a problem at the start of the chapter. How do you motivate your staff? This, as we have seen, is a key issue that organizations across the world face. Throughout the chapter we saw a number of different approaches to motivation at work. The smile card system was an attempt by Phil Weaver to apply extrinsic rewards to the staff. For some staff, including Steve Long, it certainly worked, making him more motivated. However, as we saw with goal setting theory, there were unintended consequences: think back to when Steve ran off from helping a customer to serve others in view of Simon Chance in order to get a tick on his card. John McAuley had a negative reaction, feeling like he was 'grinning like an idiot', with behaviour modification seeming inauthentic. Staff only seemed to smile when they knew they were being watched. Jane Foster rejected the smile card scheme outright, because she loves her job and was doing it 'with pride'. This form of extrinsic motivation rubbed up against her intrinsic motivation.

What could Junction Hotel have done differently? Content theories suggest that workers have needs which motivate them and for which appropriate job characteristics can be designed. Could they, for instance, have redesigned the work to give the reception staff more autonomy and room for expression? Process theories suggest that motivation is a result of subjective individual calculations and that it is important to understand workers as individuals who change over time. Finally, social theories link work motivation with the wider significance of work as a facet of our identity within society.

So what should Meg Mortimer do to increase the motivation at Junction Hotel? She cannot see any single theory of motivation in isolation as they all have their own strengths and weaknesses. However, taken together, theories of motivation outline different facets of what motivates us in the workplace.

Further reading

Dweck, C. 1986/2017. *Mindset—updated edition: Changing the way you think to fulfil your potential.* Random House: New York.

Dweck offers a fascinating concept of the growth mindset, a perspective of people who believe that even their most basic qualities such as intelligence can be changed through hard work and dedication. A highly challenging book which offers new insights into how we can change our thinking.

Herzberg, F. 2003. One more time: How do you motivate employees? *Harvard Business Review* 81 (1): 87–96.

Herzberg's explanation of his motivators and hygiene theory.

Kanfer, R., Frese, M., and Johnson, R.E. 2017. Motivation related to work: A century of progress. *Journal of Applied Psychology* 102 (3): 338.

A good overview of motivation theory from a psychological perspective.

McGee, H.M., and Johnson, D.A. 2015. Performance motivation as the behaviorist views it. *Performance Improvement* 54 (4): 15–21.

This article provides an overview of behavioural theories of workplace motivation.

References

Ackroyd, S., and Crowdy, P.A. 1990. Can culture be managed? Working with 'raw' material: the case of the English slaughtermen. *Personnel Review* 19 (5): 3–13.

Adams, J.S. 1963. Towards an understanding of inequity. *Journal of Abnormal and Social Psychology* 67 (5): 422.

Allen, D. 2015. *Getting things done: The art of stress-free productivity.* Penguin: London.

Bandura, A., Barbaranelli, C., Caprara, G.V., and Pastorelli, C. 2001. Self-efficacy beliefs as shapers of children's aspirations and career trajectories. *Child Development* 72 (1): 187–206.

BBC News. 2018a. BBC's Carrie Gracie 'could not collude' in pay discrimination, 8 January. Available at: http://www.bbc.co.uk/news/uk-42601477

BBC News. 2018b. Whistleblower prompts call for Northern trains inquiry, 18 May. Available at: https://www.bbc.co.uk/news/uk-england-manchester-44174565

Beynon, H. 1984. *Working for Ford.* Penguin: Harmondsworth.

Bridgman, T., Cummings, S., & Ballard, J. 2018. *Who built Maslow's pyramid? A history of the creation of management studies' most famous symbol and its implications for management education.* Academy of Management Learning and Education. doi.org/10.5465/amle.2017.0351

Burkeman, O. 2011. This column will change your life: Get into the habit of random rewards. *The Guardian*, 23 April.

Caven, V. 2004. Constructing a career: Women architects at work. *Career Development International* 9 (5): 518–31.

Cerasoli, C.P., Nicklin, J.M., and Ford, M.T. 2014. Intrinsic motivation and extrinsic incentives jointly predict performance: A 40-year meta-analysis. *Psychological Bulletin* 140 (4): 980–1008.

Coleman, D. 2018. Lottery-winning beauty queen turns her back on flashy lifestyle by giving away her winnings. *The Mirror*, 6 July. Available at: https://www.mirror.co.uk/news/world-news/lottery-winning-beauty-queen-shuns-12862701

Collinson, D.L. 1988. 'Engineering humour': Masculinity, joking and conflict in shop-floor relations. *Organization Studies* 9 (2): 181–99.

Colquitt, J.A., Conlon, D.E., Wesson, M.J., Porter, C.O., and Ng, K.Y. 2001. Justice at the millennium: A meta-analytic review of 25 years of organizational justice research. *Journal of Applied Psychology* 86 (3): 425–45.

Condly, S.J., Clark, R.E., and Stolovitch, H.D. 2003. The effects of incentives on workplace performance: A meta-analytic review of research studies 1. *Performance Improvement Quarterly* 16 (3): 46–63.

Covey, S. 1989. *The seven habits of highly effective people.* Simon & Schuster: London.

Cullen, D. 1997. Maslow, monkeys and motivation theory. *Organization* 4 (3): 355–73.

Cullen, D., and Gotell, L. 2002. From orgasms to organizations: Maslow, women's sexuality and the gendered foundations of the needs hierarchy. *Gender, Work and Organization* 9 (5): 537–55.

Davis, K. 1957. *Human relations in business.* McGraw-Hill: New York.

Deci, E.L. 1972. The effects of contingent and noncontingent rewards and controls on intrinsic motivation. *Organizational Behavior and Human Performance* 8: 217–29.

Deci, E., and Ryan, R.M. 1985. *Intrinsic motivation and self-determination in human behavior.* Springer Science & Business Media: New York.

De Gieter, S., De Cooman, R., Pepermans, R., Caers, R., Du Bois, C., and Jegers, M. 2006. Identifying nurses' rewards: A qualitative categorization study in Belgium. *Human Resources for Health* 4: 15.

Dewhurst, M., Guthridge, M., and Mohr, E. 2009. Motivating people: Getting beyond money. *McKinsey Quarterly*, November. Available at: https://www.mckinsey.com/business-functions/organization/our-insights/motivating-people-getting-beyond-money (last accessed 10 July 2018).

Driver, M. 2017. Motivation and identity: A psychoanalytic perspective on the turn to identity in motivation research. *Human Relations* 70 (5): 617–37.

Dweck, C. 1986/2017. *Mindset—updated edition: Changing the way you think to fulfil your potential*. Random House: New York.

Dye, J. 2017. Pandora shares rise as sales, subscriber growth picks up. *Financial Times*, 31 July. Available at: https://www.ft.com/content/8d7c1a3e-f958-3176-bca3-104373da3a76

Dye, K., Mills, A.J., and Weatherbee, T. 2005. Maslow: man interrupted: Reading management theory in context. *Management Decision* 43 (10): 1375–95.

Dymek, M., Zackariasson, P. (eds). 2016. *The business of gamification: A critical analysis*. Taylor & Francis: London.

Executive Grapevine. 2015a. Video: CEO's inspirational speech that got employees working for free, 18 June. Available at: http://www.executive-grapevine.com/board-leadership/article/2015–06–18-video-ceos-inspirational-speech-that-got-employees-working-for-free?utm_source= eshot&utm_medium = email&utm_campaign = BL%20-%20 24/06/2015 (last accessed 18 July 2015).

Executive Grapevine. 2015b. Zappos billionaire CEO lives in a trailer, 22 July. Available at: http://www.hrgrapevine.com/markets/hr/article/2015-07-22-zappos-billionaire-ceo-lives-in-a-trailer (last accessed 18 July 2015).

Fishwick, C. 2017. The big money question: would you quit work for £1m? *The Guardian*, 17 October. Available at: https://www.theguardian.com/money/shortcuts/2017/oct/17/the-big-money-question-would-you-quit-work-for-1m

Flanagan, E. 2014. Stalybridge lottery syndicate win £2.9m jackpot—but say they will stay on at work. *Manchester Evening News*, 4 November.

Foucault, M., and Rabinow, P. 1984. *The Foucault reader*. Pantheon Books: New York.

Gallup. 2017. *State of the global workplace*. Gallup Press: New York

Goldthorpe, J.H. 1968. *The affluent worker: Industrial attitudes and behaviour*. Cambridge University Press: London.

Greenberg, J. 1990a. Employee theft as a reaction to underpayment inequity: The hidden cost of pay cuts. *Journal of Applied Psychology* 75 (5): 561.

Greenberg, J. 1990b. Organizational justice: Yesterday, today, and tomorrow. *Journal of Management* 16 (2): 399–432.

Griffin, M., Harding, N., and Learmonth, M. 2017. Whistle while you work? Disney animation, organizational readiness and gendered subjugation. *Organization Studies* 38 (7): 869–94.

Griffin, M., Learmonth, M., and Piper, N. 2018. Organizational readiness: Culturally mediated learning through Disney animation. *Academy of Management Learning and Education* 17 (1): 4–23.

Griffiths, M. 1999. Gambling technologies: Prospects for problem gambling. *Journal of Gambling Studies* 15 (3): 265–83.

Hakim, C. 2000. *Work-lifestyle choices in the 21st century*. Oxford University Press: Oxford.

Harrison, J.D. 2015. When we were small: Pandora. *Washington Post*, 6 February.

Haslett, E. 2017. Here's the (surprisingly young) age at which you are the least motivated, City A.M. Available at: http://www.cityam.com/271950/heres-surprisingly-young-age-which-you-least-motivated

Herzberg, F. 1966. *Work and the nature of man*. World Pub. Co.: Cleveland, OH.

Herzberg, F. 1987. One more time: How do you motivate employees? *Harvard Business Review* September–October: 88–L 99.

Herzberg, F. 2003. One more time: How do you motivate employees? *Harvard Business Review* 81 (1): 87–96.

Hoedemaekers, C. 2009. Traversing the empty promise: Management, subjectivity and the other's desire, *Journal of Organizational Change Management* 22 (2): 181–201.

Hooker, L. 2017. Have you been nudged? BBC News, 9 October. Available at: http://www.bbc.co.uk/news/business-41549533

Huseman, R.C., Hatfield, J.D., and Miles, E.W. 1987. A new perspective on equity theory: The equity sensitivity construct. *Academy of Management Review* 12 (2): 222–34.

Kanfer, R., Frese, M., and Johnson, R.E. 2017. Motivation related to work: A century of progress. *Journal of Applied Psychology* 102 (3): 338.

King, D. 2017. Becoming business-like: Governing the nonprofit professional. *Nonprofit and Voluntary Sector Quarterly* 46 (2): 241–60.

Kingsley, P., Hickman, L., and Saner, E. 2011. What's it like to be young and looking for work in Britain? *The Guardian*, 1 November.

Kouchaki, M., Smith, I.H., and Netchaeva, E. 2015. Not all fairness is created equal: Fairness perceptions of group vs. individual decision makers. *Organization Science* 26 (5): 1301–15.

Kuvaas, B., Buch, R., Weibel, A., Dysvik, A., and Nerstad, C.G. (2017). Do intrinsic and extrinsic motivation relate differently to employee outcomes? *Journal of Economic Psychology* 61: 244–58.

Lepper, R.M., Greene, D., and Nisbett, E.R. 1973. Undermining children's intrinsic interest with extrinsic reward: A test of the 'overjustification' hypothesis. *Personality and Social Psychology* 28: 129–37.

Locke, E.A., and Latham, G.P. 1990a. *A theory of goal setting and task performance*. Prentice Hall: Harlow.

Locke, E.A. and Latham, G.P. 1990b. Work motivation and satisfaction: Light at the end of the tunnel. *Psychological Science* 1 (4): 240–6.

Locke, E.A. and Latham, G.P. 2006. New directions in goal-setting theory. *Current Directions In Psychological Science* 15 (5): 265–8.

Luthans, F., and Kreitner, R. 1985. *Organizational behaviour modification and beyond*. Scott Foresman: Glenview, IL.

Makin, P.J., and Sutherland, V.J. 1994. Reducing accidents using a behavioural approach. *Leadership and Organization Development Journal* 15 (5): 5–10.

Manville, C., Akremi, A. E., Niezborala, M., and Mignonac, K. 2016. Injustice hurts, literally: The role of sleep and emotional exhaustion in the relationship between organizational justice and musculoskeletal disorders. *Human Relations* 69 (6): 1315–39.

Martinko, M.J., and Fadil, P. 1994. Operant technologies: A theoretical foundation for organizational change and development. *Leadership and Organization Development Journal* 15 (5): 16–20.

Martinson, J. 2018. Carrie Gracie: Fearless leader of battle for equal pay at the BBC. *The Guardian*, 14 January. Available at: https://www.theguardian.com/media/2018/jan/14/carrie-gracie-fearless-leader-of-battle-for-equal-pay-at-bbc

Marx, K. 1867/1990. *Capital*, vol. 1 (transl. Fowkes, B.). Penguin Books: London.

Maslow, A.H. 1943. A theory of human motivation. *Psychological Review* 50 (4): 370–96.

Maslow, A.H. 1964. *Religions, values, and peak-experiences*. Ohio State University Press: Columbus.

Maslow, A.H. 1971. *The farther reaches of human nature*. Viking: New York.

Maslow, A.H. 1987. *Motivation and personality*. Harper and Row: New York.

Maslow, A.H. 2000. *The Maslow business reader*. John Wiley: New York, Toronto.

McDonald, M. 2018. Do your measures make employees mad? Or motivate them? Gallup, 3 January. Available at: http://news.gallup.com/opinion/gallup/224342/performance-measures-motivate-madden-employees.aspx?g_source=link_NEWSV9&g_medium=TOPIC&g_campaign=item_&g_content=Do%2520Your%2520Measures%2520Make%2520Employees%2520Mad%3f%2520Or%2520Motivate%2520Them%3f

McGee, H.M. and Johnson, D.A. 2015. Performance motivation as the behaviorist views it. *Performance Improvement* 54 (4): 15–21.

McGonigal, J. 2011. *Reality is broken: Why games make us better and how they can change the world*. Penguin: New York.

McGrath, M. 2018. Manchester City stars to earn up to £1million each in bonuses

339

if they win Premier League and Champions League. *The Sun*, 3 March. Available at: https://www.thesun.co.uk/sport/football/5718583/manchester-city-stars-to-earn-up-to-1million-each-in-bonuses-if-they-win-premier-league-and-champions-league/

Newport, C. 2016. *Deep work: Rules for focused success in a distracted world.* Hachette: London.

Nicolaou, A. (2018) Pandora to lay off 5% of staff in restructuring. *Financial Times*, 31 January. Available at: https://www.ft.com/content/8b53e08a-06de-11e8-9650-9c0ad2d7c5b5

Niemiec, C.P., Ryan, R.M., and Deci, E.L. 2009. The path taken: Consequences of attaining intrinsic and extrinsic aspirations in post-college life. *Journal of Research in Personality* 43 (3): 291–306.

Noon, M., and Blyton, P. 2007. *The realities of work: Experiencing work and employment in contemporary society.* Palgrave: Basingstoke, New York.

O'Connor, D., and Yballe, L. 2007. Maslow revisited: Constructing a road map of human nature. *Journal of Management Education* 31 (6): 738–56.

Ordóñez, L., Schweitzer, M.E., Galinsky, A., and Bazerman, M. 2009. Goals gone wild: How goals systematically harm individuals and organizations. *Academy of Management Perspectives* 23 (1): 6–16.

Özbilgin, M.F., Beauregard, T.A., Tatli, A., and Bell, M.P. 2011. Work-life, diversity and intersectionality: A critical review and research agenda. *International Journal of Management Reviews* 13 (2): 177–98.

Pavlov, I.P., and Anrep, G.V. 1927. *Conditioned reflexes: An investigation of the physiological activity of the cerebral cortex.* Oxford University Press: London.

Perrin, C. 2017. Man Utd players could get £4m bonus if they win the Premier League and Champions League. *The Express*, 1 August. Available at: https://www.express.co.uk/sport/football/835367/Manchester-United-Premier-League-Champions-League-bonuses

Pink, D. 2018. *Drive: The surprising truth about what motivates us.* Canongate Books: Edinburgh.

Raff, D., and Summers, L. 1987. Did Henry Ford pay efficiency wages? *Journal of Labour Economics* 5 (4): 557–86.

Richter, G., Raban, D.R., and Rafaeli, S. 2015. Studying gamification: The effect of rewards and incentives on motivation. In: Reiners, T., and Wood, L. (eds) *Gamification in education and business.* Springer: Cham, pp. 21–46.

Searles, M. 2018. Victory for common sense as EFL allow Accrington Stanley to keep funding £200 team trips to McDonald's. *Daily Mail*, 6 April. Available at: http://www.dailymail.co.uk/sport/football/article-5585943/Victory-common-sense-EFL-let-Accrington-Stanley-fund-McDonalds-trips.html

Shipman, T. 2018. £2 limit to curb 'crack cocaine' of gambling. *Sunday Times*, 21 January. Available at: https://www.the-times.co.uk/article/2-limit-to-curb-crack-cocaine-of-gambling-ftc6v37hr

Singh, A. 2018. John Humphrys takes pay cut as BBC targets male news presenters. *The Telegraph*, 25 January. Available at: https://www.telegraph.co.uk/news/2018/01/25/john-humphrys-co-take-pay-cuts-bbc-targets-male-news-presenters/

Skarlicki, D.P., and Folger, R. 1997. Retaliation in the workplace: The roles of distributive, procedural, and interactional justice. *Journal of Applied Psychology* 82 (3): 434–43.

Skinner, B.F. 1969. *Contingencies of reinforcement: A theoretical analysis.* Appleton-Century-Crofts: New York.

Taylor, F.W. 1911. *The principles of scientific management.* Harper: New York.

Thaler, R., and Sunstein, C. 2008. *Nudge: Improving decisions about health, wealth, and happiness.* Yale University Press: New Haven, CT.

The Economist. 2018. Labour-monitoring technologies raise efficiency—and hard questions. *The Economist*, 1 March. Available at: https://www.economist.com/news/finance-and-economics/21737507-pushing-back-against-controlling-bosses-leaves-workers-more-likely-be-replaced

Towers Watson. 2014. *The 2014 global work-force study*. Towers Watson: London.

Tyler, T.R., and Bies, R.J. 1990. Beyond formal procedures: The interpersonal context of procedural justice. In: Carroll, J. (ed.) *Applied social psychology and organizational settings*. Erlbaum: Hillsdale, NJ, pp. 77–98.

Villere, M.F., and Hartman, S.S. 1991. Reinforcement theory: A practical tool. *Leadership and Organization Development Journal* 12 (2): 27–31.

Vroom, V.H. 1964. *Work and motivation*. Wiley: New York.

Wahba, M.A., and Bridwell, L.G. 1976. Maslow reconsidered: A review of research on the need hierarchy theory. *Organizational Behavior and Human Performance* 15 (2): 212–40.

Ward, S.J., and King, L.A. 2017. Work and the good life: How work contributes to meaning in life. *Research in Organizational Behavior* 37: 59–82.

Weber, M. 1930. *The Protestant ethic and the spirit of capitalism* (transl. Parsons, T.). G. Allen & Unwin: London.

Welsh, D., and Ordóñez, L.D. 2014. The dark side of consecutive high performance goals: Linking goal setting, depletion, and unethical behavior. *Organizational Behavior and Human Decision Process* 123: 79–89.

CHAPTER 10

Knowledge and learning

Developing the individual: developing the organization

Chapter overview and learning outcomes

By the end of this chapter you should be able to:

- describe a variety of theories of individual knowledge and learning

- explain the importance of deep learning, where knowledge is learned from experience and from 'learning to learn'

- describe the importance of knowledge and learning at organizational levels

- explain and analyse the concept of the 'learning organization'

- explain the impact of artificial intelligence upon knowledge and work at individual and organizational levels

Key theorists	
Michael Polanyi	Recognized the importance of the 'tacit' dimension of knowledge which comes from personal experience, as opposed to explicit knowledge such as facts and figures
David Kolb	Devised a learning cycle which demonstrated how knowledge is gained through a cycle of experience and reflection
Howard Gardner	Outlined a theory of multiple intelligences, whereby individuals exhibit different types of intelligence, such as logical, musical, or spatial
Donna Haraway	Noted how knowledge is situated in action in social contexts
Ikujiro Nonaka	Suggested that a successful 'knowledge creating company' is adept at transforming tacit and explicit knowledge within its workforce
Chris Argyris and Donald Schön	Suggested that successful organizational learning is that which goes beyond 'single loop' to become 'double-loop' learning
Peter Senge	Outlined a model of the key characteristics of the learning organization
Jean Lave and Etienne Wenger	Noted the existence of communities of practice, and that social groups engage in learning a common area of knowledge and practice

Key terms

Explicit knowledge	Knowledge that can be expressed to other people as a set of words, facts, diagrams, or instructions
Tacit knowledge	Knowledge that is personal, a form of second nature or knowing things 'off by heart', and which is difficult to explain to others
Experiential learning	Learning that comes from experiences and reflecting on those experiences
Learning styles	Ways in which different individuals approach learning and learn more effectively
Reflective practice	A form of professional development and training where workers reflect on actual workplace experiences and events
Organizational knowledge	Knowledge that is a collective property of an organization rather than belonging to an individual
Situated knowledge	Knowledge that exists in a dynamic form in interactions between people in specific organizational contexts
Organizational learning	Sharing and transferring knowledge so that it becomes a collective property of the organization
Learning organization	An organization that is set up so as to facilitate continual learning at individual and organizational levels
Communities of practice	Social groupings that are based around a common occupational practice and set of knowledge and that develop and share that knowledge among themselves
Artificial intelligence	Knowledge in the form of data which is manipulated by algorithms to make decisions and carry out tasks

Introduction

Q Running case: an alarming experience

Simon Chance has had a busy morning dealing with a full-scale evacuation of the hotel. A faulty smoke detector set fire alarms ringing, and all guests and staff had to evacuate until the all clear.

Inside the hotel, the maintenance team are having problems. Bob Smith is their expert on the fire alarm system—he knows it inside out and can fix any problems in minutes. Unfortunately, today he is off work sick and nobody else knows how to deal with the problem. Chance sees the remaining engineers standing around the control panel, flicking through manuals and scratching their heads. None of them has ever dealt with a problem in the alarm system before.

→

At great cost, Chance brings in an outside engineer, who takes a couple of hours to arrive and a further two hours to fix the problem. In the meantime, he has to deal with a crowd of unhappy guests who are waiting outside with growing impatience.

If you were in charge of training and development of the maintenance team, what would you do to avoid a repeat of this problem?

Do you work just to get paid, or is the workplace more than that, maybe somewhere to develop as an individual? The previous two chapters have suggested that the workplace is somewhere where our personalities develop (Chapter 8) and even where we engage in our highest creative achievements through self-actualization (Chapter 9).

This chapter examines how people develop as individuals and improve their work by learning and gaining new knowledge from their workplace experience. Knowledgeable workers also benefit the organization. In recent years it has been suggested that knowledge can give organizations a competitive advantage, especially in sectors such as technology, where constant development and innovation are important. The chapter thus examines both knowledge (what people know) and learning (how people gain that knowledge).

- First we look at individual knowledge and learning, drawing a distinction between explicit knowledge, which can be learned like a set of facts, and a deeper tacit knowledge, which is learned from experience and reflection upon that experience. We look specifically at knowledge that is valuable for being a manager and how people gain that knowledge.

- Second, we move to the level of the organization. Knowledge management is concerned with how individuals learn, but also with how knowledge, both explicit and tacit, is transferred between people in and across the organization. We see how organizations that promote the sharing of knowledge become learning organizations, and how this equips them to deal with change and uncertainty.

To conclude, we look at the implications of the digitization of knowledge—will the knowledge and skills that are valued by employers today still be relevant when such work can be done through artificial intelligence?

Individual learning: knowledge, experience, and styles

Q Running case: training and development

Chance reflects upon the earlier chaos. While there is much knowledge and expertise within the maintenance team, it isn't shared—each person has their own specialist area.

The morning's events have shown how they rely on specific individuals who are the only ones with the knowledge to do key tasks. If that person is absent, the task can't be performed.

Chance decides that the maintenance staff need to learn more about each other's specialisms—to have a broader knowledge of tasks and equipment across the hotel. He sets up a training and development programme to increase knowledge and learning across the maintenance team.

We have all engaged in learning at some time, whether it is formulas for a maths exam, lines for a play, or new techniques for a sport. By reading this book you are engaged in a learning process. But what does it really mean to learn something? Is knowledge something as simple as remembering lists off by heart, or is there more to it?

In this section, we see how **experiential learning** takes us from **surface learning**, where we simply learn a set of facts, to **deep learning**, a richer form of learning where we understand knowledge in its *context* and from our own *experience*. We begin to think about the ways in which we learn best and develop our own preferred learning styles.

From lists to patterns

Running case: learning rewards

Chance audits the qualifications currently held within the maintenance team, then offers in-centives for people to add to their knowledge. Courses in plumbing, gas, and electricity, as well as workshops for particular pieces of equipment, will be offered to the maintenance team, with a bonus paid for each qualification gained. Chance calls this scheme 'learning rewards'.

One of the maintenance staff, Mike Bridges, throws himself into the scheme, gaining several certificates from a local college. He is the first to be approached when the refrigeration unit in the bar breaks down, as he has undertaken a workshop with the manufacturers of the equipment.

Unfortunately, that knowledge doesn't help him when he is faced with the task of getting the refrigeration unit working again. 'I passed that test six months ago,' explains Bridges to bar manager John Vintner. 'Took my bonus and haven't looked at the manual since. I've never actually touched one of these things before, let alone repaired one.'

 What sort of learning do you think the learning rewards scheme promoted? Is it of any value to the hotel?

To help understand individual learning, we are going to engage in a learning process ourselves. The Finnish language is unlike most other languages and one with which you will probably not be familiar. Have a look at the list of five Finnish words in Table 10.1, and their English translations, and learn them. You will be tested later: you will be given the word in English, and you will be asked to give the Finnish translation.

The Finnish flag.
Source: Lainea / Shutterstock.com

Table 10.1 Some words in Finnish, part 1

tori	market
kaupunki	town
joki	river
ulos	out
yliopisto	university

How did you go about learning the words? Did you simply read and memorize them, or did you devise some form of system? Did you think about how you have learned a language before or did you dive straight in? The strategy you adopt says a lot about how you go about learning, and also reflects some of the key learning theories.

A behaviourist view of learning

If you were offered £10 for each word you remembered correctly, would you be more likely to learn them all? Such an approach is underpinned by ideas from behavioural psychology, which, as explained Chapter 9, argues that people are motivated by rewards and punishments. Vocabulary tests from school language lessons follow this type of pattern—learn the words and you are rewarded with a good grade; fail to learn them and you may receive a punishment, for example a detention or a poor grade.

However, for behaviourist theories to work, the reward needs to be maintained. After gaining the initial £10, people will have no further incentive to retain the words in their memory. Unless further rewards come along, they will eventually forget what they have learned.

With no reward on offer besides your own satisfaction at learning the words, let's see how well your learning of the Finnish words has gone so far. Without referring back to the original list, can you say the Finnish words for the following English words listed?—no cheating or looking back!

- market
- town
- river
- out
- university

Whenever we have tried this exercise in class, people have generally remembered very few words. People may remember one or two words, but very few learn and remember all five.

Gestalt psychology: knowledge as patterns and connections

Perhaps we need a different approach to how we learn the words. Read the descriptions below. We suggest that—with no reward or punishment—there is a good chance that you will remember these words for days, weeks, months—even years—afterwards.

- The word for market is 'tori'. Margaret Thatcher was a well-known Tory prime minister. Imagine Margaret Thatcher in her blue dress and perfectly styled hair walking around a market looking at all the stalls. A famous Tory is in the market, the word for which is 'tori'.
- The word for town is 'kaupunki', pronounced cow-punk-ee. Imagine a cow with a Mohican haircut and a safety pin through its nose—a cow-punk—and it is walking down the main street in your home town. Town is cow-punk-ee.

- The word for river is 'joki', prounoced yok-ee, but let's keep it at the English pronunciation for now—jokey. Imagine you are on a boat cruising along the river, having drinks, and everyone is having a good laugh—it's quite a 'jokey' atmosphere on the river. River is joki.

- The word for out is 'ulos' or 'you-loss'. Imagine your team is out of a tournament. Why would the team be out? Because 'you-lost'.

- The Finnish word for university is 'yliopisto'—pronounced 'ill-ee-oh-pist-oh'. Imagine waking up at university one morning and you feel ill. Why are you feeling ill? Because last night you had a bit too much to drink. You are at university and you feel ill-ee-oh-pist-oh (you should be able to work this one out for yourself!).

 Go back to Table 10.1 and test yourself again on the words in Finnish. Did you do better this time? If so, what do you think helped you to remember them better?

This type of learning is through creating associations and patterns. The importance of associations and patterns is a part of **Gestalt psychology**, a branch of psychology interested in human perception (see Chapter 11) and how we structure perceptions in memory into particular patterns and connections. Gestalt psychology gives us the saying 'the whole is different than the sum of its parts' (Koffka, 1955: 176). Think of how we perceive a melody, for example. We don't think about it note by note—a B flat followed by a C; instead, we perceive the song as a whole. It's the same with a familiar face. We don't think of a friend's face in terms of each individual part—the eyes, nose, etc.; we simply recognize the overall pattern without breaking it down into its constituent parts. The whole is different from the sum of its parts.

Our method for learning the words is based on similar methods used in real life language learning programmes, such as Linkword (www.linkwordlanguages.com). Rather than take a set of individual words, devoid of any context or familiarity, we have woven them into a pattern of connections that then helps us to recall the words. We are making the word that we are learning part of an overall story, or part of a 'Gestalt', which means 'shape' or 'form' in German.

You may use similar methods when trying to memorize a list of names or items, perhaps as revision for an exam. Some people use 'mind-maps'—diagrams which show how different ideas connect—rather than just trying to learn a list of words. Another trick for memorizing items is to mentally trace out a familiar journey, placing the items to be remembered in locations along the way.

 Visit the online resources and take a look at the web links for Chapter 10 for examples of similar learning techniques.

Contextualizing knowledge as part of a pattern is a more effective way to learn than simply memorizing a list of words. However, in the next section we ask an important question about the quality of this knowledge—you may *know* some words in Finnish, but do you *know how* to speak Finnish?

From explicit to tacit knowledge

 Running case: a feel for the task

Another of the maintenance staff, Gerry Dawson, walks up to the bar to see the younger Mike Bridges staring blankly at the faulty refrigeration unit.

→

348

→

'Let me have a go,' says Dawson, rolling up his sleeves and prodding inside the unit instinctively. 'You might have all your qualifications there,' he says, pointing at Bridges's head, 'but I spent years working in a pub. I used to fix these all the time.'

'It's second nature to me. My knowledge of these machines is here,' continues Dawson, raising his hands and waving his fingers. 'I just have a feel for these things.'

Whether learning the list of Finnish words off by heart or using a Gestaltist way to remember them, so far we have learned a list of words, but could you use them in a phrase or hold a conversation in Finnish? We do not *know* every aspect of the language because, as yet, we have no *experience* of speaking the language.

The type and quality of knowledge learned is an issue that has been addressed by a number of philosophers of knowledge (e.g. Russell, 1912; Ryle, 1949; Polanyi, 1958). Based on these insights, we suggest three levels of knowledge.

- *Knowledge that* is knowing a fact: for example, that the Finnish word for market is 'tori'.
- *Knowledge how* is where there is a deeper understanding of how that fact can be used in context. For example, knowing not only that the Finnish word for market is 'tori', but also how to use it in a sentence.
- *Knowledge of*, sometimes known as acquaintance knowledge (Russell, 1912), comes from familiarity—the way in which we know a friend rather than the way in which we know a fact. This distinction is not captured well in English, where the same verb 'to know' covers both ideas. In French (and many other languages) there are two verbs meaning 'to know'—*savoir*, meaning to know a fact, and *connaître*, meaning familiarity. Thus, the phrase 'I KNOW Paris is the capital of France'—a fact—is translated as 'Je *sais* que Paris est la capitale de la France'. However, the phrase 'I KNOW Paris well', indicating familiarity with, and experience of, the city, is translated as 'Je *connais* bien Paris'. In terms of knowing Finnish, knowledge *of* suggests being a regular speaker of the language, being so well acquainted with the language that you know the slang and sayings that people use.

In learning a language, moving from knowledge *that* towards knowledge *how* and knowledge *of* requires people to actually practise speaking the language, finding out what people really say, making mistakes, being laughed at, and learning from those mistakes. Michael Polanyi (1967) recognizes this 'tacit dimension' of knowledge—where knowledge is more than just words on a page, it is something which people learn from experience. Following Polanyi, there is thus a distinction between two types of knowledge:

- **explicit knowledge** is that which can be codified or written down, and then communicated clearly to other people, for example a set of instructions, a diagram, a reference manual, a list of words, etc.;
- **tacit knowledge** is knowledge which comes from experience—from doing and practising something. It is thus much more of a personal form of knowledge that we carry within us.

We can see how explicit knowledge would relate to knowledge *that*: it is a simple set of facts that can be stated. We can also see how tacit knowledge relates to knowledge *of*—it is knowledge that can by gained only from doing and experiencing something. Knowledge *how*, the ability to do something, perhaps bridges the two. We can learn how to do something from a set of instructions

349

on a page, but it is through practising and experiencing that action that we really come to know how to perform it—when rather than having to think about it, it becomes 'second nature'.

 Real life case: learning to drive

A major learning experience for many people, which has both explicit and tacit dimensions, is learning to drive.

Part of the process of learning to drive is the theory test. This involves learning many aspects of driving theory—what road signs mean, stopping distances at different speeds, how to indicate at a roundabout, etc. This knowledge is learned as explicit knowledge from books, the Highway Code, and on websites, etc., following which the learner driver takes the theory test.

But passing a test based on explicit knowledge does not mean a learner then *knows* how to drive—there is another part of learning to drive which involves getting behind the wheel with an instructor and gaining knowledge through the experience of driving. At first a driver will be unsure, driving slowly, and possibly stalling the car often. With practice and experience, driving becomes easier.

A particular development in learning to drive is when tasks become *second nature*. For example, rather than thinking about each gear change in advance, it is done almost without consciously thinking about it.

It is this ability and knowledge—knowing how to drive in practice rather than reciting facts from a theory manual—that is tested in the actual driving test.

 Think about other common learning experiences in life, for example learning to ride a bicycle or learning to swim. To what extent can these be split into explicit and tacit knowledge? How could you teach someone else to do these activities?

Polanyi (1967: 4) sums up the nature of tacit knowledge when he says that 'we know more than we can tell'. While explicit knowledge can be written down, tacit knowledge is much harder to teach to others because it is so personal and comes only from doing and experiencing something.

With both learning a language and driving a car there is only so much knowledge that an instructor can impart. Learning the skill as tacit knowledge—until it becomes second nature—comes only from experience.

Experiential learning

It is often said that we learn from our mistakes. If we do something wrong, we learn from that experience so as not to repeat that mistake in future. However, in this section we see how all experiences—whether a mistake is made or whether we do things well—are a basis for learning when we *reflect* on those experiences.

Kolb's learning cycle

David Kolb's (1984) learning cycle is a model of **experiential learning**. It suggests that learning moves through a continuous cycle between acting, i.e. having an experience, and reflecting on that action (see Figure 10.1).

Kolb's cycle also shows how tacit and explicit aspects of knowledge are blended together in this process of learning. Table 10.2 describes the stages of Kolb's cycle and also applies them to a

Figure 10.1 Kolb's learning cycle.

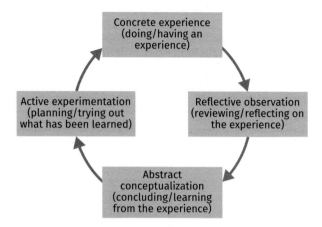

Table 10.2 Stages of Kolb's (1984) learning cycle

Stage	Definition	Example: a golfer improving her game
Concrete experience	Doing or having an experience—an action is performed.	The golfer plays a round of golf and is not happy with her score.
Reflective observation	Reviewing and reflecting on the experience. What went well? What went badly? What could be done better? etc.	She thinks back over the round and why it didn't go well, and identifies her golf swing as the main problem.
Abstract conceptualization	Concluding and learning from our reflections on the experience. After reflection, the actor makes links with theory and explicit knowledge—given what went wrong, what theory might help explain this? What explicit knowledge or theory might help to rectify the problems next time?	She refers to some explicit knowledge—maybe a golf manual written by an expert, maybe a golf coaching video, or even a golf class. From this theory and instruction she begins to identify what is wrong with the swing and what could be changed next time.
Active experimentation	Planning and trying out what has been learned from the experience. Different options are tried out for next time until the cycle goes back to the next concrete experience and then begins again.	She goes to a driving range to put what she has learned about her swing into practice—trying different ideas to see which works best with her golf swing.
Concrete experience		The golfer plays another round of golf. The score is a slight improvement from last time, but on reflection there are still areas for improvement—and so the cycle continues as the golfer continues to learn and improve ....

specific learning experience: a golf player trying to improve her game might use explicit knowledge and develop tacit knowledge as she goes through the stages of Kolb's cycle.

 Study skills: the role of feedback

What do you do when coursework is marked and returned to you? Do you just read the grade and then forget about it, or do you read the feedback and try to learn from it, applying that learning to your next assignment?

Feedback which identifies what you have done well and what you can improve for next time has been shown to be far more effective in improving future grades than a simple grade (Van der Kleij et al., 2015). However, it can only help if you both read it and act upon it. If referencing is identified as a problem, for example, then you can consult referencing guides for next time round or ask a tutor for help. You could even go back to the essay and redo the referencing in the light of the feedback and what you have learned subsequently from referencing guides. This will all help when you come to write your next piece of coursework.

In some respects, the way you use feedback as part of a process of learning as a student has similarities with Kolb's learning cycle. There is the experience—doing the coursework; the reflection—looking at and thinking about the feedback; the conceptualization—looking at guides or asking the advice of a tutor; and the experimentation—trying out things before the next piece of work is attempted.

Learning styles and multiple intelligences

Q **Running case:** different approaches

Simon Chance walks into the bar where the whole maintenance team are now standing around looking at the faulty refrigerator. He notes that each of them takes a different approach to the problem.

Some jump straight in and start fiddling with different components to see what will happen. Others stand back for a while, thinking about the problem before actually doing anything.

Furthermore, people consult different sources for information. Some look at instructions in a manual, others look at a circuit diagram, while others discuss the problem within the team, asking people about their previous experiences with similar equipment.

Chance realizes that, while he could send his maintenance staff on training courses, when it comes to actually engaging with the actual job there are many differences between how each individual learns.

While all stages of Kolb's cycle are an important part of the learning process, he suggests that people prefer certain parts of the cycle to others. Using our previous example, some golfers may prefer to spend time reflecting on the round of golf, while others may want to get straight to the driving range to start practising. People have distinct learning preferences, and this section examines how these learning styles have been categorized.

 Visit the online resources and take a look at the web links for Chapter 10 to read more on learning styles.

Figure 10.2 Honey and Mumford's learning styles.
Source: based on Honey and Mumford (2006).

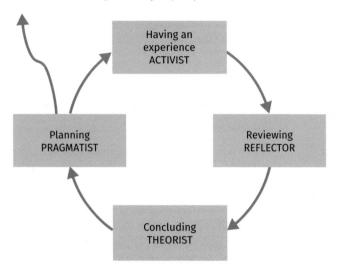

Honey and Mumford's learning styles questionnaire (LSQ)

Kolb's work was developed by Honey and Mumford (1992, 2006) into the learning styles questionnaire (LSQ). Figure 10.2 shows four stages of the cycle of learning, which are similar to Kolb's model (although, unlike the cycle of Kolb, they have an 'escape route' which recognizes that people sometimes change focus to learn something different: for instance, someone may stop learning piano and take up the guitar instead). Each of the stages is linked with one of four particular learning styles which can in turn be linked with distinct stages of Kolb's cycle, as shown in Table 10.3.

Table 10.3 Links between Honey and Mumford's learning styles and Kolb's learning cycle

Honey and Mumford's (1992) learning style	Related stage of Kolb's (1984) learning cycle	Description
Activist	Concrete experience	Prefer the actual experience—they are doers rather than thinkers. They like action and are prepared to try new things.
Reflector	Reflective observation	Spend time thinking over what they have done. Rather than being in the thick of the action they prefer to stand back, watch, and review, seeing a situation from a number of different perspectives.
Theorist	Abstract conceptualization	Rational and logical thinkers who work best with abstract knowledge such as models and theories.
Pragmatist	Active experimentation	Try out new ideas to see how they work. Rather than trying to theorize, they prefer practical actions.

Table 10.4 The VARK model (based on Fleming, 2001)

Type of learner	Description
Visual	Learns best from visual clues, e.g. from diagrams, pictures, signs, and symbols
Auditory	Learns best from listening to descriptions and explanations
Reading/writing	Learns best from reading texts and using written notes to organize that knowledge
Kinesthetic (tactile)	Learns best by doing things—actually touching and manipulating objects

The LSQ is, like some personality tests (see Chapter 8), a set of questions which help locate an individual within these four learning styles. Given that learning is seen as a cycle which needs to pass through all of the stages, it might help an individual to recognize whether they have a tendency to get caught up in one area; for example, a reflector might spend too much time thinking about what has happened without progressing further in the cycle and taking practical steps.

The LSQ also allows an organization to see the variety of learning styles that people might have, which can help with training and development in understanding that people learn in different ways. In a similar way to Belbin (see Chapter 6) it also recognizes that in a team, people will have different ways of approaching learning—some will jump in and get on with the task, while others will sit back and reflect.

The VARK model

The VARK model (Fleming, 2001) (Table 10.4) shifts the emphasis from learning styles to how people use different senses as a preferred means of learning. It suggests four preferences for how we learn and, like Honey and Mumford, is assessed by a questionnaire.

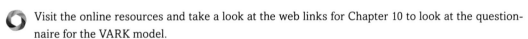 Visit the online resources and take a look at the web links for Chapter 10 to look at the questionnaire for the VARK model.

With VARK, different material will appeal to the learning abilities of different learners. For example, when fixing a car a visual learner might use a diagram of the engine, a reader/writer might look for instructions in a book or online, and a kinesthetic learner might jump in and see what happens when they physically manipulate different components.

Visit the online resources and take a look at the extension material for Chapter 10 for a discussion on how artistic and fictional material can be used in learning management theory.

Such intelligences might also be applied to our language example. An auditory learner might learn better from listening to language lessons on a tape, while a reader and writer might prefer to read the language from a book.

The implication of VARK is that people who are teaching and training people need to take account of the fact that people respond differently to different methods and materials of teaching and training. However, the model, and its associated questionnaire, also helps individuals to appreciate for themselves their own learning styles. Many of the models examined in this section, whether VARK or Honey and Mumford, feed into individual development processes of learning to learn (see later in this section).

Learning styles assessed

The idea of learning styles is certainly popular—in addition to Honey and Mumford and the VARK model there at over 70 ways of classifying learning styles. This is seen in education when teaching styles are matched to the individual learning styles of pupils, rather than a one-size-fits-all approach (Newton, 2015; Willingham et al., 2015). However, despite this popularity it is also a highly contested idea, with Riener and Willingham (2010) suggesting there is 'no credible evidence' to support learning styles. Several arguments have been made against the existence of learning styles.

- Numerous studies have shown that adapting teaching styles for the learning styles of individual pupils leads to no improvement in course results compared with teaching every pupil in exactly the same way (e.g. Pashler et al., 2008; Pilbeam and Corbridge, 2010: 189).

- There is little evidence that learning styles can be measured in a reliable and consistent way (Reynolds, 1997).

- The idea of having one preferred learning style suggests that people approach all learning in the same way; however, Willingham et al. (2015) question whether we would use the same approach in all cases—do we learn to drive a car in the same way that we learn formulas for a maths exam, for example?

- Reynolds (1997) further suggests that we may adopt different strategies of learning depending on the purpose and outcome of that learning—a reading approach might be used to learn a set of words simply to pass a language vocabulary test, but an auditory approach might be used if we wish to develop conversational ability in the language.

- Newton (2015) suggests that learning is about bringing together a lot of different types of information from various different sources rather than relying on information geared to just one preferred learning style.

The authors above accept that people do learn in different ways, but reject the idea of people having one fixed learning style as a discredited, unproved theory.

Multiple intelligences

Howard Gardner's (1983) theory of **multiple intelligences** suggests that people exhibit many different types of intelligence, each of which can be more useful in particular situations:

- *verbal/linguistic intelligence*—the ability to understand and use language to express oneself
- *musical intelligence*—performing music and understanding musical composition and pitch
- *spatial intelligence*—an awareness of space and patterns around us
- *bodily/kinesthetic intelligence*—the ability to do things with the body: sports, arts, etc.
- *logical/mathematical intelligence*—the ability to perform analytical, scientific tasks
- *interpersonal intelligence*—the ability to understand, empathize, and work with others
- *intrapersonal intelligence*—being able to understand ourselves and our feelings

Gardner (2013) notes that many people view the theory of multiple intelligences as similar to theories of learning styles, but rejects this, repeating many of the earlier criticisms. He views multiple intelligences as a list of intelligences that people possess in different combinaitons, rather than one central learning style. Different intelligences predispose us to different tasks or jobs—interpersonal intelligence is good for dealing with people, for example, whereas verbal intelligence is better for writing an essay. Some of these intelligences, such as kinesthetic intelligence, are also more tacit in nature, coming from experience and actually doing things.

The model also highlights areas of ability that we might not initially consider to be types of intelligence. For example, while playing football may not require intelligence in the traditional, academic sense of the word, you may often hear a footballer described as an 'intelligent' player. In knowing how to 'read' a pass, swerve a ball, or get into the right position, a football player draws upon kinaesthetic intelligence—bodily abilities and movements learned from experience of playing the game—and visual-spatial intelligence, which provides an awareness of the other players on the field and the formation that they fit into.

Emotional intelligence

A particular type of intelligence which has been viewed as a valuable competency for the workplace is emotional intelligence (EI). This is viewed as a form of social ability whereby we can understand and manage both our own emotions and the emotions of others. For Salovey and Mayer (1990), EI is 'the ability to monitor one's own and others' feelings and emotions, to discriminate amongst them and to use this information to guide one's own thinking and ideas', and they suggest that it links with Gardner's interpersonal and intrapersonal intelligences (see above).

The idea of EI emphasizes the ability of managers to empathize with other co-workers and subordinates (Mayer and Salovy, 1993), i.e. to be able to put yourself in their place, to understand their feelings and what makes them tick. Several benefits are claimed for EI. Understanding and harnessing emotions, which can be unpredictable, allows for flexibility and the creativity to break out of standard ways of thinking (Salovey and Mayer, 1990). Furthermore, by understanding how to generate a positive mood, EI can aid processes of leadership (see Chapter 13) by connecting with people to create a 'compelling vision' and a 'meaningful identity' for an organization (George, 2000).

As with other forms of intelligence, some people may possess more EI than others. Ashkanasy and Daus (2005) suggest that it is something that people can be trained to develop over time. However, Bolton (2005) criticizes the way that EI is presented as a scientific phenomenon even though it does not stand up to empirical scrutiny. In particular, she criticizes the work of Goleman (1998) for moving away from the human and unpredictable nature of emotion and instead seeing it as a form of mathematical variable that feeds into predictions of organizational success.

Learning to learn: from surface to deep learning and beyond

We have so far seen two broad approaches to knowledge. On the one hand, knowledge is a set of simple, *explicit* facts that we commit to memory. On the other hand, knowledge is learned in context and through experience and action, so that it becomes a deeper, more personal form of *tacit* knowledge.

The distinction is echoed in a number of approaches which distinguish between the quality of learning that people undertake (Marton and Säljö, 1976; Pask, 1976). Here, we present a commonly-used distinction between surface learning and deep learning.

- Surface learning is simply learning a set of facts by rote. The learner has no real interest in the knowledge itself; instead, it is a means to an end—to pass a test, for example.
- Deep learning is where a learner gains a deeper level of knowledge and understanding—not just learning facts, but engaging with the knowledge, making links and comparisons with other knowledge that the learner already has. This might be through using that knowledge in experience, as discussed previously in the chapter, so that it becomes a deeper, personal form of tacit knowledge.

Which of these two styles do you think you use in your university work?

The difference between surface learning and deep learning can be applied to the earlier example of learning the Finnish language. A surface learner would simply learn the words for the sake of passing an assessment. A deep learner might learn the words, but also try putting them into a sentence, relating them to words already learned, practising them in conversation with others, and even relating them to the culture of the country. Surface and deep learning can thus be compared in terms of the knowledge that is acquired from each, as shown in Table 10.5.

Models of learning styles have shown us not just how deeper levels of knowledge are acquired, but how people also have preferences for particular learning styles. **Deutero learning** (Bateson, 1973) describes levels of learning with greater depth, where the individual not only gains deeper knowledge but engages in a form of self-awareness whereby they 'learn how to learn'.

Again, think back to the Finnish learning example. Earlier in the chapter we learned some words by associating them with particular images and patterns. Learning to learn is where a learner realizes that the system works well for them and applies that same system to another learning situation—learning German, for example, or memorizing a shopping list. Learning to learn involves comparing this with other learning methods to develop an appreciation of what works best for each individual learner.

In this respect, Freire (1970) criticizes what he terms **banking education**, where learners are treated like an empty bank account to be filled passively with 'deposits' of knowledge. This type of education does not move beyond explicit knowledge and surface learning. Such theorists call for a type of learning that goes beyond the surface and engenders a greater depth of knowledge and creativity in students.

Visit the online resources and take a look at the extension material for Chapter 10 to read more about Freire's theories.

The importance of Bateson's and Freire's contributions is not to dismiss explicit knowledge and surface learning, but to see that for individuals to achieve creativity and reach their potential this needs to form part of a process of deeper learning and learning to learn. The following quote from the legendary footballer Pele suggests that this depth extends to a love of what is being learned:

> Success is no accident. It is hard work, perseverance, learning, studying, sacrifice and most of all, love of what you are doing or learning to do.

Table 10.5 Deep learning and surface learning compared

Surface learning	Deep learning
Facts and figures, learning by rote, out of context	Learning as part of a pattern or in context
Knowledge that ...	Knowledge how/knowledge of ...
Savoir	*Connaître*
Explicit knowledge only	Explicit knowledge developing into tacit knowledge through experience (e.g. Kolb's learning cycle)

Deep learning and learning to learn in the workplace: reflective practice

So far in the chapter we have examined learning at an individual level. In the remainder of this chapter we will see it applied within the workplace. Donald Schön (1983) suggested that professionals in industries such as education, health, and architecture develop their knowledge and practice of their work better—indeed, into a form of artistry—if they are reflective practitioners. Reflective practice means that a worker doesn't simply do their job, but, as with Kolb in this chapter, they see their work as an ongoing cycle of continuous learning, whereby they reflect upon their experiences in the workplace. This reflection is applied in the next two sections of the chapter, first to the job of management itself, and then to this reflection and learning across the organization as a whole.

? Review questions

Describe	What is meant by explicit and tacit knowledge?
Explain	How does learning develop through a cycle of experiential learning?
Analyse	How do the levels and quality of learning and knowledge increase as a learner moves from surface learning to deep learning to deutero learning?
Apply	How would you take account of different learning styles in developing a training programme for the maintenance staff at Junction Hotel?

Reflective practice and management knowledge

What are your expectations of a management degree? It would be a reasonable assumption that, during such a course, a student will learn and accumulate an amount of management *knowledge* that can then be applied in a management career.

This section examines what it means to 'know' how to manage. Is management *knowledge* an explicit set of facts and theories, or is it a tacit form of knowledge that comes from experience? If we can pinpoint what is meant by management knowledge, how does someone, for example a student of management, *learn* this knowledge—how does one learn how to manage?

This short section brings a reflexive approach to your study of knowledge and learning in organizations. Reflexive means that the chapter is not just describing a set of ideas and theories but invites you as both a student and a potential future manager to locate yourself personally within the subject matter of the chapter.

- As a student, the topic of this chapter—knowledge and learning—is relevant to how you engage in study. Some material may be familiar from 'study skills' or 'personal development' sessions at university, e.g., you may have taken the VARK questionnaire as a way of understanding your preferred means of learning. The aim of such techniques is to improve your quality of learning as a student, taking you from surface learning to deep learning. You are not simply approaching each learning task in isolation, to pass a test, for example; rather, you think more widely about how you learn best.

- As a student of management and, potentially, a future manager, theories of knowledge and learning are relevant to the quality of knowledge of 'how to' manage that you will take with you into a managerial career. In this section we see how this links with management knowledge being tacit and coming from experience, and how students may develop such tacit knowledge in addition to the explicit knowledge gained during their studies.

What is management knowledge?

Graduate trainees often arrive as newcomers in managerial positions to much suspicion, even sneering. The insinuation is that these wet-behind-the-ears university types may have all of the knowledge from a degree, but they lack the experience of actually doing management in the 'real world'.

This mirrors the distinction between explicit and tacit knowledge. A large amount of management knowledge comes from experience rather than from learning from books.

On the one hand, a management degree outlines a terrain of explicit management knowledge, through theories, lists and models, for example. Examples in this book might be theories of motivation, rational organizational design, management of groups and teams, management of change, etc. To see management knowledge just in these terms would, perhaps, follow Freire's (1970) 'banking education' model (Figure 10.3). A student arrives at the start of the degree as an empty vessel and, through lectures, textbooks (such as this), and other sources, is eventually filled with items of knowledge that will equip them to manage. The degree to which you, as a student, have

Figure 10.3 Freire's (1970) banking model applied to management education.

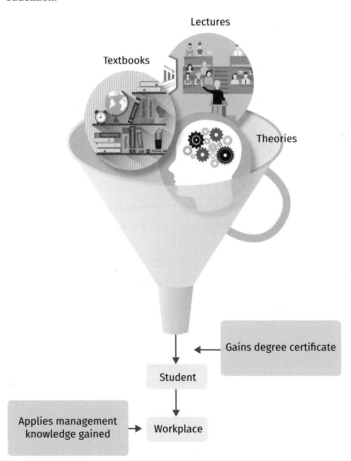

assimilated such knowledge is tested by means such as essays, examinations, presentations, and other assessments. Ultimately, a degree certificate is awarded to prove the amount of management knowledge that a student holds and which they can then go on to apply in the workplace.

But does this accumulation of management knowledge mean that a student *knows* how to manage? Has a student *learned* to be a manager, with the degree certificate as proof of this? Amanda Hay (2015: 409) suggests that management knowledge can present a 'sanitized' view of how to manage 'which avoids the complexities of the lived experiences of managers'. Rather than being a label that something like a degree certificate allows us to wear, the identity of a 'manager' is, for Hay, something that is always ongoing and developing. With management knowledge, as with the knowledge of driving a car or learning a language, there is an amount of tacit knowledge that is only learned from experience.

💡 Theory in context: origins of 'management'

It may surprise you to learn that 'management' as a word derives from the training of horses—something which requires skill, but also experience. The word can be traced back to around 1555–65 to an early Italian word *maneggiare*: to handle, train (horses). In turn, this derives from the Latin word *manus*, meaning hand (Holden and Tansley, 2008). The implication is that training horses, while a skilled job that one gets a feel for, is learned by experience and doing. As such, there is a tacit dimension to such knowledge.

The origins of management?
Source: Fotokostic/Shutterstock.com

The balance between management as explicit knowledge and management as a more tacit knowledge that comes from experience is also reflected in contemporary understandings of the word *management*.

There is a contrast between managing in the sense of a planned, controlled activity and managing in the sense of coping—just about managing to get along. This has been reflected in studies of what managers actually do in day-to-day work. Hales (1986) notes a contrast between formal and informal aspects of managerial work—the latter often involving interpersonal skills such as negotiation and dealing with conflict. Carlson (1951), in a classic study of Swedish executives, further found that the majority of their working life was spent using these interpersonal and communication skills in conversations—on the phone, in person, etc.

As we look into management as both a concept and an activity, we begin to see areas of management knowledge that are learned through experience—interpersonal skills and dealing with the 'messy' side of the organization: the politics, conflict, and negotiation that takes place (see Chapter 14). While these issues can be found within the content of a management degree, the extent to which they can be taught as explicit knowledge rather than through experience is debatable.

⊙ Employability skills: placements and work experience

Many of our students who have done placements in a workplace say that it is only through the experience of the workplace that they have come to fully understand the 'messy' and interpersonal side of the organization.

While a degree programme provides an important amount of theory and skills for management, employers increasing view this as insufficient in itself, and are interested in 'real world' experience which is gained, for example, through placements and sandwich years during a degree programme (Brooks and Kay, 2014). These placements place the explicit knowledge gained at university into a workplace context where students can enhance their learning through experience.

Even if you have not undertaken a placement, employers will be interested in what else you have done at university other than the degree itself. Work experience, such as holiday jobs, involvement in running societies or sports clubs, and voluntary work, shows evidence of management learning through experience.

This is not to say that your degree work is not important. Remember that Kolb's learning cycle recognizes the importance of both experiential and theoretical knowledge—it is the combination of both which contribute to the learning cycle.

Management as reflective practice

The idea that management learning comes from experience informs many training and development programmes, which encourage managers to become reflective practitioners. Assessment in such courses consists of keeping journals and records of work undertaken, and reflecting on this experience in the light of explicit management theory. Management knowledge is thus seen, as with Kolb's cycle, as a combination of both explicit and tacit elements, and is a knowledge which develops through experience and reflection on that experience.

Such management education aims to equip managers not only with a store of management knowledge, but also with the ability to manage in practice—where managers need to react to events, drawing upon both explicit knowledge and knowledge gained through experience when doing so.

In the next section, we see how knowledge and learning at an organizational level also help organizations to both develop knowledge and be able to use that knowledge to change and react where necessary.

❓ Review questions

Describe	What are the explicit and tacit aspects of management knowledge?
Explain	What does it mean when management is described as a reflective practice?
Analyse	To what extent does a management degree equip a student with the knowledge of how to manage? What further knowledge or experience is required?
Apply	Do you think that you approach your studies as a deep or a surface learner?

Organizational knowledge and learning: the learning organization

So far in the chapter we have seen learning as a process whereby an *individual* adds to their knowledge. In this section we examine knowledge and learning, in is explicit and tacit forms, as something that also exists at the level of the *organization*.

Organizational knowledge

There are sectors of the economy where knowledge and the development of that knowledge are vital for the competitive advantage, and even the survival, of an organization. For example, in the mobile phone industry consumers eagerly wait to upgrade to the newest smartphones with the latest technical innovations. It is important for companies to stay ahead of the game by developing this knowledge and innovating—those that get left behind can find their market share falling rapidly.

Knowledge is equally vital in industries such as pharmaceuticals, technology, and microelectronics. A key part of the strategy in these **knowledge-intensive firms** is to develop leading-edge knowledge. Workers in these sectors are described as **knowledge workers** and are valued for their particular knowledge and skills (Alvesson, 2004).

 Can you think of any other sectors of the economy that could be described as 'knowledge-intensive' or professions where workers could be described as 'knowledge workers'?

Visit the online resources and take a look at the extension material for Chapter 10 for some examples of knowledge-intensive industries.

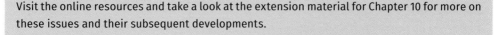

💡 Theory in context: the value of knowledge

The value of knowledge becomes apparent when we see the measures that companies take to protect their knowledge, for example through legal instruments such as patents and copyrights.

- Mobile technology companies often engage in court battles over patents; for example, there has been an ongoing series of disputes between Apple and Samsung over the intellectual properties of touch-screen features such as 'double-tap' and 'pinch to zoom' (Gibbs, 2015).

- Facebook has faced high-profile criticism of how it sells knowledge, in the form of valuable user data, to companies which use this data to target advertising. This was especially the case with Cambridge Analytica, who used user data to target political advertising during election campaigns (Greenfield, 2018).

- An ongoing debate in the academic community concerns whether or not scientific knowledge, often created from research using taxpayer funding, should be disseminated to the public freely, or whether this knowledge should remain in copyrighted journals that are accessible only through financial subscriptions (Sample, 2012; Dunn et al., 2014; Davey, 2015).

Visit the online resources and take a look at the extension material for Chapter 10 for more on these issues and their subsequent developments.

Figure 10.4 Blackler's (1995) five facets of organizational knowledge.

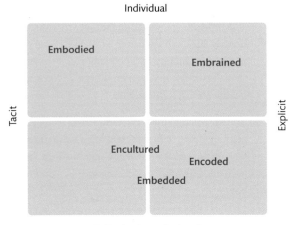

From organizational knowledge to knowing in organizations

Knowledge is located in all organizations—not just those that are involved in cutting-edge technical innovation. Knowledge of an organization's culture or day-to-day routines is as much a part of organizational knowledge as specialist skills and expert knowledge.

Furthermore, organizational knowledge is multifaceted—there are different aspects of what, collectively, makes up organizational knowledge, for example:

- Is the knowledge located in individuals within the organization, or is it more of a collective property of the organization that is shared between people?
- As with individual knowledge, is the knowledge explicit or tacit?

Blackler (1995) outlines five particular facets of knowledge located along these scales of individual/collective and tacit/explicit in Figure 10.4 (Blackler, 1995: 1023–6): embodied, embrained, encultured, encoded, and embedded. These are described in Table 10.6, where we place them in an organizational setting with an example of the types of knowledge that might be found in a restaurant kitchen.

We tend to privilege embrained knowledge: for example, the specialist knowledge of a head chef in a kitchen makes that chef a valued worker upon whose knowledge the organization depends. However, Table 10.6 shows the variety of embodied, encultured, and embedded knowledge that is found within all staff within a kitchen—there are many types and locations of organizational knowledge.

Situated knowledge: knowledge in action

For Blackler (1995), to talk of knowledge as a 'thing' misses its dynamic and social nature—it is always changing and is located within, and among, people. Rather than knowledge being in someone's head, or in books, or in databases, knowledge exists in action—there are flows of knowledge between people during the action which takes place in specific organizations (Gherardi, 2008; Nidomulu et al., 2001). Donna Haraway (1988) used the term **situated knowledge** to differentiate this view of knowledge from the ways in which we usually see knowledge as a form of neutral object that is 'out there' to be discovered.

- Knowledge is situated in specific spaces—such as organizations. There are 'local forms of knowing'—knowledge, routines, cultures, objects which are specific to the context of any one organization.

Table 10.6 Facets of organizational knowledge (based on Blackler, 1995)

Type of knowledge	Description	Example
Embrained knowledge (explicit and individual)	The individual knowledge that we hold in our brains which is explicit in nature, equating to 'knowledge that'. It is reflected in an employee's qualifications, for example.	A chef may hold a qualification from catering school and may know a set of recipes or facts about food.
Embodied knowledge (individual and tacit)	The knowledge that comes from actually doing and experiencing a task. This is tacit knowledge that an individual develops—'knowledge how'.	A chef who has made a dish many times will be able to prepare it as if it were second nature.
Encultured knowledge (organizational with tacit and explicit dimensions)	Shared understandings in the organization—the stories, traditions, values, etc. that make up an organizational culture (see Chapter 7). Often it is unwritten and tacit—described simply as 'the way things are done around here', although organizations may try to make cultures explicit by describing them in documents (see the Sloan Becker case in Chapter 11).	Different kitchens have different cultures—expected behaviours and ways of doing things. Some may be noisy and brash, some may be quieter.
Embedded knowledge (organizational with tacit and explicit dimensions)	Knowledge embedded in the routines of an organization. Routines may be formalized and explicit, but also have informal tacit elements. Think of a university timetable—at first you have to consult it regularly; it is an explicit piece of printed knowledge. After a while you get used to your timetable to the point where you automatically go to rooms at the right time—it has become tacit knowledge.	Kitchens have many rigid routines that have to be followed—prepping food before the restaurant opens for business, procedures for taking orders, etc.
Encoded knowledge (organizational and explicit)	Explicit knowledge found in books, manuals, computer databases, and sets of instructions, in the form of words, signs, symbols, lists, etc. It is also collective, as it is knowledge that can be shared and accessed by the whole organization.	A kitchen may have a library of recipe books which have step-by-step instructions for dishes, knowledge which all members of the organization may access.

- Knowledge is situated in interactions—people continually interact and communicate with each other and with objects and technologies such as computer systems. Knowledge is more like a web of interactions that a single thing.

- Knowledge is situated in the body. Similar to tacit knowledge, there is a lot of knowledge that is embodied and comes from sensory experience, and which is difficult to articulate to other people. (Based on Haraway, 1988, and Gherardi, 2008.)

For Haraway (1988), the view of knowledge as being spread across people and interactions while also specific to local organizational spaces means that knowledge is always partial or incomplete—we can never know everything because knowledge is both fragmented and constantly changing. If knowledge is always partial and incomplete, then learning in organizing is an ongoing and never-ending process.

Organizational learning

> **Q Running case:** learning at the pub
>
> Simon Chance calls in the maintenance manager, George Andrews, to review the training programme.
>
> Chance has taken account of different learning styles among the workforce and realizes how difficult it is to accommodate all of these styles.
>
> He has issued each member of the maintenance staff with a tablet computer which has access to manuals for every piece of machinery in the building, circuit diagrams, and even videos from the manufacturers. Staff can access whatever material they feel helps them most.
>
> Furthermore, the tablets give the maintenance engineers access to online forums where they can post their experiences of dealing with different problems for others to read, learn from, and search when they, too, encounter similar problems.
>
> 'It's all great,' says George Andrews. 'The tablets put a lot of information at their fingertips.'
>
> 'But, I think they learn most at the pub on a Friday evening—that's when they really talk among themselves and share experiences of what they've been doing. And, in comparison to providing training and tablet computers, that doesn't cost us a penny.'

Organizational learning is where an organization increases the amount of knowledge that it holds collectively. Knowledge is *shared*, or *transferred*, between people in the organization and, furthermore, is transferred between people and the organization itself.

For Nonaka and Takeuchi (1995: 6), the ability for an organization to create knowledge and innovate continually brings competitive advantage. There is a recognition that workers know their task best—they develop tacit knowledge the more they perform it, and thus they know all the shortcuts and tricks that help them to perform the task better. The problem for Nonaka is that this tacit knowledge is personal and comes from experience—it may be difficult to put it into words in order to share that knowledge with others. As Brown and Duguid (2000: 76) state: 'Actual work practices are full of tacit improvisations that the employees who carry them out would have trouble articulating.'

Nonaka's *knowledge-creating company* (Nonaka and Takeuchi, 1995, 2007) focuses on the ways in which particular types of knowledge are transferred. For Nonaka, it is the interaction between different types of knowledge—explicit and tacit—that creates organizational knowledge. Such knowledge can be transferred between explicit and tacit knowledge in four ways (see Table 10.7), which we again illustrate with an example of a restaurant kitchen.

Table 10.7 Knowledge transfer in Nonaka's knowledge-creating company (based on Nonaka and Takeuchi, 1995)

Type of knowledge transfer	Description	Example
From explicit to explicit: combination	Sources of encoded knowledge—manuals, databases, etc.—are added to, combined, sorted, and categorized. A library combines a number of different forms of explicit knowledge, sorted and categorized in a library catalogue, for example. Such a databank of explicit knowledge, however, does not mean that people necessarily read and learn from it.	A chef has a set of recipe books on a shelf with Indian, Chinese, and French cuisine within. More books are added, covering Italian and vegetarian cuisine. The amount of explicit knowledge has been increased, but this does not necessarily mean that the chef has tried and experimented with any of the recipes in the books.
From explicit to tacit: internalization	As in learning to drive, a learner begins with explicit instructions but continues to practise and reflect on that practice (compare with Kolb's learning cycle) until they have internalized the knowledge—it has become tacit.	A chef takes a recipe—a set of explicit instructions—and makes a dish. She continues to experiment and repeat this until she knows the dish 'off by heart'.
From tacit to explicit: externalization, articulation	An expert or person who is well-experienced in a task attempts to make their tacit knowledge explicit by writing it down as a set of instructions, diagrams, or similar encoded knowledge. The expert is trying to articulate their tacit knowledge to an external audience.	A top chef writes a recipe book featuring instructions on how to make various dishes.
From tacit to tacit: socialization	Perhaps the least controllable form of knowledge transfer, as the knowledge remains unspoken—it is never made explicit. Knowledge is acquired through observation and imitation. This might be how cultures are learned—they are absorbed from observation and experimentation rather than being told to people explicitly.	A trainee chef learns from observation under the tutelage of a kitchen's head chef.

Nonaka's model assumes that the richest form of knowledge is the tacit knowledge that exists within individuals who perform a particular job. However, for the organization to benefit fully from that knowledge it cannot just reside as tacit knowledge within one individual—what if the individual were ill or left the organization, for example? How are other members of the organization meant to learn and develop if the only experts keep their knowledge to themselves?

The key aspect of knowledge transfer, for Nonaka, is thus how tacit knowledge is made explicit—expressed in words or diagrams or in some form that other people can take on board, practise, and convert to tacit knowledge of their own. Nonaka's model suggests a form of training and knowledge transfer that is still run by the organization itself; however, the transfer of tacit, experiential knowledge has also been observed as a social phenomenon which takes place informally among workers.

This social nature of knowledge transfer was observed in a classic study of Xerox photocopier engineers in the United States (Orr, 1996). These are the people who are called out to various clients when photocopiers break down (as they often do).

The engineers had knowledge from their training and, furthermore, had encoded, explicit knowledge about each model of photocopier in the form of manuals and diagrams. This, however, was not enough—machines have their own idiosyncrasies, and complex problems can emerge that are beyond the instructions in the manual.

Using tacit knowledge.
Source: ALPA PROD / Shutterstock.com

Julian Orr discovered that a great deal of the knowledge that workers had was learned from conversations. Engineers developed tacit knowledge from their experience with machines, which they shared in social situations, such as over lunch. Orr described the sharing of 'war stories', where one engineer would tell how they dealt with a particular problem on a particular machine. Knowledge from training and the manuals was enhanced by the sharing, in a social situation, of more individual, tacit knowledge that other workers could then go away and apply to their own work.

Xerox recognized the value of this sharing of knowledge and set up a suggestions database where such knowledge could be tapped into and shared across the whole organization (Orr, 1996; Duguid, 2006). This might be familiar to people who have searched online forums if, for example, their car has broken down or if their computer has a virus. The idea is to learn from the descriptions that others have posted of how they have dealt with similar situations.

The learning organization

While the concept of organizational learning highlights how knowledge is shared and acquired, the **learning organization** is concerned with organizational characteristics which promote and facilitate this learning and knowledge transfer. Organizational learning is thus a feature of the learning organization rather than—as sometimes happens—the two terms being used interchangeably.

By being able to share learning and knowledge, an organization and its members have more abilities at their collective disposal. This goes beyond work-specific knowledge, such as how to fix a photocopier or make a particular recipe, and relates to an organization's capacity to adapt and transform when needed. Competitive advantage comes not just from knowledge as applied to product development but also from the knowledge that enables an organization to be more flexible and adaptable in the face of changing environmental conditions. The organization is seen as a 'complex organism' (Senge, 1990: 85) that constantly evolves and adjusts in response to its changing environment.

This ability to change and adapt is examined elsewhere in the book by two observations about the nature of the contemporary environment facing organizations.

- In Chapter 3 we examined post-bureaucratic organizations, where structures and communication lines are flexible rather than rigid, and where the organization can easily adapt to changes and bring together different configurations of people and knowledge so as to develop further knowledge.

- In Chapter 12, we will see an emergent approach to change which suggests that, rather than being able to plan change for the future, organizations have to react in an 'agile' manner to events as they happen, as if riding the rapids of a river.

Proponents of the learning organization emphasize a focus on the development of individual and organizational learning within organizations, but also on the organization being in a continuous process of change and transformation (Senge, 1990; Pedler et al., 1997).

Single- and double-loop learning

The process of learning and transformation at the organizational level is addressed by Argyris and Schön (1978). In particular, a move from surface learning to a more creative and deep form of learning at the organizational level is represented by the distinction between single- and double-loop learning.

- **Single-loop learning** is where an organization tries repeatedly to solve the same problem or achieve the same goal—a simple form of 'error correction' to ensure that the goal continues to be achieved. For example, an organization might have a sales target for a particular product each year. If it fails to achieve it then it takes steps the following year to correct the problem—hiring new sales staff, for example, or looking at the bonus system. The sales target itself is not questioned.

- **Double-loop learning** questions the goal itself and the underlying assumptions behind it. It wouldn't just ask how to achieve the target sales; it would ask whether the sales of that product contribute enough to profits to warrant pursuing that goal, whether the market for that product has any future, and even whether targets are a good way to motivate sales staff. In other words, rather than the simple sales target itself, just about everything is up for discussion—an organization's values, policies, and objectives (Argyris and Schön, 1978).

Characteristics of a learning organization

Double-loop learning is a more thorough and deep questioning of what an organization does. It goes beneath the surface of solving one isolated problem, developing levels of change and adaptability required for a learning organization. For Senge (1990), such a form of learning is a component of five characteristics which make up a successful learning organization (see Table 10.8).

The description of a learning organization paints a picture of an organization where there is harmony, trust, and an openness of communication between co-workers, and between workers and management, with all members of the organization unified behind the vision of the organization. To what extent this is realistic or achievable forms the basis for assessing the concept of the learning organization.

Learning organizations assessed

The development of knowledge and learning in organizations has, so far, been presented as a good thing. It gives organizations a competitive advantage in an increasingly knowledge-based economy, and it allows individual workers to develop their potential and creativity, perhaps even moving them towards 'self-actualizing' in their work (see Chapter 9).

Table 10.8 Senge's five characteristics of the learning organization (adapted from Senge, 1990: 6–11)

Personal mastery	The organization encourages the personal development and learning of individuals in the organization so that they can reach their potential.
Mental models	People are not stuck in old ways of thinking and old routines, and are open to new ideas; people engage in higher levels of learning where goals and assumptions are questioned constantly (as with double-loop learning).
Shared vision	All organizational members have a shared, mutually-agreed vision, which is reinforced through strong and inspiring leadership (see Chapter 13 on leadership).
Team learning	People work and learn together in teams with the importance of dialogue and discussion between people being highlighted, in a similar manner to the case of the Xerox photocopier engineers.
Systems thinking	People think about the organization in terms of relationships and connections (see Chapter 11), with all actions having consequences both inside and outside of the organization; systems thinking is about seeing how they fit into 'the bigger picture'.

The learning organization perspective is a far cry from the Taylorist view of individual and organizational learning presented in Chapter 3. Rather than encouraging learning, Taylor saw individual knowledge as a source of power for workers and a threat to his authority. Taylor's strategy was the absolute opposite of a learning organization—he removed knowledge from workers, placing it all in the hands of management, with individual learning reduced to learning a simple, repetitive task.

However, the view of the learning organization is not without critics; indeed, its vision of harmony in the organization, shared visions, and unhindered individual learning and development is seen by critics as an unrealistic, naïve, or 'utopian' (Coopey, 1998; Driver, 2002) view of how organizations operate. Among many critiques of the concept of the learning organization, we suggest three broad areas that may prevent the learning organization from being an ideal or achievable form of operating in organizations (see Driver, 2002, for more).

- The assumption of trust, open communication, and a sharing of knowledge ignores the influence of organizational politics (see Chapter 14) where people may choose to retain or restrict access to knowledge to retain it as a source of power for their own personal advantage.

- The idea of the learning organization assumes that people have the ability and desire to engage in constant learning and development. As seen in our discussion of orientations to work (Chapter 9), some people prefer to do repetitive and unchallenging work as a means of simply getting a wage.

- While a learning organization may not employ the forms of rationalized control that characterize Taylorism, its shared vision relies on a strong shared culture, which itself can be seen as a form of control (see Chapter 7). The idea of a shared vision also means that there is an element of control that prevents dissent against that vision (see Driver, 2002).

Visit the online resources and take a look at the extension material for Chapter 10 to consider some more critiques of the concept of the learning organization.

Open workspaces and 'collisionable hours'

While the concept of the learning organization is open to critique, in this section we outline how knowledge and learning are still important to the contemporary economy and organizations.

 Real life case: coffee stations at Telenor

Telenor is a Norwegian multinational telecommunications company, working in an industry where flexibility and constant innovation is essential for competitive advantage. As such, it has designed a workplace layout which aims to promote, in its own words, 'interaction between people, technology, and physical environment' (Telenor, 2018). The workspace is based around dynamic use—in other words constant movement of people encouraged by large open spaces, free seating rather than allocated desk spaces, and clear desks (De Paoli et al., 2013).

The design encourages collaboration and knowledge sharing. The open spaces encourage people to meet other, sometimes unexpected people, and to then talk about projects they are working on, forming groups and sharing ideas (Waber et al., 2014). These 'collisions' are encouraged by the design: in fact, Telenor removed their existing coffee stations and replaced them with bigger and fewer stations so that more people would gather around each station and more connections between people could be made (Waber et al., 2014).

The layout at Telenor is typical of many workplace designs, especially in knowledge-intensive sectors of industry such as software and telecommunications. As we saw in Chapter 2, the Googleplex has large open spaces in which employees are encouraged to circulate around, bump into each other, and then cluster in spaces such as cafés and share their ideas, all with the ultimate aim of developing innovative knowledge and products for the company overall.

This type of workplace design is similar to the learning organization, with knowledge shared freely between people. Following Nonaka and Orr, it can be seen as creating a social environment in which tacit knowledge that workers have from their own experiences can be shared. It can also be viewed, following Haraway and Gherardi, as recognizing knowledge as being situated: that is to say, it exists in interactions between people in specific spaces.

In summary, designs such as Telenor and the Googleplex recognize that knowledge and expertise are of no use to a company if they remain in the heads of workers who are then shut behind closed doors in offices—it is the interaction and sharing of knowledge that helps the company to increase its knowledge overall. To reflect this, the notion of 'collisionable hours' has been introduced by Zappos as a measure to assess the effectiveness of workspaces—those which encourage more 'collisions' of people per hour are the most effective (Waber et al., 2014; McNeill, 2017).

While workers at Telenor did feel that the workplace layout enhanced knowledge sharing and cooperation (De Paoli et al., 2013), not all similar designs have proved so effective. Common complaints about open-plan styles of workplace include too much noise and distraction (e.g. Booth, 2017) and a lack of privacy and personal space within the workspace (Congdon et al., 2014; Gapper, 2017).

 Visit the online resources and take a look at the extension material for Chapter 10 for more discussion and criticism of open workplace design.

Learning beyond the organization

Not all learning and knowledge transfer takes place with the physical confines of one organization—often it is shared across, and between, organizations. At a basic level, this happens when a person leaves an organization and joins another, taking their particular knowledge with them. The concept of the learning organization recognizes, in fact, the importance of suppliers and other stakeholders that an organization deals with (Pedler et al., 1997).

Here, we suggest three contemporary areas where work-related knowledge is shared across organizational boundaries.

- **Professional knowledge**. Professions such as medicine, architecture, and law have a knowledge base which is common to all practitioners, regardless of which organization they are based in—knowledge which they need to constantly update. A doctor, for example, needs to know about the latest medical discoveries and opinions, and about the latest drugs and treatments. Thus, there are journals, conferences, email lists, and similar networks through which professional knowledge is shared, potentially on a global scale.

- **Knowledge clusters**. Knowledge clusters occur where a number of organizations engaged in the same industry are located in close geographical proximity. They are able to collaborate, share resources, and benefit from each others' particular knowledge (see Coughlan, 2011). For example, Mediacity in Salford, UK, is a concentration of media-related organizations, bringing together large broadcasters such as the BBC and ITV, but also smaller, knowledge-intensive companies, for example manufacturers of specialist broadcast equipment or graphic design companies. Another example of a knowledge cluster is where universities set up, or are associated with, nearby 'science parks'. Academics can collaborate and share knowledge with companies and organizations engaged in the same field. Tony Hsieh of Zappos has extended the idea of collisionables (mentioned earlier in this section) to a whole district of Las Vegas which has been redeveloped to include start-ups and creative industries, with the intention that their workers will bump into each other and share knowledge within this space (McNeill, 2017).

- **Open source and online collaboration**. Open source software is computer code which is made freely available online so that anyone can apply their knowledge to it and develop it. In operating systems such as Linux, many people have applied their knowledge collaboratively to developing systems—in some cases for free as a hobby, in other cases as part of their work. A similar type of online collaboration can be seen with Wikipedia, where people have contributed their knowledge collaboratively in an open forum to create an encyclopaedia (Mulgan et al., 1995). See Chapter 16 for more on this.

Visit the online resources and take a look at the extension material for Chapter 10 for more examples of learning beyond the organization.

Communities of practice

A concept which unites these three examples of cross-boundary knowledge sharing is **communities of practice**, a term that Jean Lave and Etienne Wenger (1991) first used to describe the learning of specific areas of knowledge, especially occupational knowledge, in social contexts. The example of the photocopier engineers earlier in this chapter is an example of a community of practice within an organization—they are engaged in the same area of work, their work is based on a common set of knowledge, and they develop and share that knowledge as a form of social practice.

An organization may consist of many communities of practice within it: not just the photocopier engineers, but also the accountants, the legal staff, the gardeners, etc. who all learn and develop their knowledge within their social groups.

The three examples just above describe communities of practice which exist across organizational boundaries. For example, with medical knowledge, there may be a community of practice of people involved in treating a particular illness. Although they may all work in different institutions, and even different countries, they are involved in a common practice based on a common body of knowledge which they share and develop in social situations such as conferences. The idea of situated knowledge also relates to communities of practice—emphasizing not just the knowledge itself but the ways in which people are engaged in activities in particular spaces which bring this knowledge into action.

Collaborators in specific open-source applications can also be seen as a community of practice. Even if some of the collaborators are individuals involved as part of a hobby, it is a shared practice with a common body of knowledge, with knowledge shared and developed often through online social forums, such as discussion boards.

? Review questions

Describe	What are the different types of organizational knowledge?
Explain	What does it mean for an organization to 'learn'?
Analyse	What is the importance of converting tacit to explicit knowledge as a part of organizational learning?
Apply	How would Junction Hotel benefit from being a learning organization? What steps have already been taken towards this with the maintenance department? Would there be any negative effects of being a learning organization?

Artificial intelligence and its impact on knowledge and learning

Throughout the book we have examined the impact of the Fourth Industrial Revolution upon contemporary work and organizations. In particular, in Chapter 4 we saw the impact of automation upon work. Automation has, until recently, been viewed in the context of physical work—robots assembling cars on a factory floor, for example. However, artificial intelligence extends automation to cognitive tasks—those which are based around thought processes and manipulating knowledge and information. At the time of writing, there was a lot of media discussion about exactly which jobs will still exist within the next decade or so—not just factory jobs but also office-based jobs.

Artificial intelligence (AI) is something that many of us are familiar with in the home. Smart devices such as Google Home and Amazon Alexa allow us to ask questions or issue commands, with the response coming from interrogating data sources such as our online calendars or the internet. More recently, Google unveiled Duplex, which can automate tasks such as ringing for a hair appointment using a realistic artificial voice which then rings and speaks to a receptionist, using information in an online calendar to make the appointment (Solon, 2018).

Artificial intelligence is described by Gyton and Jefferey (2017) as a spectrum. On the one hand it can involve advanced data analytics—looking up an answer in a data set. However, by applying algorithms it has moved beyond simply retrieving data to spotting patterns in that data—making predictions about what might happen or developing new knowledge from that data.

Furthermore, these algorithms can be used to make decisions based upon this data. We are all familiar with credit scoring, which compares our own data against that of the population to assess credit risk for loans, mortgages, and mobile phone contracts. Similar algorithms can be used to draw on data to make political decisions or decisions about sentencing convicted criminals (Mols and Roberts, 2016; Cossins, 2018) and, as we saw in Chapter 8, to make decisions about recruitment and selection based on data about candidates. AI therefore combines data with algorithms, with machines learning for themselves and making decisions.

 Real life case: Cora

In the UK, NatWest Bank unveiled a digital customer assistant named Cora. Starting as a text-based chat interface, the system developed into a lifelike face and voice which customers can have a conversation with when entering a branch. The system draws upon 'AI, computing power, neuroscience and psychology' (Jones, 2018) in order to answer customer queries and is even able to detect emotion in the voices of customers. Although it can make mistakes, the algorithms which power Cora are designed to learn from those mistakes.

Visit the online resources and take a look at the web links for Chapter 10 to see a video of Cora in action.

Sources: Jones (2018); RBS (2018); BBC News (2018).

NatWest have said that Cora will complement rather than replace existing bank jobs (Jones, 2018). However, much contemporary discussion revolves around exactly which jobs can be automated by AI and therefore which jobs may be at risk, or even not exist, within a decade. Certainly, customer service work has been automated through systems such as chatbots—many banks use these on their websites, with American Express integrating the technology into Facebook Messenger (Gyton and Jefferey, 2017). Call-centre jobs are seen as one of the areas of work most at risk from AI (Wood, 2018).

Mahdawi (2017) suggests that the types of jobs that can most easily be automated by AI are those which are at some level 'routine, repetitive and predictable'. The ability to code aspects of work into data means that this now extends to many white-collar and professional jobs previously thought to be safe from automation, for example:

- in the finance industry, many accounting and tax preparation tasks
- low-level legal work, such as sorting through archives of case law
- journalistic work, such as creating articles from press agency feeds
- human resource functions, such as updating HR records
- some work done by medical consultants, for example analysing X-rays and scans

Sources: Mahdawi (2017); Gyton and Jefferey (2017); Elliot (2017); Cossins (2018).

Visit the online resources and take a look at the extension material for Chapter 10 for more examples of work that is in danger of being replaced by AI.

The increased use of AI gives us cause to rethink much of what has been said before in this chapter about the value of different types of knowledge to both individuals and organizations. We have seen how tacit knowledge is both a deeper level of knowledge for individuals, and the type of knowledge that organizations wish to share and transfer between their members. Furthermore, situated knowledge which is dynamic and suited to the context of a specific organization is also valuable. However, AI, which is taking over more and more organizational activity, is essentially, following Blackler, encoded knowledge—knowledge which may have been tacit but which has been rendered explicit in the form of computer code. This links with the form of learning that Freire criticizes in the banking model of education—it is surface learning of facts rather than a deeper understanding. Ironically, the form of learning which underpins so much of the education that we study in preparation for our working lives is the type which can be so easily replaced by AI!

 Real life case: medical knowledge and artificial intelligence

In this chapter we have seen that medical knowledge is an example of professional knowledge, shared amongst practitioners through outlets such as journals and conferences. While doctors spend years of university study to gain their qualifications, they also stress the value of experience in recognizing and treating symptoms.

This is highlighted by cases when many patients look up their symptoms on search engines, having already made a self-diagnosis. It is as if the medical knowledge of the doctor has been superseded by the amount of knowledge that can now be found online.

While the patient might be able to find a few explicit medical facts online, they lack the tacit experience that comes from years of medical practice. A doctor will have seen patients with similar symptoms; they will have learned from the diagnoses they have made previously and from the occasions when they have made a misdiagnosis.

However, while 'asking Dr Google' about symptoms can bring up a whole range of irrelevant and misleading results, more recent developments in artificial intelligence have created focused self-diagnosis apps which ask more specific and detailed questions and have a greater degree of accuracy. While they cannot replace a doctor's diagnosis, the range of data and case histories that they hold can help a doctor to spot rare illnesses that are outside of their own previous experience. Furthermore, the apps can be used in areas of the world where there is limited access to healthcare.

Artificial intelligence has also been used to automate routine medical tasks, such as the analysis of CT scans, not only to perform diagnosis, but also to learn from the data, spotting potential patients at risk, for example. However, this is not intended to replace medical staff, just to take them away from simple routine decisions and towards patients where they are more urgently needed.

While AI can automate some areas of medical practice, at the moment there are still areas where the knowledge and experience of medical professionals are required.

Sources: Tang and Ng (2006); Alexander (2012); Paddock (2012); Burgess (2018); Devlin (2018).

 Visit the online resources and take a look at the extension material for Chapter 10 for more discussion about artificial intelligence and the medical profession.

Are there any human aspects of medical care that you think could not be replaced by artificial intelligence? Are there any areas where you think AI helps healthcare?

Just as some areas of medical knowledge are still valued, there are some types of job that are not immediately under threat from AI, with some types of knowledge and learning still valued in the workplace. Based on Frey and Osborne (2017), the following are areas of work where robots and AI have difficulty and where a human touch is still needed:

- **Tasks requiring perception and manipulation**. Robots are not good at handling and movement tasks that humans find fairly simple, for example judging the firmness of grip needed between holding different objects (a robot will easily misjudge and crush an egg that it tries to carry, for example). Robots are also not good at tasks like kicking a football—they lack the embodied kinaesthetic and visual-spatial forms of intelligence necessary for this type of activity (Silcoff, 2018).

- **Tasks requiring creativity**. Work such as art and design is an obvious area here, but an area of human knowledge that is also valued is that of critical thinking and appreciation. For example, Kampfner (2016) highlights how professions such as science and engineering appreciate the perspective brought to them by job candidates with a background in arts and creative subjects. The World Economic Forum (2016) has suggested that a key skill for the Fourth Industrial Revolution is critical thinking—an ability to go beyond reciting and analysing explicit knowledge and to look at problems and situations with much more depth and originality. Bhaskar (2016) notes that while online services such as Amazon and Spotify draw upon a lot of data, using AI to make recommendations to customers, they also draw upon human judgement to curate recommended playlists of songs, or recommended book purchases.

- **Tasks requiring social intelligence and interaction**. This can include nurses dealing with patients, or people in business who need to build up networks of contacts (Mahdawi, 2017), for example. Here we see how emotional and interpersonal intelligences still remain important in a lot of work where human contact is needed. With the earlier example of Google Duplex, the initial demonstrations of the system were met with criticism that it was being 'deceitful' by pretending to be human when ringing businesses to make appointments, with the systems subsequently modified to take account of this (Hern, 2018).

- **Tasks requiring flexibility, dealing with uncertainty, or discretion**. AI is able to learn, but not at a speed where agility and flexibility are required (Mahdawi, 2017). Furthermore, AI lacks human discretion. There have been examples where AI algorithms have made decisions which are racist or sexist, based on information that they have learned and replicated from human data, and where a human judgement has been needed to prevent these decisions from being put into action (Buranyi, 2017).

AI represents interesting and ongoing developments in individual and organizational knowledge and learning. It is based in an abstracted form of knowledge—explicit and encoded knowledge as represented by computer data. At the same time, it is not yet able to replicate certain human functions, especially those which are embodied, kinaesthetic, and interactional. These aspects are key parts of situational knowledge, perhaps suggesting that AI will never be able to replicate the entirety of dynamic nature of human and social knowledge.

? Review questions

Describe	What is artificial intelligence?
Explain	How is artificial intelligence based in explicit and encoded knowledge?
Analyse	In the light of this chapter's discussion of management education, what do you think are the key skills and abilities for being a manager in the Fourth Industrial Revolution?
Apply	Think about people that you interact with daily—shop assistants, bank clerks, teaching staff, doctors, etc. How would you feel if they were replaced by AI 'chatbots'? Do you feel the same about all types of work?

Connecting case and theory

This chapter has examined knowledge and learning at both individual and organizational levels and across organizational boundaries. The importance of knowledge transfer and organizational learning is shown at the start of the chapter in Junction Hotel. There was only one person, Bob Smith, who had the expertise to fix an alarm, but he had never shared that knowledge with anyone else at the workplace. Consequently, with Bob off sick there was nobody to fix the faulty alarm, the result being a lot of unhappy guests standing out in the cold.

A distinction is made throughout the chapter between knowledge being viewed simply as a 'thing' which people and organizations accumulate, and knowledge as more of a dynamic and social process—something which exists through action. It is the latter that is generally viewed as being a better-quality and more enduring form of knowledge, a knowledge with depth rather than simply being at the surface level.

However, Simon Chance's first attempts to increase the knowledge base of his engineers wre very much based in a view of knowledge as a 'thing'. Drawing upon a **behaviourist** tradition, he offered the staff a financial reward for learning new skills. However, what happened after this demonstrates the problems associated with this kind of **surface learning**—Mike Bridges was motivated to simply pass a test and gain a bonus. With no incentive to keep that knowledge fresh in his mind, it lapsed after six months; when he was called upon to use that knowledge, he couldn't. However, his colleague Gerry Dawson proved to be much more useful by drawing on his experience and 'feel for the task'—an example of using **tacit knowledge** acquired from experience to gain further knowledge.

The staff all displayed different types of **preferred learning styles** relating to the **VARK** model, whether this is the visual style of looking at a circuit diagram, the reading style of looking at a manual, the auditory style of discussing the problem with others, or the kinaesthetic style of just getting stuck in. However, Chance realized that it would be difficult to design a training scheme that would accommodate all of these preferences. Indeed, he would be wise to look at many of the critiques of learning styles and realize that, while people may express learning style preferences, there is no advantage to tailoring education for each of these preferences.

The engineers were given an instruction manual for all of the photocopiers on a tablet. This was just **explicit knowledge**—instructions and bullet points about how each piece of machinery works. The real knowledge of how to fix the machinery came from, following **Kolb's learning cycle**, the development of **tacit knowledge** from the actual experience of fixing that machinery. Following Nonaka, the real value to Junction Hotel came not from the instruction manuals on the tablet but from the engineers sharing their tacit knowledge of their experiences of the machinery with other engineers, who then put that experience into their own practice. In a manner similar to Orr's study of the photocopier engineers, it is in the social situation of the pub that these insights from experience are shared.

Concepts such as **organizational learning** and the **learning organization** suggest that organizations which excel at this sharing of knowledge and which also undertake deeper, **double-loop learning** will gain a competitive advantage, not just through innovation in their particular sector of the economy, but also by being more capable of responding to change and adjusting their operations when required.

The knowledge of fixing machines becomes a form of **situated knowledge**—it goes beyond instructions on paper and takes in the interactions and tacit experiences of the engineers within the specific context of Junction Hotel. Furthermore, this type of knowledge transfer resonates with the idea of **collisionables**—it was in the chance meetings and conversations between engineers that vital knowledge was transferred.

The advent of AI has shifted the emphasis back to knowledge as a 'thing'—the consequences of this are only just beginning to be understood, but may have a large impact with many of today's jobs. A key point for consideration is whether or not the work of the engineers at Junction Hotel could be replaced by artificial intelligence. Certainly it is not beyond the realm of possibility that chatbots or similar software could be set up by the machinery manufacturers and could be consulted by a member of staff for any potential fault. But would this go beyond the manuals on a tablet—could it really give the type of useful knowledge that comes from experience? While discussion forums can be used to build some of that experience into that type of system, as was set up for the engineers at Junction Hotel, it is questionable whether this type of knowledge could really be a replacement for the absent Bob Smith when faced with the emergency of a faulty fire alarm.

 ## Further reading

Kolb, David A. 2014. Experiential learning: Experience as the source of learning and development. FT press: London.

A detailed introduction to and overview of Kolb's work.

Frey, C.B., and Osborne, M.A. 2017. The future of employment: How susceptible are jobs to computerisation? *Technological Forecasting and Social Change* 114: 254–80.

An investigation into the types of work and knowledge that will be valued in future, including a table showing the risks of automation of various types of work.

Nonaka, I., and Takeuchi, H. 2007. The knowledge-creating company. *Harvard Business Review* 85(7/8): 162.

An overview of knowledge creation and transfer in organizations.

Waber, B., Magnolfi, J., and Lindsay, G. 2014. Workspaces that move people. *Harvard Business Review* 92 (10): 68–77.

An introduction to open-plan workspaces and their effect on learning and innovation.

 ## References

Alexander, B. 2012. Consulting Dr Google is rarely a good idea. Here's why. *NBC News*, 20 July.

Alvesson, M. 2004. *Knowledge work and knowledge-intensive firms.* Oxford University Press: Oxford.

Argyris, C., and Schön, D.A. 1978. *Organizational learning.* Addison-Wesley Pub. Co.: Reading, MA.

Ashkanasy, N.M., and Daus, C.S. 2005. Rumors of the death of emotional intelligence in organizational behavior are vastly exaggerated. *Journal of Organizational Behavior* 26 (4): 441–52.

Bateson, G. 1973. *Steps to an ecology of mind.* Ballantine Books: New York.

BBC News. 2018. Meet Cora, your local bank avatar, 21 February. Available at: https://www.bbc.co.uk/news/av/business-43145317/meet-cora-your-local-bank-avatar

Bhaskar, M. 2016. In the age of the algorithm, the human gatekeeper is back. *The Guardian*, 22 February. Available at: https://www.theguardian.com/technology/2016/sep/30/age-of-algorithm-human-gatekeeper

Blackler, F. 1995. Knowledge, knowledge work and organizations: An overview and interpretation. *Organization Studies* 16 (6): 1021–46.

Bolton, S.C. 2005. *Emotion management in the workplace*. Macmillan International Higher Education: London.

Booth, R. 2017. Francis Crick Institute's £700m building 'too noisy to concentrate'. *The Guardian*, 21 November. Available at: https://www.theguardian.com/science/2017/nov/21/francis-crick-institutes-700m-building-too-noisy-to-concentrate

Brooks, R., and Kay, J. 2014. Enhancing employability through placements in higher education. *Higher Education, Skills and Work-based Learning* 4 (3): entire issue.

Brown, J.S., and Duguid, P. 2000. Balancing act: Capturing knowledge without killing it. *Harvard Business Review* 78 (3): 73–80.

Buranyi, S. 2017. Rise of the racist robots—how AI is learning all our worst impulses. *The Guardian*, 8 August. Available at: https://www.theguardian.com/inequality/2017/aug/08/rise-of-the-racist-robots-how-ai-is-learning-all-our-worst-impulses

Burgess, M. 2018. Stop Googling your symptoms—the smartphone doctor is here to help. *Wired*, 19 April. Available at: http://www.wired.co.uk/article/ada-smartphone-doctor-nhs-gp-video-appointment

Carlson, S. 1951. *Executive behaviour*. Arno Press: New York.

Congdon, C., Flynn, D., and Redman, M. 2014. Balancing 'we' and 'me'. *Harvard Business Review* 92 (10): 50–7.

Coopey, J. 1998. Learning to trust and trusting to learn: A role for radical theatre. *Management Learning* 29 (3): 365–82.

Cossins, D. 2018. Discriminating algorithms: 5 times AI showed prejudice. New Scientist 12 April. Available at: https://www.newscientist.com/article/2166207-discriminating-algorithms-5-times-ai-showed-prejudice/

Davey, M. 2015. Australian academics seek to challenge 'web of avarice' in scientific publishing. *The Guardian*, 14 August.

De Paoli, D., Arge, K., and Hunnes Blakstad, S. 2013. Creating business value with open space flexible offices. *Journal of Corporate Real Estate* 15 (3/4): 181–93.

Devlin, H. 2018. London hospitals to replace doctors and nurses with AI for some tasks. *The Guardian*, 21 May. Available at: https://www.theguardian.com/society/2018/may/21/london-hospitals-to-replace-doctors-and-nurses-with-ai-for-some-tasks

Driver, M. 2002. The learning organization: Foucauldian gloom or utopian sunshine? *Human Relations* 55 (1): 33–53.

Duguid, P. 2006. What talking about machines tells us. *Organization Studies* 27 (12): 1794–804.

Dunn, A., Coiera, E., and Mandl, K. 2014. Is biblioleaks inevitable? *Journal of Medical Internet Research* 16 (4). Published online, doi: 10.2196/jmir.3331.

Elliott, L. 2017. Robots will not lead to fewer jobs - but the hollowing out of the middle class. *The Guardian*, 20 August. Available at: https://www.theguardian.com/business/2017/aug/20/robots-are-not-destroying-jobs-but-they-are-hollow-out-the-middle-class

Fleming, N.D. 2001. *Teaching and learning styles: VARK strategies*. Neil Fleming: Christchurch, NZ.

Freire, P. 1970. *Pedagogy of the oppressed* (transl. Ramos, M.B.). Seabury Press: New York.

Frey, C.B., and Osborne, M.A. 2017. The future of employment: How susceptible are jobs to computerisation? *Technological Forecasting and Social Change* 114: 254–80.

Gapper, J. 2017. Tech utopias can drive workers to distraction. *Financial Times*, 13 September. Available at: https://www.ft.com/content/875d41bc-97a6-11e7-a652-cde3f882dd7b

Gardner, H. 1983. *Frames of mind: The theory of multiple intelligences*. Basic Books: New York.

Gardner, H. 2013. 'Multiple intelligences' are not 'learning styles'. *Washington Post*, 16 October. Available at: https://www.washingtonpost.com/news/answer-sheet/wp/2013/10/16/howard-gardner-multiple-intelligences-are-not-learning-styles/?utm_term=.7b636d1351a4

George, J.M. 2000. Emotions and leadership: The role of emotional intelligence. *Human Relations* 53 (8): 1027–55.

Gherardi, S. 2008. Situated knowledge and situated action: What do practice-based studies promise? In: Barry, D., and Hansen, H. (eds) *The SAGE handbook of new approaches in management and organization*. SAGE Publications: London, pp. 516–25.

Gibbs, S. 2015. Facebook, Google, Dell, HP, eBay back Samsung in patent war with Apple. *The Guardian*, 21 July.

Goleman, D. 1998. *Working with emotional intelligence*. Bantam Books: New York.

Greenfield, P. 2018. The Cambridge Analytica files: the story so far. *The Guardian*, 26 March. Available at: https://www.theguardian.com/news/2018/mar/26/the-cambridge-analytica-files-the-story-so-far

Gyton, G., and Jeffrey, R. 2017. AI vs. HR. *People Management*, 25 July. Available at: https://www.peoplemanagement.co.uk/long-reads/articles/ai-vs-hr

Hales, C.P. 1986. What do managers do? A critical review of the evidence. *Journal of Management Studies* 23 (1): 88–115.

Haraway, D. 1988. Situated knowledges: The science question in feminism and the privilege of partial perspective. *Feminist Studies* 14 (3): 575–99.

Hay, A. 2015. 'I don't know what I am doing!' Surfacing struggles of managerial identity work. *Management Learning* 45 (5): 509–24.

Hern, A. 2018. Google's 'deceitful' AI assistant to identify itself as a robot during calls. *The Guardian*, 11 May. Available at: https://www.theguardian.com/technology/2018/may/11/google-duplex-ai-identify-itself-as-robot-during-calls

Holden, N., and Tansley, C. 2008. Management in other languages: How a philological approach opens up new cross-cultural vistas. In: Tietze, S. (ed.) *International management and language*. Routledge: London, New York.

Honey, P., and Mumford, A. 1992. *The manual of learning styles*. Peter Honey Publications Ltd: Maidenhead.

Honey, P., and Mumford, A. 2006. *The learning styles helper's guide*. Peter Honey Publications Ltd: Maidenhead.

Husmann, P.R., and O'Loughlin, V.D. 2018. Another nail in the coffin for learning styles? Disparities among undergraduate anatomy students' study strategies, class performance, and reported VARK learning styles.

Anatomical Sciences Education, 13 March. Published online, doi: 10.1002/ase.1777.

Jones, R. 2018. NatWest Bank tests Cora, an AI bot that will answer customer questions. *The Guardian*, 21 February. Available at: https://www.theguardian.com/money/2018/feb/21/natwest-bank-tests-cora-an-ai-bot-that-will-answer-customer-questions

Kampfner, J. 2016. Creative subjects like art history are vital – just as engineers. I news, October 18. Available at: https://inews.co.uk/opinion/creative-subjects-like-art-history-vital-just-ask-engineers/

Koffka, K. 1955. *Principles of Gestalt psychology*. Routledge & Kegan Paul: London.

Kolb, D.A. 1984. *Experiential learning: Experience as the source of learning and development*. Prentice Hall: Englewood Cliffs, NJ.

Lave, J., and Wenger, E. 1991. *Situated learning: Legitimate peripheral participation*. Cambridge University Press: Cambridge, New York.

Mahdawi, A. 2017. What jobs will still be around in 20 years? Read this to prepare your future. *The Guardian*, 26 June. Available at: https://www.theguardian.com/us-news/2017/jun/26/jobs-future-automation-robots-skills-creative-health

Marton, F., and Säljö, R. 1976. On qualitative differences in learning. I—Outcome and Process. *British Journal of Educational Psychology* 46: 4–11.

Mayer, J.D., and Salovey, P. 1993. The intelligence of emotional intelligence. *Intelligence* 17: 433–42.

McNeill, D. 2017. Start-ups and the entrepreneurial city. *City* 21 (2): 232–9.

Mols, F. and Roberts, J. 2016. Can we replace politicians with robots? The Conversation, March 27. Available at: http://theconversation.com/can-we-replace-politicians-with-robots-56683

Mulgan, G., Steinberg, Y., and Salem, O. 1995. Wide open: Open source methods and their future potential. *Demos*. Available at: http://www.demos.co.uk/publications/wideopen (last accessed 20 August 2015).

Newton, P.M. 2015. The learning styles myth is thriving in higher education. *Frontiers in Psychology* 6: 1908.

Nidumolu, S.R., Subramani, M., and Aldrich, A. 2001. Situated learning and the situated knowledge web: Exploring the ground beneath knowledge management. *Journal of Management Information Systems* 18 (1): 115–50.

Nonaka, I., and Takeuchi, H. 1995. The knowledge-creating company: How Japanese companies create the dynamics of innovation. Oxford University Press: New York.

Nonaka, I., and Takeuchi, H. 2007. The knowledge-creating company. *Harvard Business Review* 85 (7/8): 162–71.

Orr, J.E. 1996. *Talking about machines: An ethnography of a modern job.* ILR Press: Ithaca, NY.

Paddock, C. 2012. Dr Google and the unwise practice of self-diagnosis. *Medical News Today*, 23 July.

Pashler, H., McDaniel, M., Rohrer, D., and Bjork, R. 2008. Learning styles: Concepts and evidence. *Psychological Science in the Public Interest* 9 (3): 105–19.

Pask, G. 1976. Styles and strategies of learning. *British Journal of Educational Psychology* 46: 128–48.

Pedler, M., Burgoyne, J., and Boydell, T. 1997. *The learning company: A strategy for sustainable development*, 2nd edn. McGraw-Hill: London.

Polanyi, M. 1958. *Personal knowledge: Towards a post-critical philosophy.* University of Chicago Press: Chicago.

Polanyi, M. 1967. *The tacit dimension.* Routledge & Kegan Paul: London.

RBS. 2018. NatWest begins testing AI driven 'digital human' in banking first, 21 February. Available at: https://www.rbs.com/rbs/news/2018/02/natwest-begins-testing-ai-driven-digital-human-in-banking-first.html

Reynolds, M. 1997. Learning styles: A critique. *Management Learning* 28 (2): 115–33.

Riener, C., and Willingham, D. 2010. The myth of learning styles. *Change: The Magazine of Higher Learning* 42 (5): 32–5.

Russell, B. 1912. *The problems of philosophy.* Oxford University Press: London, New York.

Ryle, G. 1949. *The concept of mind.* Hutchinson: London.

Salovey, P., and Mayer, J.D. 1990. Emotional intelligence. *Imagination, Cognition and Personality* 9 (3): 185–211.

Sample, I. 2012. Harvard University says it can't afford journal publishers' prices. *The Guardian*, 24 April.

Schön, D.A. 1983. *The reflective practitioner: How professionals think in action.* Basic Books: New York.

Senge, P.M. 1990. *The fifth discipline: The art and practice of the learning organization.* Doubleday/Currency: New York.

Silcoff, M. 2018. The world cup of robot football: No need for humans to worry (yet). *The Guardian*, 26 June. Available at: https://www.theguardian.com/science/2018/jun/26/the-world-cup-of-robot-football-no-need-for-humans-to-worry-yet

Solon, O. 2018. Google's robot assistant now makes eerily lifelike phone calls for you. *The Guardian*, 8 May. Available at: https://www.theguardian.com/technology/2018/may/08/google-duplex-assistant-phone-calls-robot-human

Tang, H., and Ng, J.H.K. 2006. Googling for a diagnosis—use of Google as a diagnostic aid: Internet based study. *British Medical Journal* 333: 1143–5.

Telenor. 2018. Workplace management. Available at: https://www.telenoreiendom.no/en/services/work-place-management/ (last accessed 17 July 2018).

Van der Kleij, F.M., Feskens, R.C.W., and Eggen, T.J.H.M. 2015. Effects of feedback in a computer-based learning environment on students' learning outcomes: A meta-analysis. *Review of Educational Research* 85 (4): 475–511.

Waber, B., Magnolfi, J., and Lindsay, G. 2014. Workspaces that move people. *Harvard Business Review* 92 (10): 68–77.

Willingham, D.T., Hughes, E.M., and Dobolyi, D.G. 2015. The scientific status of learning styles theories. *Teaching of Psychology* 42 (3): 266–71.

Wood, Z. 2018. Rise of robots threatens to terminate the UK call-centre workforce. *The Observer*, 12 May. Available at: https://www.theguardian.com/business/2018/may/12/robot-technology-threat-terminist-uk-call-centre-workforce

CHAPTER 11

Perception and communication

Is communication ever perfect?

Chapter overview and learning outcomes

By the end of this chapter you should be able to:

- explain the main theories of individual perception and how these relate to the ways we create meaning in organizations

- describe theories and processes of communication in organizations

- explain how technology mediates communication, producing a trade-off between efficiency and richness of communication

Key theorists

Max Wertheimer	Part of the Gestalt school of psychology who outlined the principles of human perceptual organization
Carol Dweck	Wrote about fixed and growth mindsets in people's attitudes to learning
Fiona Wilson	Wrote about how gender influences perceptions in organizations
Albert Mehrabian	Noted the important role of non-verbal communication in organizational settings
Richard Daft and Robert Lengel	Devised media richness theory, which examines the abilities of different media to communicate rich information and meaning

Key terms

Perception	The ways in which people actively create meaning from sensory stimuli
Selective perception	Where people foreground certain perceptions above others
Perceptual organization	The ways in which people organize perception in their minds into particular forms or patterns
Mindset	A framework that each individual develops and which then influences their future selective perception and perceptual organization
Stereotype	A form of mindset which predisposes people to attribute certain, often negative, characteristics to other people on the basis of social groupings to which they belong

Impression management	An attempt by people, including in the workplace, to manage stimuli, such as dress and digital presence, so as to encourage others to have favourable perceptions of them
Communication	The transfer of meaning or information from one person, or several, to another
Noise	Anything which disrupts and distorts communication so that the meaning perceived by the recipient is different from the meaning intended by the sender
Information and communications technologies (ICT)	A set of contemporary electronic technologies which facilitate communication between people and the sharing of information
Social presence	The degree to which the physical presence of the sender of a message can be felt in a particular communications medium
Media richness	The ability of different communications media to communicate rich, personal meanings rather than lean, impersonal information

Introduction

Running case: 'Guests First'

From: simon_chance@junctionhotel.co.uk
To: senior_management_team@junctionhotel.co.uk

Dear colleagues

As you are aware we have been facing a tough time economically, leading to some efficiencies being made in work processes and staff numbers. At the same time, we face the challenge of maintaining our position as a luxury hotel.

I believe that we can achieve this balancing act if we recognize that the key factor which adds value and luxury status to the hotel is our people and the attention to customer service that they provide.

For this reason, I am introducing our new 'Guests First' initiative. It means that, for all of us, whatever our role in the organization, we need to perform our roles with the recognition that without our guests we have no income. It is through you putting the guests first that we can maintain our status as a luxury experience.

Could you all, as senior managers, please cascade this down to the people in your departments and we can all start putting the guests first as soon as possible!

Many thanks
Simon

It is often said that we live in an age of communication which is enhanced and facilitated by the technologies of our day. ICT (information and communications technologies) describes these technologies that we use to communicate on a daily basis—the internet, smartphones etc. As we saw in Chapter 2, computer data is communicated instantly and continually through global networks; in Chapter 4 we saw how this constant communication and exchange of data underpins the cyber-physical systems of the Fourth Industrial Revolution.

However, in this chapter, we begin by seeing communication first as a human process before examining how these processes are then mediated by technology. In particular, communication is linked to human processes of **perception**. Rather than being a flawless transfer of information, like data being exchanged between two computers, it relies on the fact that people perceive and make meaning about the world around them in different ways. We will examine the related ideas of perception and communication as follows.

- First we introduce perception as the way in which people interpret and make sense of the world around them. Similarly to the chapters on personality, motivation, and learning, we see perception as an individual process—two people can perceive exactly the same thing in completely different ways. We will see how people develop mindsets—frameworks within their minds which influence the way that they perceive and make meaning from the world around them.

- Second, we examine theories of communication within organizations—the ways in which information and meaning are transferred between people. Communication is an important managerial activity, but one which is prone to *mis*communication—what a person sending a message means may not be the same as how the person receiving that message *perceives* and understands it.

- Third, we examine how technology, such as email, facilitates communication. In particular, we see that while technology can make communication more efficient, different media convey different degrees of the rich meaning that comes from face-to-face communication. This lack of rich meaning can leave communication through technology open to more instances where a message can be perceived differently from its original intention.

We conclude by noting the importance of communication to the Fourth Industrial Revolution.

Familiar communications technology.
Source: Shutterstock.

Individual perception: making sense of the world

Our senses—sight, hearing, taste, smell, touch—continually receive information, or stimuli (singular: **stimulus**). **Perception** is about what we do with these different stimuli. Rather than receiving this information passively, we actively organize and interpret these stimuli to create meaning. Perception is therefore also about how we attach meaning to the world around us. As we have seen with motivation, personality, and learning in previous chapters, the way that we create this meaning is different for different people—we all perceive the world in different ways.

Running case: different perceptions

Meg Mortimer is having a hectic day—reception is exceptionally busy, and she is stuck in the office dealing with various crises that were taking place. Peering above her glasses she sees a list of unread emails in her inbox. Just as she is about to deal with the emails, the phone rings. 'Can you come into reception please?' asks one of the receptionists, sounding flustered. 'We have a bit of a problem here.' 'I'll be there in a second,' says Meg. As she puts the phone down, she glances at the screen and inadvertently deletes a page of emails, thinking that they have been dealt with, including Chance's 'Guests First' email.

Meanwhile, accountant David Hunter is sitting in his small office doing the weekly payroll figures on his computer. The computer pings up a notification, 'New email: Simon Chance Guests First.' 'Guests!' exclaims Hunter to himself, 'I hate them—rude, ignorant, always a problem. That's why I'm an accountant—no need to even meet them, yet alone put them first.' Once again, the email is deleted without being read.

These differences in perception are evident in how different people react differently to the same things. Two people may hear the same song—one enjoying it, the other disliking it. Two people can taste the same meal but again perceive that taste in different ways. Indeed, the word 'Marmite' is used to describe things which can polarize opinion between really liking or absolutely hating something, based on the observation that the yeast spread Marmite attracts similar reactions.

Real life case: the dress

In early 2015, people across the world were obsessed with one photograph of a dress that had been posted online. Newspapers, television programmes, and social media questioned exactly what colours could be seen on the dress. Some people saw the dress as blue and

The dress.

black, while other people saw the exact same photograph as white and gold. Only 10 per cent of viewers could see the dress in both colour combinations. Although confirmed as being blue and black, reasons were given for why people might see the dress and white and gold which relate to how the brain perceives colour. Factors affecting how it is perceived include other colours surrounding the image, the device it is being viewed on, and the expectations that the viewer has (e.g. are they expecting to see it as gold and white because someone has told them it is?) (Sample, 2015; Rogers, 2015).

More recently, an auditory rather than a visual artefact achieved a similar level of global discussion. In 2018, a recording of a person saying the name 'Laurel' was perceived by many people to be saying 'Yanny'—again people tended to hear only one way or the other. The recording was said to exist on a 'perceptual boundary' (Ducharme, 2018). Both words were present in the recording, but which was perceived depended on the ways in which different people filter out different frequencies of sound.

Visit the online resources and take a look at the web links for Chapter 11 for more details about these cases.

The dress and the 'Laurel/Yanny' recording highlight a further aspect of perception. Perception is not simply about preferences for music or food: even things that we might consider to be objective facts—a colour, or a sound—can be perceived differently. The reality in front of us and what we actually perceive can be two different things.

Jane Henry (2001: 43) explains these differences in individual perception in terms of the actual physiology of the brain, which she describes as being 'malleable' in a way similar to plastic. When a stimulus reaches the brain, a cell fires a signal which communicates with neighbouring cells. The cells create paths; the next time the stimulus is received, a path has already been created that makes that particular bit of perceptual organization easier. These paths emerge differently for different people. Indeed scans have shown that different people can use different parts of the brain for the same activities. Furthermore, one act of perception is not stored in the brain, like a single, discrete piece of data on a computer disk. Different parts of the brain are responsible for different parts of perception, so what we perceive and the memories that we recall of that perception are more like a mesh which is recreated each time.

The way the brain structures perceptions explains how individuals may perceive the same stimulus differently—the stimulus triggers different paths in different brains. It also shows that perception is not a passive act, whereby we simply absorb stimuli. Perception is an active processing of what we sense, and it is through this that we understand and make sense of our world, including other people.

Factors affecting perception

A key aspect of the ways in which we each actively process perceptions is **selective perception**. Put simply, there are so many perceptual stimuli out there that it would be impossible to process them all at once. In this respect, we bring some stimuli to the foreground while pushing others to the background, effectively ignoring them. And what is in the foreground or the background can change—it is a dynamic process.

For example, when writing an essay you may concentrate on certain things—the words on the computer screen, your notes, etc. Things like the whirring of the computer hard disk, or the brightness of your lamp, or the sound of a breeze outside, equally drift into the background. However, a change to this—the doorbell ringing, for example—brings other stimuli into the foreground.

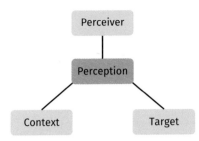

Figure 11.1 Factors that affect selective perception.

A lot of this selectivity takes place unconsciously. Henry (2001: 44) suggests that reactions to perceptual stimuli take place unconsciously around a half a second before we are conscious of them—for example, a person touching a hot oven plate may react and pull their hand away before they actually feel any pain.

There are many factors which affect how selective perception takes place, and these are usually placed into three groups (see Figure 11.1).

First, there are attributes of the perceiver (the person doing the perception) which will determine what is selected to be perceived. The person's attitudes, motivation, interests, needs, experience, and values are all aspects that might have an influence. Somebody is more likely to perceive something which interests them, for example, or immediate needs might move our essay-writer's perception away from the computer screen and towards their hunger at lunchtime.

Second, attributes of the target, i.e. the stimulus or thing potentially being perceived, are also important. Many factors can come into play here—intensity (if a light is very bright or a noise very loud), size, or closeness to us, for example. Something familiar may jump to the foreground of our perception—somebody we know in a sea of faces, for example; or conversely something novel may also grab our attention—one black swan amidst a gaggle of white swans.

Finally, the situation or context can also impact what is perceived. This could be a physical context, the social setting, the organization that we are in, or the time of day. For example, if someone were to walk past us wearing shorts and a running vest, this might attract our attention in a church, or in a business meeting where we would expect people to be dressed more formally, yet we would probably not blink an eye were this to be in a gym.

Principles of perceptual organization

While the concept of selective perception highlights the factors which determine what we might perceive, perceptual organization describes how we manage these perceptions within our minds. In this respect it refers back to the paths in the brain described by Henry—our previous experiences and perceptions, and the ways in which these have been organized, will have an impact on how we perceive stimuli in future.

Five principles of **perceptual organization** in particular structure our perceptions with our minds. These principles derive from the Gestalt tradition of psychology, which, as we saw in Chapter 10, describes the ways in which we commit learning to our minds by forming patterns and associations. The ways in which these patterns and links are organized within our brains were outlined by Max Wertheimer (1938), one of the leading members of the Gestalt school.

The figure–ground principle

This is similar to perceptual selection, where we bring particular perceptions to the foreground with others staying in the background. It can be seen particularly in a number of common optical illusions where images could be perceived in two or more different ways. Figure 11.2 shows a well-known version of this: the Rubin vase (Rubin, 1915), an image that could be perceived as either two faces in silhouette facing each other, or a blue goblet. It is very difficult to perceive both

Figure 11.2 The figure–ground principle.

at once. To stop the image from being ambiguous and having no meaning in our mind, we need to foreground one of the two possible ways of seeing it (the faces or the goblet). Our minds do not like the ambiguity of this type of image and so will try to structure it into some form of meaning. Past experience will have an impact here—if somebody shows the image and announces it is two faces, then we are more likely to see it in this way, for example; or if we had returned from a church mass where an ornate chalice was being used, we may be more likely to see the goblet.

The continuity principle

This suggests that we try to detect patterns in our perceptions and then make predictions and patterns based on these extrapolations. For example, look at the sequence below and say what the next number should be:

2, 4, 6, 8, 10, 12 ... ?

Most people would say 14, because a pattern has been detected that 2 is added to the total each time. However, there is nothing to say that this must be the case; it simply reflects the ways in which we make predictions based on patterns.

The proximity principle

This suggests that objects that are close to each other tend to be grouped together. For example, what do you see in Figure 11.3?

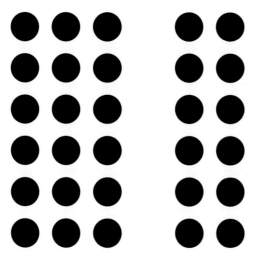

Figure 11.3 The proximity principle.

Did you say 30 dots? Or did you say two groups of dots—one with 18 dots and one with 12? Most people will say some version of the latter, indicating the tendency to group close objects together.

The closure principle

This principle applies particularly when we have incomplete information. In a similar way to the figure–ground relationship, we will try to make ambiguous or meaningless information into something meaningful. The closure principle says that we will take the information already there and try to fit it in to patterns of perceptions already formed. For example, look at Figure 11.4 and say what you see.

Figure 11.4 The closure principle—fitting information into patterns.

Many people will say a dog, particularly a dalmatian. In fact if you look again, it is just a set of black blobs, but it matches the patterns of a dalmatian we already have in our minds, and so our minds complete the closure in this incomplete information into something with which we already have familiarity.

Now look at Figure 11.5 and say what you see.

Figure 11.5 The closure principle—filling in the gaps.

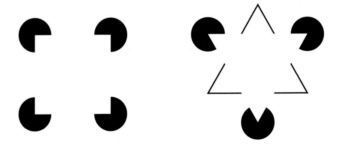

Many people would say a square (on the left) and two triangles (on the right), but again, neither is actually there in the picture. Again the closure principle applies—we look at the circles and lines that are present and 'fill in the gaps' for ourselves. In this case we can also see other principles of organization at work. The fact that we see a square and a triangle shows the proximity principle—we have perceived each of the two sets of marks separately because they are grouped close to each other. The continuity principle is also evident—we have detected the start of a pattern of drawing the triangle from the lines that are there, and we have completed those lines for ourselves in our own mind.

The similarity principle

Similar to the proximity principle, this is where we group things with similar characteristics together. Furthermore, if we see one thing with a set of characteristics, we may then attribute those characteristics to something which is similar—someone who was once bitten by a dog might, for example, react to all dogs with fear, assuming that they too will attack them.

Mindsets

The factors affecting perception and the principles of perceptual organization, which we have examined in the previous two sections, show that perception is not a random act, but that people are predisposed to perceive certain stimuli in certain ways. For example, returning to the blue-and-black (or white-and-gold) dress at the start of the section, things like the context in which the dress is presented, or what people have been told about the dress before, may predispose them to see it in one of the two ways, rather than this being a random choice between the two.

Mindsets, or **perceptual sets**, describe the ways in which we are predisposed to selectively perceive and then organize particular stimuli. We all have different ways of framing the world that we perceive and attaching meaning to those perceptions. Mindsets help us to make order of the world around us, with its many competing stimuli, by imposing ready-made frameworks on those stimuli.

The educational psychologist Carol Dweck (2006) has applied the concept of mindsets to theories about how people are motivated to learn. People with a fixed mindset tend to see their abilities as coming from innate qualities that they can do little to change. People with a growth mindset, on the other hand, believe that they can develop and improve their abilities. This will determine how people approach failure—a fixed mindset indicates that people will see failure as a negative reflection of their own abilities, whereas a growth mindset indicates that failure will be seen as a challenge from which to develop.

One perceptual phenomenon that can be explained by the concept of mindsets is **stereotyping**. In the previous chapter we saw how stereotyping is a problem in many forms of recruitment and selection, with people treated unfairly based on assumptions made about them because of characteristics such as race and gender. Stereotypes can be seen as mindsets which people use to create meaning about people based on particular characteristics. This links with a number of factors of perceptual selection and organization.

- The experience of the perceiver can influence how they perceive something. It is often said that children are born with no prejudice, but that it can be learned from what other people say about other groups—an experience that influences future perceptions.

- Stereotypes often apply a closure principle. People take a few characteristics—skin colour, accent, gender, for example—and make assumptions about intelligence or criminality.

- Stereotypes also emerge from principles of proximity and similarity: thus people might be assumed to have certain characteristics because of the city or nation they are from, the job that they do, even the office they work in ('they all enjoy a laugh in export').

Visit the online resources and take a look at the extension material for Chapter 11 for more details about the principles of perceptual organization.

Fiona Wilson has noted how stereotypes can feed into perceptions related to gender in the workplace. Just as two stimuli can be perceived differently depending on a person's mindset, gender stereotypes can be a framing device that leads to similar actions being perceived differently—for example Wilson (2003: 46) notes how displays of confidence by male managers can be perceived positively, but displays of confidence by female managers can be perceived negatively and as a threat.

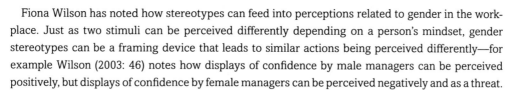

Real life case: gendered language in job adverts

A study by Seattle-based artificial intelligence consultants Textio found that the language used in job adverts is perceived differently by potential applicants depending on their gender, and that this can have the effect of deterring female applicants from applying.

For example, software company adverts which call for 'coding ninjas' create a highly masculine perception of the culture of the company which appeals more to potential male applicant and puts off female applicants.

Words in job adverts which tended to appeal to mean include 'exhaustive, enforcement, fearless, build and manage' which women preferred words such as 'transparent, catalyst, in touch with, create and develop.'

Textio give no reason for why the words appeal as they do; however, companies hiring their consultancy services have seen increases in female applicants of up to 80 per cent.

Visit the online resources and take a look at the web links for Chapter 11 to find out more about the impact of language in recruitment adverts.

Sources: Abadi (2017); Devine (2018); Silverberg (2018).

Gendered language can also influence perceptions of who might be expected to perform a particular role. For example, Barbara Czarniawska and Guje Sévon (2018) have noted how, when citations appear in academic texts and in reference lists, there is a stereotypical assumption that the author is male when only a surname and initials are present.

In Chapter 3 we discussed the work of Lillian and Frank Gilbreth, who were pioneers in time and motion studies. Lillian Gilbreth's life was particularly remarkable because of what she achieved in the early twentieth century as a woman, when women were not expected to work, let alone become academics and pioneers of industrial engineering. Lillian Gilbreth faced barriers to her groundbreaking work due to assumptions made because of her gender. She was the first woman to be awarded a doctorate in industrial engineering, but when it came to be published (Gilbreth, 1914) it was done so only with her initials, L.M. Gilbreth—the publishers feared that it would not carry credibility in engineering circles if the author were identified to be female. Stereotypical assumptions were made simple on the surface feature of her gender, despite the fact that she held a doctorate in the area and had a track record of successful consultancy and pioneering work (Lawley and Caven, 2019).

Perception in business and management

 Real life case: 'business casual'

Once, office attire was almost universally formal. Now, the suits, dark colours, and high heels are increasingly replaced with less formal 'business casual' style. Trollope (2017) notes that this informality originates from the US tech sector, where t-shirts and jeans are the predominant form of dress.

Now, only one in ten British workers report wearing a formal suit to the office (Clark, 2018) and multinational companies such as JP Morgan and Price Waterhouse Cooper have encouraged their workforces to adopt relaxed, business casual forms of dress (Stone, 2017).

However, while this may seem like freedom from the previous stuffy, formal attire, it brings its own problems. In particular, business causal is difficult to define and to get right. As Stone (2017) suggests, leggings and sportswear might be comfortable, but they are *too* casual for the office? Clark (2018) suggests that it can be difficult to judge different business contexts—when is it appropriate to wear formal shoes rather than trainers, or a tie instead of an open-neck shirt, for example? Indeed, it is a judgement that it is very easy to get wrong—walking into a meeting in jeans and a t-shirt where everyone else is wearing a suit could create an unfavourable impression.

In Chapter 10 we examined how people manage their digital presence, for example social media profiles, in order to create a favourable impression for any potential employers who may search for them. This type of impression management also takes place within the workplace. For example, clothing can be used to create an impression—what we wear may cause us to be perceived in different ways. As the 'business casual' case shows, from the perspective of selective perception, context is again important. In a room full of people wearing suits, another person in a suit will barely register, but a person in jeans and a t-shirt will. Likewise, a person in a formal suit might raise eyebrows in an open-plan office full of millennial techies wearing hoodies. Clothing might indicate conformity to the norms of the workplace, or make a bold statement of intent. In either case, it is one stimulus that workers have at their disposal in order to influence the perceptions of other workers towards them.

However, the relevance of perception to business and management goes beyond individual impression management. Given that perception is an ongoing process from second to second, there are many areas where it is relevant to business and management. Organizations involve multiple interactions, all of which might be perceived differently, with different members of the organization interpreting stimuli differently and ascribing different meanings. Furthermore, a number of different organizational factors might influence the perceptions of their members. So far in the book, we have seen several examples of this.

- In Chapters 5 and 6 we saw how group dynamics can influence the behaviour of an individual. Furthermore, they can influence perception. One aspect of selective perception is what is seen as normal or unusual in different contexts—as we saw in those chapters, group dynamics can set the values and what is seen as normal behaviour within a group.

- Chapter 7 examined organizational culture. Culture can be seen as an attempt by an organization to influence the perceptions of workers, for example by using symbols and stories to create particular meanings around the organization. However, we also saw that this does not always work: different workers might perceive these symbols and stories differently, and subcultures might emerge where people perceive cultures differently and ascribe different meanings.

- In Chapter 8, personality was viewed, from the ideographic approach, as something unique to each individual, a result of the different influences we each have throughout our lives. This mirrors Henry's description of the brain as carving out highly individual patterns in response to perceptual stimuli. This individuality was further examined in Chapter 9: process theories see motivation as a highly individual phenomenon. As we saw in this chapter, motivation, which will be different for different people, is one of the individual influences which affects selective perception.

- As noted earlier, in Chapter 10 we saw how Gestalt principles of perceptual organization also structure learning and memory.

Perception will also feed into future chapters in the book.

- In Chapter 12, about changing organizations, we will see how it is perceptions of change, rather than any objective reality, which can determine the success of change management initiatives, again drawing on Gestalt school psychology, this time of Kurt Lewin.

- In Chapter 13 we will see how leadership is a way of seeking to manage meaning and perception.

- In Chapter 15 we examine how organizations in the contemporary service sector sell themselves as an experience to customers. As such, organizations make use of emotional and aesthetic labour to control the way in which the company is perceived, which involves controlling both the behaviours and the appearance of the workers.

- In Chapter 16 on globalization we will see that many theories of cross-cultural management derive from perceptions of other cultures rooted in stereotypes that have developed from a Western perspective.

For the remainder of this chapter, we link perception to the key organizational process of communication.

? Review questions

Describe What are the principles of perceptual organization?

Explain How do mindsets help us to explain why people hold stereotypical perceptions of others?

Analyse Can you explain impression management using the terminology of perception theory?

Apply What measures could be taken to prevent the negative effects of gendered perceptions in recruitment adverts?

Communication in organizations: getting the message through

Effective **communication** is an important part of organizational success. It means that the wishes, desires, and orders of those at the top have been successfully transmitted to, and understood by, all people within the organization, who will then act upon them. Communication is therefore important for the exercise of managerial power. But is it something which always takes place flawlessly?

In this section, we examine some of the main features of communication between people in organizations, but also the ways in which **miscommunication** can occur. In other words, the meaning people intend when they send a message can be perceived completely differently by people receiving the message. We see how **noise** can interfere in the communication process, resulting in the original, intended meaning being distorted and, potentially, a completely different message being received. We question the amount of power that management actually have over the communication process and the degree to which communication allows managerial power to be exerted.

Features of communication

Rather than being a simple transfer of a **message** from a sender to a recipient, communication has many facets and features which mean that the nature of any one communication, or the way in which we pass on a particular message, will be different from another. We begin this section by examining four particular features which make up the nature of communication.

- Is it formal or informal?
- What channel does it take—is it spoken, written, symbolic, or expressed in the form of gestures?
- How long does it take to reach its intended recipient and for a reply to be received?
- What is its focus—is it between individuals or among many people?

Formal and informal channels of communication

When you think about communication in organizations, do you think of it as something official, signed by the managing director and sent on company letter-headed paper, or do you think of the conversations and gossip between workers in the staff canteen? The first feature of communication that we examine is its formal and informal aspects.

Formal communication is official communication such as memos, reports, and commands, using formalized channels. These channels can be represented by the **organization chart** (Figure 11.6), which was presented in Chapter 2 as a diagram of hierarchical structure which facilitated organizational control. However, the chart can also be seen as a map of organizational communication, showing who communicates with whom as orders and messages are passed up and down from one level to the next throughout the **hierarchy**.

As seen in Chapter 4, this form of hierarchical bureaucracy has been superseded in many organizations by more flexible structures, such as the **matrix structure** (Figure 11.7; see Chapter 4 for more explanation). Formal **channels of communication** are thus not just vertical, as with the organizational hierarchy, but can also be horizontal—with communication flowing across the organization through formally-constituted project teams.

Figure 11.6 An organizational hierarchy.

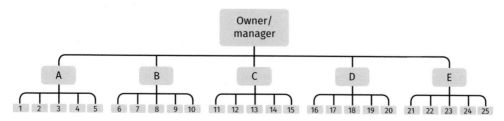

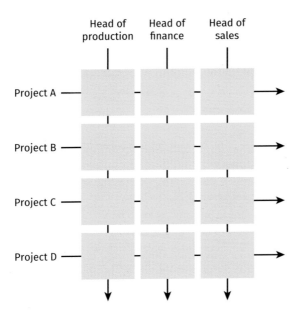

Figure 11.7 A typical matrix structure.

Alongside formal channels of communication, however, are the **informal communications** that take place: the 'water-cooler' conversations and quick chats at the photocopier, for example. Such communication is not part of the organization's authorized, formal communication, but information about the workplace is nevertheless shared.

For example, a workplace football team may bring together people from different parts of the organization—sales, accounting, production, etc.—and even from different levels in the hierarchy. Conversation in the bar after a match is likely, at some point, to turn to work-related issues. People get to learn about what is going on in other parts of the organization—information that they might not hear otherwise. And a football team is just one of potentially many informal social groups that may exist in an organization.

It is here that organizational issues might be discussed in ways that would not be mapped out by the formal channels of the organization chart. There is a 'suppleness of communication' (Deleuze and Guattari, 1987: 214) that bypasses official bureaucratic structures and communication channels.

Such communication is sometimes linked with **gossip**, where people get to find out work-related information to which they would otherwise not be party. Gossip, alongside secrecy in organizations, is an area of study in itself and has been analysed not just as a form of informal communication but also as a source of power and a means of maintaining the cohesion of groups within organizations (e.g. Noon and Delbridge, 1993; Kurland and Pelled, 2000; Fan et al., 2017).

 Visit the online resources and take a look at the extension material for Chapter 11 for more analysis of gossip in organizations.

Management are able to control the content of formal communications, such as memos and emails. To what extent can they control both the content and the accuracy of informal communications, such as gossip?

In more recent theories of organization, the distinction between formal and informal communication can become blurred. For example, **post-bureaucratic organizations** (see Chapter 2) minimize structure and formal roles and, instead, emphasize dialogue between people as the main feature of an organization. Models of organizational learning also emphasize the importance of sharing work-related knowledge through conversations, as with the case of the Xerox photocopier engineers (see Chapter 10).

Rather than communication being a discrete feature of the organization, mapped out by the organization's structure, communication is a big part of what the organization actually *is*:

> It is through the telephone calls, meetings, planning sessions, sales talks and corridor conversations that people inform, update, gossip, review, reassess, reason, instruct, revise, argue, debate, contest and actually *constitute* the moments, myths and, through time, the very *structuring* of the organization.
>
> (Boden, 1994: 8, original author's emphasis)

Communication, whether formal or informal, is thus a continual and ongoing process in organizations, or, as Broekstra (1998) states, the organization *is* a conversation.

Channels of communication

🔍 Running case: raising the bar

With the evening bar shift about to begin, John Vintner, the bar manager, is making a few announcements in the staff room. 'Oh, and finally,' he announces with a sarcastic and mocking tone, 'we have an email from Mr Chance.'

'Ooh,' reply the bar staff in mock fascination, before descending into giggles.

'We have a new initiative for customer service,' announces Vintner, his voice both grandiose and mocking. Vintner continues to read out the email, strutting around the staff room, making grand sweeping gestures with his arms, his voice becoming more mocking in tone as he continues. Each mention of the phrase 'Guests First' is telegraphed with ever more exaggerated facial mugging and, as the announcement continues, the staff fall more and more into hysterical laughter.

Finally, Vintner returns to his normal tone of voice. 'Well, guys, as far as I'm concerned you've been putting guests first for years—so off you go and do the same as always.'

 What is the bar manager communicating through his gestures and tone of voice over and above the words that he is reading out?

Have you ever found yourself giving directions to somebody while speaking on the telephone, only to realize that you are pointing and tracing out the directions with your free hand, even though the other person cannot see you? Such gestures show how communication involves factors beyond the words themselves—much of what we understand from a conversation comes from non-verbal body language.

👁 Research insight: Mehrabian's 55–38–7 ratio

Mehrabian, A. 1971. *Silent messages.* Wadsworth: Belmont, CA.

Albert Mehrabian (1971) studied communication among workers in a laboratory and was particularly interested in how people communicated emotions and attitudes. While we might think that the information conveyed in a conversation would be from words alone, Mehrabian's study discovered that much more is communicated through body language, such as hand gestures, comportment, and eye contact. In other words, communication involves more perceptual stimuli—sights, sounds etc, than just text on a page. The 55–38–7 ratio suggests that, in face-to-face conversation,

- 55 per cent of communication is from body language;
- 38 per cent of communication comes from the tone of voice;
- just 7 per cent of communication is from the actual words.

Mehrabian's work has implications for communication that does not take place in a face-to-face setting—how much meaning is lost if 55 per cent of communication is from bodily gestures?

We can identify four channels that make up much of the communication among people in an organization.

- Oral communication is through spoken words: conversations, meetings, briefings, negotiations, phone calls, etc.
- Bodily, non-verbal communication is the gestures, facial expressions, and body language that convey meaning beyond the actual words spoken.
- Written communication takes place through words on paper or on the screen of a computer, tablet, or phone; examples include letters, memos, emails, text messages, newsletters, or a noticeboard.
- Symbolic communication uses signs and symbols: e.g. drivers understand that a red circle with a white horizontal line through the middle means 'no entry'.

 Which examples of the four channels of communication have you engaged in today—either as a sender or receiver?

Synchronicity and feedback

A conversation is generally a two-way process—we take it in turns to say something, listen to or read the response, and then respond accordingly. We may also understand how a person feels about our words from the bodily, non-verbal reactions—the look on their face and their body language. This process of receiving a response to communication is **feedback**.

However, not all feedback is as instantaneous as it is with a conversation. Many of us may have experienced the frustration of sending an email or a letter only to be left waiting for a response. **Synchronicity** describes the amount of delay between sending a message and that message being received, and gives a further facet of communication.

- Synchronous communication is where transmission of the message by the sender and receipt of the message happen simultaneously, and there is thus the possibility for feedback to be instant. Misinterpretations and different perceptions of the message can be corrected immediately. Examples include face-to-face conversations, phone calls, and video calls.
- Asynchronous communication is where there is a delay between the sending and receiving of the message. Thus, feedback is not instantaneous—the sender may have a short or long delay before getting a response to their communication. Examples include letters, emails, and text messages.

Table 11.1 Different types of focus of communication

Focus	Description	Examples
One-to-one	Personal communication between two individuals	Conversation, personal email, personal letter, phone call
One-to-many (broadcasting)	One person sends a communication to many people (even a whole organization)	Bulk email, speech at a staff meeting, memo
Many-to-many	A communication to many people that doesn't come from one personal, identifiable source (e.g. it might come from the board or a marketing department)	Newsletter (although there may be individual items within this, e.g. an address from the chief executive officer)
Many-to-one	A group of people communicate to just one person	A project group might have a single email address and communicate their results collectively through this to one individual within the organization

Focus of communication

A final facet of communication is the focus of the message—whether is it directed to one person or is a more impersonal form of communication directed to many people, even the whole organization. Table 11.1 shows a number of different types of focus of communication that may take place in organizations.

Communication and miscommunication

Q Running case: misinterpretation

Chance's email is one of many in the inbox of fitness manager Carl Jones. With a busy workload to deal with, he only has time to glance at the email, picking up on the phrase 'Guests First.'

> **From:** fitnessmanager@junctionhotel.co.uk
> **To:** fitness_staff@junctionhotel.co.uk
>
> Guys,
>
> Quick message to pass on from Simon Chance—we now have to put guests first.
>
> Carl

Duty manager David Smith picks up on the email. He knows that there are some peak times when the gym is quite crowded and takes this to mean that hotel guests should have priority over external members. He conveys this instruction to his team of fitness staff.

→

> Come Monday evening at 6 pm, when the gym is usually busiest, the staff are asking pay-ing gym members to make way on the equipment for hotel guests. This leads to arguments between staff and customers and between customers. This continues throughout the week, and ten members cancel their memberships.
>
> Noticing this exodus, Chance makes his way to the fitness centre to confront the manager.
>
> 'What's the issue here? The members are leaving in their droves,' says a panicked Chance. 'I'm implementing just what you asked for—putting guests first. The members aren't happy being asked to make way for hotel guests, you know—what did you expect?' replies Smith.
>
> 'What?' asks a puzzled Chance, before realization dawns. 'No—that's not what I meant in the email. What I meant was … oh … tell you what, do you have five minutes for a quick chat?'

The four features of communication that we have examined all play a role in an overall model of the communication process. A simplified version of this model is shown in Figure 11.8.

Communication passes through the following stages, as illustrated in the model.

- The communication begins with the **source**, be this one or many people, who have a particu-lar intended meaning that they wish to communicate to one or many people.
- The source **encodes** the communication, i.e. forms a message using a verbal, bodily, written, or symbolic channel.
- The message is sent, using either formal or informal means of communication.
- The recipient (or recipients) receives and decodes the message, perceiving the message and creating their own particular meaning from it before providing feedback, either synchronous-ly or asynchronously.

Noise and miscommunication

Messages are open to misinterpretation. The intended meaning of the sender and the perceived meaning of the receiver can differ, sometimes vastly. Where there is more than one recipient, each recipient may have their own different perception of the meaning.

Figure 11.8 A model of the communication process (based on Shannon et al., 1949).

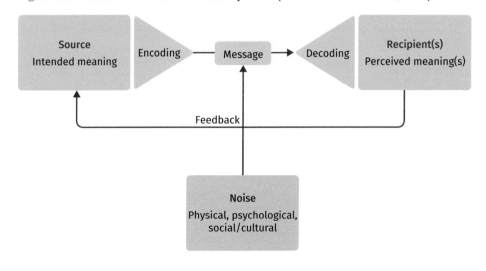

Table 11.2 Examples of noise in the communication process

Type of noise	Examples
Physical noise	Background noise getting in the way of a conversation Interference on a phone line Corruption of data in a computer file
Psychological noise	Semantics—people interpret words in different ways, attaching their own meanings to subjective ideas such as 'good', 'dedicated', etc. Perception—people may attach different degrees of importance to different parts of a message Attention—people may not give their full attention to a message, being distracted by other things
Social/cultural noise	People may speak a different language from the original communication, and mistranslations may occur Different cultures may interpret messages differently (see Chapter 16 for examples of cultural misunderstandings and differences) or people may be influenced by existing perceptual sets such as stereotypes

Anything which intervenes in the communication process and alters the original intended meaning of a message is termed 'noise' (Shannon et al., 1949), as shown in Figure 11.8. We think of noise in physical terms, perhaps such as someone shouting over a conversation so that it can't be heard; but, in the communication process, noise can take a number of forms. Examples of noise are shown in Table 11.2.

As Table 11.2 shows, perception is a key aspect of noise which might distort communication. Selective perception means that we might ignore or not pay as much attention to messages which do not interest us, or which are competing with other messages which might be louder and more immediate. Perceptual organization suggests that we will also frame messages in a particular way when we receive them. Our mindsets influence the meaning that we create from a message.

Noise exists as a barrier to communication and the effective transfer of meaning from the sender to the recipient. The model in this section shows noise intervening in a single communication. In the next section we see how the potential for noise increases as the number of stages of communication of a message increases.

 Have you ever had a situation where something you have said or a message that you have sent has been misinterpreted? What do you think was the cause of that misinterpretation?

Communication and power

Many of you have played the party game where a message is whispered from person to person, often with a wildly different message from the original appearing at the end of the line. Noise interferes as the message is passed from one person to the next, and this can happen at any stage along the way. Now think about the limited power that the first person in the line has to control the final message that appears at the end of the line. They can say the message very clearly to the next person along, but, after that, they have no control over what miscommunication and noise may happen further down the line.

A similar problem faces a manager trying to communicate a message across an organization—it has to pass from person to person and, at any stage, there is the potential for noise and miscommunication. Nichols (1962) suggested that, from top management at board level down to operators on a factory floor, only 20 per cent of the meaning of an original message remains. It would seem that management have very little **power** over how their communication is interpreted and acted upon.

 Visit the online resources and take a look at the extension material for Chapter 11 for an example of the power (or lack thereof) to communicate meaning in the lyrics of songs.

This lack of power over meaning and interpretation of communication is compared by Latour (1986) to a passing move in a rugby game. As players throw the ball to each other they each have to receive it and, with a new exertion of force, throw it to the next player. It is a fragile exercise which can fail if one player should drop the ball or throw it in the wrong direction. The power of the initial throw only lasts until the first person catches the ball—how it is then passed on is literally 'in the hands' of the next person along the line.

Latour uses this rugby metaphor to understand the movement of power in social settings such as organizations. We generally think of power being held by managers at the top of an organization and being exerted across the organization (see Chapter 14 for a discussion of this). Latour's rugby ball metaphor suggests that, in fact, the successful exercise of power is 'in the hands' of others. Each person who receives a managerial command, order, or similar communication of power will, in some way, have to perceive, decode, and interpret it in their own mind. Management can never be certain just how their acts of power, their words, commands, and deeds, will be interpreted and acted upon by individuals within the organization (Gergen, 1992).

Latour's rugby ball metaphor illustrates how noise can disrupt communication at many levels within an organization as messages are passed from person to person and department to department. The official, formal communications of the organization through which orders and power are carried out are open to being modified and disrupted in the day-to-day informal conversations and communications that take place throughout the organization.

In the next section, we see how such issues of miscommunication and noise affect an organization as it uses technology to communicate across the whole organization.

? Review questions

Describe	What are the four main features of communication in organizations?
Explain	How can noise alter the intended meaning of a message?
Analyse	In what ways do management lack the power to ensure consistent communication of a message across an organization?
Apply	What examples of noise and miscommunication can you identify in the running case throughout the chapter so far?

Technology and communication: the medium is the message

🔍 Running case: email exchange

From:	lindawilkinson@junctionhotel.co.uk
To:	reception_staff@junctionhotel.co.uk; porters@junctionhotel.co.uk
Subject:	Guests First

Hi everyone

I hope you are all well. We have a new initiative beginning this week called 'Guests First'. The aim is to make guests feel like they are the most important part of our business and, as reception area staff, you will be at the front line of this.

It's vital that we do this to maintain our reputation for customer service in these difficult times. So, can we all make that extra effort from now on to put the guests first!

Many thanks
Linda

From:	suesmith@junctionhotel.co.uk
To:	lindawilkinson@junctionhotel.co.uk
cc:	reception_staff@junctionhotel.co.uk; porters@junctionhotel.co.uk
Subject:	RE: Guests First

Dear Linda

I read with interest your email and I would be grateful if you could clarify what you mean by 'extra effort'. In particular, it implies that my effort in the job up until now has been insufficient—could you please point out the faults that you seem to think exist in my work.

Best wishes
Sue

From:	lindawilkinson@junctionhotel.co.uk
To:	suesmith@junctionhotel.co.uk
cc:	reception_staff@junctionhotel.co.uk; porters@junctionhotel.co.uk
Subject:	RE: RE: Guests First

Dear Sue

I wasn't implying that there's anything wrong with your work, but, in times like these, we all need to go that little bit further ... We really need to pull together in these difficult times rather than engaging in internecine discussions such as these.

Best
Linda

From:	suesmith@junctionhotel.co.uk
To:	lindawilkinson@junctionhotel.co.uk
cc:	reception_staff@junctionhotel.co.uk; porters@junctionhotel.co.uk
Subject:	RE: RE: RE: Guests First

Linda

I see—so now I'm the problem then, and I can't even raise a point without being branded a troublemaker. Ten years I've been here with no one saying a bad thing about my work—now it seems I don't put in enough effort and I'm a troublemaker!

Sue

From:	janedavies@junctionhotel.co.uk
To:	lindawilkinson@junctionhotel.co.uk
cc:	reception_staff@junctionhotel.co.uk; porters@junctionhotel.co.uk
Subject:	RE: RE: RE: RE: Guests First

Sue—come on, give Linda some slack. We need to try everything we can to keep afloat in this recession.

Jane

From:	bobjones@junctionhotel.co.uk
To:	janedavies@junctionhotel.co.uk
cc:	reception_staff@junctionhotel.co.uk; porters@junctionhotel.co.uk
Subject:	RE: RE: RE: RE: RE: Guests First

Could you all have this discussion in private and not use reply all—I'm fed up of seeing this nonsense in my inbox!

Thanks
Bob.

From:	gailwilliams@junctionhotel.co.uk
To:	bobjones@junctionhotel.co.uk
cc:	reception_staff@junctionhotel.co.uk; porters@junctionhotel.co.uk
Subject:	RE: RE: RE: RE: RE: RE: Guests First

Looks like a few people have gotten out of the wrong side of bed this morning:)

From:	suesmith@junctionhotel.co.uk
To:	gailwilliams@junctionhotel.co.uk
cc:	reception_staff@junctionhotel.co.uk; porters@junctionhotel.co.uk
Subject:	RE: RE: RE: RE: RE: RE: Guests First

OH SHUT UP. THIS ISN'T A JOKE

From:	lindawilkinson@junctionhotel.co.uk
To:	suesmith@junctionhotel.co.uk
cc:	reception_staff@junctionhotel.co.uk; porters@junctionhotel.co.uk
Subject:	RE: RE: RE: RE: RE: RE: RE: RE: Guests First

Look everyone—we need to calm down a bit. This doesn't help anything at all. Maybe we need to sit down and have a face-to-face meeting about this. Let's say my office at 10.30 am.

Thanks
Linda

Imagine you are a chief executive wanting to communicate an important message to all 1,000 members of your organization. How would you go about doing this? You could speak to each worker individually—but that would take a long time, especially if the message was complex. **Communication technology** or **media** might help the chief executive to communicate their message more efficiently, for example:

- a simple technology, a microphone, would allow the CEO to address all staff at once in one large auditorium;
- printing/photocopying technology would allow a letter to be sent to all employees conveying the message;
- even more efficiently, the message could be sent instantly as an email to all employees.

However, while each of these communications media allows the message to be delivered more efficiently (think of the difference in time between speaking to each employee individually, and composing and sending a mass email) this efficiency comes with a loss of **richness**, the amount and quality of information. Much of the information gained from the body language of a face-to-face conversation is lost.

How many types of communications technology can you think of? Which do you use in your daily life? Do you use different technologies for different tasks?

Research insight: what is technology?

Cooper, R. 1993. Technologies of representation. In: Ahonen, P. (ed.) *Tracing the semiotic boundaries of politics*. Mouton de Gruyter: Berlin, pp. 279–312.

We tend to think of technology in terms of the latest gadgets—smartphones, games consoles, etc.—or perhaps in terms of heavy machines. Cooper (1993) however, suggests a wider view of technology—it is any form of tool that turns a human weakness into an advantage. In other words, it facilitates human action, opening up new possibilities and potential.

Think of a communication tool such as a microphone. It is developed from the fact that the human voice is too weak to address a large crowd, but turns that weakness into an advantage whereby one speaker has the ability to communicate with many people at once. Technologies such as email allow a person to be able to communicate not only with many people, but also over a global geographical reach. Again, human potential is increased by technology.

Efficiency and richness: a trade-off

In recent years, email has come to dominate communications both within and outside organizations, replacing many forms of communication such as telephone calls and things that previously might have been written on paper (e.g. a memo).

The convenience of email can be seen by the fact that it allows global communication without the expense of telephone conversations, or the delay and expense of postage. It also means that, unlike a telephone conversation, the recipient does not have to be there physically—they can pick up emails as and when they log on to their computer network.

In this section we use email as an example to examine the trade-off that communications technology brings between efficiency and richness. Email certainly allows for efficient communication—a message can be sent to an entire workforce across the whole globe with just one click of a button. Using **social presence theory** and **media richness theory**, we examine the extent to which this is at the expense of the richness of the message and the amount of information that it can convey.

Social presence theory

Social presence theory is the degree of perceived immediacy of a person in a communication. What sense does a particular communications medium give of the person writing the message actually being there (physically present) in the room with you (Short et al., 1976; Rice, 1992)?

The most obvious form of social presence is a face-to-face conversation. As shown by Mehrabian's study, it is from this that important non-verbal aspects of communication, such as gestures and facial expressions, are gleaned. With an email, the sender is absent, and so the communication that comes from the perceptual stimuli provided by their physical presence—body language and tone of voice—is missing. In Mehrabian's analysis, this would leave just the words, which communicate a meagre 7 per cent of intended meaning.

 Real life case: the growth of emoji

Anyone who uses any form of mobile or online communication will be familiar with emoji, small pictograms which convey the meaning of an emotion (e.g. a smiling face), an object, an action (e.g. walking), or an idea. First developed in Japan in the late 1990s, the word emoji roughly translates from Japanese as 'pictograph' (Hern, 2015). In 2015, linguist Vyv Evans suggested that emoji was the fastest growing form of language in the UK, with 72 per cent of 18-to-25-year-olds finding it an easier way than words to express emotions in online communications (Lough, 2015). There is now a World Emoji Day where new emoji are released every year (BBC News, 2018).

For communication coach Robin Kermode (2015), emoji add to written words the body language and tone of voice that give meaning to face-to-face communication, telling us whether a sentence is serious, or ironic, or meant as a joke, for example. Without these pictorial clues, words can be open to misinterpretation—a picture of a smiley face clears up whether a sentence is intended as a joke or as a serious comment. For Kermode, 'The reason emojis have become the fastest growing new language is that they are merely a depiction of the body language signals that humans have been reading for centuries'.

Many of you will use particular tactics in emails which increase social presence and give more communications clues. **Emoticons**—facial expressions created out of punctuation marks, such as :) being used to denote a smiley face—are often added to emails or similar text-based communication methods, such as text messages and Twitter. Emoticons, which have developed into the more pictorial emoji described above, are a surrogate for the physical facial expression that would be seen if the person typing the email were actually present—they make up for some of the non-verbal meaning that has been lost (Lo, 2008).

The degree to which smiley faces should be used in professional workplace communication is debatable, but signatures on emails with links to web pages or that contain personal information are other examples of bringing social presence into this largely written form.

 To what extent do profiles on social media sites, such as Facebook, increase social presence by including photos and other informal aspects of the person's life?

Visit the online resources and take a look at the extension material for Chapter 11 for more analysis of emojis.

Media richness theory

The amount of social presence desirable in a particular communication depends on what is being communicated. For instance, think about the following items of information that might need to be communicated at different times within an organization:

- a single piece of data: a figure
- a summary of data, e.g. a table or a chart
- a fact
- an instruction or order
- an item of tacit knowledge about how to perform a particular task (cf. knowledge transfer in Chapter 10)
- an emotion or feeling ('I'm trying to communicate my feelings about this deal').

In some cases, basic facts are all that need to be communicated. In others, a richer, more personal form of communication that puts across information, such as a person's feelings and attitudes, is required. Daft and Lengel's (1986) theory of media richness recognizes two particular contingencies of information which might make different communications media more or less appropriate at different times.

- **Uncertainty** relates to an absence of information. This uncertainty can be reduced by providing basic facts and data. For example, a head of sales looking to produce a sales forecast would reduce uncertainty by reading an email with sales figures for the past year. The lack of gestures and facial expressions does not alter the value of information in this email for someone who simply needs to know the basic facts.

- **Equivocality** is the extent to which a communication is open to interpretation, in other words the degree to which it can be perceived differently by different people. It involves attitudes, feelings, and items of disagreement, something which can't be resolved by the provision of basic facts alone. For example, an email to workers which outlines complaints about customer service might need to be carefully worded. Workers could misinterpret it: a member of staff who is working well might think it applies to them, for example, and take unnecessary offence. A manager may decide that email is not the best way to communicate such a complex message that might affect people emotionally and might instead have a quiet word with a few individuals.

Can the emoticons and emoji described in the previous section be viewed in terms of reducing equivocality? While emoticons and emoji might bring richer meaning to text-based communication, are they appropriate for workplace and professional communication?

Daft and Lengel (1986) provide a continuum between rich and lean media (see Figure 11.9). Richer media are those that provide more of the personal, face-to-face qualities of communication, which might be needed in situations of equivocality where feelings and attitudes are being expressed, while leaner media provide more basic information and facts.

The amount of richness of a particular medium can be described in terms of the four features of communication explored in the previous section. Are verbal, bodily, or written channels used? Is the communication personal or addressed to many people? Is feedback immediate or is the communication asynchronous? From Figure 11.9 we see the different levels of richness in different media, with aspects of richness lost as the diagram moves down towards leaner, more efficient modes of communication.

- Face-to-face communication is the richest form of communication. It is personal, contains bodily gestures and vocal tone clues, and provides immediate feedback.

- A telephone conversation is personal and may give rich communication information and feedback from the tone of voice, but it lacks the bodily gestures of a face-to-face conversation.

- An email addressed to a specific person is an example of a written personal document which lacks the richness of communications forms such as a conversation face to face or by telephone. The sender has to formulate the words in such a way as to best convey their intention, but this might be difficult for the reader to interpret, for example whether a comment is made as a joke or seriously. Furthermore, there is no opportunity to clarify the meaning of a communication instantly through feedback, and thus misunderstandings, for which there is already more potential, may go uncorrected.

- Bulk emails, those sent to a group of recipients, are an example of a written, impersonal document. Richness is lost further as the communication moves from being personal to impersonal. Think about how many bulk or 'spam' emails you receive—do you even open all of them, let alone read the message contained within?

- Numerical documents, such as spreadsheets or a set of accounts, are the leanest and least rich medium, containing basic facts and information.

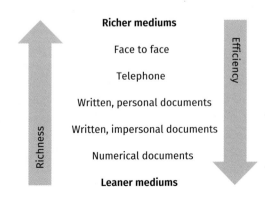

Figure 11.9 Media richness theory.
Source: Based on Daft and Lengel (1986).

Think about specific communications technologies that you use—email, SMS, social media. Where would you place them on the media richness continuum in Figure 11.9?

We can see in this model the trade-off between efficiency and richness of communication: for example, while a bulk email may be an efficient form of communication, it lacks richness—and some people may not even open and read the email. Conversely, while a face-to-face conversation may provide rich communication, useful in situations of an equivocal nature, it is time-consuming and inefficient if communication needs to be over a wide scale.

The importance of media richness theory is not necessarily to choose the richest medium for all communication, but to choose the medium appropriate for what is being communicated.

The medium is the message

 Real life case: Fired by text message

Stories regularly appear in the news about workers who, rather than being told face to face that they are to lose their jobs, have been fired more insensitively by text message.

- A digger driver in Devon, UK, caused £100,000 of damage when he went on a rampage after being sacked by text message (*Metro*, 2017).

- Chelsea football manager Antonio Conte fired striker Diego Costa by text, an action suggested to be one of the reasons for his own eventual dismissal (Johnson, 2018; Law, 2017).

- A restaurant in Sydney, Australia, was fined AUD 200,000 for firing a worker by text who had taken a day of sick leave after not being paid for four months (Patty, 2018).

Visit the online resources and take a look at the web links for Chapter 11 for more details about these cases.

407

In all of the cases of firing by text, the problem is not necessarily the sacking in itself, but the way that it was done, with an impersonal text message seen as being insensitive for such a potentially upsetting piece of news. In this respect, the context element of selective perception is important—communications media that are inappropriate for their context are more likely to meet a hostile perception. Furthermore, the choice of communication medium might in and of itself contribute to the message and how it is perceived, as Marshall McLuhan (1964) stated: 'The medium is the message'. Thus, a letter might seem too formal as a way to ask a friend out for a night out, when a text message might suffice. Likewise, an email might be too distant as a means to deliver bad news when a face-to-face conversation might communicate more sincerity and concern.

While face-to-face conversation might be the richest form of communication, it doesn't follow that it is the most appropriate in all cases. Think about getting driving directions—would you prefer someone to tell you every twist and turn of the journey face to face, or would you prefer to simply look at it on a map? The map might be a leaner form of communication—it is impersonal, with symbols, but it gets the message across concisely and efficiently.

Thus, on occasion, leaner forms of communication might be more appropriate for communicating information in organizations—it is simpler to see a summary of sales figures as a table than have somebody recite them face to face.

What do you think would be the most appropriate ways to communicate the following within an organization?

- Facts about a project
- Figures, such as accounts
- Instructions for repairing a piece of machinery
- Directions to the head office
- Feedback to members of a project team
- Praise to an individual who has secured a new contract
- Anger at a colleague who is stirring up trouble
- An idea for a new product
- A new culture

Research insight: communicating a culture

Gergen, K.J., and Whitney, D. 1996. Technologies of representation in the global corporation: Power and polyphony. In: Boje, D.M., Gephart, R.P., Jr, and Thatchenkery, T.J. (eds) *Postmodern management and organization theory*. Sage: Thousand Oaks, CA, pp. 331–57.

Gergen and Whitney's (1996) study of culture change in a recently merged multinational firm, Sloan Becker, highlights the relevance of media richness in communicating something as open to interpretation as an organizational culture.

In a bid to integrate the two newly-merged firms and their cultures, it was decided to implement a common set of principles or a common culture. This came under the slogan 'Simply Better', summing up the idea that workers should improve their 'performance' continually to reach the potential and promise within Sloan Becker. The new culture would be disseminated globally through a printed booklet.

However, as a relatively lean medium, lacking the richness of information that would come from the presence of the original authors, much of the culture was left open to the interpretation of the workers receiving and reading the booklet. Terms such as 'performance' are equivocal—they mean different things to different people; however, there was no opportunity for feedback for workers to ask about, and clarify, the meaning of terms and statements in the booklet.

The recipients were left to make their own interpretations of the culture, in discussion with familiar people around them. What emerged at Sloan Becker was not the one unified culture that management desired, but a whole patchwork of different cultures and meanings across the organization.

Gergen and Whitney's case highlights the problem of using a relatively lean medium, in this case printed text, to communicate richer, more equivocal ideas, such as culture and corporate values. The leaner medium cannot communicate every nuance of the culture, and it allows more possibility for noise to intervene in the communication process and for people's perceived meanings of the culture to be different to the original intended meaning. As with the lyrics of a song (see the extension material in the online resources), the original author lacks power over the interpretation that others will make—the meaning of the culture here is passed on by others and redirected in a manner similar to Latour's rugby ball metaphor.

The Fourth Industrial Revolution: a triumph for lean communication

So far in this chapter we have examined communication, and how technology is used as a medium to enhance the abilities of people to communicate in organizations. However, in Chapter 2 we saw how such technologies not only communicate information but in fact *create* information. Zuboff's (1988) concept of the **informated** organization suggests that more and more of what an organization actually does—its processes and the information that it holds—is stored as computerized data.

In Chapter 4 we saw than in the Fourth Industrial Revolution, this data becomes vast databanks of big data, to which algorithms are applied to control workers and organizational processes and, ultimately, to create yet more data.

So far, in examining communication, we have seen information largely in terms of communications such as words, gestures, and diagrams, etc. Leaner communications media gain efficiency at the expense of richness. However, it is worthy of note that it is the leanest possible form of data—numerical, digital data that boils down to binary zeroes and ones—which makes up the communication which take place in informated organizations and the cyber-physical systems of the Fourth Industrial Revolution.

As we saw in Chapters 2 and 3, this means that the command and control of workers in, for example, the gig economy, can be done entirely through data and algorithms—your phone becomes your boss. There is no human contact. Supervisory feedback can boil down to numerical ratings based on performance metrics. As we will see in Chapter 15, even nuanced ideas such as the quality of customer service can be represented by simple digital data.

So, on the one hand, the Fourth Industrial Revolution uses lean data to manage and control people efficiently and on a large scale. On the other hand, much of the meaning that is usually transferred in the rich data settings of face-to-face managerial control is lost.

? Review questions

Describe   What are the main features of media richness theory?

Explain   How do different communications media convey the social presence of the sender of the message?

Analyse   How is communication a trade-off between efficiency and richness?

Apply   How can the miscommunication in the email chain at Junction Hotel be analysed in terms of media richness and social presence theories?

Connecting case and theory

This chapter began by examining **perception** as a property of the individual, and indeed the chapter concludes the section of the book entitled 'Managing the individual'. As with the other chapters in the section, we see that individual traits and processes such as personality, motivation, and learning also highlight how we are all different as individuals. With perception, we all have different mindsets which lead us to perceive the same things in different ways.

However, while perception is a phenomenon of the individual, it also shows how we are linked as individuals to the wider world. An examination of perception demonstrates how we take sensory stimuli from the world around us, and selectively organize them to make sense and meaning of that world.

The links between the individual and the wider world are demonstrated further when we link perception with communication. Communication refers to how meaning is created among and between people and how this meaning can be changed and interpreted differently, with different people perceiving what is being communicated in different ways.

At the start of the chapter, Simon Chance sent out an email outlining his 'Guests First' initiative. Throughout the chapter we saw how other people interpreted this initiative, generally in ways not originally intended by Chance. From the point of view of perception, we saw how different people perceived the idea of 'Guests First' differently, taking a different meaning from the one intended by Chance. From the perspective of communication, we saw how the idea was miscommunicated as it passed from person to person. The processes are interlinked—communication involves some form of perception of the message, and this perception can later change the interpretation of the original meaning of the message.

We first saw this when the email reached Meg Mortimer, or more accurately it failed to reach her. Selective perception here explains how stimuli such as the ringing phone were brought to the foreground and the emails disappeared into the background such that she deleted them almost without actively perceiving their presence. David Hunter, on the other hand, deleted the email after making an instant judgement about the word 'Guests' in the header. This could be seen to follow some of the principles of perceptual organization: for example, the proximity principle is in evidence in that he sees the guests as a group apart from himself in his office, and he applied a similarity principle, viewing all guests in the same way. Overall, he showed a mindset which led to him forming stereotypes of guests being bad people that he does not wish to be around.

In both cases, the communication failed because neither Mortimer nor Hunter even read the original message. At the squash club we saw that Graham Effingham had read the email, but that the communication was distorted through the lens of gossip, or informal communication, with people adding their own stories and assumptions about Chance's private life to the formal communication of the email.

We have seen how technology acts as a double-edged sword in terms of communication. On the one hand, it amplifies the power of individuals to communicate—over long distances, for example, or to many people at once. At the same time, this technology takes away some of the richness of communication, a loss of meaning which leaves more room for individuals to perceive the message in their own way, making meanings which distort the original intention of the sender.

In the bar we saw how a lot of the meaning of communication can be lost when it is written in a textual form, such as an email, without the perceptual stimuli of the tone of voice and body language. Mehrabian's 55-38-7 ratio was much in evidence when John Vinter read the email in an exaggerated mocking style, his vocal and bodily expressions creating a more readily-perceived impression and meaning different from that intended by Chance.

When gym Manager David Smith received the email, we saw an example of noise distorting the message, in this case psychological noise, with Smith creating a different meaning of 'Guests First' from Chance's original intention. Again we could view this in terms of selective perception, this time from the point of view of context. In the context of the hotel, 'Guests' implies the only hotel guests; however, in the gym 'Guests' suggests a division between hotel guests and external members. The context thus directs the perception of 'Guests First' towards some form of choice about who to prioritize.

We could also use media richness theory to analyse the miscommunication between Chance and Smith. As we saw, the email is just text: it was missing the further perceptual stimuli of tone of voice and body language. Email is a leaner medium, in terms of media richness theory, than the richer face-to-face conversation that Chance suggested they have in order to clear up any confusion from the miscommunication.

The same can be said of the email exchange initiated by Linda Wilkinson, which rapidly spiraled out of control. We saw that the email lacked the immediate feedback of face-to-face conversation, with staff unable to clarify what was meant by 'extra effort'. Furthermore, without a face-to-face presence and tone of voice, staff easily jumped to assumptions, making their own perceptions of words and phrases as being some form of admonishment. Again, the solution to the miscommunication was to convene a face-to-face meeting. Social presence theory here would say that the decontextualized text of the short emails lacked the perceptual stimuli that come from being in the actual presence of the person speaking.

Overall, very few people, if any, seemed to receive and perceive the 'Guests First' message in the way that Chance originally intended. Once Chance released the communication, he seems to have had little power over how people actually perceived it, much like the rugby ball being passed on as discussed by Latour.

411

Further reading

Brewer, E., and Westerman, J. 2017. *Organizational communication: Today's professional life in context*. Oxford University Press: Oxford.

A more in-depth introduction to organizational communication.

Rice, R.E. 1992. Task analyzability, use of new media, and effectiveness: A multi-site exploration of media richness. *Organization Science* 3 (4): 475–500.

Introduces and critiques social presence theory and media richness theory.

Jensen, U.T., Moynihan, D.P., and Houlberg Salomonsen, H. 2018. Communicating the vision: How face-to-face dialogue facilitates transformational leadership. *Public Administration Review* 78 (3): 350–61.

Applies media richness theory to theories of leadership.

Wagemans, J., Elder, J.H., Kubovy, M., Palmer, S.E., Peterson, M.A., Singh, M., and von der Heydt, R. 2012. A century of Gestalt psychology in visual perception: I. Perceptual grouping and figure–ground organization. *Psychological Bulletin* 138 (6): 1172.

A detailed overview of the Gestalt principles of perceptual organization.

References

Abadi, M. 2017. For an inside look at Facebook, Amazon, and Apple, scrutinize something most people overlook: the words used in their job postings. *Business Insider*, 14 December. Available at: http://uk.businessinsider.com/words-companies-use-in-job-listings-reveal-company-culture-2017-12

BBC News. 2018. Apple unveils its latest emojis on World Emoji Day, 17 July. Available at: https://www.bbc.co.uk/news/world-44856509

Boden, D. 1994. *The business of talk: Organizations in action*. Polity Press: London, Cambridge, MA.

Broekstra, G. 1998. An organization is a conversation. In: Grant, D., Keenoy, T., and Oswick, C. (eds) *Discourse and Organization*. Sage: London, pp. 152–76.

Clark, P. 2018. What are we meant to wear to work? *Financial Times*, 1 April. Available at: https://www.ft.com/content/6e593a04-329c-11e8-b5bf-23cb17fd1498

Cooper, R. 1993. Technologies of representation. In: Ahonen, P. (ed.) *Tracing the semiotic boundaries of politics*. Mouton de Gruyter: Berlin, pp. 279–312.

Czarniawska, B., and Sevón, G. 2018. Gendered references in organization studies. *Qualitative Research in Organizations and Management* 13 (2): 196–200.

Daft, R.L., and Lengel, R.H. 1986. Organizational information requirements, media richness and structural design. *Management Science* 32 (5): 554–71.

Deleuze, G., and Guattari, F. 1987. *A thousand plateaus: Capitalism and schizophrenia*. University of Minnesota Press: Minneapolis.

Devine, L. 2018. How the language used in job adverts discourages women from applying. *Evening Standard*, 13 June. Available at: https://www.standard.co.uk/lifestyle/job-adverts-women-language-gender-bias-a3861811.html

Ducharme, J. 2018. An audiologist explains why you hear 'Yanny' or 'Laurel'—or both. *Time Magazine*, 16 May. Available at: http://time.com/5279069/yanny-laurel-explanation/

Dweck, C.S. 2006. *Mindset: The new psychology of success*. Random House: New York.

Fan, Z., Costas, J., and Grey, C. 2017. Secrecy and communication: Towards a research agenda. *Corporate Communications* 22 (4): 562–6.

Gergen, K.J. 1992. Organization theory in the postmodern era. In: Reed, M., and Hughes, M.D. (eds) *Rethinking organisation: New directions in organization theory and analysis*. Sage: London, pp. 207–26.

Gergen, K., and Whitney, D. 1996. Technologies of representation in the global corporation: Power and polyphony. In: Boje, R., Gephart, R., Jr, and Thatchenkery, T. (eds) *Postmodern management and organization theory*. Sage: London, pp. 331–57.

Gilbreth, L.M. 1914. *The psychology of management: The function of the mind in determining, teaching and installing methods of least waste*. Sturgis & Walton: New York.

Henry, J. 2001. *Creativity and perception in management*. Sage: London.

Hern, A. 2015. Don't know the difference between emoji and emoticons? Let me explain. *The Guardian*, 6 February.

Johnson, S. 2018. Antonio Conte to sue Chelsea: Sacked manager will take legal action after dismissal. *Evening Standard*, 20 July. Available at: https://www.standard.co.uk/sport/football/antonio-conte-to-sue-chelsea-sacked-manager-will-take-legal-action-after-dismissal-a3892516.html

Kermode, R. 2015. Emoji invasion: The end of language as we know it. *The Guardian*, 25 June.

Kurland, N.B., and Pelled, L.H. 2000. Passing the word: Toward a model of gossip and power in the workplace. *Academy of Management Review* 25 (2): 428–38.

Latour, B. 1986. The powers of association. *Psychological Review* 32: 264–80.

Law, M. 2017. Antonio Conte's decision to dump Diego Costa by text threatens to cost Chelsea millions. *Daily Telegraph*, 8 June. Available at: https://www.telegraph.co.uk/football/2017/06/08/antonio-contes-decision-dump-diego-costa-text-threatens-cost/

Lawley, S. and Caven, V. 2019. Lillian Moller Gilbreth. In: McMurray, R., and Pullen, A. (eds) *Routledge focus on women writers in organization studies: Beyond rationality in organization and management.* Routledge: London.

Lo, S.K. 2008. The nonverbal communication functions of emoticons in computer-mediated communication. *CyberPsychology and Behavior* 11 (5): 595–7.

Lough, K. 2015. Emoji is the fastest growing new language ever—but the over 40s feel left behind. *Evening Standard*, 19 May.

McLuhan, M. 1964. *Understanding media: The extensions of man.* McGraw-Hill: New York.

Mehrabian, A. 1971. *Silent messages.* Wadsworth Pub. Co.: Belmont, CA.

Metro. 2017. Digger driver goes on £100,000 rampage after he is sacked by text message, 23 May. Available at: https://metro.co.uk/2017/05/23/digger-driver-goes-on-100000-rampage-after-he-is-sacked-by-text-message-6653937/

Nichols, R.G. 1962. Listening is good business. *Human Resource Management* 1 (2): 1–10.

Noon, M., and Delbridge, R. 1993. News from behind my hand: Gossip in organizations. *Organization Studies* 14 (1): 23–36.

Patty, A. 2018. Worker sacked by text message after taking one day of sick leave. *Sydney Morning Herald*, 27 March. Available at: https://www.smh.com.au/business/workplace/worker-sacked-by-text-message-after-taking-one-day-of-sick-leave-20180327-p4z6go.html

Rice, R.E. 1992. Task analyzability, use of new media, and effectiveness: A multi-site exploration of media richness. *Organization Science* 3 (4): 475–500.

Rogers, A. 2015. The science of why no-one agrees on the color of this dress. *Wired*, 26 February. Available at: https://www.wired.com/2015/02/science-one-agrees-color-dress/

Rubin, E. 1915. *Synsoplevede Figurer: Studier i psykologisk Analyse.* Gyldendalske Boghandel: Copenhagen.

Sample, I. 2015. #TheDress: Have researchers solved the mystery of its colour? *The Guardian*, 14 May. Available at: https://www.theguardian.com/science/2015/may/14/thedress-have-researchers-solved-the-mystery-of-its-colour

Shannon, C.E., Weaver, W., and Blahut, R.E. 1949. *The mathematical theory of communication*, vol. 117. University of Illinois Press: Urbana.

Short, J., Williams, E., and Christie, B. 1976. *The social psychology of telecommunications.* Wiley: London, New York.

Silverberg, D. 2018. Why do some job adverts put women off applying? *BBC News*, 12 June Available at: https://www.bbc.co.uk/news/business-44399028

Stone, M. 2017. This is the biggest mistake you can make when dressing 'business casual'. *The Independent*, 27 March. Available at: https://www.independent.co.uk/life-style/fashion/this-is-the-biggest-mistake-you-can-make-when-dressing-business-casual-a7652646.html

Trollope, J. 2017. Opinion: City women showed me how the office uniform has changed. *Financial Times*, 7 March. Available at: https://www.ft.com/content/de118e60-fce1-11e6-96f8-3700c5664d30

Wertheimer, M. 1938. Laws of organization in perceptual forms. In: Ellis, W. (ed.) *A source book of Gestalt psychology.* Routledge & Kegan Paul: London, pp. 71–88.

Wilson, F. 2003. *Organizational behaviour and gender.* Ashgate: Aldershot.

Zuboff, S. 1988. *In the age of the smart machine: The future of work and power.* Heinemann Professional: Oxford.

413

PART 4

Managing the organization

CHAPTER 12
Changing the organization
Planning and emergence

Chapter overview and learning outcomes

By the end of this chapter you should be able to:

- describe a range of triggers for change and factors that resist against change

- explain how change can be messy, causing conflict and resistance

- describe three approaches to the management of change: naïve, planned, and emergent approaches

- analyse the different perspectives that these three approaches give of the nature of an organization and how it might be changed

Key theorists	
Kurt Lewin	Psychologist whose work on group dynamics has been applied to many areas of planned change, including force-field analysis, the three-step model of change, and organization development
Sara Ahmed	Has written about the differences between official diversity policy and bringing about change within the depths of an organization
Ralph Stacey	Has applied chaos and complexity theories to organizational change
Rosabeth Moss Kanter	Has written prolifically about change management, focusing on the attributes of companies that have undergone successful change programmes
Bernard Burnes	Has analysed the work of Lewin and advocates its relevance to contemporary organizational change
Thomas Cummings and Christopher Worley	Have outlined the wide variety of change management techniques which are used in organizational settings

Key terms	
Naïve approach to change	An approach to change which sees the organization in simplistic terms, as if it were a set of building blocks which can be rearranged easily
Planned approach to change	An approach which sees change as planned over a long-term series of steps; pays attention to human and social aspects of change, which are seen as 'hidden aspects' below the surface, as if the organization were an iceberg
Emergent approach to change	An approach to change which sees the organization as being like a river, in constant flow, and suggests that in such an environment change emerges rather than being planned in advance
Force-field analysis	A technique whereby triggers for, and resistance against, change are plotted on a diagram in order to identify areas on which to focus a change-management programme
Three-step model	A model of change based on three stages of unfreezing, movement, and freezing
Complexity theory	An emergent approach to organizational change, suggesting that small changes can have unpredictable and potentially limitless consequences

Introduction

Running case: successful change at 'Coral Reef?'

Six months after taking over at the fitness centre, manager Carl Jones is sipping champagne with the hotel's management team in the boardroom. The toast is to the success of the fitness centre. Jones had been brought in as a 'new broom' to turn around the ailing fortunes of the fitness centre. Six months on, the results speak for themselves.

- The centre has been refurbished and rebranded as 'Coral Reef', projecting an image and ambience of a warm, tropical beach environment.

- Turnover has trebled, and the fitness centre is beginning to make profits and a financial contribution to the hotel.

- The percentage of hotel guests using the centre has doubled from 20 per cent to 40 per cent.

→

- Full-time membership of the club, from people living locally, has doubled.

- A new range of beauty and health services is offered.

- Many more female guests are using the centre, where previously the clientele was 95 per cent male.

These achievements, especially the profit figures, are seen as outstanding by Simon Chance. Leading the toast to Jones, he praises his 'authoritative, decisive, and, ultimately, successful programme of change'.

We all encounter change in our lives, whether it is a major decision—to move house or change jobs, for example—or something as minor as a change of hairstyle. Change might be forced upon us by particular circumstances or something that we do of our own volition.

In organizations, **change management** is any form of effort or initiative undertaken to alter a particular aspect of the organization. This might be to improve the current situation of the organization or, as we have seen with recent economic and political events, to respond to circumstances that necessitate some form of change for the survival of the organization.

We begin the chapter by seeing how people have different perspectives on change. On the one hand, change might be seen by managers as a reasonable action to take in response to certain triggers or pressures—moving to larger premises, for example, if the current premises are crowded. On the other hand, change can cause anxiety, fear, and upset among the workforce that it affects—the new premises might necessitate a longer commute for the workforce, even resulting in some having to give up their jobs. Rather than being a smooth process which runs exactly as managers desire, change can be messy and can meet with conflict and resistance.

We present three broad approaches which examine the implementation of change against the backdrop of such conflicting perspectives. These approaches are derived from three particular metaphors or ways of seeing the organization, which we suggest offer different insights into the subject.

- Firstly, we examine a **naïve approach to change** which stems from viewing the organization in simplistic terms, as a set of building blocks. This approach, where managers can change the organization by rearranging elements of it at will, is one that we suggest is misguided and misses out on many important aspects of the organization within the change process.

- Secondly, we suggest that viewing the organization as an iceberg shows its *hidden depths* which affect the implementation of change. These hidden depths are the human and social aspects of the organization, within which resistance and anxiety can develop. The **planned approach to change** suggests that, using knowledge from behavioural psychology, change can be implemented in a set of steps using techniques which overcome that resistance and bring about attitude change.

- Finally, an **emergent approach to change** sees the organization as a river, constantly in flow. The organization is never still for long enough for change to be a planned process; change is what emerges in the course of events.

The three approaches take us from managers being in absolute control *of* change, to managers being controlled *by* change, having to react to events as they happen.

Conflicting perspectives of change: triggers and resistance

> 🔍 **Running case:** 'Coral Grief'
>
> The boardroom celebrations do not extend to the Coral Reef fitness centre. The long-standing staff have seen their jobs and workplace change out of all recognition in the past six months, and this has made them unhappy.
>
> Egged on by his colleagues, one of the trainers walks up to the grinning photograph in the fitness centre entrance, underneath which reads 'Carl Jones, Fitness Centre Manager.' He draws on a moustache and spectacles; then, applying his marker pen to the fitness centre entrance sign, 'Coral Reef' is rechristened as 'Coral Grief'.
>
> Later, with the staff having long left the building, Meg Mortimer leaves the party to check that the fitness suite is locked up. Noticing the doctored photograph and sign she smiles to herself. Of course, she cleans it up before it can be discovered, but after the six months she's had coping with the fallout from Jones's changes, she isn't going to pursue the culprits any further.

When change takes place, it can be a messy process. People may have conflicting views and opinions of the change, perceiving the reasons for the change differently and having different ways of framing and making sense of the change process (Helms-Mills, 2003). What might seem like a perfectly rational and necessary change to a senior manager may upset other workers who are happy as they are and do not see that need, or the change process may leave them anxious about their job security or working conditions.

King (2001) noticed this in a study of change in a financial services organization, where a building society was adopting a more risk-taking, sales-driven culture. When asked to draw pictures of their attitudes to the change, managers drew optimistic pictures of bridges leading to sunnier destinations. Conversely, the staff drew pictures of themselves swamped by paperwork, with managers depicted as Nazis. Clearly there were conflicting opinions of the change.

 Visit the online resources and take a look at the extension material for Chapter 12 for more about this financial services case.

In this section we see change as a process that takes place amidst conflicting perspectives across the organization. On the one hand, there are a number of **triggers** which provide an impetus for managers to make a change. On the other hand, reaction to that change might take the form of different types of **resistance**.

Triggers for change

> 🔍 **Running case:** flashback—embarking on change
>
> Six months before the boardroom celebrations, Carl Jones had started his first day as the new fitness centre director. His brief: the centre was a loss-maker—it needed not only to hold its own, but to start making money for the hotel. Jones saw two main areas of potential for income growth.
>
> 1. External memberships—Junction Hotel offered fitness centre membership to non-residents within the local population; however, take-up was low. The fitness industry was highly
>
> →

competitive and dominated by a number of large-scale branded chains. Junction Hotel needed its own, smaller-scale gym to trade on its more personal atmosphere, while matching the offerings of its larger competitors.

2. Income from hotel guests—hotel guests could use the gym facilities for free and Jones was not allowed to change this. However, he thought that the fitness centre could provide paid extras for the guests—classes, beauty treatments, etc. Indeed, the fitness centre could become a reason for people to stay at the hotel per se, with spa weekend packages being offered.

Jones had started by listing the current features of the gym.

- The fitness centre had no separate brand identity of its own—it was not marketed within the hotel nor externally to the local population.

- The décor was somewhat basic (cold, plain walls); the gym had basic equipment (none of the electronic machinery found in competitors' gyms); showers were provided, but no sauna or spa facilities, as found in competitors' gyms.

- Opening hours: the fitness centre was open from 7 am until 7 pm, but competitors were open earlier and later.

- There was a reception desk at the entrance, but it was largely unstaffed, and extras, such as towels, were not provided; staff would be on hand to give advice if asked, although, in practice, this was given mainly to a number of regular members who had devised workout programmes with the staff.

- Unlike competitors, the gym offered no exercise classes or lessons. There were two treatment rooms—some of the staff had physiotherapy qualifications and would provide treatments, charging separately for this and pocketing the money themselves. For much of the time, the treatment rooms lay unused—with one of them even being used as an informal staff room.

- The five fitness centre staff worked as a team, all working a nine-to-five shift, Monday to Saturday, with the centre unstaffed at other times.

- Work tasks were arranged informally. Tasks included the maintenance and cleaning of gym equipment, pool life-guarding duties, general monitoring of the gym floor and the safety of users, and checking membership cards when people entered—this was the closest there was to any form of reception duties. All staff had a sports science qualification, which they were proud of. No staff uniforms were worn.

- The basic nature of the gym floor gave it a 'spit and sawdust' feel. Regular members tended to be male and heavily into weight training. Casual users, such as hotel guests, and people considering gym membership, said that they found the atmosphere to be intimidating and overwhelmingly macho. The staff found no problem with the culture and enjoyed working with the regular members. The fewer new members the better, otherwise it might disrupt the way that things were run.

Jones had started to think of what changes he could make to turn around the fitness centre. He was working within two financial parameters.

1. There was a healthy budget for investment—equipment, building works, etc. Whatever needed to be done, should be done.

421

2. While the investment budget was plentiful, Jones had to keep increases in running costs to a minimum. Day to day, the fitness centre had to be making a profit. In particular, there was little room to increase staff costs.

 What changes would you make in Carl Jones's position?

Triggers for change are forces which give an impetus for a change to occur, whether they are external triggers from outside the organization, or internal triggers from within. Potentially, the number of triggers for change in an organization is limitless.

Senior and Swailes (2016) suggest that external triggers for change can be identified using the PEST (political, economic, socio-cultural, and technological) model, introduced in Chapter 2, to think more broadly about the sectors of the organization's external environment from which these triggers might originate (Figure 12.1).

Some, or indeed all, of these sectors of the environment may be acting on an organization at any one time. For example, in UK universities, triggers from all four sectors of the external environment have, perhaps, pushed universities towards a more commercial and student-focused way of operating, and away from more traditional, academic 'ivory tower' cultures (Figure 12.2).

The impetus for change can also come from internal triggers—a reorganization or restructuring, for example, may come from a recognition of problems within the organization itself, such as poor communication or coordination between departments. Based on Senior and Swailes (2016: 21), we suggest a number of potential internal triggers to change.

- New senior staff may bring in their own ideas and vision for how the organization should be run—a new broom sweeps clean.

- Aspects of the organization's current performance (e.g. sales, employee morale) may give cause for concern.

- Unions within the organization may bring their own pressure and action for changes.

- The politics and power of particular groups, individuals, and coalitions within an organization, including the vision of management (see Chapter 14), may be a force towards change.

Figure 12.1 The PEST model and external triggers for change.

Political	Economic
• Policies and laws made at an international, national, or local level	• Economic conditions, e.g. growth, competition, interest rates, unemployment levels

Organization

Social	Technological
• Social attitudes and values, e.g. towards the environment, healthy eating, equality	• Technology in other organizations giving a competetive advantage for new technologies

Figure 12.2 Aspects of the external environment acting as triggers for change in UK universities.

Political	Economic
• Increase in tuition fees may reduce demand for university places and intensify competition between universities	• Recession and increased unemployment may increase demand for university places

University

Social	Technological
• Greater sense of consumer rights among student body	• Online learning and access to library materials

- Changes may be required as an organization grows in size: for instance, new premises to cope with increased capacity.

- A redesign of technology, jobs, or even the physical layout of the organization may bring with it a need for further changes.

Visit the online resources and take a look at the extension material for Chapter 12 for further examples of potential internal triggers to change.

Resistance to change

While triggers for change may exist, change is often resisted strongly by individuals, by groups of individuals, or, indeed, by organizational forces as a whole.

Change can arouse very strong and powerful human emotions and feelings, which are displayed as **resistance to change**. Based on Drafke (2009: 431–7), we can set out some examples of why people resist change.

- Generally, people do not like change—they are comfortable with their everyday routine and dislike any disruption to this.

- People worry about job security or pay issues, i.e. they perceive that they will lose out in some way as a result of the change.

- Change may disrupt social and informal ties, e.g. being moved from an office with people whose company they enjoy to one where they dislike the people.

- People may not recognize or understand the need for the change which is being proposed and which may have a considerable effect upon them.

- The change may go against the values held by individuals, e.g. a clash of professional and commercial values.

Taking all of the points mentioned, change can create anxiety when people are unsure of what is about to happen.

Visit the online resources and take a look at the extension material for Chapter 12 to see further reasons why people resist change.

Resistance to change may also occur at an organization-wide level, where organizational factors cause **inertia**, a tendency to resist change. In this chapter we will see that groups and cultures can cause resistance within the organization (the organization as an iceberg), as can the systemic nature of organizations that causes unpredictable knock-on effects (the organization as a river).

At a more practical level, the organization may also be shackled against undergoing a particular change, for example owing to contractual obligations or fixed investments. Furthermore, an organization may simply lack the capability to change. This may be because of a lack of finance or other resources for the change, a lack of space or equipment, or a lack of capability or skills within the organization's workforce (Senior and Fleming, 2006: 286).

Force-field analysis

The multitude of triggers and resisting factors show that there are a number of different factors influencing any change scenario. The whole situation in any one organization can become very complicated to understand. **Force-field analysis** is a technique which provides a snapshot of the factors at work in a change situation. The triggers and resisting factors are shown on a diagram (Figure 12.3) as arrows converging on one point—the current position. At this point the organization is in a 'quasi-stationary equilibrium'. To move to a desired situation, i.e. to change, the organization needs to strengthen the triggers to change and weaken the resisting forces.

Force-field analysis derives from the psychology of Kurt Lewin. In Chapter 6 we saw how Lewin analysed the influence of group dynamics, or peer pressure, upon individual behaviour. For Lewin (1943), group dynamics is one of many forces in an individual's **life space**: the combination of factors that influence their behaviour. While consisting mainly of psychological forces as perceived by the individual, this life space may also contain factors from the physical and social world that a person encounters. Such forces can be plotted on a force-field analysis diagram to help an individual to understand and then change their behaviour (Burnes and Cooke, 2013).

Take, for example, an individual who wishes to give up smoking. A similar diagram can be drawn (Figure 12.4) which shows the triggers pushing the individual towards that change (e.g. family pressure, health concerns, the cost, the unpleasant nature of smoking) pitted against forces resistant to giving up smoking (e.g. its addictive nature, peer pressure in social situations, stress in work and life in general).

Figure 12.3 Force-field analysis.

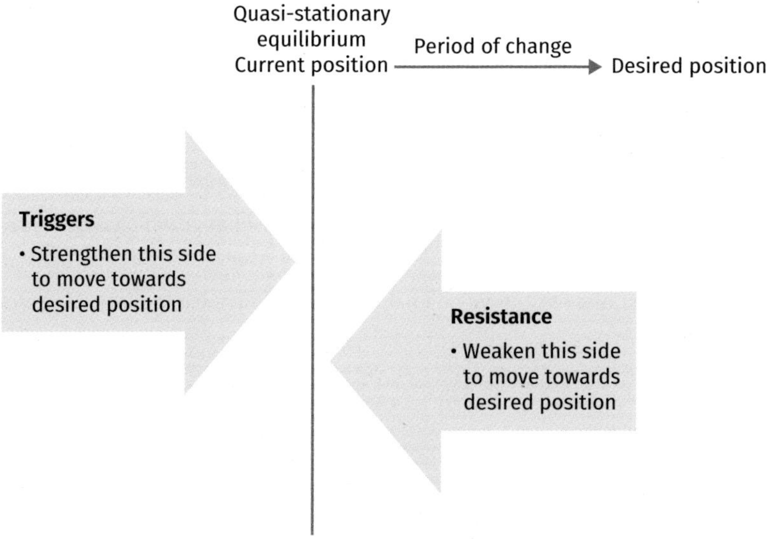

Quasi-stationary equilibrium
Current position —— Period of change ——→ Desired position

Triggers
• Strengthen this side to move towards desired position

Resistance
• Weaken this side to move towards desired position

Figure 12.4 Force-field analysis for an individual giving up smoking.

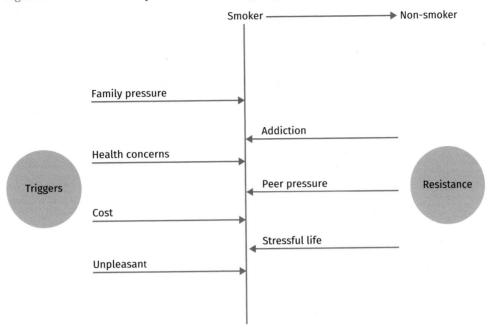

There are more triggers than there are resisting factors, so will the change happen inevitably? Possibly not, as the addictive nature of smoking is a major factor and a considerable weight in preventing the change to being a non-smoker. Another aspect of force-field analysis is that different forces can be given different strengths—as in Figure 12.5—by showing the different arrows with different weights.

The change to being a non-smoker might come about by attention to reducing the resisting factors, for example by avoiding socializing with the people who smoke or by taking some form of treatment for the nicotine addiction. Viewing this situation from the point of view of a government wanting to implement a national programme to stop people from smoking, they might also pay attention to strengthening some of the triggers—increasing the cost of cigarettes, for example, or placing pictures of diseased lungs on cigarette packets to prompt health concerns (compare these tactics with behaviour modification as discussed in Chapter 10).

How might the more recent development of vaping appear as a factor on the smoking force-field analysis diagram?

Although Lewin derived force-field analysis from his work in individual psychology and behaviour, he also used it as a basis for understanding and changing group behaviours (Burnes and Cooke, 2013), and it has since been adapted on a wider scale as a means of understanding organizational and even social situations of potential, or desired, change. In that 'any event is the resultant of a multitude of factors' (Lewin, 1943: 293), the value of the force-field analysis diagram is that it provides a snapshot of the conflicting factors and perspectives in a change situation, and suggests areas where the implementation of a change management process might focus.

Visit the online resources and take a look at the extension material for Chapter 12 for further examples of force-field analysis diagrams.

Figure 12.5 Weighted forces in a force-field analysis diagram.

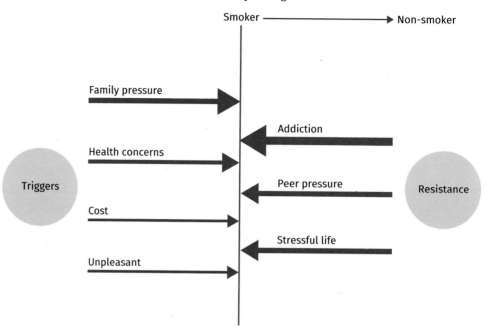

? Review questions

Describe What is meant by triggers for change and resistance against change?

Explain How does a force-field analysis diagram plot out the forces at work in a change situation?

Apply Using the information in Figures 12.4 and 12.5, what actions might you take when designing a programme to persuade people to stop smoking?

Apply Using the information about the change in the fitness centre, draw a similar force-field analysis diagram for the situation facing Carl Jones (see the online resources for a suggested answer).

Types of change and the nature of the organization

Q Running case: Jones's action plan

Fitness centre action plan

1. Identity and marketing
   - rebrand as Coral Reef—extensive marketing campaign to accompany this

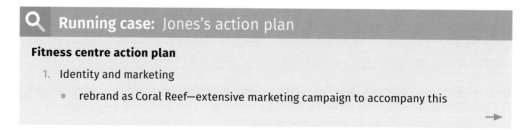

2. Decor and equipment
   - decor in coral reef style—redesign pool area with tropical island theme and develop part of changing area into health spa
   - redecorate gym and replace equipment—I suggest electronic card-controlled equipment and the card can double up as the entrance key at reception
   - build extension to create a studio for classes

3. Customer service
   - extend opening: 6 am to 11 pm daily, with centre, including reception desk, staffed at all times; towels to be provided at the reception desk, and customers greeted and handed towel on arrival
   - staff to maintain presence on the gym floor and pool for safety purposes, but should also welcome and encourage guests

4. Classes and treatments
   - provide beauty and health treatments in the treatment rooms
   - no recruitment allowed, so slots within the treatment rooms to be rented to local practitioners—hairdressers, beauticians, etc.
   - classes, e.g. pilates in the new studio; pool to offer swimming lessons and aqua aerobics—existing staff to do this, but bring in local expertise on a freelance basis as and when needed

5. Staff
   - expected to work flexibly within the 6 am to 11 pm working day, including weekends, according to a rota; staff to always present an upbeat, friendly image
   - will promote the paid treatments and classes—some sort of bonus incentive for this
   - one qualified member of staff should be on duty at all times; as this will stretch existing staff across the new opening hours, employ local students to work alongside qualified staff as and when needed
   - Staff to work as a team and also to mentor new temporary staff

6. Culture and atmosphere
   - *must* change from 'spit and sawdust' to 'upmarket, tropical luxury'—changes to decor will help
   - staff to get new uniforms; they are expected to be the embodiment of this culture—motivating people to exercise but, at the same time, creating a relaxing atmosphere
   - culture *must* be less aggressively masculine and less intimidating to potential members and hotel guests

427

When we speak about 'change' we could be speaking about a whole variety of activities where something is done differently—from a small change in one worker's rota, to a department relocating to a different office, to an overall corporate rebranding. All are examples of change in an organization. Cummings and Worley (2015) suggest four main categories of change management, focusing on different aspects of organizational life.

- *Strategic change interventions* are major shifts in the overall focus and direction of the organization. Areas of focus might be corporate strategy, products and services offered, culture change, rebranding, or organizational learning.

- *Technostructural interventions* look at areas of technology and the organization's structure. Examples include the design and division of work, downsizing, bringing in new technology, and redesigning the organization's bureaucratic structure.

- *Human process interventions* are concerned with human social issues in the organization—how people relate to each other, communication, decision making, and leadership. They are based around group dynamics and team-building activities.

- *Human resource management interventions* are focused on people at a more individual level. Examples include performance management, recruitment, appraisal, reward management, motivation, and managing diversity.

This list touches on many topics covered in other chapters in this book, and it shows that the focus of change may be wide and far-reaching; indeed, change is potentially infinite in its scope.

Further categorization can be made in terms of the scale of change from small to large: from fine-tuning to corporate transformation (Senior and Swailes, 2016: 36–7). Senior and Swailes also suggest that the degree of change that an organization faces may be predictable or a complete surprise, depending on the turbulence of the environment (see Chapter 2) that the organization faces.

Taking into account the variety of both types and scale of change, and the differences in the environmental turbulence encountered by organizations, change management theories tend to divide into two broad approaches: a *planned approach*, which sees change managed through a series of steps from one point to another (as with force-field analysis), and an *emergent approach*, which sees change as more unpredictable, likely to be carried along by the flow of events within the organization and unforeseen influences from the environment.

Change and the nature of organization

What is an organization? This might seem like an obvious question to ask, but we suggest that to understand the nature of change and its implementation, a step back needs to be taken to see the nature of what is actually being changed—the organization itself. Whether change can be planned or whether change is emergent, for example, depends very much on the nature of the organization itself.

In this section we introduce three **metaphors** which provide three different ways of answering the question 'what is an organization?' These metaphors portray the organization as either a set of building blocks, an iceberg, or a river (see Table 12.1).

Study skills: the use of metaphors

Metaphors are ways of visualizing or imagining the world around us in order to gain new insights. For example, Morgan (2006) constructs his whole book *Images of organization* around different metaphors to understand different aspects of organizational life and theory. One chapter depicts 'organizations as machines' as a means of visualizing the rational, Taylorist organization (which we examine in Chapter 2), while 'organizations as brains' is the metaphor used to envisage learning organizations (which we examine in Chapter 10).

The three metaphors used in this chapter—building blocks, iceberg, and river—are different ways in which we can view the nature of what an organization is, which lead to different ways of approaching the change process.

The metaphors are not necessarily mutually exclusive—there is no need to choose one as being better or more truthful than the other two. Instead, each uncovers different aspects of

→

an organization's nature—each tells us something different and new about what an organization is. They provide a set of lenses to view and understand the nature of an organization, each of which may inform our knowledge about implementing change in an organization in different ways.

Table 12.1 Metaphors of change and the nature of organizations

Metaphor	Description	Related approach to change
The organization as a set of building blocks	The organization has a solid *structure* that management have complete *power* to control and change at will. Managing change is as easy as rearranging a set of children's building blocks. This takes a very mechanical view of how we gain *knowledge* of the organization, and there is little account taken of human elements. *Resistance* to change and to management power is seen as being alien to the organization.	Naïve approach to change
The organization as an iceberg	Like an iceberg, the *structure* of the organization has hidden depths lurking beneath the surface—the human and social aspects of the organization. *Knowledge* of these hidden, human depths is harder to uncover and the change agent relies on human sciences, such as psychology, to understand the organization. *Resistance* is an understandable human reaction to change, but, ultimately, psychologically-informed techniques, which are planned and implemented over a period of time, give management *power* to bring about change.	Planned approach to change
The organization as a river	The organization is in a constant state of flux and flow, like rapids on a river. As such, it is never still long enough to have a stable *structure*. Management has little *power* over an organization that is changing constantly and evading its grasp. *Resistance* is continual—think of trying to paddle against the rapids. *Knowledge* is something that comes from experience and action, from jumping in and riding the rapids.	Emergent approach to change

Sources: Shutterstock

These metaphors help us to put ourselves in the place of someone who has the job of implementing change within an organization, a so-called **change agent**: a manager, consultant, or other person who initiates and manages change. They help us to ask four questions about the nature of an organization that inform the nature and implementation of change in that organization:

- Is the *structure* of the organization stable, or is the organization constantly changing?
- How does a change agent gain *knowledge* about what is going on in the organization, e.g. when trying to identify and understand the triggers and resisting forces that might be shown in a force-field analysis diagram?
- How does *power* operate in the organization, e.g. what ability does a change agent have to control and bring about change in an organization?
- To what extent is *resistance* a challenge to power in the organization, and how might that resistance be overcome?

Using the metaphors to address these questions leads us to three approaches to change that we examine in the remainder of this chapter, as shown in Table 12.1.

? Review questions

Describe	What are the categories of change outlined by Cummings and Worley?
Explain	How do metaphors help us to understand the nature of an organization?
Analyse	How are structure, knowledge, power, and resistance key features of the organization which influence different approaches to change?
Apply	Using Cummings and Worley's categories, what types of change are being attempted in the fitness centre? (Visit the online resources for a suggested answer.)

The organization as a set of building blocks: a naïve approach to change?

Q Running case: letter to employees

Dear Fitness Staff,

As loyal employees of the fitness centre, I'm sure you will be excited by the changes that will transform our centre into a leading gym and health spa facility. From this week, the fitness centre will be known as Coral Reef. To match the name change we are undertaking a massive refurbishment programme.

It's not just the buildings and equipment that will change, however. We aim to attract new customers and hotel guests with a set of activities and treatments

→

with our new unique selling point of 'tropical luxury'. To make this work we need to change the culture of Coral Reef, and this can only be done through you—the staff.

For this, we are introducing our 'simply the best' culture change programme. You, as staff, will become 'simply the best' at carrying our new culture in the following ways.

- You will give 'simply the best' customer service, greeting customers when they arrive, smiling at all times, and making conversation with customers on the gym floor.

- You will encourage customers to be 'simply the best' by motivating them to achieve their fitness goals and providing encouragement to all customers on the gym floor.

- You will become 'simply the best' at generating revenue for Coral Reef by promoting our new courses and treatments—each month there will be a bonus for the best at selling.

There will be some changes to working arrangements, with flexible rostering during an extended working day. To cover extra hours, new part-time staff will be brought in along with freelance instructors and treatment practitioners. I'm sure you will welcome them all in due course and help them to also be 'simply the best'.

Best wishes,
Carl

 How do you think the fitness centre staff will react to receiving this letter?

Imagine yourself as a manager implementing a change. The ideal situation, with the least amount of hassle, would be if you could simply rearrange the elements of the organization as if you were playing with a set of children's building blocks. Our first way of seeing the nature of an organization is that it is like a set of building blocks that fit together and can be rearranged at will.

The organization as a set of building blocks.
Source: koya979/Shutterstock.com

A change that focuses purely on structural or technological features of the organization (see Cummings and Worley's (2015) technostructural interventions in the previous section) can be seen as taking this building block view of the organization. However, this may be seen as a naïve view, based on a number of simplistic assumptions that it makes about the nature of an organization.

- The *structure* is simple and solid, where every conceivable element is visible—there are no hidden aspects to the organization.
- *Knowledge* is simply what can be measured, calculated, or represented as some form of model, equation, or diagram; it is a view of the organization almost as if it were a machine (think of similarities here with Taylor and Ford from Chapter 3).
- Management have total *power* over the organization from the top down.
- *Resistance* has no place in the organization; change is thus a matter of simply issuing orders and commands which will then be followed.

It is a very clean and simple view of what an organization is, but we know from previous chapters that organizational life is not this simple—it can be complex, messy, and unpredictable. This view fails to note how change is often perceived differently by workers and management, and thus often meets resistance. By paying attention to just the building blocks aspects of the change, management are blinkered to other human and social issues which ensue as a result, and which may make an important difference between the success and failure of that change.

This is not to say that change involving technostructural elements is naïve and simplistic per se—there are times when technology needs to be changed or an organization restructured. What is naïve is the assumption that this is all that needs to be changed while ignoring human processes and interactions. We could say that this approach concentrates only on the triggers to change and remains ignorant of any potential resisting forces, such as the fears and anxieties that often accompany change.

And yet how many managers see their organization in these terms, for example by planning to restructure a bureaucracy without thinking about how people will fit into the new system? Or, perhaps, by making changes to technology or the buildings without thinking about how people will actually use them or interact within them? Or even announcing a new culture without understanding that the culture has to work through people?

⟳ Real life case: Wimbledon FC / AFC Wimbledon / MK Dons

Football fans in England may be familiar with two professional teams from different cities: AFC Wimbledon, from south London, and MK Dons, from Milton Keynes. However, both of these teams have a common origin from a team called Wimbledon FC, from which a split took place in 2002. The split was so bitter and acrimonious that matches between the two teams remain 'emotionally charged' (Jenkins, 2017) to this day.

Wimbledon FC had been a successful club, but also had fairly small crowds. In 2002, the club directors club moved to Milton Keynes, renaming the club Milton Keynes Dons and eventually building its own stadium. What it couldn't take to Milton Keynes, however, were the existing fans, who were had a strong culture and were known as the 'crazy gang'. Rather than travel to Milton Keynes, the fans set up their own alternative football club in Wimbledon, known as AFC Wimbledon.

Despite starting as a new club, AFC Wimbledon has grown and in 2018 was playing in the same league as MK Dons, with the two teams having played each other on several occasions. However, the acrimony from the original split remains: for example, AFC Wimbledon refuse to acknowledge the legitimacy of MK Dons as a club and do not print their name on the cover of their matchday programme when they host them in league matches, and they refer to the club simply by its location, 'Milton Keynes', refusing it the cultural associations of the name 'Dons.'

Visit the online resources and take a look at the extension material for Chapter 12 for more about the Wimbledon case and about naïve approaches to change.

Sources: Hutchins et al. (2009); Nakrani (2011); Hognestad (2012); Tynan (2012); Jenkins (2017).

The move to Milton Keynes could be seen as a perfectly rational business decision, made with the aim of taking advantage of potentially larger crowds and gaining more income. However, it can also be interpreted as an example of a naïve building blocks approach to change. The change involves simply the visible, structural elements of the organization—the buildings, league position, name, etc. It is ignorant of or blinkered to other more intangible aspects—the culture, ties with the community, traditions, etc. Yet it is these with which the fans identified as being the essence of the club, not the building blocks such as the ground. It is this aspect over which the management had no power—they could move the building blocks to a new location, but they couldn't get that culture to follow them in the same direction.

? Review questions

Describe	What is meant by a naïve approach to change?
Explain	What important aspects of organizational life are ignored by a naïve approach to change?
Apply	In what ways could the management of the original Wimbledon be seen to have taken a naïve approach to change?

The organization as an iceberg: the planned approach to change

🔍 Running case: culture clashes

The new culture was at odds with the spit and sawdust culture that the original staff were used to. They wanted nothing to do with the 'simply the best' culture, and they felt that the constant smiling and upbeat small-talk trivialized their professional qualifications and commitment to fitness. As much as possible they tried to avoid the new culture, giving perfunctory smiles only when in view of the boss. The fact that the new rota had disrupted their personal lives, meaning they couldn't work together as a group, didn't help.

Conversely, the new staff—part-timers and freelance instructors—were inducted into the culture from the start and identified with it a lot more. This irritated the older staff, who started to refer to the new staff as the 'grinners'. Two groups emerged who would lunch, socialize, and chat separately. The grinners began to refer to the original staff as the 'oldies'. Contact between them was minimal.

The divisions were more than obvious at a launch night for the new fitness centre. With staff seated (in their oldies and grinners groups) Carl Jones stormed on to a makeshift stage with 'Simply the Best' blaring out over a loudspeaker. After some speeches about the new culture, Jones brought on some staff to model the new uniform. Based around the tropical theme, it consisted of a Coral Reef plain top with garish patterned beach shorts.

The oldies looked aghast and their hearts sank—it went against every professional and cultural value that they held. The grinners, however, were jumping up and down and whooping at their 'cool' new uniforms and swarmed Carl Jones to get their hands on their own uniforms to try on.

Think of the trouble that an iceberg can cause for a passing ship. It's not the part of the iceberg that is visible above the surface that causes the problems—it's the vast bulk of the iceberg that is hidden from view beneath the surface of the water that can cause a ship to run aground.

The organization as an iceberg.
Source: Volodymyr Goinyk / Shutterstock.com

The metaphor of an iceberg portrays the organization as having hidden depths that lie beneath the surface. The technical and structural features which make up the building blocks of an organization are merely the tip of the iceberg—the part that is easily visible and may appear easiest, at first glance, to manage and control. Hidden below the surface, in the bulk of the iceberg, are the more intangible aspects of the organization (Figure 12.6).

Figure 12.6 Aspects of the organization above and below the surface.

The building blocks
of the organization, e.g. buildings,
technology, structure, rules, procedures

Social aspects,
e.g. cultures, group dynamics

Human aspects, e.g. attitudes,
anxieties, values, feelings, emotions

These hidden features include human aspects, such as anxieties, attitudes, values, and emotions; and social aspects, such as cultures and group dynamics. In a similar manner, Edgar Schein (2010) used an iceberg metaphor to describe layers and depths of organizational culture (see Chapter 7).

While hard to uncover at first, human and social aspects are an important part of the organization and, if ignored, could potentially cause a change management initiative to be met with resistance and potentially to run aground. The iceberg metaphor highlights the following aspects of an organization relevant to the change process, which make up the key assumptions behind the planned approach to change.

- As with the building blocks approach, the *structure* is solid, but it also has hidden depths consisting of the human and social elements, which make up a considerable part of the organization beneath the surface.

- Gaining *knowledge* of the organization, therefore, means getting beneath the surface to the hidden depths. Psychologically-based techniques are used to get to know and understand these human and social aspects of the organization.

- A manager, or change agent, using a set of psychologically-informed techniques, ultimately has *power* to bring about top-down change in the organization. It is not as instant, simple, and neat as the building blocks approach would suggest; instead, it is a wide-ranging and long-term process.

- *Resistance* is understandable—it is a natural human and social reaction to change. Part of the job of overcoming resistance to change is to understand why it occurs in the first place before implementing a plan to overcome that resistance.

The planned approach to change

Unlike the naïve approach, the planned approach recognizes that change is not a simple and straightforward process, and that resistance to change can be expected. Given that such resistance resides in human and social aspects of the organization, psychological knowledge and techniques are used to overcome that resistance. In this respect the planned approach to change draws heavily upon the work of Kurt Lewin, whose field theory has been used in plotting out the triggers and resisting forces at work in a change situation. In this section we see how Lewin's work is also valuable in putting this change into action. First, we see a common but simplistic application of Lewin's work which sees change as a series of carefully planned and managed steps to take an organization, or a part of the organization, from point A to point B. Second, we adopt a more complex view of Lewin's work which emphasizes the importance of group dynamics (discussed in Chapter 6) in bringing about successful change. Third, we look at a more holistic, organization-wide change in the form of organization development. Finally, we put all of Lewin's work together to show how, in the light of Lewin's own background in social change, his work is relevant today to issues of culture change associated with workplace and institutional discrimination.

The three-step model of change

Many models of change view the process as a series of planned steps or changes, an idea which was first outlined in Lewin's (1947) work on changing group behaviours which saw the process as going through three broad steps of unfreezing, moving, and freezing. This **three-step model** was only a small part of Lewin's work (Cummings et al., 2016), and he never applied it directly to change in organizations. Nevertheless, it has taken on a life of its own as a model of organizational change. For example, Goodstein and Burke (1991) used the three-step model to analyse a major change undertaken by British Airways in the 1980s, moving from being a nationalized loss-making

Table 12.2 Lewin's (1947) three-step model of changing group behaviours

Stage	Explanation	Examples at British Airways (Goodstein and Burke, 1991)
Unfreezing	The current situation is outlined, perhaps using a force-field analysis diagram, and the organization is shaken out of its current state and made aware the need for change	Downsizing, bringing in a new top management team, and redefining the purpose of the company as service and not transportation
Moving	The organization moves and changes slowly towards the desired state	Attention to communications, peer support groups, a new training centre, and off-site team-building activities
Freezing	Once the change has been achieved, it is consolidated and reinforced so as to avoid slipping back into the previous ways of doing things	Promoting staff who demonstrated the new values, new reward and appraisal systems, and continued development and training

airline with a bureaucratic, militaristic culture, to a private, commercial enterprise with a culture focused on customer service. Table 12.2 outlines the main features of each of the three stages alongside how they were implemented at British Airways.

Many authors have extended the three-step model to provide more detail about what each of the three stages entails. As Collins (1998: 84) notes, these 'n-step' models all view change management as being formed of 'a number of relatively discrete, yet simple and easily manageable steps and phases.' For example, for Lippitt et al. (1958) the three steps became seven phases; more recently, Kotter (1996) outlined an eight-stage process of leading change. Bullock and Batten (1985) noted the existence of over 30 different such stage models of change, and helpfully synthesized them into a four-phase model of their own! The key features of each of these models are shown in Table 12.3, with the stages of each mapped onto the original three-step model.

Group dynamics and T-groups

A critique of n-step models of change, such as the three-step model, is that they provide an over-simplified view of the change process. They neglect the complexities of the social side of change (Collins, 1998), while presenting a 'quaintly linear and static' notion (Kanter et al., 1992: 10) that an organization can exist in 'frozen' states which bear no relation to the complex and fast-moving nature of organizational life. However, these critiques are very much aimed at ways in which Lewin's work has been simplified beyond his original writing. Lewin's work was firmly based in the social aspects of group dynamics—he saw the group as a 'primary focus' of analysis (Cummings et al., 2016: 50). Furthermore, rather than a set of linear, sequential stages, he saw group dynamics as being an ever-changing and complex set of contradictory variables all acting at the same time—as with the force-field analysis diagram (Cummings et al., 2016: 51). Indeed, the idea of a 'quasi-stationary equilibrium' suggests that instead of the solid states of freezing and unfreezing, group dynamics are in a constant state of flux and tension (Burnes, 2004a: 993; Cummings et al., 2016: 36).

 Visit the online resources and take a look at the web links for Chapter 12 to see a video discussion of Cummings et al.'s work in this area.

Table 12.3 Comparison of stepped models of change

Lewin (1947)	Lippitt et al. (1958)	Bullock and Batten (1985)	Kotter (1996)
Unfreezing	Diagnose problem Assess motivation and capacity for change	Exploration *Awareness of need for change* *Search* *Contracting*	Establishing a sense of urgency Creating the guiding coalition Developing a vision and strategy
Moving	Assess abilities of change agent Develop action plans and strategies Assign clear roles to change agents	Planning *Diagnosis* *Design* *Decision* Action *Implementation* *Evaluation*	Communicating the change vision Empowering employees for broad-based action Generating short-term wins
Freezing	Maintain the change through communication, feedback, and group coordination Terminate the change relationship when the change becomes part of the organizational culture	Integration *Stabilization* *Diffusion* *Renewal*	Consolidating gains Anchoring new approaches in the culture

To understand the significance of group dynamics in Lewin's work on change, it is important to understand the background to his work. While Lewin is today associated with management and organizational change, very little of Lewin's work actually took place in organizations and, indeed, his political leanings were to the left and to Marxism, rather than towards capitalism and the quest for effective management (Cooke, 1999). His key interests were in social change and the role of groups in achieving this.

Theory in context: Kurt Lewin and social change

Lewin was a Jewish refugee from Nazi Germany, and this experience shaped his interests towards removing discrimination and promoting harmonious relations within society. His work in America was in attitude change with respect to social conflict and discrimination faced by different religious and ethnic groups (Burnes, 2017: 754). This work had an initial aim of creating practical outcomes for disadvantaged groups, for example with housing or employment opportunities, but it soon recognized the power of the groups within this process (Burnes and Cooke, 2012: 1398). It was in unstructured group activities that the real change in attitudes was taking place, especially when the groups gained an insight into how their own dynamics work.

Visit the online resources and take a look at the videos for Chapter 12 for an interview with Bill Cooke about the background to Lewin's work and its modern-day relevance.

One of the main techniques developed from Lewin is the **T-group** (or sensitivity training group). A small group of participants learns, with a facilitator, about its own group dynamics and interpersonal processes. The group develops a 'sensitivity' to the intangible values and attitudes that guide group behaviours, including those of group leaders—the process is about getting to the intangible depths beneath the surface which guide behaviour. By understanding how the group works, it can thus strengthen itself, and negative behaviours and resistance can be changed. A key finding of Lewin is that change is only successful when there is a 'felt need' within the group: in other words, the group feels a sense of ownership and participation in the change (Burnes, 2017: 756). The group level is the key to successful organizational change; indeed, the T-group is the forerunner of many of the group- and team-building activities commonplace in contemporary organizations, as discussed in Chapter 6.

Organization development

Lewin's work on social change had laid the foundation for an all-encompassing approach to change known as **organization development** (OD). He founded the National Training Laboratories (NTL), a behavioural science institute, shortly before his death in 1947 (Burnes, 2004a). The NTL continued to develop his ideas, especially with respect to applying his ideas of attitude change in organizational and workplace contexts. In particular, organization development is based in Lewin's participative and democratic approach as exemplified in his group dynamics work. Lewin believed that democratic rather than autocratic leaders (see Chapter 13) got the best results (Burnes, 2017: 755). While OD draws upon the behavioural science knowledge and techniques developed by Lewin, it has since become a system-wide approach to organizational change (Burnes and Cooke, 2012), combining behavioural science insights with other, potentially limitless techniques (see the list from Cummings and Worley earlier in this chapter) to address change at an organization-wide level:

> Organization Development is an effort (1) planned, (2) organization-wide and (3) managed from the top to (4) increase organization effectiveness and health through (5) planned interventions in the organization's processes using behavioural science knowledge.
>
> (Beckhard, 1969: 9)

OD doesn't rule out the type of technostructural interventions addressed in the building-blocks approach, but sets them alongside more psychologically-informed techniques aimed at the aspects of the organization below the surface. While OD and the planned approach to change have been criticized for being too slow for the contemporary world (Burnes and Cooke, 2012), this chapter's 'Real life case' discussing institutional racism shows how, when linked with Lewin's original concerns for social justice, OD still has relevance for change management issues today.

 Real life case: institutional racism—from coffee shops to police canteens

At the time of writing, a number of social movements, reflected in Twitter hashtags, were highlighting the extent to which sexism (#metoo, #timesup, #everydaysexism) and racism (#blacklivesmatter) affect people on a daily basis, both in society and the workplace. Such discrimination exists even though national laws and workplace anti-discrimination policies are in place aimed at preventing it from happening.

⟶

Sara Ahmed (2007, 2012) has noted that there is a difference between the official policy and paperwork and more hidden experience of discrimination that can be found 'beneath the surface', institutionalized in everyday interactions such as offhand comments, unconscious biases, and informal cultures within organizations (Konrad and Linnehan, 1995; Odum, 2016; Simms, 2016; Faragher, 2017).

Such bias has been shown in recent cases. For example, in the USA two black men in Starbucks waiting for a friend were assumed to be enaged in criminal activity and arrested, despite doing nothing wrong. A number of similar cases of racism based upon often hidden assumptions has led to the term 'coffee shop racism' (Hinsliff, 2018; Gabbatt, 2018; BBC News, 2018).

Such hidden discrimination was identified as a feature of UK police forces in the late 1990s, and led to large-scale organization-wide attitude and culture change programmes in response to 'institutional racism'. The term was used in the Macpherson Report (1999), which investigated the handling of the murder of black teenager Stephen Lawrence in London in 1993 and a series of failures by the Metropolitan Police in bringing a prosecution. The murder and the subsequent report had such an impact on the public consciousness in the UK that in 2018, 25 years after the murder, the British prime minister Theresa May announced that 22 April, the anniversary of the murder, would be commemorated annually as Stephen Lawrence Day (Sherwood, 2018).

The Macpherson Report concluded that the police force was not explicitly racist, but institutional racism could be detected at the level of cultures and individual attitudes, defined as:

> The collective failure of an organisation to provide an appropriate and professional service to people because of colour, culture or ethnic origin. It can be seen or detected in processes, attitudes and behaviour which amount to discrimination through unwitting prejudice, ignorance, thoughtlessness and racist stereotyping. (Macpherson, 1999)

In other words, while the police did not have policies that promoted racism—indeed, their policies said the opposite—there was still discrimination taking place in the hidden workings of the organization: the cultures, attitudes, and everyday interactions, for example in the staff canteen. These discriminatory attitudes at the levels of groups and interactions are similar to the race relations problems that Lewin addressed in his work, and the changes which took place within the police have some similarities with Lewin's work.

How could the police force draw upon OD methods to increase the effectiveness of attitude change?

439

The work on attitude and culture change carried out by the Metropolitan Police would seem to have been an ideal application of Lewin's ideas, based, as it was, in race relations and social attitude change. However, the case also highlights one of the critiques of Lewin's work and of the planned approach to change. Attitude change, such as that in the police force, does not happen overnight—attitudes and cultures take time to change, in some cases generations.

Visit the online resources and take a look at the extension material for Chapter 12 for more discussion of police force change, including some of the training methods used to bring about change, and for a wider discussion of links between change management and culture change.

A critique of the planned approach is therefore that it is too long-term and slow-moving, a drawn-out process which requires consensus among groups (Burnes, 2004a). In Chapter 2 we saw that the environment faced by contemporary organizations is volatile and unpredictable, and organizations therefore need to be nimble and react quickly to change. Furthermore, the idea that change takes place as a set of discrete stages, as seen in the various n-step models, has been criticized as being far removed from the realities of organizational life (Kanter et al., 1992; Appelbaum et al., 2012). A different approach, where the organization is seen as if it were a river, is examined in the following section.

? Review questions

Describe	What are the main features of the planned approach to change?
Explain	How does the planned approach to change address features of the organization 'below the surface'?
Analyse	How might an organization development approach help to bring about attitude and culture change?
Apply	How might the three-step model have been used to implement the change in the fitness centre at Junction Hotel?

The organization as a river: the emergent approach to change

🔍 Running case: unintended consequences

A number of unintended and unpredicted consequences emerged as a result of the changes at the fitness centre, which had knock-on effects on the hotel and beyond.

- The information technology system at the fitness reception was unable to handle bookings for the freelance treatment providers and for the fitness classes. Eventually, this function was handed over to the main hotel reception, who were not happy with the additional work. As bookings became more popular, this got in the way of checking in hotel guests, who started to complain about the waiting times.

- It became increasingly difficult to coordinate the times of freelance treatment providers, as they started to outnumber the two treatment rooms available. Some refused to use one of the rooms because the 'oldies' were still using it as their unofficial room for lunch breaks. As a result, Chance decided to block out three of the guest rooms and use them as treatment rooms—with a loss in revenue for the hotel.

- Reception staff were having to deal with irate fitness customers as the freelancers became unreliable, cancelling bookings at the last minute. Meg Mortimer became more and more exasperated with the situation, especially because when one member of staff went off ill with stress she then had to cover her work.

→

→

- The new health spa and showers were installed hurriedly. It turned out that they put a strain on the hotel boiler, which broke down on a number of occasions, meaning that there was no hot water for the hotel rooms. As well as bringing more complaints to the already overworked reception, it also meant that laundry had to be outsourced temporarily, at an extra cost.

- As memberships grew, so did the demand for hotel car park spaces. Guests complained (at reception again) about the lack of spaces. More concerned, however, were the local council, who received complaints from residents about overspill car parking on their streets.

Simon Chance had known there were problems and had had to play a mediating role between Meg Mortimer, who seemed to bear the brunt of things, and Carl Jones. Mortimer constantly plotted and briefed against Jones with other managers, but Chance wanted this project to work; he therefore supported Jones, and he eventually issued an informal warning to Mortimer that her job would be at risk if she didn't go along with the new systems. Chance had also had a meeting with the council's residential services division to deal with the parking issues.

If you were white-water rafting on a river, of course you would plan ahead—working out your route and making sure you had the appropriate safety equipment, etc. But the precise, step-by-step details of the journey are impossible to plan—part of the skill of rafting is reacting *on the spot* to the twists and turns of the water beneath you. No two journeys will be the same; the ever-moving and ever-changing nature of the river is unpredictable.

441

> You cannot step twice into the same river, for other waters are continually flowing on ... Everything flows and nothing abides; everything gives way and nothing stays fixed.
>
> (Heraclitus, *c*.500 BC, quoted in Morgan, 2006: 241)

The river metaphor suggests something which is in constant *flow*, never the same from one moment to the next. As such, it emphasizes the dynamic, complex, and ever-changing nature of organization, with *change as the constant natural state of the organization*. The organization is not a stable entity that is occasionally 'moved around' by management, as with the planned approach—the organization never stays still long enough to be 'unfrozen' and 'frozen': 'change never starts because it never stops' (Applebaum et al., 2012: 764). This gives a radically different view of the nature of the organization from that of the building blocks or the iceberg.

- An organization never stays still for long enough to be described as a *structure*, such as an iceberg or a set of building blocks. Complex, hidden depths exist, but their dynamic nature makes them difficult to even begin to grasp.

- It is never possible to have complete *knowledge* of every aspect of the organization to use as a basis for planning owing to the continually-changing nature of the organization—it is always beyond our grasp.

- Without complete knowledge of the organization, *power* is much more difficult for management to exert. Power is not top-down and in the hands of management, but exists within the movement of the organization itself. You may be in charge of the raft, but you are very much controlled by the movement of the river beneath it.

The organization as a river.
Source: bikeriderlondon/Shutterstock.com

- Wherever management tries to exert power over an organization it will always meet with natural *resistance*, just as trying to exert power over the course of a river by setting up a dam, for example, will always meet with resistance from the flow of the water. The resistance within the river is always there as a challenge to those who seek to exert power over it.

The emergent approach to change

The metaphor of the river suggests a complex and messy situation for management to deal with, one that is both fast-flowing and with complex murky depths—potentially beyond management knowledge and power. Change is not a discrete period of upheaval planned in advance to take an organization from point A to B; instead, change is the norm and is always present. With the emergent approach, change is managed in a much more ad hoc fashion, reacting to events as and when they occur. Change is what *emerges* along with the flow of the river.

The emergent approach to change is not one specific approach to change, but a number of approaches which recognize the complex and interconnected nature of organizations. Two particular approaches are the processual approach and the systemic approach.

The processual approach to change—political consequences

The **processual approach to change** paints change as an 'untidy cocktail' (Burnes, 2004a: 989) of individual perceptions and political struggles. This reflects change as a political and messy process. It also emphasizes that there may be no single, individual cause of change and that in the change process there is an interconnectedness and inter-relatedness of individuals, groups, organizations, and society.

Earlier in the chapter we discussed how change causes anxiety and upset. The planned approach would see this as elements of resistance 'beneath the surface' to be overcome by psychological means. In a processual approach, human and social elements, such as fear, anxiety, and the power of different groups and subcultures within the organization, become the basis for political battles—rather than being overcome there is active resistance to change (see Chapter 14 for more on these political aspects of the organization).

The systemic approach to change—knock-on effects

The processual approach recognizes the interconnectedness of different aspects of an organization. A similar approach comes from an understanding of an organization as a system (**systemic approach to change**), defined by Evered (1980) as 'a set of different parts which combine and work together as an organized whole'. This approach recognizes the organization as an interconnected system whereby change in one area can have consequences and knock-on effects in other areas. If one part of the system breaks down then it can affect the functioning of the system as a whole. Think, for example, of a car. It is a system in that different parts and components function together as a whole. If one of the components fails, the interdependency of the parts of the system means that the system as a whole—the car—can stop functioning.

A simple example of this systemic interdependence can be seen within a rail network. You may well have been standing on a station platform and heard that your service is late because of a signal failure elsewhere in the country. A rail network is a system with a number of inter-related parts—tracks, points, signals, trains, and drivers—all elements that work together to make the rail network function. Rather than being a problem in isolation, the broken signal causes trains to block the track, affecting any services behind them. These knock-on effects can carry on down the line—the effects can be felt throughout the network (Meek, 2001).

Changing a system

If we see the organization as an interconnected system, it follows that making a change will have knock-on effects and consequences, but to what extent can such consequences be managed? The emergent approach would suggest that, rather than managers being in control of the consequences of a change, such consequences are unpredictable and uncontrollable, as if the managers were being carried along by the flow of the river.

The watchmaker and the surgeon

Collins (1998: 148) highlights the degree to which we can change one part of a system without affecting its overall functioning. We can consider whether the organizational change manager is more like a 'watchmaker' or a 'surgeon'—whether change is a simple mechanical job, or whether the systemic interdependencies make it a much more complex and emergent phenomenon.

- The watchmaker can identify a component which is not working and simply replace it—the system will then begin working again. There is no problem in shutting down the system for a while, making some changes and then restarting it.

- For the surgeon, however, this luxury is not available. Say a heart needs replacing—it's not possible to shut down the body temporarily to do this. The interdependencies it has with the rest of the system means that it must maintain its action for the rest of the system to survive. The knock-on effects of changing one part of the system have to be considered. Therefore, the surgeon has to make arrangements to ensure that the heart's role within the system (i.e. circulating blood) is somehow maintained while attending to that one component.

While organizational change managers are not surgeons, they have to think about the effects that making a change might have. To return to the rail example, there are often planned engineering works on railways. Unlike a watch, the railway system cannot simply be shut down. The railway manager has to maintain a flow of passengers by providing, for example, alternative bus services or timetabling alternative rail routes.

 Visit the online resources and take a look at the extension material for Chapter 12 for some suggestions for answers to this library question.

 Imagine if your university library building closed for six months for refurbishment. What effects would it have on the rest of the university and how might the university deal with those effects to keep the university running?

Open and closed systems

In describing the nature of a system, we can make a further distinction between an open and a closed system (Jackson and Carter, 2007: 211).

- A closed system has a distinct boundary around it and operates fully within that boundary—there is no movement across the boundary.
- An open system interacts with its environment—there is movement across the boundary.

As we have seen, and as common sense might suggest, organizations are open systems. They are affected by activity in their environment (think of the PEST model earlier in this chapter and in Chapter 2). In the opposite direction, organizations can affect their own environment. Think of the effects of pollution or an organization creating extra traffic on the streets around it and thus causing those streets to be congested. Many people are affected by, and have an interest in, the activities of particular organizations.

The Gaia hypothesis (see Jackson and Carter, 2007: 214) or a 'systems view of the world' (Capra, 1992) sees *all aspects of the world* being potentially interconnected. The nature of organizations as both dynamic and open systems means that the 'ripples and knock-on effects' (Collins, 1998: 149) or 'waves of consequences' (Darwin et al., 2002: 177) of any change or intervention within the system have to be considered. The interdependencies of parts of a system, both inside and out, mean that the consequences of a particular change could, potentially, be limitless. Thus, as discussed in Chapter 17, the concept of corporate social responsibility suggests that organizations have a responsibility for the effects of their actions on the world around them—if their activities cause harm to the environment, for example.

Chaos and complexity theory—the butterfly effect

The idea of knock-on effects and consequences is mirrored in studies of scientific and natural systems. Chaos theory emphasizes the unpredictable and interconnected nature of many scientific systems. Small changes in a natural system can have unpredictable knock-on effects of a disproportionate magnitude. Lorenz (1972) noted this with his famous question: 'Does the flap of a butterfly's wings in Brazil set off a tornado in Texas?' A minute change in the natural ecosystem— the air disturbances of a butterfly's wings—has the potential to set up a series of knock-on effects such that it might actually alter weather patterns. Lorenz's butterfly effect is perhaps one of the best-known aspects of chaos theory.

Complexity theory has extended the ideas of chaos theory beyond purely scientific systems into systems in general. The recent financial crisis, as examined in Chapter 16 on globalization, is an example of such interconnectedness where a change in one small area—the collapse of one bank—had knock-on effects that led to the near-collapse of the world's financial systems. In a similar manner, complexity theory would suggest that, because an organization is a system, small changes in one area of an organization can have disproportionate effects.

Real life case: the knock-on effects of Brexit

At the time of writing the final Brexit deal was uncertain, and discussion was taking place between whether or not there should be a 'soft Brexit', with some degree of customs union between the UK and European Union, or whether there should be a clean-break 'hard Brexit'.

Reports suggested that the clean break would lead to increased time for customs checks at Channel ports and that this would cause a number of knock-on effects.

- The delays would cause tailbacks of lorries along on roads outside of ferry ports. This has led to plans to build lorry parks to remove the congestion, which in turn has led to complaints from local residents about areas of green pasture being covered in tarmac.

- Parts for manufacturing could be held up, leading to a breakdown in just-in-time production systems which rely on parts being delivered promptly, e.g. in car manufacturing (see Chapter 3).

- Companies and organizations may need to stockpile food and medicines in case the delays cause shortages in these.

Whatever the end result of Brexit, these predictions show the complex interconnections in the economy and beyond and how a change in just one small area—the ports—can have considerable knock-on effects.

Sources: Peck (2017); Pickard et al. (2018); Sparrow (2018).

An implication of chaos theory is that long-term predictions in systems are impossible to make (Tsoukas, 1998). Take a system like the weather. We know that weather forecasting is not a precise science. Meteorologists can model the system and have a good stab at predicting the weather for the next few days, but beyond that, the system is so complex and open to so many knock-on effects and changes that prediction is impossible, and, indeed, very few forecasters now provide long-range forecasts.

In Stacey's (1992) terms, it is not that the future is *unknown*, it is the fact that the future is inherently *unknowable*. There are no equations or models that can tell us precisely what the long-term weather will be—it is something that will emerge in the future.

Stacey suggests that the idea of the future being 'unknowable' applies to organizations. As such, this emergent approach to change dismisses the idea that change is a 'planned' activity where the change manager can work towards a particular desired outcome—the consequences of a change intervention are yet to emerge when action is taken. Rather than being planned, change is unpredictable—its knock-on effects and ultimate outcomes are unknowable.

Managing with emergence

Using the river metaphor, we see the organization as an emergent phenomenon. This presents a picture of knock-on effects of action which become uncontrollable and unplannable, and a murky world of political processes and power struggles lie within this. To plan change precisely becomes impossible, just as it is impossible to predict the weather beyond the very short term.

Does this mean that we can do without management and leadership if they are so evidently powerless to control change? For Jenner (1994), managers still have a role in guiding the system; rather than managing change, managers are, in effect, managing *with* change—they are carried along by the flow of the river as much as the rest of the organization.

One value of the emergent approach is simply for management to appreciate the systemic nature of an organization (Stacey, 1992) and the fact that a change will have knock-on effects—an appreciation beyond the simplistic view of change that is arranging a set of building blocks.

Furthermore, the emergent approach suggests ways in which management can create opportunities for creativity and innovation among their workforce. Rather than the river being something to be feared and coped with, it is something to be embraced for the potential that it offers. In Chapter 2 we looked at post-bureaucratic approaches to organizations which minimize structure, and in Chapter 10 we saw how such organizations, as found in the Googleplex and Telenor, promoted 'collisions' of people so that they might swap ideas and thus increase knowledge within the organization. These organizations can be seen as being like rivers in that they promote constant movement as a way of generating knowledge and innovation.

 Real life case: the agile manifesto

A flexible form of working that constantly anticipates and responds to change was first developed in the software industry, which is characterized by constant innovation and development, under the 'Manifesto for agile software development' (Beck et al., 2001). The four principles which it values are:

- Individuals and interactions over processes and tools
- Working software over comprehensive documentation
- Customer collaboration over contract negotiation
- Responding to change over following a plan

The philosophy behind this is that the company should be constantly responding to customer needs to produce useful products, rather than being held back in more structural issues such as processes, contracts, and documentation. In this respect, an organization seems to gain its flexibility by pursuing post-bureaucratic rather than rationalized structures and processes (see Chapter 2). However, the manifesto also valuees efficiency, in particular minimizing waste. In a means similar to the Gilbreths (see Chapter 3), the manifesto goes on to state that 'Simplicity—the art of maximizing the amount of work not done—is essential.' In this respect, agile methods have also been linked with lean techniques in manufacturing—neo-Fordist techniques (see Chapter 3) which allow constant changes to the process to be made in order to meet customer demands.

In wider organizational contexts, this 'operational agility,' the ability of organizational process and structures to adapt to change, is also found alongside 'workforce agility'—seen in people being flexible with their working hours and locations (CIPD, 2014) as seen in Chapter 2. This, according to the CIPD (2014), can present challenges in finding the right skilled workers who are available at short notice to meet changes in demand. Furthermore, the CIPD note that such working can often require a change of culture, from internally-focused and highly controlled environments, which are found in most organizations, to the rarer external- (customer-) focused culture with a flexible rather than a highly controlled environment.

 Visit the online resources and take a look at the web links for Chapter 12 for other examples of companies that use such emergent approaches to promote innovation.

Describe	What are the main features of the emergent approach to change?
Explain	What does it mean to take a systemic view of an organization?
Analyse	How can the butterfly effect be used to analyse the ways in which small changes in an organization lead to unpredictable consequences?
Apply	Would the agile manifesto be suitable for all organizations? Would it work in a fast-food restaurant, for example?

The three approaches considered together

🔍 Running case: denouement

Back in the present day, Meg Mortimer returns to the boardroom where the party is in full swing and Carl Jones is the man of the moment. He is being fêted as a great manager and implementer of change. 'Easy to say once it's all been done and dusted,' thinks Meg, 'but if it weren't for me coping with the fall-out it would never have happened.'

Meanwhile, the five 'oldies' have moved away from defacing the picture of Carl Jones. They are in a pub, meeting a representative of an upmarket residential development with gym facilities. They sign on the dotted line to go into partnership to run the facilities themselves as a gym and personal-training business. They too raise their glasses to toast change—and the change they are looking forward to most is going into work the next day to hand in their notices to Carl Jones.

 Knowing the full story, how well do you think Carl Jones managed change at the fitness centre? Do you think the change can be described as the naïve, planned, or emergent approach (or any combination thereof?)

447

Once the upheaval of a period of change is out of the way and a change has been achieved, it can often be presented as having been successful. This, however, might mask a lot of upset, resistance, and unintended consequences that have happened along the way.

In this chapter we have seen how change can be a messy process. What might seem like perfectly rational triggers to change from one perspective may cause fear and anxiety from another, leading to resistance to that change.

We have seen that a naïve view of change would ignore this resistance, seeing the organization simply as a set of building blocks that can be rearranged at will. A planned approach to change recognizes this resistance as existing in the 'hidden depths' of the organization, beneath its surface, and would use techniques based in psychology to overcome that resistance. An emergent approach—the organization as a river—views resistance as part and parcel of the dynamic, interconnected, and political nature of the organization, part of the course of events that managers have to deal with.

While it is argued that the emergent approach is more in tune with the dynamic, changeable nature of our contemporary world, all three approaches contribute to our understanding of the nature of change. The planned approach, for example, is suited to changing deeply-held attitudes and cultures, as were found in the Metropolitan Police after the Stephen Lawrence case, and even a building-blocks approach might be appropriate when quick and drastic action is required. And there is some overlap between the three approaches. For example, Kotter (2014) updated his eight-step process of change to allow for the stages to run concurrently rather than in sequence, and to see change as a constant and flexible process. Burnes (2004b) suggests that there are similarities between emergent approaches and Lewin's planned change approach: in particular, the idea of a 'quasi-stationary equilibrium' mirrors some of the balance between order and unpredictability found in complexity theory. And, while agile working might be within the emergent perspective, it draws on language and ideas found in Lewin's approach to planned change, particularly by prioritizing 'interactions' (Beck et al., 2001) and aiming to 'anticipate and address the *forces* affecting the business' (CIPD, 2014: 2). All three approaches uncover, and make us aware of, different characteristics of the organization which are important when engaging in change.

Connecting case and theory

At the start of the case we saw a seemingly successful change being celebrated within the boardroom, but it was not long before it became obvious that, as we have seen with reactions to change, different people and groups had different views of the change. The staff in the leisure centre had a far from positive view of the change, judging by the way they defaced the image of Carl Jones. Meg Mortimer's reluctance to celebrate also showed how change that seems to be successful can be the result of a messy process, and it was she that had to deal with many of the problems which happened along the way.

Going back six months, Jones had been faced with a number of **triggers for change** within the leisure centre—areas of potential growth, the better offering of competitors, the lack of classes, the intimidating macho culture, to name but a few, along with the impetus from the top management for change to take place. Jones's action plan was wide ranging, covering all four of Cummings and Worley's (2015) categories of change management (Table 12.4).

However, while the plan was detailed, Jones's implementation of the plan, through a letter to all of the staff, could be described as a **naïve** approach to the change. As with the Wimbledon FC case, the change was implemented without an understanding of the current culture and how people might react. In fact, there was a lot of **resistance** to the change from the existing gym staff—the 'oldies'—both because of their distaste for the new 'simply the best' culture, and also because they could no longer work together as a group. The fact that the newer staff, the 'grinners', identified with the new culture straight away shows how it is existing, long-held cultures and attitudes which can be much harder to change.

Rather than simply ordering the staff to change by means of a letter, Jones could have learned from Lewin's approach to **planned change**. The older staff simply didn't see a

Table 12.4 Categories of change management as applied at Junction Hotel

Category of change management (Cummings and Worley, 2015)	Example from Jones's action plan
Strategic change interventions	New identity and new, less aggressive culture New range of classes and services
Technostructural interventions	New gym equipment and key card entrance system New extension to be built
Human process interventions	Teamworking and mentoring of new staff
Human resource interventions	New flexible working hours Bonus and incentive scheme

need to change—there had been no unfreezing. Bringing in their involvement earlier and explaining the need for change would have helped. There emerged two completely separated groups, the 'oldies' and the 'grinners.' Lewin's work was based on reconciling differences between groups. In the gym at Junction Hotel, group work which integrated the two groups and got them to become sensitive to each other's attitudes and values could have helped the 'movement' part of the process.

Jones was also naïve to the **emergent** and unpredictable elements of change. For example, the **systemic** nature of change had been overlooked, with changes in the fitness centre having knock-on effects in the hotel, for example on the boiler system and on the queues in reception. The knock-on effects even extended to car parking in the local area, showing how the hotel is an open system with consequences beyond the organization. The **processual**, political nature of change was evident in Meg Mortimer plotting against the change because of the negative impact on her work, and Simon Chance warning her against this because of his own personal investment in the project.

The denouement of the case shows that while the change was being celebrated as successful, it left a lot of bad feeling, with Mortimer resenting the problems that were forced upon her, and the five oldies taking the ultimate form of resistance and leaving the organization. How successful the change process was may depend on which of the metaphors you use to judge the change. From a 'building blocks' perspective, maybe it was successful: if the oldies dislike the new culture then perhaps the hotel is better off without them, and there are plenty of new grinners who can come in and who are much more malleable to the new culture. From an 'iceberg' approach, the change ignored all of the feelings and attitudes beneath the surface—if the management had taken account of these they might have been able, eventually, to bring the oldies on board with the new culture. From the 'river' approach, knock-on effects are inevitable, and Jones's mistake was to not understand how the fitness centre operated as part of the overall hotel system. The case has shown how change is messy and unpredictable. Given this, do you feel that Carl Jones was a successful manager of change?

Further reading

Cummings, T.G., and Worley, C.G. 2015. *Organization development and change*, 10th edn. South-Western/Cengage Learning: Mason, OH.

A practical overview of a wide range of change management techniques and interventions.

Ahmed, S. 2012. *On being included: Racism and diversity in institutional life.* Duke University Press: London.

Highlights the tensions between diversity policies and actual discrimination 'beneath the surface'.

Kotter, J.P. 1996. *Leading change.* Harvard Business Press: Cambridge, MA.

Kotter's eight-step model of change, with each stage explained in detail.

Senior, B., and Swailes, S. 2016. *Organizational change*, 5th edn. Pearson Education: Harlow.

An accessible introduction to and overview of the wide field of change management.

 References

Ahmed, S. 2007. 'You end up doing the document rather than doing the doing': Diversity, race equality and the politics of documentation. *Ethnic and Racial Studies* 30 (4): 590–609.

Ahmed, S. 2012. *On being included: Racism and diversity in institutional life.* London: Duke University Press.

Appelbaum, S.H., Habashy, S., Malo, J.L. and Shafiq, H. 2012. Back to the future: Revisiting Kotter's 1996 change model. *Journal of Management Development* 31 (8): 764–82.

BBC News. 2018. How Starbucks hopes to end staff racism, 29 May. Available at: https://www.bbc.co.uk/news/av/world-us-canada-44259850/how-starbucks-hopes-to-end-staff-racism

Beck, K., Beedle, M., Bennekum, A. van, Cockburn, A., Cunningham, W., Fowler, M., Martin, R.C., Mellor, S., Grenning, J., Highsmith, J., Hunt, A., Jeffries, R., Kern, J., Marick, B., Schwaber, K., Sutherland, J., and Thomas, D. 2001. Manifesto for agile software development. Available at: https://www.agilealliance.org/agile101/the-agile-manifesto/

Beckhard, R. 1969. *Organization development: Strategies and models.* Addison-Wesley: Reading, MA.

Bullock, R.J., and Batten, D., 1985. It's just a phase we're going through: A review and synthesis of OD phase analysis. *Group and Organization Studies* 10 (4): 383–412.

Burnes, B. 2004a. Kurt Lewin and the planned approach to change: A re-appraisal. *Journal of Management Studies* 41 (6): 977–1002.

Burnes, B. 2004b. Kurt Lewin and complexity theories: Back to the future? *Journal of Change Management* 4 (4): 309–25.

Burnes, B. 2017. Kurt Lewin (1890–1947): The practical theorist. In: Szabla, D., Pasmore, W., Barnes, M., and Gipson, A. (eds) *The Palgrave handbook of organizational change thinkers.* Palgrave Macmillan: Cham.

Burnes, B., and Cooke, B. 2012. The past, present and future of organization development: Taking the long view. *Human Relations* 65 (11): 1395–429.

Burnes, B., and Bill Cooke, B. 2013. Kurt Lewin's field theory: A review and re-evaluation. *International Journal of Management Reviews* 15 (4): 408–25.

Capra, F. 1992. A systems view of the world. *Resurgence Magazine* 151: 34–37.

CIPD. 2014. HR: Getting smart about agile working. Available at: https://www.cipd.co.uk/knowledge/strategy/change/agile-working-report

Collins, D. 1998. *Organizational change: Sociological perspectives.* Routledge: London.

Cooke, B. 1999. Writing the left out of management theory: The historiography of the management of change. *Organization* 6 (1): 81–105.

Cummings, S., Bridgman, T. and Brown, K.G. 2016. Unfreezing change as three steps: Rethinking Kurt Lewin's legacy for change management. *Human Relations* 69 (1): 33–60.

Cummings, T.G., and Worley, C.G. 2015. *Organization development and change*, 10th edn. South-Western/Cengage Learning: Mason, OH.

Darwin, J., Johnson, P., and McAuley, J. 2002. *Developing strategies for change*. Financial Times/Prentice Hall: Harlow.

Drafke, M.W. 2009. *The human side of organizations*. Pearson/Prentice Hall: Upper Saddle River, NJ.

Evered, R. 1980. Consequences of and prospects for systems thinking in organizational change. In: Cummings, T.G. (ed.) *Systems theory for organization development*. John Wiley and Sons: New York, pp. 5–13.

Faragher, J. 2017. Still think there isn't a problem with bias in your workplace? *People Management*, May: 33–6.

Gabbatt, A. 2018. Coffee shop racism: Where America's racial divisions are exposed. *The Guardian*, 28 May. Available at: https://www.theguardian.com/world/2018/may/28/coffee-shop-racism-starbucks-arrests

Goodstein, L.D., and Warner Burke, W. 1991. Creating successful organization change. *Organizational Dynamics* 19 (4): 5–17.

Helms-Mills, J. 2003. *Making sense of organizational change*. Routledge: London.

Hinsliff, G. 2018. Training Starbucks staff won't fix racism—but changing the rules will. *The Guardian*, 29 May. Available at: https://www.theguardian.com/commentisfree/2018/may/29/training-starbucks-racism-rules-unconscious-bias

Hognestad, H. 2012. Split loyalties: Football is a community business. *Soccer and Society* 13 (3): 377–91.

Hutchins, B., Rowe, D., and Ruddock, A. 2009. 'It's fantasy football made real': Networked media sport, the internet, and the hybrid reality of MyFootballClub. *Sociology of Sport Journal* 26: 89–106.

Jackson, N., and Carter, P. 2007. *Rethinking organisational behaviour*. Financial Times/Prentice Hall: Harlow.

Jenkins, T., 2017. A weekend of football passion, rivalry and animosity—photo essay. *The Guardian*, 25 September. Available at: https://www.theguardian.com/football/2017/sep/25/a-weekend-of-football-passion-rivalry-and-animosity-photo-essay

Jenner, R. 1994. Changing patterns of power: Chaotic dynamics and the emergence of a post-modern organizational paradigm. *Journal of Organizational Change Management* 7 (3): 8–21.

Kanter, R.M., Stein, B., and Jick, T. 1992. *The challenge of organizational change: How companies experience it and leaders guide it*. Free Press: New York.

King, D. 2001. *Devils and Nazis: Representations of change through postmodern research*. British Academy of Management, University of Edinburgh: Edinburgh.

Konrad, A.M., and Linnehan, F. 1995. Formalized HRM structures: Coordinating equal employment opportunity or concealing organizational practices? *Academy of Management Journal* 38 (3): 787–820.

Kotter, J.P. 1996. *Leading change*. Harvard Business Press: Cambridge, MA.

Kotter, J.P. 2014. *Accelerate: Building strategic agility for a faster-moving world*. Harvard Business Review Press: Cambridge, MA.

Lewin, K. 1943. Defining the 'field at a given time'. *Psychological Review* 50 (3): 292.

Lewin, K. 1947. Frontiers in group dynamics. *Human Relations* 1 (2): 143–53.

Lippitt, R., Watson, J., and Westley, B. 1958. *Planned change: A comparative study of principles and techniques*. Harcourt, Brace & World: New York.

Lorenz, E. 1972. *Does the flap of a butterfly's wings in Brazil set off a tornado in Texas?* Speech before the American Academy for the Advancement of Science, December.

Macpherson, W. 1999. *The Stephen Lawrence Inquiry: Report of an inquiry*. The Stationery Office: London.

Meek, J. 2001. 'Things fall apart'. *The Guardian*, 1 March.

Morgan, G. 2006. *Images of organization*. Sage Publications: Thousand Oaks, CA.

451

Nakrani, S. 2011. AFC Wimbledon celebrate 'phenomenal' rise to League Two. *The Guardian*, 22 May.

Odum, S. 2016. Has the City solved sexism? *People Management*, October: 8–9.

Peck, T. 2017. Brexit: UK must start preparing for Dover no-deal chaos (and build a 1,000 strong lorry park). *The Independent*, 11 November. Available at: https://www.independent.co.uk/news/uk/politics/brexit-uk-must-start-preparing-for-dover-chaos-in-event-of-a-no-deal-a8023976.html

Pickard, J., Blitz, J., Daneshkhu, D., and Neville, S. 2018. Britain steps up dooms-day planning for no-deal Brexit. *Financial Times*, 20 July. Available at: https://www.ft.com/content/9f494eea-8b77-11e8-b18d-0181731a0340

Schein, E. 2010. *Organizational culture and leadership*. Jossey Bass: San Francisco.

Senior, B., and Fleming, J.D. 2006. *Organizational change*, 3rd edn. Pearson Education: Harlow.

Senior, B., and Swailes, S. 2016. *Organizational change*, 5th edn. Pearson Education: Harlow.

Sherwood, H. 2018. Stephen Lawrence Day to be created in tribute to murdered teenager. *The Guardian*, 23 April. Available at: https://www.theguardian.com/uk-news/2018/apr/23/prince-harry-and-meghan-attend-stephen-lawrence-memorial-service

Simms, J. 2016. Thank goodness times have changed … *People Management*, July: 31–6.

Sparrow, A. 2018. Brussels 'irresponsible' for flagging risks of no-deal Brexit, says Raab. *The Guardian*, 22 July. Available at: https://www.theguardian.com/politics/2018/jul/22/brexit-no-divorce-payment-without-trade-deal-says-dominic-raab

Stacey, R.D. 1992. *Managing chaos: Dynamic business strategies in an unpredictable world*. Kogan Page: London.

Tsoukas, H. 1998. Introduction: Chaos, complexity and organization theory. *Organization* 5 (3): 291–313.

Tynan, G. 2012. FA Cup: MK Dons book grudge tie against AFC Wimbledon. *The Independent*, 14 November.

CHAPTER 13
Leadership
Leading the way

Chapter overview and learning outcomes

By the end of this chapter you should be able to:

- describe the key leadership theories
- explain why contingency theory argues that there is no best leadership style
- explain the differences between leadership and management
- analyse whether there is too much emphasis on the individual leader and explore the importance of followers
- explain the key principles of distributive leadership

Key theorists

Paul Hersey and Ken Blanchard	Key writers who developed the situational leadership perspective, which argues that the appropriate leadership style depends on the situation
James Meindl	A key critic of the heroic leadership perspective who argues that there is a romanticism of leadership
Rosabeth Moss Kanter	A Harvard Business School professor who specializes in leadership for change; has written widely and is considered to be highly influential
Nancy Harding and Jackie Ford	Two critical management studies scholars who have questioned many of the assumptions of leadership and followership theory

Key terms

Behaviourism	Drawn from psychology, behaviourism is the theory that behaviour is determined by conditioning, not by thoughts and feelings, and that personal and interpersonal problems may be solved by altering behaviour
Contingency theory	States that the type of leadership style adopted is dependent (contingent) on the situation
Trait	A characteristic of a person: the behaviour, thoughts, and emotions that the person exhibits considered stable over time
Post-heroic	A perspective which argues that we need to move beyond seeing the leader as hero
Followership	A theoretical perspective which stresses the importance of followers
Glass ceiling	A barrier that a particular group (e.g. women) cannot move beyond

Introduction

Simon Chance knows that this is an important day for him and Junction Hotel. This evening some of the key investors are having a tour of Junction Hotel to hear about the changes Chance has already made, and the plans he has developed for the future. As chief executive officer (CEO) of the Second-Chance Consortium, Chance knows that how the investors respond to the meal and their visit to the hotel is going to really shape the board meeting next month, and their reactions to his investment plans. Chance feels it is important—actually his duty—to give his followers a clear sense of vision about where they are taking Junction Hotel. He is running the staff meeting this morning, followed by one-to-one meetings with Linda Wilkinson and Graham Effingham—two quite different characters. After a smallish lunch with the investors Chance will then spend the afternoon making sure that everything is ready for the big one: the meeting with the investors.

As he settles down to write his pitch for the investors, and the staff meeting before that, Chance looks at his bookshelf lined with the biographies of so-called 'great' leaders, among them Nelson Mandela, Winston Churchill, and Gandhi; he wonders what they would make of Junction Hotel. Suddenly drawing him out of his daydream, his phone rings. 'Hi, it's Meg.' Meg Mortimer's voice is sounding panicked down the phone. 'Three of my reception staff have phoned in sick! I'm covering the reception desk and I can't find any replacements. What are we going to do, Simon?' Chance feels crestfallen. 'Today of all days, why is this happening to me?' he thinks to himself.

Leaders as heroes and villains

Does your organization have a problem? Then call in a great leader to sort it out. Great leaders are seen as the solution to all sorts of organizational problems. Like knights in shining armour, great leaders are the default solution to any organizational crisis. With vision, courage, determination, and insight, the traits that ordinary people are seen not to have, great authentic leaders can transform any organizational situation from crisis to prosperity. Little wonder, therefore, that they get paid so much and are in high demand. Leaders are often presented as either heroes, visionaries who are courageous, and principled individuals who lead their people to better futures; or failures, lacking moral courage, knowledge, or insight, resulting in bad decisions that lead to disaster (see Table 13.1). If you have a problem in the organization, then look to 'the man' (for it still normally is the man) at the top of the organization to sort it out.

 Visit the online resources and take a look at the extension material for Chapter 13 for further examples of leaders as heroes and villains.

This image of great leaders being single-handedly responsible for their organization's success or failure is commonplace in the news, and in some academic literature. It has led to considerable energy being directed at examining the characteristics of great leaders and trying to discover how to develop them. Yet despite decades of research, the field is inconclusive, with little agreement on how important certain characteristics are, or what traits make great leaders. Indeed, arguably there is too much emphasis on the leader as a hero or villain, and not enough attention focused on leader*ship* as a process that goes on throughout the organization and that is done by

Table 13.1 Examples of leaders as 'heroes' or 'villains'

Heroes	Villains
During their successful run in the 2018 World Cup, the England manager Gareth Southgate was widely praised for his calm, confident manner, people management, and attention to detail (Stern, 2018).	In 2017 officials in England's Football Association were called upon to resign, having failed to deal with accusations of racism within the England women's football team (Taylor, 2017).
Arundhati Bhattacharya is credited with transforming SBI, India's largest bank, through plain speaking, financial acumen, and an entrepreneurial approach. Her visionary outlook helped her understand the changing nature of technology and transform the 200-year-old bank (Majumdar, 2015).	Samsung's CEO and vice-chair Kwon Oh-Hyun resigned in what he called an 'unprecedented crisis', which included the new Note 7 smartphone bursting into flames. Oh-Hyun stated that Samsung needed 'a new leader more than ever' (Lee and Jin, 2017).
Stock in the semiconductor maker AMD has almost quadrupled thanks to Lisa Su's leadership. She is known for technical prowess, vision in simplifying the business, and tackling really difficult problems (Gharib, 2017).	One month after Deutsche Bank was fined $2.5bn and ordered to fire seven employees for their role in the Libor rate-fixing scandal, the bank's joint CEOs, Jürgen Fitschen and Anshu Jain, resigned. While not implicated themselves, as heads of the bank they were deemed liable for its actions (Henning and Strasburg, 2015).

many people. Indeed, Tesla's CEO, Elon Musk, is often praised as a hero, described as a visionary, ideologue, and risk-taker by trying to create a carbon-free world and a human colony on Mars (Korosec, 2017); yet he is also criticized as a villain for bad working conditions and being anti-union (White, 2018).

Theories of leadership

This chapter starts with the individualist great man and trait theories. These theories focus on the individual at the top of the organization and seek to work out what makes such an individual great and successful. While this focus on 'superstars' is intuitively appealing and still common-place in the press and some academic theory, we will see that it is too narrow, focusing on an individual and not looking at their behaviour. We next look at behavioural theories, which are broader in that they look at the interactions between leaders and followers, beginning to examine what leaders actually do. Yet these theories do not take into account the situation that a leader faces, which is what situational leadership explores. However, all the above still predominantly focus on the leader as individual rather than leaders*hip* as an activity. Transformational leadership offers workers a vision of the future. More recent theories seek to disrupt our fascination with great leaders. The concept of post-heroic leadership draws our attention to the social processes of leadership. Distributive leadership theory explores where leadership occurs throughout the organization. Those studying democratic leadership seek to explore ways in which power and control can be spread throughout the organization, potentially increasing both the autonomy and the commitment of everyone involved.

Employability skills: developing your leadership skills—insights from prominent business leaders

Stephen Hester, CEO of RSA Insurance Group and former CEO of the Royal Bank of Scotland, states that he worked on developing his skills over the course of his career. In his exclusive interview for this book, Hester states that he realized early in his career that his

> strongest skills were analytical skills and communication skills, my weaker skills were dealing nicely with people or managing people well. And I got a long way with just analytical and communication skills, but I did not get as far as I wanted to get. So, I needed to spend a point in the middle bit of my career working really hard to improve my ability to manage people.

So how did he go about this?

> Concentrating on it, thinking about it; I actually took on an external coach for a couple of years to help work with me on those things, getting feedback from other people, the same way anyone would learn about anything.

Stephen Hester, former CEO of the Royal Bank of Scotland.
Source: Facundo Arrizabalaga / Shutterstock.com

Joe Greenwell, the former chairman of Ford in Britain, echoes many of these sentiments, stating that you need the capacity to 'learn all the time', to use data well, and to understand the marketplace and the customer. Fundamentally, you need to have energy and enthusiasm, a passion for what you do, an acute awareness of your strengths and weaknesses, and an ability to overcome your weaknesses. Listen and learn from others, particularly good leaders. Above all you need to focus on the essentials of the business—revenue, costs, and profit.

Sources: Author interview with Stephen Hester (2012); author interview with Joe Greenwell (2012).

 Visit the online resources and take a look at the videos and transcripts for the full interviews with Stephen Hester and Joe Greenwell.

 What skills and experience do you have of leadership and what areas do you need to improve? Identify one or two areas that you want to work on and spend some time considering how you can develop.

Definitions of leadership

What do we mean by leadership? The following are some popular definitions of leadership.

> Leadership has traditionally been seen as the ability and capacity to influence others.
>
> (Bass, 1985)

> The ability of an individual to influence, motivate, and enable others to contribute towards the effectiveness and success of the organisations of which they are members.
>
> (House et al., 2004: 56)

> Managers are people who do things right and leaders are people who do the right thing.
>
> (Bennis and Nanus, 1985: 21)

Differences between leadership and management

So what are leadership and management? While some commentators use the words 'leadership' and 'management' interchangeably, Grint and Holt (2011) argue that they are different. **Management** is concerned with organizations running smoothly, creating stability, and following the rules; **leadership** focuses on the vision of the future of the organization and creating new rules. Management is, therefore, business-as-usual, or as Bennis and Nanus have it 'do[ing] things right', whereas leadership is concerned with the future of the business, or in Bennis and Nanus's terms 'do[ing] the right thing' (1985). These differences are summarized in Table 13.2.

This definition impacts not just particular organizations but whole sectors. Grint and Holt cite the US car industry, which they say focused on the efficiency of sports utility vehicles (SUVs), which is a tame problem, rather than questioning whether these are appropriate vehicles for the twenty-first century (Grint and Holt, 2011: 90). Thus leadership is about asking the right questions, acting with vision, and rethinking the status quo. Leadership does not necessarily coincide with a formal position in the organization, but is more a way of thinking about how to solve organizational problems.

457

Table 13.2 The differences between leadership and management (based on Grint and Holt, 2011)

	Leadership	Management
Type of problem	Uncertain	Certain, knowable problems
	Vu jàdé (never seen this before)	Déjà vu (seen this before)
	Wicked problems (complex problem, not a simple cause and effect)	Tame problems (complicated, but resolvable through unilinear acts and is likely to have occurred before)
Response	Ask right questions	Give correct answers
	Innovative response to the novel problem	Same process or standard operating procedure that resolved the problem the last time it emerged
Outlook	Art	Science
	Vision	Operational
Example	Creating a transport strategy	Timetabling the railways

© Grint & Holt, *Followership in the NHS*, 2011. Available at http://www.kingsfund.org.uk/publications/articles/leadership_papers/nhs_followership.html

The individualistic leader: great man theory and trait theory

Chance rushes into the staff meeting a little out of breath. He has managed to get Saffron, one of the restaurant servers, to cover the reception, but he knows that this is only until lunchtime, when she has to return to her normal job. At least it is covered for now, he thinks to himself. With the meeting room full, Chance goes to the front to give his speech to the staff at Junction Hotel. He loves these moments—laying out the vision and mission of the hotel, reminding the staff of the direction that they are going in, and rallying the troops. At times like this, he imagines what other leaders would do. He loves the innovation of Steve Jobs and his drive and determination, and the passionate outlook of Howard Schultz (see Schultz, 2011; BBC, 2011; Groth, 2011), but he is happiest and feels most leader-like when he imagines himself as Winston Churchill. As he concludes his speech about how the hotel will overcome adversity and move into a brighter future, particularly if the investors' meal goes well, Chance declares with gusto, in Churchillian tones, that Junction Hotel will never be defeated.

 Make a list of who you think are great leaders—what makes them great? Are there any common characteristics that make them great?

What do successful leaders do before breakfast? Laura Vanderkam asks this in a book promising to reveal the secrets of successful leaders (2013). Vanderkam is not alone in her interest. Books such as *Alibaba: The house that Jack Ma built* (Clark, 2018); *Elon Musk: How the billionaire ECO of SpaceX and Tesla is shaping our future* (Vance, 2015); and *Lean in: Women, work, and the will to lead* by Sheryl Sandberg (2015) of Facebook, tantalize the reader with the promise to expose the secrets of leadership.

 Visit the online resources and take a look at the extension material for Chapter 13 for a further list of biographies of leaders.

This interest in what makes leaders great is hardly new. Over 150 years ago **great man theory**, first proposed by historian Thomas Carlyle, and **trait theory**, explained by Victorian sociologist and proto-geneticist Sir Francis Galton, attempted to understand what makes leaders great. Thomas Carlyle believed history was created by great men, 'who alone,' he argued, 'turn the wheel of history' (Collinson et al. 2017: 7). Both Carlyle and Galton thought that great leaders have innate characteristics putting them above normal people, due to their background, personal and physical character, key actions, and philosophy. Carlyle and Galton provided heroic accounts emphasizing great leaders' wisdom, charm, intelligence, insight, or political savvy.

The multi-Oscar-nominated film *Darkest hour* (dir. Joe Wright, 2017) tells the story of Winston Churchill in the midst of World War II. Neville Chamberlain had just been forced to resign as the UK prime minister for being too weak, so Winston Churchill stepped up in a time of crisis, leading Britain when it 'stood alone' against Nazi Germany. The film portrays Churchill as a strong leader with moral courage, consulting with the public and members of parliament before deciding to continue to fight.

→

Darkest Hour is in a long line of portrayals of Winston Churchill depicting him as the greatest statesman of the twentieth century. The International Churchill Society and numerous biographies aim to study the personality, background, and skills of Churchill to uncover the sources of his greatness and unique character. Churchill is widely presented (e.g. Roberts, 2003) as having a 'sense of destiny' and superior insight into the potential danger that Hitler posed. He is described as a visionary: inspirational, courageous, and an innovative leader with good people-management and listening skills. A strong public orator, he also impacted those he met personally, leaving them feeling braver after the meeting.

Understanding his life and background is seen as relevant to modern-day leadership. 'Churchill's leadership principles have proved both timeless and to be a continual source of inspiration to modern-day leaders, in both politics and business at a time when effective leadership has never been more essential' (Longstaffe, 2005: 83).

Winston Churchill.
Source: AF archive / Alamy Stock Photo

Yet such accounts often present a one-sided view stressing the good characteristics. Alternative accounts highlight how Churchill opposed Gandhi's peaceful protests for Indian independence and presided over one of the worst famines in human history (Oppenheim, 2017). Churchill, Shashi Tharoor argues, diverted food, on his personal orders, away from Bengal to British soldiers and countries such as Greece while a deadly famine swept through Bengal in which four million starved to death (Tharoor, 2018). Tharoor writes:

> Ships laden with wheat were coming in from Australia docking in Calcutta and were instructed by Churchill not to disembark their cargo but sail on to Europe ... And when conscience-stricken British officials wrote to the Prime Minister in London pointing out that his policies were causing needless loss of life all he could do was write peevishly in the margin of the report, 'Why hasn't Gandhi died yet?'

(Tharoor, cited in Oppenheim, 2017)

Sources: Roberts (2003); Longstaffe (2005); https://winstonchurchill.org/the-life-of-churchill/life/churchill-leader-and-statesman/

So what makes an ideal leader? Trait theory seeks list all the traits that an ideal leader would possess. For instance, John Gardner states that they include physical vitality and stamina, intelligence, being action-oriented, judgement, eagerness to accept responsibility, task competence, understanding followers and their needs, people management skills, need for achievement, motivational skills, courage and resolution, trustworthiness, decisiveness, self-confidence, assertiveness, and adaptability/flexibility (Gardner, 1989).

 Read through the traits listed. Do you think that any one individual could hold all these traits?

The individualistic (heroic) leader assessed

The focus on individual leaders continues to be popular, with top business leaders celebrated, presented as critical to organizational success and people we can learn from. However, the assumptions that individualistic leadership theories are based upon are problematic. In the first account of trait theory, Sir Francis Galton's *Hereditary genius* (1869) presented these traits as genetic, linked almost exclusively with the aristocracy and arising from 'breeding', with certain individuals *born* as good leaders. This view is now largely dismissed as being elitist (particularly as eugenics is often associated with Nazi Germany). While few hold such views today, many still assume that certain people are born *natural* leaders, stating 'it is unequivocally clear that leaders are not like other people' (Kirkpatrick and Locke, 1991: 59). Indeed, these special qualities are cited to provide the justification for business leaders earning substantially more than most people (see Chapter 17 for a discussion). The 'big five' personality traits (see Chapter 8 on personality) have been linked to leadership, with leaders seen to be more extravert, more conscientious in terms of the emergence of leaders (but not their effectiveness), and more open to experience because they are more analytical. Agreeableness was more mixed, and leaders were less neurotic (Bono et al., 2014: 201–4). More recently, trait theorists have argued that individuals can cultivate certain traits and therefore develop their leadership skills by learning from successful people.

Individualistic models suffer from difficulty in defining what makes a great leader. It is hard to imagine one person having all the traits a great leader should possess. Indeed, as far back as 1948, Stogdill concluded that there was no universal list of traits that could be defined for all leaders, making the concept inconclusive at best and, arguably, meaningless. Moreover, leadership traits that are successful in one situation might prove counterproductive in another. For instance, Winston Churchill was widely seen as one of the greatest wartime leaders, with approval ratings of over 78 per cent; however, after the war he led the Conservative Party to one of its heaviest defeats (Addison, 2011). His traits, as a strong and determined personality that everyone could rally round, may have worked in wartime, but in peacetime, without a clear common enemy or collective vision for the country, his strong-willed personality was unsuited for the environment.

Many researchers have also questioned whether these traits are objective and measurable. Complex personalities, they argue, cannot be simply reduced down to a list of definable characteristics (see Chapter 8 on personality). These traits do not actually exist in an objective sense but are a result of researchers interpreting the actions of the leaders.

Many of the key traits such as individualism, assertiveness, and control are often associated with a masculine personality (Calás and Smircich, 1993). Individualistic theory reinforces dominant, masculine images of the heroic leader (Bryman et al., 1988) and, as Badaracco (2001) argues, downplays the quiet, less heroic, but often more effective, aspects of leadership.

? Review questions

Describe	What are the key principles behind great man and trait theories?
Explain	What are the differences between leadership and management?
Analyse	What are the strengths and weaknesses of the great man theory?

Table 13.3 sets out some of the strengths and weaknesses of individualistic leadership theories.

Table 13.3 Strengths and weaknesses of individualistic leadership theories

Strengths	Weaknesses
Focused research on leadership	Lacks empirical evidence
Some evidence, as there are a number of great leaders throughout history	Lacks explanatory value
Still popular with some	Masculine and Western bias
	Stogdill (1948) points out that there is no universal list—inconclusive
	Class bias—breeding
	Not necessarily applicable to work organization
	Post-hoc rationalization
	Dated

Behavioural theory

Q Running case: the kitchen in preparation for the investors' meal

In the kitchen, Effingham is pacing up and down barking orders like a sergeant major: he knows this meal is critical to the hotel's success. 'Right, everyone, we have a big dinner to-night, with members of the board, the mayor, potential investors, and the press. I don't want anyone to put a foot wrong. Clem, start peeling the potatoes and then cut them into chips like I showed you last week; Josh, corkscrew the carrots—I want 100 of them by 4 pm; and, Toby, start marinating the pork. Come on! What are you waiting for?'

'But ... ,' begins Toby, quickly trailing off. 'I don't want to hear any "buts," Effingham snaps back, 'just do what I say.' Feeling the force of Effingham barking out his orders, Toby looks to Clem in a worried way. 'Saffron says the mayor is a vegetarian,' Toby whispers to Clem. 'And I don't want to hear any more talking, just get on with it!' Effingham roars.

As a response to the criticisms of the individualistic perspective, academic research began to focus on what leaders actually do. Behavioural theories drawing on **behaviourism**, particularly behavioural psychology (see Chapters 9 and 10), focus on how a leader's behaviour shapes their followers. Behaviour theories begin with the premise that all behaviour is a result of what they call **conditioning** (Figure 13.1). How we behave is thus a result of learned reacting to positive signs (rewards) or negative ones (punishment), and then adjusting our behaviour accordingly (see Chapter 9). Consequently, the actions of followers emerge from how the leader responds to their behaviour and the signals that they exhibit.

One of the earliest focuses of the impact of a leader's behaviour was developed in the late 1940s by the **Michigan studies**, and in the 1950s and early 1960s by the **Ohio State studies**. They stated that leaders are either employee- or task-focused, as shown in Table 13.4.

The Ohio studies have led to the conclusion that the most effective leaders combine task- and employee-focused approaches. This approach was developed in 1964 by Robert Blake and Jane

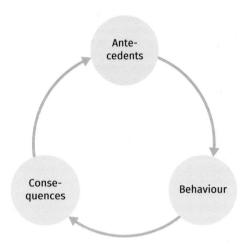

Figure 13.1 Skinner's A–B–C of behavioural conditioning.

Table 13.4 Differences between employee-centred and task-centred leadership (based on the Ohio State leadership studies)

Overall focus	Employee-centred	Task-centred
Leadership style	Listens to the subordinates, encourages participation, has a friendly manner that aims to enhance self-esteem, and builds an environment of trust, warmth, and concern; social sensitivity	Focuses on the task, provides clear expectations, instructions, and deadlines, focusing on maintaining standards
Leader's focus	Towards satisfying emotional and social needs of employees	Towards goals
Inspired by	Human relations theory	Taylorism
McGregor's Theory X or Theory Y (visit the online resources for a discussion)	Theory Y	Theory X
Leader's primary aim	Increased satisfaction	Higher production
Potential problems	Lower production	Increased turnover, absenteeism, and grievances of employees

Mouton, who developed the Leadership Grid®. They argued that the team management style, which combines a high concern for both people and production, was most effective, whereas the worst style is the impoverished management style, which has low concern for both (Blake and Mouton, 1964).

Autocratic, democratic, and laissez-faire leadership styles

A related approach to leaders' behaviour was developed in the late 1930s by Kurt Lewin and colleagues. They claimed there were three key styles of leadership: autocratic, democratic, and laissez-faire. See Table 13.5 for a summary.

Table 13.5 Lewin's three leadership styles (Lewin et al., 1939)

Name	Decision making	Role of group	Advantages	Disadvantages
Autocratic	Centralized	Followers	Quick decision making	Can hinder creativity
Participative	With group, leader overall	Participating and involved	Involvement and originality	Can be slow in time of crisis
Laissez-faire	Left to the group	Have full autonomy	Freedom of group members	Slow decision making and often unproductive

The autocratic style emphasizes **command and control**. All decisions are made by the leader, one step at a time, with little input from the group, so that the followers never know for certain what the next step will be. The leader is personal in his praise and criticism of the followers, but aloof from the group unless demonstrating what the next step is.

While this approach is good for rapid decision making, it tends to be dysfunctional, creating discontentment, hostility, scapegoating, and aggression within the group, and blocking creativity. Such groups tended to 'develop a pattern of aggressive domination towards one another, and their relation to the leader was one of submission or of persistent demands for attention' (Lewin et al., 1939: 277).

In many senses, the laissez-faire approach offers the complete opposite perspective. The group has *complete freedom to act without any participation of the leader.* The leader provides the resources and information but does not participate or interfere outside of this. Lewin et al. (1939) state that the laissez-faire approach is highly inefficient and unproductive, resulting in discontent, hostility, scapegoating, and aggression as the groups feel they lack direction.

The democratic approach makes *all policy matters a subject for group discussion.* The leader facilitates group discussions but does not dominate. The aim is to involve all the group members and allow them to make decisions, as they will implement them and be impacted by them. The democratic approach, Lewin et al. claim, is the most effective. There is less aggression, change is more easily accepted, relations between the group members are friendlier, and the group is more creative. It creates a sense of belonging and participation within the group.

Visit the online resources and take a look at the extension material for Chapter 13 to take the Lewin quiz and find out your leadership style.

 Theory in context: Lewin's leadership styles

Like many of the theories that we use in organizational behaviour, Lewin's did not start out as business and management theories. Lewin's three leadership styles actually started life as Lewin assessed the reactions of ten-year-old children to a group leader in 'theatrical mask-making for a period of three months' (Lewin et al., 1939: 271). Therefore, it is questionable if this research can be applied easily to understanding management practice, as the context is quite different.

→

→

Bill Cooke, an expert on Kurt Lewin's work, argues that the styles were also part of Lewin's left-wing political project. Lewin, he claims, saw these three leadership styles as representing three different political systems.

- Autocratic style: fascism, dictatorship, and control
- Participative style: social democracy, a left-wing reform movement embracing socialism and government intervention for the good of society
- Laissez-faire: free-market capitalism

Lewin, a German Jew who left Germany when Hitler came to power, had an obvious opposition to autocratic leadership styles. As a socialist he was also opposed to the laissez-faire approaches, as he thought that the capitalist market should not be left to itself because the poor and weak suffer in such systems. Lewin wanted to demonstrate that it was 'right, proper and possible to intervene to effect social change on behalf of the disadvantaged' (Cooke, 1999: 92). Therefore, the superiority of the democratic model was, for Lewin, support for the social democratic model of government (Thelen, 1992). This model of leadership, therefore, could be read as a political project to further a more democratic and fairer society rather than simply as three categories of leadership.

Behavioural approaches assessed

These behavioural approaches have focused attention on how a leader's actions impact followers, bringing in followers to research for the first time. They also offer the potential for leadership skills to be learned and developed over time.

However, they still search for a 'one best way'—an ideal form of leadership that should be used by all leaders in all situations. Behaviourism also offers a simplistic and mechanical understanding of followers' behaviour, as simply a reaction to stimulus with little free will. See Table 13.6 for a summary.

Table 13.6 Strengths and weaknesses of behaviourism

Strengths	Weaknesses
More subtle than many previous theories	Hard to measure
Examines the interaction of the leader and follower and the impact the leader has on the group	Presents a 'one best way' approach and does not take into account the situation
Practice of leadership	Male and Western bias
Possibility of training	Questionable validity of research
	Overemphasis on taxonomies
	Simplistic
	Examines only behaviour, not its impact

? **Review questions**

Describe	What are behavioural theories of leadership?
Explain	Why do behaviourists believe the leader's behaviour impacts the followers?
Analyse	Why is it important that Lewin's original study was about mask-making by ten-year-old children rather than about practising managers? How might knowing this background be useful in your essay/exam? What are the implications that Lewin's political leanings might have on his theory of leadership?
Apply	How would you describe Effingham's leadership style? Do you think it is appropriate for working in the kitchen at Junction Hotel?

Situation and contingency leadership theories

Q **Running case:** Chance prepares for his one-to-one meetings

Returning to his office, Chance gathers his notes for his one-to-one sessions. First, he is meeting Linda Wilkinson, his keen, committed, but sometimes anxious domestic manager. Although she is experienced, Chance sometimes feels he has to be careful what he says to her as she has a habit of taking things the wrong way. They have to have a tricky discussion over why the maintenance staff are not fixing rooms up to the standard that some customers require. Wilkinson, though, can be defensive of her team, and Chance wonders quite how to put it.

Being direct with Effingham, though, is never a problem. The boisterous and outspoken chef is the complete opposite and obsessed with the restaurant. However, Chance wonders if this style always works well with others in the hotel, as Effingham has a reputation for falling out with other members of staff. It is this issue that Chance needs to raise with Effingham. He wonders if he should just come out and say it.

Visit the online resources and take a look at the extension material for Chapter 13 to read our online profiles of Wilkinson and Effingham. How do you think Chance will treat these two? Make up your own mind after reading their online profiles.

Why are some leaders more effective in some situations than others? Contingency theory argues that leaders are effective when their leadership style is appropriate for the situation that they face. A leader's success will be dependent on two factors: (1) the leader's preferred leadership style—their typical way of interacting with followers; (2) situational control—the degree of control the leader has over the situation. Effective leadership depends on getting the perfect match between the situation and the leadership style (Figure 13.2).

The Least Preferred Co-worker scale

One of the most well-known contingency theorists is Fred Fiedler. Fiedler argued that everyone has a preferred leadership style and they are most successful when their style matches the situation. It is vital therefore to work out your preferred leadership style.

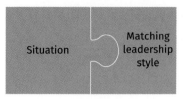

Figure 13.2 Leadership style to match the situation.

But how do you discover your preferred leadership style? To find this out Fiedler developed the Least Preferred Co-worker scale, a series of questions about the person you work least well with (LPC). It works like this: you are asked to think of the one person in your life you find hardest to work with. You then give them a rating between 1 and 8 on a range of adjectives: friendly/unfriendly, pleasant/unpleasant, interesting/boring, etc. (Fiedler and Chemers, 1984). If you rate them very harshly, then Fiedler states that you are task-oriented, because you value the task more highly. However, if you are more lenient then you are more relationship-oriented.

Fiedler suggests that the score you give says more about you, and in particular your attitudes to work and people, than it says about the LPC, because he assumes that all the least preferred co-workers are equally unpleasant. He also says that neither task- nor relationship-orientated leaders are better. Rather, Fiedler argued, the most effective leadership style depends on the situation, based on the quality of the relationship the leader has with the followers; the nature of the task; and the degree of formal authority the leader has (see Table 13.7). Fiedler argued that it is easier to be a leader when the group accepts and trusts its leader, when the task is highly structured, and when the leader has formal authority than when the group distrusts the leader, tasks are vague,

Table 13.7 Key factors in Fiedler's (1967) Least Preferred Co-worker scale

Leader–member relations	Good—the group tends to trust the leader and accept them
	Poor—the group tends to distrust the leader and does not accept the leader's position
Task structure	Structured—with clear goals; highly standardized and predictable, with only a few ways to carry it out
	Unstructured—ambiguous goals, many ways of undertaking the task, and unclear criteria to judge success
Leader position power	Strong—the leader has considerable formal authority and has the power to influence the group
	Weak—the leader has little formal authority and little power to influence the group

and the leader has little formal authority. As we all have a preferred leadership approach, we can try to match the right leader to the right situation.

Visit the online resources and take a look at the extension material for Chapter 13 to see the LPC diagram, take the LPC questionnaire, and discover what your leadership style is.

Situational leadership

A more flexible contingency leadership theory is offered by Hersey and Blanchard (1988). They say that leaders can adapt their style to the situation rather than simply having a fixed style that needs to be matched to the appropriate situation. They call this situational leadership.

Hersey and Blanchard present their model as a two-by-two matrix. The horizontal axis is the complexity of the task (either low or high) and the amount of direction the leader gives to the group. On the vertical axis is the relationship focus: how supportive the leader needs to be. Their model (see Table 13.8) argues that groups go through stages as they mature, and the leader needs to adjust their behaviour to match the situation of the group.

- Stage 1: *telling or directing*. High task- and low relationship-focused. In this stage the group are new, they are committed (they want to be seen as doing well), but they have low levels of competency (do not have many skills). The leader is highly directive, telling the subordinates what to do and how to do it. The leader has very little relationship with the followers.

- Stage 2: *selling or coaching*. High task and high relationship. At this stage the group increase their competency (they have started learning to do things), but, as a result, they begin to lose confidence and their motivation drops as they become aware of what they cannot do. In this situation the leader remains quite directive, telling them what to do, but is more encouraging and therefore focused on building up personal relationships.

- Stage 3: *participating or encouraging*. Low task and high relationship. As the group develops, its members increase their levels of skill and confidence, and their commitment levels begin to rise again. To support this stage the leader becomes less focused on the task and more on helping to support and encourage the group through adopting a facilitation style.

- Stage 4: *delegating and empowering*. Low task and low relationship. At this final stage the group have matured and have high levels of skill and confidence. As a result, the leader can allow them to run things on a daily basis and is only really involved in problem solving and key decisions.

Visit the online resources and take a look at the web links for Chapter 13 to see a diagram illustrating this.

How it works

The leader diagnoses the commitment and competency of the followers and then shapes a leadership style accordingly. For instance, faced with an inexperienced but highly motivated group (D1), the leader needs to adopt a direct and goal-focused approach, providing clear tasks with clear instructions (S1). The followers, having low skill levels, will appreciate clear tasks as this removes ambiguity.

As the group members learn new skills (D2), they become increasingly uncertain and can thus lose motivation. The leader therefore needs to develop the group's confidence by focusing on relationship and commitment, using two-way dialogue to increase involvement. As their skills increase (S3) the group need less direction but more encouragement to maintain confidence in their skills (D3).

467

468

Table 13.8 Situational leadership model (based on Hersey and Blanchard, 1988)

Title	Leader's focus		Followers'			Appropriate communication style	Appropriate leadership style
	Task	Relationship	Commitment	Competency			
S1 Telling/ directing	High	Low	High	Low D1		Top-down Announced as the followers are after certainty	Goal focused Clear, well-defined task: what is to be done, how to do it, and who is responsible Closely supervised
S2 Selling/ coaching/ explaining	High	High	Lack (lost initial motivation) Aim to build self-esteem	Some competent D2		Two-way to involve and motivate the employees and develop their competency	Leader provides some direction as followers are still relatively inexperience
S3 Participating/ supporting/ asking	Low	High	Lack (as unsure of their skill)	Moderate to high D3		Facilitation model	Day-to-day decision making by followers as they have experience, but involvement by leader to bolster confidence and motivation
S4 Delegating/ empowering	Low	Low	High	High D4		Little support or facilitation needed	Leaders are still involved in decisions and problem solving, but control is with the followers

An experienced, motivated, and confident group (D4) works best with more autonomy, with the leader only involved in problem solving and key decisions (S4).

More recently, Hersey and Blanchard have argued that the leader also needs to explain to the group why the leadership style is changing; otherwise the group can be left feeling isolated, believing that the leader does not care (compare this model to Tuckman's group formation in Chapter 6).

 Study skills: leadership in group work

During your time at university, you will probably spend time working in groups. While it is unlikely your group will officially appoint a 'leader', you will, at times, take on leadership roles, both in terms of organizing your group and by supporting and encouraging other group members. As you read through this chapter, consider your own leadership style and how it can be adjusted to meet different situations.

Path–goal and congruence model

One of the primary problems of early contingency theory is that it sees leadership style as simply matching the leader's focus on task and/or relationships to the followers' commitment and competency, ignoring wider factors such as culture, power and politics, and identity.

To overcome this narrow perspective, House (1996) developed **path–goal theory**, and Nadler and Tushman (1997) developed the congruence model. These theories broaden the analysis to include factors such as the organization's environment, the resources available to the leader, and the organization's history (visit the online resources for Chapter 13 for more details). By taking into account more variables, they offer a more subtle and far-reaching understanding of the environment the leader faces. However, they also become more complicated and mathematical as they try to deal with almost every factor the organization faces.

Situational and contingency leadership theories assessed

Situational and contingency theories have been used regularly in training programmes for future leaders because they offer practical guidelines and tools to help leaders assess and adapt their leadership styles to meet the situations they face. For instance, recent leadership theories suggest that a leader's style needs to fit with the culture of the organization that they are working in and that they should provide consistent cues for the employees on how to behave in keeping with this culture (Hartnell et al., 2016). Therefore situational theories offer a more subtle understanding than individualistic and behavioural approaches, as they increase attention to leaders' impact on followers. However, they do little to explain how leaders move from low to high development levels (Northouse, 2010). There is also a lack of empirical evidence to support situational and contingency theories (Bryman, 1986).

One underlying problem is that all contingency theories work on the assumption that the context of the group, including the skill levels, motivation, leader–follower relations, organizational history, etc., is an objective reality which the leader can know 'transparent[ly] through scientific analysis' (Grint, 2005: 1470). However, human behaviour is far more unpredictable and complex than these models suggest.

Also, although these perspectives challenge the notion there is one best leadership style, they still assume that each situation demands a particular leadership style, thus moving from the *one best way* to *one best response*. Table 13.9 summarizes the pros and cons of such theories.

Table 13.9 Pros and cons of contingency theory

Pros	Cons
Understand situation	Neat models, but applicable to real life?
No ideal leader	Still limited view on the group
Variety of leadership styles	Potentially normative
More flexible models	North-American and gender bias
Impact on followers	Limited look at structure, politics, etc.

Visit the online resources and take a look at the extension material for Chapter 13 for more details on these models.

? Review questions

Describe   What is meant by contingency leadership theory?

Explain   Why does contingency theory offer a more flexible approach to leadership?

Analyse   How could contingency theory be criticized as still representing a 'one best way'?

Transformational leadership

Q Running case: Linda Wilkinson's one-to-one

As their meeting progresses Simon Chance realizes that Linda Wilkinson is struggling with managing the maintenance team. 'They just ignore some of my requests,' she says honestly. 'You know, I ask them to do things, try to offer them incentives to fix the rooms, but they just don't seem to make it a priority. I've even tried just pulling rank on them and telling them—it works OK for a day or so and then they go back to their old ways.' Chance listens intently and then leans forward. 'You need to inspire them—they need to want to do a good job.' 'Easier said than done,' thinks Wilkinson.

A recent study by Dinh et al. (2014) argued that charismatic and transformational leadership theories are the most common within leadership studies. These studies, much like great man theory, seek to discover what makes certain leaders outstanding. At their heart they argue that such leaders have a future orientation, which offers a positive vision of the way the organization is going which motivates others. One of the founders of this theoretical perspective is Burns (1978) who argues Transformational leaders are those who offer a better vision of the world that employees can buy into. He contrasts this with Transactional leaders who try to control followers and cut deals with them. Table 13.10 summarizes the main differences between these two approaches.

Transformational leaders lead by inspiring, causing a change in the followers, creating a shared mission, and encouraging followers to take ownership of their work. Drawing from

Table 13.10 Transactional and transformational leadership styles (based on Burns, 1978)

Transactional	Transformational
Cut deals with employees	Transform institutions
Exchange with workers	Offer a vision of the future that people want to buy into
Monitor and control workers	Let workers feel part of the solution
Extrinsic motivation	Intrinsic motivation
Short-term self-interest	Long-term substantive goals
Works best with inexperienced followers	Works best with experienced followers
Contingency theory	Charismatic leadership
Manager	Leader
Tame problems	Wicked problems
Preserver/trustee	Insurgent entrepreneur
Organizational man [*sic*]	Maverick

Maslow's hierarchy of needs (see Chapter 9), Burns argued that great leaders focus attention away from low-level needs (such as pay) towards loftier goals, such as self-esteem and self-actualization. They help followers achieve their goals and motivate them along the way (Bass and Riggio, 2006). According to Tichy and Davanna, transformational leaders are visionary change agents (see Chapter 11) who are courageous, are driven by values, have a strong belief in people, can cope with complexity, and are life-long learners. Similarly, Bass (1985) identified the following characteristics of transformational leaders:

- *idealized influence*—high moral and ethical standards, and therefore respected by the followers which creates loyalty

- *inspirational motivation*—strong vision for future based on values and ideals, which builds confidence and inspires followers

- *intellectual stimulation*—challenges organizational norms and encourages alternative thinking

- *individual consideration*—recognizes unique growth and developmental needs of followers.

By contrast, **transactional leaders** believe their followers are motivated by rewards and punishment, so they lead by offering exchanges or transactions (promises of higher pay, promotion, or status) for increased effort. The primary focus of transactional leaders is to plan, organize tasks, monitor progress, and fix problems as they arise. According to Bass (1985), the following characteristics define transactional leaders:

- *contingent reward*—tangible or intangible support or resources for effort and support

- *management by exception: active*—monitor performance and take corrective action when necessary

- *management by exception: passive*—monitor performance and only take action when really serious

- *laissez-faire*—avoidance of leadership responsibility.

Transformational leaders, therefore, are best at dealing with wicked problems, whereas transactional leaders are similar to managers as they focus on finding answers to everyday, tame problems. As Kanter (1992) states, for an organization to be successful it needs a mix of both of these types. Too many questioners and everything gets confused; too many people who follow the same old patterns and organizations get stuck in dead ends.

Transformative theory assessed

The transformative theory reignites the idea of the heroic leader, often using masculine traits to describe their personality, presenting them as having almost superhuman characteristics, inspiring their followers with passion to go the extra mile. However, evidence indicates that such charismatic and transformational leaders are only really effective in certain situations, for instance in highly bureaucratic organizations or in times of organizational crisis (Mumford et al., 2008). In such times of crisis charismatic leaders can provide followers with a story which gives them a sense of meaning and purpose, making sense of the messiness and confusion that they are experiencing.

While transformative and charismatic leaders might be seen as inspiring, they have been criticized for ignoring the more mundane activities of planning and decision-making that are central for organizational success (Yukl, 1999). From a critical perspective, transformative leadership could be seen as a form of control, manipulating the workers' desires and interests (as in the work of Stephen Lukes, discussed in Chapter 14) or inspiring them with a vision to get them to work harder against their real interests (see Chapter 7).

Leadership scandals and responses to them

Research insight: toxic leadership and authoritarian followers

Padilla, A., Hogan, R., and Kaiser, R.B. 2007. The toxic triangle: Destructive leaders, susceptible followers, and conducive environments. *Leadership Quarterly* 18 (3): 176–94.

Leadership is often presented as a *good thing*, something that organizations need and people desire. However, this view downplays another side of leadership: the destructive side. Art Padilla and colleagues call this the toxic triangle (Figure 13.3), a combination of destructive leaders, susceptible followers (who either conform or collude), and a conducive environment, particularly in unstable circumstances or where the followers perceive that there is a threat.

While the authors argue that not all charismatic leaders are destructive, 'destructive leaders typically are charismatic' (2007: 180). They also have a personal need for power; use their position for self-promotion; isolate and demonize opposing groups; and are narcissistic and at times sadistic, 'demand[ing] unquestioning obedience' (p. 181). They tend also to have had troubled early lives and to maintain an ideology of hate, 'vanquishing rivals and destroying despised enemies' (p. 182).

For these leaders to become destructive, Padilla et al. argue, they also need susceptible followers. These followers often have unmet needs (see the discussion of Maslow in Chapter 9), negative self-evaluation—'individuals with low self-esteem often wish to be someone more desirable, which prompts them to identify with charismatic leaders' (p. 183)—and low maturity. They might also be highly ambitious and willing to follow if they believe they will get personal advantage.

Figure 13.3 The toxic triangle: elements in three domains related to destructive leadership.
Source: Padilla et al. (2007: 180).

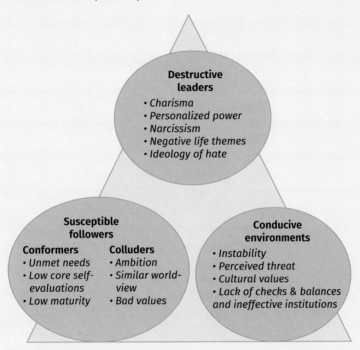

The final part of the triangle is the environment, which is more conducive where there is instability and/or a perceived threat so that people look to a strong leader to restore order. Having an absence of checks and balances can allow the leader more control and therefore room for destructiveness.

Padilla et al. argue that to limit the potential for destructive leadership, psychometric assessment should be used to identify potentially destructive leaders, more checks and balances should be put in to reduce the potential for destructiveness, and cultural values should be encouraged to support uncertainty avoidance and to reduce power distance.

 Real life case: emissions scandal at Volkswagen

On 18 September 2015, the United States Environmental Protection Agency issued German car manufacturer Volkswagen with a notice that they had violated the USA's Clean Air Act. Their tests had revealed that rather than passing the emissions tests, as had previously been thought, the cars failed. Under normal driving conditions the performance was better (more fuel efficient), but they released up to 40 times more nitrous oxides (which cause breathing difficulties for people) than had been asserted. Even more worrying was that the cars had appeared to pass the tests because software in the engines, known as 'defeat devices', had been programmed to recognize when the car was being tested, and only when this was happening did they turn on the emission controls. In other words, Volkswagen were cheating

→

the system. A worldwide scandal followed. At first approximately 482,000 US diesel vehicles were identified as having defeat devices, a figure that ultimately rose to around 11 million worldwide. The scandal is estimated to have cost Volkswagen $23.9bn (Rauwald, 2017), making it one of the largest business scandals to have ever occurred (Taylor and Schwartz, 2017). Following the diesel emissions scandal, Volkswagen's CEO Martin Winterkorn resigned, stating that he takes 'responsibility for the irregularities that have been found in diesel engines' (Ewing, 2015).

So why did Winterkorn have to resign, though he himself did not design the emissions-cheating software? First, as other leaders have done, he has taken personal responsibility for what occurred within Volkswagen and how they operated. Second, and a more troubling issue from an ethical position, he, alongside the board, were the ones that set the overall targets for the company and their strategic direction. In 2007 Winterkorn set highly ambitious targets, which 'critics at the time had ridiculed as delusional', announcing that by 2018 they would be 'the world's most profitable, fascinating and sustainable automobile manufacturer' (Rhodes, 2016: 1502). While we do not know what went on within Volkswagen itself, one can only imagine the pressure that the designers, engineers and production team were under to make a 'sustainable', i.e. fuel efficient, car, at an affordable price.

 How much responsibility should a leader of a large corporation have for the actions of their company?

Over the past few years, numerous corporate scandals have hit the headlines with business leaders in the spotlight. Revelations of unethical working practices at such firms as Uber, Sports Direct, and Volkswagen have rocked confidence in the values of business leadership. In response, a number of theories of leadership, including authentic leadership, servant leadership, and environmental leadership, have sought to make the values of the leader central.

Authentic leadership

Authentic leadership is an approach which emphasizes leadership through use of personal experiences, emotions, needs, and beliefs. Authentic leadership, seen as a valuable alternative to leaders who emphasize profit over people, prioritizes ethics and people as it emphasizes the legitimacy that leaders gain through having honest relationships with their followers. Avolio and Gardner argue that this is a more positive version of leadership (2005) that can guide leaders' behaviour towards more ethical ends (Gardner et al., 2011), giving leadership a moral foundation. Therefore there should be a link between the words and deeds of leaders, and leaders should be true to themselves and their own moral beliefs (Sendjaya et al., 2016). Authentic leadership means being self-aware and acting in line with your core beliefs, rather than using followers to further your own personal ends. However, in response to this emphasis on authentic leadership, Ford and Harding argue that such a position is impossible and that it is a more subtle way of controlling people (2011). An authentic leader, Ford and Harding state, would be so absorbed into the organization that they would lack subjectivity (consciousness).

While a focus on transformational leaders has been popular in recent years, a more balanced approach is offered by the C-I-P model (Table 13.11). This model suggests that charismatic,

Table 13.11 The C-I-P model

Style	Charismatic	Ideological	Pragmatic
Orientation	Vision of future	Idealizing the past	Problem solving in the present
Outlook	Constantly positive outlook	Rigid worldview reliant on personal values	Shaped by the environment
Use of emotions	Constantly positive	React with negative emotions, perceived injustice	Largely does not attempt to influence large groups, focuses on small group of trusted elite
Example	Herbert Hoover or Jack Welch	Steve Jobs or Donald Trump	Larry Page or Rupert Murdoch

Source: based on Griffith et al. (2015).

ideological, and pragmatic leadership styles all offer pathways to outstanding leadership with related strengths and weaknesses.

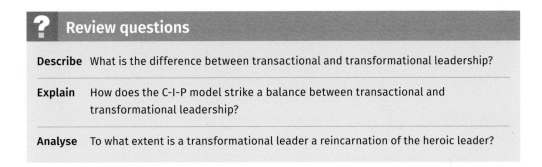

? Review questions

Describe What is the difference between transactional and transformational leadership?

Explain How does the C-I-P model strike a balance between transactional and transformational leadership?

Analyse To what extent is a transformational leader a reincarnation of the heroic leader?

Servant leadership and environmental leadership

Another approach that seeks to recover the moral purpose of leadership is **servant leadership** (Greenleaf, 1970). Servant leadership states that leaders should set aside personal interest for the betterment of their followers and the organization. It is a bottom-up perspective which sees the leader being their most effective when they support followers to enable them to do their jobs: the leader should give priority to the needs of their followers and colleagues, aiming to serve rather than to be served. To do this, the servant leader needs to know about each individual follower's unique characteristics and assist them to achieve their potential. This is done through encouragement and support. This is a dramatic change in the model of leadership. The leader is humble and acts to bring the best out of the employees:

> The difference manifests itself in the care taken by the servant—first to make sure that other people's highest priority needs are being served. The best test, and difficult to administer, is: Do those served grow as persons? Do they, while being served, become healthier, wiser, freer, more autonomous, more likely themselves to become servants? And, what is the effect on the least privileged in society? Will they benefit or at least not be further deprived?
>
> (Greenleaf, 1970: 7)

Greenleaf argues that servant leaders have 'moral authority' and follow truth. Fry talks in glowing terms about such leaders, arguing they embody the key values of 'patience, kindness, lack of envy, forgiveness, humility, selflessness, self-control, trust, loyalty, and truthfulness' (Fry, 2003: 712). In a recent review of 39 studies, Parris and Peachey argue that servant leadership is a viable leadership theory as it helps organizations improve *and* increase the well-being of the followers (2013). Liden et al. (2014) argue that servant leaders tend to be more respected by their followers and consequently they have a stronger influence on changing their culture. Similarly, environmental leadership aims to cultivate a self-sustaining group where employees find gratification through the group and task. These perspectives aim to create a more egalitarian and less hierarchical culture where the relationship between the leader and follower are more collaborative in nature.

Recent leadership theories assessed

Authentic leadership, servant leadership, and environmental leadership all share the same romantic view (see below) of leaders as positive and natural (Collinson et al., 2017). While such approaches appear to seek to offer a more positive vision of leadership, like transformative leadership theory, the central goal of this approach is to increase the productivity of the followers, to make them work harder (but not necessarily to gain more reward). They also can lead to over-estimating the power and importance of leaders, the issue to which we now turn.

 Look at Fry's list of the values of a servant leader. Do you think many leaders exhibit such values?

476

 Real life case: Vineet Nayar

Vineet Nayar is the former CEO of HCL Technologies, one of India's largest IT companies. During his time at HCL, the company's revenue almost tripled. But it was also praised for being highly democratic. Nayar argues that while traditional command and control structures might be the easiest, they are often not the most effective. The aim should be to decentralize power, responsibility, and accountability. This resulted in HCL being voted the Number One Best Employer in India 2009 and the Best Employer in Asia and the United Kingdom in 2017 and listed as one of the World's Most Attractive Employers 2016.

At the heart of Nayar's approach was a challenge to conventional business wisdom. He called it 'Employees First, Customers Second'. This is not designed to be nice to employees, but rather a way of being more effective. Traditional hierarchy, Nayar argued, often got in the way of teams that were trying to work together. 'The senior managers, sitting at their lofty remove from the real action, are the ones who can exercise the Hand of God decision that often puts at risk everything that is happening in the value zone' (Nayar, 2010: 96). Nayar also reversed accountability, so that if an issue came up or they wanted more information, an employee could open a 'ticket', meaning that the managers became responsible for solving the problem. Managers were also subject to 360-degree appraisal: they were appraised not only by their managers but also by their employees. HCL also had opinion polls on the company strategy and online forums so that employees could talk directly to Nayar.

Sources: *USA Today* (2007); Nayar (2010); Frauenheim (2014).

Challenging the leader-centric view

As Effingham goes in for his one-to-one, a call comes through to the kitchen. It's the mayor; he is a vegetarian, and they didn't know. With only 40 minutes until they arrive and Effingham in his meeting, there is panic in the kitchen as there is nothing prepared and there are no ingredients for vegetarians. Suddenly, Josh springs into action. 'We could do risotto,' he declares. 'We could use some of the veg we prepared for the roast.' Sensing Josh's idea, Toby chips in, 'Yes, and we could add the finely chopped onion on top—that would make it really nice.' Excited by their decisions, taken without Effingham there, they get to work.

All the theories we have presented so far are leader-centric. They are based on the assumption that the leader is central to an organization's success: a superman (or, occasionally, superwoman), with extraordinary powers to transform the organization virtually single-handedly. They achieve this either through force of character (great man, trait, and transformational theory) or through skill in working with the group (in contingency theory). This leader-centric lens portrays leaders as powerful, whereas the followers are simply passive, merely responding to leaders' actions. However, is such a picture accurate? Some leadership scholars have argued not: the leaders' significance is overstated, producing what Meindl et al. (1985) call a 'romanticism of leadership'.

477

Meindl, J.R., Ehrlich, S.B., and Dukerich, J.M. 1985. The romance of leadership. *Administrative Science Quarterly* 30 (1): 78–102.

Pillai, R., and Meindl, J.R. 1991. The impact of a performance crisis on attributions of charismatic leadership: A preliminary study. In: *Proceedings of the 1991 Eastern Academy of Management Meetings*, Hartford, CT.

In a series of influential studies, Meindl and colleagues argue that we overestimate the power and control of leaders. Using attribution theory (how people look for causes for events), they argue that often we over-attribute the success (or failure) of an organization to the leadership.

An early study (Meindl et al., 1985) found when reading 33,248 press articles that there was a significant correlation between references to the organizational leader in the article title and strong company performance. They found that in the years that the firms did well, these articles emphasized the leader more.

In a later study, Pillai and Meindl (1991) gave a group of people an identical CV of a male CEO but different information about the company's success. In the scenario, when there was a sudden increase in performance, the CEO was considered charismatic, but when performance declined, they stated he lacked charisma. In other words, the performance of the firm changed the way the leader's personality was viewed.

The implication is that leaders get credit (or the blame) even when there is little evidence that they have done anything remarkable.

 Why do you feel the 'romanticism of leadership' has been such an enduring concept?

This romanticism presents leaders as saviours of the organization, solely responsible for its fate, justifying the often incredibly large salaries (and bonuses) and high status which leaders receive (as discussed in Chapter 17). Indeed, followers often collude in this image, looking to leaders and investing hopes and fears in the leader to be saviours or scapegoats if things go wrong (see Grint, 2010). The problem that Meindl and colleagues identified is that there is a widespread tendency, in both academic and popular thinking, to exaggerate leaders' contribution to the success or failure of organizations. While truly incompetent leaders can make very harmful decisions (Goel and Thakor, 2008), in practice the success or failure of an organization is more constrained and linked to external factors which are outside of the leaders' control (Collinson et al., 2017). These factors can include the actions of employees, suppliers, or competitors; luck in terms of research and development breakthroughs; a changing political environment; or significant world events. Moreover, organizational employees rarely blindly follow a leader's actions, as they are often driven by professional codes of conduct which shape their actions. Thus, however good a leader's decision-making process may be, numerous unforeseen outcomes can impact the implementation of the decision.

These romantic theories tend to focus on the leader, their traits or behaviours, rather than the practice of leader*ship*, which involves followers. This infatuation with great leaders means that we have lost sight of followers (Uhl-Bien et al., 2014), what Bjerke calls followership (1999). Followership theory argues that followers are essential to leadership. Moreover, followers are not passive, simply responding to the behaviour of the leader, but have their own ways of thinking and acting.

Real life case: followers care about their work but are not engaged

The 2017 Gallup *State of the global workplace* survey (Gallup, 2017) explored the attitudes and perceptions of employees for 155 countries. They found that only 15 per cent of all adults in full-time work (and only 10 per cent in Western Europe) said they were highly involved in and enthusiastic about their work and workplace. These figures are worse than a 2014 survey by Towers Watson, who found that workers wanted to be engaged in their work and have a passion for what they did: 40 per cent were highly engaged and would 'go the extra mile' for their job, up from only 21 per cent in 2007; 24 per cent felt were actually disengaged because they did not have an emotional connection with the company; and a further 36 per cent felt unsupported or detached, meaning that a total of 60 per cent did not feel fully engaged (Figure 13.4).

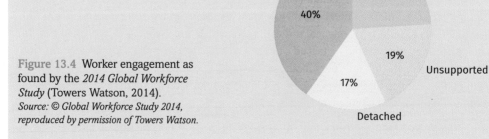

Figure 13.4 Worker engagement as found by the *2014 Global Workforce Study* (Towers Watson, 2014).
Source: © Global Workforce Study 2014, reproduced by permission of Towers Watson.

→

Both surveys demonstrate an 'engagement gap', which occurs because organizations are not tapping into the full potential of their staff or creating an energized workforce. The top driver in increasing worker engagement was senior management being seen as effective.

Sources: Towers Watson (2014); Gallup (2017).

The post-heroic perspective and the importance of followers

In the following sections we will look at ideas and leadership theories that draw the focus away from the leader as hero: the social constructionist perspective; the importance of followers; leadership-as-practice; distributive leadership; and finally leadership as 'muddling through'.

Social constructionist theory of leadership

The social constructionist perspective (see the online resources for Chapter 13 for more details) challenges the leader-centric view. It argues that what counts as good leadership is determined by the followers' perceptions as well as by the intentions of the leader.

For a leader to be considered successful (or at least accepted), they need to live up to (or potentially redefine) the followers' beliefs or expectations of them. For instance, all professions have social and cultural expectations of how they should be treated and led. Doctors tend not to respond well to just being told what to do, because part of their identity and training is tied up in being autonomous (Dent, 2003). Consequently, a leader needs to respond to these expectations in order to be accepted. The followers have to actually want to follow the leader.

The missing followers

Our obsession with leaders, as identified by Meindl and colleagues (1995), means that we ignore the other critical side of this relationship, the followers. Followers are vital for leadership. Leaders are charismatic only if the followers see them as charismatic; leaders can be motivational only if the followers see them as motivational; and leaders can make things happen only if followers follow their lead and put their ideas into practice. Without followers there can be nobody to lead. Followers, however, for a long time received very little attention in the academic literature and where they did appear, followers were often presented in a rather negative light, as 'passive, helpless, conforming individuals, with little or no drive or aspiration until they are persuaded out of their sloth by the leader' (Ford and Harding, 2018: 4).

Followers have more recently become an important subject of study in their own right. These studies have looked at followers' identities and styles (Collinson, 2006) and how followers can exhibit many of the behaviours that are traditionally seen to be associated with leaders (Cunha et al., 2013). Some of this recent research (i.e. Carsten et al., 2017) explores how followers shape the behaviour of leaders. Indeed, building on some of the work by Meindl this work suggests that the mere title 'leader' makes the follower see the leader differently. One approach is to understand the different orientations of the followers and how these orientations shape the relationship with the leader. Followers, for instance, might see themselves as co-producing the outcomes, collaborating with a leader as a partner; or, at the opposite extreme, followers may see themselves as simply passive recipients of instructions (Carsten et al., 2017). These beliefs or orientations shape the way that leaders can act. Followership theory presents a two-way dynamic process, where the leaders and followers shape each other and, by doing so, shape the possibile outcomes for both the follower *and* the leader.

This attention on followers is certainly welcome, as it opens up discussion of the relationship between leaders and followers. However, despite the authors' attempts to portray followers more positively, they still present them as largely passive (Ford and Harding, 2011; 2018). Often, within the literature, leaders are praised and followers are seen more as obstacles to getting things done (as discussed in Chapter 12).

Leadership-as-practice

Another related view that seeks to disrupt the focus on the heroic leader is leadership-as-practice. Traditional and many contemporary perspectives (i.e. transformational and servant leadership) are preoccupied with the individual leader, their traits or behaviours. In doing so they ignore two highly important aspects of leadership: practices and relationships. Leadership-as-practice looks at *where*, *how*, and *why* leadership occurs rather than, as most leadership theories do, *who* is doing it. It is concerneds less about what a single individual thinks or does and instead focuses on what people achieve together. Leadership, therefore, is seen as a cooperative activity (Raelin, 2011), as 'a complex web of relationships, practices and structures' (Chreim, 2015: 518).

The focus of this perspective, therefore, is social relations: the interactions between people which shape meaning. The distinction between leaders and followers is seen as somewhat artificial (Collinson, 2005). Instead, leadership is seen as a social practice, a *process*, creating shared meaning and understanding by using symbols, forming shared language, and shaping values (see, for instance, Smircich and Morgan, 1982).

From this perspective, leadership should be thought of as an act that can be done by anyone throughout the organization. Many engage in acts of leadership—for example, an administrative assistant 'showing the ropes' to a new employee (Raelin, 2005), a shop worker solving a customer's problem, or an engineer designing a new tool. Everyone has the capacity to take a lead at certain points, which Raelin calls being leaderful (2005). This perspective shifts the focus away from the leader's personal characteristics and on to the act of leading, where everyone has the capacity to be a leader or take a lead through their actions.

Theory in context: the changing nature of society needing alternative forms of leadership

Over the last 50 years there have been dramatic changes, particularly in the West, in the nature of society and the economy, which challenge traditional leadership theories. First, since the 1960s there has been a gradual loss of faith in the abilities of authority figures to solve our problems. Second, the shift from manufacturing to the information or knowledge economy has meant that the nature of jobs has changed. Third, these better-educated 'knowledge workers' desire more autonomy and use of their skills. Fourth, there is a change in organizational structure, with flatter organizations based more around teamwork.

The 'knowledge worker' holds specialized skills, meaning that their ideas and input are essential for organizational success. They are employed to think rather than to be told what to do. As Niall FitzGerald, deputy chairman of Thomson Reuters, puts it:

[T]he way in which the world has developed means authority is no longer to be given. It must be earned. People will only give their loyalty to those they respect—they will not give it to the position ... You have to engage people.

(Thomson and Lloyd, 2011: 31)

Leadership is an activity that takes place throughout the organization. This is particularly important in knowledge-intensive, creative, or customer-service-focused industries where traditional command and control leadership styles are less effective.

Such shifts require different approaches to leadership. Instead of top-down, command and control leadership, this new economy requires involving the workers by getting their ideas and input. Organizational success is built upon the experience and knowledge of the workforce.

The question therefore emerges of how to create the right conditions to encourage and enhance the actions of organizational members. Rather than the leader standing at the front of the organization directing and controlling the passive followers, the leader's role is to create the environment in which followers can flourish.

Distributive leadership

Distributive leadership argues that leadership does not simply follow a formal position in the hierarchy but can be seen throughout the organization (Gronn, 2002). Gronn seeks to get rid of the leader-follower distinction, by arguing that all organizational members potentially can be leaders and that leadership is an *outcome* of the interactions process. There are no followers in that, at a given time, different people can emerge and take a lead in a situation because they have a better view of what needs to be done and how to do it. This perspective argues that organizational success is usually the product of a collective effort, rather than the effort of one (heroic) individual alone.

One result of this perspective is that teamworking, empowerment, and more participatory approaches are encouraged as they create a more inclusive, motivated, and involved workforce, utilizing everyone's skills and abilities within the organization. Changes in technology mean that there is a significant reduction in the need for one individual to be at the top of the organization telling others what to do. Proponents of this perspective argue that top-down leadership can be a source of frustration, particularly for professionals who generally desire autonomy and input into decision making processes. Not engaging followers or using their passion, ideas, and knowledge can be experienced as demotivating, particularly when the followers feel that decisions are being imposed on them.

Rather than tying people to formal roles or positions, distributive leadership works on the premise that different people can take on leadership responsibilities at different points, largely linked to their knowledge and expertise. Leadership therefore works on a rotational basis, with members of the group stepping forward and leading the group when their specialism or skills demand it and then acting as normal members of the group the rest of the time. This is particularly effective in situations where other members of the group recognize that a particular individual has the knowledge to respond to that particular situation.

 Real life case: distributing the power and getting results

Ricardo Semler was Latin American Businessman of the Year in 1990. He is widely heralded as leading one of the most innovative and democratic organizations in the world. Semler argues he treats Semco's 800 employees as responsible adults. Workers can set their own hours, chose their own information technology, share all information, and even set their own salary. Semco has three core values: democracy, profit-sharing, and information. Twice a year subordinates evaluate their managers, and they even interview their future managers. Key decisions are made collectively via a vote. Letting people participate in decisions that affect their lives has positive effects on their motivation and morale, Semler claims (Semler, 1999).

Leadership as muddling through

After his meeting with Effingham, Chance hears a knock on the door. 'Come in, David,' Chance says, showing Hunter to a seat. 'Have you heard the good news? We've got the mayor tonight.' 'Yes, that's why I've come,' responds Hunter hesitantly. 'I fear it is not good news.' 'What?' asks Chance, somewhat confused. 'Have you not heard the stories?' Hunter continues. 'The mayor has had a falling-out with City Investments.' 'Oh dear, that's one of our top potential investors,' Chance responds. 'What are we going to do?'

What do leaders actually do in practice? Our common-sense views, which are derived from such writers as Henri Fayol (see Chapter 2) and emphasized in mainstream leadership theory, present leadership and management as a rational activity conducted by heroic characters—reflecting and having creative visions and strategies. However, as Alvesson and Sveningsson (2003) argue, much of what managers and leaders actually do in practice is mundane and involves everyday activities, such as listening and chatting.

One of the first writers to bring this to the attention of management theory was Henry Mintzberg. In a famous article in 1975, he compared the folklore (the stories of myths about managers and leaders) to what he called the fact (the actual practices). His theory is summarized in Table 13.12.

Mintzberg discovered that leadership practice is more messy, confused, and disjointed than the idealized image presented in leadership theories. Much of leadership and management work is political (see Chapter 14 of this book) and involves dealing with competing priorities. Mintzberg also found that, far from resembling the work of an idealized reflective planner, the average day of managers he studied was characterized by brevity and discontinuity. Most of the managers surveyed 'worked without interruption for a half hour or more only about once every two days'. He concluded the current system of 'managing does not breed reflective planners; managers respond to stimuli'.

Furthermore, in contrast to the heroic image of the leader as the all-knowing individual who is in complete control, Mintzberg's work acknowledges that much of leadership is conducted through improvisation and coping with situations that the leader faces. More recently, a number of researchers have discovered that the overwhelming majority of decisions are taken 'on the hoof' (Chia and Holt, 2006: 643) and therefore leaders need to be 'skilled [at] improvised in-situ coping' (Chia, 2004: 33). Holmberg and Tyrstrup (2010) argue that more of management and leadership

Table 13.12 What managers really do—folklore and fact (based on Mintzberg, 1975)

Folklore	Fact
Systematic, reflective planner	Brevity, discontinuous activity, orientation to action
No regular duties, but is a coordinator and then sits back	Regular duties, such as presiding over rituals, ceremonies, and negotiations
Uses formal management information system	Does not use them but prefers verbal communication instead of documents
Management is a science	Little has really changed over the last 100 years but has become a little more scientific

activity is event-driven—responding to situations rather than planning for the future. Classic leadership theory of the reflective planner or heroic visionary could therefore be seen as a romanticized fantasy, as reality is far more messy and confusing (Sveningsson and Larsson, 2006). In her analysis of interviews with MBA graduates, Amanda Hay found that many struggled with their role as organizational leaders and often felt they didn't know what they were doing (2014). She illustrates how they were involved in *practical coping*, and argues that management (and leadership) education should be focused on challenging the fantasy view of leaders and understanding the actual everyday challenges that real leaders face.

While this might come as a disappointment in comparison to the classic fantasy view of leaders and managers, the revelation that reality is more messy and confusing can be comforting. Reflecting on Mintzberg's article some 15 years later, one manager stated that it was a relief to discover that most managers do not spend their time planning and coordinating as in the idealized image, but rather were 'keeping a lid on the chaos'.

? Review questions

Describe What are the key principles behind post-heroic leadership?

Explain Why do post-heroic leadership theorists argue that it is important to focus attention on followership?

Analyse Why do post-heroic leadership theorists argue that shifting from command and control to distributive leadership could increase productivity in the organization?

Analyse Why is the idealized view of leadership challenged by seeing what managers actually do in practice?

Post-heroic leadership theory assessed

Post-heroic leadership theory has therefore sought to redress the balance that has over-emphasized the role of individual leaders at the top of the organization's hierarchy by drawing attention to the real everyday practices of leadership. However, such theory often ignores issues of gender and race and does little to really transform the power relations within organizations, as we will discuss in the next section.

Breaking the glass ceiling

 Real life case: Uber

Uber was in crisis, having hit the headlines when former employee Susan Fowler released her blog accusing the company of a culture of sexism (Fowler, 2017) and when Uber's founder and CEO Travis Kalanick took a leave of absence, saying he needed to mourn the death of his mother and 'work on himself'. Uber had arranged for former US attorney general Eric Holder to investigate claims of sexism and to offer recommendations for changing the way they

→

→

operated. Yet in the middle of an all-staff meeting led by board member Arianna Huffington—ironically, a meeting about the importance of diversity on boards of directors—David Bonderman made his infamous remarks. Huffington was reported to have said 'There's a lot of data that shows when there's one woman on the board, it's much more likely that there will be a second woman on the board,' to which Bonderman responded: 'Actually, what it shows is that it's much more likely to be more talking' (Somerville and Menn, 2017). Bonderman's comments sparked another wave of controversy, leading him to resign and Travis Kalanick to resign a few days later.

Uber are hardly alone in lacking representation of women or ethic minorities on boards. In 2011, a UK government-commissioned report, *Women on boards* (Davies, 2011), called for higher representation of women in the boardroom, with a target of 25 per cent of women serving on the boards of FTSE 100 companies by 2015 and all chairmen of FTSE 250 companies setting out the percentage of women that they aim to have on their boards by 2013 and 2015. The problems are stark: in 2015 it was revealed that the CEO of a FTSE 100 is more likely to be called John than to be a woman (Rankin, 2015). By 2017 Davies' target was met, but the increase has largely been among non-executive positions (Gale, 2017) than in positions of power on the boards.

In 2017 Sir John Parker undertook a review of the ethnic diversity of company boards, finding that only 85 out of 1,050 director positions in the FTSE 100 were held by people from ethnic minorities (Treanor, 2017).

Some companies, among them Diageo and Intercontinental Hotels Group, have led the way with 45.45 per cent of women on their boards, whereas Coca-Cola Hellenic Bottling Company was bottom of the list with only one female board member. Some of the major US firms have progressed, with General Motors, IBM, PepsiCo, Lockheed Martin, and DuPont all having women CEOs (*The Economist*, 2015).

The problems run deeper than simply not enough women at board level. In a survey by O2 that was widely publicized in the human resource management trade press, nearly half of women said they believed that all the decision makers in their organizations were men and 17 per cent believed it was 'impossible' for a woman to reach a senior management position (Newbery, 2015). An O2 human resources director stated:

> While the diversity debate has moved on outside of the office, not enough women are actually seeing this progress at work. If we're to achieve sustainable and long-lasting change, we can't just look at women already at the top; we need to focus our efforts on women at every level, creating a strong pipeline of female talent across British businesses.

> (quoted in Newbery, 2015)

A 2017 survey of approximately 900 directors by PricewaterhouseCoopers (PwC) found that 73 per cent believe that diversity is beneficial, with 94 per cent stating that it brings unique perspectives to the boardroom and 82 per cent saying it improves board performance. However, related findings showed that among 18- to 29-year-olds, 49 per cent believe that diversity is a barrier to progression within their organization (whereas only 20 per cent of those over 60 considered it a barrier) (PwC, 2017).

The report cited Norway as the prime example—it has over 44 per cent of board positions occupied by women. It was not always like this. In 2002 only 6.8 per cent of board posts were filled by women, rising to 18 per cent by 2005. Concerned by this, the Norwegian government drafted legislation giving companies until 2008 to meet their quota, with the threat of fines, and even liquidation,

Figure 13.5 Comparison of percentage of female new appointees in seven European countries, 2015.
Source: © Vinnicombe, Doldor, Sealy, Pryce, Turner, Cranfield University, 2015.

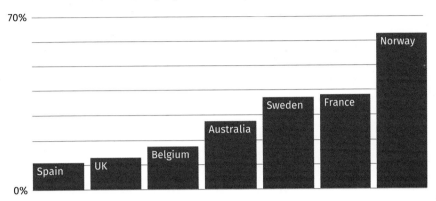

if they missed them. Norway has a training programme for women, as well as well-supported child-care, a welfare state, and maternity and paternity leave. With the right pressure, things can change.

Visit the online resources and take a look at the web links for Chapter 13 for more statistics on the representation of women in companies.

The lack of women in senior positions has long been identified as a problem and has been labelled the **glass ceiling** effect: an invisible barrier that minority groups and women cannot pass through to progress beyond middle management and get to senior positions in the organization (Kanter, 1977; Davidson and Cooper, 1992). Internationally, the UK is in a weak position when it comes to appointing women, with countries including Sweden, France, and Norway being far more successful (Figure 13.5).

Furthermore, men are able to accelerate their careers through the **glass escalator**, a metaphor for when men enter female-dominated professions and glide past women to more senior positions (Williams, 1992). Female managers, Wood and Newton (2006) have argued, have to work twice as hard to reach the top as they face many challenges within organizations and owing to their position in society, which can limit their capacity to rise up the career ladder. Men, therefore, despite considerable advances by women in junior and middle management, continue to monopolize senior positions of power and authority (Wajcman, 1998), and the women who reach senior positions exist in a male-dominated world.

Similar challenges can be seen for BAME (black, Asian and minority ethnic) employees. In a recent article Wyatt and Silverster state that while in the UK 12.4 per cent of the total working population are BAME employees, only 8.4 per cent are managers and 5 per cent senior managers (2015: 1244). This situation is sometimes called the *concrete* ceiling as it is denser and less easily shattered than the *glass* ceiling, but also seen as a labyrinth, in that it requires persistence and careful analysis to get through. Some of the problems that BAME employees and some women experience include exclusion from social networks, stereotyping, and the problem of 'similarity-attraction': senior leaders are likely to recruit people who have similar values and attitudes and come from a similar demographic to themselves (Wyatt and Silvester, 2015).

The *Women on boards* (Davies, 2011) report identifies reasons for the existence of the glass ceiling, including:

- problems with maintaining work/life balance
- masculine culture and poor networks for women
- maternity issues/leave

- traditional bias

- lack of opportunities

- tendency to recruit men.

They propose the following solutions:

- mentoring and support that helps overcome some of the gender issues

- changing corporate and societal attitudes

- challenging stereotypes about male and female roles (particularly those which suggest women cannot lead)

- childcare, flexible work arrangements, career breaks, and sabbaticals

- affirmative action, creating informal support and providing senior management sponsorship

- working with head-hunters to make women more visible in the recruitment process.

Research insight: are women really less visionary than men?

Painter-Morland, M., and Deslandes, G. 2014. Gender and visionary leading: Rethinking 'vision' with Bergson, Deleuze and Guattari. *Organization* 21 (6): 844–66.

Vision is seen as one of the key traits that sets great leaders apart from other people (see for instance the Winston Churchill case above). Visionary leaders are said to inspire their followers, creating social change as well as organizational success, and therefore vision it is often seen as a great trait to have. A commonly-held assumption is that women are less visionary than their male counterparts, and that this makes them less effective leaders. Mollie Painter-Morland and Ghislain Deslandes challenge this concept of 'vision', arguing that it draws on particular gender stereotypes. They argue that the 'stereotypical description of the female leader does not include attributes that are considered ideal for leadership positions' and that what is perceived to be 'female is defined as the inferior part of binary terms, i.e. as that which is not-male, that which is therefore not-efficient, not analytical, not visionary'. They go on to say that 'ideal traits, such as being analytical, competent, confident, convincing, decisive, efficient, fore-sighted, independent, etc. are associated with the male stereotype' (2014: 847). The consequence of this is that many women are caught in a trap. If they display what are seen as male behaviours such as 'aggressive, ambitious, dominant, self-confident and forceful, as well as self-reliant and individualistic, they are seen as not communal enough, and often, this is associated with inauthenticity' (2014: 847–8); yet if they do not display these traits they are seen as not visionary. The authors argue that we should rethink our preoccupation with vision and explore alternative ideas around leadership.

Alternatives to hierarchical leadership

Running case: Effingham returns to the kitchen

'OK, everyone, I've just heard we have the mayor tonight, and he's vegetarian. I want you, Toby, to start preparing another main course and Josh another starter.' Looking up he notices that none of them move. 'Come on, everyone!' Effingham shouts in exasperation. 'It's OK,' Josh smiles,

'we knew about this one because Saffron overheard Hunter on the phone—we've already got it sorted.' Effingham looks confused. 'What's this?' he says pointing at the starter. 'It's meant to be pork.' 'But we knew the mayor is vegetarian,' Toby declares proudly. Josh pipes up confidently: 'Look, we have it all under control.' Looking round the kitchen, Effingham is forced to agree.

Out in the restaurant things seem to be going well. 'Well, I must say,' declares the mayor, 'that is one of the finest meals I have had in a long time. To have produced that at such short notice you must have a wonderful chef.' 'I agree,' declares Steph, one of the potential investors, 'it was an individual meal, full of character and style.' Chance feels chuffed to lead Junction Hotel and is pleased to see the team pulling together.

Real life case: the problem with top-down leadership at Toshiba

In July 2015 the president and CEO of the Japanese company Toshiba, Hisao Tanaka, stepped down amid accusations that the company had inflated profits by $1.2 billion (Farrell, 2015). One of the fundamental problems was that the company had a top-down culture where followers did not question their leaders. As one report stated: 'Within Toshiba, there was a corporate culture in which one could not go against the wishes of superiors.' It went on to say: 'Therefore, when top management presented "challenges", division presidents, line managers and employees below them continually carried out inappropriate accounting practices to meet targets in line with the wishes of their superiors' (cited by Ando, 2015). It was clear that senior managers had too much power and not enough accountability. As a response, Toshiba planned to hire more independent directors, lawyers, and accountants (*Executive Grapevine*, 2015).

487

The leadership theories we have presented so far include organizational leaders as a natural and inevitable feature of the hierarchical structures that they are a part of, a view that can be traced back to Robert Michels' 'iron law of oligarchy' (Michels, 1915/2001; for a critique see Diefenbach, 2018). These assumptions about the superiority of hierarchical management, Blaug argues, are 'so ingrained into our political culture as to severely limit the set of possible strategic and procedural solutions available to us' (1999: 35). Yet some question such taken-for-granted assumptions.

Critical studies argue that hierarchical workplaces can generate systemic inequality and disempowerment for the majority of employees (Acker, 1990; Alvesson and Willmott, 1992). Hierarchy 'restricts people's freedom of action and expression' (Child, 2009: 504),

> undermin[ing] the freedom of large numbers of working people to adequately control their own lives. ... [Hierarchies are] based on structural inequality in a way that gives employers significant and unaccountable power over their employees, and are therefore deeply damaging to most workers' freedom.

(Malleson, 2014: 27 and 29)

Such structures work in favour of organizational elites, largely to the detriment of those lower down the hierarchy. Even leadership theories such as authentic leadership and servant leadership, which claim to be for the benefit of workers, are justified only to the extent that they can make the employees work harder and therefore can be seen as just a more effective way of exploiting workers. Such hierarchical systems not only harm workers but also managers, who 'frequently feel frustrated and abused by the systems which they supposedly control' (Alvesson and Willmott, 1996: 11).

As our real life case with Toshiba illustrates, top-down, hierarchical systems can produce significant problems. Theories deriving from anarchist literature, cooperative movements, and Scandinavian social theory question the assumptions that support such systems and argue that alternative, non-hierarchical, and non-leader-centred ways of organizing are not only possible but preferable. They state that worker-owned and worker-run organizations can not only produce benefits for society but also be more effective, creative, and motivational than traditional top-down organizations (e.g. Brown and Hosking, 1986; Land and King, 2014; Reedy et al., 2016).

Such approaches are not new. The Rochdale Pioneers, founded in 1844, were one of the first cooperative organizations, and many building societies started as mutual societies. However, these organizations still retain the traditional command and control structures.

More radical worker-run organizations do away with formal hierarchy altogether, in the belief that all members of the organization should be involved in decision making as it is more democratic, increases involvement, and results in better, more representative decision making. They are self-managed, built around consensus decision making, and conducted in the interests of the workers and wider society. All members of the organization have their say in how things are run and all have a share of the profits (Schwabenland, 2006; Parker et al., 2007).

This view goes beyond the participative approach of post-heroic leadership (and empowerment, which we will examine in the next chapter) as all the power resides with the members, who, on an equal basis, decide how the organization is run and receive the benefits. Generally, these organizations have a social purpose and seek to make products or sell services that people need. They work on a completely different value structure, as shown in Table 13.13.

While small in number, there are varied examples of this approach, from manufacturing and housing cooperatives through to youth groups. For example, Suma is a wholefoods cooperative that has a democratic management structure. The cooperative is jointly owned by all the members and everyone within the organization gets paid the same. They are committed to being ethical, ecological, and vegetarian (Suma, 2015).

Table 13.13 Differences between worker-run and shareholder-run organizations

Worker-run organizations	Shareholder/management-run organizations
Cooperation	Competition
Collective decision making	Senior management make decisions
Bottom-up decision making	Top-down decision making
Individual freedom	Economic freedom
Network	Command and control
Consensus decision making	Leader decides
Self-governing	Leader-governed
Workers' democracy	Share-owning democracy
Self-management	Hierarchical management
Vertical	Horizontal
Socially-driven	Shareholder-driven
Profit-sharing	Profit-driven
Self-help	Economic benefit

One of the key aims for these groups is to change the way that organizations are run, basing them on more democratic, participatory lines with the purpose of social progress.

One group which aims to develop such an approach is called Radical Routes. They state:

> We want to see a world based on equality and co-operation, where people give according to their ability and receive according to their needs, where work is fulfilling and useful and creativity is encouraged, where decision making is open to everyone with no hierarchies, where the environment is valued and respected in its own right rather than exploited.

(http://www.radicalroutes.org.uk/aims-and-principles.html)

Workers take control of the means of production, organize themselves, and decide the aims and purposes of the organization. By getting rid of the organization's leader, who makes decisions, they work in a more cooperative, consensus-driven, and democratic manner.

Consensus-based approaches offer alternatives to hierarchical, management-led approaches, aiming towards a shared solution. Consensus-based approaches build on the group's knowledge and insight, founded on learning from each other, and creating a shared understanding of the problem and the solution. The aim is to get overwhelming agreement and informed consensus, striving for everyone to say yes, but, where this is not possible, getting support from most of the group. The aim is for informed consent—they can live with the proposed settlement.

There is an obvious challenge in getting more people involved—many reject the potential for large-scale group discussions. However, techniques such as World Café (Brown et al., 2005) and Open Space Technology (Owen, 2008) can be used to hold meetings between only a handful or a few thousand people. They allow members of the organization to propose subjects to discuss, focus on the topics that matter to them, and build consensus through conversations. They have been used for cultural change programmes, business planning, and international conferences in for-profit organizations, social enterprises, and government agencies. Supporters of these systems argue that they are more democratic and participative and that they create better decisions that everyone can buy into by engaging with a much wider range of decision making.

Visit the online resources and take a look at the extension material for Chapter 13 for further discussion of these systems.

Real life case: Europace using Sociocracy

Europace Ltd are Germany's largest financial marketplace for financing real estate, providing saving schemes and private loans. What makes them unusual is how they organize themselves. Europace use sociocracy. Sociocracy, sometimes called dynamic governance, is a new, more empowering and relational way of organizing. Instead of operating using a hierarchical system, within sociocracy the organization is made up of a series of circles. Each circle has clear lines of responsibility and its members have autonomy to make decisions in their own right. They also work by consensus, where the circle makes decisions collectively so that everyone can *live with* the decision that is made. Sociocracy does not strive for perfect decisions, rather for decisions that have few objections so that action can be taken. If the decision is seen as 'good enough for now' then it goes ahead, with the view that it can be reviewed and changed later. Meetings at Europace occur using 'rounds', in which everyone gets the opportunity to speak; this is aimed at preventing unnecessary debates or only a few people dominating. They keep decision making to small but transparent groups, so that decisions can be made quickly. Europace say that this structure is helping them grow as a business.

Source: tech.europace.de

While these more democratic forms of organizing offer significant opportunities for greater levels of participation and control of workers' own lives, the responsibility which they bring can be challenging; indeed, workers sometimes reject opportunities for greater democratic control (King and Land, 2018). It is arguable that we have been so schooled into hierarchical forms of society, from education through to work, that we expect and in some senses crave a leader to tell us what to do, even when we also want autonomy and self-control.

? Review questions

Describe	What are worker-run organizations?
Explain	Why do worker-run organizations require different leadership styles and decision-making processes?
Analyse	Why would alternative organizational structures require a different attitude for everyone in the organization?
Apply	What type of leadership takes place at Europace (see the real life case above)? What are the advantages and disadvantages of this?

Connecting case and theory

Throughout this chapter we have seen different images of leadership at work. We opened with Simon Chance, the CEO of the Second Chance Consortium, preparing for his day, thinking of himself as a strategist and musing on an idealized view of leaders as heroic figures, leading from the front.

Chance drew on this heroic imagery in his presentation to the staff meeting, particularly referring to the biographies of Jobs, Schultz, and Churchill. These male leaders often provide us with our everyday assumptions of what leaders should be. Yet such a view of the heroic leader, which is used in great man theory and trait theory, is problematic, not least because it is too focused on the individual leader and does not take enough notice of the way the leader's actions impact the followers.

As behavioural theories argue, we need to understand more about the impact of the leader's behaviour on their followers. Think back to Effingham barking orders in an autocratic (Lewin et al., 1939) manner like a sergeant major, demanding obedience of the followers to his every command. While this might be good in a pressured environment such as the kitchen, it is less effective at getting the best from the staff where more creative input is required, for instance with the marketing team at the hotel. It also means that vital information can get missed, an issue we looked at later in the chapter. Notice how Toby reacted to Effingham's orders, becoming almost passive; his reaction can be seen as a result of conditioning, learnt responses to previous experiences. Toby knew that when Effingham was in this mood, he was not worth arguing with (so without telling Effingham they prepared a vegetarian option, just in case). We also saw how Effingham is highly task focused, a focus that is concerned, as Blake and Mouton's Leadership Grid® (1964) illustrates, with productivity rather than with people. Had Effingham been more concerned with the people he works with then potentially he would be able to get more out of them in the long run.

When we returned to Simon Chance we saw him preparing for his meetings with Effingham and Wilkinson. Due to their different personalities and the different challenges that they face, Chance realizes that he needs to adapt his leadership approach to the situation. This introduces us to **situational** (and **contingency**) **leadership theory**, which states that the leadership style that is used depends on the situation the leader faces. Hersey and Blanchard's model (1988) might be of interest to Effingham, who is in the *directing* phase. As his kitchen staff become more skilled, Hersey and Blanchard would argue, he should focus more on building the relationships and finding ways to motivate his staff, ultimately moving to facilitating and then delegating decisions to them.

In his one-to-one with Linda Wilkinson, Chance sought to encourage her to act as a **transformational leader**, inspiring the workers, instead of continuing with the **transactional** approach she has been using. This brought us to some contemporary theories including **authentic** leadership, where the leader inspires through using personal experiences, emotions, needs, and beliefs. However, as we have argued in this chapter, this simply returns us back to the image of the heroic leader, albeit with moral values seen as core. What it does ignore is the significance of followers.

We saw the importance of followers when we returned to the kitchen. Effingham had been unaware that the mayor was a vegetarian, so he is rescued by Toby, who had actually already produced a vegetarian main meal. Toby's actions challenge the **heroic** and **romantic** view of organizational leaders as all-knowing individuals. These **post-heroic** perspectives stress the importance of **followers** in the organization, not only in getting things done, but also in shaping the actions of the leaders. Followers such as Toby may have many good ideas that will be missed if the focus is solely on the leader.

We also saw throughout the chapter the idea of **leadership as a practice**, a perspective which sees leadership as a social process rather than about traits or behaviours. One version of this is **distributive leadership**, which seeks to pay less attention to the individual leader but rather explores how leadership occurs throughout the organization (such as when Toby takes initiative and prepares a vegetarian meal). Leadership is thus seen as a process of muddling through, dealing with constant interruption and workplace politics.

The running case therefore challenges the assumptions of the idealized vision of leadership by all-knowing great men, illustrating many of the everyday challenges that leaders face. As we have seen from the running case, followers are incredibly important (but often ignored in leadership literature) as is the practice of leadership as a way of coping with everyday situations. Leadership might indeed be thought of as 'keeping a lid on the chaos'.

Further reading

Bass, B.M. 1985. *Leadership and performance beyond expectation*. Free Press: New York.

This is one of the most influential mainstream leadership texts; it explores why certain leaders outperform others. This book was central in the establishment of the transformational view of leadership.

Meindl, J.R., Ehrlich, S.B., and Dukerich, J.M. 1985. The romance of leadership. *Administrative Science Quarterly* 30 (1): 78–102.

This highly influential article presents a telling critique of the heroic leadership model and provides the opening to the post-heroic.

Pettigrew, A., and McNulty, T. 1995. Power and influence in and around the boardroom. *Human Relations* 48 (8): 845–73.

This article examines the power and influence of board members of some of the top 200 companies and asks some interesting critical questions about the influence that this elite group have.

Griffith, J., Connelly, S., Thiel, C., and Johnson, G. 2015. How outstanding leaders lead with affect: An examination of charismatic, ideological, and pragmatic leaders. *Leadership Quarterly* 26 (4): 502–17.

This article provides an interesting overview of charismatic, ideological, and pragmatic leadership styles.

Uhl-Bien, M., Riggio, R.E., Lowe, K.B., and Carsten, M.K. 2014. Followership theory: A review and research agenda. *Leadership Quarterly* 25 (1): 83–104.

This article gives a good overview of leadership theory and the importance of followership, stating the need for more research in this area.

Klein, M. 2016. *Democratizing leadership: Counter-hegemonic democracy in organizations, institutions and communities.* Information Age Publishing Inc: Charlotte, NC.

A challenging book which offers a different vision of leadership away from the classic top-down style to one that is designed to work alongside oppressed people (including workers) to create new democratic spaces.

References

Acker, J. 1990. Hierarchies, jobs, bodies: A theory of gendered organizations. *Gender & Society* 4(2): 139–158.

Addison, P. 2011. Why Churchill lost in 1945. BBC Online. Available at: http://www.bbc.co.uk/history/worldwars/wwtwo/election_01.shtml (last accessed 30 November 2012).

Alvesson, M., and Sveningsson, S. 2003. Good visions, bad micro-management and ugly ambiguity: Contradictions of (non-) leadership in a knowledge-intensive organization. *Organization Studies* 24 (6): 961–88.

Alvesson, M., and Willmott, H. 1992. On the idea of emancipation in management and organization studies. *Academy of Management Review* 17 (3): 432–64.

Alvesson, M., and Willmott, H. 1996. Making Sense of Management: A Critical Introduction. SAGE: London.

Ando, R. 2015. UPDATE 2-Toshiba inflated profits by $1.2 bln with top execs' knowledge—investigation. *Reuters*, 20 July.

Avolio, B.J., and Gardner, W.L. 2005. Authentic leadership development: Getting to the root of positive forms of leadership. *Leadership Quarterly* 16 (3): 315–38.

Badaracco, J.L. 2001. We don't need another hero. *Harvard Business Review* 79 (8): 120–6.

Bass, B.M. 1985. *Leadership and performance beyond expectations.* Free Press: New York.

Bass, B., and Riggio, R. 2006. *Transformational leadership*, 2nd edn. Lawrence Erlbaum Associates: London.

BBC. 2011. Howard Schultz—CEO of Starbucks [radio interview]. BBC Radio 4, 12 May. Available at: http://www.bbc.co.uk/programmes/p00gwwkb (last accessed 5 July 2012).

Bennis, W., and Nanus, B. 1985. *Leaders: The strategies for taking charge.* Harper Collins: New York.

Bjerke, B. 1999. *Business leadership and culture: National management styles in the global economy.* Edward Elgar: Northampton, MA.

Blake, R., and Mouton, J. 1964. *The managerial grid.* Gulf: Houston, TX.

Bono, J.E., Shen, W., and Yoon, D.J. 2014. Personality and leadership: Looking back, looking ahead. In: Day, D. (ed.) *The Oxford handbook of leadership and organizations.*: Oxford Handbooks: Oxford, pp. 199–220.

Brown, J., and Isaacs, D. 2005. *World Café: Shaping our futures through conversations that matter*. Berrett-Koehler Publishers Inc.: San Francisco.

Brown, M.H., and Hosking, D.M. 1986. Distributed leadership and skilled performance as successful organization in social movements. *Human Relations* 39 (1): 65–79.

Bryman, A. 1986. *Leadership and organizations*. Routledge: London.

Bryman, A., Bresnen, M., Beardworth, A., and Keil, T.T. 1988. Qualitative research and the study of leadership. *Human Relations* 41 (1): 13–30.

Burns, J.M. 1978. *Leadership*. Harper & Row: New York.

Calás, M., and Smircich, L. 1993. Dangerous liaisons: The feminine-in-management meets globalization. *Business Horizons* 36 (2): 71–81.

Carsten, M. K., Uhl-Bien, M., & Huang, L. 2017. Leader perceptions and motivation as outcomes of followership role orientation and behavior. *Leadership* doi: 1742715017720306.

Chia, R. 2004. Strategy-as-practice: Reflections on the research agenda. *European Management Review* 1 (1): 29–34.

Chia, R., and Holt, R. 2006. Strategy as practical coping: A Heideggerian perspective. *Organization Studies* 27 (5): 635–55.

Child, J. 2009. Challenging hierarchy. In: Alvesson, M., Bridgman, T., and Willmott, H. (eds) *The Oxford handbook of critical management studies*. Oxford University Press: Oxford, pp. 501–14.

Chreim, S. 2015. The (non) distribution of leadership roles: Considering leadership practices and configurations. *Human Relations* 68 (4): 517–43.

Clark, D. 2018. *Alibaba: The house that Jack Ma built*. HarperCollins: New York.

Collinson, D. 2005. Questions of distance. *Leadership* 1 (2): 235–50.

Collinson, D. 2006. Rethinking followership: A post-structuralist analysis of follower identities. *Leadership Quarterly* 17 (2): 179–89.

Collinson, D., Jones, O. S. and Grint, K. 2018. 'No More Heroes': Critical Perspectives on Leadership Romanticism.

Organization Studies 39(11): 1625–47. doi: 10.1177/0170840617727784.

Cooke, B. 1999. Writing the left out of management theory: The historiography of the management of change. *Organization* 6 (1): 81–105.

Covington and Burling LLP. 2017. Recommendations. Available at: https://drive.google.com/file/d/0B1s08BdVqCgrUVM4UHBpTGROLXM/view

e Cunha, M. P., Rego, A., Clegg, S., & Neves, P. 2013. The case for transcendent followership. *Leadership* 9 (1): 87–106. https://doi.org/10.1177/1742715012447006

Davidson, M., and Cooper, C. 1992. *Shattering the glass ceiling: The woman manager*. Paul Chapman Publishing: London.

Davies, E. 2011. Women on boards. Department for Business Innovation and Skills. Available at: http://www.bis.gov.uk/assets/biscore/business-law/docs/w/11-745-women-on-boards

Dent, M. 2003. Managing doctors and saving a hospital: Irony, rhetoric and actor-networks. *Organization* 10 (1): 107–27.

Diefenbach, T. 2018. Why Michels' 'iron law of oligarchy' is not an iron law—and how democratic organisations can stay 'oligarchy-free'. *Organization Studies*, published online: https://doi.org/10.1177/0170840617751007.

Dinh, J.E., Lord, R.G., Gardner, W.L., Meuser, J.D., Liden, R.C., and Hu, J. 2014. Leadership theory and research in the new millennium: Current theoretical trends and changing perspectives. *Leadership Quarterly* 25 (1): 36–62.

Ewing, J. 2015. Volkswagen C.E.O. Martin Winterkorn resigns amid emissions scandal. *New York Times*, 24 September. Available at: https://www.nytimes.com/2015/09/24/business/international/volkswagen-chief-martin-winterkorn-resigns-amid-emissions-scandal.html

Executive Grapevine. 2015. Toshiba to cut interim CEOs' pay by 90%, 20 July.

Farrell, S. 2015. Toshiba boss quits over £780m accounting scandal. *The Guardian*, 21 July.

Fiedler, F. 1967. *A theory of leadership effectiveness*. McGraw-Hill: New York.

Fiedler, F., and Chemers, M. 1984. *Improving leadership effectiveness: The leader match concept*. John Wiley and Sons: Chichester.

Ford, J., and Harding, N. 2011. The impossibility of the 'true self' of authentic leadership. *Leadership* 7 (4): 463–79.

Ford, J., and Harding, N. 2018. Followers in leadership theory: Fiction, fantasy and illusion. *Leadership* 14 (1): 3–24.

Fowler, S. 2017. Reflecting on one very, very strange year at Uber. susanjfowler.com [blog], 19 February. Available at: https://www.susanjfowler.com/blog/2017/2/19/reflecting-on-one-very-strange-year-at-uber

Frauenheim, E. 2014. Vineet Nayar's happy feet. Workforce. Available at: http://www.workforce.com/articles/20311-vineet-nayars-happy-feet (last accessed 18 June 2015).

Fry, L.W. 2003. Toward a theory of spiritual leadership. *Leadership Quarterly* 14 (6): 693–727.

Gale, A. 2017. Revealed: The FTSE 100 companies where women do and don't succeed. *Management Today*, 24 April. Available at: http://www.management-today.co.uk/revealed-ftse-100-companies-women-dont-succeed/women-in-business/article/1431348

Gallup. 2017. *State of the global workplace*. Available at: https://www.gallup.com/services/178517/state-global-workplace.aspx

Gardner, J. 1989. *On leadership*. Free Press: New York.

Gardner, W.L., Cogliser, C.C., Davis, K.M., and Dickens, M.P. 2011. Authentic leadership: A review of the literature and research agenda. *Leadership Quarterly* 22 (6): 1120–45.

Gharib, S. 2017. AMD's CEO says to embrace work challenges. *Fortune Magazine*, 6 August. Available at: http://fortune.com/video/2017/01/03/amd-ceo-advice-at-work/

Goel, A.M., and Thakor, A.V. 2008. Overconfidence, CEO selection, and corporate governance. *Journal of Finance* 63 (6): 2737–84.

Greenleaf, R.K. 1970. *The servant as leader*. Robert K. Greenleaf Center: Newton Center, MA.

Griffith, J., Connelly, S., Thiel, C., and Johnson, G. 2015. How outstanding leaders lead with affect: An examination of charismatic, ideological, and pragmatic leaders. *Leadership Quarterly* 26 (4): 502–17.

Grint, K. 2005. Problems, problems, problems: The social construction of 'leadership'. *Human Relations* 58 (11): 1467–94.

Grint, K. 2010. The sacred in leadership: Separation, sacrifice and silence. *Organization Studies* 31 (1): 89–107.

Grint, K., and Holt, C. 2011. Leading questions: If 'Total Place', 'Big Society' and local leadership are the answers, what's the question? *Leadership* 7 (1): 85–98.

Gronn, P. 2002. Distributed leadership as a unit of analysis. *Leadership Quarterly* 13 (4): 423–51.

Groth, A. 2011. 19 amazing ways CEO Howard Schultz saved Starbucks. *Business Insider*, 19 June. Available at: http://www.businessinsider.com/howard-schultz-turned-starbucks-around-2011-6?op=1

Hartnell, C.A., Kinicki, A.J., Lambert, L.S., Fugate, M., and Doyle Corner, P. (2016). Do similarities or differences between CEO leadership and organizational culture have a more positive effect on firm performance? A test of competing predictions. *Journal of Applied Psychology* 101 (6): 846.

Hay, A. 2014. 'I don't know what I am doing!' Surfacing struggles of managerial identity work. *Management Learning* 45 (5): 509–24.

Henning, E., Enrich, D., and Strasburg, J. 2015. Deutsche Bank co-CEOs Jain and Fitschen resign. *Wall Street Journal*, 7 June. Available at: https://www.wsj.com/articles/deutsche-bank-co-ceos-to-announce-resignations-1433674815

Hersey, P., and Blanchard, K.H. 1988. *Management of organizational behaviour: Utilizing human resources*. Prentice Hall: Englewood Cliffs, NJ.

Holmberg, I., and Tyrstrup, M. 2010. Well then—what now? An everyday approach to managerial leadership. *Leadership* 6 (4): 353–72.

House, R. 1996. Path-goal theory of leadership: Lessons, legacy, and a reformulated theory. *Leadership Quarterly* 7 (3): 323–52.

House, R.J., Hanges, P.W., Javidan, M., Dorfman, P., and Gupta, V. (eds) 2004. *Culture, leadership, and organizations: The GLOBE study of 62 societies*. Sage: London.

Kanter, R. 1977. *Men and women of the corporation*. Basic Books: London.

Kanter, R.M. 1992. *The change masters: Corporate entrepreneurs at work*. Cengage Learning: London.

King, D., and Land, C. 2018. The democratic rejection of democracy: Performative failure and the limits of critical performativity in an organizational change project. *Human Relations*, published online: https://doi.org/10.1177/0018726717751841.

Kirkpatrick, S.A., and Locke, E.A. 1991. Leadership: Do traits matter? *Academy of Management Executive* 5 (2): 48–60.

Korosec, K. 2017. Why Tesla CEO Elon Musk is among the world's greatest leaders. *Fortune Magazine*, 24 March. Available at: http://fortune.com/2017/03/24/tesla-elon-musk-worlds-greatest-leaders/

Land, C., and King, D. 2014. Organizing otherwise: Translating anarchism in a voluntary sector organization. *Ephemera* 14 (4): 923–50.

Lee, Y., and Jin, H. 2017. Samsung Electronics CEO Kwon announces shock resignation as profits surge. Reuters. Available at: https://www.reuters.com/article/us-samsung-elec-kwon/samsung-electronics-ceo-kwon-announces-shock-resignation-as-profits-surge-idUSKBN1CI03P

Lewin, K., Lippitt, R., and White, R. 1939. Patterns of aggressive behavior in experimentally created social climates. *Journal of Social Psychology* 10: 271–301.

Liden, R.C., Wayne, S.J., Liao, C., and Meuser, J.D. 2014. Servant leadership and serving culture: Influence on individual and unit performance. *Academy of Management Journal* 57 (5): 1434–52.

Longstaffe, C. 2005. Winston Churchill, a leader from history or an inspiration for the future? *Industrial and Commercial Training* 37 (2): 80–83.

Majumdar, S. 2015. Arundhati Bhattacharya: Madam chairman. Forbes India, 15 October. Available at: http://www.forbesindia.com/article/leadership-awards-2015/arundhati-bhattacharya-madam-chairman/41249/1

Malleson, T. 2014. After Occupy: Economic Democracy for the 21st Century. New York: Oxford University Press.

Meindl, J.R., Ehrlich, S.B., and Dukerich, J.M. 1985. The romance of leadership. *Administrative Science Quarterly* 30 (1): 78–102.

Mintzberg, H. 1975. The manager's job: Folklore and fact. *Harvard Business Review* 53 (4): 29–61.

Mumford, M.D., Antes, A.L., Caughron, J.J., & Friedrich, T.L. 2008. Charismatic, ideological, and pragmatic leadership: Multi-level influences on emergence and performance. *Leadership Quarterly* 19 (2): 144–60

Nadler, D.A., and Tushman, M.L. 1997. *Competing by design: The power of organizational architecture*. Oxford University Press: Oxford.

Nayar, V. 2010. *Employees first, customers second: Turning conventional management upside down*. Harvard Business Press: Boston.

Newbery, C. 2015. A fifth of women believe it's 'impossible' to attain a top job. *People Management*, 20 January.

Northouse, P. 2010. *Leadership: Theory and practice*. Sage: London.

Oppenheim, M. 2017. Winston Churchill has as much blood on his hands as the worst genocidal dictators, claims Indian politician. *The Independent*, 8 September. Available at: https://www.independent.co.uk/news/world/world-history/winston-churchill-genocide-dictator-shashi-tharoor-melbourne-writers-festival-a7936141.html

Owen, H. 2008. *Open space technology: A user's guide*. Berrett-Koehler Publishers Inc.: San Francisco.

Parker, M., Fournier, V., and Reedy, P. 2007. *The dictionary of alternatives*. Zed Books: London.

Parris, D.L., and Peachey, J.W. 2013. A systematic literature review of servant leadership theory in organizational contexts. *Journal of Business Ethics* 113 (3): 377–93.

Pillai, R., and Meindl, J.R. 1991. The impact of a performance crisis on attributions of charismatic leadership: A preliminary study. In: *Proceedings of the 1991 Eastern Academy of Management Meetings*, Hartford, CT.

PwC. 2017. Global diversity and inclusion survey. Available at: https://www.pwc.com/gx/en/services/people-organisation/global-diversity-and-inclusion-survey.html

Raelin, J. 2005. We the leaders: In order to form a leaderful organization. *Journal of Leadership and Organizational Studies* 12 (2): 18–31.

Raelin, J. 2011. From leadership-as-practice to leaderful practice. *Leadership* 7 (2): 195–211.

Rankin, J. 2015. Fewer women leading FTSE firms than men called John. *The Guardian*, 6 March. Available at: https://www.theguardian.com/business/2015/mar/06/johns-davids-and-ians-outnumber-female-chief-executives-in-ftse-100

Rauwald, C. 2017. VW's costs keep adding up from its worst crisis ever. Bloomberg. Available at: www.bloomberg.com/news/articles/2017-02-24/vw-s-profit-boost-clouded-by-6-8-billion-diesel-crisis-charge

Reedy, P., King, D., and Coupland, C. 2016. Organizing for individuation: Alternative organizing, politics and new identities. *Organization Studies* 37 (11): 1553–73.

Rhodes, C. 2016. Democratic business ethics: Volkswagen's emissions scandal and the disruption of corporate sovereignty. *Organization Studies* 37 (10): 1501–18.

Roberts, A. 2003. *Hitler and Churchill: Secrets of leadership*. Weidenfeld & Nicolson: London.

Sandberg, S. 2015. *Lean in: Women, work, and the will to lead*. WH Allen: London.

Schultz, H. 2011. *Onward: How Starbucks fought for its life without losing its soul*. John Wiley and Sons: Chichester.

Schwabenland, C. 2006. *Stories, visions and values in voluntary organisations*. Ashgate: Farnham.

Semler, R. 1999. *Maverick! The success story behind the world's most unusual workplace*. Random House: London.

Sendjaya, S., Pekerti, A., Härtel, C., Hirst, G., and Butarbutar, I. 2016. Are authentic leaders always moral? The role of Machiavellianism in the relationship between authentic leadership and morality. *Journal of Business Ethics* 133 (1): 125–39.

Smircich, L., and Morgan, G. 1982. Leadership: The management of meaning. *Journal of Applied Behavioral Science* 18 (3): 257–73.

Somerville, H., and Menn, J. 2017. Uber board member apologizes for 'inappropriate' remark about women. Reuters. Available at: http://www.reuters.com/article/us-uber-board-bonderman/uber-board-member-apologizes-for-inappropriate-remark-about-women-idUSKBN1942ZD

Stern, S. 2018. Steppe change: How Gareth Southgate became a management guru in Russia. *The Guardian*, 28 June. Available at: https://www.theguardian.com/commentisfree/2018/jun/28/gareth-southgate-harvard-business-school-england-manager-football

Stogdill, R.M. 1948. Personal factors associated with leadership: A survey of the literature. *Journal of Psychology* 25: 35–71.

Suma. 2015. About Suma. Available at: http://www.suma.coop/about/ (last accessed 23 August 2015).

Sveningsson, S., and Larsson, M. 2006. Fantasies of leadership: Identity work. *Leadership* 2 (2): 203–24.

Taylor, D. 2017. Calls for FA officials to resign as Aluko says treatment 'bordered on blackmail'. *The Guardian*, 18 October. Available at: https://www.theguardian.com/football/2017/oct/18/fa-apologises-eni-aluko-drew-spence-mark-sampson-racial-remarks

Taylor, E., and Schwartz, J. 2017. VW bosses were told costs of emissions cheating scandal a month before investors. *The Independent*, 10 July. Available at: www.independent.co.uk/news/business/news/vw-volkswagen-diesel-emissions-cheating-scandal-bosses-told-costs-month-before-investors-illegal-a7832836.html

Tharoor, S. 2018. *Inglorious empire: What the British did to India*. Penguin: London.

The Economist. 2015. Sex in the boardroom, 6 June.

Thelen, H. 1992. *Research with Bion's concepts*. In: Pines, M. (ed.) *Bion and group psychotherapy*. Tavistock/Routledge: London.

Thomson, P., and Lloyd, T. 2011. *Women and the new business leadership*. Palgrave Macmillan: Basingstoke.

Towers Watson. 2014. *The 2014 Global Workforce Study*. Towers Watson: London.

Treanor, J. 2017. Top firms given four years to appoint ethnic minority directors. *The Guardian*, 12 October. Available at: https://www.theguardian.com/business/2017/oct/12/ftse-100-firms-deadline-ethnic-minority-directors

Uhl-Bien, M., Riggio, R.E., Lowe, K.B., and Carsten, M.K. 2014. Followership theory: A review and research agenda. *Leadership Quarterly* 25 (1): 83–104.

USA Today. 2007. CEO's bold experiment: Management by democracy, 16 December. Available at: http://usatoday30.usatoday.com/money/companies/management/2007-12-16-workplace-democracy_N.htm (last accessed 18 June 2015).

Vance, A. 2015. *Elon Musk: How the billionaire ECO of SpaceX and Tesla is shaping our future*. Virgin Books: London.

Vinnicombe, S., Doldor, E., Sealy, R., Pryce, P., and Turner, C. 2015. *The female FTSE board report 2015*. Cranfield School of Management: Cranfield.

Wajcman, J. 1998. *Managing like a man: Women and men in corporate management*. Polity Press: Cambridge.

White, J. 2018. Elon Musk anti-union tweet spurs labour law violation charge. *The Independent*, 24 May. Available at: https://www.independent.co.uk/life-style/gadgets-and-tech/news/elon-musk-tesla-twitter-union-uaw-organizing-labor-nlrb-fremont-plant-a8368111.html

Williams, C. 1992. The glass escalator: Hidden advantages for men in the 'female' professions. *Social Problems* 39 (3): 253–67.

Wood, G., and Newton, J. 2006. Childnessness and women managers: 'Choice' context and discourses. *Gender, Work and Organization* 13 (4): 338–58.

Wright, J. 2017. *Darkest hour* (film). Perfect World Pictures / Working Title Films.

Wyatt, M., & Silvester, J. 2015. Reflections on the labyrinth: Investigating black and minority ethnic leaders' career experiences. *Human Relations* 68 (8): 1243–69.

Yukl, G. 1999. An evaluation of conceptual weaknesses in transformational and charismatic leadership theories. *Leadership Quarterly* 10 (2): 285–305.

497

CHAPTER 14

Power and politics

The murky world of organizational life

Chapter overview and learning outcomes

By the end of this chapter you should be able to:

- describe the 'power as property' view

- explain why power and politics exist within organizations

- explain why power and politics challenge the image of organizations as rational places

- explain why Lukes and Foucault believe that power shapes how people see the world

- analyse the different underlying assumptions of 'power as property', 'structure as power', and 'power as productive'

Key theorists	
Stephen Lukes	Marxist theorist who argues that power works in often invisible ways, defining the choices that people make in ways they are often not aware of
Jeffrey Pfeffer	US management theorist who has investigated power in organizations and is a leading proponent of the 'power as property' view
John French and Bertram Raven	US social psychologists who argue that individuals can have several different sources of power
Rosabeth Moss Kanter	A professor at Harvard Business School, Kanter is one of the most influential business academics in the world, highly regarded for her work on change, gender, leadership, and empowerment
Michel Foucault	French historian and philosopher who presents a challenging interpretation of how power operates, seeing it as productive rather than repressive
Max Weber	German sociologist who argues that there are three categories of authority

Key terms

Power	A highly contested term, but can be seen as the capacity to get things done or to influence others
Office politics	Often seen as game-playing or manipulation, but can also be seen as an essential part of organizational life
Influence	The capacity to impact others, directly or indirectly
Emancipation	Literally—freedom from slavery; freedom from (often onerous) levels of control
False consciousness	A Marxist term—false beliefs held by the proletariat (workers) who do not know their true position in society as the revolutionary force to overthrow capitalism; instead, they see the current structure of society as unchangeable and largely fair
Empowerment	To be delegated power or authority to make (some) decisions

Introduction: politics at work

🔍 Running case: the staff development planning meeting

The middle managers of Junction Hotel are just finishing meeting to discuss their plans for the 'staff development week' (in reality only three days) which traditionally takes place in the last week of January when the hotel is closed for a refurbishment. 'Well, I think that's settled,' declares Meg Mortimer with considerable satisfaction in her voice. 'I think we have a really good programme of activities for the staff this year.'

'Yes,' agrees Linda Wilkinson, 'we have three packed days that I think will really improve the customer service of Junction Hotel. It is particularly good this year because the managers have organized some excellent big names to come to and speak to staff, and for the drama group to provide a more interesting way of training the staff in Gold Standard Service.'

'Well,' smiles Effingham, 'we know that what everyone really looks forward to is the tasting menu. This hotel's reputation, as Chance keeps telling me, is built on the quality of its restaurant. So I want to make sure that everyone this year really gets to taste everything as they need to promote it to all our customers—it only really works if they have sampled the food. I don't want what happened last year, when, you know, it got cut ... again!'

→

> →
>
> 'Look,' says Mortimer, 'you know that was a one-off. Linda didn't mean to book the outside caterers, that was just a communication breakdown. Anyway, you were not the only one that got stuff cut last year. My session on cleaning also got cut last year, despite it being every-one's responsibility, and we can't have that again.'
>
> 'Cleaning, how dull', Effingham mutters to himself.
>
> 'It might not matter to you if the hotel isn't kept clean,' retorts Wilkinson, 'but then we won't have any customers'.
>
> Mortimer looks crossly at Wilkinson and Effingham. 'Stop it, you two. Look, the programme has been agreed. Let's not reopen old wounds.'

We like to think of organizations as rational places, where decisions are made on merit, following rational and logical procedures, taken in the organizations' long-term best interests. We like to believe everyone involved in decision making leaves aside their personal interest to work for the common good and that we, as individual employees, are judged on our merits, and can get pro-moted or praised in line with our hard work and performance. In our idealized view, organizations are meritocracies, free of power and politics.

Jeffrey Pfeffer (2010) claims this idealized view is a fantasy. 'Power and politics is an essen-tial feature of organizational life. It takes more than good performance to do well in organiza-tions,' he states; 'being politically savvy and seeking power are related to career success and even managerial performance' (Pfeffer, 2010: 4). Pfeffer argues that as organizations have only one chief executive officer (CEO), and other senior positions are limited, competition to get to the top can be ferocious and highly politically charged. The result can be that 'Some of the individuals competing for advancement bend the rules of fair play or ignore them completely. Don't complain about this or wish the world were different,' Pfeffer (2010: 4–5) counsels. 'You can compete and even triumph if you understand the principles of power and are willing to use them' (ibid.: 5).

Power and politics are daily activities, Pfeffer argues, and may include various tactics: 'show-ing up opponents at meetings, getting access to some critical information, making a point with the boss ... forming alliances' (Pfeffer, 1981: 369). Even lower down the organization power and politics have impacts, such as getting the shift you want or being given a bonus. We need to be aware of power and politics and the impact that they can have on what goes on within the working environment, on organizational success, and on our individual careers.

This chapter argues that power and politics are central features of organizational life. Like organizational culture, power and politics are subterranean, below the surface, often invisible, but impacting everything. This observation reveals a shadow organization where decisions are made for alternative reasons than those officially stated. If you want to get on in organizations or under-stand how they work, then you need to understand power and politics.

501

> Consider an organization that you know well, somewhere you have worked, a club or society you have been involved in, or even your family. Are there any features that you would class as political? How did you feel about this?

This chapter starts with defining power and politics before moving on to explore office politics in everyday situations. We will then explore three key theoretical perspectives to understand power: *power as property* (which sees power as the possession of an individual or group), *structure as power* (which sees how the social structure shapes the way people think), and *power as productive* (which examines how power operates within everyday relations between people and organizations). Finally, we will explore how some writers and managers have sought to produce more equal and balanced management practices.

While power and politics are important to organizational life, until relatively recently these subjects did not receive much attention from organizational researchers, who preferred to view organizations as rational and bureaucratic (see Chapters 2–4) (Clegg and Haugaard, 2012). Consequently, many of the following theories did not arise from studying management, but rather came from political and social science, and, therefore, ask slightly broader questions about the way that power works in influencing society.

 Real life case: the dark side of power: sexual harassment in Hollywood

In late 2017 Hollywood was rocked by a series of scandals involving sexual harassment, sexual assaults, and rape. In particular, film producer and studio executive Harvey Weinstein, cofounder of Miramax, was implicated in a large number of allegations of sexual misconduct (Kantor and Twohey, 2017), and was quickly fired by his company's board of directors and expelled from the Academy of Motion Picture Arts and Sciences. Weinstein was not alone. By late 2017 thirty Hollywood actors, directors, and executives, including actor Kevin Spacey, were implicated, accused of inappropriate behaviour (Weaver and Convery, 2017). Across the Atlantic in the UK, a Conservative government minister was being investigated after allegedly asking his personal assistant to buy him sex toys (Jordan et al., 2017).

One of the underlying features of these stories is the imbalance of power that exists in these elite occupations. According to a 2017 report, 87 per cent of screenwriting credits and 79 per cent of producers in Hollywood are men, giving them significant power. Film producer Christine Vachon stated that this creates a certain culture: 'powerful men in any business could do what they wanted' (James and Blake, 2017). Speaking about this issue on BBC Radio 4's Today programme, Labour MP Lucy Powell stated that when you have many people wanting to work in an area but very few jobs 'you have an imbalance of power between those that might be able to offer you employment and also those who might be able to give you a leg-up in terms of advancement … this sort of power abuse can thrive' (BBC, 2017).

 Why do you think these scandals were allowed to continue for so long without being challenged? What impact did the power imbalance play between the powerful men and the women they are alleged to have abused? What would you have done if you were the victim of such attacks, particularly given the potential career costs of speaking out? What significance do you think the #MeToo movement has had in enabling victims to be able to speak out about these issues?

What is power?

Recent allegations of sexual harassment by public figures throw light on one of the most significant, but under-discussed, issues in organizational life: power. They demonstrate the power imbalance between the victim and the harasser that exist in these high-profile industries. The victims were almost universally in a weaker position in terms of career, prestige, and status, meaning not only were they less likely to have been believed, but making the accusations could have had potentially disastrous consequences for their career (Berlingieri, 2015). As such, sexual harassment, alongside other forms of bullying and abuse, are often invisible, representing dark forms of power that exist within organizations.

When we think of power in organizational life it is often with such negative connotations. Power is seen as a destructive force, making people do things that they do not want to do. Indeed, the classical view of organizational studies presents power in this light. Power breaks down the social order and causes problems to those within the organization. Yet this is a narrow view of power. While there are certainly exceptions (such as the cases of sexual harassment), power can be a positive force. To get virtually anything done in our society involves bringing people together (often in organizations) and this, in and of itself, is going to require a form of power: harnessing the wills of a collection of individuals for common purposes. Power is 'the ability to get things done, to mobilize resources, to get and use whatever it is that a person needs for the goals he or she is attempting to meet' (Kanter, 1977: 166). Power in an organization may therefore be legitimate and can be 'defined as the capacity to effect (or affect) organizational outcomes' (Mintzberg, 1983).

Power is an essential feature of everyday organizational life. As Clegg et al. state, 'Power is to organization as oxygen is to breathing' (2006: 3). While power is at its most visible when it is coercive, forcing people to do what they do not want to do (Fleming and Spicer, 2014), it is also present in invisible ways such as a system, a process, ideas, and the shaping of identities. Power exists in relationships, in all organizations and even through the invisible things that we rarely question: in rules, in taken-for-granted assumptions that we carry around with us, and in what we consider normal and acceptable ways of acting and behaving.

Power is part of our everyday selves. Consider a situation when you are driving along the road and then you see a police car: what do you do? Even if you are driving perfectly legally and within the speed limit, most of us slow down. Power shapes the way we experience the world and how we see ourselves as people (Fleming and Spicer, 2014). It is inherent within social relations, shaped by factors such as race, class, and gender, that impact on how we feel and behave at work. Power also operates within and between groups. As we saw in Chapters 5 and 6, the feeling of the need to belong, or to gain status within a group, is a powerful one that shapes peoples' behaviour.

Definitions of power and politics

- 'A has power over B to the extent that he can get B to do something that B would not otherwise do' (Dahl, 1957).
- Power is 'the probability that one actor within a social relationship will be in a position to carry out his own will despite resistance, regardless of the basis on which this probability rests' (Weber, 1978: 53).
- 'Power is a property of the system at rest; politics is the study of power in action' (Pfeffer, 1981: 7).
- Politics is 'the observable, but often covert, actions by which executives enhance their power to influence a decision' (Eisenhardt and Bourgeois III, 1988: 737).

Office politics—political skills

Meg Mortimer returns to her office with her notes from the meeting and looks with pleasure at the timetable that they have created. 'Three days of essential training', she thinks to herself.

	Tuesday	Wednesday	Thursday
10	You matter: Welcome to the Staff Development Week (Chance)	Face the future: The changing face of the hotel industry (Weaver)	Junction Hotel: Our mission for the year ahead (Chance)
11	Senior management briefing	Department briefings (Effingham, Hunter)	Developing your career (Mortimer)
12	(Weaver, Mortimer, Wilkinson)		Know your dishes (Effingham)
13	Tasting Menu 1	Tasting Menu 2	Tasting Menu 3
14	Cleaning, it is everybody's responsibility (Wilkinson)	Gold Standard Service (Mortimer)	Junction Hotel as an efficient hotel (Weaver)
15			
16			

As she finishes typing it up, the phone rings. 'Meg, it's Simon,' the voice on the phone states. 'We have a problem with the staff development week. We have a booking on the Thursday. One of the investor's daughter is getting married and wants to use the hotel for the reception. I couldn't possibly say no.'

Mortimer's heart sinks as she hears this. 'We can't do that,' she thinks to herself. 'Yes, of course, Mr Chance. I will start changing the timetable now,' she replies.

- In April 2017, the Indian consultancy and IT experts Infosys appointed Ravi Venkatesan to join R Seshasayee as co-chairman of the company, in a move that was seen by business commentators as 'confirmation that boardroom politics has become mainstream for the company' (Narayanan, 2017). According to Narayanan, Infosys were in a tussle between board members who have a 'socially conscious mindset' and those that have more a 'capitalist' perspective. The introduction of the new co-chair was seen as particularly challenging for Vishal Sikka, the managing director and CEO of Infosys, who Narayanan claims 'would rather deal with artificial intelligence in computers than natural politics in the boardroom' (2017). This claim seems to have been borne out when in August 2017 Sikka resigned. In his resignation letter Sikka cited distractions of the 'constant drumbeat of the same issues over and over again', 'have all been besieged by false, baseless, malicious and increasingly personal attacks', amplified, he said, by the very people he thought should have been supporting him which he said, took the 'excitement and passion out of this amazing journey' (*Economic Times*, 2017).

- Following a 'bust-up with a colleague' (Bird and Williams, 2017) the executive chairman of the Automobile Association, Bob Mackenzie, was sacked for gross misconduct. Mackenzie is reported to have been caught on camera physically attacking a colleague for up to two minutes and as a result of being fired was likely to lose shares worth between £68 and £95 million. Mackenzie's lawyers cite the level of stress and workload as mitigating factors that led to the attack (Mendick, 2017).

- All seemed rosy in August 2015 for Canadian pharmaceuticals giant Valeant. Their share price had risen to an all-time high of $262.52 and their CEO, Michael Pearson, was celebrating having 'delivered our fourth consecutive quarter of greater than 15 percent organic growth' (quoted in Morgenson, 2016). Yet within months, they lost 90 per cent of their share price and Pearson was removed with reports of bust-ups within the board (Crow, 2016). The troubled company had grown rapidly under Person's leadership based on debt-fuelled acquisitions (Crow and Platt, 2016) and a controversial pricing strategy where the prices of life-saving drugs were significantly increased. For instance Glumetza, a diabetes drug, price was increased from $572 to $3,432 and then one month later to $5,148 (Morgenson, 2016). The *Financial Times* reported that two of the biggest shareholders had a long-held rivalry over the direction of the company, causing divisions between the executives and directors about where the company was going (Crow, 2016).

- In October 2014 Chris Viehbacher resigned after receiving a payoff of, reportedly, approximately €3m and €250,000 per month (Ward, 2015) from the French pharmaceutical company Sanofi. The German-Canadian had clashed with Serge Weinberg, the chairman, 'over his management style and alleged communications problems with the board' (Ward, 2015). Mr Weinberg had told the *Financial Times*: 'We had some worries about management style, about execution, focus and also about the nature of the relationship with the board' (Thomson, 2014). Furthermore, the *Financial Times* reported, 'Mr Viehbacher's decisive character and quick decision-making had irritated some board members, and its chairman, in particular' (Thomson, 2014).

- Australian oil and gas company Tap Oil have been subject to continued speculation about the relationship between the CEO and the principal Thai shareholder (Macdonald-Smith, 2015), with rumours that the company would be split and some of the directors replaced with the Thai owners' own directors (Tap Oil, 2015).

 Can you think of any examples of office politics either that are in the news or that you have seen at work?

505

The advice pages of the business press are regularly filled with stories of treacherous personalities, sucking up to the boss, personal feuds, managers placing unrealistic pressures on employees, and less talented people getting promoted. These accounts demonstrate that organizations are not as rational as we like to think and that office politics is a key feature of organizational life.

Office politics rarely makes it into the public arena, and when it does it is often major boardroom disagreements which hit the headlines. Yet office politics can take many forms, including being humiliated by one's boss, being subject to gossip, and being offered support that never materializes. Popular management advice books present tips about how to succeed, negotiate, or just

Table 14.1 Examples of situations in office politics and suggested solutions

Situations in office politics	Suggested solutions
Regularly falling out of favour with the boss or with colleagues	Think about how you present yourself at work and how others might interpret your comments
Being the scapegoat for decisions	Build alliances with others and get a mentor
Swamped with work while a colleague slacks	Be more assertive at work and ask your colleague politely, but firmly, to take on some tasks
Having a boss that does not solve problems in a team and instead follows the line of least resistance	Do not expect the boss to be the saviour and try to tackle the problem yourself

survive office politics. These include learning the unspoken rules of the game, standing up for oneself, being seen in a positive light, being associated with a successful project, and ingratiating oneself to key people—all seen to be essential for office politics. Many claim that office politics is at least as important as being good at your job for career progression. Table 14.1 lists some examples of issues arising from office politics and suggested solutions.

 Visit the online resources and take a look at the extension material for Chapter 14 to see more examples of office politics.

Niccoló Machiavelli's *The prince*

Running case: a bun fight?

'I don't want to turn this into a departmental bun fight,' states Phil Weaver, as he and Linda Wilkinson stand outside the meeting room waiting for Meg Mortimer to arrive. 'I mean,' he continues, 'some people would make this type of event a battle between different sections of the hotel, and that's just not my style.'

'What's actually happened?' asks Wilkinson, looking a little perplexed. 'The last I knew we had all agreed the programme for the staff development week, and I've already been working on putting together my training programme for my sections.'

'Orders from on high,' replies Weaver, pointing to Chance's office. 'One of the daughters of our biggest investor is getting married on the Thursday, and they are going to use the hotel for the reception. That means that we have to do the training in two days, not three, because everyone will need to be working on Thursday morning to get the hotel looking spick and span for the reception that evening.

'You know what I would cut?' continues Weaver. 'All that stuff on customer service being everyone's responsibility and on communication skills. I mean have you ever heard such twaddle? You know,' Weaver continues, speaking in a whisper, 'I heard that Mortimer wants to cut your session on cleaning being everyone's responsibility. But if you support me, then I can support you in keeping it on the agenda.'

 How would you describe Weaver's behaviour towards Wilkinson? What types of office politics are at work here?

506

Office politics is often a shorthand way of describing the behaviour of someone who is manipulative, dishonest, controlling, cunning, and duplicitous. Such people are often labelled 'Machiavellian' (Wilson et al., 1996). Based on Italian philosopher Niccolò Machiavelli's work *The Prince* (1532/1984), someone who is Machiavellian is seen as an unscrupulous character who stops at nothing to gain, and retain, power and influence.

Source: feeling lucky / Shutterstock.com

Machiavelli's writings on power, however, are subtler than is popularly portrayed. Machiavelli provided one of the earliest accounts of how power actually works in organizations. Rather than taking an idealized view (what we would like to happen) of leaders as good people anointed by God or born with authority, Machiavelli took a realist view (a description of what really happens) by examining how power was actually gained (and lost) by the elite. He therefore challenged the view that leaders are necessarily good simply because of their position (a dominant view at that time). Rather, he argued, to get to the top and maintain their power, leaders need to perform sometimes ethically questionable acts.

A key question for Machiavelli (1532/1984) is: Is it better to be loved or feared? He replied:

> The answer is that one would like to be both the one and the other; but because it is difficult to combine them, it is far safer to be feared than loved if you cannot be both.

He argued that people obey because they fear the consequences of not doing so. Therefore, the leader should use coercive power and be prepared to do evil; to produce good, sometimes the leader has to do evil. For Machiavelli, the end justifies the means.

Research insight: Machiavellian leaders using ethical leadership

Den Hartog, D.N., and Belschak, F.D. 2012. Work engagement and Machiavellianism in the ethical leadership process. *Journal of Business Ethics* 107 (1): 35–47.

As we have seen in Chapter 12 and will see in Chapter 17, as a response to criticism of various corporate scandals, in recent years there has been greater emphasis on business leaders acting in more ethical ways. Ethical and authentic leadership should 'send clear messages about ethical values' and model good behaviour (Den Hartog and Belschak, 2012: 36). This is seen to have benefits for the firm, as having a strong set of values makes the work feel more meaningful to the followers, increasing their motivation. However, Den Hartog and Belschak argue, 'highly manipulative Machiavellians may try to enact an ethical image if they feel this benefits them' (ibid.: 39). In other words, they *act* publicly in a way that appears ethical but privately they continue with a 'deceitful and unethical value system' (ibid.: 39). They state that it is 'likely that Machiavellian leaders will increasingly see maintaining their ethical image at work as important for their success in the organization' (ibid.: 44). However, they also found that 'followers do seem to distinguish between authentic and inauthentic displays of ethical leadership' (ibid.: 45): this surface acting (discussed in Chapter 16) does not always convince followers, which may, the authors suggest, 'make their leadership less impactful' (ibid.: 45).

◎ Employability skills: enhance your political skills

While being manipulative at work is not something to aspire to, understanding the need for political skills is very important for organizational success. Political skill has been defined as 'the ability to effectively understand others at work, and to use such knowledge to influence others to act in ways that enhance one's personal and/or organizational objectives' (Ferris et al., 2005: 127).

Academic articles (see Ferris et al., 2007), popular business books, newspaper columns (for instance *The Guardian*'s 'Work' section), and websites offer advice as to how to be a good political operator or just how to survive at work. Some of the overall advice is included in Table 14.2.

Table 14.2 Ways to build your political skills (adapted from Ferris et al., 2007, www.office-politics.com, and Yeung, 2009)

Political skill	Description	Example
Accept that office politics exists	Accept and understand that organizations are not simply meritocracies, but office politics exists and is vital for survival (and career)	Understand the political landscape and informal rules of your organization
Develop social skills	Listen to, and be sensitive to, others and adapt your ideas to fit their worldview	Have a convincing personal style that influences others and elicits the desired response from others
Networking ability	Develop diverse contacts within, and outside, the organization that are useful for personal and organizational purposes	Attach yourself to potential high-flyers and get a mentor to support your development; go to lunch with people and for a drink after work

(*Continued*)

Political skill	Description	Example
Appearing sincere	Appear authentic, sincere, genuine, and as though you have no ulterior motives	Make sure that you do not appear to have political motives for your actions
Political nous	Learn how things really work	Watch what is deemed acceptable and unacceptable behaviour, and the unwritten rules of what is a success
Personal characteristics	Self-confidence, self-awareness, with a strong locus of control and an outgoing and likeable personality	Have the type of personality that others want to be with and charm people
Self-promotion	Demonstrate how accomplished you are, presenting yourself, and your successes, in the best possible light	Get on flagship projects that the boss pays attention to; appear in company newsletters, etc.
Building coalitions	Build power bases either with peers (alliances) or subordinates (empire-building)	Bring a range of people on to your side and make them feel they will benefit from your projects

 Are you skilled in any of these areas and are there some that you would like to improve? From what you have read, what advice would you offer Linda Wilkinson in dealing with her situation?

Implications of office politics at work

🔍 Running case: building coalitions

'Right,' begins Mortimer. 'I guess you all know what's happened. We have to cut the staff development week down to two days.'

'But that's ridiculous,' protests Wilkinson. 'I mean it was meant to be a week. Three days was bad enough but two days is laughable.'

Meg Mortimer bristles. 'Well, we have two days now, so we have to get on with it. Don't shoot the messenger. I'm just doing what I've been told. Look,' continues Mortimer, 'we need to make some decisions. It's obvious that we have to maintain the Gold Standard Service section, as it's so core to the hotel's mission and I've already booked the train for the afternoon. But I wanted your views on what activities we could merge or drop.'

Weaver gives Wilkinson a knowing glance.

The existence of office politics demonstrates that work is not always meritocratic. This impacts on the way people feel about work. Zivnuska et al. suggests that organizational politics is often disliked by employees because it means that rewards such as increased pay or promotion are not simply produced through effort, merit, and contribution, but through other factors—particularly politics (2004). However, more recently Kane-Frieder et al. have argued that engaged employees often see organizational politics not as a hindrance, but a challenge to be worked through: it offers a strategic advantages because employees less engaged with work are less willing to play political games whereas more engaged employees do (Kane-Frieder et al., 2014).

Organizational politics also reveals that organizations are sites where individuals (and groups) have different interests, goals, and visions of the organization's future. Power is an essential and normal part of everyday life. It is to this topic that we now turn.

? Review questions	
Describe	What is meant by politics in organizations?
Explain	Why do theorists suggest that office politics is common in organizations?
Explain	What are some of the key strategies for dealing with office politics?
Analyse	Machiavelli wrote about politics at a governmental level, so why is his analysis also relevant to politics in organizations?

Levels of power in organizations

Who has the power in an organization? Our first impression is generally that the power is held by those at the top: organizational leaders making decisions, controlling the resources, and setting the organization's strategic direction. Yet if we look closer, we can see it is not that clear-cut. Organizational leaders rely on workers to implement their plans. For 'despite senior management's apparent authority to speak and enact strategy, other groups of employees are [often] critical to how it actually plays out in an organization, providing a much better understanding of why some strategies … work while others fail' (Dick and Collings, 2014: 1517). Power, therefore, is distributed across the organization (see Table 14.3).

While employees potentially have substantial power (e.g. to withhold their labour, quit, withhold information), they rarely use it. As Jeffrey Pfeffer argues, 'most of the time in most work settings the authority of the manager to direct the work activities is so legitimated and taken for granted, that issues of relative power and sanctions seldom become consciously considered' (1981: 5–6). Equally, managers rarely use their power to fire employees or impact their promotion opportunities. Most of the time managerial authority is taken for granted, so power is often not visible with the labour–capital relationship (Figure 14.1; see also Chapter 3) and is rarely questioned.

Organizations therefore can be seen as more complicated than a formal organizational chart would indicate. As Whittle et al. state, 'Formal structures, then, do not determine organizational processes or outcomes, and organizational behaviour cannot be "read off" from the formal structure chart' (Whittle et al., 2015: 381). To understand why this is the case and how power operates in organizations, we need to explore deeper theoretical perspectives.

Table 14.3 Levels of power

Executive power	Management power	Worker power
Set wider operational goals	Make operational decisions	Specialist knowledge that managers or co-workers do not have
Strategic direction of the company	Individual career progression	Specialist skills that make the employee valuable
Set key overall policies	Conduct appraisals	Implement management requests
Hire and fire key management	Allocate work	Work-to-rule and go-slow, do the job poorly
Open and close key stores/factories	Set targets/pace of the machine	Withhold information
Agree major purchasing decisions (e.g. a new IT system)	Give rewards and punishment	Resist management control

Figure 14.1 The capitalist wage–labour relationship.

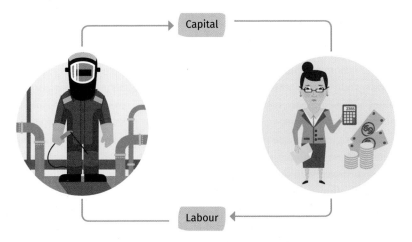

Theoretical interpretations of power

In the following section we will discuss the three main ways of looking at power:

- *power as possession*—sees power as something that is owned or possessed by individuals or groups
- *power through structure*—sees power as something that is a product of the social structure
- *power as productive*—sees power as something that produces new ways of thinking and acting, rather than a negative force which prevents action.

They each present alternative views of what power is and how it impacts organizational members. They come from different ideological viewpoints and therefore provide not only different views of power but also beliefs about how society should work.

Power as a possession

> **Q Running case:** can three go into two?
>
> 'Ok,' says Weaver, 'it is obvious that we need to start with our priories as a hotel. Obviously, given the changes that we have been bringing through, we have to work on making the hotel more efficient. I mean, if we're to compete against all these new budget hotels, with our high cost-base we need to make efficiency a priority. What do you think, Linda?' he concludes, looking over to Wilkinson.
>
> 'Oh yes,' Wilkinson stutters, 'that does make sense. We also need to make sure that we have a full session on cleaning as everyone's responsibility. We did really badly on that on the last customer satisfaction survey, so we need the full session on that'.
>
> Mortimer looks concerned. 'But we can't do all three, something needs to go. Three into two just doesn't go.'

Our common-sense view of power is something that belongs to an individual, a position (e.g. the CEO), or a group (e.g. the human resources department). The underlying metaphor for this view of power is as a possession, a physical thing that belongs to or is held by an individual or group. Steven Lukes states that this view leads people to 'discuss its location and its extent, who has more and who less, how to gain, resist, seize, harness, secure, tame, share, spread, distribute, equalize or maximize it, how to render it more effective and how to limit or avoid its effects' (2005: 61).

So how do individuals acquire power? Jeffrey Pfeffer argues it is by 'having something that someone else wants or needs, and being in control of the performance or resources so that there are few alternative sources, or no alternative sources, for obtaining what is desired' (1981: 99). This can include doing *jobs vital to organizational success* requiring rare skills; *controlling resources*, however small, used strategically, to get others *dependent* on you; being good at *solving important problems* to the organization and *reducing uncertainty* (McNulty et al., 2011); *controlling information* that others need; and *controlling the information about alternatives* and the premises upon which decisions are made. The key underlying principle of Pfeffer's view is that power is created by having something that others need without a suitable alternative and being able to withdraw this at any given point.

Personal characteristics such as *energy and endurance*, an understanding of the political dynamics within the organization, and a willingness to use this insight all further someone's power. This is easier for those higher up, as those 'with relatively more power are better able to get their perception of the problem and the environment accepted' (Pfeffer, 1981: 141).

French and Raven: bases of power

> **Q Running case:** Chance meets with Mortimer to discuss the staff development week agenda
>
> 'So the issue is, Meg,' Simon Chance smiles at Meg Mortimer, 'that we need to make some adjustments to the programme and the area that has been adjusted is the Gold Standard Service. I'm sure it would be great to have it,' continues Chance, noting the look of disgust on Mortimer's face, 'but in situations like this we all need to make sacrifices.'
>
> 'But with the greatest of respect,' Mortimer begins firmly, 'the Gold Standard Service training is not something that we can drop. Gaining the Gold Standard Service accreditation is one

of the Key Performance Indicators for Junction Hotel for the next year, and we have to do the full three hours of training by their accredited trainers. In any case, we have already paid for it, and I doubt we would be able to cancel at this late stage. Also,' Mortimer continues, getting into her stride, 'how would this look to the Gold Standard Service accreditation panel if we pull out now? I do know a few on the panel but I think it is going to look bad if we pull out of the training right now'.

 Who has the power in this situation? Is that power reflected in their positions in the hierarchy? What form of power does Mortimer use in this situation?

John French and Bertram Raven (1958) argued there are six common sources, or, as they put it, the 'bases of power', that individuals can hold (Raven, 1965, 1993; see Table 14.4). They can be divided between hard power, which constrains the individual because they have to comply with the leaders' demands, and soft power, which provides followers with more freedom and autonomy (Pierro et al., 2013).

Power is possessed by particular individuals, but for it to be really effective the powerless person needs to perceive that the powerful person has power. For instance, it does not matter if the

Table 14.4 French and Raven's six bases of power (based on French and Raven, 1958; extended in Raven, 1965, 1993)

	Type	Description	Example
Hierarchical	Legitimate	Extent to which an individual is socialized and has internalized the belief that certain groups (e.g. managers) have a legitimate right to command. This belief is set by cultural values and acceptance of current social structure.	You respond to a request because it is a manager telling you rather than because you think it is a good idea.
	Reward	Extent to which an individual can use rewards from the organization. The employee must desire the reward in order for it to work. If they do not want the reward it will have no sway over them.	You take on a task because you believe that you will get a promotion out of it.
	Coercive	Perception that one's boss has the power to punish. This can be strong punishments, such as sacking, through to more symbolic forms such as withdrawing positive interaction. The more legitimate this approach, the more it will be accepted.	You aim to hit your sales targets because they are part of your appraisal and you do not want to fail.

Hard power

Type	Description	Example	
Expert (Personal)	Knowledge that another person needs but does not have: for instance, a lawyer's advice as to whether an advertising campaign is legal. What is essential for it to be valid is that the recipient trusts the advice of the giver.	You require an IT specialist in order to fix your computer.	
Referent (Personal)	Being the type of person that others want to emulate. Being friendly/supportive towards others.	A colleague you want to emulate asks you to take on a task which you do not want to do but, because you want to emulate them, you do it anyway.	Soft power
Informational (Personal)	Changes in perspective as a result of being given information.	You hold information that others want and can present it in such a way that they change how they see a situation.	

leader actually has the power to withhold promotion, so long as the follower believes they do. The strength of the power base is also dependent on how much the follower desires the item offered. For instance, a threat to sack someone will hold far less sway over an employee who does not really want the job and believes that they will have better job prospects elsewhere.

The follower's perception is produced primarily by two things. First, the follower's upbringing and socialization shape how they perceive the power base. For instance, some followers will believe that the management have an automatic right to lead and will accept their authority unquestioningly, whereas others will believe that the leaders need to earn this right or will even be hostile towards leaders. This perception is a product of socialization, such as the follower's schooling, previous experiences (i.e. of authority), and the wider culture they are a part of. In the 1950s, when French and Raven were writing, authority was accepted more readily than it is today. Second, this perception is dynamic and changes over time based on experience of the actions of an individual. Therefore, if a person uses expert power but is proved to be wrong on a number of occasions, this basis of power will diminish over time. Power also shapes how the less powerful see the more powerful. Holding power (particularly hard power) tends to make people see the role holder as cold, dominant, assertive, and forceful, whereas the less powerful are associated more with warmth, cooperation, and agreeableness (Zheng et al., 2016).

The basis of power can also be divided up into that which is hierarchical, derived from the leader's position in the organization, and that which is more influenced by the perception of personal skills and characteristics. Therefore, while someone can be senior in the organization, if they lack the skill or knowledge that an expert holds then they can be beholden to that expert.

Weber's three ideal types of authority

One of the founders of the power as possession perspective was Max Weber (2004) (whose views on bureaucracy we saw in Chapter 3). Weber argued there are three ideal types of authority.

- *Charismatic*—based on a heroic leader, where people unquestioningly follow the leader. One of the problems with this type is that it relies on a single leader for its survival. The followers also become subservient.

- *Traditional*—based on tradition or custom. The leader holds their authority based on the status they are given or have inherited (such as the monarchy).

- *Rational–legal*—based on formalized laws and regulation, akin to bureaucracy. Weber saw this form as superior, as it does not rely on the charisma of a single leader or the unquestioning following of tradition.

Therefore, while bureaucracy sometimes has a bad reputation, Weber considered that well-constructed rules can produce the best form of authority.

'Power as a possession' assessed

While the perspective that power is the property of an individual or group is intuitively appealing, it suffers from some key problems. First, it tends to individualize power—seeing it as something that is solely the possession of an individual or group, as a zero-sum game, where some people have power (often the managers) and others do not. Yet power is not something that an individual holds, nor is there a fixed quantity of it. Second, this perspective ignores more societal reasons for why people think how they do. Although French and Raven describe how individuals are socialized into seeing the world in a particular way, this view of power downplays issues such as gender and the labour–capital divide, which others, such as Steven Lukes, feel are essential. It is to this perspective that we now turn.

515

? Review questions

Describe   What are French and Raven's six bases of power?

Explain   What are the key principles of the 'power as a possession' perspective?

Apply   Which of the six bases of power does Effingham hold in the case study?

Power as structure: Steven Lukes' three dimensions of power

In 1974 Steven Lukes, a Marxist political scientist, wrote a highly influential account of power (republished and updated in a second edition in 2005). He aimed to offer a more comprehensive view of how power operates, presenting three dimensions or what he called faces of power: observable conflict, agenda setting, and social structure (Figure 14.2). Drawing on Marxist theory (see Chapter 3 for a discussion of Karl Marx's theory), Lukes asked: why do the powerful, i.e. managers or leaders, achieve compliance from the less powerful, i.e. the workers, particularly when workers are acting against their own best interests? The first two dimensions, he concluded, were inadequate in answering this question and, therefore, the third dimension offered a deeper understanding of how power operates in practice.

Figure 14.2 Lukes' (2005) three levels of power.

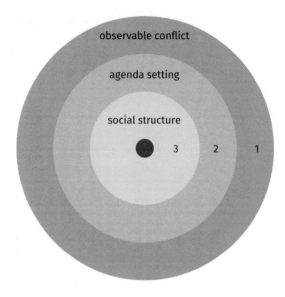

Dimension 1 is direct observable conflict which sees power as a possession. This perspective draws from the political theorist Robert Dahl, who defined power as: 'A has power over B to the extent that he can get B to do something that B would not otherwise do.' Dahl (1957: 202–3) focused on decision making by the US political elite and provided one of the first rigorous explorations of how power works in practice. For Dahl 'who[ever] prevails in decision making [provides] the best way to determine which individuals and groups have more power' (1958: 4, cited in Lukes, 2005: 18). Dahl, who had a pluralist outlook, saw different groups having preferences which can lead to conflict when they clash. Dahl argued that the one who comes out on top has the power. While Dahl believed power can be present even when no opposition appears, his methods and assumptions focus only on overt, observable behaviour and, therefore, when there is actual, visible conflict.

Dimension 1 assessed: the advantage of dimension 1 is that it focuses on the actual processes involved in decision making. However, Lukes argued this perspective is overly narrow, focusing only on observable power, and ignores many covert, less observable aspects. This aspect is examined by dimension 2.

Dimension 2 sees power as the ability to determine what can or cannot be spoken about—what Lukes calls behind-the-scenes agenda setting. Those with power can limit the range of topics that can be discussed and, by doing so, can keep certain controversial issues 'off limits'. Consequently certain things, such as employees pay rises, managerial incompetence, or a proposal by a competing group, are not spoken about, and therefore cannot be decided upon. Leading supporters of this view, Bachrach and Baratz, state a person or group has power to the extent he or she—'consciously or unconsciously—creates or reinforces barriers to the public airing of policy conflicts' (1970: 8, cited in Lukes, 2005: 6). Dimension 2 thus broadens the definition of power away from purely observable conflict to non-decision processes where the powerful can ignore the grievances of the less powerful. This may involve the use of rules, both formal and informal, which are often built around masculine norms (Kanter, 1977). For instance, Whittle and her colleagues reported that in a US-headquartered multinational corporation, those lower down in the organizational hierarchy censored the information they presented to their superiors and did not act on their plans (strategic inaction) because of the way they interpreted the power dynamics at the organization. This meant

Real life case: limiting the agenda—the Hutton Inquiry

After the second Iraq war, Tony Blair's government set up the Hutton Inquiry into the death of the government scientist Dr David Kelly. Many criticized this inquiry, arguing that they limited the scope of decision making to a far too narrow remit and therefore did not examine fairly the real reasons behind the war or Dr Kelly's death. This could be seen as a classic example of keeping certain controversial issues off the agenda.

Sources: *Daily Telegraph* (2003); Runciman (2004); Wheeler (2006).

 How did the government keep certain issues off the agenda of the Hutton Inquiry? Can you think of any examples you have seen in organizations where someone more powerful has kept issues off the agenda?

that 'proposals, issues and agendas do not even get "on the table" (Lukes, 2005, p. 40), and can therefore not even receive a hearing' (Whittle et al., 2015: 1342).

Dimension 2 assessed: this view of power is more subtle and provides a deeper understanding of how power operates in practice. Power can be covert (concealed), allowing the powerful to maintain their position through establishing the 'rules of the game' that privilege certain groups at the expense of others. However, dimension 2 still assumes that power only occurs if there is a conflict or grievance. According to Bachrach and Baratz, 'if there is no conflict, overt or covert, the presumption must be that there is consensus on the prevailing allocation of values, in which case nondecision-making is impossible' (1970: 49, cited in Lukes, 2005: 23). It is this view that dimension 3 challenges.

Dimension 3 states that power shapes not only our behaviours, but also our desires and beliefs. Therefore, while it might appear that there is consensus or that certain individuals and groups have no grievances, dimension 3 argues this gives a false perception of harmony. Workers, owing to their position in the capitalist working relationship, are often not conscious of their *true* interests, and therefore conflict between labour and capital (the workers and managers) rarely materializes. It remains latent—present but rarely visible.

Dimension 3 assessed: this dimension goes beyond behaviourism (Lukes, 2005), as it argues that just because you cannot observe the conflict does not mean it does not exist. Rather, the powerful (i.e. management) influence, shape, or determine the very wants and desires of the less powerful (i.e. workers), distracting them from their true interests. Conflict, therefore, does not materialize (become visible) because the workers have been socialized (taught) to believe that they do not have different interests from management. This is achieved through processes of socialization, including schooling, company induction programmes, and wider culture, where the worker is taught to see their interests as being the same as the organization's. To quote Karl Marx (1859/2012: 11–12): 'It is not the consciousness of men that determines their existence, but, on the contrary, their social existence determines their consciousness.' In other words, how people see the world (their consciousness) is shaped by the society in which they live and its values, a process influenced by economic interests of the powerful. Consequently, according to Lukes (2005), not only do workers not know that they are oppressed, but they enthusiastically participate in their own oppression.

Visit the online resources and take a look at the extension material for Chapter 14 for further information on Lukes' three dimensions.

> **Running case:** Weaver meets Chance for their weekly game of squash
>
> 'Well, that was a great game. You pushed me all the way,' declares Chance to Weaver as they get changed following their weekly squash game.
>
> 'Thanks. I am improving thanks to my training,' smiles Weaver. 'I've been working on the efficiency of my strokes. Talking of efficiency,' he continues, 'this thing about the staff development week …'
>
> 'Oh, that,' signs Chance wearily. 'It's been a real headache.'
>
> 'Yes, I understand,' interrupts Weaver. 'It's just that rumours are going round that Meg wants to cut the session on efficiency, and we can't allow this to happen. If we are to achieve the changes that we set out to do when we took over Junction Hotel, then we must have a full session on efficiency. Anything less, I am worried what signal that gives to the rest of the staff'.

Power as structure assessed

Lukes' theory is helpful because he alerts us to the often invisible processes of power within organizations, providing a compelling explanation of how the more powerful can gain compliance from the less powerful. He thus moves beyond the study of individualistic power to explore the wider structural aspects, i.e. how the individual is shaped by society.

As with any Marxist analysis of its type, Lukes believes employees suffer from false consciousness. This creates a state of mind where workers do not recognize their 'true' interests or their oppression and exploitation because they get distracted by everyday issues. Workers are thus unable to think of alternative ways of doing things (i.e. self-management) because they are socialized into believing that the current way society runs is fixed and is the only way things can be (i.e. that we must have management-led organizations).

This view is based on the assumption that employees, collectively, have 'true' interests which they are not aware of, but the Marxist theoretician is. However, many, particularly from the post-structuralist viewpoint, have argued that there is no universal interest that all employees share and the Marxist theorist is not necessarily better placed to identify what these interests are. As a response, in the more recent edition, Lukes recognizes that he implied that everyone of a particular class has the same interest, whereas he now argues that workers have multiple, and sometimes contradictory, interests and needs.

Have you ever considered the alternatives to capitalism? Why do we tend to take for granted managers' right to manage?

? Review questions

Explain	What are the three dimensions of power as outlined by Lukes?
Explain	Why does Lukes consider the first two dimensions inadequate? Why does he consider that the third dimension captures the true nature of power?
Analyse	Do workers really know their true interests? Is it possible to really know your true interests? How do different theories of power answer this question?
Apply	From Lukes' perspective, do the workers at Junction Hotel really know their true interests? If not, how might they act differently if they did?

Power as productive: Michel Foucault

Linda Wilkinson stares into her glass of wine as she has her regular 'girls' night out' with her friend Sarah. 'I just don't know if I trust him,' Linda says to herself as much to her friend. 'I'm mean he has a reputation for double-crossing people. I really need this training session, not just for the hotel but my own position as well. If the session on cleaning as everyone's responsibility gets cancelled, then what does that say about my position in the hotel? As senior managers we're all meant to be on a par, but if those two each get a full session but I only get an hour, or worse still nothing, then what does that say about me?'

Sarah smiles at her long-standing friend. 'You need to be more assertive. Stop letting them dictate things. Look at this,' Sarah continues, opening up an app on her phone. 'You can develop your assertiveness skills using this app. If you do the activities every day, working on your self-talk and improving the ways that you talk to people, no end of opportunities await you. It's transformed my life.'

Visit the online resources and take a look at the web links for Chapter 14 to try the assertiveness quiz. How do you feel about completing it?

In his most recent edition of *Power: A radical view*, Lukes argues that Michel Foucault's work explores the fourth dimension of power (Lukes, 2005). Foucault was a French philosopher and historian who aimed at rethinking our assumptions about how power operates, providing a radical departure from the previously discussed theorists. His views on power, however, are complex and he never presented a full theory of power; therefore, we present a summary in Table 14.5.

Foucault (1977) asks us to think differently from traditional perspectives about how power operates. Power is not something that one group possesses and which forces the powerless to do things against their own interests. Rather, for Foucault, power is a creative, positive force that brings certain ways of thinking and behaving into being and, through that, introduces a new reality. He offers this view as a result of three key theoretical perspectives.

- *Power/knowledge*—for Foucault, knowledge is intertwined with power. He argued the 'human sciences' such as sociology and psychology (which feature heavily as the underpinnings of many of the theories in this book—see Chapter 1) produce new techniques of power. For instance, psychology creates personality tests used in recruitment and selection, and Belbin's teamwork framework (see Chapter 6). These techniques are powerful, not only in helping management, but also in claiming to enable us to discover the truth about ourselves. Knowledge, for instance in work psychology, offers to reveal how we really think in a way that allows us to change how we act (Rose, 1998). For Foucault, this knowledge cannot be thought of as neutral, but is linked fundamentally to power because it is created and used to transform how we understand ourselves. This extends the investigation of power to the role that knowledge plays in how we understand ourselves at work.

- *Power relations*—for Foucault (1981), power exists in relations between people and occurs when power is exercised (used). Foucault sees power as a relationship where both sides have some power and each person has some choice in what they do. Therefore, for Foucault, there must always be the opportunity for resistance, otherwise it is domination. For example, a manager might ask one of their team to write a report which is additional to their existing workload. The employee has a number of options, including completely ignoring the request,

Table 14.5 Foucault's reconceptualization of power (drawn from Foucault, 1981 and 1977)

Classic view	Foucault's view
Power is a repressive, coercive, controlling, authoritarian force	Power is also productive and creative; it produces new knowledge and behaviours, and, through this, new realities
Power forces people to do things that they do not want to do	Power also works in a positive fashion by guiding individuals, giving them choices, and shaping how they see things and their identity
Power is a property, a thing that certain groups possess	Power has no essence—it is not a thing that one group possesses and other (weaker) groups do not possess; rather, power is relational—it exists in the relationship between people and only when it is exercised (i.e. used)
Power is top-down, possessed by an elite and held over the powerless (such as the workers)	Power also is bottom-up; rather than being possessed by a small elite, power is everywhere—it is like a net, a system of relations spread throughout society; it is also constantly shifting; one group does not always hold it—it changes over time
Power crushes resistance	Where there is power there is resistance, which is the production of alternative discourses; if there is no possibility of resistance then there is no power, as this is domination
Control through direct repression	Control through invisible strategies of normalization
Knowledge is seen as either objective and disinterested—it does not take sides (mainstream view)—or emancipatory (critical view), freeing people from power	Knowledge is linked fundamentally to power; new knowledge (such as sociology) produces new techniques of power (Foucault used the phrase power/knowledge to indicate this link)
Individuals or groups have true interests that exist outside of power	Who we think we are—our identity—is a product of knowledge and of power; power is everywhere and in all relations with people
Asks who has power and how they gain and maintain their position and use or abuse power	Investigates specific techniques and practices through which power operates

doing it very slowly, or not writing it in the way the manager would like. The important point here is that both the employee and the manager have a range of options available to them, and therefore power is more a relationship than a one-way process. The employee can always resist the manager's request.

- *Disciplinary power and normalization* provides the third area where Foucault (1977) rethought power. Disciplinary power operates through hierarchical observation, normalizing judgement, and examination—observing people and judging them against a series of norms, standards, and values which separates the normal from abnormal. These norms provide the standards by which we learn to judge ourselves. We do this in many areas of life, from testing ourselves against what 'level' we are at—for instance we judge ourselves at school and compare averages for height and weight using the Body Mass Index (BMI)—through to sales targets that workers judge themselves by. Power through normalization is often not conducted in a domineering or controlling manner. Rather, it can be experienced as positive in that we decide how to engage with it. For instance, you might wear a FitBit to monitor how many steps you take a day, or use Strava to measure how far you have run. We judge ourselves against a norm (for instance 10,000 steps a day), and failing to achieve these steps can be seen as a failure for which the individual is blamed. This form of power is invisible, as we tend to treat these norms as unquestionable facts, designed by experts for our own good. Foucault's view reveals how power shapes seemingly neutral everyday practices that are missed by other approaches.

We can see all three of these accounts of power at work in Foucault's most famous book, *Discipline and punish* (1977). This book examines the history of prison and starts with a graphic scene of the botched torture and execution of 'Damiens the regicide'. Foucault describes how this criminal was placed on a scaffold, his 'flesh torn from his breasts, arms, thighs and calves with red-hot pincers … [and] his body drawn and quartered by four horses and his limbs and body consumed by fire' (1977: 3). Ultimately, six horses were needed to pull Damiens apart and still the executioner struggled to tear his limbs off him, requiring the executioner to cut his limbs off.

Foucault then presents a description of a criminal who is being reformed, which takes place a mere eight years later. His day includes getting up at 6 am, working for 9 hours, and receiving 2 hours of schooling (reading, writing, drawing, and arithmetic, and then listening to an instructional text). The aim of this style of punishment is to reform the prisoner, i.e. to make them a better person.

When thinking about the form of power in the two accounts of the prisoners, our initial reaction is that the first one is brutal and the second is more humane. These cases demonstrate not only two different styles of punishment, but also two types of power—the public execution (physical force) and the timetable (reform). However, Foucault questions the assumption that the second, reforming the prisoner, is necessarily better. He argues that while the first prisoner had violence (and power) directed on the body, the second has this power internalized within him, with the one doing the punishment seeking to control the values and the beliefs of the prisoner; in short, changing who they are. The second form of power is a key example of what Foucault called disciplinary power, which was most evident in his discussion of the Panopticon.

Visit the online resources and take a look at the web links for Chapter 14 for pictures of the Panopticon.

The Panopticon (which literally means all-seeing-eye; see Chapter 4) was a prison devised by the English philosopher and social theorist Jeremy Bentham for the purposes of reforming the prisoner in a cost-effective manner. It could achieve a high level of efficiency, as in the centre of the prison stood the prison guard, who could see into every prison cell at all times. In theory, therefore, it only required one prison guard who could watch all the prisoners at one time. This was achieved because the prisoner was unable to tell if they were being watched and therefore had to always assume that they were. There are two key implications for this.

First, this image of the Panopticon has been used to make the claim that a key area of modern power is through surveillance, overt or covert observation of people to gain information or control over them. The power of the Panopticon was that the prisoner never knew if they were being watched and therefore they had to act in the right way at all times. It is therefore used to render (make) visible key aspects of someone's behaviour. A modern example of this is the call centre, where all of the call-centre operatives are monitored constantly for such things as their call length and success rates, as well as the time taken between calls and even toilet breaks. They can also be listened to at any stage of their call, meaning that they always need to perform because they never know when they might be being heard. Similarly, shop workers can be investigated by mystery shoppers who judge whether they are smiling at the right point. Even university lecturers are now increasingly subject to surveillance practices such as student feedback and evaluation surveys, or fellow staff members watching a lecture or seminar. This is then fed into lecturers' performance appraisals and can impact their careers (see Chapter 15 for a discussion of the reputation economy).

The second key development of this form of power is how it is used to reform the prisoner through a series of routines and practices in order to make them a better person. Seemingly everyday practices, such as timetables, filling in forms, or types of training, are used to change the prisoner in how they understand themselves and the way that they act. This form of power is at its strongest when it is internalized by the prisoner as self-discipline, a form of internalized control. A series of experts (social workers, probation officers, mentors, etc.) work with the prisoner to help them transform themselves. Rather than forcing them to change through coercive force, reform and self-discipline are used to train the prisoner to change their behaviour and become a better person. It works best where the prisoner wants to become a better person. The prisoner thus internalizes the power and monitors themselves against these particular standards. In this sense, discipline does not just mean punishment, but comes from the Latin and means training to produce a specific character or pattern of behaviour, particularly a form of training that produces moral or mental improvement.

This form of self-discipline is often seen as essential for those who want to be successful. For instance, a successful boxer needs to follow a strict timetable with set times for exercise and rest, eat particular types of food, and avoid certain activities. They will follow the advice of experts (trainers, nutritionists, psychologists) and work on particular areas of physical and mental development (power/knowledge). By following this regime and being self-disciplined (discipline and normalization) the boxer is able to develop certain capabilities and skills and is moulded into becoming a particular type of person. However, they are also limiting the development of other skills and outlooks. By going through this training the boxer is transformed and could, arguably, become a different person. Power therefore works in a positive way—creating a new type of person—but it also stops other possibilities into which the individual could develop.

◎ Study skills: the power of university

Going to university to gain your degree is another example of this form of self-discipline. Many claim that if they go to university, study the subjects, and meet new people, the university changes who they are—that they come out as someone different from the person that went in. Part of this will involve reading certain texts and debating particular ideas that might change how you think. You might train yourself to go to the library regularly, turn up to 9 am lectures, read around the subject, plan your assignments, and do your work on time. You might use tools such as the Pomodoro technique to keep yourself focused while you are doing your work, or apps such as Offtime to block you from distractions such as Facebook or Instagram. It is unlikely that you will have someone watching over you telling you what to do; rather, you will have internalized the power and become self-disciplined. This form of power should not necessarily be seen as something oppressive—forcing you to do work against your will. Rather, you may begin to identify yourself as a different person who studies hard to get good grades.

How self-disciplined are you?
Source: Wavebreak Media Ltd/123RF.

At work, this form of power operates on us through such techniques as training, appraisal, and management development. The power of normalization is most evident in appraisal systems where employees are asked to 'confess' their strengths and weaknesses and judge themselves against a series of categories of what is considered normal behaviour. In particular, they are asked to define areas they do well in and those that require development. They are then made responsible for their own improvement, for example by writing self-development plans. In this sense employees engage in their own self-surveillance, judging themselves against these set categories (power/knowledge) with the view to self-improvement. Employees, therefore, act as their own supervisors by monitoring and judging themselves against particular norms (Townley, 1994). (Compare with how people internalize the labels bestowed by personality tests, as described in Chapter 8.)

The same argument could be made about management. We might find some of the techniques used by Taylorism controlling, oppressive, at times brutal, and often dehumanizing (see Chapter 3). However, under Taylorism workers are not expected to actually believe in the cause of the organization. In contrast, the so-called more humane developments of the human relations school (see Chapter 5) appear more sympathetic to the interests of the staff, as people feel that they belong. However, according to Foucault's reading of power these workers are actually more controlled. Through processes such as teamwork, motivation, and culture, workers are expected to act as though they believe in the purpose of the organization and want to progress and develop themselves into better kinds of employees. Employees are more controlled because they believe in the organization and therefore have no possibility to resist it. (For a very interesting discussion of this topic see Cederström and Fleming, 2012.)

Therefore, like Lukes, Foucault argued that people actively participate in practices which involve invisible power. However, unlike Lukes, Foucault does not necessarily see this form of power as coercion—forcing people into changes against their will. Rather, they participate actively in practices that change them into new types of people. The question is: Do we like the people that we have become?

523

The 'power as productive' view assessed

Running case: Linda Wilkinson reviews her progress with Sarah

Linda Wilkinson decides to phone Sarah. 'Hi, Sarah, it's Linda. Is now a good time to talk?' 'Sure,' Sarah replies. 'I have ten minutes before my next appointment, but, until then, I'm all yours. How was the App?' 'Brilliant,' enthuses Linda, 'amazing. It really made me think—I feel like a new me!' 'That's great,' replies Sarah. 'It works, doesn't it?' 'Yes,' acknowledges Linda. 'I did the assertiveness quiz you recommended and I came out OK, but not that strong, so I started work on those exercises and I've changed the way that I speak to people. I'm much more direct, but not aggressive. I learned those phrases and I'm using them all the time.' 'How have people reacted to you?' asks Sarah. 'I'm amazed ... really differently. I feel much more confident in putting my case at the planning meeting tomorrow.'

According to Foucault, how might power/knowledge, power relations, and normalization be occurring in this case?

While Foucault has produced a powerful re-reading of power, his theories have been criticized for a number of reasons. Firstly, because Foucault sees power everywhere, his critics argue that Foucault presents a world of complete domination without hope for a better world. This, his critics state, creates despair as there is no escape from power (McNay, 1994; Thompson and Ackroyd,

1995). Secondly, they claim Foucault's theory seems to discount human agency (i.e. the capacity of individuals to exist independently of the social structure). There is little account in Foucault's theory of those that can resist power. Finally, because Foucault does not offer a set of values by which to judge the use of power, many have questioned the political benefits of his work. Without a clear set of values to judge power, Foucault's critics argue that he does not give us the capacity to resist (e.g. Callaghan and Thompson, 2001).

? Review questions

Describe	What is meant, for Foucault, by the term Panopticon?
Explain	What are Foucault's key views on power?
Analyse	Why does Foucault see power as productive rather than repressive?
Apply	What type of power is the assertiveness quiz exerting on Linda Wilkinson? Do you see this as being repressive or productive for Wilkinson?

Obedience to authority

Would you electrically shock someone just because a scientist told you to? The infamous experiment by Stanley Milgram (1974) predicts that you probably would. Milgram wanted to find out whether normal, law-abiding citizens would give a lethal electric shock because they were following authority. He discovered that almost two-thirds of people would.

The participants were university students who thought they were taking part in a study of memory and learning, and received a small payment for their participation. Initially they were met by a scientist and another 'volunteer' (who actually worked for the experiment), and were told they were studying the effects of punishment on learning (a behaviourist approach). They drew lots, with one person acting as the learner to receive the shocks and the other as the teacher who applied them. While it appeared random, it was actually a fix so that the person who was the genuine volunteer ended up as the teacher.

The teacher then saw the learner strapped to an electric shock device and the generator, which had power up to 450 volts. They were then told that the learner had been given a list of word-pairs to memorize. Whenever the learner got it wrong the teacher had to administer electric shocks, starting at 15 volts and increasing to 450 volts (twice the household level). When they administered the shock they could hear what they thought was the learner (but was actually a tape recording) shouting things like 'I cannot go on'. Two-thirds of the subjects continued to do this past the switch marked 'fatal'.

The results dismayed Milgram. Indeed, before the experiment all the psychiatrists that Milgram questioned had stated that most people would stop early. Why did most give a potentially fatal shock? The answer, for Milgram, lay in their acceptance of authority. After a while the screams became very loud and they would often worry they were harming the learner, but the scientist would reassure, saying 'the experiment requires it'. It was not that they were uncaring; indeed, many of the experimenters voiced concerns, but they were willing to obey the commands of the scientist over their own judgement.

Another experiment which revealed how people respond to authority was Zimbardo's prison experiment. Zimbardo wanted to test good people versus an evil situation. Unfortunately, he found that the unpleasant situation won (Zimbardo, 2007).

Zimbardo set up a mock jail and selected 21 normal, healthy, and emotionally stable men and placed them into two groups: ten as prisoners and eleven as guards. The guards wore uniforms, including special glasses to prevent eye contact. Unexpectedly, the prisoners were picked up from home, put in a police car, finger-printed, blindfolded, placed in prison uniforms, and had nylons put on their head to give the appearance of baldness. They were also given identification numbers instead of names.

After only six days into the fourteen-day experiment, it was abandoned. The relationship between the guards and the prisoners was vicious, with three of the guards using their power in sadistic ways, developing techniques to break the prisoners, and making them feel worthless. The prisoners felt dehumanized and some even had breakdowns. Zimbardo's experiment indicated that being given the label 'prisoner' or 'guard' shaped the way individuals behaved, demonstrating the power of the social environment on individual behaviour (2007).

The two studies make us ask fundamental questions about ourselves (would we be a sadistic guard or electrocute someone if we were participant in the study?) and also wider society (are bad events not a product of bad people but of the type of society that we have?). The results show the uncomfortable reality that 'we ourselves could be perpetrators' (Reicher et al., 2014: 397). Both these experiments argue (as do the insights of Zygmunt Bauman, 1989) there are dangerous effects when people unquestioningly follow authority. Instead of using their own judgement, people regularly defer to authority figures (Milgram, 1974), who, when in this position, can abuse their power (Zimbardo, 2007) or simply say they are following the rules (Bauman, 1989). Critical theorists therefore look for less hierarchical and more empowering organizations.

 Study skills: dealing with controversial research

Problem with research design

While Milgram's and Zimbardo's studies are very famous, they have been heavily criticized, not only for their results but their research methods. The following are some of the key criticisms of both experiments.

- The treatment of the participants was unethical. It is highly unlikely that such research would be allowed by modern university ethics processes (Reicher et al., 2014).

- The studies have not been replicated (Lovibond and Adams, 1979; Reicher and Haslam, 2006), which critics argue makes the results less valid. Indeed, in one of the few attempts to replicate the prison study Haslam and Reicher concluded that people do not automatically assume the roles given to them, as Zimbardo suggested.

- As the research took place in 'laboratory conditions', did the participants act like they would in the real world? Kaposi argues 'the learner did by no reasonable standard protest continuously and despite the occasional outbursts never engaged in argumentations about his own existential or moral status' (2017: 397). Their screams might be a less powerful or persuasive force than Milgram claimed. Kaposi also claims we cannot assume the participants felt they had a free choice (a core assumption by Milgram), and they made have assumed 'that any decision to disengage may result in some destructive consequences regarding their own wellbeing' (2017: 398).

- Similarly, in the prison experiment Griggs argues that it 'seems plausible that most of the participants in the SPE would have guessed how Zimbardo and his colleagues wanted them to behave' and to have adjusted their behaviour accordingly (2014: 196).

→

Indeed, one of the guards, David Eshelman, stated he 'arrived independently at the conclusion that this experiment must have been put together to prove a point about prisons being a cruel and inhumane place ... and therefore I would do my part of help those results come about' (Duke, 2006: 8:00 min, cited in Bartels, 2015: 41). Zimbardo also encouraged his guards to behave in a tyrannical fashion, telling them how to behave (Reicher and Haslam, 2017).

- There are issues with how the participants were selected as they were very similar to each other, so it unsurprising they acted in similar ways (Bartels, 2015).

Problems with textbook interpretation

It is not only the original research that has been criticized but also the way many textbooks have reported it. In studies of psychology textbooks, Griggs (2014) and Bartels (2015) found that nearly all the accounts reported that all the guards were sadistic, whereas in fact the original study reported that only three of the eleven guards acted with excessive abuse (Zimbardo, 2007). Furthermore, despite the large volume of criticism of these experiments, Griggs found that almost half of the textbooks did not include any of the criticisms of the prison experiment. Those that did offer criticisms presented only minimal ones that were largely presented without any references to the original texts (2014).

It is not only Zimbardo and Milgram's studies that have suffered the fate of being poorly interpreted. Maslow's hierarchy of needs often gets reduced to little more than a triangle, with many of the nuances ignored (see Chapter 9 for a review). Similarly, the contested nature of Mayo's interpretation of the Hawthorne studies is often downplayed (see Chapter 5).

Why is this? Introductory textbooks (including this one) have to cover a large number of topics and therefore they cannot give them all the depth that they need. Textbooks have to try to simplify and so by their nature cannot provide complete coverage of all the topics they include. Therefore, while good textbooks offer a helpful starting-point and overview of studies, highlighting seminal works in a field and up-to-date debates, they cannot be seen as the final word on the subject.

So should you use textbooks? Yes. Textbooks act as a primer—a way of introducing you to the topic, to important writers, and to key ideas—and they usually do so in accessible language. But they should not be seen as ends in themselves. Our hope in writing this textbook is that we give you a starting-point to understand organizational behaviour, but it is only an introduction through which to get into the literature.

Using textbooks: tips for students

Textbooks can be great starting-points into topics and give you an overview of the field. It is important, if you are drawing directly on an idea from a textbook, to cite that textbook as your source. This way not only do you acknowledge the source that you have used, but you also indicate whose interpretation you are using. As a good starting-point to conducting research, make full use of the recommended readings at the end of each chapter, the reference lists, the online resources, and the knowledge of your lecturer and your subject librarian.

 Visit the online resources and take a look at the web links for Chapter 14 for more analysis of these studies.

Empowering workers

> ### 🔍 Running case: planning the staff development week
>
> 'So,' begins Meg Mortimer, 'we need to decide today on the programme for the staff development week. I have spoken to Simon and he said that it is up to us how we arrange the programme. So I would like us to have an open, frank, and creative meeting to come up with the plan. I have a bunch of post-it notes so we can move things around. Who would like to go first?'
>
> 'Well, it is obvious,' begins Weaver. 'Efficiency is at the centre of our transformation of Junction Hotel and therefore it is essential that it is part of the training for everyone.'
>
> 'I disagree with you. I see the situation this way,' interjects Wilkinson, with new-found confidence based on her assertiveness training. 'I appreciate that efficiency is important, but we need to have the certified training on cleaning as everyone's responsibility to achieve the Gold Standard Service award which we have to start next month. So I propose we run daytime training sessions in future weeks on efficiency in specific areas of the hotel, as necessary.'

So far in this chapter we have focused on how people gain and use power in organizations. However, many workers feel powerless and unable to make key decisions that impact their work. Heavily bureaucratic organizations create systems and cultures in which workers must follow prescriptive rules over which they have little say (see Chapter 4). Heroic leadership styles (see Chapter 13) concentrate power in the leaders' hands. They then dictate decisions, resulting in many employees having little authority or control, and, consequently, they feel powerless. This can be frustrating—not only do they feel dehumanized (see Braverman's critique of Taylorism in Chapter 3) but also this situation can be counterproductive, as it could be argued that workers often have better ideas of how to complete a task than their managers.

Supervisors, in particular, suffer from this position. As Rosabeth Moss Kanter states, supervisors are 'caught in the middle' between the managers that demand their targets be met and the workers who 'have the power to slack, to slouch, to take too much time' (a supervisor quoted in Kanter, 1977: 187). The supervisor in this position has little power to actually influence the work because they do not have access to rewards or punishment that can influence the employees' behaviour or the processes that shape how the activities occur.

Kanter argues that this feeling of powerlessness significantly impacts the mindset of workers. Drawing on psychoanalysis by Karen Horney, Kanter claims that powerless people tend to become 'critical, bossy, and controlling' (1977: 189) and neurotic (excessively anxious about everything), and therefore attempt to dominate (control) everything around them. This behaviour, Kanter argues, despite appearances, is rational because acting in this controlling and neurotic way is the only power available to them. Such behaviour, though, can result in more controlling leadership behaviour, creating a 'vicious cycle: powerless authority figures who use coercive tactics, provoke resistance and aggression, which prompts them to become even more coercive, controlling, and behaviourally restrictive' (1977: 190).

Powerlessness can make people overly focused on rules. As we saw in Chapter 2, highly bureaucratic organizations can lead people to remove themselves from taking personal responsibility and to follow the rules regardless of the effect on customers or clients. They do only the minimum they need in order to get things done. Finally, those with less power guard their territory more jealously as they seek to protect their domain. This can result, Kanter argues, in competitiveness, sectarianism, and hostility between sections, resulting in the powerless being less effective and feeling less satisfied with their work.

To tackle this situation she argues that workers should be empowered. Empowerment distributes power away from being solely in the hands of managers to the people actually doing the job. They get to define how to achieve their tasks and, in negotiation with their manager, what overall goals are. Consequently, 'when more people are empowered—that is, allowed to have control over the conditions that make their actions possible—then more is accomplished' (Kanter, 1977: 166).

Empowerment is a post-bureaucratic form of management in that it aims to move away from command and control to more participatory forms of management and decision making (see Chapters 13 and 17). Empowered workers have the capacity to make on-the-spot decisions that can satisfy customers rather than having to refer to managers or the rule book, have more opportunities to participate in decision making, and can be more self-determined. This frees people up to do their jobs in response to customer needs, which is particularly important in the service sector (see Chapter 15).

Empowerment is said to increase engagement and commitment: employees feel they have more control over their work because they are implementing their own ideas. Proponents of this approach say that empowered employees quickly take responsibility, have increased motivation, commitment, and skills, and move away from a blame culture, all of which results in a more positive outlook. Employees can become less cynical, and this can improve their relationships with their leaders (Lorinkova and Perry, 2014).

In order for empowerment to work, three key factors are often considered important. Firstly, it requires employees to understand the production process or how things currently operate (with a view to changing them); secondly, it requires trust from management to give over key information; and, thirdly, it requires a high level of teamwork and cooperation among the members.

Quality circles provide an example of empowerment in action. They started in the Japanese car industry, where they began as a grass-roots movement of workers who wanted to take more responsibility for their work. A quality circle often has around ten volunteers who come together to solve a problem of mutual concern, such as how to improve their products, the production process, or other related aspects. The members aim to identify the root of the problem, devise solutions, and disseminate the results to the relevant people in the organization. Rather than seeking to produce large-scale changes, these are often incremental (step-by-step) changes designed by the same people that will implement them (see Chapter 12). Workers in these situations have been very successful not only in empowering themselves but also in improving the production line.

However, this approach has been less successful in the UK. Some have put this down to cultural differences between Japan (which is more collectivist) and the UK (which is more individualistic; see Chapter 16 for more details on national cultural differences). Often, empowerment programmes are said to fail because senior management fail to let go of control or to trust the workers to make decisions (Jensen and Raver, 2012). Similarly, employees can be resistant to change as they do not want to take on the extra responsibility that the empowerment programme produces. As a result, empowerment programmes sound very good in principle, but in many cases they do not live up to their supporters' hopes (Cunningham and Hyman, 1999).

Critique of empowerment

Writers from the critical management studies perspective have argued that while empowerment sounds positive in principle, rather than workers having more autonomy they could, in fact, be seen as being under more subtle forms of control (Alvesson and Willmott, 1992a). Such critics argue that most empowerment programmes increase workers' responsibility but do not give workers wider power to set organizational aims and objectives (Humborstad, 2014). Therefore, workers are made responsible for all aspects of the implementation, which results in workers internalizing the blame, believing that if they do not achieve the task it is their fault. Empowerment, critical theorists argue, gives the illusion of autonomy, but it actually elicits a more subtle form of control as employees become their own supervisors (think back to the image of the Panopticon earlier in the chapter).

Emancipation

For Kanter, empowerment was important not simply in giving the powerless more discretion and influence, but also as a step towards changing the 'fabric of job relationships' (1977: 11). She argued that real change requires a more substantial overturning of the way organizations and society operate in order to produce a truly equal and fair workplace.

Marxists, such as Lukes, would agree. Within their perspective they argue that capitalist working relationships always produce power dynamics which act in favour of management. Therefore, while systems such as empowerment might produce changes that can benefit workers, they ultimately will always favour management. Marxists argue that the entire basis of capitalism needs to be overthrown and a new society with a new economic system created. It is only when this change happens and power is truly in the hands of workers who can determine their own ends that a more equal, fair, and effective distribution of power can occur.

Those of the critical management studies perspective are generally not optimistic that the whole of capitalism will be overthrown. Alvesson and Willmott (1992b) argue that a more realistic objective is what they call 'microemancipation'. Microemancipation involves small-scale changes that help the individual or group to take control of their own destiny. For these writers 'emancipation is not a gift bestowed upon employees; rather it necessitates the (often painful) resistance to, and overcoming of, socially unnecessary restrictions' (1992b: 433). In other words, power cannot be given by managers (because it always comes with strings attached); rather, it needs to be fought for actively to produce a fairer system.

According to this view, workers therefore need to try to achieve microemancipation by working on small-scale changes that they choose themselves. Workers (and indeed management) can thus temporarily escape from domination and control through small changes in how they work. 'Inherent in the concept of microemancipation is an emphasis on partial, temporary movements that break away from diverse forms of oppression, rather than successive moves toward a predetermined state of liberation' (1992b: 447). Microemancipation therefore aims for little breaks with the normal ways of doing things in order to think and act differently.

Microemancipation, however, does not come without a cost. It might mean a reduction in productivity; workers might be less work-focused and, therefore, might not get promotions or might even lose their jobs. Microemancipation has its costs as well as benefits. Furthermore, as King and Learmonth argue, it is challenging to practise microemancipation: even small changes are hard to achieve or think of when one is a manager (King and Learmonth, 2015). More recent critical work therefore explores the possibilities of non-domination (Griffin et al., 2015) or of *creating* emancipation through actualizing equality and through dissent to transform society and organizations now, rather than in a distant future (Huault et al., 2014).

Connecting case and theory

Throughout the chapter we saw power and politics at work between some of the senior managers at Junction Hotel. While setting up a staff training session might be thought of as a question of trying to work out what are the gaps in knowledge of the staff, in practice we saw struggles not only between individuals but also departments as well. The struggles around which sessions to pick reflected a battle for resources, the status and position of each department and individual, but also their underlying beliefs as to what each department should consider as important. These struggles demonstrate the nature of everyday office politics. Each senior manager saw their part of the business as the most important (cleanliness, efficiency, or customer service) which caused a struggle for control.

One way of making sense of this case is through the power as a position perspective. This perspective sees Simon Chance, as the CEO of Junction Hotel, having the power, due to his position, to impose the cut from three to two days for the staff development week. His interactions with Meg Mortimer demonstrated French and Raven's legitimate power and coercive power, but Meg Mortimer, with her knowledge of the awarding bodies, demonstrated expert power.

The power as structure perspective can explain Weaver's conversation with Chance through Lukes' second dimension of power, behind-the-scenes agenda setting. For Lukes, as a Marxist, the more significant question would be why so little direct power was demonstrated in the case. It particular this perspective draws attention to the lack of confrontation that the management team had with Simon Chance: despite all their work in developing the training programme, they all accepted his right to impose a sudden change on their plans, and in turn Chance did not question why the investor had the right to book the wedding at short notice and therefore to change the training dates. The third dimension of power alerts us to wider structural issues of power and how we are shaped by society.

The power as productive perspective, however, alerts us to how power produces certain ways of being. Linda Wilkinson's response to the challenges she faced was to become more assertive, training herself to act differently. Power, as Foucault argues, therefore can shift how we see ourselves. It also works through self-disciplining and normalizing.

While, throughout this case, the middle managers were *empowered*, in that they received little direct instruction from Simon Chance, we also see that they ultimately had little control. They had freedom in how they solved the problem of fitting three days' training into two days, but little opportunity to change the wider goals or resources of Junction Hotel. They are therefore largely responsible for solving a problem that was not of their own making. We leave the chapter with a potential resolution—but will Weaver concede?

? Review questions

Describe	How would you define empowerment?
Explain	What negative reactions can feeling powerless produce?
Analyse	Why do some critical theorists argue that empowerment increases control over workers?

Further reading

Clegg, S.R., and Haugaard, M. (eds). 2012. *Power and organizations*, vols 1–4. SAGE Publications Ltd: London.

This comprehensive collection includes many of the key articles from the last 50 years about power and organizations. This book is a useful resource if you want to find influential articles to get an in-depth understanding of the topic.

McNay, L. 1994. *Foucault: A critical introduction*. Blackwell: Cambridge.

A very readable introduction to Foucault's work which provides a good explanation of his views on power.

Lukes, S. 2005. *Power: A radical view*. Palgrave Macmillan: Basingstoke.

This gives a good overview of the issues of power and politics—particularly the three faces of power. It presents an interesting Marxist view of power that demonstrates how it is structural and often invisible.

Pfeffer, J. 1992. *Managing with power: Politics and influence in organizations*. Harvard Business School Press: Boston.

Pfeffer is in the 'power as a possession' camp, and this book is his key text on the subject. It explores how managers can use power and politics in organizations.

Ou, A.Y., Waldman, D.A., and Peterson, S.J. 2018. Do humble CEOs matter? An examination of CEO humility and firm outcomes. *Journal of Management* 44 (3): 1147–73.

This goes against some of our assumptions about powerful leaders.

References

Alvesson, M., and Willmott, H. 1992a. *Making sense of management*. Sage: London.

Alvesson, M., and Willmott, H. 1992b. On the idea of emancipation in management and organization studies. *Academy of Management Review* 17 (3): 432–64.

Bartels, J.M. 2015. The Stanford prison experiment in introductory psychology textbooks: A content analysis. *Psychology Learning and Teaching* 14 (1): 36–50.

Bauman, Z. 1989. *Modernity and the holocaust*. Polity Press: Cambridge.

BBC. 2017. Today, 30 October. Available at: http://www.bbc.co.uk/programmes/b09bxk32

Berlingieri, A. 2015. Workplace bullying: Exploring an emerging framework. *Work, Employment and Society* 29 (2): 342-353.

Bird, S., and Williams, C. 2017. AA chief fired for 'Clarkson moment' could lose nearly £100million in share options. *The Telegraph*, 2 August. Available at: http://www.telegraph.co.uk/news/2017/08/02/aa-chief-fired-clarkson-moment-could-lose-valuable-multi-million/

Callaghan, G., and Thompson, P. 2001. Edwards revisited: Technical control and call centres. *Economic and Industrial Democracy* 22 (1): 13–37.

Cederström, C., and Fleming, P. 2012. *Dead man working*. Zer0 Books: Winchester.

Clegg, S., and Haugaard, M. (eds) 2012. *Power and organizations*, vols 1–4. SAGE Publications Ltd: London.

Crow, D. 2016. The boardroom bust-up behind the worst day in Valeant's history. *Financial Times*, 16 March. Available at: https://www.ft.com/content/8f670e56-eafa-11e5-888e-2eadd5fbc4a4

Crow, D., and Platt, E. 2016. Valeant halves in value on default alarm. *Financial Times*, 15 March. Available at: https://www.ft.com/content/4fd955b6-eaa8-11e5-888e-2eadd5fbc4a4

Cunningham, I., and Hyman, J. 1999. The poverty of empowerment? A critical case study. *Personnel Review* 28 (3): 192–207.

Dahl, R. 1957. The concept of power. *Behavioral Science* 2: 201–25.

Dahl, R. 1958. A critique of the ruling elite model. *American Political Science Review* 52: 463–9.

Daily Telegraph. 2003. The truth about Dr Kelly, 22 July.

Den Hartog, D.N., and Belschak, F.D. 2012. Work engagement and Machiavellianism in the ethical leadership process. *Journal of Business Ethics* 107 (1): 35–47.

Dick, P., and Collings, D.G. 2014. Discipline and punish? Strategy discourse, senior manager subjectivity and contradictory power effects. *Human Relations* 67 (12): 1513–36.

Economic Times, 2017. Why Vishal Sikka quit as Infosys MD: Full text of his resignation letter, 18 August. Available at: https://economictimes.indiatimes.com/markets/stocks/news/full-text-vishal-sikkas-resignation-letter/articleshow/60113647.cms

Eisenhardt, K.M., & Bourgeois III, L.J. 1988. Politics of strategic decision making in high-velocity environments: Toward a midrange theory. *Academy of Management Journal* 31 (4): 737–70.

Ferris, G., Treadway, D., Kolodinsky, R., Hochwarter, W., Kacmar, C., Douglas, C., and Frink, D. 2005. Development and validation of the political skill inventory. *Journal of Management* 31: 126–52.

Ferris, G., Treadway, D., Perrewé, P., Brouer, R., Douglas, C., and Lux, S. 2007. Political skill in organizations. *Journal of Management* 33 (3): 290–320.

Fleming, P. & Spicer, A. 2014. Power in management and organization science. *Academy of Management Annals* 8 (1): 237–98.

Foucault, M. 1977. *Discipline and punish: The birth of the prison* (transl. Sheridan, A.). Penguin Books: London.

Foucault, M. 1981. *The history of sexuality: The will to knowledge*, vol. 1. Penguin: London.

French, J., and Raven, B. 1958. *The bases of social power*. In: Cartwright, D. (ed.) *Introducing social psychology*. Institute for Social Research, University of Michigan Press: Ann Arbor, MI, pp. 150–67.

Griffin, M., Learmonth, M., and Elliott, C. 2015. Non-domination, contestation and freedom: The contribution of Philip Pettit to learning and democracy in organisations. *Management Learning* 46 (3): 317–36.

Griggs, R.A. 2014. Coverage of the Stanford Prison Experiment in introductory psychology textbooks. *Teaching of Psychology* 41 (3): 195–203.

Huault, I., Perret, V., and Spicer, A. 2014. Beyond macro- and micro-emancipation: Rethinking emancipation in organization studies. *Organization* 21 (1): 22–49.

Humborstad, S.I.W. 2014. When industrial democracy and empowerment go hand-in-hand: A co-power approach. *Economic and Industrial Democracy* 35 (3): 391–411.

James, M., and Blake, M. 2017. Hollywood's man problem may be a matter of simple math. *Los Angeles Times*, 30 October. Available at: http://www.latimes.com/business/hollywood/la-fi-ct-hollywood-gender-imbalance-20171030-story.html

Jensen, J.M., and Raver, J.L. 2012. When self-management and surveillance collide: Consequences for employees' organizational citizenship and counterproductive work behaviors. *Group and Organization Management* 37 (3): 308–46.

Jordan, C., McGann, H., and Dewan, A. 2017. UK minister investigated after sex toy allegations. CNN, 29 October. Available at: http://edition.cnn.com/2017/10/29/europe/mark-garnier-uk-trade-minister-allegations/index.html

Kane-Frieder, R.E., Hochwarter, W.A., and Ferris, G.R. 2014. Terms of engagement: Political boundaries of work engagement-work outcomes relationships. *Human Relations* 67 (3): 357–82.

Kanter, R. 1977. *Men and women of the corporation*. Basic Books: London.

Kantor, J., and Twohey, M. 2017. Harvey Weinstein paid off sexual harassment accusers for decades. *New York Times*, 5 October. Available at: https://www.nytimes.com/2017/10/05/us/harvey-weinstein-harassment-allegations.html?_r=0

King, D., and Learmonth, M. 2015. Can critical management studies ever be 'practical'? A case study in engaged scholarship. *Human Relations* 68 (3): 353–75.

Lorinkova, N.M., and Perry, S.J. 2014. When is empowerment effective? The role of leader–leader exchange in empowering leadership, cynicism, and time theft. *Journal of Management*, 26 November, doi: 10.1177/0149206314560411.

Lovibond, S., and Adams, W. 1979. The effects of three experimental prison environments on the behaviour of non-convict volunteer subjects. *Australian Psychologist* 14 (3): 273–87.

Lukes, S. 2005. *Power: A radical view.* Palgrave Macmillan: Basingstoke.

Macdonald-Smith, A. 2015. Tap Oil CEO seeks deals in bid to ward off Thai shareholder; assets for sale. *Sydney Morning Herald*, 15 March.

Machiavelli, N. 1532/1984. *The prince.* Oxford University Press: Oxford.

Marx, K. 1859/2012. *A contribution to the critique of political economy.* Forgotten Books: London.

McNay, L. 1994. *Foucault: A critical introduction.* Polity Press: Cambridge.

McNulty, T., Pettigrew, A., Jobome, G., and Morris, C. 2011. The role, power and influence of company chairs. *Journal of Management and Governance* 15 (1): 91–121.

Mendick, R. 2017. AA boss fired over hotel punch-up blames booze and pills for 'sustained attack'. *The Telegraph*, 12 September. Available at: http://www.telegraph.co.uk/news/2017/09/12/aa-boss-fired-hotel-punch-up-blames-booze-pills-sustained-attack/

Milgram, S. 1974. *Obedience to authority: An experimental view.* Travistock: London.

Mintzberg, H. 1983. *Power in and around organizations.* Prentice Hall: Englewood Cliffs, NJ.

Morgenson, G. 2016. How Valeant cashed in twice on higher drug prices. *New York Times*, 31 July. Available at: https://www.nytimes.com/2016/07/31/business/how-valeant-cashed-in-twice-on-higher-drug-prices.html

Narayanan, M. 2017. Will Ravi Venkatesan as Infosys co-chairman hinder Vishal Sikka's cutting-edge thinking? Firstpost, 14 April. Available at: http://www.firstpost.com/business/will-ravi-venkatesan-as-infosys-co-chairman-hinder-vishal-sikkas-cutting-edge-thinking-3383832.html

Pfeffer, J. 1981. *Power in organizations.* Harper Collins: New York.

Pfeffer, J. 2010. *Power: Why some people have it—and others don't.* Harper Collins: New York.

Pierro, A., Raven, B.H., Amato, C., and Bélanger, J.J. 2013. Bases of social power, leadership styles, and organizational commitment. *International Journal of Psychology* 48 (6): 1122–34.

Raven, B.H. 1965. Social influence and power. In: Steiner, D., and Fishbein, M. (eds) *Current studies in social psychology.* Holt, Rinehart, Winston: New York.

Raven, B.H. 1993. The bases of power: Origins and recent developments. *Journal of Social Issues* 49 (4): 227–51.

Reicher, S.D., and Haslam, S.A. 2006. Rethinking the psychology of tyranny: The BBC prison study. *British Journal of Social Psychology* 45 (1): 1.

Reicher, S.D., Haslam, S.A., and Miller, A.G. 2014. What makes a person a perpetrator? The intellectual, moral, and methodological arguments for revisiting Milgram's research on the influence of authority. *Journal of Social Issues* 70 (3): 393–408.

Reicher, S and Haslam, S.A. 2017. Tyranny: Revisiting Zimbardo's Stanford Prison Experiment. In Smith, J.R. and Haslam, S.A. *Social Psychology Revisiting the Classic Studies.* SAGE: London, pp. 130–45.

Rose, N. 1998. *Inventing our selves: Psychology, power, and personhood.* Cambridge University Press: Cambridge.

Runciman, W. 2004. *Hutton and Butler: Lifting the lid on the workings of power.* Oxford University Press: Oxford.

Tap Oil. 2015. Letter to shareholders. Available at: http://www.tapoil.com.au/site/PDF/2056_0/NoticeofAGMProxyFormand-LettertoShareholders (last accessed 11 October 2018).

Thompson, P., and Ackroyd, S. 1995. All quiet on the workplace front? A critique of recent trends in British industrial sociology. *Sociology* 29: 615–33.

Thomson, A. 2014. Sanofi board ousts chief executive Chris Viehbacher. *Financial Times*, 29 October.

Townley, B. 1994. *Reframing human resource management: Power, ethics and the subject at work.* Sage: London.

Ward, A. 2015. Sanofi's ousted CEO Vieh-bacher received €3m pay-off. *Financial Times*, 22 January.

Weaver, M., and Convery, S. 2017. Kevin Spacey criticised over link between homosexuality and abuse. *The Guardian*, 30 October. Available at: https://www.theguardian.com/culture/2017/oct/30/kevin-spacey-criticised-over-link-between-abuse-and-homosexuality

Weber, M. 1978. *Economy and society*. University of California Press: Berkeley.

Weber, M. 2004. *The essential Weber* (ed. Whimster, S.). Routledge: London.

Wheeler, B. 2006. MP investigates Dr Kelly's death. BBC News, 19 May. Available at: http://news.bbc.co.uk/1/hi/uk_politics/4995076.stm (last accessed 24 November 2012).

Whittle, A., Housley, W., Gilchrist, A., Mueller, F., and Lenney, P. 2015. Category predication work, discursive leadership and strategic sensemaking. *Human Relations* 68 (3): 377–407.

Wilson, D.S., Near, D., and Miller, R.R. 1996. Machiavellianism: A synthesis of the evolutionary and psychological literatures. *Psychological Bulletin* 119 (2): 285.

Yeung, R. 2009. *Office politics: The new rules*. Marshall Cavendish: London.

Zheng, X., Van Dijke, M., Leunissen, J.M., Giurge, L.M., and De Cremer, D. 2016. When saying sorry may not help: Transgressor power moderates the effect of an apology on forgiveness in the workplace. *Human Relations* 69 (6): 1387–418.

Zimbardo, P. 2007. Revisiting the Stanford Prison experiment: A lesson in the power of situation. *Chronicle of Higher Education* 53 (30): B6–B7.

Zivnuska, S., Kacmar, K.M., Witt, L., Carlson, D.S., and Bratton, V.K. 2004. Interactive effects of impression management and organizational politics on job performance. *Journal of Organizational Behavior* 25 (5): 627–40.

PART 5

The organization and its environment

CHAPTER 15

Work, emotion, and aesthetics

Organizations as an experience, work as a performance

Chapter overview and learning outcomes

By the end of this chapter you should be able to:

- explain how many service-sector organizations create an 'experience' rather than a product which is consumed

- describe the main features of 'Disneyized' organizations (Bryman, 2004) within the service-sector and leisure industries

- explain what is meant by 'performative labour' as an aspect of the service-sector labour process

- describe the main features of emotional and aesthetic labour

- analyse how emotional and aesthetic labour impacts workers differently depending upon their gender

- explain how emotional labour is managed in the reputation economy, as typified by the rating systems of the Fourth Industrial Revolution

Key theorists	
Alan Bryman	Developed the idea of the 'Disneyization of society' to suggest that characteristics of Disney theme parks are widespread in other service and leisure organizations
Arlie Hochschild	From research into the work of air hostesses, developed the term 'emotional labour' to show how workers are expected to manage their emotions in return for a wage
Pierre Bourdieu	Used the term 'habitus' to suggest that people have deeply-held dispositions which they demonstrate unwittingly in their behaviour and which are difficult to change
Erving Goffman	Used theatrical analogies in his 1959 book *The presentation of self in everyday life* to suggest that people put on different performances in different social contexts
Anne Witz, Chris Warhurst, and Dennis Nickson	Identified aesthetic labour in customer-facing service industries, where people manage their appearance and behavioural dispositions in return for a wage
Sharon Bolton	Examined how emotional performances are managed throughout an organization and not just in front of customers

CHAPTER 15

Key terms	
Disneyization (of society)	As noted by Alan Bryman, the adoption of certain characteristics of the Disney theme park in a large number of service and leisure organizations, especially in organizations which are experienced by consumers as destinations in their own right
Performative labour	Cited by Bryman as an aspect of Disneyization whereby workers are on show in front of consumers and are required to put on some form of performance; such performance encompasses both emotional and aesthetic labour
Emotional labour	Workers managing the emotions that they display in front of customers and clients in return for the wage that they are paid
Aesthetic labour	Workers adhering to certain requirements of appearance and comportment in return for the wage that they are paid
Reputation economy	Describes how the reputation and trustworthiness of workers and organizations in the Fourth Industrial Revolution are determined by online scores and ranking

Introduction

Running case: a bad reputation

At a senior management meeting, Phil Weaver raised concerns about a decrease in bookings. 'I know that other hotels in the area are full to capacity. Why aren't we?'

'This might be the reason,' suggested Linda Wilkinson, linking her computer to a projector. On the screen, she called up TripAdvisor, a hotel listing site, with ratings and comments from previous guests. A search for Junction Hotel revealed a score of 2.9 out of 5.

'Surely that's not bad?' asked Simon Chance. 'More people like it than not.'

'Yes, but look at the other hotels close to us: Grand Hotel 4 out of 5; Luxury Retreat 4.5 out of 5—even the budget hotels get better scores than us because they offer value for money,' Wilkinson replied. As if to emphasize the point, the hotel with a score of 4 and above had a green smiling face next to the score. Next to Junction Hotel, however, was a red frowning face, with the word 'Poor'.

'Looks like we have a really bad reputation compared to other hotels.' said Weaver. 'We need to find out why.'

When we use websites and apps to buy or investigate products or services, they regularly ask us to rate the **experience** that we have had. Usually they relate to service-sector organizations—bars, restaurants, banks etc.—which, in many Western economies, have replaced manufacturing as the dominant areas of employment. In the UK, for example, service industries account for almost 80 per cent of economic and employment activity (Office for National Statistics, 2018).

In this chapter we see why the quality of the experience is so important to service work, in particular aspects of service work defined variously as front-line, customer-facing, or **interactive service work**. This might include retail work or leisure work, such as bars and restaurants, but can include any job where work is performed in front of customers or clients, including much of the work which now takes place in the gig economy.

In this chapter we explore how even within this shift away from manufacturing towards services, much of this work is still rationalized, drawing on Tayloristic and bureaucratic forms of efficiency and control. Call centres, supermarkets, budget hotels, and the fast-food restaurant are all contemporary examples of efficient, rationalized organizations, and all are located in the service sector. However, while service-sector organizations employ rationalized techniques, they also display their own particular characteristics, which we suggest are a result of consumers engaging with organizations as an experience—in a way that they would not do with manufacturing organizations.

- Service-sector organizations, such as bars, restaurants, and shopping malls, often create a theme, environment, or experience for the consumer in a similar way to a theme park. Bryman (2004) uses the term 'Disneyization' to describe characteristics of Disney theme parks which can be found in contemporary service and leisure organizations.

- If a theme or experience is part of what an organization is selling, then workers play a role in creating that experience. Unlike workers on an assembly line, service workers are 'on show'. Gabriel (2005) uses the metaphor of the 'glass cage' to at invoke the McDonaldized, rationalized nature of much service but also to highlight workers being constantly on display as if they were in a glass cabinet.

Organizations become like theatres, with workers putting on a performance in front of customers and clients. Bryman (2004) suggests that workers undertake **performative labour** in exchange for the wages they are paid. In this chapter we examine two particular aspects of this type of work.

- **Emotional labour** (Hochschild, 1983) is concerned with how workers behave and interact with customers and clients. This is often by smiling and being pleasant to customers, but we will see that other service work might demand different types of emotional display.

- **Aesthetic labour** (Witz et al., 2003) is concerned with aspects of appearance, e.g. through dress codes, and how workers present and 'carry' themselves in front of customers.

We will see how emotional and aesthetic labour are not gender neutral. The burden of performative labour falls disproportionately upon women, to the point where women are seen to be objectified or sexually 'commodified' (Adkins, 1995) in service work.

While service work has long existed, the importance of organizations as an experience has been highlighted recently with high-street shops forced to compete with online shopping, and therefore paying attention to the 'experience' that they provide in order to win customers back through their doors (Thomas, 2018). Emotional and aesthetic labour play a part in creating this experience. Furthermore, Bank of England governor Mark Carney suggests that 'emotional intelligence' is vital for jobs in areas such as leisure and care industries, where the need for a human touch has resisted the automation typical of the Fourth Industrial Revolution (Drury, 2018; see also Chapter 10). Nevertheless, towards the end of this chapter we will see how these requirements for emotional labour have also become coded into the algorithms which are used to rate workers within the gig economy (see Chapter 4). A **reputation economy**, based on these ratings and rankings, can ultimately decide whether or not gig economy workers are given any future work.

? Review questions

Describe	How is service-sector work rationalized? (You may wish to look back to Chapter 4.)
Explain	What is meant by 'putting on a performance' at work?
Analyse	What similarities and differences exist between manufacturing and service-sector work?
Apply	What characteristics of customer-facing service work can you identify in the Junction Hotel case?

The organization as an experience

🔍 Running case: poor ratings

Weaver and Chance look at the TripAdvisor site in more detail, and are shocked to find poor ratings, with critical comments from previous guests.

★★☆☆☆ 'Ruined by poor service'
Stayed here for a weekend. Really good food, but it was ruined by the service—servers were really rude to us, almost threw the food at us and snatched plates away. They were dressed a bit scruffily too—not what I would expect for this class of hotel.

★☆☆☆☆ 'Spoiled our wedding reception.'
Paid a fortune for our wedding reception here. The room itself was great and they really decorated it well for the occasion. The bar staff were a problem though, they looked bored, as if they would rather be somewhere else. None of them could smile, in fact one of them got into a row with the best man—I know he'd had a few drinks, but you expect that when people pay so much for a wedding.

★★★☆☆ 'Perfunctory'
Room was fine but overall the hotel was lacking something. At check-in the receptionists did the bare minimum, we felt like we were being processed rather than being welcomed to a luxury hotel. You would think the staff could go that extra mile given the amount we paid.

The problem didn't seem to be with the products offered by Junction Hotel—in fact, the rooms were fine and the food in the restaurant was praised as being exemplary. It was the behaviour and the appearance of the staff that was ruining the experience for the guests.

In this section we suggest that there is a fundamental difference between manufacturing and service organizations. When we buy manufactured goods, such as a television, we don't actually see the work that has gone into making them. It is highly unlikely that we will have stood and watched the television being assembled in a factory—**production** took place in another place at another time, and our enjoyment of the product is none the worse for this. In service organizations it is much more than the product itself that determines whether or not customers are satisfied and happy with what they have received. They are also judging the organization on the experience that they have while there, with the staff a key part of that experience.

⟳ Real life case: dining out as an experience

When you go to a restaurant it is not just the food that determines your enjoyment of the visit, but also the atmosphere, the decor, the attitude of the waiting staff, etc. Many restaurants advertise their offer as a dining *experience* rather than emphasizing the food alone.

US retail consultancy PSFK (2018) suggest that many restaurants are 'repositioning the experience' that they offer, providing 'additional lifestyle, immersive and family-oriented experiences that help complement the expected meal'. The restaurant becomes a destination and experience in itself alongside the food consumed, or as Portuguese chef Nuno Mendes suggests the restaurant creates memories, not just sustenance (Whittle, 2017).

Fred Sirieix, a maître d' known for his role on the UK television programme *First dates*, suggests that good hospitality can make the food taste better. He sees his role as maître d' to be one that greets the guest and guides their 'journey' through the restaurant experience, stating that diners should receive five smiles from the staff en route. His key recommendation for restaurant staff to provide good hospitality is simple: 'being human' (Rayner and Lewis, 2016).

Of course there are also many things that can spoil the dining experience at a restaurant. Rude and inattentive staff is one element. A Canadian study showed that even something like the presence of smartphones can ruin the experience for diners (Petter, 2018).

The focus on the organization as an experience brings about a fundamental change in the relationship between production and consumption, and the roles of workers within this. In manufacturing, production takes place in one particular place (the factory), whereas **consumption** of that product—using and enjoying the product—takes place elsewhere (e.g. the customer's home) and at a different time. There is a 'temporal and spatial buffer' (Korczynski and Ott, 2004: 576) between the labour performed in producing the item and the consumption of that item (see Figure 15.1).

Figure 15.1 The gap between production and consumption in manufacturing industries.

Figure 15.2 Simultaneous production and consumption in the 'experience' of service and leisure organizations.

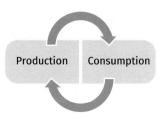

In service industries, such as a restaurant, however, the product on offer is not a just a tangible good, i.e. a meal; rather it is the overall experience within the restaurant that is consumed. Production and consumption are intertwined, both happening simultaneously (see Figure 15.2).

Real life case: American Dream Mall

Plans have been submitted for the American Dream Mall in Miami, planned to be the largest shopping mall in the US. Its more than half a million square metres will contain more than just shops—the mall will also have a water park, a theme park, a luxury hotel, a sports centre, and even an outdoor fishing area. The mall claims a ratio of 55 per cent entertainment to 45 per cent retail, and even the shopping areas will be themed around famous international shopping districts.

The mall is an example of a 'destination mall'—one which attracts visitors from its wider region as a destination in its own right, with other attractions such as bars and movie theatres keeping shoppers in for longer—and away from online shopping.

Sources: American Dream (2018); Garfield (2018); Hanks (2018).

Visit the online resources and take a look at the web links for Chapter 15 to learn more about destination malls.

In that consumption takes place within the organization itself, a characteristic of many service and leisure organizations is that they are created as locations *in their own right*, to be experienced by consumers. As seen with the American Dream Mall, shopping malls are destinations to be experienced for themselves rather than simply somewhere to shop. For Gottdiener (1998) the mall has to advertise itself as an attractive location or experience to compete with the town centre that it aims to replace, with other shopping malls, and with online retailing.

> As a result, almost every mall has an overarching motif that attempts to convey it as a unique and desirable location for its own sake. (Gottdiener, 1998: 80)

It is not just large shopping malls where this type of experience is provided. The growth of online retailing means that individual physical stores are having to compete by delivering an 'engaging, theatrical and memorable retail experience' (Ruth Jacobs, MD Ranstad Business Support, quoted in Lavelle, 2018).

Visit the online resources and take a look at the extension material for Chapter 15 to learn more about the ways in which museums also market themselves as 'experiences'.

The Disneyization of society

An organization whose main focus is to create an experience for its visitors is the Disney theme park. We think of a Disney theme park as a place to visit on a special occasion to experience its spectacular images and sights. However, Bryman (2004) suggests that the characteristics of Disney theme parks can also be found in more mundane, everyday service and leisure organizations. Bryman suggests four characteristics which make up this **Disneyization** of society.

Disneyland.
Source: iStock.com / MarKord

- Many service and leisure organizations engage in **theming**. Pubs are presented as sports bars or Irish pubs. Restaurants are themed around food (e.g. Chinese or Indian) or take other themes, e.g. the Hard Rock Café themed around music (Beardsworth and Bryman, 1999). Even tourist areas are themed, e.g. 'Shakespeare country' around Stratford-upon-Avon in England, or Santa Claus Land in Finland (Pretes, 1995).

- A theme park encompasses different types of consumption—shops, restaurants, leisure rides, etc. Such **hybrid consumption**, whereby different activities take place under the same roof, is also found in service and leisure organizations. Shopping malls are often combined with other activities, such as bars, restaurants, and cinemas. Sports stadium developments often encompass hotels and fast-food restaurants or are built as part of a retail park.

- Goods are produced using the name or image of a particular organization. Disney **merchandising** (films, soft toys, etc.) is familiar and there may even be cross-promotion, with, for example, a new Disney film being promoted at a fast-food restaurant. Top sports clubs also produce merchandise—think of a Real Madrid duvet or a Manchester United pencil case.

- As we will see later in the chapter, workers are expected—through the management of emotion and appearance—to engage in performative labour as if they were on a stage.

The earlier example of the American Dream Mall demonstrates at least three examples of Disneyization. There is theming of some of the areas; there is hybrid consumption with different types of consumption in one place, such as retail, entertainment, and hotels; and with interactive service work in the various attractions within the mall, we can presume that performative labour takes place too. There is no merchandising of the mall as such—although a Disney store within a mall means that merchandising is not entirely absent!

Not all service and leisure organizations exhibit all of the characteristics of Disneyization, and some will exhibit more than others.

Visit the online resources and take a look at the web links for Chapter 15 for more examples of Disneyized organizations.

Controlling organizational realities

When we enter a theme park, museum, shopping mall, or similar organization, we are effectively leaving our everyday lives behind for a few hours and immersing ourselves in the experience that they create. The organizations meticulously create their own particular 'realities', especially in a themed environment. Indeed, the experience that they create is often so much better than the reality it is meant to imitate that it has been described as **hyper-reality** (Baudrillard, 1983; Eco, 1986), an artificial reality better than anything that could be experienced in the actual reality that it aims to reproduce. Referring to the painstaking recreation of a tropical rain forest at Disneyland, Eco states: 'A real crocodile can be found in the zoo, and as a rule it is dozing or hiding, but Disneyland tells us that faked nature corresponds much more to our daydream demands' (Eco, 1986: 44).

We might expect something spectacular from a theme park, but the experience of a more mundane place, such as a shopping centre, also aims to create something of a 'perfect world'. For example, in a town centre the weather can provide all manner of unpleasant experiences—rain, snow, and cold temperatures. In shopping centres, technology provides a constant perfect climate within its walls—much better than a 'real' climate outdoors (Ritzer, 2019: 106).

Technology and organizational control can also help to make the mall better than the world outside by reducing the instances of crime. Surveillance technology, such as closed circuit television (CCTV) cameras, along with private security forces are designed to ensure that the mall remains a safe space.

In such organizations, the environment is totally organized or 'climatized'—a 'total conditioning of actions and time' (Baudrillard, 1970: 23–4, author's translation). The better-than-perfect experience comes from very tight levels of organizational control.

Bryman (1995: 181) notes how the themed experience and hyper-reality created by Disney theme parks is also achieved by tight control over workers. Many of the techniques used are familiar techniques of rational management, including manuals to control the work process, job roles delineated by different uniforms, and highly structured work routines. The magical experience of the theme park would seem to bear the rationalized hallmarks of Taylor and Ford.

? Review questions

Describe	What are the four main features of Disneyization?
Explain	How do organizations create 'hyper-real' environments?
Analyse	How does the nature of consumption differ between manufacturing and service-sector products?
Apply	Think of a service organization that you use regularly—can you describe it in terms of the four features of Disneyization?

Work as a performance: emotional and aesthetic labour

It sounds obvious to say that service work should be customer-focused, but looking back at Figures 15.1 and 15.2 gives us an idea of why. Workers in the service sector interact directly with customers—there is no distance in time or space between the work done and the consumption of that work. A bar worker or a restaurant worker is on show to the customers. Whether they are friendly, rude, well-groomed, or unkempt, they are a part of the customer's 'experience' of the organization.

Have you ever complained about the service you have received in an organization or maybe even not gone back to that organization because of bad service?

Jane Grimes, a university student, has recently started part-time bar work at Junction Hotel. At the weekend, Grimes likes to go out around town with friends. This Saturday, however, she is on the rota to work.

At 7 pm, the bar is quiet. Grimes catches sight of the painting hanging on the wall—Édouard Manet's *A bar at the Folies-Bergère*. It has become her favourite, and after several weekend shifts she realizes why. The facial expression sums up her feelings—she is bored. She would much rather be having a laugh with her friends than be stuck behind the bar.

To compound matters, unlike the barmaid in the painting, she isn't allowed to look bored for too long. However she feels—bored, sad, angry—she has to put on a show: smile, be pleas- ant, show interest in the customers. As the bar manager keeps reminding her, she is a part of the decoration and an unhappy face spoils things for customers.

Keeping a happy face becomes more of a test as the night wears on.

The first man to arrive tells her 'how lovely' she looks. She smiles and says 'thank you,' but, inside, feels disgust. Her skin crawls at the thought that she is some sort of object for him to ogle at. Besides, she doesn't feel 'lovely' at all. The bar has a dress code, which she hates, and rules on make-up and hair that she feels make her look like a doll rather than a real person.

As the night continues and customers drink more, they become ruder and the compliments on her looks become more suggestive. The regular bar-room bore sits at one end of the bar, unburdening his tales of marital woe to Grimes. She wants to tell him what a sad individual he is, but, instead, she has to smile and humour him. This is particularly difficult for her because his drawling, incoherent sentences are keeping her from serving others, and these gaps in service will show up on the printout from the till at the end of the shift.

Jane Grimes looks up again at the woman in the painting and the bored expression on her face. 'If only I could show my true feelings like she does; just drop the mask for a while,' she thinks. 'Instead, I have to keep up this performance for the rest of the shift.'

Édouard Manet's *A bar at the Folies-Bergère*.
Source: © The Samuel Courtauld Trust, The Courtauld Gallery, London.

 What aspects of this case do you recognize from your own experiences of work?

Performative labour

Disney views its staff as an important part of the experience that the organization creates, and exerts considerable control over their behaviour and appearance to ensure their 'performance' as a standardized 'product'.

Performance time.
Source: Alain Lauga / Shutterstock.com

Performative labour describes customer- and client-facing service work which is 'akin to a theatrical performance in which the workplace is construed as similar to a stage' Bryman (2004: 104). Work is a performance, and managers are the directors of that performance: the whole experience offered by Disney is show business (Peters and Waterman, 1982). **Performative labour** draws together two strands of control over the service-sector labour process, which we examine in the remainder of this chapter: **emotional labour**, where people control their behaviour and feelings in front of customers, and **aesthetic labour**, where workers adhere to particular requirements of dress, appearance, and comportment.

The presentation of the self

Goffman (1959) used metaphors of theatre and performance to analyse how people present themselves in different social situations, including the workplace. He noted how people put on different emotional and behavioural 'performances', including their use of dress, props, and appearance, depending on the situation.

Goffman suggested that in different teams, for example with colleagues, family members, or university friends, we might offer a different 'presentation of the self', that is to say we may modify our behaviour and appearance accordingly.

 Do you act differently in these different situations, e.g. at work, at university, in a sports club? How do you *know* the appropriate performance to maintain in each?

Goffman (1959) outlines three particular areas:

- frontstage—where members of a team are involved in a performance and must maintain that performance;
- backstage—where the team is out of view; the performance does not need to be maintained, but issues relating to the performance might be discussed among the team (similar to the wings or the rehearsal room in a theatre);
- outside—away from the situation completely.

Goffman's theatrical metaphor resonates with the service industry; indeed, similar metaphors are even used in some service organizations. Disney, for example, refers to theme park workers as 'cast members' and speaks of **frontstage** areas as being in front of theme park visitors and **backstage** areas being out of view of the visitors. Similarly, service organizations, such as cinemas or hotels, have 'front-of-house staff' who deal directly with customers and 'backroom staff' who work out of view of customers in offices or kitchens, for example.

> ### ⟳ Real life case: Peter Street Kitchen
>
> Peter Street Kitchen, a new restaurant opening in Manchester, UK, engaged in a 'ground-breaking' campaign to recruit staff. Stating that the restaurant would 'premiere' in 2018, notices outside the premises and on their website announced a 'casting call' with opportunities for all areas of food and beverage in 'Front of House, Back of House and Kitchen'. Several 'casting days' were held at the premises in order to attract the best hospitality staff for the new venture.
>
> Sources: Peter Street Kitchen (2018); Barlow (2018).

We can make a direct link between Goffman's theatrical metaphors of society and the workplace, especially in the service sector.

- Frontstage areas are areas where workers are facing and interacting with customers, and where some form of performance might be expected—at the counter, in the aeroplane cabin, on the gym floor, or on the phones in a call centre, for example.

- Backstage areas are in the workplace but out of view of customers—the offices, the staff room, the smoking area at the back of the building, or the galley in an aeroplane, for example.

- Outside areas are away from work—at home, out with non-work friends; they represent private life rather than working life.

Performance and the wage–labour relationship: from the iron cage to the glass cage

While service-sector work differs from manufacturing work in many ways, they may share a common feature of being highly **rationalized**. In Chapter 4 we discussed the McDonaldization of society, showing how fast-food restaurants developed and intensified Taylorist and bureaucratic techniques in a service-sector environment. For example, a till in a bar is designed to combine the efficiency of service of a fast-food restaurant with the surveillance and control of the call centre. Like a till in a fast-food restaurant it has a set of simple buttons for each product to make recording a sale quick and straightforward, which is useful in a busy bar when fast service is needed. It also allows for control and surveillance (see Chapter 4) to be exerted over bar workers. It can record the number, time, and amount of transactions for each member of staff and this can be examined at a later date—just as, in a call centre, staff can be monitored by the data held on them in the computer system (see Chapter 4). By recording the flow of drinks through the pumps, the system can even identify if staff are adding a free drink to a round for a friend.

Korczynski and Ott (2004: 578) suggest that while rationalization is undoubtedly present in service work, there is little evidence of pure McDonaldization or Taylorism in practice; instead, rationalization is blended with customer-focused work. Frontstage performances therefore become important to the organization—the service interaction is a part of what the organization offers, and emotional and aesthetic performances of workers are a part of this. Service work therefore combines Taylorist rationalization of the work process with extra burdens to 'perform' and to be on show.

547

Figure 15.3 The capitalist wage–labour relationship.

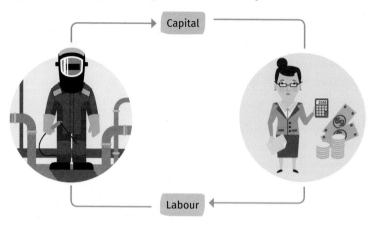

It is worthwhile recalling the specific meaning of 'labour' as it applies to these performance aspects of work. We repeat here the diagram from Chapter 3 outlining the nature of the capitalist wage–labour relationship (Figure 15.3).

Workers receive a wage and, in return, provide their labour. So, labour has a specific meaning: it is that which is provided (or done) by workers in exchange for the wage paid to them. We saw in Chapter 3 how Taylorism rationalizes and intensifies this labour process, getting more work in return for the wages paid. There are two types of labour with which we are familiar.

- Manual labour involves using physical abilities in return for the wage paid. It could be argued that Taylor and Ford's factory techniques relied on manual labour as they reduced work to simple, repetitive tasks.

- Intellectual labour is where a worker uses their knowledge, skill, or some other similar intellectual ability in order to carry out a task for which they are paid a wage.

While both of these types of labour might be required in service-sector work, performative labour is where a particular emotional performance or standards of appearance are prescribed as part of what the worker does in return for their wage, or where there is an expectation that they will be performed as a part of the job.

So, while a member of bar staff may have to carry crates up from the cellar (physical labour) and operate till equipment (intellectual labour), they also have the additional burdens of smiling at customers (emotional labour) and adhering to a particular dress code (aesthetic labour). Performance is thus a further aspect of labour expected in exchange for the wage paid in service-sector work. Performative labour can be seen as an extra level of control, with emotional and aesthetic performances being demanded on top of rationalized efficiency as part of the wage–labour relationship.

Increasingly, the recruitment and selection process for retail work is reflecting this demand for performances. While the Taylorist, rationalized element of work is easy to perform and requires little special skill or training, the recruitment process seeks to uncover the extrovert personalities (see Chapter 8) that will perform well on stage. Lavelle (2018) outlines how interviews become more like auditions, with some sort of speech or performance required, in some ways mirroring TV talent shows where candidates are 'eliminated' and sent home at various stages throughout the process.

Gabriel (2005) develops Weber's concept of the iron cage of society to take account of this immediate visibility of people's work. The concept of the iron cage (see Chapters 2 and 4) suggested that bureaucracy and rationalization were so commonplace that they trapped people in their monotonous routines. Ritzer (2019) later used the iron cage metaphor to describe the prevalence of McDonaldization in contemporary society.

Gabriel's **glass cage** metaphor recognizes this McDonaldized, iron cage aspect of rationalization in contemporary service work. The visibility of being behind glass equates to the visibility that rational forms of surveillance bring to the work that people do. The bar till, for example, records every transaction made by a worker and when it took place. The transparency of glass also refers to the further visibility of constantly being on show—doing service work in an organization is like being on display in a glass cage.

This creates a further level of control in the capitalist wage–labour relationship. However, as with resistance in the capitalist wage–labour relationship, we will see how frontstage performances of emotional labour also create spaces where resistance against that control may take place.

? Review questions

Describe	What is performative labour?
Explain	Using Goffman's concepts, explain what is meant by front- and backstage areas of an organization.
Analyse	How does performative labour affect the nature of the wage–labour relationship in the service-sector labour process?
Apply	How can both aspects of the glass cage (rationalization and being on display) be seen in bar work?

549

Emotional labour

Q Running case: 'don't expect a tip'

'Get me a gin,' snarls a customer later in the evening. Jane Grimes has to change the optic before pouring the drink, and the customer starts shouting: 'Come on, what type of amateurs are you? Get me my drink now.' Flustered, but trying not to show it, she serves the drink, smiles, and says: 'There you go, Sir, that will be £4.50 please.' The customer hands over the exact money and tells Grimes not to expect a tip. Her smile remains.

Anybody who has had to work in front of clients or customers will be familiar with the mantra that 'The customer is always right.' No matter how wrong, impatient, rude, or downright abusive the customer might be, you treat them as if they are right. You might want to shout or swear at the abusive customer, but these feelings have to be suppressed—the expectation is that you will smile and remain pleasant.

You may have your own feelings that you have brought into work that particular day—personal events may have made you sad, upset, or angry. But, in front of customers, you are again expected to put these personal emotions into the background and perform the emotional display required by the organization.

Such a performance, where emotions are managed to project a particular set of feelings, potentially different from the feeling being held deeply within, is what Arlie Hochschild (1983) termed **emotional labour**, defining it as 'the management of feeling to create a publicly observable facial and bodily display [which] is sold for a wage' (Hochschild, 1983: 7).

Research insight: emotional labour

Hochschild, A.R. 1983. *The managed heart: Commercialization of human feeling.* University of California Press: Berkeley.

Arlie Hochschild's concept of 'emotional labour' derived from her research into the work of air cabin crew. She noted how the smile of the air hostess was something that seemed to be 'bought' by the airline as part of the wages paid. Maintaining a smile was a part of the wage-labour relationship as much as other aspects of the work of cabin crew, such as pushing trolleys and performing safety demonstrations.

Cabin crew are expected to maintain the appearance of a particular set of feelings—smiling and being pleasant to passengers, no matter how rude the passengers may be. This management of feeling and emotion as part and parcel of paid employment gives the title of Hochschild's (1983) text *The managed heart.*

 Visit the online resources and take a look at the extension material for Chapter 15 for a discussion of the TV comedy character Basil Fawlty, whose rudeness as a hotel manager is the exact opposite of what we would expect from someone performing emotional labour.

The nature of cabin-crew work, where emotions and feelings have to be controlled in front of passengers as a part of the work done for wages, will be familiar to many people who have worked in customer-facing jobs. It is often characterized as retaining a smile in the face of the abusive customer, but there are a variety of ways in which workers might be expected to manage their emotions to give a particular form of emotional display (see Ward and McMurray, 2015, for some examples of the 'darker side' of emotional labour').

- *Smiling and being pleasant to customers.* This is the type of behaviour that people most associate with emotional labour—shop workers, bar staff, cabin crew, any job where workers maintain a smile and pleasant manner in front of customers, no matter how rude or abusive the customer may be.

- *Presenting an upbeat, motivational personality.* Gym instructors (Bryman, 2004: 120), tour reps (Guerrier and Adib, 2003), and teachers are all examples of workers who may have to put on an upbeat performance at work to motivate and interest others.

- *Presenting a respectful and sombre personality.* In some work very different displays are needed. Nurses delivering bad news are discussed later in this chapter; funeral directors and social workers (Karabanow, 1999) are examples where, even if a worker is personally happy, they may need to manage emotions to put on a more serious display.

- *Remaining calm during tense situations.* Police officers and nightclub bouncers have to deal with situations that could be inflamed easily. They may even be on the receiving end of verbal abuse or physical threats. Emotions have to be managed so as not to retaliate to such threats, but to stay calm and not let the situation get out of hand.

Deep and surface acting

Emotional labour involves putting on some form of act, and so it fits in with the performance and theatrical metaphors discussed earlier. As customers, we may sometimes be well aware that an act is taking place. When we are encouraged to 'have a nice day' accompanied by a toothsome, sickly grin, it can feel fake and inauthentic.

Hochschild (1983) noted such a distinction between fake and authentic in how emotional labourers themselves approach their work.

- **Surface acting** is where the emotional display is fake and superficial—the smile and pleasantness are deliberately put on, like a mask. The worker is not acting as their 'authentic self' and, instead, is consciously acting and putting on a display in front of customers.

- **Deep acting** is where a worker deceives themselves as much as the customer. The feelings displayed are much more authentic—the display comes from within. This might mean that the worker is displaying their authentic feelings, or that they have taken on board the performance so much that it has become their authentic behaviour rather than a superficial performance.

The distinction is not clear cut. Think of a situation where a nurse has to deliver bad news. On the one hand, if the nurse appeared superficial and artificial in delivering the news (i.e. surface acting), it could come across as crass and insensitive. A nurse would be expected to display genuine sensitivity and empathy in delivering such news, i.e. there is an expectation of acting with much more depth.

However, if a nurse were to get deeply emotionally involved in all cases that they handled, it would have a detrimental effect on their own ability to cope with the job: the emotion would overwhelm them. There is thus a delicate balance between displaying deep emotional sensitivity but keeping this at such a surface level that it allows the nurse to remain unaffected while not appearing artificial.

Such difficulties in maintaining a balance of appropriate emotional performances, while maintaining a suitable distance so as not to be personally affected, means that the performance of emotional labour is often associated with stress.

Stress, coping, and emotional labour

551

Q Running case: 'all kicking off'

Simon Chance has arranged, through his football club directorship, some deals at the hotel for travelling away supporters. Jane Grimes can hear a set of supporters in the restaurant being drunk, loud, and generally abusive to the waiting staff—as if the waiting staff didn't get enough abuse from the head chef.

After dinner, the football party makes their way into the bar area. At first, the raucous behaviour—singing, chanting, and dancing on the table—is confined to their corner of the bar. Then, two of the party stagger up to the bar to buy a round.

As they slump against the bar, Grimes feels intimidated. They start to make lewd suggestions about what she might like to do once her shift has finished. She tries as hard as she can to smile and humour them, but, as it becomes obvious she will not be acquiescing to their requests, things turn nasty. Pointing at her, one of the men starts yelling at the top of his voice, shouting a stream of the worst insults and expletives possible.

Grimes can take it no longer, bursts into tears, and runs behind the bar into the staff room.

> Imagine performing a job, day in, day out, where you are required to remain calm and pleasant in the face of abusive customers—a constant onslaught of unpleasant remarks, swearing, and even violent threats. How much of this could you take before you snapped back at the customer? How would you cope?

Visit the online resources and take a look at the web links for Chapter 15 to listen to a recording of such a phone call in a call centre.

As described earlier, emotional labour often accompanies service-sector jobs which are already subject to intensified forms of rationalization, such as numerical targets in the case of the call centre. Pugliesi (1999: 134) describes this emotional labour as a 'hidden workload' on top of existing work.

Pugliesi (1999) further suggests that emotional labour is stressful, lowering job satisfaction and increasing psychological distress. To what extent workers are expected to deal with unpleasant behaviour, even abuse, as part of their work, varies in different professions.

- Korczynski and Bishop (2009) highlighted how workers in UK job centres faced regular threats, abuse, and often violence in their work. This, however, was 'normalized and routinized' (ibid.: 84) with neutral, euphemistic language used in training and by management—abusive customers became 'challenging customers', for example. At the same time, the workers were expected to perform emotional labour. Requirements to be helpful and friendly could be enforced by 'mystery shopper' visits.

- Taylor (1998) noted how airline sales call centre workers were monitored both by hard numerical targets, e.g. the number of calls handled per hour, and by soft targets relating to the way they spoke to and interacted with customers. Their performance could be monitored by listening into conversations—staff would be found out if they let their emotions get the better of them and shouted or snapped back at rude or abusive callers.

In other cases, management might intervene more in protecting front-line staff. In UK railway stations, posters can be seen which uphold the right of staff to work 'without fear', stressing to passengers the unacceptability of abusive behaviour.

 What responsibility do you think management have to help workers manage and cope with stress caused by performing emotional labour?

Q Running case: backstage

Jane Grimes is in tears in the staff room, with a small group of staff gathered around to comfort her.

'Poor you,' said one of the bar staff. 'You're new, aren't you—not experienced that before. Don't worry, you'll get used to it. You'll be able to keep that smile fixed pretty soon.'

'But why should I have to put up with that?' asks Grimes. 'They were just horrible to me.'

'We shouldn't have to put up with it, but unfortunately we have to, otherwise we'd be out of a job,' is the reply. 'Look, we get no help on this from the management, so we have to help each other—don't let the punters get the better of us. When we are back here we can help each other and be ourselves—remember out there it's all an act.'

'Look over there,' says one of the bar staff, pointing at the now highly inebriated man who had been making suggestive comments to Grimes earlier on, 'I mean, as if someone as gorgeous as you would go near him. He's in here a lot—we've all had those approaches from him. We're convinced that's a wig he wears.' Grimes peers through a gap in the staff room door to see another member of staff clearing glasses next to the supporter. She smiles at him as she takes the glass, then turns to the staff room, touches the top of her head as if to indicate a wig, and winks towards the others in the staff room.

Grimes starts to laugh and the women in the staff room join in, pulling apart the character of the football fan and imagining the inadequacies that lead him to behave in such a way. Feeling better, she thanks the other staff for helping her to cope.

→

> → 'Don't worry,' replies one, 'we all have our ways of dealing with it.' 'Just remember,' adds another, 'they have no idea who you are so don't take it personally. In fact, most of us put on an act, almost taking on a different personality in front of the punters. As long as you don't lose sight of who you are when you get back here then you'll be OK. Just think of yourself as an actor, and out there is your stage, and you can even begin to enjoy it, let alone cope with it.'

Whether or not management helps workers to cope with the stress of emotional labour, studies have shown how workers help each other on a more informal basis. Such emotional support among colleagues is often focused around camaraderie and the use of humour as a means of coping with the stress of such work (Bolton and Boyd, 2003; Bolton, 2005).

- Hochschild (1983) noted the use of 'upbeat banter' among cabin crew when in 'backstage' areas, out of sight of passengers. This may be to offer support to each other or may be to make jokes at the expense of passengers to help 'laugh off' the stresses of abusive or rude behaviour.

- Korczynski (2003: 58) studied emotional labour in call centres and used the term **communities of coping** to describe informal, backstage groupings that provide mutual emotional support and which become a 'crucial part of the social relations of the service workplace'.

- Lively (2000) notes similar forms of 'reciprocal emotion management'—colleagues listening and offering emotional support—among paralegals in private law firms.

Emotional labour and emotion management

The management of our emotions is not confined to what happens in the workplace when serving customers. When a casual acquaintance passes in the street and enquires how we are, we may smile and say 'very well, thank you,' rather than reveal all of our tales of woe.

Hochschild (1983) made a distinction between emotional labour and other, wider forms of emotion work or **emotion management**. When saying 'very well' to an acquaintance, we are engaging in the management of our emotions, but we are not performing emotional labour—the reason being that we are not receiving a wage for that particular performance.

Earlier in the chapter we saw performative labour, of which emotional labour is an example, located within the capitalist wage–labour relationship. Hochschild, too, located emotional labour within this relationship—it is work performed specifically and explicitly for a wage.

Emotion management is a general term for the control of emotions, of which emotional labour is one specific type that has an exchange value—it attracts a wage (Callahan and McCollum, 2002). The backstage banter and mutual coping strategies seen previously are a form of emotion management, but they are not emotional labour as they are not done for a wage. However, it is not a clear-cut distinction to say that emotional labour is that which takes place frontstage and emotion management is a coping strategy which takes place backstage.

Bolton and Boyd (2003), drawing from Goffman's earlier terminology, use the term 'presentational self' to describe the sort of emotion management that takes place not only backstage, but occasionally front of stage too—the nudges and winks that workers use to help each other cope with stresses of emotional labour: 'A put down comment, a secret smile—these are small, but important moments ... offering important intervals in organizational control for the maintenance of organizational identities' (Bolton and Boyd, 2003: 102).

While such emotion management does not attract a wage, it does, nevertheless, play a part in the wage–labour relationship in the sense that it affects the balance of control in that relationship. The organization 'no longer controls the emotional agenda' (Bolton and Boyd, 2003: 291).

While management may wish to control workers into particular emotional performances, the emotion management of the workers can be seen as a form of coping with stress and, furthermore, as a form of collective resistance against these organizationally prescribed 'feeling rules' (Bolton and Boyd, 2003).

Taylor and Tyler (2000), like Hochschild, studied air cabin crew and noted a number of individualized acts of coping and resistance. Some attendants spoke of faking smiles, deliberately maintaining a personal level of distance behind the look that the organization required of them—a psychological act of distancing in order to maintain their own identities. The suggestion is that workers maintain a degree of control, even when frontstage, such that control of emotions by management is not total.

By bringing in the role of emotion work in backstage areas, and its slippage into the behaviour and gestures of the team while in frontstage areas, we see that the boundaries between frontstage and backstage are not necessarily permanent. Bolton (2005) has suggested that many forms of emotional displays take place within different spaces in organizations, not just between frontstage and backstage, but also between workers. As Goffman (1959: 78) states: 'All the world is not, of course, a stage, but the crucial ways in which it is are not easy to specify.'

? Review questions

Describe	What is meant by emotional labour?
Explain	What is the difference between deep and surface acting?
Analyse	How can emotional labour be used as a form of resistance by workers?
Apply	How does backstage emotion management help workers in the bar at Junction Hotel cope with the stress of their work?

Aesthetic labour

Q Running case: dress code

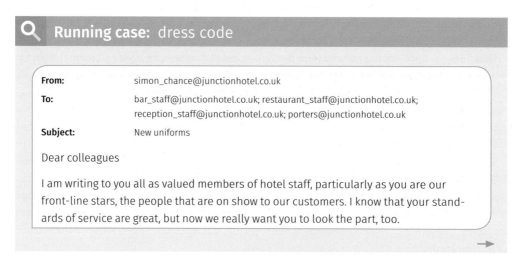

From:	simon_chance@junctionhotel.co.uk
To:	bar_staff@junctionhotel.co.uk; restaurant_staff@junctionhotel.co.uk; reception_staff@junctionhotel.co.uk; porters@junctionhotel.co.uk
Subject:	New uniforms

Dear colleagues

I am writing to you all as valued members of hotel staff, particularly as you are our front-line stars, the people that are on show to our customers. I know that your standards of service are great, but now we really want you to look the part, too.

Tomorrow, new uniforms will arrive for all customer-facing staff. I hope that you will like them and, when wearing the Junction Hotel uniform, feel that you are a living, breathing part of the brand itself.

It's not just the uniform which is important here—it's the way you are the look of the hotel. Service is sleek and professional, polite and unhurried, yet efficient.

May I here remind you of other aspects of our dress code which have been slipping recently, but which are important in presenting the look of Junction Hotel that you are here to perform.

- Women: wear make-up to be elegant—it is there to enhance your professional image. Too little and you look unkempt, but, at the same time, don't lay it on with a trowel. Hair is to be in a neat, professional style—nothing too extreme in colour or styling. Some jewellery looks good, but, as with the make-up, not too much.

- Men: hair should be neatly styled and short—full stop. Facial hair is absolutely discouraged. This is a slick, luxurious hotel, not a gathering of geography teachers. No jewellery is the preferred option—it is a distraction.

- For both men and women it goes without saying that basic levels of hygiene are required—nails and the like are to be clipped to appropriately professional lengths. And remember—absolutely no tattoos to be on show at all.

You will be called out from shifts tomorrow to collect your new uniforms—wear them proudly and exude the Junction Hotel image throughout your working day!

Best wishes,

Simon

Performance aspects of service work involve not just the management of emotions, but of appearance too—if work is like a stage, then costume is a part of the performance. An example might be dress codes, which specify what workers should wear, and other aspects of appearance, such as hair or fingernail length.

Aesthetic labour (Witz et al., 2003) describes those demands upon a worker's appearance which form part of the wage–labour relationship—just as there are demands on emotional performances front of stage in service industries, so it is that workers are also expected to dress and look the part. However, aesthetic labour goes beyond surface appearance—clothes and grooming—to bodily movements and comportment, almost the way that the look and image of an organization is performed.

Workplace dress codes

Uniforms are common in many workplace environments. We might not think of a police officer, a professional footballer, or a nurse as adhering to a dress code, but they are being instructed what to wear while undertaking paid employment. At the most basic level, uniforms are thus an aspect of aesthetic labour.

However, **dress codes** often go further than just providing a particular set of clothes to wear. They may also give guidance as to how a uniform should be supplemented with particular aspects of grooming. Thus Lainsbury (2000), quoted in Bryman (2004: 124), notes appearance standards that might supplement uniforms at Disneyland Paris:

> We have appearance standards that are a condition of being hired. For men it means no facial hair, a conservative haircut with no hair over the ears or the collar, no earrings, no exposed tattoos, and no jeans. For women, no extremes in dying hair or in makeup, and no long fingernails. We want a conservative, professional look; we want our employees to be warm, outgoing and sincere. We don't want guests to be distracted by oddities or mannerisms of the cast members.

Even without there being a specified uniform, guidance on the type of clothing to wear, as well as grooming standards, might be given. This might be in routine service work or in professional jobs where workers deal with clients.

 Visit the online resources and take a look at the extension material for Chapter 15 for a discussion about the extensive dress code given to workers at the financial services company UBS.

While dress codes can set standards and advice for workplace appearance, they may also be used both to preclude people from gaining employment and exclude people from current employment. Nickson et al. (2003: 193) give a list of reasons for dismissal from work or the refusal of employment in the first place. They included a man refused bar employment for having a ponytail, people being dismissed for appearing too old, and a designer boutique manager not employing women who wore larger than a dress size 16. Such cases have formed the basis of legal action.

Real life case: legal action over workplace appearance

- In the USA a number of cases have considered whether an employer can make demands on the hairstyle of employees. The cases have concluded that, while employers can reasonably demand a 'professional' appearance, e.g. with no extremes of dying, they cannot make demands which might impinge on hairstyles which form part of religious expression (Hyman, 2018; Cohen, 2018).

- In Egypt, a court ruled against a police force dress code which banned male police officers from having beards (Middle East Monitor, 2018).

- In the USA, a class action led to clothing retailer Abercromie and Fitch removing its 'look policy', which described its store staff as 'models'—employing staff who conveyed the attractive, young look of the customers that they hoped to attract (Kaplan, 2015).

 Visit the online resources and take a look at the extension material for Chapter 15 for more discussion of these cases.

As we will see later in the chapter, often these requirements impinge unequally on women, as do the standards of appearance by which they are judged compared with those applied to men.

Aesthetic skills and embodiment

While dress and appearance form a part of aesthetic labour, Witz et al. (2003), who originally coined the term, suggested that it is about more than just surface 'costume'. Rather, aesthetic labour is about how we 'embody' deep down a particular 'look' or aesthetic.

The suggestion is that much service work requires more than the performance of a robotic fast-food worker repeating phrases at the till. Service work may involve a lot of feeling in the interaction: for example, in a hotel or restaurant the interaction is judged a lot more, and it is in movements and looks, as well as costumes, that this is demonstrated—it comes from much deeper within the body. The concept of aesthetic labour, as outlined by Witz et al. (2003), suggests that aesthetic labourers do more than put on an act: they begin to embody the dispositions as demanded of them by their workplace.

 Theory in context: Pierre Bourdieu and habitus

The idea of embodiment, or **embodied dispositions**, derives from Pierre Bourdieu (1984), whose concept of **habitus** described how aspects of our social being are deeply ingrained and are manifested in such things as our dispositions—the way we instinctively act and react in social situations. This is not just a product of the feeling and emotional mind, nor reducible to a product of learning—it is a product of much deeper levels of socialization.

Bourdieu's work is most strongly associated with social class. He suggests that our up-bringing creates deeply embodied markers of class that are shown in our mannerisms and dispositions. It is when we try to adopt the mannerisms of a different class group that we betray our background.

You may hear people pour scorn on other people for being 'new money'—lottery winners or self-made business people, for example. The implication is while they have the money, they do not have the 'breeding'—the tastes and mannerisms associated with the upper class. Despite having the money being associated with the upper class they give away their working class origins in their tastes and behaviours.

Such examples illustrate the idea of habitus—the social signs of class are so ingrained that it is difficult to achieve mobility between the classes while not betraying class origins in mannerisms and behaviour: in our embodied dispositions.

Think of nightclub bouncers. They don't just have to dress the part—wearing a dark suit and tie maybe; a key skill of their job is that they also have to embody the part. Thus we would not only expect a bouncer to have certain physical characteristics—size and strength—but we would also expect them to 'carry' that body in a certain way, with an authoritative demeanour. Such a demeanour would also be carried through in interactions—the way in which a situation is responded to, for example. In the face of a fight, a calm authority can be displayed through bodily movements and mannerisms as much as words. Of course, such a performance also links with emotional labour, as described earlier. The bouncer would be expected to remain calm, even if others were in a heightened emotional state and, perhaps, being abusive.

 Can you think of any other jobs where you would have expectations of the appropriate demeanour that a worker would display?

The suggestion of Witz et al. is that a similar set of embodied dispositions are expected more and more in service work—workers are expected to embody the image or 'look' of the company in their actions and movements. Workers arrive with a set of 'embodied dispositions'—those which are desirable will have been encouraged, for instance, through imagery in recruitment advertising.

Such dispositions are never a completed project and so, through training, workers are 'corporately made up' (Witz et al., 2003: 37)—trained not just in appearance and social/emotional interaction, but also in the style of the service encounter or 'specific modes of embodiment' (ibid.: 44). Thus, the workers themselves become part of the organizational aesthetic that is presented to customers, part of the 'experience' created by service- and leisure-sector organizations as examined earlier in the chapter.

This embodied notion of aesthetic labour draws both on Bourdieu, to show the deep nature of embodied dispositions, and Goffman, to demonstrate how these are presented in 'action' when front of stage.

Nickson et al. (2003) note specific class issues in this type of aesthetic labour in service encounters, namely that the types of dispositions sought are increasingly those typical of the middle class. In areas where manufacturing industry has declined, those made unemployed, generally from a working-class background, have found themselves at a disadvantage in gaining employment in service work, where it is the characteristics of students from middle-class backgrounds performing part-time service work which are valued more by employers.

Class is not the only area where aesthetic labour has a disproportionate impact. In the following section we see how both emotional and aesthetic labour have a different impact when gender is considered.

? Review questions

Describe	What is meant by aesthetic labour?
Explain	How does aesthetic labour go beyond surface-level appearance to embodied dispositions?
Analyse	How might aesthetic labour exclude people from certain jobs?
Apply	What dress and appearance codes have you had to follow, both in work and elsewhere?

Performative labour and gender

🔍 Running case: 'sexing up'

Staff reactions to the new uniforms are mixed. The receptionists have business suit outfits, whereas in the bar and restaurant women are expected to wear outfits described by one female member of the waiting staff as 'a bit revealing'.

'Lucky you,' replies a receptionist, 'you get to be feminine, do yourself up a bit. We have to stand behind reception looking like we're working in a bank.' 'No, lucky you,' replies the female member of waiting staff, 'those customers are like rampant tom-cats at the best of times—we're just going to be objects for their desires in these outfits.'

In contrast, the male staff in all areas have the same outfit: a regular fitting shirt, trousers and tie, with a jacket for any staff on duty in the reception area—certainly not an outfit that could also be described as 'revealing'.

→

> In the bar, the first shift wearing the new uniform starts. While the male bar staff are allowed to get on with their work, Simon Chance calls Jane Grimes over. 'Come on love, do the outfit some justice,' he says in an encouraging tone. 'Go and have a bit of banter with them—it will make their night. You've got the outfit—go and sex it up a bit with them.'
>
> Grimes has had enough—she already has to deal with the unpleasant behaviour of customers that often borders on harassment, and now she is expected to positively encourage it. She removes her name badge and throws it on to the floor in front of Simon Chance. 'I quit,' she shouts. 'I thought I had come to work in a hotel, but it seems like I'm working in a brothel!'

Statistically, service work is gendered (Kerfoot and Korczynski, 2005: 389) and the types of performative labour demanded in service work suggest that the burden of emotional and aesthetic labour impinges unequally on women rather than men.

For Steve Taylor (1998) the increase of women in the service workforce has been paralleled by an increase in emotional labour. As Hochschild suggests: 'Schooled in emotion management at home, women have entered in disproportionate numbers those jobs that call for emotional labour outside the home' (1983: 181).

Within the wage–labour relationship, emotional labour is not rewarded financially to the same extent as other workplace competencies. A worker might expect a qualification, such as a degree, to be rewarded financially as part of the wage–labour exchange, but emotional skills seem to be considered merely a natural part of being female, learned as a part of growing up. Women are employed as 'women' with various assumed natural resources (Adkins and Lury, 1999), but these resources are not rewarded in the market place.

As with emotional labour, many of the requirements of aesthetic labour seem to impinge more on women. Studies on appearance at work have focused on how it is often an unrewarded burden that falls upon women as part of a perceived 'natural femininity', an embodied knowledge, or habitus, about what 'feminine' behaviour and aesthetics entails. Taylor and Tyler (2000: 86) note how, in addition to norms of feminine 'aesthetically pleasing' appearance, flight attendants' emotional work in caring for and interacting with people were seen as 'natural' feminine abilities or as 'women's work'.

Gender and sexual commodification

Furthermore, aesthetic labour, with its concerns with appearance, can lead to the sexualization and objectification of women in service work. Sexual attractiveness becomes a part of what is expected in return for a wage; in other words, sex sells. For example, Caven et al. (2013) noted how female recruitment workers in the construction industry were encouraged to play up their femininity in front of (overwhelmingly male) clients. This included wearing pink safety helmets, wearing high heels which were unsuitable for the terrain of building sites, and being encouraged to use flirting as a means of engaging with clients. Earlier studies have also noted how women are expected to use appearance and sexuality to engage with clients (e.g. Filby, 1992; Adkins, 1995).

In her original work, Hochschild (1983: 181) noted how female flight attendants were expected to embody both 'motherly' emotional qualities and more appearance-bound 'sexual' qualities. Or, as Tyler and Abbott (1998: 440) state more bluntly, the air stewardess combines three emotional, aesthetic, and sexually-commodified roles—'part mother, part servant, part tart'. Hochschild repeats a quote from one air hostess in her original study:

> You have a married man with three kids getting on a plane and suddenly they feel anything goes. It's like they leave that reality on the ground, and you fit into their fantasy as some geisha girl.
>
> (Hochschild, 1983: 93)

In such professions where smiles, ego massaging, and 'entering into the spirit' take place, Adkins suggest that women are being expected, as part of their paid work, to enter into a form of 'sexual servicing' of men. This involves not only maintaining an attractive appearance and complying with a dress code, but also engaging in sexualized jokes and banter, or 'giving men what they want' (1985: 133). In this respect, Adkins states that women become **sexually commodified**—it is part of the 'arrangement of service labour' (Adkins, 2000: 207). Brewis and Linstead (2000: 172) suggest that in some areas of service work, women may 'genuinely prostitute' themselves.

More recently, the UK government have issued guidance to employers which suggests that uneven demands on workplace appearance between genders, for example by stipulating the wearing of high heels, make-up, or revealing clothing, could fall foul of workplace legislation (Government Equalities Office, 2018). Nevertheless, examples of this sexual commodification have been found in high-profile cases.

- The Presidents Club scandal in 2018 saw undercover reporters infiltrate a charity event at the Dorchester hotel in London. Leading businessmen, entertainers, and politicians were in attendance and invited to bid for various auctions. However, attention focused on the female hostesses employed to entertain the all-male attendees. The uniform requirements included 'black sexy shoes, black underwear, and … hair and makeup as they would go to a smart, sexy place' (Marriage, 2018). Stories emerged of the women being treated as sexual objects, with both verbal and physical harassment including some of the hostesses being groped and subject to suggestive remarks. The scandal led to charities returning donations from the event and the Presidents Club eventually folding (Bulman, 2018; Davies et al., 2018).

- Theme restaurant Hooters is marketed around female sex appeal based on the image of an American cheerleader. A contract from Hooters in the USA was leaked on to the internet. It emphasized just how much Hooters 'girls' were expected to see their 'sex appeal' as a part and parcel of their everyday job for which they are paid, including signing an acknowledgement that they accept an amount of joking, banter, and sexual innuendo based upon this (Hyde, 2008; Walker, 2014). While this has attracted protests (Brown, 2008; Walker, 2014; Blair, 2017, Hooters have defended themselves. They note a vigorous anti-harrassment policy and suggest that

> Claims that Hooters exploits attractive women are as ridiculous as saying the NFL exploits men who are big and fast. Hooters Girls have the same right to use their natural female sex appeal to earn a living as do super models Cindy Crawford and Naomi Campbell. To Hooters, the women's rights movement is important because it guarantees women have the right to choose their own careers, be it a Supreme Court Justice or Hooters Girl.
>
> (quoted in *The Guardian*, 2010; and Ferrell and Hartline, 2011)

 Visit the online resources and take a look at the web links for Chapter 15 for more information about these cases of sexual commodification.

 Do you think that it is legitimate for a company to expect people to perform this type of work for a wage?

Review questions

Describe	What is meant by sexual commodification in service work?
Explain	To what extent are expectations for emotional and aesthetic labour placed more on women than they are on men?
Analyse	What do you understand by Brewis and Linstead's (2000) statement that some women 'genuinely prostitute' themselves in service work?
Apply	Are there jobs where emotional and aesthetic labour are expected mainly of men?

The reputation economy: performative labour in the Fourth Industrial Revolution

🔍 Running case: push the button

Chance and Weaver realized that their attempts to influence the dress and behaviour of the staff had not been received well. If anything they were making the staff unhappier, making the original problem worse, not better.

Weaver made another suggestion, and one that could be implemented in a more distant way. Key areas of the hotel were identified—the reception desk, the restaurant, the gym etc. At the exit to each was placed a console with a notice saying 'Please rate your experience with us today'. There were three buttons which guests could choose from—a green one for a great experience, orange for neutral, and red for bad. Helpfully, the buttons also had the smiling or frowning faces that were originally seen on the ratings of the TripAdvisor website.

'This is how we are rated on those websites, so we can mirror it in each department and see how they contribute directly to our online reputation. Departments with lots of smiley green buttons can get a bonus, but if there are loads of frowning red we'll get their manager in and tell them to get it sorted out.'

We are used to being asked to rate many things in life. It might be someone who has sold us something on eBay, an Airbnb host, a restaurant on its Facebook page, books on Amazon, or even modules at university. Usually we are asked to give some sort of score out of 5 or 10, and then add comments. It feels as if we are asked to rate almost everything that we do in life, and on a more frequent and ongoing basis.

💡 Theory in context: *Black mirror*—'Nosedive'

An episode of the Netflix science-fiction series *Black mirror* presented a world in the not-too-distant future where ratings apply to just about all aspects of human activity. In 'Nosedive', people swipe a smartphone app to rate each other on every minute social interaction—not

→

→

just customer service, but short chats in a lift, or someone at work bringing round drinks. People walk around with permanent grins, being nice to people they otherwise dislike for fear of receiving a low rating.

People monitor their ratings continuously. Not only do they signal a particular social standing, they can have significant consequences in life: slip below a certain level and you could lose your job, for example. The main character in the programme is trying to increase her rating to 4.5 in order to qualify for an apartment in a high-end housing development. The pursuit of ratings directs her actions in life, not just smiling, but seeking out approval from people with high ratings whose opinion counts for more within the algorithm. Those with low ratings become a form of underclass within the society, finding it increasingly difficult to raise their own ratings.

 Visit the online resources and take a look at the extension material for Chapter 15 for a discussion about how such personal ratings are becoming a reality in China.

How do you modify your behaviours in response to potential online ratings?

In the *Black mirror* example, reputations are represented by a single figure, calculated by an algorithm based on the many ratings given. While it is science fiction, it is not too different to the types of ratings that we see today. Hotels, restaurants, eBay sellers—in fact a whole range of organizations and individuals have their reputation represented by a single-figure rating which brings together the various reviews that have been received.

Such rankings and ratings have been called part of a **reputation economy** (Hearn, 2010; Gandini, 2016), which is particularly appropriate to the digital world of the Fourth Industrial Revolution (see Chapter 4). When we book an Airbnb room, buy from an eBay seller, or book a seat at a restaurant, we take a risk. Is the total stranger whose apartment I will stay in trustworthy? Will the seller actually send the goods? Is the food in the restaurant good? If we see that somebody has a five-star ranking, we will be more inclined to trust them, but what if a restaurant had a ranking of only 1 out of 5? Rankings give a measure of value to the reputation of the person that we intend doing business with, and this serves as 'both a measure of trustworthiness and an approximation of risk among individuals who interact with each other as quasi-strangers' (Arcidiacono et al., 2018).

In the Fourth Industrial Revolution these ratings have been integrated into performance measurement algorithms. In Chapter 4 we saw how workers in the gig economy are constantly having their performance measured, monitored, and evaluated through the data about their work that is analysed by the platform that they work on. For example, Uber drivers are assessed by measures such as the number of journeys they accept, but also by the ratings given to them by passengers. In this respect, a requirement for emotional labour is built into the performance management system. Rosenblat and Stark (2016) suggest that this causes Uber drivers to modify their behaviour in a way similar to emotional labour, suppressing their own emotions in order to act in a way which invites positive passenger feedback. This change in behaviour is brought about without any interaction with managers—it is entirely the pursuit of the rating which drives the change in behaviour. There are many similarities to *Black mirror* here: if a rating drops below a certain level, a driver can find that they are 'deactivated' and will receive no further work—in effect being fired. Fourth Industrial Revolution technology makes the *Black mirror* fiction increasingly a reality (Hvistendahl, 2017).

Connecting case and theory

This chapter has examined emotional and aesthetic 'performances' that take place in customer-facing service work in order to contribute to the 'experience' that is consumed in many service-sector organizations. Such work sits alongside rational management techniques as part of the service-sector labour process. Both rationalized working techniques and performances where the worker is 'on show' are aspects of the service-sector working relationship for which a wage is paid.

The reputation economy in many ways draws performative labour further into the rationalized labour process. Ratings become part of the cyber-physical system whose algorithms exert control over gig economy workers. The reputation economy goes beyond the gig economy, however, and various ratings sites provide publicly available calculations of the experience provided by just about every organization within the service sector.

The management meeting at the start of the chapter showed the power of the **reputation economy**. The Jouneyhelp website was like many of the sites that we all use when planning a holiday—we want to know if we should book a hotel and so we rely on the **ratings** of other guests to help us make that judgement.

Clearly the ratings for Junction Hotel were not good. The comments demonstrated that it was the **experience** overall which determined people's views of the organization. Junction Hotel seemed to be providing perfectly good, if not excellent, rooms and food, but it was the attitude of the staff which was creating a bad experience for the guests. In this respect, Junction Hotel is just like many other **service-sector** organizations—the experience they provide is just as important as other work which takes place. From the comments, it seemed that both the behaviour and the appearance of the staff were part of the negative experience, suggesting that **emotional labour** and **aesthetic labour** were not being performed as one might have expected in a hotel.

However, in the chapter we saw that performative labour creates inequalities in terms of class and gender, for example, and can be seen as an extra element of control over workers by management. At the same time, it is also an area where worker resistance, which starts with strategies of coping in backstage areas of the organization, can find its way into frontstage workplace performances.

The story of Jane Grimes gives this perspective of emotional labour from the point of view of the workers who have to perform it. She had to perform emotional labour by masking her feelings and putting on a smile, even if people were being rude and obnoxious to her; she felt as if she was having to keep up a performance when standing behind the bar. When the football crowd arrived and things turned nasty, we could question whether the management should have been doing more to support the staff: some sort of zero-tolerance policy to the levels of abuse, as illustrated in other organizations, might be needed here. The stress of performing emotional labour in such circumstances became too much for Grimes, who broke down.

Later, she received support backstage, in the staff room, from her colleagues. This mirrors Korczynski's **communities of coping**, whereby it is colleagues rather than management that help each other through the stresses of emotional labour, and also reflects some of the **emotion management**—the nudges and winks—that Bolton and Boyd suggest move between the **frontstage** and backstage in service work.

Chance's new **dress code** clearly responded to some of the online comments about the appearance of staff—he wanted them to smarten up. However, it seemed to work only at surface levels of appearance—clothes, hair, make-up etc. Much of the original research on **aesthetic labour** undertaken by Witz, Nickson, and Warhurst actually took place in the luxury hotel sector in Glasgow, where they found that the presentations required to create the experience of a luxury hotel were much more **embodied** characteristics rather than surface appearance—maybe Chance would do well to turn his attention to developing a **habitus** of luxury service amongst the employees?

Sadly, the hotel instead engaged in the **sexual commodification** of female workers, who felt sexualized in a similar way to workers in the Presidents Club and Hooters. It was not just the demands for a sexualized appearance; the expectations placed on the female staff resembled the many other demands for sexualized interaction discussed in the chapter, for example as Hochschild noted with air cabin crew. This is the final straw which causes Grimes to quit.

At the end of the case we saw Chance and Weaver returning to tactics in line with the ratings system which began the chapter. The button system was a means of monitoring individual departments, placing the responsibility for delivering the right kind of emotional and aesthetic labour with their managers, assessed using the data from the button system. While Junction Hotel is not a **gig economy** organization, we can question how far away technology is from allowing the hotel to apply this system to individual members of staff, creating a situation similar to *Black mirror*, where staff interaction is evaluated and fed into an ongoing performance management algorithm that evaluates not just their efficiency but also their ability, through emotional and aesthetic labour, to create an experience for guests that will increase the reputation of the hotel.

 ## Further reading

Bryman, A. 2004. The Disneyization of society. Sage: London.

Covers all aspects of Disneyization; the chapter on performative labour looks at both emotional and aesthetic labour.

Caven, V., Lawley, S., and Baker, J. 2013. Performance, gender and sexualised work: Beyond management control, beyond legislation? A case study of work in a recruitment company. *Equality, Diversity and Inclusion* 32 (5): 475–90.

A case study of sexual commodification in the construction industry, also with a review of key literature on gender and aesthetic labour.

Ward, J., and McMurray, R. 2015. *The dark side of emotional labour.* Routledge: London.

This book includes studies of emotional labour in different professions.

Gandini, A. 2016. *The reputation economy: Understanding knowledge work in digital society.* Palgrave Macmillan: London.

An introduction to the reputation economy.

 ## References

Adkins, L. 1995. *Gendered work: Sexuality, family and the labour market.* Open University Press: Buckingham.

Adkins, L. 2000. Mobile desire: Aesthetics, sexuality and the 'lesbian' at work. *Sexualities* 3 (2): 201–18.

Adkins, L., and Lury, C. 1999. The labour of identity: Performing identities, performing economies. *Economy and Society* 28 (4): 598–614.

American Dream. 2018. Website. Available at: http://www.americandream.com/ (last accessed 18 July 2018).

Arcidiacono, D., Gandini, A., and Pais, I. 2018. Sharing what? The 'sharing economy' in the sociological debate. *Sociological Review* 66 (2): 275–88.

Barlow, N. 2018. Ground-breaking recruitment initiative for Peter Street Kitchen. *About Manchester*, 7 June. Available at: http://aboutmanchester.co.uk/ground-breaking-recruitment-initiative-for-peter-street-kitchen/

Baudrillard, J. 1970. *La société de consommation: Ses mythes, ses structures*. Denoël: Paris.

Baudrillard, J. 1983. *Simulations*. Semiotext(e) Inc.: New York.

Beardsworth, A., and Bryman, A. 1999. Late modernity and the dynamics of quasification: The case of the themed restaurant. *Sociological Review* 47 (2): 228–57.

Blair, O. 2017. Hooters opens first restaurant that doesn't 'objectify' women—and employs men. *The Independent*, 1 February. Available at: https://www.independent.co.uk/life-style/food-and-drink/hooters-hoots-new-restaurant-women-uniforms-men-illinios-a7556616.html

Bolton, S. 2005. *Emotion management in the workplace*. Palgrave Macmillan: Basingstoke.

Bolton, S.C., and Boyd, C. 2003. Trolley dolly or skilled emotion manager? Moving on from Hochschild's *Managed Heart*. *Work, Employment and Society* 17 (2): 289–308.

Bourdieu, P. 1984. *Distinction: A social critique of the judgement of taste*. Harvard University Press: Cambridge, MA.

Brewis, J., and Linstead, S. 2000. The worst thing is the screwing (2): Context and career in sex work. *Gender, Work and Organization* 7 (3): 168–80.

Brown, J. 2008. Hooters: Over the top, underdressed and over here. *The Independent*, 12 April. Available at: http://www.independent.co.uk/life-style/food-and-drink/features/hooters-over-the-top-underdressed-and-over-here-808160.html

Bryman, A. 1995. *Disney and his worlds*. Routledge: London, New York.

Bryman, A. 2004. *The Disneyization of society*. Sage: London.

Bulman, M. 2018. President's Club: Great Ormond Street to return cash from all-male charity gala where guests 'groped' hostesses. *The Independent*, 24 January. Available at: https://www.independent.co.uk/news/uk/home-news/presidents-club-great-ormond-street-hospital-money-return-dorchester-hotel-all-men-charity-a8175361.html

Callahan, J.L., and McCollum, E.E. 2002. Obscured variability: The distinction between emotion work and emotional labor. In: Rafaeli, A., Ashkanasy, N.M., Zerbe, W.J., and Hartel, C.E.J. (eds) *Managing emotions in the workplace*. Sharpe: Armonk, NY, pp. 219–31.

Caven, V., Lawley, S., and Baker, J. 2013. Performance, gender and sexualised work: Beyond management control, beyond legislation? A case study of work in a recruitment company. *Equality, Diversity and Inclusion* 32 (5): 475–90.

Cohen, R. 2018. 5 Incredible things about hair in the workplace. *Above the Law*, 8 March. Available at: https://abovethelaw.com/2018/03/5-incredible-things-about-hair-in-the-workplace/

Davies, R., Weaver, M., and Stewart, H. 2018. Presidents Club to close down after claims of harassment at 'hostess' gala. *The Guardian*, 24 January. Available at: https://www.theguardian.com/society/2018/jan/24/great-ormond-street-return-presidents-club-donations-harassment-claims

Drury, C. 2018. Mark Carney warns robots taking jobs could lead to rise of Marxism. *The Independent*, 14 April. Available at: https://www.independent.co.uk/news/uk/home-news/mark-carney-marxism-automation-bank-of-england-governor-job-losses-capitalism-a8304706.html

Eco, U. 1986. *Travels in hyper-reality: Essays*. Harcourt Brace Jovanovich: San Diego.

Ferrell, O.C., and Hartline, M.D. 2011. *Marketing strategy*, 5th edn. South-Western Cengage Learning: Mason, OH.

Filby, M.P. 1992. The figures, the personality and the bums: Service work and sexuality. *Work, Employment and Society* 6 (1): 23–42.

565

Gabriel, Y. 2005. Glass cages and glass palaces: Images of organization in image-conscious times. *Organization* 12 (1): 9–27.

Gandini, A. 2016. *The reputation economy: Understanding knowledge work in digital society.* Springer: London.

Garfield, L. 2018. The largest mall in the US is coming to Miami, and it will have a massive indoor water park and ice rink. *Business Insider*, 25 May. Available at: http://uk.businessinsider.com/largest-mall-us-american-dream-miami-2018-5

Goffman, E. 1959. *The presentation of self in everyday life.* Doubleday: Garden City, NY.

Gottdiener, M. 1998. Themed environments of everyday life: Restaurants and malls. In: Berger, A.A. (ed.) *The postmodern presence: Readings on postmodernism in American culture and society.* Alta Mira Press: Walnut Creek, CA, pp. 74–87.

Government Equalities Office. 2018. Dress codes and sex discrimination—what you need to know, May 2018. Available at: https://www.gov.uk/government/publications/dress-codes-and-sex-discrimination-what-you-need-to-know

Guerrier, Y., and Adib, A. 2003. Work at leisure and leisure at work: A study of the emotional labour of tour reps. *Human Relations* 56 (11): 1399–417.

Hanks, D. 2018. Nation's largest mall wins Miami-Dade approval as county backs American Dream Miami. *Miami Herald*, 17 May. Available at: https://www.miamiherald.com/news/local/community/miami-dade/article211306649.html

Hearn, A. 2010. Structuring feeling: Web 2.0, online ranking and rating, and the digital 'reputation' economy. *Ephemera: Theory and Politics in Organization* 10 (3/4): 421–38.

Hochschild, A.R. 1983. *The managed heart: Commercialization of human feeling.* University of California Press: Berkeley.

Hvistendahl, M. 2017. Inside China's vast new experiment in social ranking. *Wired*, 14 December. Available at: https://www.wired.com/story/age-of-social-credit/?mbid=synd_digg

Hyde, M. 2008. Buffalo duck wings and a dash of orange tempt Beijing palates. *The Guardian*, 12 August.

Hyman, J. 2018. Hair discrimination: Not a thing. *Workforce*, 30 April. Available at: http://www.workforce.com/2018/04/30/hair-discrimination-not-thing/

Kaplan, S. 2015. The rise and fall of Abercrombie's 'look policy'. *Washington Post*, 2 June. Available at: https://www.washingtonpost.com/news/morning-mix/wp/2015/06/02/the-rise-and-fall-of-abercrombies-look-policy/?utm_term=.ad5865d98888

Karabanow, J. 1999. When caring is not enough: Emotional labor and youth shelter workers. *Social Service Review* 73 (3): 340–57.

Kerfoot, D., and Korczynski, M. 2005. Gender and service: New directions for the study of 'front-line' service work. *Gender, Work and Organization* 12 (5): 387–99.

Korczynski, M. 2003. Communities of coping: Collective emotional labour in service work. *Organization* 10 (1): 55–79.

Korczynski, M., and Bishop, V. 2009. Abuse, violence and fear on the front line: Implications of the rise of the enchanting myth of consumer sovereignty. In: Fineman, S. (ed.) *The emotional organization: Passions and power.* Blackwell Publishing: Oxford, pp. 74–87.

Korczynski, M., and Ott, U. 2004. When production and consumption meet: Cultural contradictions and the enchanting myth of customer sovereignty. *Journal of Management Studies* 41 (4): 575–99.

Lavelle, D. 2018. Want a shop job? You've got to have the X Factor. *The Guardian*, 27 February. Available at: https://www.theguardian.com/money/2018/feb/27/x-factor-want-a-shop-job-auditions

Lively, K.J. 2000. Reciprocal emotion management: Working together to maintain stratification in private law firms. *Work and Occupations* 27 (1): 32–63.

Marriage, M. 2018. Men only: Inside the charity fundraiser where hostesses are put on show. *Financial Times*, 23 January. Available at: https://www.ft.com/content/075d679e-0033-11e8-9650-9c0ad2d7c5b5

Middle East Monitor. 2018. Egypt court upholds police officers' right to have beards, 4 July. Available at: https://www.middleeastmonitor.com/20180704-egypt-court-upholds-police-officers-right-to-have-beards/

Nickson, D., Warhurst, C., and Cullen, A.M. 2003. Bringing in the excluded? Aesthetic labour, skills and training in the 'new' economy. *Journal of Education and Work* 16 (2): 185–203.

Office for National Statistics (ONS) 2018. *Index of services, UK: May 2018*. Available at: https://www.ons.gov.uk/economy/economicoutputandproductivity/output/bulletins/indexofservices/may2018 (last accessed 18 July 2018).

Peter Street Kitchen. 2018. Website. Available at: http://www.peterstreetkitchen.co.uk/ (last accessed 18 July 2018).

Peters, T.J., and Waterman, R.H., Jr. 1982. *In search of excellence: Lessons from America's best run companies.* Harper Row: London.

Petter, O. 2018. Smartphones are ruining the dining out experience, study finds. *The Independent*, 28 February. Available at: https://www.independent.co.uk/life-style/smartphones-dining-out-experience-ruin-meaningful-conversation-study-british-columbia-a8232176.html

Pretes, M. 1995. Postmodern tourism: The Santa Claus industry. *Annals of Tourism Research* 22 (1): 1–15.

PSFK. 2018. Designing the new dining experience: A PFSK research paper, April. Available at: https://www.psfk.com/report/designing-the-new-dining-experience

Pugliesi, K. 1999. The consequences of emotional labor: Effects on work stress, job satisfaction, and well-being. *Motivation and Emotion* 23 (2):125–54.

Rayner, J. and Lewis, T. 2016. The art of service: Secrets of the maître d'. *The Guardian*, 17 April. Available at: https://www.theguardian.com/lifeandstyle/2016/apr/17/the-art-of-service-maitre-ds-secrets-fred-sirieix

Ritzer, G. 2019. *The McDonaldization of society*, 9th edn. Sage Publications: Thousand Oaks, CA.

Rosenblat, A., and Stark, L. 2016. Algorithmic labor and information asymmetries: A case study of Uber's drivers, 30 July. *International Journal of Communication* 10 (27). Available at: https://ssrn.com/abstract=2686227 or http://dx.doi.org/10.2139/ssrn.2686227

Taylor, S. 1998. Emotional labour and the new workplace. In: Thompson, P., and Warhurst, C. (eds) *Workplaces of the future*. Palgrave Macmillan: Basingstoke, pp. 84–103.

Taylor, S., and Tyler, M. 2000. Emotional labour and sexual difference in the airline industry. *Work, Employment and Society* 14 (1): 77–95.

The Guardian. 2010. Feminist activists protest against Hooters in Cardiff, 11 August. Available at: http://www.guardian.co.uk/cardiff/2010/aug/11/cardiff-feminist-network-say-no-to-hooters-campaign-city-centre-protest

Thomas, D. 2018. Why we no longer love department stores. BBC News. 7 June. Available at: https://www.bbc.co.uk/news/business-44358704

Tyler, M., and Abbott, P. 1998. Chocs away: Weight watching in the contemporary airline industry. *Sociology* 32 (3): 433–50.

Walker, T. 2014. Grim second life of the 'breastaurant': The oft-loathed sector is booming in the States thanks to Hooters, Twin Peaks and Tilted Kilt. *The Independent*, 12 December 2014.

Ward, J., and McMurray, R. 2015. *The dark side of emotional labour.* Routledge: London.

Whittle, N. 2017. Dining is about experience, not expense, says Nuno Mendes. *Financial Times*, 15 May. Available at: https://www.ft.com/content/1bb15674-12f4-11e7-b0c1-37e417ee6c76

Witz, A., Warhurst, C., and Nickson, D. 2003. The labour of aesthetics and the aesthetics of organization. *Organization* 10 (1): 33–54.

CHAPTER 16

Globalization
Managing between the global and the local

Chapter overview and learning outcomes

By the end of this chapter you should be able to:

- describe the key features of globalization

- explain how contemporary globalization can be described as being in a 'global village'

- explain how organizations operate on a global scale

- describe the history of globalization from the colonial era, and how postcolonial perspectives suggest that this still leads to global inequalities today

- explain how national and local cultures influence the ways in which organizations operate globally

Key theorists

Marshall McLuhan	A theorist of media who first described the effects of globalization as a 'global village'
Roland Robertson	A sociologist who has analysed globalization from the perspective of global consciousness and the relationship between the global and the local
Edward Said	An early postcolonial writer who notes how perspectives on global cultural values are largely influenced by a Western, colonial perspective
Naomi Klein	Author of *No logo*, one of the earliest and most popular manifestos of the anti-globalization movement
Geert Hofstede	Attempted to outline national managerial cultures on a set of four numerical scales

Key terms

Globalization	Activities, both organizational and in wider society, taking place on a global scale
Global village	A perceived shrinking of the globe and increased sense of global proximity due to the effects of transport and communications technologies
Global culture	A homogeneous, worldwide culture that emerges as a result of globalization and the activities of global organizations

Colonialism	A period between the fifteenth and twentieth centuries when European countries invaded and occupied other parts of the globe
Postcolonialism	A perspective which suggests that, while the colonial era has ended, the global inequalities that it created still remain with us today
National culture, local culture	Individual and distinct cultures as seen in individual nations or territories
Glocalization	Adapting global practices to local cultures and contexts

Introduction

🔍 Running case: 'Junction International'

Simon Chance is discussing Junction Hotel's global ambitions with his investors. The hotel has joined an online booking website; this means that it is showing up on global searches with more guests coming from around the world.

Chance has tried to give the hotel a more international feel. So far, it has all been fairly superficial—hanging welcome signs on the doors in different languages, displaying a set of clocks with world times behind reception, and a providing a selection of international newspapers in the lobby.

Chance wants to take his international strategy further. As an independent hotel, Junction doesn't have the global presence of some of the big-name chains, but nevertheless, Chance still wants to be an international player.

At the meeting, it is decided to work towards an internationalization plan, named 'Junction International'.

You often hear that we live in a 'globalized' society and that contemporary business has global horizons. The global nature of our own existence, and the array of products and services that we consume, is summed up in the following statement:

> Being British is about driving in a German car to an Irish pub for a Belgian beer, and then travelling home, grabbing an Indian curry or a Turkish kebab on the way, to sit on Swedish furniture and watch American shows on a Japanese TV. And the most British thing of all? Suspicion of anything foreign.
>
> (quoted in Race, 2015)

Although humorous in its intent, the quote highlights the global nature of the economy, and also how this global variety can be seen in the goods and services available within one particular country, the UK.

As individuals we are more aware and in touch with the globe as a whole. Films, videos, and television programmes bring to life situations from other countries, and the internet allows us to communicate directly and instantaneously with people in those countries.

 In your day-to-day internet and media activity, which countries do you come into contact with?

Globalization is a complex and multifaceted process which commands full books in its own right. In this chapter we examine some of the key features of the process. We begin with the commonly held view of globalization which suggests that we have become one, united globe with individual nations becoming less relevant; with the economy, business, and politics increasingly interconnected; and, at the same time, with global culture becoming increasingly homogeneous. We examine the move towards what McLuhan (1964) termed a 'global village' and the features of globalization that contribute to this trend, including the role of organizations.

We then examine two perspectives which argue against this unified view of the globe.

- First, we will see that globalization brings with it many inequalities—while some people in one part of the globe enjoy its benefits, there are other areas of the globe where most people live in poverty and, as ongoing migrant crises have shown, may be desperate to escape political and economic instability. We examine the history of globalization as a violent and oppressive history of colonialism. While this era has ended, postcolonialism suggests that its legacy still exists in the form of these enduring inequalities.

- Second, we will explore how, despite trends towards globalization, individual nations, and the differences between them, are still important—their laws, cultures, customs, etc., still exert an influence on how management is practised within their borders. We thus look at the implications of national and cultural differences for managing and organizing on a global basis.

 Do an inventory of all the goods that you own or have in your house—clothes, food, electronic goods, white goods, transport, etc. Where was each made? Think also about companies whose services you use—banks, insurance, utilities, etc. Who owns these companies and in what countries are they based?

Globalization: a global village?

Q Running case: globally connected

A hotel trade association—Global Luxury—catches Chance's attention. Membership of Global Luxury is exclusive and subject to a number of stringent tests to earn the label of 'luxury hotel'.

While hotels in this association remain independent, their people meet regularly to discuss common issues. Furthermore, the hotels engage in cross-promotion, producing a joint brochure and a website from which bookings for any of the hotels can be made. Marketing and booking is pooled between the member hotels, while each individual hotel remains independent.

For European meetings, Chance leaves on the 6 am flight to Amsterdam and is in a meeting room at the airport for 8.30 am. Representatives from other European hotels in the network will also be there. None of them will actually leave the airport during the day. Instead they will get on return flights in the evening and Chance will be back home in time for supper.

→

Global meetings are rare, at least in person, as there are greater distances to travel. Meetings tend to take place by phone or video conferencing—even then the time has to be chosen carefully, as morning in the USA can be the middle of the night elsewhere.

Chance feels more globally connected than he was in his previous life as a football club chairman. Looking at his email inbox, he used to have a list of clubs from various small-sized English towns. Now his inbox spans the globe, with messages from Australia, Germany, Brazil, and China, among others, sitting next to each other.

While global organization and activity is not a new phenomenon, in this section we examine how we experience globalization differently now from in the past. In particular, there is a feeling that the world is a lot smaller and more immediate. This does not mean that the planet is literally shrinking in size, but that the world *feels to us* as if it is getting smaller.

For example, it takes less time to travel across the globe than it did even a few decades ago and we can communicate instantly with people on the other side of the planet. This contrasts with transport around the time of the Second Industrial Revolution. The Gilbreths, who were pioneers of scientific management (see Chapter 3), often travelled from the USA to Europe to attend conferences and undertake consultancy work. However, in the 1920s the only option for this travel was by boat. At best a journey took a week, meaning that any movement of goods or labour took a round trip of at least two weeks at the time. Similarly, it would take a fortnight for a letter or other documentation to be sent from the USA to Europe and a reply received.

> How might the changes in transport and communications technology since the Second Industrial Revolution have facilitated trading and business between the UK and USA? What types of business and organizational activity are possible now that would not have been in the early 1900s?

In 1964, transport and communication technology had advanced to such a level that Marshall McLuhan (1964) described the world as a global village. When he was writing, this related to the role of the media which brought images from across the world to our attention—we could see other people and cultures as if they were our neighbours, as if the globe were a village. For example, for many parts of the world US life is familiar through its extensive film and television industry. Global news, issues, and events are also seen throughout the world via news broadcasts.

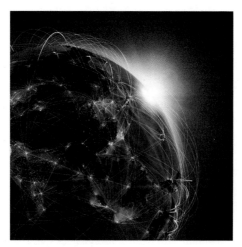

The global village.
Source: Anton Balazh / Shutterstock.com

More than 50 years since McLuhan first used the term, the world is even more of a global village. News broadcasts switch seamlessly between live images from different parts of the globe, budget airlines make international travel available to more of us, and the internet allows us not just to communicate instantly across the globe, but to see the minutiae of everyday life across the planet through applications such as Google Street View and videos posted on YouTube. Many of the companies of the Fourth Industrial Revolution operate through their cyber-physical systems on a global scale (see Chapter 4): for example, Amazon and eBay provide global marketplaces for their goods and services.

 How many people do you communicate with globally, either personally, through email and messaging apps, or through online forums?

Robertson (1992: 8) describes globalization as 'the compression of the world and the **intensification of consciousness** of the world as a whole'. This idea pulls together the compression or shrinking of journey times, and times for communicating with people, alongside people having a greater awareness and perception of what goes on elsewhere within the globe (see Figure 16.1).

In a similar vein, Waters (2001: 5) defines globalization as 'a social process in which the constraints of geography on social and cultural arrangements recede and in which people become increasingly aware that they are receding'. Again, this encompasses the idea that geography (physical space) is less of an issue in separating people across the globe and that we are aware of the world feeling much more immediate to us. We live in a global village *and we are more than aware that we live in that global village.*

Aspects of globalization

Waters's definition highlights globalization as a 'process' rather than a distinct 'thing'. Rather than being one single, distinct phenomenon, it is multifaceted and encompasses many different trends and phenomena.

Parker and Clegg (2006) suggest six aspects (see Figure 16.2) which together contribute to the multifaceted nature of globalization or, more specifically, 'global interconnectedness' (ibid.: 655). Each of these does not constitute globalization in itself; they are inter-related aspects which combine in the processes of globalization that we experience today and within which organizations operate. In this section we examine how four of these—the economy, politics, technology, and the natural environment—contribute to globalization. Later in the chapter we examine the importance of global business and organizations and of global culture.

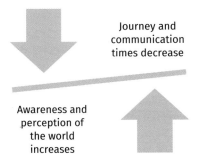

Journey and communication times decrease

Awareness and perception of the world increases

Figure 16.1 Robertson's (1992) 'intensification of consciousness'.
Source: Based on Robertson, Globalization, 1992.

Figure 16.2 Parker and Clegg's (2006) six aspects of global interconnectedness.
Source: Based on Parker and Clegg (2006).

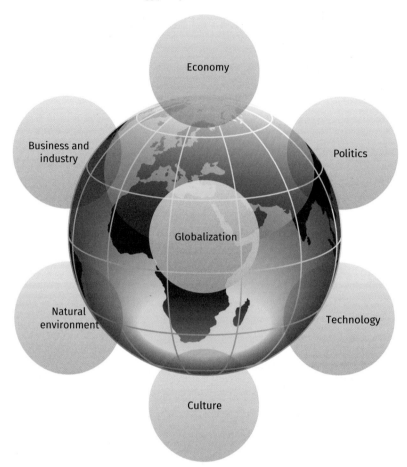

The global economy

There is a saying that 'When America sneezes, Britain catches cold'. The USA is the world's largest economy and is also the largest purchaser of UK exports (see Table 16.1). A recession or other economic problem in the USA will affect the demand for UK exports and affect UK businesses that export to the USA. Many other countries will have a similar set of global dependencies for their export trade. Global economies are interconnected.

There are other influences on the global economy too. China is rapidly catching up with the USA as the world's largest economy and, as Table 16.1 shows, the UK is dependent on the economies of many other countries.

Recent events in the global economy have demonstrated that interdependency is not just about trading and exports, but also about the global interconnectedness of financial institutions and financial products. The 2008 financial crisis was a global phenomenon which hit countries and continents across the globe and from which the consequences and knock-on effects are still being felt.

 Visit the online resources and the extension material for Chapter 16 for a discussion of recent problems with the global economy.

Global politics

Politics is often seen as an activity which takes place at a national level—general elections, national prime ministers, presidents, etc. However, politics also increasingly takes place at

Table 16.1 UK exports 2017 (£ millions)

USA	46,967
Germany	36,030
France	25,491
Netherlands	21,215
Ireland	19,374
China	16,807
Switzerland	16,437
Belgium	13,680
Spain	10,394
Italy	10,220

Source: HM Revenue and Customs (2018).

international levels, partly because of the global nature of the economy and its importance to individual nations.

Many global political groupings and agencies have an effect upon the global economy and the conditions for individual organizations within that economy. For example, the World Trade Organization (WTO) in effect sets the rules and regulations for world trade (and, as we will see later in the chapter, comes under criticism for how it does this). The European Union, which has 28 members at the time of writing, began as a free-trade area and engages in a number of activities which impact on business and organizations in its member nations: for example, through the single currency (the Euro), the freedom of movement of goods and people, the standardization of aspects of employment law, and investment in socioeconomically deprived areas.

 Real life case: Brexit and interconnectedness

At the time of writing the European Union had 28 countries; however, the vote by the United Kingdom to leave the EU—known as Brexit—means that this could be 27 countries at the time of publication. Also at the time of writing the exact development of Brexit was unclear, with discussions ongoing about how closely the UK should remain linked to the EU—for example through a customs union or through membership of a wider European Economic Area, or whether there should be a clean break with the EU and the UK, with interactions between them then operating under World Trade Organization rules.

The ongoing negotiations revealed how closely the countries of the European Union were tied both politically and economically, and how difficult these ties were to unravel. In the financial sector, cross-border transactions take place continually through computer networks; in such industries as car manufacturing, supply chains mean that components are continually moving between countries. The common regulations and open borders of the European Union allow this to take place efficiently. A key issue in the Brexit negotiation will be whether it is practical for a country to operate in isolation in today's globalized world, or whether the interconnectedness of politics and economies needs to be maintained.

Sources: House of Lords (2016); Pooler (2017); Brunsden (2018).

Global technology

Global technology refers to technologies which contribute to the aforementioned 'global village': they allow barriers of geography to be overcome so that people can travel the globe or communicate globally with much more ease. Examples of such technologies include:

- transport—cars, planes, trains, etc. and their associated infrastructures, such as roads and railway lines
- communications technologies—e.g. the telephone and the infrastructure through which it works
- media technologies—television transmitters, satellites, etc. which allow the dissemination of words and images, such as news, film, and television shows
- computer networks—the internet allows an instantaneous transmission and reception of images, words, data, communication, etc.

Such technologies obviously have an impact on what organizations can do on a global scale. The internet and computer networks, and how they affect organizations, have already been examined in Chapters 2 and 4.

Globalization of the natural environment

Another aspect of globalization is the natural environment and its resources, which become commodities to be traded on a global basis. Such resources are important because of their value and, in many cases, their finite nature—think of the importance of fuel to the world economy, for example.

 Real life case: carbon trading

Carbon dioxide is one of the greenhouse gases which contribute to environmental damage, including global warming, and is a by-product of many industrial processes. Such gases do not respect national borders, and so a solution to the problem needs to be global.

Carbon trading is a scheme where governments attempt to limit the amount of carbon dioxide that companies can emit. Governments issue or auction licences for the maximum amount of carbon that a firm can emit. Companies that emit less than their allocation can sell the excess to companies that wish to pollute more.

It has been noted that, in effect, this is a market in an intangible good—selling the right to pollute. In this respect it can be difficult to set the right price so that the market acts as a disincentive to pollute. Furthermore, the market is not yet an international market. While the European Union has a fairly advanced market, a similar scheme in the massive power market of China has only recently been launched.

 Visit the online resources and take a look at the web links for Chapter 16 for more on carbon trading.

Sources: BBC News (2015); Feng (2017); World Economic Forum (2017).

Depletion of natural resources and climate change are aspects of damage to the environment that are viewed as global problems. Workers, too, can be seen as natural resources that are now employed on a global scale. For example, a global division of labour has emerged because in the developing world, where manufacturing now tends to be concentrated, labour is cheaper—in some cases employed in sweatshop conditions. Such problematic issues have further fuelled the anti-globalization movement. Issues of corporate social responsibility with respect to workers and the environment are further examined in Chapter 17.

Physical and intangible spaces of globalization

Earlier in this section, it was suggested that we now experience a 'global village' where the world feels smaller and more immediate. We suggest that this is the result of a shift in emphasis—from globalization primarily of physical space to one which is supplemented by a global, intangible space.

- Globalization of **physical space** refers to the actual land of the globe itself—the *terra firma* on which we stand. As we will see, colonization was about physically moving products across the globe to trade them, and conquering land to create empires.
- Global **intangible space** is that which brings about some form of global connectedness without movement over actual land—data in computer networks and television signals, etc. It is these abstract elements which bring about global consciousness, the immediacy of communication, and the global images that we are now afforded.

Visit the online resources and take a look at the web links for Chapter 16 for a discussion of 'soft power', the global intangible influence that is wielded by some countries through, for example, their media and cultural activities.

Globalization has both physical and intangible elements, and these are reflected in Parker and Clegg's aspects of globalization that we examined earlier.

- The global economy has physical aspects—the physical goods which are produced and then exported across land and sea; equally, it has intangible elements, the 'symbol economy' (Clegg and Gray, 1996: 303) of financial transactions and data flow between financial institutions.
- Global technology has physical aspects (transport which crosses land) and intangible aspects (the signals and data which are beamed through communications, computer, and media networks).

Among these various physical and intangible elements lie organizations. While organizations are affected by the aspects of globalization listed previously, Parker notes that they are not simply passive bystanders; rather, they play their part in making globalization happen: 'Organizations are not simply affected by globalization: the combined activities of all kinds of organizations stimulate, facilitate, sustain and extend globalization' (Parker, 1996: 484).

We now turn to organizations themselves—their role in both the global economy and global culture, noting how they contribute to physical and intangible elements of globalization.

? Review questions

Describe	What are the physical and intangible aspects of globalization?
Explain	What is meant by the phrase 'global village'?
Analyse	What is meant by globalization being experienced as an 'intensification of consciousness'?
Apply	Think of an organization that you know. How do Parker and Clegg's aspects of globalization affect this organization?

577

Global organizations

Simon Chance is enjoying the new status of Junction Hotel being part of Global Luxury group, but he feels that while it has brought an undoubted cachet to the hotel, it is not generating revenue. Indeed, it is creating extra cost and expense to keep up to the luxury standards required to stay within the group.

Chance wonders whether there are other ways to have a global reach but also maintain efficiency and cost-competitiveness.

At his regular meeting with the board of investors, an option put on the table is to buy a similar hotel that is for sale in France. While the board of investors like the sound of 'Junction Paris' and see it as a possible start for a whole chain of Junction Hotels, they soon realize that the costs for this form of expansion will be prohibitive.

Another option presented is to become a *franchise* of a global hotel chain. A number of these franchises exist; the one with the best reputation for quality is the US Luxonational chain.

Luxonational don't own their own hotels; instead, independent hotels apply to become franchise holders, which they achieve after passing a set of standard requirements. The business belongs to the franchise holder in return for an annual fee, based on the size of the hotel, being paid to Luxonational in return for the right to run the franchise. The franchise has to be renewed annually, subject to maintaining the standard requirements.

Being part of the Luxonational franchise would certainly make the hotel part of a global chain, but at what cost to the hotel? Chance is asked to investigate and bring his findings to the next board meeting.

When we think of global organizations, we tend to think of huge companies with recognizable brands. Certainly, a glance (*Fortune*, 2018) at the world's top multinationals by their annual income shows some familiar names, which tend to be concentrated in a number of industries:

- energy companies, such as Royal Dutch Shell (Netherlands), Sinopec (China), and BP (UK)

- automobile companies, such as Toyota (Japan), Volkswagen (Germany), and Ford (USA)

- finance companies, such as AXA (France), Bank of China (China), and Banco Santander (Spain)

- telecommunications and electronics companies, such as AT&T (USA), Apple (USA), Siemens (Germany), and Samsung (South Korea)

- retailing companies, both physical retailers such as Walmart (USA) and Tesco (UK) and online retailers such as Amazon (USA) and Alibaba (China)

 Is there anything in the nature of the products and services in the list here which makes them more likely to be traded on a global scale? Would they benefit from economies of scale?

Such organizations can be so huge as to be bigger than the economies of individual nations. For example, US retailer Walmart, the largest multinational by income, has an income larger than individual medium-sized nations such as Belgium and South Africa (*Fortune*, 2018; Nationmaster, 2018).

Visit the online resources and take a look at the web links for Chapter 16 for a full list of the top multinational companies and a comparison of the largest with national economies.

While many global organizations are massive conglomerates, there are many different ways in which organizations are able to grow their operations to become global players, including possibilities for small-scale organizations to use technology to operate globally. Using the terminology of the previous section we see how global organizations move from growing through physical means, such as goods, people, and premises, to growing through more intangible means, such as brands, licences, and computer networks.

The structure and spread of global organizations

Organizations are not born global; instead, they extend and expand their activities internationally through a number of different types of activity: for example, exporting; overseas investment and expansion; mergers, acquisitions, and joint ventures; franchising and licensing; and subcontracting.

Exporting

This is the most basic form of international activity—selling and shipping a product to another country. In its simplest form, this would mean a company operating in just one country selling goods that it distributes to other countries while not having any premises or operations in those countries. In practice, **exporting** may be combined with some of the activities discussed next.

Overseas investment and expansion

If an organization exports frequently to a particular country or area, it may find a benefit in setting up premises in that area. For example, to generate exports a company may open sales offices in different countries, or a company might operate after-sales service centres for different national markets.

Foreign direct investment is an example of overseas investment where, rather than exporting goods, an organization sets up a production plant in an overseas territory directly. Examples of this might be car firms setting up production plants closer to different markets globally. This happened in the 1980s when a number of Japanese firms, such as Sony and Nissan, set up production plants in the UK.

Mergers, acquisitions, and joint ventures

Rather than setting up brand new operations in overseas territories, another way of expanding operations globally is by buying or **acquiring** companies overseas. This might be by buying a similar organization so as to expand operations internationally (e.g. a supermarket chain buys a supermarket chain in another country) or it may involve buying an organization at another point in the production chain (e.g. a food manufacturer buys an overseas supplier, or a film company buys an overseas distributor).

In some cases, two companies may feel it in their best interests to **merge**, perhaps to gain economies of scale by pooling certain operations. In 2017, chemical conglomerates Dow and Du Pont merged to form DowDuPont, with the intention of pooling resources to dominate their areas of industry (Reuters, 2017).

Real life case: the overseas expansion of Tesco

The UK supermarket Tesco has used a number of different methods to expand into international territories.

- In Hungary, Tesco acquired and rebranded the local S-market chain of stores. Similar acquisitions have taken place in Ireland and the Czech Republic.

- In many Asian countries, such as China and Thailand, Tesco has partnered with local businesses, entering joint ventures to take advantage of the local market knowledge of those firms.

- In Slovakia, Tesco began by acquiring some stores of a local supermarket chain, but has since engaged in direct investment, building new stores.

- A different type of joint venture sees Tesco supplying their goods to overseas supermarkets. For example, a joint venture with Tata in India sees Tesco provide goods and distribution services to the Star Bazaar chain, supplying 80 per cent of their stock. The joint venture has since developed into online retailing.

Sources: *The Guardian* (2015); Tesco plc. (2018); Saha (2018).

Sometimes organizations in different countries find it in their best interests to cooperate in some way without merging their own operations—a joint venture. In 2017, car manufacturers Nissan and Renault teamed up with Chinese manufacturers Dongfeng to create a joint venture to develop electric cars. The cars use existing design and technology from Renault and Nissan, but are manufactured in China under the Dongfeng brand and then sold to the Chinese market (Tovey, 2017).

Franchising and licensing

A company might not want the upfront expense that direct investment or an acquisition might necessitate. Franchising is where a company allows another organization to operate its business on its behalf using its brand and products. This will be for some form of fee, and will come with specific conditions as to how the franchisee operates and uses the brand. McDonald's, for example, do not own their restaurants. Their global expansion has come from their restaurants being run independently by franchise holders, albeit these franchise holders have to adhere to numerous conditions. For example, a franchise holder could not, of their own volition, change the menu offered. Sometimes in a McDonald's restaurant, the name of the actual business holder—the franchisee—will be on display in the restaurant.

Licensing is similar to franchising; however, here, a company grants a licence to produce its good (and sell it under their brand) in another territory. For example, adverts for Fosters beer play very much on the Australian origin of the product, but a small caption at the bottom of the advert indicates it to have been 'brewed under licence in the UK'. The strategy makes sense—it would be impractical to brew beer in Australia and export it to the UK. Licensing is a means to expand the brand globally. This is how Coca-Cola operates on a global scale—by licensing its syrup to overseas plants who then produce and sell it in their local markets.

Subcontracting

With subcontracting, an organization employs the services of another organization to conduct an aspect of its work. This has become a global activity whereby an organization not only subcontracts, but does so to an organization in a different country—often where the costs of this are cheaper. Clothing and manufacturing organizations subcontract production of their items to a factory in a different country, leading to criticism in instances where the cost of labour is so cheap that people are employed in 'sweatshop' conditions (see Chapter 17).

Global technology has allowed for administrative tasks, in addition to manufacturing, to be subcontracted globally. The Indian call centre industry is a well-known example of subcontracting on a global scale, handling calls for credit card companies, insurance companies, technical helplines—any organizations that use a call centre to handle enquiries. Organizations will exist purely as subcontractors—an organization could run contracts for firms across the globe (UK, USA, Australia) in one building, for example.

Other subcontracted administrative tasks include handling paperwork, such as the typing up of medical notes which are scanned and emailed to workers performing the task. More recently, the Fourth Industrial Revolution has facilitated the development of 'clickwork' as a part of the gig economy, where workers perform small simple tasks on their computers, such as transcription, or identifying objects in photographs. In effect, companies subcontract these tasks on a global scale (see Chapter 4 for more on clickwork).

Visit the online resources and take a look at the web links for Chapter 16 for more discussion of global subcontracting.

Global industries and labour markets

Subcontracting shows that it is not just organizations that are globalized—labour markets, too, are global. In the case of manufacturing and call centres, cheaper labour elsewhere in the world is used by global organizations. Global labour markets could also refer to large multinationals hiring their top staff or valued knowledge workers with key skills (see Chapter 10) from a global pool of labour. A university department, for example, will often be made up of an international variety of leading professors.

Industries, too, can be seen as global, with different organizations within an industry contributing to that globalization in different ways. These forms of global activity show that both physical aspects (setting up premises, exporting goods, etc.) and more intangible aspects (e.g. licensing a brand) contribute to organizations and industries extending their activities globally.

Technology and the potential for globalization

While global organization tends to be associated with large-scale global expansion, as described in the previous section, another aspect of global organizational activity is the ability of small-scale organizations, even individuals, to have a global presence. This is made possible by global technology, in particular that provided by the internet.

⟳ Real life case: Skype

The video messaging service Skype is now used by hundreds of millions of people globally for both business and personal communication, indeed many meetings during the writing of this book took place through Skype for Business. The company is now owned by the multinational Microsoft, but it had much smaller beginnings in Estonia.

The original developers wanted to develop file sharing software into a communication tool. At its launch in August 2003, the business started to gain millions of users in its first month. Even though Estonia was far from established technology centres such as Silicon valley, ac-

→

cess to the internet meant that the application could still go viral. Skype shows how, with internet technology, small-scale start-ups can become global in their reach.

Sources: Warnick (2013); Walt (2017); Hunt (2018).

Visit the online resources and take a look at the extension material for Chapter 16 for a discussion of how Estonia has developed many more global technology companies in addition to Skype.

The example of Skype shows how larger-scale organizations—in particular those which provide some form of global network infrastructure—facilitate the global spread of smaller organizations. The global scale of the downloading comes from the intangible global technologies of computer networks and, furthermore, from being available through existing organizations, such as mobile phone download stores. It is as if a form of 'piggy-back' is provided by the larger organization—itself global—to enable the smaller organization to also achieve a global presence (see Chapter 4 for more on the merging of an organization's operations through computer networks).

❓ Review questions

Describe	What are the different ways in which organizations might extend their activities internationally?
Explain	How does global technology allow small-scale organizations to operate on a global scale?
Analyse	What are the advantages and disadvantages of the different types of international organizational activity, such as franchising or subcontracting?
Apply	Look at websites for a number of small and large organizations. In what ways do those specific organizations operate globally?

Organizations and global culture

🔍 Running case: franchise requirements

From:	simon_chance@junctionhotel.co.uk
To:	board_members@junctionhotel.co.uk;
	senior_management_team@junctionhotel.co.uk
Subject:	Re: Franchising

As requested, I've done some research into what becoming a franchise of Luxonational would entail. Here are the main points:

- *Branding.* Junction Hotel would lose its independent identity. It would be re-branded as 'Luxonational Junction'. All marketing and logos to be replaced by those of Luxonational.

- *Booking and marketing.* Common booking and marketing procedure with other franchises in the Luxonational chain. We would be marketed through the international Luxonational website and appear in their marketing materials—a much wider reach than before. We would do some local marketing, but this would have to adhere to a Luxonational 'template'. Information technology upgrade needed at reception to fit in with the standard booking procedure.

- *Hotel furnishings.* Standard Luxonational 'look'. Furniture in rooms, carpets, curtains, the reception layout—all fixtures and fittings would be those supplied by Luxonational. This will cost, but we are due for a refurbishment. Taking the standard Luxonational items will be cheaper owing to their bulk purchasing power.

- *Staff procedures.* Just like the furnishings, the staff will be branded as Luxonational staff, with new uniforms provided similar to the rest of the chain. Furthermore, certain staff procedures would be expected to be brought into line with the rest of the chain, including human resources issues, such as pay and holiday entitlements (not quite as generous as we currently operate). Training provided by Luxonational manual or at a number of regional training centres that the head office run. Expectation of certain cultural behaviours and a brand 'look' that the workers will embody.

- *Purchasing.* Items such as towels, toiletries for rooms, toilet paper, pens, and many other consumables bought on a regular basis would have to be purchased from Luxonational. Restricts choice, but would bring economies of scale as such items are produced for the global range of hotels. Furthermore, the drinks in the bar, food supplies, and many other catering items would have to be sourced from Luxonational's preferred suppliers—this would give discount but dictates to the hotel what drinks and food they can serve.

583

From:	meg_mortimer@junctionhotel.co.uk
To:	simon_chance@junctionhotel.co.uk
Subject:	Re: Re: Franchising

Simon, I've stayed at one of those Luxonational places before: identikit, sterile, characterless, bland—need I go on?

So far in the chapter we have seen how multinational companies are able to extend their reach across the globe, to dominate the globe in economic and business terms. In this section we examine claims that this dominance is also cultural, to the extent that there is a global culture that overrides cultures at a national and local level.

The media is seen as one aspect in this cultural homogenization. Across the globe we all watch the same films and television shows, listen to the same music, and play the same computer games. In many cases, these reflect a Western, predominantly US, culture. This global culture is shown by the following statement made in 1998 by Michael Eisner, then Chairman and Chief Executive of Disney: 'It doesn't matter whether it comes in by cable, telephone lines, computer, or satellite. Everyone's going to have to deal with Disney' (quoted in *New Internationalist*, 1998).

Eisner is speaking here about the global prevalence of Disney films, media, and even imagery through merchandising. It is a global cultural presence, achieved through intangible means—television signals and computer networks rather than physical means.

Such media are usually presented in English, and a further element of global culture is the emergence of English as a global language (Bryson, 1990). While English is not the most widespread language by first speakers (indeed, it is not even second—the top three languages are Mandarin, Spanish, and then English), it nevertheless is the second language of choice in many business and cultural areas.

Real life case: from Globish to global English

The common use of English as a second language means that in many areas of life, including the business world, English is often spoken between non-native English speakers. As Skapinker (2012) notes: 'When a Japanese employee met a Belgian, a Chilean and an Italian, they managed. None spoke English brilliantly but each knew the others were making mistakes too.'

This particular use of English had been observed by Jean-Paul Nerrière, a vice-president of IBM, during his business travels. He created a standard simplified form of global English, named Globish. With a basic vocabulary of 1,500 words and a simplified grammatical structure, Globish was designed as a common language for global business use, especially among non-native English speakers.

However, while Globish aids international communication, other commentators argue that is it limits the learning of English. Skapinker (2012) suggests that a form of English spoken by executives emerges which has no jokes or figurative language. This appears stilted compared to much more fluent speakers. Kuper (2018) further suggests that Globish is not sufficient in a world where more and more people speak fluent, flawless English. Kuper highlights presentations from the French President Emmanuel Macron and the videos of Swedish YouTube star PewDiePie as examples of where the simplified Globish is being superseded by an international cohort of people speaking perfect English as a second language.

There are many examples of industries where English is used as a common global language.

- In air travel, all communications between pilots and air traffic controllers, wherever they may be in the world, are in English. This is even the case where the participants share a common language; thus a Spanish pilot will speak to a (Spanish-speaking) Argentinian air-traffic controller in English.

- International conferences, more often than not, choose English as their language of business. An example of this is academic conferences. Conferences set in a non-English-speaking country will transact their proceedings in English. Speeches, presentations, handouts, email communications, and websites are all in English, regardless of the native language of the host country.

 Visit the online resources and take a look at the extension material for Chapter 16 for a video introduction to Globish—in Globish.

Sources: Skapinker (2012); Globish.com (2018); Kuper (2018).

Global brands

Beyond the media and the use of English, multinationals can be seen to contribute to global culture through their brand imagery. Brands are viewed as 'icons of culture and signifying devices' (Yakhlef, 2004: 238)—that is to say, they give an identity to an organization and even create a meaning to people who consume them (as may be the case when people buy a particular pair of trainers for the brand).

Where brands create meaning and identity, they also contribute to global culture. Much of the global value of Coca-Cola, for example, comes from its widely recognized brand (Interbrand, 2018).

Disney is, again, significant here. As we have seen, Bryman (2004) suggests that the Disney theme park, and the way it creates particular imagery that is experienced within that organization, is a model for other types of service and leisure organizations. Organizations want to create a particular feeling that reflects their brand through the decoration, the atmosphere, and even the behaviour of the staff within their premises (Witz et al., 2003; Yakhlef, 2004).

The standardized airport.
Source: ssray/Shutterstock.com

In Chapter 4 we saw how the 'McDonaldization of society' (Ritzer, 2019) brings about standardization on a global scale. A key element of McDonaldization is global predictability—there is a standard global product range (a Big Mac can be bought in McDonald's restaurants worldwide), and a standard brand and layout of the restaurants (the McDonald's arches have, in some surveys, been deemed to be a global symbol recognized more than the Christian cross).

Taken together, McDonaldization and Disneyization are representative of organizations that supply a standard experience and atmosphere on a global scale. One hotel, fast-food restaurant, airport, or multiplex cinema feels the same wherever in the world you happen to be. It is as if, when in these organizational spaces, one could forget which country lies outside—such is their standardized nature that there is a global homogenous space created within organizations. Many of these spaces are branded, and thus global brands contribute to a standardized global culture not just through the ubiquitous presence of those brands but also through the organizational environments that they create.

? Review questions

Describe	What is meant by global culture?
Explain	How do global organizations contribute to global culture?
Analyse	What roles do brands play in creating global culture? How do they help to create standardized organizational spaces?
Apply	What are the advantages and disadvantages that Junction Hotel should consider in thinking about becoming a franchise of Luxonation?

Colonialism and postcolonialism

In the previous section we presented a view of globalization as a phenomenon which is creating a unified, interconnected world. While this may be the experience for many people in the Western world, it is not a shared experience globally. In this section we address two important assumptions about globalization. First is the assumption that globalization is a recent phenomenon of the last few decades, one which is a part of our modern era of international travel and instant global communication through the internet. In fact globalization has a history which goes back centuries, and it is an unpleasant history of violence and exploitation through colonization. This leads to a second assumption—that globalization is an evenly-spread phenomenon across the globe. As we will see, many inequalities across the globe are an ongoing consequence of colonialism. We explore a postcolonial perspective which sees the inequalities that are experienced today as a legacy of earlier colonialism.

Colonialism and the history of globalization

Colonialism refers to a period between the fifteenth century and the early twentieth when a group of western European nations (chiefly Belgium, France, Germany, Great Britain, Italy, the Netherlands, Portugal, and Spain) set about exploring the globe to discover 'new' lands in Asia, Africa, and the Americas. These discoveries made international trade possible, with newly-discovered goods brought to European markets. For example, the East India Company, founded in 1600, one of the earliest global companies, traded cotton, tea, and opium, moving goods between China, India, and the UK (Chaudhuri, 1965).

In the nineteenth and twentieth centuries, these countries developed empires: they turned countries and regions in Africa, Asia, and the Americas into colonies, exploited the natural resources of these countries, and in some cases forced their inhabitants into slavery. Jack and Westwood (2009: 7) describe this as a 'period of violence, conquest and racism associated with the expansion of spheres of influence of a small number of Western European countries'. As recently as the beginning of the twentieth century, Western colonial empires covered 84.6 per cent of the global economy (Loomba, 1998).

While the colonial era has 'formally' ended, a postcolonial perspective recognizes that its legacy still remains. The inequalities developed during the colonial era haven't simply disappeared, and indeed are still replicated in the Western capitalist system which emerged from colonialism (Jack and Westwood, 2009). Postcolonialism is a set of theories which recognize the troubled history of globalization and how this legacy still creates global inequalities today, where the interests of globalization are 'weighted to the global superpowers and industry' (Jack, 2015: 151). We highlight some of these inequalities before examining the relevance of postcolonial perspectives to global culture and to business education.

Inequalities of the global economy

The global economy is one area where inequality remains as a legacy of colonialism. Former colonial powers and areas such as North America and East Asia, which have more recently benefited from its colonialism's capitalist, industrialist legacy, are far richer than areas of the globe which were subject to colonialism. These inequalities can be seen through a calculation of GDP per capita, i.e. national income per person.

Figure 16.3 Gross domestic product (GDP) per capita, 2007–11.
Source: Based on data from the World Bank, http://data.worldbank.org

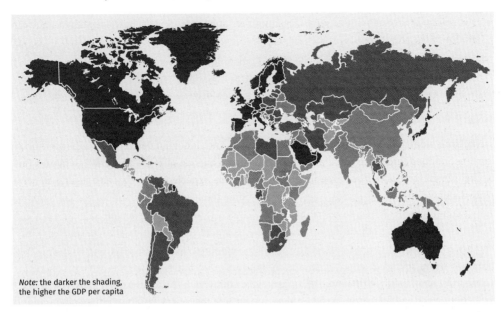

Note: the darker the shading, the higher the GDP per capita

Figure 16.3 shows that this income is unevenly distributed—the higher incomes per person are enjoyed mainly in North America, Western Europe, and other developed countries. There are much lower incomes, in some cases below the poverty line, in Africa, large parts of Asia, and South America.

The economic divide is further illustrated when looking at the distribution of headquarters of the top fifty multinational companies worldwide (see Figure 16.4). This mirrors the inequalities shown by GDP per capita distribution.

Figure 16.4 Location of headquarters of the top 50 multinational companies.
Source: Based on CNN Money (2012).

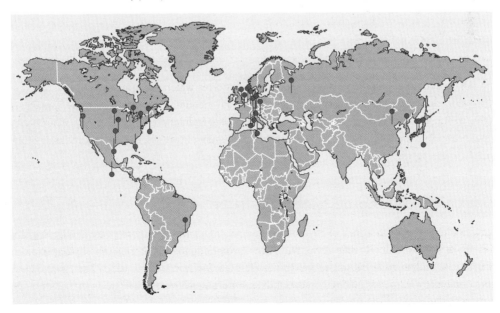

In Chapter 17 we will see how this economic inequality also takes place in a context that, in many cases, still replicates the exploitation of the colonial era, for example:

- sweatshop labour conditions, often arising from global brands subcontracting manufacturing labour to the third world;
- global commodity chains, dominated by Western multinational firms, which pay below subsistence prices to third world suppliers.

Inequalities of global politics

A criticism made of global politics is that it reinforces and, indeed, creates inequalities within the global economy. Institutions such as the World Trade Organization (WTO) and the World Bank are dominated largely by rich countries who can decide on policies which tend to suit their purposes. As Laurence Brahm puts it, 'the WTO has come to be seen as a forum for the G8 to extract trading conditions from less-developed nations' (2009: 71) for their own benefit. This view is even more strongly expressed by anti-globalization campaigner Walden Bello, who states the WTO is 'patently a method for the US and the EU to institutionalize their hegemony [leadership/power]' (cited in Brahm, 2009: 72).

Anti-globalization campaigners therefore state that these institutions promote and, indeed, force countries to adopt a free market model by, for instance, only lending money when an individual country promises to sell off formally nationalized industries. In doing so, not only are they promoting a particular form of capitalism, but they also erode the power of the nation state (i.e. an individual government's options and choices) by imposing sanctions if they do not act in the required way, therefore reducing their autonomy as they need to work in accordance with the rules and regulations of institutions such as the International Monetary Fund.

Campaigners argue that these rules serve the interests of global elites, as the privatized industries are often sold to rich multinationals who cream off the profits and move them out of these countries. They also argue that trade laws promote the free movement of capital but protect the interests of the richest nations. They argue that these policies have 'left a trail of destroyed economies, ruined nations and marginalized people' (Brahm, 2009: 16).

 Visit the online resources and take a look at the web links for Chapter 16 for more discussion of the anti-globalization movement.

Inequalities and global technology

While the modern era of globalization might be experienced as a 'global village' by some parts of the world, the lack of access to this global village deepens inequalities for others. The digital divide describes the inequalities between those people who have plentiful access to internet and media technologies, and those who have little or no access.

Postcolonialism and global culture

Postcolonialism sees the legacy of colonialism not only in terms of economic inequalities, but also in terms of a cultural dominance of the West over former colonial territories. An obvious example of this is language, as discussed earlier in the chapter. Many countries which have long gained independence from former colonial powers still bear the signs of that power through the languages that they speak—Spanish and Portuguese in South America; English in India and Pakistan; and French in areas of Africa and the Caribbean. In some cases the languages sit alongside local, indigenous languages, while in other cases they still have an official role in governance and education over and above local languages.

Edward Said's *Orientalism* (1978) is a key foundational text in postcolonialism which argues that the economic and territorial power of colonizing countries also allowed Western and European cultural values to be imposed on the rest of the world. These values are created on the terms of the powerful, a situation that 'sets the agenda' (Jack, 2015) for how the rest of the world—those without power—are spoken about. Ideas are constructed which privilege Western culture as 'superior, civilised, developed, moral and scientific', and cast non-Western cultures as 'inferior, uncivilised, backward, immoral and superstitious' (Jack et al., 2011: 279).

Postcolonialism further highlights how non-Western voices become suppressed. The way that we come to understand the world and its cultures is exclusively through a Western lens that bears the hallmarks of colonialism—languages, values, knowledge, and cultural identities which have developed in non-Western context do not get the chance to speak and to be identified (Spivak, 1999). Postcolonialism therefore tries to bring to the fore these cultural identities and knowledges that have been suppressed as a legacy of colonialism.

Inequalities in global culture

Walk along your local high street and you will probably see the same shops as in any other high street in the country. You may drink coffee in Starbucks, get your food from Tesco, and buy clothes from H&M. Indeed, if you travel abroad, many of the shops and products inside them will be very familiar to you. Naomi Klein (2001) suggests that there has been a return to colonization under the dominance of global brands. This is colonization not so much of physical space but more of an intangible cultural space, and it is the large brands that are performing this colonization. Indeed, looking at Coca-Cola as the world's first globally-advertised brand, the phrase 'coca-colonization' has been used to suggest this dominance of global brands across the globe (Pendergrast, 1993).

George Ritzer, whose work we encountered in Chapter 4 and who argued that society had become McDonaldized, extends this thesis to state that the whole world has become globalized, centralized, and standardized. Through this process, Ritzer (2007) argues that local products, with their distinctive character and qualities, have become swallowed up by these standardized global products. As a result, distinctiveness (*something* in Ritzer's language) becomes lost to standardization (which Ritzer calls *nothing*).

Klein (2001) uses Starbucks as an example of a firm that hastens this standardization by setting up their coffee shops in every community, squeezing out alternative, local providers. While their supporters argue that this is simply a result of offering something that people want—good coffee in a pleasant environment—their critics claim that they have developed tactics of flooding the market to drive local coffee shops out of business, and then reducing the number of their shops once they control the market. This criticism was recognized by Howard Schultz, who, when taking control of Starbucks as chief executive officer (CEO), stated that they should only work in communities that welcome them in, for fear that customers would reject them outright (Schultz, 2011).

Postcolonialism and business education

This Western bias can also be found in business education. Joy and Poonamallee (2013: 399) suggest that the US was instrumental in the redevelopment of many countries following the Second World War, including the development of business schools. In this respect, the agenda and knowledge of business schools very much reflects the interests of America and the West. Jack and Westwood (2009) note how international management books and journals tend to be published by academics

589

from the US and Western Europe, from within universities in these countries, again propagating a view of management that is based in a Western colonial legacy and suppresses other types of knowledge about management.

What we come to know as management knowledge—the various theories and ideas that you learn—is in fact a very narrow set of privileged Western knowledge which ignores other types of management styles and knowledge in other parts of the world. For example, Mika and O'Sullivan (2014) note the role of kinship in Maori forms of management in Aotearoa/New Zealand, which builds in a sustainability ethic (see Chapter 17) by focusing on the needs of future generations. Furthermore, Stella Nkomo (2011) notes how management in South Africa draws on the philosophy of Ubuntu which not only emphasizes collectivity, caring, and community but sees these as 'superior approaches' to managing organizations: 'Organizations infused with humaneness, a pervasive spirit of caring and community, harmony and hospitality, respect and responsiveness will enjoy more sustainable competitive advantage' (Nkomo, 2011: 377).

These ideas are widely practised in their parts of the world, but barely recognized, if at all, by Western business studies. Fougere and Moulettes (2012) have noted how such ideas receive little coverage in business textbooks, which instead promote Western-dominated views of international business cultures.

Such critiques of course also apply to this textbook, written by two UK-based academics from within a UK business school. While we have tried to highlight the legacy of colonialism and its inequalities, we also realize that this chapter (and indeed the rest of the textbook) covers theories of globalization that emerge from a largely Western perspective. There is a dilemma when writing a textbook such as this, and in management education more broadly, that on the one hand we would like to demonstrate an awareness of alternative theories from different contexts, however on the other we need to reflect and work within the Western traditions that we are teaching within. Our approach is to highlight, where appropriate, some of the legacy of colonialism and encourage you to read beyond this book to look towards other theories and perspectives as your knowledge grows.

? Review questions

Describe	What inequalities exist within the global economy?
Explain	What is meant by a postcolonial perspective, and how does it relate to global inequalities today?
Analyse	What is meant by the postcolonial critique that suggests globalization is seen through a Western lens?
Apply	What can a small organization like Junction Hotel do to help minimize and overcome global inequalities?

Globalization and national differences

Q Running case: cultural misunderstandings

The franchise idea has been rejected—it was felt that it would create a bland space that would lose the distinctiveness of Junction Hotel. The international strategy continues, however, and being on a few booking websites has brought more international visitors to Junction Hotel.

→

This includes a group of Japanese tourists who booked through the website and are trying to check in. They speak little English and the receptionists don't speak a word of Japanese. Even basic cultural niceties, such as greetings, are not understood between the two groups, with gestures being misunderstood. Flustered, the receptionists have asked the guests to sit in the bar and wait for a while. Simon Chance tries to smooth over the situation, and thinks to himself that some cross-cultural training for the staff might be needed. A global strategy will have to start much closer to home—within the hotel itself.

There is a saying that 'travel broadens the mind', and any of you that have visited countries either near to, or far away from, home will have experienced different ways of life. It's not just the language that might be different—the food, mannerisms, and daily routines may also seem unfamiliar. It can take time to adjust to, and understand, the cultural differences between life at home and life in the new country. There might even be cultural misunderstandings—what is considered acceptable at home may offend people in other cultures or be seen as inappropriate behaviour. More formally, local laws may prohibit activities that you can do freely at home, or vice versa.

Anyone experiencing such legal, linguistic, or cultural differences might be sceptical that we live in a 'global village' with a standard, homogenized global culture. In this section we examine the extent to which national differences are still noticeable and still exert an influence on the way business is done, and the challenges of cross-cultural management, i.e. being sensitive to these cultural differences, that this creates for organizations operating in a global environment.

Visit the online resources and take a look at the extension material for Chapter 16 for an example of cultural differences within a few metres of the German and Polish border.

591

From linguistic to cultural differences

An obvious aspect of national and cultural difference is that people speak different languages. As explored earlier, a legacy of colonialism is that English is widely used as a global *lingua franca* for business and organizations; however, linguistic differences—and the difficulties in translating between languages—are evident.

For example, while we have examined the presence of global brands and global advertising campaigns, their ability to convey a global message or identity can be undermined by mistranslations.

- The French pronunciation of the Toyota MR2, 'MR deux', sounds like a vulgar word in the French language (CNN Money, 2008).

- Coors' advertising slogan 'Turn it loose' was translated into Spanish as 'Get loose bowels' (CNN Money, 2008).

- KFC's slogan 'finger licking good' was translated into Chinese as 'eat your fingers off' (Adler, 2003).

Translation brings particular practical issues to global organizations. Try using an online translation service or translation software. Put a paragraph in your own language, translate it into another language, then translate that back into your own language. The chances are that what you will have is clumsy—at times incomprehensible, at times amusing like the mistranslations listed earlier—but certainly not a perfect rendition of your original paragraph.

However, translation—and mistranslation—is about more than a simple technical issue or transposing words from one language into another. Blenkinsopp and Pajouh (2010) suggest that this 'mechanical perspective' on translation—translating word for word—often misses out on the cultural meaning of what was originally said. The meaning of words can be embedded in the culture from which they come, leading to some words being 'untranslatable'. For example, the German word *Schadenfreude*, which means a sense of pleasure in the misfortune of others, has no equivalent single word in English that conveys the same idea, and so in English the original German word is used.

In the business sphere, Blenkinsopp and Pajouh (2010) offer two 'untranslatable' words, *guanxi* in Chinese, often translated as 'relationship' in English, and a Farsi word *tarouf*, which refers to a form of superficial politeness. However, rather than simple translations, both words refer to particular types of behaviours, trust, politeness, and relationship-building that are particular to their own culture and impact on how business relationships are carried out. The cultural and interpersonal behaviours suggested by these words in their original cultural context would be missed if one relied on a simple, mechanistic translation of the words.

Blenkinsopp and Pajouh's work on translation suggests that differences between nations are more than linguistic—there is a cultural element to language. Indeed, there may be aspects of different languages and cultures that simply cannot be captured from a Western cultural and linguistic frame of reference—and vice versa. As we saw earlier, a postcolonial perspective suggests that, because most business education is created from this Western perspective, many other ways of doing business and management in other cultures are simply not noticed by this, or are adapted to fit a Western frame of reference, thus losing their particular cultural nuances.

For example, Al-Husan et al. (2009) examine cultural differences which mean that Western human resources management practices do not transfer exactly to a Middle Eastern context. Elsewehere, Japanese management techniques which work well in a Japanese context, where there is a strong cultural attachment to the organization, need to be adapted for Western contexts where people are much more individualistic (also discussed in Chapter 3 and later in this chapter) (Lohr, 1987; Imai, 1986).

 Visit the online resources and take a look at the extension material for Chapter 16 for a discussion of differences between approaches to teamwork as they are influenced by UK and Japanese cultural perspectives.

 Real life case: the 'rude' waiter

Guillaume Rey, formerly a waiter in a Vancouver restaurant, has launched an appeal against his dismissal from that job. He was fired for being 'aggressive, rude and disrespectful'. However, he suggests that there is a perfectly reasonable explanation for his behaviour—he is French. Rey suggests that French culture tends to be more 'direct and expressive' and that this demeanour was instilled into him when training in the French hospitality industry.

Differences between French service culture and that of countries such as the UK and USA have been noted elsewhere. Kirby (2010) suggests that French service is based on a relationship of equals: 'I'm not your slave.' This can lead to service which is formal and detached, rather than fawning, and which can result in 'blunt honesty' rather than grinning platitudes. For Le Conte (2018) 'getting barked at by a sour waiter is part of the experience … as is being terrified by the possibility of a knowing frown when ordering the wrong wine with the wrong course.'

Sources: Kirby (2010); Le Conte (2018); BBC News (2018); *The Guardian* (2018).

The case of the French waiter shows how service cultures based around emotional labour (see Chapter 15) can differ, even between near geographical neighbours such as the UK and France. Euro Disney in Paris is another example where differing cultural perspectives can be found—from a view of Disney being an icon of US global culture, to a cynical viewpoint in France of its cultural inferiority, a 'cultural Chernobyl' (Hamnett, 1999). Such differences could be found among the workers. Disneyland relies on a very American form of service culture, where workers are putting on an act in front of theme park guests (see Chapter 15). Curwen suggests that, again, a cultural mismatch led to high labour turnover at Disneyland Paris where 'French youth refused to see the need to cut their hair, dress uniformly and smile incessantly' (Curwen, 1995: 17).

Can national cultures be measured?

One of the most influential studies in cross-cultural management is from Dutch researcher Geert Hofstede (1980). Hofstede saw national cultures in a similar manner to organizational cultures (see Chapter 7) in that they demonstrated a set of values, attitudes, and sensitivities that amounted to the 'collective programming of the mind' (Hofstede, 1980). As such, he suggested that differences between national cultures, and specifically national management cultures, could be measured and quantified.

Hofstede's study comes from over 100,000 attitude surveys of managers in over 50 national offices of the computer firm IBM. From this, he devised a formal, numerical means of identifying and describing individual management cultures, which were plotted out on four dimensions, known as Hofstede's dimensions of culture (adapted from Hofstede, 1980).

- *Power distance* concerns the mobility of people with regard to positions of power. Does power come from social status—who you are, who you were born to, and who you know—or is promotion more about merit, your proven abilities, and what you know? This also covers the way in which managers and subordinates interact—is a lot of deference shown to authority, or do management and workers interact more as equals?

- *Uncertainty avoidance* is the extent to which people are comfortable with risk and insecurity, or whether or not they tend to prefer stability and predictability.

- *Masculinity/femininity* concerns the level of assertiveness and aggressiveness within the organization, which Hofstede saw as a masculine trait, as opposed to a more feminine view of the organization based around concepts of welfare and nurture. It is also reflected in the level of equality between the genders.

- *Individualism/collectivism* is the extent to which the organization is seen as a community or a family to which a worker 'belongs' and has loyalty, or whether people work more as individuals, more interested in a sense of getting ahead than a sense of belonging.

According to Hofstede's analysis, the UK and USA have very similar characteristics. Both have highly individualistic approaches to work—workers are there for their own career rather than a sense of loyalty to an organization. Low power distance suggests that promotion on merit to the top of organizations is possible, perhaps reflected in the 'American dream' that anyone can become president. Both countries are also comfortable with risk and uncertainty. Overall, it suggests a forward-looking, individual-achievement-based culture.

France has much higher power distance and uncertainty avoidance. A characteristic of the latter is a large amount of bureaucracy in French public and organizational life. Combined with high power distance, this brings about a more formal working environment with greater deference to seniority and perhaps explains the unwillingness to engage in more informal service interactions, as highlighted in the case of the French waiter discussed earlier.

A notable feature of Swedish management culture is its high femininity. Sweden is known for its egalitarian work legislation and practices between the genders; however, femininity also feeds into a management style that is less aggressive and abrasive, and more nurturing, phlegmatic (see Chapter 8), and focused on practical outcomes.

Table 16.2 Selected results of Hofstede's (1980) dimensions of national culture

	Power distance	Uncertainty avoidance	Masculinity	Individualism
USA	40	46	62	91
UK	35	35	66	89
Japan	54	92	95	46
Sweden	31	29	5	71
France	68	86	43	71
India	77	40	56	48
Top-ranked	Malaysia	Greece	Japan	USA
Bottom-ranked	Austria	Singapore	Sweden	Guatemala

Source: Based on Hickson and Pugh (1995: 33–5).

Japan has a unique set of characteristics, contributing to its very culturally-specific management style. There is very high uncertainty avoidance—decision making is time-consuming, conservative, and avoids risk (Kono, 1982). Individualism is low—Japanese workers have very high loyalty to the organization and will work long hours of unpaid overtime. Masculinity is also high—there are few women in senior management positions.

Indian management has very high power distance and low individualism. It is characterized by 'paternalistic centralization'—managers will exert strong, centralized control in a way that shows concern for workers, too. There is loyalty to the workplace, but not the sense of devotion found in Japan.

Table 16.2 gives some further results from Hofstede's survey. Some particular cultural features of different countries are highlighted by these scales (adapted from Hickson and Pugh, 1995).

Hofstede was one of the first to draw attention to the importance of recognizing cultural differences when managing an international workforce, and his work has been developed and replicated many times since. The scales, which allow national cultures to be compared easily, give the model an 'appealing simplicity' (Nyíri and Ybemi, 2015: 39); however, this also leaves them open to considerable criticism.

One area of critique is that the scales do not give a proper measurement of culture. We might question whether culture is something that can be reduced to numbers (cf. critiques of numerical personality scales in Chapter 8); whether surveys adequately measure rich and complex phenomena, such as cultures; and, indeed, whether a view of an overall national culture can be gained from a survey of just one organization—IBM. McSweeney (2002) gives a thorough critique of the methodology and conclusions of the work of Hofstede, and his 'limited characterization' (2002: 112) of the concept of culture.

A further critique suggests that Hofstede has a simplistic understanding of national cultures 'based on dimension scores which provide at best a minimal, static and monolithic sketch of national cultures and, at worst, a false and misleading representation' (Nyíri and Ybemi, 2015: 39). This is saying that it is too simplistic to say that a whole country has one culture, and that in fact many different cultures can be found within one country (e.g. Beugelsdijk et al., 2017). Furthermore, as we saw in Chapter 7, the perspective that organizations 'are' cultures (Smircich,

1983) suggests that cultures are always changing and evolving, as are national cultures—they are not a fixed figure, as in Hofstede's scales.

A final critique takes a postcolonial approach and suggests that Hofstede reproduces views of culture based in a dominant Western cultural perspective—in other words, other cultures are seen through a Western lens (Kwek, 2003; Ailon, 2008; Fougere and Moulettes, 2007, 2012). Drawing on Said's approach, these critiques suggest that Hofstede imposes a definition of cultures from a Western perspective, with other cultures unable to contribute to this definition from their own cultural perspective. Furthermore, by analysing Hofstede's descriptions of his scales it is suggested that he reproduced a colonial legacy which views non-Western cultures as inferior. For example, with power distance, Hofstede suggests that low power distance is superior, and is typical of more modern (i.e. Western) countries rather than parts of the world where more traditional forms of authority exist. Similarly, with individualism, Hofstede sees high individualism, typical of Western cultures, as superior (Fougeres and Moulettes, 2007; Ailon, 2008).

An example of the postcolonial critique is provided by Ailon (2008: 890), who notes the irony that South Africa has a low power distance score. This might reflect the original research from a global technology company such as IBM, but ignores the wider context of power imbalances in South African society that emerged in the apartheid regime. Nkomo (2011) further notes how non-Western cultures are ignored: for example, 'West Africa' is listed as one country with one set of scores, even though it is actually a region comprising several countries, each with different cultures.

Managing across the global and the local

🔍 Running case: 'Don't patronize us!'

595

Chance gathered the staff together and called up a website on 'Japanese culture'. It painted a picture of a polite and unassuming nation, people who would keep themselves to themselves. 'Treat them with kid gloves,' said Chance.

Suddenly a look of horror came across Chance's face as he remembered that he had one of his football crowds booked into the hotel that afternoon—and they usually got drunk and very rowdy. 'We need to keep the two groups apart,' said Chance. 'Keep the football crowd in the bar and the Japanese tourists in the function room—we need two areas with distinct and separate atmospheres.'

Already Chance could hear chanting coming from the football crowd, so he sprinted towards the bar to separate the two groups. Flinging open the door, he was surprised to see the football crowd and the Japanese tourists all mingling—drinking, chanting, and singing together. Chance approached the tour leader, who could speak English well. 'Are you sure you are OK here?' asked Chance, 'I thought you might prefer somewhere quieter, more subdued, you know?'

'Don't patronize us!' replied the tour leader boisterously. 'You've been reading some guide, haven't you—you think we are all the same. Actually this is great—now don't hang about—go to the bar for us and get drinks all round. Cheers!'

While the rigid numerical calculation of Hofstede's scales should be treated with caution in terms of giving an absolute mapping of national managerial cultures, it suggests that national differences and cultures are important and exert an effect on how business and management operate. In the final part of this section we examine two particular ways in which organizations manage globally, but taking account of the local; namely managing people and cultures, and managing strategies.

Managing people and cultures

The first implication of national cultural differences is that, in a multinational workforce, they might impact differently on how individuals are managed. For example, an assertive, ambitious, individualistic worker might be motivated differently to one whose culture suggests loyalty to the organization and belonging.

 Real life case: cultural diversity in a football team

Top-level football teams are an example of a multinational workforce, with players from many different countries and continents. Maderer et al. (2014) found that this cultural diversity can be a strength for a team, with different football traditions, skills, and training methods brought together to increase the creativity of a team overall.

However, it can also bring about challenges, such as sub-groups forming within the team and conflict arising. A skilled manager with intercultural experience is needed in order to harness the strengths of cultural diversity and avoid its problems.

Sir Alex Ferguson, former manager of Manchester United, has noted how sensitivity to different cultural backgrounds is needed in managing across cultures within a team, where people not only have a different way of seeing the world, but also even basic things, like times for eating and sleeping, may be different (BBC Sport, 2011).

 Visit the online resources and take a look at the extension material for Chapter 16 for more discussion of cross-cultural issues in football.

These differences extend to the management of culture across organizations. Gergen and Whitney (1996) argue that the implementation of a global culture is simply impossible, given the effects of different cultures in national context; instead, culture is seen through the lens of local cultures at a national level.

Furthermore, personal cultural differences extend beyond management over the organization, to relationships across organizations—dealing with clients, customers, and colleagues in different countries. Crace (2003) outlines the role of 'cultural consultants' in advising firms on cultural differences that might cause problems from seemingly innocuous behaviours: for example, a polite enquiry about somebody's family might be seen in Arab countries as planning an affair with a customer's wife; and putting a business card into a back pocket would cause offence in Japan.

Managing structure and strategies

 Real life case: the limits of McDonaldization

While McDonald's and its brand are globally ubiquitous and the company employs global standardized practices, it is not true to say that McDonald's, as it exists from country to country, is uniform globally; for example:

- in France beer is served in McDonald's restaurants, as local culture associates dining out with drinking (Breen, 2016);

- in India, the menu has been adapted both for religious reasons, avoiding pork and beef in the menu, and for a wider vegetarian diet in the area (Kannan, 2014);

- alongside the standard global range, such as the Big Mac, Mcdonald's offers national specialities which reflect local cuisine, such as the Koroke burger in Japan—made with mashed potato, cabbage, and katsu sauce—or gazpacho soup served in a carton in Spain (Kelly, 2012).

Glocalization (Robertson, 1995) is a term which captures both the global activities of multinational firms and, at the same time, their adaptation of strategies for local markets as discussed in the previous section—at once acting globally and locally.

The highlighted case shows how an organization like McDonald's, while seemingly a contributor to a global, standardized culture, in fact adapts for local tastes, sensitivities, laws, and cultures. There are adaptations to McDonald's menus in different national markets.

Similarly, in a set of adverts, the global bank HSBC describes itself as 'The world's local bank'. The suggestion is that, while it operates on a global scale, it understands and responds to different national markets. Indeed, many of the national subsidiaries operate independently, with a knowledge of their national market, while carrying the global HSBC branding.

Visit the online resources and take a look at the web links for Chapter 16 to see this HSBC advertisement and to read more about how McDonald's adapts its offering in different countries.

Different degrees of glocalization are encompassed in Bartlett and Ghoshal's (1989) model of multinational structures and strategies, based around two particular dimensions:

- corporate integration—the extent to which the organization is standardized and controlled across its global operations: is it an integrated, bureaucratic whole, or do individual national units operate relatively independently?

- responsiveness to local markets—to what extent are the goods, services, and branding of an organization standardized globally, or are they adjusted to be more responsive to local needs and requirements?

Figure 16.5 Bartlett and Ghoshal's (1989) model.
Source: Based on Bartlett and Ghoshal, Managing across borders (1989).

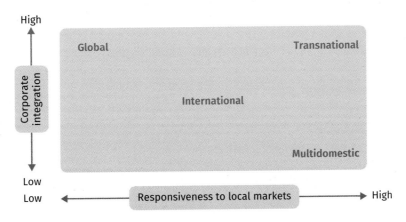

Figure 16.5 shows different types of organization along the dimensions suggested by Bartlett and Ghoshal. This gives four particular types of global firm.

- Global firms benefit from high economies of scale through a globalized and highly standardized offering. There is a great deal of standardized control across the globe and little alteration of products to suit local markets. This is found in consumer electronics: for example, an iPad is the same standard product wherever it is sold. Look also at the international website of Swedish clothes retailer H&M—the websites for each national territory where it operates offer the exact same range of (mass-produced) clothing.

- Transnational firms have economies of scale, especially through standardized control mechanisms; however, there is some responsiveness to local markets, e.g. by adapting products, services, or marketing strategies. The organization is seen as a set of international subsidiaries with some independence, but also a sharing of learning across the global organization. The standardized bureaucratic control of McDonald's, coupled with its responsiveness to local markets, as described previously, would be an example of this.

- A multinational or multidomestic firm is a global organization which runs more like a set of independent national subsidiaries. Different national subsidiaries may have different identities or product ranges: e.g. it is the national context which is important rather than standardized, global control. The earlier example of Tesco would fit into this category—it runs a number of differently branded chains in different countries.

- An international firm uses knowledge from head office, but in a more autonomous way. People might be trained at head office, but they are then free to operate relatively autonomously once they have that knowledge.

As with other theories discussed in this chapter, we should treat these ideas of glocalization with some caution. Although they can be seen as examples of responsiveness to different cultures, a postcolonial perspective suggests that this still produces signals of Western dominance. It is Western companies with Western business models which are seen as the overarching global norm that is then 'tweaked' in order to adapt to other local cultures. Rather than elements of non-Western cultures being seen as valid cultural perspectives in their own right, they are simply seen as 'oddities' to which the Western norm must be adapted.

? Review questions

Describe	What are Hofstede's four dimensions of national culture?
Explain	What is meant by cultural differences?
Analyse	How do organizations respond to national and cultural differences in the ways that they manage people and develop organizational strategies?
Apply	How would you advise Junction Hotel about dealing with cultural differences?

Connecting case and theory

In this chapter, we have seen that globalization is a complex process, involving both physical and intangible spaces, and encompassing areas of society such as the economy, politics, culture, technology, and the natural environment. Organizations play a role in this, using a number of strategies to act globally, whether on a large or small scale.

Furthermore, globalization is an unequal process which bears the legacy of the colonial area. At the start of the chapter, Simon Chance was looking at ways in which the hotel could become more global, something which is difficult to do as a small, independent hotel. The main global players are massive multinational chains, and it would be difficult to compete with these.

On the one hand, there is an argument that globalization is a process that brings us together as a global village, leading to a homogeneous global culture with the differences between individual nations and their cultures becoming less and less pronounced. This global village was evident when the hotel joined the Global Luxury group as a first step towards this. The physical space of the globe becomes smaller, as evidence by people converging on an airport for a meeting. In addition, communications technologies facilitate meetings and interaction for the members of the group across intangible spaces of globalization.

Junction Hotel's proposal to join a franchise demonstrates one of the ways in which companies start to operate on a global scale. Chance originally considered buying a hotel in France—an acquisition strategy which was deemed to be too costly. The franchise option would rely little extra expense. It would mean the hotel would carry an internationally-recognized brand, but this would be at the expense of autonomy—they would have to used the standardized rules and branding of the Luxonational chain. As Meg Mortimer noted, it would make the hotel look exactly the same as every other hotel in the brand worldwide—a form of bland cultural homogenization where culture starts to become the same globally.

The arrival of Japanese tourists brought home to the hotel just what is meant by globalization. Rather than standardizing decor or communicating through videoconferencing, it actually involves real people with different languages and cultures. National and cultural differences could be seen to still exist and, indeed, influence the global strategies that organizations undertake.

Chance's immediate reaction was to engage in a form of cross-cultural management. He got the staff to try to understand what Japanese culture is like from websites. By separating the tourists and the football crowd, Chance could be seen to be engaging in glocalization—adapting the offering of the hotel to meet different cultural values.

However, Chance's efforts also demonstrate some of the problems with cross-cultural management, especially when they rely on characterizations of measurements of national cultures. From a postcolonial perspective, Chance could be seen to be viewing Japanese culture through a Western lens which paints a particular stereotype. In fact, by joining in with the football crowd wholeheartedly, the tourists showed that there can be many differences within national cultures.

 ## Further reading

Hickson, D.J., and Pugh, D.S. 1995. *Management worldwide: Distinctive styles amid globalization*. Penguin Books Ltd: London.

A good introduction to Hofstede's scales, with examples of national cultures in a wide variety of countries worldwide.

Jack, G., and Westwood, R. 2009. International and cross-cultural management studies: A postcolonial reading. Palgrave Macmillan: London.

An introduction to and overview of the postcolonial perspective on globalization.

Nyíri, P., and Ybema, S. 2015. The Hofstede factor: The consequences of *Culture's Consequences*. In: Holden, N., Michaelova, S., and Tietze, S. (eds) *The Routledge Companion to Cross-Cultural Management*. Routledge: Abingdon, pp. 87–98.

A critical overview of Hofstede's work.

House of Lords. 2016. European Union Committee report, Brexit: financial services, 15 December. Available at: https://publications.parliament.uk/pa/ld201617/ldselect/ldeucom/81/8102.htm

Gives an overview of the global interconnectedness of financial services.

 ## References

Adler, C. 2003. Colonel Sanders' march on China. *Time Magazine*, 17 November.

Ailon, G. 2008. Mirror, mirror on the wall: *Culture's consequences* in a value test of its own design. *Academy of Management Review* 33 (4): 885–904.

Al-Husan, F.Z.B., Brennan, R., and James, P. 2009. Transferring Western HRM practices to developing countries: The case of a privatized utility in Jordan. *Personnel Review* 38 (2): 104–23.

Bartlett, C.A., and Ghoshal, S. 1989. *Managing across borders: The transnational solution*. Harvard Business School Press: Boston.

BBC News. 2015. Carbon trading: How does it work? 25 September. Available at: https://www.bbc.com/news/science-environment-34356604

BBC News. 2018. Fired Vancouver waiter: I'm not rude, just French, 26 March. Available at: https://www.bbc.com/news/world-us-canada-43507949

BBC Sport. 2011. In-depth interview—Sir Alex Ferguson on TV, youth policy, hairdryers and more. Available at: http://www.bbc.co.uk/sport/0/football/15064028 (last accessed 20 August 2015).

Beugelsdijk, S., Kostova, T., and Roth, K. 2017. An overview of Hofstede-inspired country-level culture research in international business since 2006. *Journal of International Business Studies* 48 (1): 30–47.

Blenkinsopp, J., and Pajouh, M.S. 2010. Lost in translation? Culture, language and the role of the translator in international business. *Critical Perspectives on International Business* 6 (1): 38–52.

Brahm, L.J. 2009. *The anti-globalization breakfast club manifesto for a peaceful revolution*. John Wiley & Sons (Asia): Singapore.

Breen, M. 2016. McDonald's starts selling beer in world's most 'spirited' nation. NBC News, 17 February. Available at: https://www.nbcnews.com/business/business-news/mcdonald-s-starts-selling-beer-world-s-most-spirited-nation-n519681

Brunsden, J. 2018. Brussels rejects UK's financial services Brexit plan. *Financial Times*, 22 July. Available at: https://www.ft.com/content/0df20cc6-8c43-11e8-b18d-0181731a0340

Bryman, A. 2004. *The Disneyization of society*. Sage: London.

Bryson, B. 1990. *Mother tongue: The English language*. Penguin: London.

Chaudhuri, K.N. 1965. *The English East India Company: The study of an early joint-stock company, 1600–1640*. Cass: London.

Clegg, S.R., and Gray, J.T. 1996. Metaphors of globalization. In: Boje, D., Gephart, R., and Thatchenkery, T. (eds) *Postmodern management and organization theory*. Sage: Thousand Oaks, CA, pp. 293–307.

CNN Money. 2008. How not to sell abroad. Available at: http://money.cnn.com/galleries/2008/fsb/0807/gallery.bad_translations.fsb/index.html (last accessed 20 August 2015).

Crace, J. 2003. Crossing cultures. *The Guardian*, 14 October.

Curwen, P. 1995. EuroDisney: The mouse that roared (not!). *European Business Review* 95 (5): 15–20.

Feng, E. 2017. China moves towards launch of carbon trading scheme. *Financial Times*,

19 December. Available at: https://www.ft.com/content/cd549b9a-e088-11e7-a8a4-0a1e63a52f9c

Fortune. 2018. Global 500. Available at: http://fortune.com/global500/ (last accessed 30 May 2018).

Fougère, M., and Moulettes, A. 2007. The construction of the modern West and the backward rest: Studying the discourse of Hofstede's Culture's consequences. Journal of Multicultural Discourses 2 (1): 1–19.

Fougère, M., and Moulettes, A. 2012. Disclaimers, dichotomies and disappearances in international business textbooks: A postcolonial deconstruction. Management Learning 43 (1): 5–24.

Gergen, K., and Whitney, D. 1996. Technologies of representation in the global corporation: Power and polyphony. In: Boje, D., Gephart, R.P., and Tatchenkery, T.J. (eds) Postmodern management and organization theory. Sage: London, pp. 331–57.

Globish.com. 2018. Website. Available at http://www.globish.com (last accessed 18 July 2018).

Hamnett, J.L. 1999. Euro Disney: A cross-cultural communications failure? In: Goodman, R.A., Atkin, I., Barry, J., and Pettersen, E. (eds) Modern organizations and emerging conundrums: Exploring the postindustrial subculture of the third millennium. Lexington Books: Lanham, MD, p. 240.

Hickson, D.J., and Pugh, D.S. 1995. Management worldwide. Penguin Books: Harmondsworth.

HM Revenue and Customs. 2018. Annual trade. Available at: https://www.uktradeinfo.com/Statistics/Pages/Annual-Tables.aspx (last accessed 30 May 2018).

Hofstede, G.H. 1980. Culture's consequences: International differences in work-related values. Sage: Beverly Hills, CA.

House of Lords. 2016. European Union Committee report, Brexit: financial services, 15 December. Available at: https://publications.parliament.uk/pa/ld201617/ldselect/ldeucom/81/8102.htm

Hunt, E. 2018. Estonian president delights in country's high proportion of unicorns. The Guardian, 29 June. Available at: https://www.theguardian.com/world/2018/jun/29/estonia-unicorns-president-kersti-kaljulaid-delight

Imai, M. 1986. KAIZEN—the key to Japan's competitive success. Random House: New York.

Interbrand. 2018. Best global brands 2017. Available at: http://bestglobalbrands.com (last accessed 30 May 2018).

Jack, G. 2015. Postcolonial theory. In: Mir, R., Willmott, H., and Greenwood, M. (eds) The Routledge companion to philosophy in organization studies. Routledge: Abingdon, pp. 151–70.

Jack, G., and Westwood, R. 2009. International and cross-cultural management studies: A postcolonial reading. Springer: London.

Jack, G., Westwood, R., Srinivas, N., and Sardar, Z. 2011. Deepening, broadening and re-asserting a postcolonial interrogative space in organization studies. Organization 18 (3): 275–302.

Joy, S., and Poonamallee, L. Cross-cultural teaching in globalized management classrooms: Time to move from functionalist to postcolonial approaches? Academy of Management Learning and Education 12 (3): 396–413.

Kannan, S. 2014. How McDonald's conquered India. BBC News, 19 November. Available at: https://www.bbc.com/news/business-30115555

Kelly, N. 2012. McDonald's' local strategy, from El McPollo to Le McWrap Chèvre. Harvard Business Review, 8 October. Available at: https://hbr.org/2012/10/mcdonalds-local-strategy-from

Kirby, E. 2010. In Paris, the customer is not always right. From our own correspondent, BBC Radio 4, 6 February. Available at: http://news.bbc.co.uk/2/hi/programmes/from_our_own_correspondent/8500246.stm

Klein, N. 2001. No logo: No space, no choice, no jobs. Flamingo: London.

Kono, T. 1982. Japanese management philosophy: Can it be exported? Long Range Planning 15 (3): 90–102.

Kuper, S. 2018. Globish just doesn't cut it anymore. *Financial Times*, 11 January. Available at: https://www.ft.com/content/981379a8-f58f-11e7-88f7-5465a6ce1a00

Kwek, D. 2003. Decolonizing and re-presenting *Culture's consequences*: A postcolonial critique of cross-cultural studies in management 1. In Prasad, A. (ed.) *Postcolonial theory and organizational analysis: A critical engagement*. Palgrave Macmillan: New York, pp. 121–46.

Le Conte, M. 2018. Vive l'indifférence: why rude French waiters should be celebrated. *The Guardian*, 27 March. Available at: https://www.theguardian.com/lifeandstyle/shortcuts/2018/mar/27/vive-lindifference-why-rude-french-waiters-should-be-celebrated-vancouver

Lohr, S. 1987. Nissan's revolution in Britain. *New York Times*, 2 June.

Loomba, A. 1998. *Colonialism–postcolonialism*. Routledge: London.

Maderer, D., Holtbrügge, D., and Schuster, T. 2014. Professional football squads as multicultural teams: Cultural diversity, intercultural experience, and team performance. *International Journal of Cross Cultural Management* 14 (2): 215–38.

McLuhan, M. 1964. *Understanding media: The extensions of man*. McGraw-Hill: New York.

McSweeney, B. 2002. Hofstede's model of national cultural differences and their consequences: A triumph of faith—a failure of analysis. *Human Relations* 55 (1): 89–118.

Mika, J.P., and O'Sullivan, J.G. 2014. A Māori approach to management: Contrasting traditional and modern Māori management practices in Aotearoa New Zealand. *Journal of Management and Organization* 20 (5): 648–70.

Nationmaster. 2018. GDP: Countries compared. Available at: http://www.nationmaster.com/country-info/stats/Economy/GDP (last accessed 30 May 2018).

New Internationalist. 1998. The mousetrap—Inside Disney's dream machine, 5 December.

Nkomo, S.M. 2011. A postcolonial and anti-colonial reading of 'African' leadership and management in organization studies: Tensions, contradictions and possibilities. *Organization* 18 (3): 365–86.

Nyíri, Pál, and Ybema, S. 2015. The Hofstede factor: The consequences of *Culture's consequences*. In: Holden, N., Michailova, S., and Tietze, S. (eds) *The Routledge companion to cross-cultural management*. Routledge: Abingdon, pp. 87–98.

Parker, B. 1996. Evolution and revolution: From international business to globalization. In: Clegg, S.R., Hardy, C., and Nord, W.R. (eds) *Handbook of organization studies*. Sage: London, pp. 484–506.

Parker, B., and Clegg, S.R. 2006. Globalization. In: Clegg, S.R., Hardy, C., Lawrence, T., and Nord, W.R. (eds) *The Sage handbook of organization studies*. Sage: London, pp. 651–74.

Pendergrast, M, 1993. A brief history of Coca-colonization. *New York Times*, 15 August, Available at https://www.nytimes.com/1993/08/15/business/viewpoints-a-brief-history-of-coca-colonization.html

Pooler, M. 2017. Brexit adds to challenges facing car parts suppliers. *Financial Times*, 14 September. Available at: https://www.ft.com/content/44589a00-582d-11e7-80b6-9bfa4c1f83d2

Race, R. 2015. *Multiculturalism and education*, 2nd edn. Bloomsburg: London.

Reuters. 2017. Dow, DuPont complete planned merger to form DowDuPont, 1 September. Available at: https://www.reuters.com/article/us-dow-m-a-dupont/dow-dupont-complete-planned-merger-to-form-dowdupont-idUSKCN1BC4MO

Ritzer, G. 2007. *The globalization of nothing 2*. Pine Forge Press: Thousand Oaks, CA.

Ritzer, G. 2019. *The McDonaldization of society*, 9th edn. Sage Publications: Thousand Oaks, CA.

Robertson, R. 1992. *Globalization: Social theory and global culture*. Sage: London.

Robertson, R. 1995. Glocalization: Time–space and homogeneity–heterogeneity. In: Featherstone, M., Lash, S., and Robertson, R. (eds) *Global modernities*. Sage: London, pp. 25–44.

Saha, S. 2018. Trent gears up for online challenge. *Telegraph India*, 19 May. Available at: https://www.telegraphindia.com/business/trent-gears-up-for-online-challenge-231502

Said, E. 1978. *Orientalism: Western conceptions of the orient*. New York: Pantheon.

Schultz, H. 2011. *Onward: How Starbucks fought for its life without losing its soul*. John Wiley and Sons: Chichester.

Skapinker, M. 2012. Executives speak a language of their own. *Financial Times*, 29 February. Available at: https://www.ft.com/content/634db9a6-57eb-11e1-ae89-00144feabdc0#ixzz1nsiQ1vP7

Smircich, L. 1983. Concepts of culture and organizational analysis. *Administrative Science Quarterly* 28 (3): 339–58.

Spivak, G.C. 1999. *A critique of postcolonial reason*. Harvard University Press: Cambridge, MA.

Tesco plc. 2018. Our business. Available at: https://www.tescoplc.com/index.asp?pageid=8 (last accessed 30 May 2018).

The Guardian. 2015. Tesco timeline—the retail giant's rise and fall, 23 April. Available at: https://www.theguardian.com/business/2014/dec/09/tesco-timeline-the-retail-giants-rise-and-fall

The Guardian. 2018. French waiter says firing for rudeness is 'discrimination against my culture', 26 March. Available at: https://www.theguardian.com/world/2018/mar/26/french-waiter-says-firing-for-rudeness-is-discrimination-against-my-culture

Tovey, A. 2017. Renault-Nissan plugs into Chinese electric car market with joint venture. *Daily Telegraph*, 29 August. Available at: https://www.telegraph.co.uk/business/2017/08/29/renault-nissan-plugs-chinese-electric-car-market-joint-venture/

Walt, V. 2017. Is this tiny European nation a preview of our tech future? *Fortune*, 27 April. Available at: http://fortune.com/2017/04/27/estonia-digital-life-tech-startups/

Warnick, J. 2013. Skype at 10: How an Estonian startup transformed itself (and the world). Available at: https://www.microsoft.com/en-us/stories/skype/skype-chapter-1-skype-at-10.aspx

Waters, M. 2001. *Globalization*, 2nd edn. Routledge: London, New York.

Witz, A., Warhurst, C., and Nickson, D. 2003. The labour of aesthetics and the aesthetics of organization. *Organization* 10 (1): 33–54.

World Economic Forum, 2017. How does carbon trading work? 28 September. Available at: https://www.weforum.org/agenda/2017/09/everything-you-need-to-know-about-carbon-trading/

Yakhlef, A. 2004. Global brands as embodied 'generic spaces'. *Space and Culture* 7 (2): 237–48.

CHAPTER 17

Corporate social responsibility, sustainability, and business ethics

Can businesses act sustainably, ethically, and responsibly?

Chapter overview and learning outcomes

By the end of this chapter you should be able to:

- describe some of the key principles of corporate social responsibility, business ethics, and sustainability

- explain why Milton Friedman argued that firms have no corporate social responsibility

- explain the principles behind shareholder capitalism

- analyse what the key critiques of capitalism are

Key theorists	
R. Edward Freeman	Freeman is one of the leading proponents of stakeholder theory, which argues that successful businesses build their strategy around their relationships with key stakeholders
Karl Marx	Philosopher, economist, activist, and revolutionary, Karl Marx is famous for his hard-hitting critiques of capitalism and support for communism; his works continue to be widely read and debated today
Milton Friedman	The Nobel-Prize-winning economist who famously argued that corporate social responsibility is 'unethical'
Naomi Klein	Social activist, author, and filmmaker Naomi Klein first became famous for her book *No logo* (1999), critiquing consumer and brand culture; she has continued to popularize the critiques of capitalism and been a leading voice for alternatives to capitalism
Gibson-Graham	The pen name for feminist economic geographers Julie Graham and Katherine Gibson. Gibson-Graham argue that we need to rethink our understanding of the economy by highlighting how many non-capitalist economic practices exist

Key terms

Business ethics	The application of ethical principles to organizations to either understand, judge, or direct individual and organizational ethical decision making
Corporate social responsibility	A perspective which stresses the responsibilities that corporations have towards society and other stakeholders
Sustainability	A complex term; it often stresses the long-term viability of the environment and/or the corporation
Capitalism	The dominant economic system, which is based on private ownership of the means of production of goods and services for the purposes of making profit
Philanthropy	Originally meaning 'for the love of humanity', it is now taken as meaning the giving of time or, more commonly, money for good causes

Introduction: scandals and corruption

Running case: expansion plans

With Junction Hotel now finally doing well, Simon Chance begins to think about expansion. Booking rates are near capacity, the hotel now regularly holds five weddings a weekend with, on average, 150 people for a full sit-down meal, and the bar takings have doubled. Profits are increasing and, for the first time, he is looking forward to writing the yearly report.

With this success Chance has started to consider building an extension at the front of the hotel. A new conservatory would add much-needed space and allow them to host 250 people per wedding and for the big Christmas parties—boosting potential profit. An architect has said it should be feasible, as long as they can get planning consent.

Flicking through his emails he notices a couple from Linda Wilkinson entitled 'Complaints from local residents'. In the email she explains how two of the local residents came in over the weekend, while the wedding was in full swing, complaining about the noise. Another email—'More complaints'—was, this time, about the aggressive behaviour of the guests as they left the wedding. While he wished such things didn't happen, he thinks, 'What can Junction Hotel do? People come to the hotel to have a good time and it is our job to give it to them.' With that, he goes back to the architect's plans.

It seems that we are never far away from stories of corporate corruption or scandals.

Stories of corporate corruption and miscommunication have been commonplace in the news in recent years.

- Mark Zuckerberg was questioned by US Congress for 10 hours over the right to privacy, the links to Cambridge Analytica, and how Facebook stores and uses personal data (Watson, 2018).

- Film producer Harvey Weinstein has been accused by more than 50 women of sexual harassment and rape. This led to a wider #MeToo campaign highlighting sexual harassment and assault in business and society (Izadi, 2018).

- The Peer-to-peer ride-sharing service has faced numerous scandals involving false advertising, sexual harassment, lawsuits from Google, and underpayment of drivers (Levin, 2017).

- Malaysian developers 1MDB were involved in one of the world's biggest financial scandals, where 'at least $3.5bn has been stolen from 1MDB' (for a full review read Ramesh, 2016).

- Oxfam were accused of a cover-up following allegations that its staff paid for sex in Haiti (Gayle, 2018).

Trust in business, government, and even charities is low. The 2018 Edelman 'trust barometer', an international survey of experts and the general population, reveals that worldwide only 52 per cent of the general population has trust in business and NGOs, whereas government and media are even lower at just 43 per cent. Technical experts are the most trusted people (closely followed by academics), whereas government and journalists are the least trusted people. CEOs have risen in the perception of people, due, the report suggests, to being seen speaking out on issues of public concern (Edelman, 2018). America saw one of the biggest declines in trust in institutions, whereas in China trust in institutions remains high. The 2008 financial crisis put the social responsibility of business firmly in the spotlight, and, along with climate change and human rights issues in developing countries, such concerns can be expected to exist for many years to come. Indeed, as we will contend in this chapter, corporate reputation is likely to form one of the biggest contemporary issues throughout your career.

 Real life case: should you think twice about buying a KitKat? How Nestlé responded to Greenpeace's campaign

Eating a KitKat might seem an innocent pleasure, a chance to have a break from some hard work. But what if it is killing orangutans?

Why might it be doing this? A small ingredient that you might not have noticed in the chocolate, palm oil. Palm oil is an edible vegetable oil which comes from the fruit of oil palms. It is in lots of different products, including cosmetics, cleaning products, fuels, and food, and is the most commonly produced vegetable oil in the world, found in 'half of all supermarket products' (Rainforest Rescue, 2018). Why? Because it is cheap.

Yet this comes at a cost. To grow the palm oil, vast areas of rainforest have been cut down, and with it the habitat of orangutans (Packham, 2018). The result of this is that in a 16-year period, 100,000 orangutans have been killed (Gill, 2018). 90 per cent of the world's palm oil is from Indonesia and Malaysia which, over the last 60 years, have lost a portion of rainforest three times larger than the UK; this, according to the UN, is a significant reason why Indonesia is the third largest emitter of carbon in the world. Charities such as International Animal Rescue are trying to rescue these amazing creatures, who we share 97 per cent of our DNA with.

But why focus on a KitKat? In March 2010, Greenpeace launched a campaign claiming a key ingredient, palm oil, was killing orangutans. To highlight the issue, Greenpeace produced a short advert of an office-worker biting into a KitKat finger in the shape of an orangutan, which then dripped blood on to his computer keyboard. The advert went viral on Facebook and YouTube, with tens of thousands of hits. Greenpeace campaigners posted messages on Nestlé's Facebook page and dressed as orangutans to meet shareholders at Nestlé's annual general meeting.

At first, Greenpeace claim, Nestlé tried to censor the advert, but within three months, and after substantial public pressure, they promised to change. Their head of stakeholder engagement in sustainability says deforestation is complex but 'now we're seeing a wave of ambition to tackle this that is sweeping the industry' (cited in Gies, 2014). Nestlé, in 2010, were a member of the Consumer Goods Forum, whose vision is 'Better lives through better business'.

→

They committed to a 'No Deforestation' declaration, including sourcing traceable palm oil and buying all their products in line with their 'High Conservation Value' (Nestlé, 2018). KitKats are also Fairtrade—and so maybe it is now possible to eat them with a clear conscience?

Yet Greenpeace are sceptical of such claims. In a new report, *Moment of Truth*, Greenpeace argue that no company is sourcing 100 per cent 'clean palm oil'. They say that firms must state where their palm oil comes from, an approach that Nestlé have committed to. There is still a long way to go, but with pressure from Greenpeace, activists, and consumers, and with large firms taking the lead, change is slowly occurring.

Source: Hermiadi Eher / Shutterstock.com.

Sources: Hickman (2009); Greenpeace (2010, 2013); Tabacek (2010); Nestlé (2018).

 Why do you think Nestlé felt the need to respond to this campaign? Look through other ingredients of your food, and even cleaning products—do they include palm oil? How do you feel about this?

The humble KitKat connects us to many of the key features that this chapter examines.

- Nestlé are not alone in being the subject of protest campaigns; many other companies have been criticized for using unsustainable palm oil (Bates, 2015). Indeed, recent years have seen numerous corporations under scrutiny about their practices. At stake is their corporate reputation and brand image, prevention of increased legislation, and the maintenance of ties with key stakeholders.

- Getting these features wrong, as we will see, can cost firms millions of pounds in fines (such as those that the banking industry has received) and, more significantly, goodwill from customers, suppliers, and the government. Getting it right can open up to new customers or give the firm a competitive advantage.

- As we will see later in the chapter, corporate social responsibility (CSR) statements have become standard practice and many organizations are now also producing sustainability reports. Business ethics and sustainability have become core aspects on many business degrees and are increasingly seen as critical competences for business leaders.

A word on definitions and terms

Attentive readers will have noticed that so far we have used three key phrases: business ethics, sustainability, and CSR (Figure 17.1). We could also have used, among others, the phrases 'stakeholder

Figure 17.1 The three overlapping theoretical frameworks.

theory', 'corporate governance', and 'global citizens'. Each phrase captures a particular aspect of business practice.

Business ethics deals primarily with the principles that should be used to govern business conduct, how people should act, and the underlying philosophies behind ethical actions. It focuses on decision making and is often taught using case studies. One of its central aims is to sensitize students and managers to the need for ethical awareness in business and (in some versions at least) to attempt to lay out a moral code of conduct for business people.

CSR, which stands for corporate social responsibility, looks at the wider social and environmental responsibilities that businesses have and how they should meet them. Based on stakeholder theory (discussed later in the chapter), the CSR perspective argues that it is often in the firm's interest to meet the needs of its stakeholders in order to ensure its long-term survival.

Sustainability focuses on increasing concerns with the environment (particularly climate change), but it has the wider meaning of the long-term sustainability of the firm itself. This can lead to confusion, but it does demonstrate the challenges of balancing environmental and profit concerns.

While each has their different meaning and focus, for the purposes of this chapter we will not spend too long distinguishing between these terms, rather drawing on the ideas from each area where appropriate.

This chapter will set out why ethics matters before moving on to examine the four key ethical perspectives. This discussion will then lay the foundation for the central questions which preoccupy this chapter. Should privately-owned, profit-seeking companies be concerned with acting in a socially responsible, moral, and humane way? Should they exist for their own purposes or for the good of society? The response that one makes to this question is moral and depends, to a large degree, on one's beliefs as to the central purpose and responsibility of businesses, which we have summed up in the following five categories:

- shareholder capitalism
- stakeholder capitalism
- ethical capitalism
- ethical within capitalism
- ethical against capitalism.

While each category covers a particular perspective, they also overlap and do not necessarily capture all the views of each perspective. They therefore should be seen as heuristic devices—an approach to simplify a theory to make it more understandable and which broadly captures these positions— rather than as fixed categories.

The need for business ethics

 Real life case: corporate scandals in the news

Dutch retail chain Hema have been ordered to pay a €4.5m fine for selling jeans that look rather to similar to Levi's. The jeans were deemed to look far too similar, including the well-known stitching on the back pocket and a very similar design to the world-famous red tag (DutchNews, 2018).

Swedish holding company Industrivärden, which owns Volvo, Ericsson, and SCA (a Swedish forestry and paper company), was caught up in scandal around its senior management. In late 2014 it was revealed SCA president and CEO Jan Johansson had been using private jets to fly around, often flying alone: not a good impression for the company's sustainability image. What happened next was more worrying. Reports then started coming out of wives and children being flown to the SCA-owned hunting lodge (which cost an estimated 100 million krona), the London Olympics, and European football championships (Milne, 2015). In 2017 Fredrik Lundberg, the chairman of Industrivärden, was then put under investigation for 'suspected bribery relating to a series of elk hunts' (Milne, 2017). These revelations showed a level of corporate extravagance at odds with the egalitarian values that Sweden holds (Crouch, 2015). Since then, 10 chief executive and chairman posts in almost every one of Industrivärden's companies have changed hands (Milne, 2016).

While backpacking around Australia might be a dream for many, it can also turn into a nightmare of exploitation. The 88-day rule requires tourists who want a visa extension for a second year to do 88 days in specific types of work, such as harvesting fruit and vegetables, scaffolding, or herding cattle. This can be a source of exploitation on the part of farm owners:

> Routine underpayment, crowding backpackers into rundown houses and pubs with an inadequate number of bathrooms and sexual harassment are common. The Australian Workers' Union, which covers fruit pickers and farm labourers, says the incentives inherent in the scheme make backpackers extremely vulnerable.

(Davies, 2018)

Farm workers put up with illegal wages and poor conditions just to make sure that they meet the 88-day rule, working in temperatures often exceeding 40 degrees.

Petrobras, the Brazilian state-run oil giant, is one of Latin America's most prominent firms. They are now involved in one of the largest corruption scandals ever in Brazil (Costas, 2014). The investigation started when investigators discovered that Alberto Youseff had given a Land Rover to Paulo Roberto Costa, the former Petrobras executive (Bawden and Sheffield, 2015). Prosecutors claim that in an arrangement commonly referred to as 'Operation Car Wash', Petrobras executives took bribes from construction firms and overpaid for contracts; other accusations include bribes to government officials and politicians and the fixing of contracts (Smith et al., 2015). They have also been accused of transferring $1.4 million to

Europe by wrapping money into plastic packages and concealing them in clothing and socks and 'underneath a baggy suit' (Bawden and Sheffield, 2015). In April 2015 Petrobras wrote off approximately $17 billion in corruption-related costs (Connors and Trevisani, 2015). Petrobras says that they are now tackling the problem. Petrobras chief Aldemir Bendine states 'Today is an important day, not only for us but for the whole company. We are cleaning up mistakes' (cited in Bawden and Sheffield, 2015).

Australian financial services firm AMP have continued to be embroiled in a 'fees for no service' scandal where clients were still paying for services despite not receiving the service. CEO Craig Meller resigned and more than $1 billion was lost in share value. Furthermore, after the scandal broke only female directors resigned, which Elana Rubin, former chairwoman of Australian Super, argued was a reflection of 'deep cultural issues' within the wealth manager (Yeates, 2018).

Visit the online resources and take a look at the extension material for Chapter 17 to read about other scandals.

If you have a cynical attitude, then you might expect this chapter to be a very short one—the phrase 'business ethics' could be seen as an oxymoron, a phrase that appears to contradict itself. You might think that businesses are only worried about making a profit. Indeed, the phrase 'business is business' is often used to suggest that you have made a 'hardnosed', 'rational' decision where morals and feelings did not come into it.

But, on closer examination, all business at its most basic level requires some degree of ethical behaviour; otherwise business quickly becomes impossible. What would happen, for instance, if you knew that your university canteen, to save costs, were using ingredients that might kill you? Similarly, how likely would a business be to sell to someone they believe has no intention of paying? Also, given the choice, would you want to work for a company that you knew treated its workers badly and even physically abused them? All business activity, to be able to survive, requires a level of trust and moral action—otherwise the entire system quickly disintegrates.

The question, therefore, is not whether firms should act in an ethical way, but rather what is the ethical basis for their actions and how do they balance wider social responsibilities with concerns for profit?

Ethical decision making

As customers we face ethical decisions every day: from streaming music for free to choosing whether to pay more for organic food. At work we also face ethical decisions, from how we treat customers and colleagues through to being pressured to do things that go against our personal values. As many of the business scandals we have listed above demonstrate, ethical decision making is an important issue. Ethical issues at work do not just relate to large headline-hitting scandals; they can also be everyday and seemingly innocuous acts, as shown in Table 17.1.

Ethical dilemmas are therefore all around us. While we may think that unethical decisions are made by 'bad' people, John Boatright (2013) argues that ethically questionable actions are often carried out by people that do not set out to act badly. He claims that they often start on a 'slippery slope' where they convince themselves that so long as it is legal, it is acceptable. This can eventually lead to more substantial unethical acts. Boatright argues: 'Recent graduates just entering the investment profession are especially vulnerable to ethical missteps because they are often naive and may

Table 17.1 Ethical dilemmas in the workplace

Issue	Example
Cheating on the company	Leaving work early, stealing pens from work, or small-scale fiddling of expenses
Cheating on clients	Misleading customers about how good a product is in order to get a sale, hiding the true costs of a service agreement, or encouraging them to buy something that they don't really need so that you win your monthly bonus
Working in unethical industries	Companies spamming customers with fake payment protection insurance and 'accident claim' calls
Turning a blind eye to unethical acts of co-workers or managers	Seeing, but not confronting or reporting, a manager who over-reports figures to meet targets, or a fellow employee who treats a customer badly or takes short-cuts on product safety to get the job done on time
Producing or selling products that are bad for the planet or people	A cashier at a petrol station selling products that will contribute to global warming, a customer service assistant at a discount retailer selling clothes made in sweatshop conditions, or a fast-food chef making burgers that are unhealthy

not see the ethical aspects of situations they confront' (2013: 8). They can feel pressure from middle managers to hit targets. Such middle managers might not have told them to act unethically, but 'they often turn a blind eye to how an objective is achieved so long as it is achieved' (2013: 8). Boatright argues that the aim of teaching business ethics should not be to stop 'bad people' acting unethically but should be to sensitize good people to what might be unethical decisions.

However, individual awareness is not enough. Often such unethical acts are 'known' but collectively we choose not to see them. This is called 'wilful blindness' (Heffernan, 2011), where 'a group of people tacitly agree to outwardly ignore something of which they are all personally aware' (Zerubavel, 2006: 2). Ethics therefore needs to impact culture, and unethical acts need to be challenged by people (sometimes called whistleblowers, as discussed later in the chapter) who are prepared to say what everyone knows but does not feel able to say.

These ethical issues are important, not only for companies' reputations but also for the lives of the people that are affected by the decisions they make. Some of the most serious scandals have resulted in people losing their lives. Organizations therefore play a part in shaping our society.

An ethical framework

Business ethics is a complex field drawing on many different theories. The following sections will introduce the main ethical theories, which are summarized neatly in Figure 17.2.

To better understand how to make ethical decisions, we first have to turn to the field of business ethics (see Table 17.2).

Teleological ethics

Taken from the Greek telos meaning ends, teleological ethics states that an action can only be judged by its consequences. For our purposes, the most important teleological perspective is

Figure 17.2 An ethical framework.
Source: © Business Ethics & Values: Individual, Corporate and International Perspectives, C. Fisher and A. Lovell, Pearson Education Limited (2006).

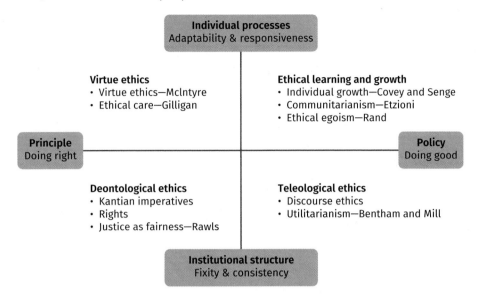

utilitarianism, which was summed up by Jeremy Bentham (the inventor of the Panopticon—see Chapters 4 and 15) as 'The greatest happiness of the greatest number is the foundation of morals and legislation' (cited in Fisher and Lovell, 2009: 129).

Within this view, actions are not good or bad because of their character or intention; rather it is their effect on how much overall benefit they produce. For utilitarians, something is good if it increases the overall well-being of people. A moral act is thus one that increases pleasure (good) more than it produces pain (bad). Utilitarians therefore argue that you can calculate the cost–benefit of a particular action. Bentham assumed all humans are motivated by the desire to create pleasure and avoid pain, and therefore they will do things that increase pleasure.

In a business sense, pleasure is often equated with profit maximization and is used to justify shareholder capitalism (see the following sections), the belief being that if everyone follows their self-interest, overall it will benefit the whole of society. A wider interpretation, however, might be used to justify stakeholder capitalism (see later in the chapter), as the impact on the whole of society needs to be calculated.

Table 17.2   Key areas of business ethics

Type of ethics	Description
Normative ethics	Tells us what we *should* do. These ethical frameworks seek to separate out good from bad practice and make moral judgements on how people should act.
Descriptive ethics	Tells us what people *actually* do and seek to provide an explanation of *why* they do it.
Managing ethics	Ways in which companies seek to manage the behaviour of their staff. This can be through a variety of techniques such as mission statements, codes of practice, and training.

613

Deontological ethics

Taken from the Greek *deon*, meaning duty, deontological ethics asks whether the action is right, fair, and honest. It is not concerned with the consequences of an action, but the reasons behind it. Within this perspective, acts are ethical only if they are conducted based on duty and not if there is a reward.

The deontological perspective looks to create universal rules and sees ethics as an end in itself. Ethical principles, particularly for the philosopher Kant, exist a priori; in other words, they exist independently of the particular circumstance or the outcome and are worked out on the basis of pure reason, and there is one universal code, regardless of culture and belief, which everyone should follow. Kant, in what he called the 'categorical imperative', argued you should always act based on the assumption your action will become a universal law of human behaviour. (For a review, see Fisher et al., 2013.) This approach sees people not as a means to an end, but an end in themselves, an approach which supports the notion of stakeholder theory (see below) (van der Linden and Freeman, 2017).

While this view might seem appealing, it is also seen as very rigid. For instance, while most of us would consider lying as wrong, what if you had to lie to save someone's life? For Kant, this then raises the question over which duty should come first (such as lying or preserving someone's life). However, it becomes difficult to come up with universal laws that fit all circumstances.

👁 Research insight: what happens to whistleblowers?

Kenny, K. 2018. Censored: Whistleblowers and impossible speech. *Human Relations* 71 (8): 1025–48.

Society needs whistleblowers (Latan et al., 2018). According to the UK government a whistle-blower is someone who 'report[s] certain types of wrongdoing … in the public interest' (Gov. uk, 2018). This can include reporting concerns about danger to health, damage to the environment, fraud, or a company not obeying the law or covering up wrongdoing. Whistleblowers therefore act in the public good, for which they shouldn't be treated unfairly e.g. by losing their job—yet often this is the case (PCAW, 2015).

A study by Kate Kenny investigates the fate of 15 senior managers and auditors in major banks, based in the UK, Ireland, Switzerland, and the USA, all of whom were involved in whistleblowing. By interviewing them, Kenny got them to reveal their experiences of being whistleblowers, including what led them to take action and what impact it had on their lives. None of them had set out to be whistleblowers, but for all of them it had profound impacts.

The whistleblowers all saw examples of major misdemeanours in their work, from 'regularly mis-selling financial insurance products in order to boost profits, to systematically overcharging business clients and facilitating money-laundering by overseas drug dealers' (Kenny, 2018: 1036). They first tried to speak out internally, contacting bosses, board members, or human resource departments, but realized after a while they were not being heard, so 'felt compelled to go outside of their organization, disclosing to a regulator, a journalist or the police' (Kenny, 2018: 1036). At this point things often changed for them, and they experienced retaliation, being ostracized by their colleagues, demoted, bullied, or sacked. Many were shunned by former colleagues and even friends. Indeed, a recent report has stated that half of all whistleblowers who contacted the report's authors had either been dismissed or resigned after raising their concern.

The impact on the whistleblowers as individuals was significant. Many began to suffer self-doubt, even about what they knew they saw. They were often portrayed as disgruntled, as

→

lunatics, or as prickly, difficult people with personal issues. They, however, saw themselves as true professionals, 'merely fulfilling their professional obligations by highlighting the problems they witnessed', or as obeying the law, speaking up when others were afraid to (Kenny, 2018: 1040). This mirrors other research, which states that people are more likely to become whistleblowers when they feel that they are fulfilling a role requirement (Lam et al., 2016).

To tackle this problem around the world, calls have been made to protect whistleblowers. Unions in India have been calling for more protection in the banking industry (Muringatheri, 2015), and in the UK the Bank of England said that in the Libor rate scandal whistleblowers were largely ineffective (Grant, 2015). The NHS in Scotland will employ 'whistleblowing champions': 'Scotland's Health Secretary Shona Robison wanted all NHS staff to "have the confidence to speak up without fear" about patient safety' (BBC News, 2015). Furthermore, Lin et al. suggest that humble leaders are more likely to create the conditions in which individuals feel more able to speak up, an approach which might prevent people having to become whistleblowers (Lin et al., 2017).

 What would it take for you to become a whistleblower? How much would you be prepared to risk to speak out for what you think is right? How would you act differently if you knew that everyone would follow your actions?

Another deontological perspective is that of justice and rights. The libertarian view, which stresses individual freedom above all other concerns, particularly as developed by Robert Nozick, argues that the essential right people have is freedom, particularly freedom from government interference and freedom to own property. People, he argued, have the right to free choice and to act how they want so long as they are not breaking the law. In business, this justifies shareholder capitalism (discussed later in the chapter), as shareholders are seen as having the right to use their property in whatever way they like providing they act within the law.

An alternative deontological perspective is social justice. This perspective is most strongly associated with John Rawls and is linked to communitarianism (discussed later in the chapter). Rawls asks us to imagine what a 'just' society would look like if we did not know our position in the world. In other words, you could be anyone, rich or poor, male or female, in the developed world or from a developing nation. From this position of 'total ignorance' we then need to imagine what we would like the world to be like. Believing that we are risk-averse individuals, Rawls thinks we would design a world of fairness based upon the same civil and political rights for all and a system of meritocracy (this supports the stakeholder approach).

Virtue ethics

 Real life case: PRME

PRME—the Principles of Responsible Management Education—is an organized relationship between the United Nations and management-related academic institutions, business schools, and universities (UNPRME, 2015). It was launched in 2007 to provide a framework for

→

academic institutions to advance corporate sustainability and social responsibility by building PRME values into teaching and research. It is based around six key principles.

1. **Purpose**: Developing the capabilities of students to be future generators of sustainable value for business and society, to create a more inclusive and sustainable global economy.
2. **Values**: Building the values into teaching and organizational practices.
3. **Method**: Creating educational materials to enable learning responsible leadership.
4. **Research**: Creating research that helps understand how corporations can create sustainable social, environmental, and economic value.
5. **Partnership**: With businesses to meet social and environmental responsibilities.
6. **Dialogue**: Between educators, students, business, government, customers and media etc., around social responsible business and sustainability.

To date over 600 institutions have signed up and are integrating PRME principles into their teaching and learning and also their research. This might include learning about sustainability, business ethics, and responsible management on courses such as the one that you are doing now. One approach, therefore, is helping to create sustainability mindsets (Cohen and King, 2017).

A key challenge, though, as Paul Hibbert and Ann Cunliffe have argued, is that simply helping students, like yourself, to know about the principles of responsible management is not enough if such learning is disconnected from practice. Being aware of ethical concerns alone does not mean that you are able to know how to act differently (Hibbert and Cunliffe, 2015). Indeed, as one of us (Daniel) has found, being aware of the critiques of management does not mean that you are able to know what to do in practice (King and Learmonth, 2015). PRME and other initiatives like it, therefore, are a good start in that they put responsible management on the agenda, but initiatives like this alone cannot bring about change.

 Do you know if your university has signed up for PRME? Have you seen any evidence of it in the teaching you have received? Check out the UNPRME website and see if you can get involved. http://www.unprme.org/

Virtue-based ethics focuses on the individual, particularly their personal characteristics. Drawing on Aristotle, it looks at the individual character—how it is formed and develops to achieve 'eudaimonia' (life-long development of well-being, or human flourishing). (For a review, see Fisher et al., 2013.) It focuses on means, not ends (unlike teleological ethics), and personal characteristics rather than rules (unlike deontological ethics). Advocates of virtue-based ethics believe that if practised in the right way it will lead the individual to make the right choices.

In the business context, virtue ethics focuses on the character of the individual and their capacity to make the right choices (see MacIntyre, 1967). Proponents would argue that the moral education of managers is therefore vital to help them cope with the ethical complexity of modern life. PRME (see the 'Real life case') is an example of the way modern-day business schools have responded to this approach.

Indeed, increasingly there is an expectation within the public for business leaders to speak out on issues of public importance. The results of the 2018 Edelman Trust Barometer stated that 84 per cent of the general public expect CEOs to inform policy debates on societal issues, and 56 per cent of people had no respect for CEOs who do not speak out (Edelman, 2018). Chatterji and Toffel argue that this is producing a new brand of what they call CEO activists (2018). These CEOs are speaking out on issues such as gun control, climate change, gender discrimination, and race. While such speaking out by CEOs used to be thought of as something that could harm sales, increasingly business leaders including Apple's Tim Cook, Starbucks' Howard Schultz, and Marc Benioff of Salesforce are speaking out, acting as the voice for shareholders and employees. In part this is linked to ideas of authentic leadership (see Chapter 13), as not speaking up is seen as 'insincere'. This can involve such gestures as signing open letters calling for action, but also taking action that has economic consequences, such as PayPal's refusal to locate a new office in the US state of North Carolina because of a new law on discrimination.

A related concept, drawing on feminist philosophy, is the 'ethics of care'. It argues that most philosophy (and therefore ethics) is written by, and based on, male ideals. For instance, Gilligan (1982) argues that women demonstrate a different way of moral reasoning, particularly due to early socialization, and tend to seek compromise and ways of avoiding blaming one side exclusively in a dispute so that everyone gets something, rather than looking for the black-and-white morals that men tend to look for (for a review, see Fisher and Lovell, 2009: 107).

Virtue ethics, however, can overemphasize the importance of the individual, either by praising heroic individuals or by blaming so-called bad apples, saying that bad actions occur because of a few bad individuals rather than because of wider problems.

 Real life case: whose fault was the banking crisis? A case of 'bad apples', says deputy governor of the Bank of England

Recent years have seen numerous scandals within the financial services industry, with mis-selling and rate fixing being reported. To date, these scandals have cost the industry an estimated £264 billion in fines and compensation worldwide (Treanor, 2017). But whose fault was it?

Minouche Shafik, the deputy governor of the Bank of England, said more should be done to punish what she called 'bad apples' (BBC News, 2014). This view is echoed by Tim Sloan, CEO of the US financial firm Wells Fargo CEO, who (according to Stephen Gandel) 'wants to paint the bank's regulatory missteps, and the resulting fines, as the actions of a few bad apples that have been picked clean from the bank' (Gandel, 2018). Yet while many would welcome punishment for bad individuals, many others have questioned if it is really a result of a few 'bad apples' or a product of a wider culture of corruption (Arnold and Binham, 2015).

A problem with the 'bad apples' argument is that companies can then blame a few individuals (who often leave with good payouts) which means that they can avoid getting to the root cause of the problem (Jago and Pfeffer, 2018: 13). A report by André Spicer of the Cass Business School states that what is needed is not necessarily punishment of a few individuals but wholesale cultural change (Spicer et al., 2016). In an interview for this book, Spicer told us that this should include changing the symbols and signs which are prominently displayed within the banks. For instance, some large banks prominently displayed the share price in the lobby of their headquarters. This reminded employees that the only thing which counted was increasing the share price of the bank. Now some large banks prominently display values and ethical statements in the headquarters—this communicates a different message. But symbolism is not enough. Banks have also had to transform day-to-day practices—this means

→

encouraging people to engage in different ways of doing things. In the past, interactions with customers were mainly based around a routine of sales: for example, in the case of a customer taking out a loan from a bank. This has been replaced with routines based on customer support and educating the customer about the risks they are taking on when they get a loan.

Finally, changing culture means shifting deeper values of people within the bank. Often senior management try to do this through inspirational speeches and training programmes. But this is often not enough—tone from the top counts for very little when it is not matched by 'message from the middle'. Getting the latter right is difficult—often because middle managers face competing pressure to both cut costs and build a more ethical culture at once. The result is they find it difficult to change culture as quickly as regulators and senior management might like (Spicer et al., 2016).

Individual growth and organizational learning

Our final ethical perspective emphasizes the importance of learning and development (see Chapter 10) as part of ethical development. It focuses on how to be more effective in one's job while developing an ethical character. A particularly popular (and inspiring) example is provided by Stephen Covey's book *The 7 habits of highly effective people* (2004). On the surface, this book appears to be a conventional time-management and self-help book, with charts for how to plan a week and habits to be successful. However, it goes further by asking the reader to define what they consider being successful really means, and what sort of character and life they want. This stresses a number of things, including the importance of having a personal vision not just in work, but also in terms of balancing personal, family, and professional responsibilities. At the heart is developing an ethical character and focusing on priorities based upon principles rather than quick fixes. Having sold over 15 million copies, Covey's book has proved highly influential, particularly during the 1990s. It does, however, reinforce the image of the heroic ethical individual able to overcome all adversity.

A different individual growth perspective is communitarianism. This perspective argues that the community should be considered more important than individuals or the state. Communitarianism stresses the importance of social relations and suggests that human life will improve if the community and public values guide our decision making. In other words, we do things for the good of the community rather than for ourselves. We will have more to say on communitarianism later in the chapter.

? Review questions

Describe	What are the key principles of each of the ethical frameworks?
Explain	What are the strengths and weaknesses of each of the ethical frameworks?
Analyse	Which of the frameworks do you consider more useful when tackling business dilemmas? What is your reasoning for this?
Apply	In the 'bad apples' case, how much impact do you think it would make to change the symbols displayed in the banks from live share price updates to ethical statements?

The economic framework for ethical action

While ethical frameworks are important in guiding individual and organizational behaviour, the choices that we have and the possibilities for ethical action are also shaped by the economic system in which we live. For the rest of the chapter we will examine the five main perspectives that exist currently, at least within Western countries.

Karl Marx (1859/2012) argued that the economic structure (which he called the base) shapes the nature of society (which he called the superstructure), and society exists to maintain and legitimize the economic system (Figure 17.3). For instance, this Marxist framework argues that within our society schooling exists primarily to support the economy, not only in providing skilled workers but also in establishing the values and attitudes these workers should have (to accept authority, turn up on time, want to achieve high grades—like promotion at work—and accept discipline).

Consequently, for ethics, our central ideas are a product of the superstructure (our family, education, religion, reading of mass media, politics, etc.) and our actions are constrained by the base— the economic system in which we operate. According to this view, while it is important to look to individual organizations and people, our ethical beliefs and the choices (we think) we have are more political or ideological in nature than we tend to believe.

The first three frameworks discussed here accept the economic system of capitalism as their basis, although they have different interpretations and emphasis within it. The latter two could broadly be said to be against capitalism as an economic system, but they offer two different responses to the problems they perceive that capitalism creates (Figure 17.4).

Figure 17.3 The base and superstructure model (based on Marx, 1859/2012).

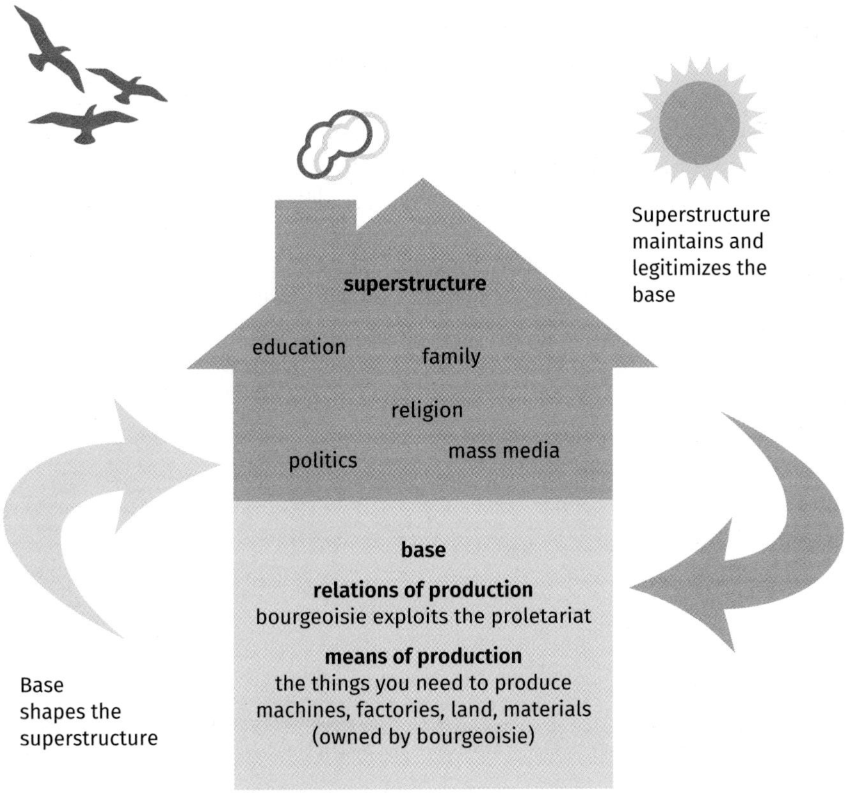

619

Figure 17.4 The five frameworks featured in this chapter.

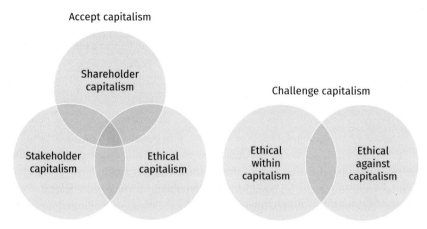

For the purposes of this chapter, capitalism is understood to be the economic system in which we (in the West) live, where one group—the capitalists (shareholders or owners of the firm)—owns the means of production, and another group—labour (workers)—sell their labour. We have featured this in the capitalist working relationship.

Shareholder capitalism

🔍 **Running case:** hitting the headlines

While Simon Chance is still musing over his hotel expansion plans, Linda Wilkinson comes rushing into his office looking flustered. 'Do we have an appointment?' Chance looks at her quizzically and with slight annoyance.

'Look at this,' Wilkinson cuts across him, pointing to the front page of the local paper. 'It's worse than I predicted.'

Still not really understanding what is going on, Chance snatches the paper from her. 'What are you talking about? ... Oh, I see,' Chance says, seeing the headline 'Junction Rubbish' accompanied by a big photo of the hotel with litter strewn across the road. '"Weddings at local hotel are causing mayhem, say local residents",' Chance reads out, '"drunken yobs making noise throughout the night ... traffic blocking up local streets ... guests being sick in neighbour's front garden ... litter being dumped on the street." This is not good,' Chance declares, looking up from the paper.

Chance's office door opens and in comes Weaver. 'Have you seen this?' Chance asks, handing the paper to Weaver. With only a quick glance, Weaver hands the paper back.

'Newspaper tittle-tattle,' Weaver declares. 'Look, the weddings make us a lot of money. Sure, they make a lot of noise, but then they are having fun.'

Wilkinson looks shocked: 'But it's a really bad story—front page, too.'

Weaver smiles at her. 'It's just paper talk. It will all blow over in a week and be forgotten about. News today, but tomorrow it's just fish and chip paper. You have to be strong and withstand these stories. When the profits come through, the investors will be thanking you.'

Milton Friedman: the social responsibility of business is to increase its profits

Nobel-Prize-winning economist Milton Friedman was the most prominent and outspoken critic of corporate social responsibility and a defender of shareholder capitalism. In a widely discussed article published in 1970 he claimed:

> [T]here is one and only one social responsibility of business—to use its resources and engage in activities designed to increase its profits so long as it stays within the rules of the game, which is to say, engages in open and free competition without deception or fraud.

> (Friedman, 1970: 126)

Anything else, he states, not only is not the purpose of organizations, but is actually unethical.

Drawing on libertarianism, Friedman put forward a profit-maximizing argument: that firms should seek to maximize their profits at all times. He argued that companies are the shareholders' property and therefore should be run exclusively in their interest. This interest, he stated, is 'to make as much money as possible while conforming to their basic rules of the society'. For instance, a company should not spend money 'on reducing pollution beyond the amount that is in the best interests of the corporation or that is required by law', as it would lower profit for the shareholders.

This libertarian perspective also calls for less control by the government, as people (including shareholders and therefore corporations) should be free to live their lives in a way that maximizes freedom. In this way, these profit maximizers argue, the market runs at its most efficient (see Van Der Linden and Freeman, 2017, for a discussion). Finally, Friedman also argues that because managers are not trained in solving social problems, they should not be required to tackle them. Businesses, therefore, should not have responsibilities for solving society's problems because it dilutes what they are good at—running in an efficient and profitable manner.

Visit the online resources and take a look at the extension material for Chapter 17 to read more about Milton Friedman's theories.

 Do you think companies should be run exclusively in shareholders' interests? Can you see any problems with the position that Friedman outlines? Can you think of any examples that would question Friedman's assertions?

621

Adam Smith: the invisible hand

The shareholder capitalism perspective also takes a particular reading of utilitarianism, using ethical egoism. This perspective claims that you should act in your own self-interest because doing so is the best way of promoting the maximum overall level of happiness. The philosopher Adam Smith wrote:

> It is not from the benevolence of the butcher, the brewer, or the baker, that we expect our dinner, but from their regard to their own interest. We address ourselves, not to their humanity but to their self-love, and never talk to them of our own necessities but of their advantages

> (*Wealth of nations*, I.ii.2: Smith, 1776/2012)

Because trading is beneficial to both parties, it will increase the good for all. Collective interest, it is claimed, is best promoted through self-interest. Intentions reached individually will be the best decisions for the entire society.

Smith argues that you are likely to work harder, spend your money more carefully, and invest it more wisely if it is for your own interest. Similarly, workers will seek to maximize their skills and work as hard as possible to maximize their wages, buyers will look to purchase goods for the lowest amount possible, and sellers will thus be forced to compete with each other to offer the best goods at the lowest price. Self-interest supports society as a whole, 'led by an invisible hand to promote an end which was no part of his intention ... By pursuing his own interest he frequently promotes that of the society more effectually than when he really intends to promote it' (*Wealth of nations* IV.ii.9: Smith, 1776/2012). According to this view, the market has an 'invisible hand' that promotes the greatest good for all.

Economic growth is good for all: the rising tide raises all ships

 Real life case: Stephen Hester's bonus

In January 2012 Stephen Hester, the then CEO of Royal Bank of Scotland (RBS), turned down a bonus of just under £1 million. Hester had come under considerable public and political pressure, particularly because RBS were by that time predominantly a government-owned company. Many members of the public considered his pay excessive, particularly at a time of austerity that meant the majority of public and private sector workers were experiencing pay freezes and even job cuts (Neate, 2012).

In an interview we conducted with Hester, he said that although it 'may not be the job of a business person specifically', everyone needs to understand the issues surrounding high pay and inequality. However, he argues that capitalism is 'the most effective way of increasing the wealth and opportunities of most people'. It is effective because it increases the size of the 'economic pie' which

unleashes different people's motivations and talents in different ways, which can accentuate financial differences. The biggest income differences on the planet at the moment are in China and India today, which are the fastest-growing, biggest producers of economic pie growth out there.

... If you want, as a society, to have some wealth to go round, you need to allow, or even encourage, the efforts that lead to some people having a lot more money than others because of their business success. And then you need to rein some of that back through taxation in order to make acceptable to everyone the way that the pie is ultimately distributed ... and that is the trick. So, if we were to instigate a rule that said that pay differences cannot be more than X, then, simply, we will be less successful economically and there will be less of the pie to go round for everyone. But, equally, if the people that do well out of the current system are ignorant of everyone else and offensive, then the system won't last either.

Source: Author interview with Stephen Hester, former CEO of Royal Bank of Scotland, February 2012.

 Visit the online resources and take a look at the extension material for Chapter 17 to read the full interview with Stephen Hester.

Stephen Hester's arguments draw on utilitarianism and libertarianism. Both hinge on the assumption that shareholder capitalism is the most effective way of increasing overall wealth and produces increased benefits for all. This argument is sometimes known as the 'trickle-down effect': in US president Franklin D. Roosevelt's metaphor, 'the rising tide raises all ships'. This argument claims that although capitalism might produce more inequality (as the rich will get proportionally richer than the poor), it will 'drag up the poor people, because there are the resources to do so' (Robinson, 2012: 204), as British prime minister Margaret Thatcher once famously claimed. According to this view, the goal of the economy should be wealth creation rather than wealth redistribution as, in the long run, everyone will benefit.

Philanthropy: giving something back to society

 Real life case: Mark Zuckerberg and Priscilla Chan's letter to their newborn child

In December 2015 Mark Zuckerberg and Priscilla Chan wrote an open letter to Max, their new-born child.

In it they explained their wish to promote equality and human potential, including increasing access to the internet around the world. To do this they said they would donate 99 per cent of their Facebook shares, at the time worth $45 billion, to a new foundation called the Chan Zuckerberg Initiative. One of the central aims of the foundation is to 'unlock the gifts of every person around the world' (https://www.chanzuckerberg.com/).

Zuckerberg and Chan are not the first to donate large amounts of their fortunes. In 2010, Bill Gates and Warren Buffett launched a campaign called the Giving Pledge 'to invite the wealthiest individuals and families in America to commit to giving the majority [at least half] of their wealth to philanthropy' (Carlyle, 2012; Giving Pledge, 2018). By 2018, 175 had signed up, all billionaires who committed to donate the majority of their wealth to good causes.

Visit the online resources and take a look at the web links for Chapter 17 for more detail about these campaigns.

The shareholder capitalism model argues that individual shareholders have the right, indeed in countries like the USA almost a duty, to give some of their wealth away. Chan and Zuckerberg are not the first. Henry Ford set up one of the first such foundations, and David Packard, the founder of Hewlett Packard, gave money to set up a hospital, university, and aquarium (Ford Foundation, 2018; Packard Foundation, 2018).

Philanthropy was at its strongest in the UK in the Victorian era, when many successful business people were often driven by Christian belief that money is the root of all evil and that it was a necessity to help the poor. Many were Quakers, including the founders of Barclays Bank and Lloyds Bank and of the chocolate manufacturer Cadbury's. They gave away vast fortunes to help the needy; they also set up schools and hospitals and funded the arts (Dellheim, 1987; Ackrill and Hannah, 2001).

Today, many corporations have a philanthropic arm, giving money back to society, investing in the arts and local community projects, sponsoring local sports teams, and allowing staff to volunteer their time and skills to local charities. While such actions are highly commendable, questions remain about the role of philanthropy. First, there is a concern that it is undemocratic, as certain causes might be more appealing to rich people, giving them more power than if the money was distributed through general taxation (BBC Television, 2011a). For instance, Victorian philanthropist George Peabody, whose aim was to help the poor of London to have somewhere to live, only wanted people he considered of 'excellent moral character' who he thought were worthy of help (BBC Television, 2011b).

Second, giving these large amounts diverts attention away from potentially less ethical activities, for example donating money to a local good cause to gain public support for a potentially controversial activity. One of us (Daniel) went on a training day for artists in business and was told of a business that put on an arts event to give them some positive publicity when applying for planning permission. The impression they gave was that using the arts was a cheap way of buying public support for their new development. Philanthropy, therefore, is about redistributing wealth rather than exploring how wealth is created in the first place and some of the inequalities that are produced through this process.

Third, some of these donations are not as altruistic as they at first seem. While it would appear that Mark Zuckerberg donated most of his wealth to charity, the Chan Zuckerberg Initiative was in fact 'a limited liability company'. The implication of this is that '[as] a company, the Initiative can do much more than charitable activity … [which] means that Zuckerberg can control the company's investments as he sees fit, while accruing significant commercial, tax and political benefits' (Rhodes and Bloom, 2018). This kind of activity gives CEOs considerable power to influence the way that society works.

Problems with the shareholder capitalism model

While shareholder capitalism has been very popular with many politicians and business leaders, substantial questions remain over its ethical status and the assumptions on which it is based. First, it is based on the assumption of the 'economic person' who always acts in a rational manner. As we discussed in Chapter 5, people do not always act rationally or seek to maximize their own interests. Second, it assumes that self-interest is good for all—an assumption that is challenged by the 'tragedy of the commons' (see the 'Research insight'). Third, it assumes that acting in self-interest has no negative effects on others, something economists call externalities. Fourth, challenges have been presented to the 'rising tide' thesis by arguments that income inequalities produce social problems. Finally, the supreme rights of shareholders are being challenged by placing more attention on them.

Assumption 1: self-interest is good for all

Hardin, G. 1968. The tragedy of the commons. *Science* 162 (3859): 1243–8.

In this seminal article, ecologist Garrett Hardin describes a fictional situation where cattle herders graze their cows on common land. Hardin states that, unconsciously, each herdsman will ask 'What is the **utility** [a marginal personal benefit] *to me* of adding one more animal to my herd?' By putting another cow on the land, a herdsman increases his personal wealth as he benefits from the proceeds of the sale of the cow, but it has a negative effect on the grass that will be spread across all the herdsmen. Therefore, by acting in his individual interests each herdsman will add more cattle to the land, which will ultimately destroy the quality of the land—thus the tragedy of the commons.

Self-interest versus common interest.
Source: Vibrant Image Studio/Shutterstock.com

While Hardin's work has been criticized for its historical inaccuracies (Hawkshaw et al., 2012), it does provide a powerful riposte to the utilitarian argument that everyone should act in their own self-interest. It demonstrates that if they do, our common interests are not always served. As the KitKat example which opened this chapter demonstrates, while it might have been in Nestlé's private interest to obtain supplies from the cheapest possible source, the long-term interests of the whole of humanity would be better served by maintaining the rainforest. Such failures are sometimes called 'market failures', when negative effects of a transaction can fall on a third party—again, the occurrences that economists call externalities (Bakan, 2005).

One solution some economists, accountants, and governments have tried is to put a price on nature through 'natural capital accounts', an attempt to incorporate nature into accounts, thereby putting the environment at the heart of the economy. Without such a price, the argument goes, irrational decisions will be made by not valuing nature. However, environmental campaigner George Monbiot argues this whole approach is based on the false logic 'that nature exists to serve us; that its value consists of the instrumental benefits we can extract; that this value can be measured in cash terms; and that what can't be measured does not matter', and that such logic may prove 'lethal to the rest of life on Earth' (Monbiot, 2018). The whole logic of seeing nature only in terms of (albeit broader) economic value, Monbiot argues, is wrong.

Assumption 2: individuals should be free to pursue their own interests

The premise of shareholder capitalism, that business leaders have responsibilities only to shareholders, is justified on the grounds that business activity is positive—creating jobs, goods, and services—or, at best, benign (not harmful) for society. However, upon closer examination, this position is hard to sustain in every instance.

To maximize profits, critics argue, businesses in fact transfer the true cost of transactions to society. For instance, firms do not pay for the pollution they cause, the unemployment benefit of workers made redundant, the building of new roads needed for a new factory, or the extra health costs caused by their products, e.g. smoking. These other costs fall on a third party who is not involved in the decision making process.

Economists call these costs externalities or spillover costs. 'Externalities arise when firms create social costs that they do not have to bear, such as pollution' Porter and Kramer argue. Because these costs need to be made, 'society must impose taxes, regulations, and penalties so that firms "internalize" these externalities—a belief influencing many government policy decisions' (2011: 5). This creates a problem, particularly in an increasingly globalized world where large corporations are able to move around to achieve the best deal and thus externalize more costs.

Governments are faced with the need to deal with externalities, such as reducing carbon emissions back to the socially optimal level. Either the government could impose regulation to overcome any negative effects on society, for instance making it more expensive to emit carbon by imposing a carbon tax, or it could make firms internalize the negative costs, e.g. the clean-up costs, which is an incentive to reduce pollution (for a critique see Böhm et al., 2012). Climate change, many critical theorists argue, is not simply a technical issue but one that requires political solutions (Wittneben et al., 2012), which require new ways of seeing the world (Levy and Spicer, 2013).

Assumption 3: economic growth is good for all

 Real life case: executive pay

In recent years one of the strongest areas of criticism of large corporations has been the levels of executive pay.

- In the USA the average CEO-to-worker pay ratio is 339:1; in the UK it is 129:1. At some firms in the USA, the gap is as large as 5000:1.

- The McDonald's CEO's annual salary could be used to pay the year's wages for 3,101 workers.

→

→

- The average income of a FTSE 100 CEO is estimated at £4.5 million.

- The average CEO earns more in three days than the average employee makes in a year, which is 129 times the average worker.

- Executives of the failed company Carillon received £4 million in bonuses during the period when the company was collapsing (Burt, 2018).

- The average male CEO earns 77 per cent more than their female counterpart.

- Amazon's CEO and Founder Jeff Bezos is estimated to be worth $131 billion (Forbes, 2018).

- The average individual worker at Walmart earns $19,177 per year, meaning they would have to work for more than a thousand years to earn the $22.2 million that Doug McMillon, the company's chief executive, was awarded in 2017 (Gelles, 2018).

- Forecasters predict, at current levels of increase, that by 2035 the top 0.1 per cent of people will take home 14 per cent of national income.

Sources: CIPD (2017); Ellison (2018).

 Visit the online resources and take a look at the web links for Chapter 17 to see these reports.

Real life case: Lloyds Bank faces a shareholder revolt

An annual general meeting is not a place in which is normally the place of intrigue and revolt, but the Lloyds Bank Group AGM of May 2018 threatened to be just that. António Horta Osório, who previously was famous for taking sick leave in 2011 for exhaustion some nine months into the job, faced a shareholder rebellion because his salary was 95 times that of the average worker in the bank. The advisory group Institutional Shareholders Services took the unusual step of recommending shareholders not to approve his pay of £6.4m (*The Guardian*, 2018).

Osório was not the first CEO to be put under pressure because of their pay. Sir Martin Sorrell, CEO of an advertising company, saw his pay drop from £70.4m to £48.1m in 2016, although he is still the highest paid CEO in the UK. In December 2017 the chairman of house builders Persimmon resigned because of a badly designed incentive scheme which saw CEO Jeff Fairburn receive a bonus of around £100m. While the house builder was making much higher than expected profits, this was widely seen as a result of a government-funded help-to-buy scheme. Fairburn's bonus was 'preposterous,' said Euan Stirling of Aberdeen Standard Investments, and his 'insistence in extracting such a high proportion of the value that has been created is damaging, both financially and reputationally, to the company' (Pratley, 2018). Universities have also come under criticism: Christina Slade, vice-chancellor of Bath Spa University, one of the smallest UK universities, received £808,000 when she left the post, including a payoff of £429,000 for 'compensation for loss of office' (Grove, 2017).

What do you think about the levels of executive pay illustrated by these examples? Does it matter if these executives are earning high amounts if their companies are doing well?

Figure 17.5 The impact of income inequality on child mortality.
Source: From Wilkinson and Pickett, The Spirit Level (2010). Reproduced by permission of Penguin.

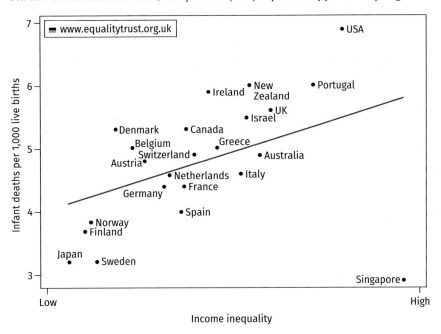

The belief that as long as everyone gets richer the level of inequality does not matter has been challenged in *The spirit level: Why equality is better for everyone* (Wilkinson and Pickett, 2010). Drawing on large amounts of statistical evidence, Wilkinson and Pickett argue that it is not the overall level of wealth which matters (as shareholder capitalism has it), but the level of inequality.

Looking at societal issues, such as physical health, mental health, drug abuse, imprisonment, obesity, trust, and violence, they found that the countries with the highest levels of social inequality fared worse in these measures. For instance, on the one hand, the USA is the world's richest country, and they have vast inequalities of income, high crime, and even high infant deaths per head of population (see Figure 17.5). On the other hand, Scandinavian countries have greater equality and lower social problems. Wilkinson and Pickett therefore conclude that the greater the gap between the rich and the poor, the higher the levels of crime, health problems, unhappiness, drug addiction, and environmental problems.

A report by Oxfam stated that 42 people have as much wealth as 3.7 billion combined, which is about half the world's population (Elliott, 2018). According to a report published by French economist Thomas Piketty, inequality is on the rise worldwide, almost doubling in such countries as India over the last 25 years (Alvaredo et al., 2018).

While inequality is high now, a major concern developing with the Fourth Industrial Revolution, particularly with the growth of automation and AI, is that inequality could grow to even higher levels. In early 2018 Mark Carney, the then governor of the Bank of England, made headlines through his claims that automation might claim millions of jobs, seeing a hollowing-out of lower- and middle-level jobs, which could result in mass unemployment and wage stagnation. He argued that 'increases in artificial intelligence, big data and high-tech machines could create huge inequalities between the high-skilled workers who benefit from the advances and those who are sidelined by them' (Drury, 2018). This could cause big issues in society, as a relatively limited number of people benefit from these changes and many people would suffer. What would these people, displaced from work by the Fourth Industrial Revolution, then do? Mark Carney argued that this could lead to a situation where 'Marx and Engels [authors of the Communist Manifesto] may again become relevant' and ordinary people might create social unrest (cited in Drury, 2018).

Carney is hardly the first to raise concerns that the Fourth Industrial Revolution will see a rise in social problems. Bill Gates, the founder of Microsoft, has argued that robots should be taxed and the money put to 'communities where this has a particularly big impact', and Benoît Hamon, a French presidential candidate, also called for a tax on robots to fund a universal basic income (Waters, 2017). It is clear that everyone needs to benefit from teleological change in order to get a cohesive and stable society.

How much should the average CEO earn compared to an ordinary worker? According to a recent survey the British public said the ideal ratio should be 7:1 (Pratley, 2018). This is significantly lower than the British current average but actually much closer to what Greek philosopher Plato believed. Plato stated that the best paid in society should not receive more than five times the lowest in society.

 What would society be like if a 7:1 policy was introduced? Does the amount of money you have matter more, or the gap between rich and poor? How might equity theory (which we examined in Chapter 9) apply here?

Assumption 4: shareholders' interests are the only important ones

The final underlying assumption of shareholder capitalism is that because they (the shareholders) own the firm, it is their property to do with as they like. The business should be run exclusively in shareholders' interests, and the consequences for others are, at best, secondary and, at worst, disregarded if they harm the shareholders' interest. As we will see later, however, it could be argued that from a moral point of view such a perspective is problematic and can even be detrimental to the long-term interests of the shareholders.

 Real life cases: harm to stakeholders

In recent years there have been numerous cases of the harmful impacts that large (and sometimes small) organizations have had. Business supporters often reject them as examples of a few bad apples and state that we should also be aware of the vast amount of good that businesses do (primarily in supplying jobs, goods, and services that people need, and also giving things back to society). However, for campaigners and anti-capitalism protestors, such cases are examples of fundamental problems with the structure of capitalism.

Asbestos

Asbestos was presented as a miracle product. Fire retardant, sound absorbent, strong, and affordable, it was put into countless buildings and lagging in things like power reactors and even schools. Yet, unbeknown to many of the people living or working in buildings that used it, it is also a killer. Inhaling the asbestos fibres can lead to lung cancer, mesothelioma, and asbestosis. More people died from asbestos in the UK than from road traffic accidents (Devlin, 2018). Yet asbestos was only banned in the UK in 1990, despite the first death being known to have occurred in 1909. This meant that many within the industry knew about its dangers for 80 years, continuing to sell it. Because of this, the asbestos industry had to pay substantial levels of compensation. To date there have been around $64bn in insurance claims from

→

→

former workers and customers who have had their lives cut short by the cancer that asbestos causes, with a further $21bn held in reserve (Gray, 2017).

Harm to customers—sugar tax

If you have tried Ribena recently, it probably has tasted different from what it was a few years ago. This is because Ribena's manufacturer decided to reformulate the product rather than paying the controversial sugar tax. Throughout the world, sugar taxes are being brought in as a way of tackling the obesity crisis. We are increasingly told we are facing an obesity crisis, as many adults and even children are overweight. One of the root causes for this is said to be sugar, which is in many everyday items from breakfast cereals through to yoghurts, fast food, and energy drinks. To tackle this, Public Health England had called for cutting 20 per cent of sugar by 2020. Everyday products are harming people's health.

Harm to the environment—the last straw?

Around the world the plastic straw is now under threat. For years, a soft drink from a café or McDonald's would be accompanied by a plastic straw, but now the plastic straw's days may be numbered. An estimated 8.5bn straws are thrown away annually in the UK alone (Hancock, 2018), part of 150m tonnes of plastic waste which end up in the sea each year (Perkins, 2018). This is following the lead of such places as Delhi, India, that have already banned plastic straws.

These sorts of situations presented in the 'Real life cases' challenge Milton Friedman's and Adam Smith's argument that unfettered self-interest produces good for everyone. Organizations can produce *externalities* which harm others. Furthermore, simply focusing on short-term profits can have significant long-term costs (for instance the estimated $85bn costs for compensation for people who have died early due to asbestos), the reputational harms that can come with scandals, and the dangers of legislation clampdowns that can occur if firms are seen to do harm to society. Moreover, leaders, as Mesdaghinia et al. argue, who are focused on the bottom line can create a toxic environment, which has long-term costs to the organization (2018). Organizations therefore have a responsibility to wider society. This is where stakeholder perspective comes in.

? Review questions

Describe	What is the shareholder capitalism perspective?
Explain	What are the key arguments for and critiques of this perspective?
Analyse	What do you think of Andrew Carnegie's statement: 'The man who dies rich, dies disgraced' (quoted in Partington, 1998: 181)?
Apply	How would you advise Junction Hotel to deal with the negative newspaper headlines? Should the income from weddings be their main concern?

Stakeholder capitalism

> ### 🔍 Running case: the letters column
>
> Having hoped that the media storm would blow over, Chance is horrified to see that in the following day's paper the letters column is full of letters from the local community complaining that Junction Hotel is affecting their lives. Oliver Price from the local neighbourhood committee writes to complain of the 'loutish' behaviour of wedding guests and the 'excessive noise' made at weekends. Ronald Farley also writes in complaining that, despite his emails, the management of the hotel do not seem to care.
>
> Thinking that nothing else could go wrong, Chance picks up his ringing telephone. On the other end is Ian Terry, one of Second Chance Consortium's biggest investors and a local in the town. Terry has also seen the letters column in the paper and says that he is horrified that the hotel is receiving such negative publicity. Recalling Weaver's words, Chance tries to calm his fears by saying that the storm will quickly blow over and once the profits come in from the larger weddings all of this will be forgotten. 'I live in this community,' Terry protests, 'and, anyway, do you really think that we have a chance of getting the extension through planning with stories going on in the press like this? We will get kicked out at the first stage if this is kept up. You need to sort it out, and fast.' With that, he slams the phone down.

It is quickly apparent that the shareholders are not the only ones to be affected by an organization's actions. Even such profit maximizers as Milton Friedman recognized that firms need to stay 'within the rules of the game' and may need to consider some other values alongside the bottom line. Van Der Linden and Freeman argue that maybe 'profit maximizers could even agree that values such as safety, privacy, and work-life balance also can require consideration simultaneously with profit' (2017: 359). The question therefore becomes which values should be taken into account.

Stakeholder theory argues that many groups or individuals have a stake (a claim, or interest) in any action a business takes and therefore, it could be argued, should be considered when decisions are made. For instance, a full-time employee spends a large part of their waking hours at work and is, generally, financially dependent on the job, so, arguably, has more at stake than an individual shareholder who might only have some of their savings tied up in the company. Similarly, many customers rely on the services a company offers. For instance, when care home provider Southern Cross ran into financial difficulties after their rents increased, not only were staff going to potentially lose their jobs but also the accommodation of thousands of vulnerable pensioners was at risk, causing anxiety for them and their families (Snell, 2011; BBC News, 2011). Equally, local communities can be impacted by issues such as noise pollution or an increase in traffic. In short, many other parties are impacted by the actions of a single organization. These groups include, but are not limited to, those shown in Figure 17.6.

Within academic literature and business terminology these groups are often called stakeholders. Freeman defines stakeholders as 'those groups who can affect or are affected by the achievement of an organization's purpose' (1984: 49). The challenge is to identify who the stakeholders are and what responsibilities the organization has to them, and to balance the competing interests of these stakeholders.

Firms have to act within the interests of society because otherwise society will withdraw its support and prevent them from existing. As Davis argues, 'Society gave business its charter to exist, and that charter could be amended or revoked at any time that business fails to live up to society's expectations' (1973: 314). This charter, often called the 'licence to operate', stated that any business

Figure 17.6 Organizations' stakeholders.

631

needs to make sure everyone's rights are respected in a community. Furthermore, governments impose or loosen controls, make investment in infrastructure, provide workers with training and education, and provide regulation against unfair competition and (in the UK) healthcare for sick employees. Corporations are socially sanctioned and are able to operate provided that they contribute to society in return (Skilton and Purdy, 2017). Therefore a firm 'owes an obligation [to stakeholders] based on their participation in the cooperative scheme that constitutes the organization and makes it a going concern' (Phillips, cited in Van Der Linden and Freeman, 2017: 356). Indeed, in recent years, throughout the world, governments have even been bailing out banks because of the negative impact that their failure would have had on other businesses. As a consequence, businesses must maintain enough trust in order to not be put under extra legislation.

One of the central challenges, therefore, is to define who the stakeholders are and how much to privilege them. Different versions of stakeholder theory present alternative approaches to this issue. The legal view presents a narrow list of only the legal duties a firm has; the strategic view stresses what is good for the firm, therefore privileging the importance of customers or those whose actions will impact trade (e.g. maintaining a good relationship with a key supplier and paying them on time); whereas the full stakeholder view looks at everyone the firm can impact, even if they are not likely to affect or be affected by trade (Figure 17.7). Even this wider view can have business benefits. Consider the KitKat case from the beginning of the chapter. The orangutan is not a consumer of Nestlé products and the activists who campaigned against Nestlé were still a small minority of consumers, but the wider impact of this campaign had the potential to damage Nestlé's long-term reputation. Furthermore, stakeholders rarely fit into neat categories: someone might simultaneously be an employee, a shareholder, and a member of the local community (Hejjas et al., 2018).

Figure 17.7 How wide should stakeholder theory go?

Stakeholder theory also draws on business ethics. From a social justice (deontological) view-point, it argues that business actions should be fair. Drawing on communitarian ethics, it stresses the importance of placing the community above individual interests.

Certainly, from an ethical viewpoint stakeholder theory offers the potential for a more well-rounded view of the ethical responsibilities than the rather narrow definition of shareholder capitalism because it asks businesses to consider the overall benefits to society. Yet questions remain about how much organizations fully apply these principles.

Corporate social responsibility (CSR)

Few people and, in particular, few large-scale organizations today (at least publicly) support Friedman's claim that the only responsibility businesses have is to their shareholders. Increasing attention by the press, public awareness, and campaign groups have meant that firms have to respond to issues such as sweatshop labour and environmental pollution to protect their reputation and brand image. Many large firms are now ranked on their CSR ratings (Giamporcaro and Gold, 2016). Consequently, it is increasingly important to consider CSR (Freeman and Liedtka, 1991).

Aguinis and Gravas suggest, based on a review of 588 journal articles and 102 books and book chapters, that there are three main reasons for CSR:

1) instrumental or self-interest—it is good for the company in the long term;

2) relational—concern for the relationships that the firm has with others, i.e. customers and suppliers;

3) moral concerns—supporting ethical standards.

Companies such as Ford now stress their CSR credentials. In an interview with us, Joe Greenwell, the chairman of Ford in Britain, states that Henry Ford saw his purpose as 'broader than just making money', but in 'serving mankind' (Author interview with Joe Greenwell, Ford in Britain, 2012). Ford paid for schools and hospitals and got involved in the local community—something that lives on in Ford as a company. Greenwell states that all leaders within Ford throughout the world are engaged in some aspect of CSR. Ford, Greenwell says, 'clearly went beyond Milton Friedman' as he 'wanted to make the world a better place'. The pillars of Ford today—'quality, green, safe and smart'—carry on this legacy. 'Ford has given us such good opportunities and we want others to think well of it'. This is not just to do social good, but there 'is a certain amount of enlightened self-interest about it'.

 Visit the online resources and take a look at the extension material for Chapter 17 to see the full interview with Ford's Joe Greenwell.

Indeed, Adam Smith, who we met earlier, as well as writing *The wealth of nations* (1776/2012), also wrote *The theory of moral sentiments* (1759/1976), a book which suggested combining ethics with capitalism. In the Victorian era many business owners, particularly because of their Christian faith, became concerned about the ethics of their wealth, resulting in them setting up charities or, like Cadbury's, running their firms in a way that also looked after their workers. However, it was not until the 1950s that CSR became a serious concern within business and academia, starting with Howard Bowen (1953).

Bowen is considered the founder of CSR (Carroll, 1999). He argued that because business leaders have decision making power which impacts citizens, they have a responsibility to act in ways beyond money making but 'which are desirable in terms of the objectives and values of our society' (Bowen, 1953: 6). Interestingly, when surveyed, 93.5 per cent of business leaders agreed with this statement (Bowen, 1953).

Since Bowen's work was published, CSR has grown enormously as an academic discipline and business practice. Most businesses now consider it an important part of their practice (Carroll, 1999)—essential for building (or protecting) their reputation and demonstrating the positive impact they can have on society. Thus it has now become almost an obligatory requirement for most medium and large companies to issue CSR statements and reports and even to establish departments dedicated to CSR.

CSR draws on the ideas of Scottish industrialist and philanthropist Andrew Carnegie, the founder of US Steel. He believed that business is a positive force as it increases society's wealth. However, it required two key principles to be in place in order to work: (i) the charitable principle, where the more fortunate help the less fortunate; and (ii) the stewardship principle, where the rich hold the wealth 'in trust' for the rest of society (Fisher et al., 2013). Belief in these basic principles, combined with the belief that acting appropriately results in limited government intervention (particularly rules and regulations), has given CSR considerable credence in business circles (Freeman and Liedtka, 1991).

While there is no agreed definition of CSR (Carroll, 1999), there are a few common themes (Figure 17.8). Most definitions argue that businesses have obligations (something that an organization has to do) beyond their legal obligations (following the law) and economic obligations (making money for shareholders), towards society (for a discussion, see Carroll, 1999).

In this section we will argue that there are two main forms of enlightened self-interest. One is the damage limitation model, which sees CSR as a way of limiting the negative side-effects of the

Figure 17.8 Carroll's (1991) levels of corporate social responsibility (CSR).

Figure 17.9 Minimal and integrated corporate social responsibility (CSR).

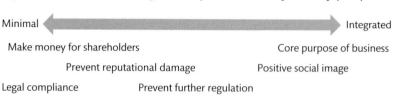

Minimal ⟵⟶ Integrated

Make money for shareholders   Core purpose of business

Prevent reputational damage   Positive social image

Legal compliance   Prevent further regulation

firm's activity. This view sees CSR coming into play only when there is a potential impact on the firm. The other is the model called ethical capitalism, which tries to integrate CSR into the heart of the firm's activities and trade on the benefits (Figure 17.9). Firms such as Innocent Smoothies, Yeo Valley milk, and Ben and Jerry's ice cream set themselves up as being more ethical in their approach, with the intention of customers buying into (and paying a premium for) more ethical and sustainable products.

These two positions can really be seen on a continuum, with many firms operating somewhere between them. The minimal CSR perspective argues that it is in a firm's self-interest to act in a responsible way because it will save money, avoid legislation, and prevent the brand being stained.

The rise of corporate social responsibility is said to produce numerous benefits for the firm. This is sometimes called the enlightened self-interest model. This could be seen as positive CSR (Kim et al., 2018) and may have various benefits.

- *Attracting better employees*—as companies compete in a 'war for talent', top employees are more likely to go to a company with good CSR credentials. Mesdaghinia et al. argue that unethical leaders have much higher levels of turnover, which in turn can lower productivity, cause drift, and even lead to a company's demise (2018). Sustainability can be inspiring to employees and increase motivation (Renwick et al., 2013). Anthony Carey, a partner with accountancy and audit firm Mazars, argues that this makes good business sense. 'If you want the most talented team members then you need a good ethical reputation. The most talented employees want to work for ethical businesses' (Carey, 2015). This is particularly important for attracting millennials, he claims, who have ethical values 'hardwired' into them.

- *Gaining more affluent customers*—having products that are Fairtrade, more sustainable, and ethically supported is often seen as attracting more affluent customers who can afford to pay more for ethical products. This can raise customer satisfaction (Agunis and Glavas, 2012) and firms with a good reputation with their customers also cope better with scandals and negative events and therefore protect the value of the firm (Kim et al., 2018).

- *Attracting shareholders* who do not want to be associated with unethical companies—in recent times ethical investment funds have emerged: for instance, those that do not invest in arms companies or tobacco producers.

- *Building long-term reputation*—speaking on BBC Radio 4 in 2011, Sir Martin Sorrell argued that if businesses are only interested in short-term profit then CSR does not matter. However, 'if you are in the business of building brands in the long term ... you will not do things that offend society, the environment and other stakeholders'. CSR should not be an add-on or a separate department or statement. CSR should be 'embedded in the strategy of the company. CSR therefore is an essential prerequisite for success, ensuring that the firm continues to be trusted by the public' (BBC Radio, 2011).

- *Avoiding legislation*—for instance, firms avoid giving off too much pollution in order to prevent more stringent legislation from being enacted. This is a critical reason for putting CSR in place and is seen in the long term as a way of reducing costs.

Does being ethical reduce profits?

CSR scholars (e.g. Aras and Crowther, 2012) argue that CSR and profitability are not only compatible but also essential. While unethical practices might, in the short term, produce a profit, in the long term they can have devastating impacts on a firm through negative implications on reputation, legislation, and employee commitment. In particular, as Carberry et al. argue, when unethical actions are revealed this can lead to the share price falling and often the CEO resigning as well (Carberry et al., 2018).

Evidence seems to suggest (see Capaldi, 2005) that firms that apply some CSR to their practices do better than those that are completely unethical, but also do better than those that really try to integrate their ethical practices. Overall 'firms with high social performance achieve better financial performance than firms with poor social performance' (Candi et al., 2018: 10). Melvin Tumin calls this the 'principle of least morality' (1964). It costs to be seen as really bad, but it is also expensive to do very good activity. The most financially prudent and successful way is to do just enough to be seen as not negative. CSR therefore could be seen as a source of competitive advantage. Firms need to weigh up the costs and benefits of positive and negative CSR to see which is the best option (Kim et al., 2018). It is arguable that enlightened self-interest is not really ethical at all. According to this view, doing a good act because it is for your own benefit could simply be considered as self-interest and does little to challenge the dominance of large-scale corporations (Banerjee, 2008).

Should organizational leaders be ethical?

Organizational leaders play an important role in setting organizational context and tone, as well as the expectations of their followers, and thus in setting the framework and culture for the ethical actions of their organizations. In recent years there has been increased interest in the idea of ethical leaders, examining the way that leaders conduct their personal actions, communication, and decision making and how this is connected with the outcomes of the organization. Ethical leaders are seen to be important as they provide their followers with a voice. Lam et al. argue 'Because ethical leaders emphasize two-way communication, voice should emerge because ethical leaders are more willing to listen to employees' (Lam et al., 2016: 278). These ethical leaders, Lam et al. state, reduce the turnover of staff and the cost of unethical behaviour throughout the organization, and they motivate workers better because jobs feel more meaningful (2016). These are seen in contrast to unethical leaders who simply pursue the bottom line (Mesdaghinia et al., 2018).

However, this focus on ethical leaders is also problematic. Munro and Thanem argue that the regularity of ethical scandals challenges the presupposition that leaders are more likely to be morally superior (Munro and Thanem, 2018). In an argument which echoes the critics of the romantic review of leadership (see Chapter 13), they argue that we should not be looking only to leaders, or assuming that replacing unethical leaders with more ethical ones will solve all our problems, as this reinforces problematic reliance on the leader–follower relationship. Instead they stress the room and possibilities for collective use of reason and therefore enhancing our understanding of the importance of followers.

Sustainability

Concern over climate change has put sustainability on the agenda for many organizations. While this is, in part, an environmental concern (using the earth's natural resources in a sustainable manner) it has also come to mean sustainability of the organization. It has therefore become quite a woolly concept and means different things to different people. However, a good working definition

635

has been provided by a Norwegian prime minister, Gro Harlem Brundtland: 'meeting the needs of the present without compromising the ability of future generations to meet their own needs' (World Commission on Environment and Development, 1987: 43).

↻ Real life case: car makers tell Trump that climate change is real

In May 2018 many of the top executives of the leading car producers in America went to the White House to tell President Trump to impose national standards over fuel efficiency and carbon-dioxide emissions. While some lobbyists were trying to reduce regulation, others were seeking to hold or even improve the standards. David Schwietert, executive vice president of federal government relations at the trade group, stated: 'Automakers remain committed to increasing fuel efficiency requirements, which yield everyday fuel savings for consumers while also reducing emissions—because climate change is real and we have a continuing role in reducing greenhouse gases and improving fuel efficiency' (quoted by Beene, 2018). Meanwhile in Europe a number of countries have sought to ban diesel and petrol cars by 2040, meaning that cars going into production now might not be able to be driven in their lifetime.

Every car manufacturer is now producing more environmentally friendly cars. We turn again to the author's interview with Joe Greenwell, chairman of Ford in Britain, who argues that the car industry 'bought the science [on climate change] a while back' and has been working on reducing the CO2 emissions of cars for many years.

It is necessary to comply with European legislation, but in our interview, Greenwell stated that it is 'not a compliance issue but a competitive race … as the customer in general sees the benefits'. He said climate change groups see the automobile industry as a good example of where 'regulation has been useful in encouraging us as a manufacturing group to compete with each other to get CO2 emissions down'.

Customers, however, have not bought into all eco-cars, largely because some are expensive, and Greenwell states that the industry believes there is more that it needs to do to convince them. 'The customer has to see value.' It has moved from compliance to competitive advantage as customers become more interested in eco-cars. He argued that low carbon technology is a tremendous opportunity for growth for car manufacturers.

Source: Author interview with Joe Greenwell, Ford in Britain, 2012.

 Visit the online resources and take a look at the extension material for Chapter 17 for the full interview with Joe Greenwell.

Triple bottom line

Whereas shareholder capitalism looks only to the 'bottom line' of profit, the idea of the 'triple bottom line' extends the organization's focus to include people and the planet (Figure 17.10).

Developed by John Elkington of consultancy firm SustainAbility, this approach works on the basis of measuring performance to improve the focus on people and planet. It aims to create a set of measures, called metrics, for all of a firm's activities. By measuring them the belief is that it will change the firm's behaviour. While profit is easy to measure, the impact on people and the planet is harder. Balancing the different bottom lines is also a challenge. However, this does represent an interesting way of putting into 'hard' terms (i.e. numbers) many of the social and environmental concerns that CSR and sustainability raise.

Figure 17.10 The triple bottom line.

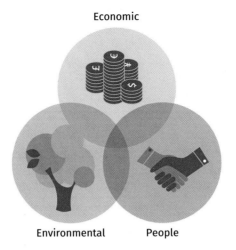

Economic

Environmental   People

Ethical capitalism

🔍 **Running case:** Chance needs to decide between money and reputation

Chance realizes that he is on the horns of a dilemma. Yes, the weddings are making a lot of money, but they are beginning to create a bad reputation for Junction Hotel, and this is hitting the business. He had heard that at a recent wedding fair at least two couples had said they did not want to get married at the hotel because of what they'd read in the papers about people getting drunk and aggressive. 'We need to turn this around,' he thinks, 'but how?' So, he calls in Linda Wilkinson for a meeting.

'We need to grab hold of the agenda and show that we are putting something back into the local economy,' Wilkinson suggests. 'How about we get all our food locally—sustainably, and seasonally. You know, local beef and pork, freshly-picked vegetables … people really go for that sort of thing. We could buy in local beer from the microbrewery and also start offering eco-weddings. Then, get it out in the paper to show that we are doing good things for this area—creating jobs and supporting the environment. You never know, we might even get a better class of customer and not have the same problems.'

Our third perspective extends the CSR/sustainability issue by arguing that rather than being an add-on to existing practice, ethics needs to be at the heart of business. A firm can no longer simply 'appear' ethical—they have to actually practise ethical behaviour; otherwise, in the world of social media, they will be found out. For instance, in his book *Who cares wins* David Jones claims that 'Consumers now know more about companies and expect more of them' (2012: 4). He argues that in the world of social media greater attention is placed on companies' ethical standards. It is not enough to appear ethical—they need to be ethical. Similarly, in *Screw business as usual* Sir Richard Branson (2011) argues that businesses should be a force for good in the world. He claims the boundaries between doing good and doing well are becoming merged. He writes that if he had 'one message' to help the next generation of entrepreneurs it is 'doing good can help improve your prospects, your profits and your business; and it can change the world' (2011: 2). The idea of a conflict between profits and being ethical is a 'false dilemma', Branson claims; 'business as usual isn't working. In fact, it's "business as usual" that's wrecking our planet. Resources are being used up; the air, the sea, the land—are all heavily polluted. The poor are getting poorer.' While capitalism has 'created economic growth in the world and brought many wonderful benefits to people [it has] come at a cost that is not reflected on the balance sheet' (2011: 20–1). Capitalism needs to adjust, Pfeffer and Kramer argue, to not be focused just on the bottom line but on wider issues, simply if it is to survive (2011).

Employability skills: put ethical actions on your CV

Both David Jones (2012) and Richard Branson (2011) argue that ethical capitalism is on the rise and, in the future, numerous jobs and businesses will focus on this emerging area of business. Branson claims that successful entrepreneurs will combine ethics and business, and Jones claims that consumers are driving businesses to greater social responsibility. These views are backed up by the professional services company KPMG, who state 'Business leaders are increasingly realizing the need to integrate environmental and social issues within the business strategy' (KPMG, 2011: 1). As we saw in the KitKat example, many feel that there is a need for businesses to be more aware of the ethical dimensions of their actions. Therefore, CSR and employability do not, necessarily, have to be seen in opposition.

As you develop your CV, including something that demonstrates a good understanding of CSR can be very useful. As Lord Michael Hastings (2008), KPMG's global head of citizenship and diversity, states: 'I think that any of the big FTSE 100 companies is utterly and expectantly approachable on CSR'. He goes on to say that when putting together your CV you should highlight things that you have done that have done good, not as extras under CSR but as an integral part of your CV. In doing so you will demonstrate that you 'love making a difference'. Finally, find a job where you feel you can make a positive impact on the world. This will turn your job from being a 'duty' to 'an opportunity to make a powerful difference in the world' around you.

? Review questions

Describe	What are the key principles behind stakeholder capitalism?
Explain	What is meant by the 'triple bottom line'?
Analyse	Why do stakeholder capitalism and ethical capitalism see shareholder capitalism as unsustainable, both for the planet *and* for the businesses concerned? Which position do you consider stronger, and why?
Apply	Consider a company that you know well and try to list all the stakeholders that you can think of (remember to include those in the supply chain and those who are indirectly impacted by the organization or might have an interest in it). Using the three models listed, which ones would fit in a legal, strategic, or wide definition of stakeholders? Which would you consider the most important and why?

'Ethical within capitalism'

While CSR and ethical capitalism have brought with them a number of benefits, for many academics and campaigners they do not go far enough. They state that an organization's primary purpose should be not to make money but to do social good: for example, to help particular communities and the environment, to promote particular causes, or to create more humane work practices.

 Real life case: Leeds Bread Coop

The Leeds Bread Coop are a social enterprise and worker coop who make artisan bread. Their values are at the heart of how they operate. They seek to make bread as socially and environmentally friendly as possible by ethically and where possible locally sourcing all their ingredients, minimizing packaging, and sourcing as much energy as possible from renewable sources. They also encourage all staff to have an input into developing new products so 'everyone has an intellectual stake in the business'. They have a flat wage structure and use consensus-based decision making. The members describe working for the coop as rewarding, feeling like a community rather than a company, and feeling collective, where people are genuinely concerned about your wellbeing.

https://leedsbread.coop/ and https://www.youtube.com/watch?v=UyNZ-RpAWMw&t=1s

Many of these alternative organizations are run on a not-for-profit basis, either reinvesting their surpluses back into the community or running things on a cost-only basis. Many are run as workers' cooperatives, which seek to make the workers central to the decision making processes (Parker et al., 2007; Cheney et al., 2014; Radical Routes, 2018).

Cooperatives have a long tradition. One of the most famous is the Rochdale Pioneers, a group of textile and other workers who came together to pool their resources in order to buy food and other household items. They were responding to the high prices that the mill owners charged and came together with a common goal of good service over profit.

The Rochdale Pioneers were working-class people who came together to offer self-help and tackle their own problems (rather than receiving handouts from middle-class philanthropists). They offered an alternative model of production and exchange. The principles of the Rochdale Pioneers continues to inform the core covalues of self-help, self-responsibility, democracy, equality, equity, and solidarity and the seven core co-operative principles stated by the Coop International Co-operative Alliance:

- Voluntary and Open Membership
- Democratic Member Control
- Member Economic Participation
- Autonomy and Independence
- Education, Training and Information
- Co-operation among Co-operatives
- Concern for Community

'Ethical within capitalism' organizations are not only driven by social purpose but, based on the idea of prefiguration, they seek to embody their values in how they operate (Reedy et al., 2016). One of the key ways this is done is by increasing participation in decision making. Many are run non-hierarchically so that power is distributed throughout the organization and decisions are based upon consensus rather than through orders from the leader (Parker, 2012; King and Land, 2018). Consensus-based decision making is not based on voting but involves reaching a genuine, informed agreement which everyone supports or can live with (Reedy et al., 2016). It aims to weave together the best ideas to allow the group to collectively formulate the most creative solutions (Reedy and King, 2017). The Seeds for Change activist group is one of the key trainers and proponents for consensus-based decision making. A group that wishes to use consensus could aim to put in place the following qualities:

- Common goal that everyone wants to be a part of.
- Commitment to reaching consensus by honestly listening to each other and being willing to shift your position to accommodate others.
- Trust and openness: everyone respects each other's opinions and right to express them.
- Sufficient time given for consensus making so that the right decisions are made.
- Clear process: making sure everyone understands the process.
- Active participation: create a situation where everyone can feel involved.

(Source: adapted from http://seedsforchange.org.uk/free/shortconsensus)

In doing so, these alternative organizations provide a direct challenge to many of the 'mainstream' practices that we have covered in this book (see Land and King, 2014; Parker et al., 2014; Griffin et al., 2015). They turn the pursuit of profit on its head by making the ambition for the organization to work for social good or to create employment opportunities where, in conventional terms, they would not exist.

 Real life case: alternative ways of organizing in Greece

Greece was one of the countries most severely hit by the 2007–8 economic crisis. Its sovereign debt crisis led to austerity, tax increases, large wage cuts, and very high levels of unemployment, particularly among young people, where official rates reached 51.9 per cent (Daskalaki and Kokkinidis, 2017). Due to these changes, not only did Greece see mass protests against the government, but also a number of experiments in alternative ways of organizing, including 'workers' occupied workplaces, art collectives, self-organized cooperatives, squats and alternative eco-communities' (Daskalaki, 2018: 155). These collectives and self-organized cooperatives set out to create employment, but also new ways of living and working. For instance, Pagkaki, a worker run café, says 'instead of surrendering to the defeat of poverty and despair, people attempt to provide collective solutions to the problem of daily survival' (http://pagkaki.org/en, 2018). Running as a worker collective, something not yet represented in Greek law, they all have taken a risk in setting it up but can also all benefit from its success. Not only do they run a café but they have a bookshop and also work with other cooperatives in the Worker Cooperatives' Network of Athens, a network of mutual support (Varkarolis and King, 2017). Another example is workers taking control and reopening factories which had previously shut down. One such factory, Vio.Me.SI, has over 1,000 'solidarity supporters' who commit to buying a certain number of products from the factory, ensuring that it can survive. These experiments show that other ways of organizing are possible, although they can be hard to achieve.

'Ethical within capitalism' models do not focus primarily on what is most effective or efficient in traditional management terms (i.e. profit) but, instead, direct their attention to what maximizes human freedom, growth, and personal autonomy. They therefore offer a different model not only of what organizations can be, but also of the type of society and culture that they would like to create (Parker et al., 2014). As Richard Wolff argues, reorganizing workplaces to make them more participatory and democratic 'would effectively end capitalism' (Wolff, 2012: 13). The focus on mutual aid, community, personal growth, expression, and empowerment is often seen by members as working in direct opposition to the consumerism of much of Western society (Parker et al., 2007; Radical Routes, 2018).

While small in number in comparison with the power and influence of large corporations that tend to dominate society and business, these organizations do cover a wide variety of areas including housing, food, transport, and even construction. Many work in education, often teaching people long-forgotten skills to help them become more independent in their lives and build up community bonds to become less reliant on large-scale corporations. In doing so they aim for more sustainable and ethical organizations and, with them, a reform of society.

This perspective, therefore, challenges most of the underlying assumptions of business and management education. Most business and management education takes for granted the large-scale corporation as the default way of organizing and maximizing profit for shareholders as the primary (and largely unquestioned) purpose of the organization. In a recent book, provocatively titled *Shut down the business school: What's wrong with management education*, Martin Parker argues that the education provided within business schools has created a culture of short-termism and greed which is bad for workers, society, and the environment (2018). He argues that business and management schools should be transformed as 'schools for organizing', opening up alternative forms of organizing to even include focusing on other forms of organization such as circuses, gangs, Occupy, the Mafia, and utopias. Parker therefore encourages us to think again about our assumptions of what we learn about as normal and taken-for-granted at university.

Visit the online resources and take a look at the web links for Chapter 17 for a list of alternative organizations.

641

'Ethical within capitalism' assessed

> **Q Running case:** Chance tries to balance ethics and profits
>
> Chance considers Wilkinson's views—they make sense. The more he thinks about it the more he begins to see possibilities for environmental and social improvements within the hotel. Some, he comes to realize, could actually save money: better loft insulation, eco-lights, reduction of food waste, key-cards for rooms to switch off electricity, and reducing the washing of towels. Others, though, might be more expensive, such as trying to get the hotel to reach zero carbon emissions (which would require refitting the whole hotel), insulating the whole building, or buying only organic food. 'There's only so far I can go, really,' Chance thinks to himself. 'It is a challenge balancing profits with ethics.'

Non-capitalist organizations place their emphasis on community, empowerment, personal growth, and social change and offer us a fascinating and exciting vision of how organizations and society could be (Reedy et al., 2016). However, sometimes they fail to live up to their ideals, having their own prejudices and blind spots. For instance, Sherryl Kleinman (1996) describes a holistic health centre which, while run on alternative grounds, allegedly ends up reproducing the same practices of exclusion, power, and gendered relations that many accuse mainstream organizations of doing. Such schemes can also be hard to implement, as Daniel found when he tried to introduce democracy into a small charity (King and Land, 2018). Despite the chair and most of the workers wanting democratic organization, they could not reach a consensus over what they wanted. They therefore faced a contradiction: they needed some form of power to impose democracy on them.

'Ethical against capitalism'

Think about some of the big issues that are in the news at the moment: climate change, the housing crisis and 'generation rent', automation and the potential loss of countless jobs. While these are often seen as individual issues for many campaigners and some academics, particularly those of the critical management and Marxist perspectives, the underlying cause of all these problems may be found in the economic system. Inspired by critics of capitalism, such as Marx and Engels, and anarchists, such as Proudhon (2011), many thinkers argue that the capitalist system is fundamentally exploitative and destructive: with its relentless focus on growth and profit, it is destructive to the environment, to people, and to society. It breeds inequality, exploitation, and social division and, through this, makes everyone poorer. It makes humans compete with each other rather than cooperate. According to this view, we are all trapped in an economic system that we have very little control over. It also holds us back from reaching our true human creative potential. Capitalism also perpetuates inequality by drawing wealth towards the rich and away from the poor.

One of the most well-known critics of mainstream capitalism is Naomi Klein. Her first book *No logo* critiqued the modern obsession with consumerism and the way massive corporations, such as McDonald's, continually bombard us with advertising and branding. Similarly she demonstrated how workers are exploited by these large corporations moving their production to ever cheaper countries (Klein, 1999). In 2007, at the time of the global financial crisis, Klein provided an alternative economic history by showing how ideas of free-market, neo-liberal capitalism, particularly as supported by Milton Friedman, resulted in economic crisis, debt, hyperinflation and the devastating impacts that these events have (Klein, 2008). Her most recent book, *No is not enough*, argues not only for a critique of capitalism but that we as individuals and collectively can produce a better society (Klein, 2018).

While many of the 'ethical against capitalism' perspectives stress the problems of capitalism and the need to overturn it, radical feminist geographers who go by the pen name Gibson-Graham argue that we tend to think of capitalism as one monolithic system that dominates, but that in fact there are multiple different forms of economic activity that are not 'capitalist' and that we should explore and develop these (Gibson-Graham, 2006). In developing them and acting in them, we can become different (non-capitalist) people who see and act in the world in a different way. For Gibson-Graham this offers us a more economical, ecological, and fulfilling future.

 Connecting case and theory

Throughout this chapter Simon Chance faced a struggle between the desire to make profits for shareholders and the concerns of the local community. The weddings held at Junction Hotel were bringing in money, but also 'drunken yobs' and 'blocked traffic' and with it complaints from the local residents and also unwanted newspaper headlines. While Phil Weaver dismissed it as unimportant, in a view that echoed Milton Friedman's that the sole goal of the organization is to make money for shareholders, Linda Wilkinson and significantly Ian Terry, one of the investors, were concerned that it was impacting the reputation and potentially profits of the hotel. Notably, Terry is also a resident in the local area. Shareholders therefore do not just have their interest in the profits of an organization, but are also other forms of stakeholders, including resident of the local community. As R. Edward Freeman argues, organizations have multiple stakeholders, including local communities, the environment, employees, etc., not least because share-holders can often be other stakeholders as well.

One way of working through the hotel's dilemma between making profits and the interest of other stakeholders was provided by Linda Wilkinson. In an approach that drew on ideas of sustainability, Wilkinson argued that Junction Hotel should support the local economy by buying from local suppliers and also emphasizing this practice to cus-tomers (who might pay more for these products). Simon Chance, taking on this approach, also looked at more sustainable ways of managing the hotel, including better-quality insulation, that might actually save money in the future.

The balance between the different needs of stakeholders is a challenge for managers in organizations. Therefore, as Martin Parker has recently argued (2018), management education needs to go beyond simply thinking about maximizing profit for shareholders and to consider the wider interests of society and also alternative ways of organizing.

Further reading

Boje, D.M. 1998. Nike, Greek goddess of victory or cruelty? Women's stories of Asian factory life. *Journal of Organizational Change Management* 11 (6): 461–80.

In this controversial article, David Boje describes some of the key criticisms made of a factory making Nike products, including physical and verbal abuse of the workers, long hours, and low pay. What is most fascinating is that the article was originally withdrawn by the journal—visit the online resources for links to the original article and to read Boje's own explanation of what happened.

Klein, N. 2018. No is not enough: Defeating the new shock politics. Penguin: London.

Naomi Klein offers a far-reaching critique of capitalism and conventional society, challenging many of our assumptions and also offering some possibilities for producing new forms of society.

Ngai, P. 2004. Women workers and precarious employment in Shenzhen Special Economic Zone, China. *Gender and Development* 12 (2): 29–36.

This interesting article describes the difficult working conditions of garment workers in China. While it is a little dated, recent case studies have shown that these conditions continue in many developing countries.

Parker, M. 2018. *Shut down the business school: What's wrong with management education.* Pluto Press: London.

A polemical critique of the business school and the education that is provided within it. Parker challenges the assumptions of mainstream management theory and practice and offers an alternative: the school for organizing.

References

Ackrill, M., and Hannah, L. 2001. *Barclays: The business of banking, 1690–1996.* Cambridge University Press: Cambridge.

Aguinis, H., & Glavas, A. 2012. What we know and don't know about corporate social re-sponsibility: A review and research agenda. *Journal of Management* 38 (4): 932–68.

Alvaredo, F., Chancel, L., Piketty, T., Saez, E., and Zucman, G. 2018. World Inequality Report 2018. Available at: http://wir2018.wid.world/files/download/wir2018-full-report-english.pdf

643

Aras, G., and Crowther, D. 2012. *Governance and social responsibility: International perspectives*. Palgrave: London.

Arnold, M., and Binham, C. 2015. City of London 'black book' is called for to track 'bad apple' traders. *Financial Times*, 19 February.

Bakan, J. 2005. *The corporation: The pathological pursuit of profit and power*. Constable and Robinson: London.

Banerjee, S. 2008. Corporate social responsibility: The good, the bad and the ugly. *Critical Sociology* 34 (1): 51–79.

Bates, D. 2015. The chocolate companies on the hunt for a sustainable Easter egg. *The Guardian*, 27 March.

Bawden, T., and Sheffield, H. 2015. Petrobras scandal adds to $16.8b losses: How gang allegedly used Spanx and cling film to smuggle millions. *The Independent*, 23 April.

BBC News. 2014. Penalise 'bad apple' traders, suggests Bank of England, 27 October. Available at: https://www.bbc.co.uk/news/business-29788270

BBC News. 2015. New measures pledge to make Scottish NHS whistleblowing easier. Available at: http://www.bbc.co.uk/news/uk-scotland-scotland-politics-33224516 (last accessed 2 July 2015).

BBC Radio 4. 2011. Desert island discs: Martin Sorrell. Available at: http://www.bbc.co.uk/radio/player/b017vjlw (last accessed 28 November 2012).

BBC Television. 2011a. *Newsnight*. BBC 2, 13 June.

BBC Television. 2011b. When bankers were good. BBC2, 23 November.

Beene, R. 2018. 'Climate change is real,' carmakers tell White House in letter. Bloomberg. Available at: https://www.bloomberg.com/news/articles/2018-05-21/carmakers-tell-white-house-that-climate-change-is-real-in-letter

Boatright, J.R. 2013. Confronting ethical dilemmas in the workplace. *Financial Analysts Journal* 69 (5): 6–9.

Böhm, S., Misoczky, M.C., and Moog, S. 2012. Greening capitalism? A Marxist critique of carbon markets. *Organization Studies* 33 (11): 1617–38.

Bowen, H. 1953. *Social responsibilities of the businessman*. Harper & Row: New York.

Branson, R. 2011. *Screw business as usual*. Virgin Books: London.

Burt, E. 2018. Anger as Carillion bosses share £4m bonuses despite liquidation. *People Management*, 16 January. Available at: https://www.peoplemanagement.co.uk/news/articles/carillion-bosses-share-bonuses

Candi, M., Melia, M., and Colurcio, M. 2018. Two birds with one stone: The quest for addressing both business goals and social needs with innovation. *Journal of Business Ethics*, published online: https://doi.org/10.1007/s10551-018-3853-y.

Capaldi, N. 2005. Corporate social responsibility and the bottom line. *International Journal of Social Economics* 32 (5): 408–23.

Carberry, E.J., Engelen, P.J., and Van Essen, M. 2018. Which firms get punished for unethical behavior? Explaining variation in stock market reactions to corporate misconduct. *Business Ethics Quarterly* 28 (2): 119–51.

Carey, A. 2015. The board charter. Interview with Daniel King.

Carlyle, E. 2012. Meet the eight Forbes 400 billionaires who just signed the Giving Pledge. Forbes. Available at: http://www.forbes.com/sites/erincarlyle/2012/09/18/forbes-400-billionaires-whove-signed-the-giving-pledge/ (last accessed 24 November 2012).

Carroll, A. 1991. The pyramid of corporate social responsibility: Toward the moral management of organizational stakeholders. *Business Horizons* 34: 39–48.

Carroll, A. 1999. Corporate social responsibility: Evolution of a definitional construct. *Business Society* 38: 268–95.

Chatterji, A., and Toffel, M. 2018. The new CEO activists. *Harvard Business Review* 96 (1) (January–February): 78–89.

Cheney, G., Santa Cruz, I., Peredo, A.M., and Nazareno, E. 2014. Worker cooperatives as an organizational alternative: Challenges, achievements and promise in business governance and ownership. *Organization* 21 (5): 591–603.

CIPD. 2017. Executive pay review of FTSE 100 executive pay packages. High Pay Centre. Available at: http://highpaycentre.org/files/7571_CEO_pay_in_the_FTSE100_report_%28FINAL%29.pdf

Cohen, E. and King, D. 2017. Human resource management: Developing sustainability mindsets. In: Molthan-Hill, P. (ed.) *The business student's guide to sustainable management: Principles and practice*. Greenleaf Publishing: Sheffield, pp. 259–85.

Connors, W., and Trevisani, P. 2015. World News: Brazil 'carwash' shrugs off ties to corruption scandal. *Wall Street Journal, Europe*, 23 June.

Costas, R. 2014. Petrobras scandal: Brazil's energy giant under pressure. Available at: http://www.bbc.co.uk/news/business-30129184 (last accessed 2 July 2015).

Covey, S. 2004. *The 7 habits of highly effective people*. Simon and Schuster: London.

Crouch, D. 2015. Swedish private jet scandal claims seventh scalp. *The Guardian*, 11 February.

Daskalaki, M. 2018. Alternative organizing in times of crisis: Resistance assemblages and socio-spatial solidarity. *European Urban and Regional Studies* 25 (2): 155–70.

Daskalaki, M., and Kokkinidis, G. 2017. Organizing solidarity initiatives: A socio-spatial conceptualization of resistance. *Organization Studies* 38 (9): 1303–25.

Davies, A. 2018. Death in the sun: Australia's 88-day law leaves backpackers exploited and exposed. *The Guardian*, 21 May. Available at: https://www.theguardian.com/australia-news/2018/may/21/death-in-the-sun-australias-88-day-law-leaves-backpackers-exploited-and-exposed

Davis, K. 1973. The case for and against business assumption of social responsibilities. *Academy of Management Journal* 16 (2): 312–22.

Dellheim, C. 1987. The creation of a company culture: Cadburys 1861–1931. *American Historical Review* 92 (1): 13–44.

Devlin, H. 2018. Why is asbestos still killing people? *The Guardian*, 18 May. Available at: https://www.theguardian.com/science/audio/2018/may/18/why-is-asbestos-still-killing-people-science-weekly-podcast

Drury, C. 2018. Mark Carney warns robots taking jobs could lead to rise of Marxism. *The Independent*, 14 April. Available at: https://www.independent.co.uk/news/uk/home-news/mark-carney-marxism-automation-bank-of-england-governor-job-losses-capitalism-a8304706.html

DutchNews. 2018. Hema fined €4.5m for selling jeans which look too much like Levi's. *DutchNews*, 17 May. Available at: https://www.dutchnews.nl/news/2018/05/hema-fined-e4-5m-for-selling-jeans-which-look-too-much-like-levis/

Edelman. 2018. 2018 Edelman trust barometer: Expectations for CEOs. Available at: https://www.edelman.com/sites/default/files/2018-04/Edelman_Trust_Barometer_Implications_for_CEOs_2018.pdf

Elliott, L. 2018. Inequality gap widens as 42 people hold same wealth as 3.7bn poorest. *The Guardian*, 22 January. Available at: https://www.theguardian.com/inequality/2018/jan/22/inequality-gap-widens-as-42-people-hold-same-wealth-as-37bn-poorest

Ellison, K. 2018. Rewarding or hoarding: An examination of pay ratios revealed by Dodd-Frank. Available at: https://ellison.house.gov/sites/ellison.house.gov/files/Rewarding%20Or%20Hoarding%20Full%20Report.pdf

Fisher, C., and Lovell, A. 2009. *Business ethics and values: Individual, corporate and international perspectives*. Prentice Hall: Harlow.

Fisher, C., Lovell, A., and Valero-Silva, N. 2013. *Business ethics and values*. Prentice Hall: Harlow.

Forbes. 2018. Jeff Bezos. Available at: https://www.forbes.com/profile/jeff-bezos/

Ford Foundation. 2018. History. Available at: https://www.fordfoundation.org/regions/united-states/history/ (last accessed 22 May 2018).

Freeman, E., and Liedtka, J. 1991. Corporate social responsibility: A critical approach. *Business Horizons* 34 (4): 92–8.

Friedman, M. 1970. The social responsibility of business is to increase its profits. *New York Times Magazine*, 13 September.

Gandel, S. 2018. Wells Fargo leaves a potential subprime smudge on its way to squeaky clean. Bloomberg. Available at: https://www.bloomberg.com/gadfly/articles/2018-04-24/wells-fargo-leaves-a-potential-smudge-in-squeaky-clean

Gayle, D. 2018. Timeline: Oxfam sexual exploitation scandal in Haiti. *The Guardian*, 15 June. Available at: https://www.theguardian.com/world/2018/jun/15/timeline-oxfam-sexual-exploitation-scandal-in-haiti

Gelles, D. 2018. Want to make money like a C.E.O.? Work for 275 years. *New York Times*, 25 May. Available at: https://www.nytimes.com/2018/05/25/business/highest-paid-ceos-2017.html

Giamporcaro, S., and Gond, J.-P. 2016. Calculability as politics in the construction of markets: The case of socially responsible investment in France. *Organization Studies* 37 (4): 465–95.

Gibson-Graham, J.K. 2006. *A postcapitalist politics*. University of Minnesota Press: Minneapolis.

Gies, E. 2014. Greenpeace report on P&G's palm oil sources could spur industry change. *The Guardian*, 31 March.

Gill, V. 2018. '100,00 orangutans' killed in 16 years. BBC News. Available at: http://www.bbc.co.uk/news/science-environment-42994630

Gilligan, C. 1982. *In a different voice: Psychological theory and women's development*. Harvard University Press: Cambridge, MA.

Giving Pledge. 2018. Website. Available at: http://givingpledge.org/ (last accessed 17 July 2018).

Gov.uk. 2018. Whistleblowing for employees. Available at: https://www.gov.uk/whistleblowing (last accessed 21 May 2018).

Grant, J. 2015. Bank of England acts to encourage whistleblowers. *Financial Times*, 11 June.

Gray, A. 2017. Berkshire takes on $1.5bn asbestos risk from Hartford. *Financial Times*, 3 January. Available at: https://www.ft.com/content/a218bc54-d1cf-11e6-9341-7393bb2e1b51

Greenpeace. 2010. Ask Nestlé CEO to stop buying palm oil from destroyed rainforest. Available at: http://www.youtube.com/watch?v=1BCA8dQfGi0 (last accessed 28 November 2012).

Greenpeace. 2013. Certifying destruction. http://www.greenpeace.org/international/Global/international/publications/forests/2013/Indonesia/RSPO-Certifying-Destruction.pdf (last accessed 5 July 2015).

Griffin, M., Learmonth, M., and Elliott, C. 2015. Non-domination, contestation and freedom: The contribution of Philip Pettit to learning and democracy in organisations. *Management Learning* 46 (3): 317–36.

Grove, J. 2017. Departing Bath Spa v-c paid £808K in final year. *Time Higher Education*, 6 December. Available at: https://www.timeshighereducation.com/news/departing-bath-spa-v-c-paid-ps808k-final-year

Hancock, E. 2018. Plastic straws could be banned throughout England. Drinks Business, April. Available at: https://www.thedrinksbusiness.com/2018/04/plastic-straws-could-be-banned-throughout-england/

Hardin, G. 1968. The tragedy of the commons. *Science* 162 (3859): 1243–8.

Hastings, M. 2008. Everyone's talking about corporate social responsibility. YouTube. Available at: http://www.youtube.com/watch?v=TNKn93VViUc (last accessed 24 November 2012).

Hawkshaw, R., Hawkshaw, S., and Sumaila, U.R. 2012. The tragedy of the 'Tragedy of the commons': Why coining too good a phrase can be dangerous. *Sustainability* 4 (11): 3141–50.

Heffernan, M. 2011. *Wilful blindness: Why we ignore the obvious*. Simon and Schuster: New York.

Hejjas, K., Miller, G., and Scarles, C. 2018. 'It's like hating puppies!' Employee disengagement and corporate social responsibility. *Journal of Business Ethics*, published online: https://doi.org/10.1007/s10551-018-3791-8.

Hibbert, P., and Cunliffe, A. 2015. Responsible management: Engaging moral reflexive practice through threshold concepts. *Journal of Business Ethics* 127 (1): 177–88.

Hickman, M. 2009. Have a break—have an ethical Kit Kat. *The Independent*, 23 October. Available at: http://www.independent.co.uk/life-style/food-and-drink/news/have-a-breakndash-have-an-ethical-kit-kat-1835608.html (last accessed 11 July 2012).

Izadi, E. 2018. Harvey Weinstein indicted on new sexual assault charges, could face life in prison. *Washington Post*, 2 July. Available at: https://www.washingtonpost.com/news/arts-and-entertainment/wp/2018/07/02/harvey-weinstein-indicted-on-new-sexual-assault-charges-could-face-life-in-prison/?noredirect=on&utm_term=.e34b6cee675d

Jago, A.S., and Pfeffer, J. 2018. Organizations appear more unethical than individuals. *Journal of Business Ethics*, published online: https://doi.org/10.1007/s10551-018-3811-8.

Jones, D. 2012. *Who cares wins: Why good business is better business*. FT Publishing: London.

Kenny, K. 2018. Censored: Whistleblowers and impossible speech. *Human Relations* 71 (8): 1025–48.

Klein, N. 1999. *No logo: Taking aim at the brand bullies*. Picador: New York.

Klein, N. 2008. *The shock doctrine: The rise of disaster capitalism*. Picador: New York.

Klein, N. 2018. *No is not enough: Defeating the new shock politics*. Penguin: London.

Kleinman, S. 1996. *Opposing ambitions: Gender and identity in an alternative organization*. University of Chicago Press: Chicago.

Kim, K.H., Kim, M., and Qian, C. 2018. Effects of corporate social responsibility on corporate financial performance: A competitive-action perspective. *Journal of Management* 44 (3): 1097–118.

King, D., and Land, C. 2018. The democratic rejection of democracy: Performative failure and the limits of critical performativity in an organizational change project. *Human Relations* 71 (11): 1535–57.

King, D., and Learmonth, M. 2015. Can critical management studies ever be 'practical'? A case study in engaged scholarship. *Human Relations* 68 (3): 353–75.

KPMG. 2011. *Corporate responsibility survey 2011: Marching towards embracing sustainability development*. KPMG: India. Available at: http://www.kpmg.com/IN/en/IssuesAndInsights/ArticlesPublications/Documents/Corporate-Responsibilty-Survey-Report.pdf (last accessed 24 November 2012).

Lam, L.W., Loi, R., Chan, K.W., and Liu, Y. 2016. Voice more and stay longer: How ethical leaders influence employee voice and exit intentions. *Business Ethics Quarterly* 26 (3): 277–300.

Land, C., and King, D. 2014. Organizing otherwise: Translating anarchism in a voluntary sector organization. *Ephemera* 14 (4): 923–50.

Latan, H., Jabbour, C.J.C., and de Sousa Jabbour, A.B.L. 2018. 'Whistleblowing triangle': Framework and empirical evidence. *Journal of Business Ethics*, published online: https://doi.org/10.1007/s10551-018-3862-x.

Levin, S. 2017. Uber's scandals, blunders and PR disasters: The full list. *The Guardian*, 18 June. Available at: https://www.theguardian.com/technology/2017/jun/18/uber-travis-kalanick-scandal-pr-disaster-timeline

Levy, D.L., and Spicer, A. 2013. Contested imaginaries and the cultural political economy of climate change. *Organization* 20 (5): 659–78.

Lin, X., Chen, Z.X., Herman, H.M., Wei, W., and Ma, C. 2017. Why and when employees like to speak up more under humble leaders? The roles of personal sense of power and power distance. *Journal of Business Ethics*, published online: https://doi.org/10.1007/s10551-017-3704-2.

MacIntyre, A. 1967. *A short history of ethics: A history of moral philosophy from the Homeric age to the twentieth century*. Routledge: London.

Marx, K. 1859/2012. *A contribution to the critique of political economy.* Forgotten Books: London.

Mesdaghinia, S., Rawat, A., and Nadavulakere, S. 2018. Why moral followers quit: Examining the role of leader bottom-line mentality and unethical pro-leader behavior. *Journal of Business Ethics,* published online: https://doi.org/10.1007/s10551-018-3812-7.

Milne, R. 2015. Sweden flies into a corporate storm. *Financial Times,* 21 January.

Milne, R. 2016. Jet scandal redraws Sweden's corporate landscape. *Financial Times,* 29 August. Available at: https://www.ft.com/content/926d90e2-6b7a-11e6-a0b1-d87a9fea034f

Milne, R. 2017. Top Swedish executive probed for suspected elk hunting bribery. *Financial Times,* 27 January. Available at: https://www.ft.com/content/a88bd06a-e455-11e6-8405-9e5580d6e5fb

Monbiot, G. 2018. The UK government wants to put a price on nature—but that will destroy it. *The Guardian,* 15 May. Available at: https://www.theguardian.com/commentisfree/2018/may/15/price-natural-world-destruction-natural-capital

Munro, I., and Thanem, T. 2018. The ethics of affective leadership: Organizing good encounters without leaders. *Business Ethics Quarterly* 28 (1): 51–69.

Muringatheri, M. 2015. Protect whistle-blowers, says bank union. *The Hindu,* 29 June.

Neate, R. 2012. RBS boss Stephen Hester waives bonus: Reaction. *The Guardian,* 30 January. Available at: http://www.guardian.co.uk/business/2012/jan/30/rbs-stephen-hester-bonus-reaction (last accessed 26 November 2012).

Nestlé. 2018. Response to author query from Nestlé. Customer Services. Enquiry 14853040, May 2018.

Packard Foundation. 2018. Website. Available at: https://www.packard.org/

Packham, C. 2018. Palm oil producers are wiping out orangutans—despite multinationals' promises. *The Guardian,* 10 May. Available at: https://www.theguardian.com/commentisfree/2018/may/10/palm-oil-orangutans-multinationals-promises-deforestation

Parker, M. 2012. Super flat: Hierarchy, culture and dimensions of organizing. *Research in the Sociology of Organizations* 35: 229–47.

Parker, M., Cheney, G., Fournier, V., and Land, C. (eds) 2014. *The Routledge companion to alternative organization.* Routledge: London.

Parker, M., Fournier, V., and Reedy, P. 2007. *The dictionary of alternatives.* Zed Books: London.

Partington, A. 1998. *The Oxford dictionary of quotations.* Oxford University Press: Oxford.

PCAW. 2015. The UK whistleblowing report: Public concern at work, 20 May.

Perkins, A. 2018. Cotton buds and plastic straws could be banned in England next year. *The Guardian,* 19 April. Available at: https://www.theguardian.com/environment/2018/apr/18/single-use-plastics-could-be-banned-in-england-next-year

Porter, M.E., and Kramer, M.R. 2011. The big idea: Creating shared value. *Harvard Business Review* (1): 2.

Pratley, N. 2018. Jeff Fairburn's tin ear makes Persimmon the home of executive greed. *The Guardian,* 23 February. Available at: https://www.theguardian.com/business/2018/feb/23/jeff-fairburns-tin-ear-makes-persimmon-the-home-of-executive-greed

Proudhon, P. 2011. *Property is theft! A Pierre-Joseph Proudhon reader.* AK Press: London.

Radical Routes. 2018. Aims and principles. Available at: http://www.radicalroutes.org.uk/aims-and-principles.html (last accessed 17 July 2018).

Rainforest Rescue. 2018. 5-minute info—palm oil. Available at: https://www.rainforest-rescue.org/topics/palm-oil#start

Ramesh, R. 2016. 1MDB: The inside story of the world's biggest financial scandal. *The Guardian,* 28 July. Available at: https://www.theguardian.com/world/2016/jul/28/1mdb-inside-story-worlds-biggest-financial-scandal-malaysia

Reedy, P.C., and King, D.R. 2017. Critical performativity in the field: Methodological principles for activist ethnographers. *Organizational Research Methods*, published online: https://doi.org/10.1177/1094428117744881

Reedy, P., King, D., and Coupland, C. 2016. Organizing for individuation: Alternative organizing, politics and new identities. *Organization Studies* 37 (11): 1553–73.

Renwick, D.W., Redman, T., and Maguire, S. 2013. Green human resource management: A review and research agenda. *International Journal of Management Reviews* 15 (1): 1–14.

Rhodes, C., and Bloom, P. 2018. The trouble with charitable billionaires. *The Guardian*, 24 May. Available at: https://www.theguardian.com/news/2018/may/24/the-trouble-with-charitable-billionaires-philanthrocapitalism?CMP=share_btn_link

Robinson, N. 2012. *Live from Downing Street: The inside story of politics, power and the media*. Bantam Press: London.

Skilton, P.F., and Purdy, J.M. 2017. Authenticity, power, and pluralism: A framework for understanding stakeholder evaluations of corporate social responsibility activities. *Business Ethics Quarterly* 27 (1): 99–123.

Smith, A. 1759/1976. *The theory of moral sentiments*. Clarendon Press: Oxford.

Smith, A. 1776/2012. *The wealth of nations*. Wordsworth Editions Ltd: Ware.

Smith, M., Valle, S., and Schmidt, B. 2015. The betrayal of Brazil. *Bloomberg Business*, 8 May.

Snell, J. 2011. Why a critic of institutional care is taking over from Southern Cross. *The Guardian*, 19 October. Available at: http://www.guardian.co.uk/society/2011/oct/19/interview-anne-williams-hc-one?newsfeed=true (last accessed 24 November 2012).

Spicer, A., Lindley, D., Gond, J-P., Mosonyi, S., Jaser, Z., Marti, E., Petersen, H., and Edwards, A. 2016. *Cultural change in the FCA, PRA & Bank of England: Practising what they preach?* New City Agenda/Cass Business School: London.

Tabacek, K. 2010. Nestlé stars in smear campaign over Indonesian palm oil. *The Guardian*, 18 March. Available at: http://www.guardian.co.uk/sustainable-business/nestleindonesian-palm-oil (last accessed 11 July 2012).

The Guardian. 2018. Lloyds faces shareholder revolt as CEO's pay is 95 times that of average worker, 18 May. Available at: https://www.theguardian.com/business/2018/may/18/lloyds-faces-shareholder-revolt-as-ceo-pay-is-95-times-that-of-average-worker

Treanor, J. 2017. World's biggest banks face £264bn bill for poor conduct. *The Guardian*, 14 August. Available at: https://www.theguardian.com/business/2017/aug/14/worlds-biggest-banks-face-264bn-bill-for-poor-conduct

Tumin, M. 1964. Business as a social system. *Behavioral Science* 9 (2): 120–30.

UNPRME. 2015. Six principles. Available at: http://www.unprme.org/about-prme/the-six-principles.php

Van Der Linden, B., and Freeman, R.E. 2017. Profit and other values: Thick evaluation in decision making. *Business Ethics Quarterly* 27 (3): 353–79.

Varkarolis, O., and King, D. 2017. Voicing researched activists with responsive action research. *Qualitative Research in Organizations and Management* 12 (4): 315–34.

Waters, R. 2017. Bill Gates calls for income tax on robots. *Financial Times*, 19 February. Available at: https://www.ft.com/content/d04a89c2-f6c8-11e6-9516-2d969e0d3b65

Watson, C. 2018. The key moments from Mark Zuckerberg's testimony to Congress. *The Guardian*, 11 April. Available at: https://www.theguardian.com/technology/2018/apr/11/mark-zuckerbergs-testimony-to-congress-the-key-moments

Wilkinson, R., and Pickett, K. 2010. *The spirit level: Why equality is better for everyone*. Allen Lane, Penguin: London.

Wittneben, B.B., Okereke, C., Banerjee, S.B., and Levy, D.L. 2012. Climate change and the emergence of new organizational landscapes. *Organization Studies* 33 (11): 1431–50.

649

Wolff, R.D. 2012. *Democracy at work: A cure for capitalism*. Haymarket books: Chicago.

World Commission on Environment and Development (WCED). 1987. *Our common future*. Oxford University Press: Oxford.

Yeates, C. 2018. Female-only AMP board resignations reflect 'cultural issues': Rubin.

Sydney Morning Herald, 17 May. Available at: https://www.smh.com.au/business/banking-and-finance/female-only-amp-board-resignations-reflect-cultural-issues-rubin-20180517-p4zfyl.html

Zerubavel, E. 2006. *The elephant in the room: Silence and denial in everyday life*. Oxford University Press: Oxford.

CHAPTER 18
Bringing it all together
Fond farewells

Chapter overview and learning outcomes

By the end of this chapter you should be able to:

- explain the importance of connecting organizational behaviour theories together

- apply some of the study skill strategies to developing your assessments

- analyse why it is important to develop your lifelong learning skills

Bringing everything together

Q Running case: Meg Mortimer's last day

'It is 6 am and you are listening to Calm FM,' Meg Mortimer's radio blurts out in the same way as it has every morning for the last 40 years. 'The headlines today ...,' the presenter drones on in his usual way, with Meg playing little attention. For her, today there is only one headline ... it is her last day at work.

It feels surreal knowing that this routine, which she has come to know so well, is going to be her last: getting up at 6 am and having breakfast—two slices of toast; shower at 6:20 am; walking the dog at 6:40 am; driving to work at 7 am (she'll be pleased not to have to battle through the traffic and that queue on London Road again); in the cubbyhole-cum-office at 7.45 am reading her emails, seeing the reception girls, and catching up with the gossip with the cleaners; beginning her daily inspection at 9 am; looking at the daily statistics for room bookings at 10 am; attending the daily senior management meeting at 10.30 am; attending the restaurant meeting at 11.30 am; and having lunch at 12:30 am. Then, in the afternoons, tackling emergencies, dealing with maintenance issues, having meetings with staff to solve their problems, and—the bit that she really likes—listening to them as people. Today, though, will be different. Today she is having her leaving party.

Mortimer begins to reflect on the last year. It has been a year of changes, what with the new structure, all the new procedures, and the culture that the Second Chance Consortium has tried to bring in.

She is surprised at how successful they have been. Occupancy rates are up, cleaning times are down, the restaurant has gone from strength to strength, and the new staff are certainly professional and hard-working. Yet some of the magic, the things that she really used to love about the hotel, seem to have been lost. Yes, they are more effective and efficient, more businesslike in their approach, and have clearly stated objectives, but it is somehow different.

With all these changes she wonders whether Junction Hotel, the one that she really loves, is still there.

→

→

Simon Chance reflects on a year in charge of Junction Hotel

Today is also a strange day for Simon Chance: it is his one-year anniversary at Junction Hotel. 'How time flies,' he thinks. It only seemed yesterday he first sat in this office and began what has proved to be one of his hardest, but also most interesting, years in management. Chance looks around his office again. 'Those wooden panels are still loose,' he thinks to himself. 'It is about time that I got them fixed.'

The year began with such optimism: Weaver's A3s, their new work processes, business reports, targets, and change programmes. These initiatives had worked—well, if he was honest, sort of worked. The rationalized cleaning system had been successful. Yes, a few people had left, but you don't make an omelette without breaking eggs, as his mother used to say. Yet many of these changes seemed so much more difficult than they originally had thought. When he and Weaver had developed their plans prior to taking on the hotel, they thought they would just need to introduce a few quick fixes, tools he had used elsewhere, and off they would go—the hotel would become profitable again; another dose of the Second Chance magic.

Yet, in practice, it all seemed so much harder. Things just did not fit the master plan. Indeed, things rarely seemed to go to plan. Numerous issues that he and Weaver had not even considered kept disrupting their plans. People did not react the way they expected, and systems that had worked so well elsewhere seemed to fail here: the usual motivational tools just seemed to not work at Junction Hotel.

At first, he had got really frustrated with this and blamed the staff for not wanting to change. But, gradually, his respect for them began to grow. They cared about the hotel, he realized, not just their jobs. They just had different values and objectives from his.

Maybe Meg Mortimer was right after all. At first, Chance had thought Mortimer a silly old fool for saying that Junction Hotel was special. However, a year on, he really feels he is beginning to understand what she meant. He has grown to love the place. Yes, it is a business, but he feels increasingly that it is more than that.

Simon Chance has come to realize how complicated and multifaceted management and working in organizations really is. Even the seemingly simplest change involves working with numerous people that have their own perspectives, with groups that have their established hierarchies and political agendas, and within (or sometimes even against) the established organizational culture. He began, as we often do, with the rational metaphor of the organization which sees it as a well-oiled machine (Morgan, 2006), running like clockwork to get the job done. This gives us the image that organizations are always logical and simple, that people follow predictable patterns, and that with just some effective management things would go smoothly. Yet this machine metaphor is limited. It gives the impression that organizational problems are fairly easy to solve—just implement a few simple procedures, steps, or theories. However, as we have seen throughout this book, in practice it can be far harder to do. The rationalized approach ignores the issues of culture, motivation, power, and politics; it ignores the fact that people have different personalities and perspectives; it ignores possible conflict between workers and management. In short it ignores the human element.

From the decisions that people make through to the challenges of communication and change, human factors shape everything that goes on in organizations. The study of organizational behaviour is about these human factors. It is about seeking to understand how different people see the world and how their perspectives are shaped by their personalities, culture, and position within the organization. Organizational behaviour is often thought about, researched, and taught as a collection of separate topics. Issues such as motivation, culture, or teamwork often draw on different theorists and are presented as independent issues. Yet, to really understand how things work in practice, we need to see the connections between these elements. To understand how these topics connect it is useful to have a worked example.

Connecting things together: a worked example

In Chapter 3 we saw Phil Weaver trying to change how the cleaners work. Weaver considered their approach inefficient, and using the logic and principles of Taylorist rational work design, he set about to conduct time and motion studies to design a work process that he considered efficient. Using these Taylorist techniques, driven by the belief in the 'one best way', he created a blueprint for how the cleaners should deal with the room, in one *standardized* way. Workers, through this perspective, are seen as merely cogs in the machine, replaceable parts devoid of individual characteristics.

What this narrow perspective ignores, however, are many of the human factors that other perspectives in organizational behaviour theory reveal. For instance, motivation theory (Chapter 9) would draw our attention to how, since losing the ability to conduct the cleaning in the way they see fit, the intrinsic motivation of doing the job might get lost. For Amy Turtle, who took pride in how she worked, this loss of control and autonomy led her to want to retire. Change management theory (Chapter 12) would provide a perspective on the way Weaver instigated the change, in a top-down and naïve approach, seeing the organization simply as a set of building blocks and taking little account of the human elements involved in the change, such as how the employees might feel about, and indeed react and resist to, such changes.

Seeing Junction Hotel as more like an iceberg or river, understanding the psychology of the workers (see Chapter 8 on personality and individual differences) and the power relations (see Chapter 14), would have helped Weaver to understand the extent and also limitations of his power and control to enact the change the way he wanted. Theories of knowledge and learning (Chapter 10) would also have alerted Weaver to the way that certain forms of knowledge, for example that of Amy Turtle, got lost in this 'one best way' approach. This would also have challenged the idea that all forms of knowledge can be made explicit, to be written down in the way that Weaver's plan assumes, and instead have emphasized that some tacit skills are important. Some of the theoretical consequences of the Hawthorne Studies (Chapter 5), which stress the importance of the social side of the organization, might have challenged Weaver's more narrow view which ignored the social needs. Indeed, taking this perspective could have allowed Weaver to look at options such as teamwork (Chapter 6) as a way of increasing productivity.

Understanding these connections is important in practice and also in developing essays and answers to exam questions. Strong answers and essays go beyond focusing on one particular topic, and instead look more deeply at the underlying assumptions that shape the actions of individuals.

This chapter brings together some of the key topics we have covered, drawing links between them. In doing so it aims to help you develop some of the skills and critical thinking skills (see Chapter 1) which are important for doing well in essays and exams. Organizational behaviour is a highly interconnected discipline.

Study skills: the importance of connecting the themes together

It is tempting when completing an essay or exam question to just look at the topics closely associated with that particular question and only read the chapter concerned. However, in practice, and indeed to really understand the theory, it is important to understand how each aspect of organizational behaviour (OB) connects to other aspects. Strong answers show an awareness of the connection between themes. Intelligent management understands the connections between one intervention and other aspects of the organization.

It is therefore essential to appreciate the connections between the themes. By showing these connections you are able to present a stronger level of understanding of the particular topic, demonstrating an awareness of how the individual theory is impacted by the wider field of OB and the deeper issues that theorists are seeking to explore. Therefore, when you come to write an essay or study for an exam, do not simply focus on one topic alone, but try to make connections back to other themes.

? Review questions

Describe	What is meant by OB being an 'interconnected' discipline?
Explain	Why is it important to link the key themes in OB together?
Analyse	What are the dangers of viewing a topic in isolation? What important organizational issues might be missed by doing this?
Apply	What themes from the book can you identify in the reflections of Meg Mortimer and Simon Chance in this chapter so far?

Recurring themes

As well as various interconnected topics, throughout the book we have explored a number of recurring themes and issues, which have underpinned many of the debates we have covered. Exploring these recurring themes is important not only to gain a deeper understanding of organizational behaviour, but also as an effective way to develop your critical analysis (see Figure 18.1 and Chapter 1 for discussion). By engaging in this deeper critical analysis, we go beyond exploring just one topic: rather, these recurring themes open up more fundamental questions about human nature, questions about the type of society we live in and the purpose and nature of organizations. This gives opportunities to develop critical analysis—and with it the possibilities for getting higher grades. The rest of the chapter will bring out a number of these recurring debates, which you can use to reflect on and consider how they might apply to the questions and issues that you explore in any assessment or studies you are undertaking. They are not meant to be comprehensive, but rather a starting-point for you to develop your own analysis.

Figure 18.1 Levels of critical thinking.

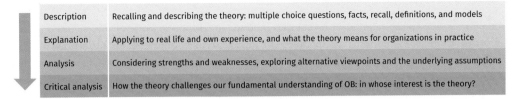

Description	Recalling and describing the theory: multiple choice questions, facts, recall, definitions, and models
Explanation	Applying to real life and own experience, and what the theory means for organizations in practice
Analysis	Considering strengths and weaknesses, exploring alternative viewpoints and the underlying assumptions
Critical analysis	How the theory challenges our fundamental understanding of OB: in whose interest is the theory?

Rational or social perspective

One of the recurring debates throughout the book is the contrast between the rational and social perspectives. The rational perspective emphasizes the logical, structural, and official organizational forms, which seek to design organizations in the most technically efficient manner. Exemplified by the work of Frederick Taylor, this perspective emphasizes mechanisms such as organizational charts and time and motion studies that seek to achieve maximum efficiency and reduce cost through technically efficient means. This perspective sees organizations more like machines (Morgan, 2006). Human nature is seen as 'rational', where individuals do cost-benefit analysis for all decisions and people are motivated through instrumental means such as pay (see, for instance, Henry Ford's $5 a day).

The social perspective, in contrast, emphasizes the human side of the organization. Rather than looking at formal mechanisms, like organizational charts, it accentuates the informal, often more messy human factors. This social person was 'discovered' in the Hawthorne studies (see Chapter 5) and is important for understanding teamwork, culture, leadership, and power and politics. This social perspective has a different take on human nature, seeing us driven by needs, particularly around the need to belong and be part of a group (see for instance Mayo's reading of the Hawthorne Studies in Chapter 5). The social perspective often does seek to increase productivity, but rather than through efficiency and cutting costs, this is achieved through getting people to work more effectively together, through increasing motivation, or through being inspired by the values and beliefs of the organization (see for instance Chapter 7 on organizational culture).

These two perspectives therefore have different underlying views on human nature. The rational perspective assumption is the economic person: economically motivated and naturally lazy (see Taylor's views in Chapter 3). This is in contrast to the social perspective, which sees people as motivated by the need to belong, influenced by group norms, and often driven by emotion (see Chapter 5 for a discussion).

Some things to consider: How do the rationalization and social perspectives understand human nature, organizational practice, and the way to manage people differently? How do they see similar situations (such as low levels of productivity) and produce different solutions? To what extent can the social perspective, with its emphasis on the human experience within the organization, overcome the difficulties of the rationalization perspective, such as dehumanization? Do the rationalization perspective and the social perspective really have different objectives, given that they are both ultimately trying to increase productivity within the organization?

It can also be helpful to examine how the underlying metaphors, such as the machine metaphor in rationalization (Morgan, 2006), present different interpretations of the organization. How do these metaphors present particular views of the organization? What do they allow you do see, and what do they hide?

Formal or informal

In a similar way to the rational or social perspective we can look at organizations through the lens of the formal and informal organization. The formal organization, from organizational charts, mission statements, and official channels of communication, emphasizes the official way that the organization is run. This formal organization presents the management's view of an organization, largely giving an ordered and controlled depiction of the organization. In contrast, the informal organization represents the unofficial everyday occurrences. The informal organization approach captures issues such as power and politics, informal means of communication such as gossip and joking, and informal hierarchies set by expertise rather than formal positions. The informal organization perspective tends to emphasize the messier, emergent, and unofficial ways of working, giving a broader understanding of how people might experience work.

Some things to consider: How important is the concept of the informal organization in really understanding what is going on in organizational practice? How might informal structures and hierarchies be at least as significant as the official hierarchy, if not more so? Consider the way that the informal organization challenges the idea of total managerial control.

Freedom or control

One of the underlying goals of many 'mainstream' management theories has been to get greater control over the work. This has been through approaches such as time and motion studies (see Chapter 3) where all the movements of workers are assessed and monitored, or in very visible forms of surveillance, such as the targets that call handlers have in call centres. Some theorists see being controlled by management as an inevitable sacrifice that workers need to make in exchange for their wage. Again, we can see this in Henry Ford's famous $5 a day.

Theorists and practitioners have, however, criticized this approach to control. From an efficiency and productivity viewpoint, such high levels of control are seen as potentially counterproductive: often workers find them oppressive and seek ways to resist. Also, from a productivity viewpoint, although tight control may have worked relatively well for the more mechanical approaches of the early-twentieth-century factory, it appears less effective for twenty-first century knowledge workers or emotional labourers, who need to not only comply with management instructions but to bring their personal ideas, their emotions, or indeed their 'whole selves' to work: tight control crushes the creativity and imagination that they need. Motivation theorists, therefore, have argued for us to move away from narrow carrot-and-stick approaches and towards more intrinsic forms of motivation that redesign the work in a way that is more meaningful and engaging for the individuals themselves. Teamwork theorists have argued that too much hierarchical control can limit the creativity of experienced workers, and some leadership theorists argue this can lead to slow and unresponsive decision-making. For instance, the situational leadership model argues that more experienced workers need increased say in decision making that impacts their work.

Giving workers more freedom not only can be a good way of motivating them, but is also important in fast-moving sectors where continual learning (as we saw in Chapter 10) is essential to success. Furthermore, it is simply not possible, particularly in industries which need a lot of creativity or continual learning, for managers to be able to understand, let alone control, every aspect of what workers do.

Disempowering workers can have major impacts on their sense of well-being and satisfaction at work. As we saw in Chapter 3, Braverman argued that tight managerial control left workers feeling deskilled and alienated, a view symbolized by Charlie Chaplin getting swallowed into the machine in his classic film *Modern times*. Managing workers through culture and values, as Peters and Waterman (1982) argued, is a way of giving freedom and autonomy, creating a new form of society (see Chapter 7). Empowering workers (see Chapter 14) by giving greater freedom and autonomy can help to overcome some of these problems. A fuller view is provided by Karl Marx, who argues that emancipation—freedom from slavery and having more autonomy and control over your working life—is a driving force in the human spirit.

However, more recent critical theorists suggest that what initially looks like it might produce freedom can also be more subtle forms of control. Take organizational culture: while Peters and Waterman talk about cultural change bringing about increased freedom (1992), Hugh Willmott (1993) argues that it really is more about control. Workers either need to buy into the management norms or get out. Furthermore, whereas Taylorism was about controlling bodies, within cultural and other wider social forms of organizing, workers also need to bring their hearts, minds, and souls to the organization. Workers may be told they need to 'be themselves' (Fleming and Sturdy, 2011) or bring their whole self to work (Cederström and Fleming, 2012).

Some things to consider: If you get paid to go to work, should you give up all your freedom in exchange for your wage? Should workers have more freedom only to the extent that they are more productive, or is freedom, particularly in the form of emancipation, a fundamental goal for humanity? Is the social organization perspective, such as organizational culture, a more subtle form of control?

Harmony or conflict

Do managers and workers have similar interests? Many of the theorists we have explored in this book implicitly present managers and workers as having similar goals and interests. Exemplified by Elton Mayo, management theorists have sought to present workers and managers working to the same objectives (such as increased productivity, higher levels of customer satisfaction, or better organizational products). Cultural theorists such as Peters and Waterman argue for greater worker autonomy, governed by shared values, where there is no longer a conflict between the interests of workers and organizations (1992). Most mainstream change management theorists see resistance as an aberration to be overcome, and many management theorists see hierarchy as inevitable and managers unquestionably having the right to manage (for a review see Alvesson and Willmott, 1992).

Some management theorists, however, challenge this view. Taylor believed there was a fundamental conflict between workers and management, and therefore he sought to shift control from the worker to management (see Chapter 3). Critical theorists also challenge the idea that there is harmony between workers and management, by seeking to reveal their different interests. For instance, Stephen Lukes argues that even when there appears to be harmony of interests (due to the lack of conflict), this is because workers are not fully aware of their own real interests (Lukes, 2005). From this perspective, the labour–capital relationship is always one of tension and conflict, even when the workers accept management requests and perspectives.

Some things to consider: Do managers and workers share the same interests, or are their goals ultimately different? If they are different, why is it that we rarely see the sort of conflict between workers and owners (labour and capital) that critical theorists, particularly Marxists, would predict?

Workers' or managers' perspective: whose side are you on?

Whose interest should organizational behaviour theory serve? Many of the theories that we have covered in this book have had the goal of increasing efficiency and productivity in order to increase profits. This is quite explicit in the work of Frederick Taylor, who designed work in a way that was designed to give control over all the movements of workers in order to help managers maximize profit, but also appears in areas such as motivation, leadership, and organizational culture, where theorists specifically argue that they can help managers increase productivity. These 'mainstream' theorists often take it for granted that management theory should be in the interests of management. However, critical theorists question the idea that any theory is neutral, arguing that all theory represents a particular perspective and is written for specific interests. Most organizational behaviour theory is written for or to support managers. These critical theorists are often more up-front about their values, beliefs, and political viewpoints (Alvesson and Willmott, 1996). They argue that to be critical is 'to say that there is something wrong with management ... and it should be changed' (Fournier and Grey, 2000: 16). Critical theorists argue instead that research should be done in the interests of wider society, such as for workers or the environment, with some even intervening directly into management practice to try to change it (King and Land, 2018).

Core questions to examine: Look at different theories and ask yourself if they are written from a 'mainstream' or a 'critical' perspective. You can do this by asking: Whose interest are they written for (i.e. managers or workers)? What goals are they trying to achieve (increased productivity or greater freedom)? What assumptions do they hold?

 Study skills: bringing out the underlying perspectives and debates

Critical thinking, as we first explored in the introduction, is an essential skill at university. Rather than simply describing theories, critical thinking is an approach which looks to explain and analyse the theory. To get to these more fundamental levels, a core skill is to explore the underlying assumptions that the theorists hold. These are the taken-for-granted assumptions that the theorists might not themselves explicitly state, but include the beliefs that they hold around areas such as human nature, the role and purpose of the organization (i.e. profit for shareholders or for the betterment of society), or issues around the way that people should be managed. The above themes are a useful starting-point for beginning your analysis. Asking these questions, and using them to start developing your own questions, is a way of beginning to develop a deeper perspective on the topic. This will not come overnight. It is a way of thinking about academic material to help you develop arguments that go beyond simple description.

Endings

 Running case: farewell

As Meg walks nervously into the conference room she is greeted by a massive round of applause from Junction Hotel staff—past and present. 'Grab yourself a drink,' Simon Chance declares in a jovial way, greeting his adversary and friend. 'I want you to enjoy today.' It seems odd, but in many ways comforting, to Mortimer that through all their disagreements, at least Chance has been nice to her as a person—their disagreements have been largely professional rather than personal.

As she picks up a glass of Prosecco, she looks around the room. 'I'm going to miss you lot,' she thinks. Sam from reception comes up to her and they exchange pleasantries for a while.

→

'I bet you can't wait to retire,' Sam beams. 'Particularly no more putting up with him,' Meg says, looking in the direction of Weaver. Weaver had certainly been difficult, or, in his management-speak, 'a challenge,' with all his systems and efficiency practices. Yet, she must concede, the hotel is now running better that it had ever done. However, in some areas it has gone too far, like those changes to the fitness centre. If Weaver had had his way, then the whole hotel would have been running on a great big flow-chart.

Then there was Chance himself. Meg has grown to respect him over the year. They did not see eye to eye on a lot of things and it had felt as though he was taking her hotel away from her. But, she has to admit it: ultimately, the guy seems to care about what goes on here. The way he tried to change the culture of Junction Hotel and get them working in teams was different from how she would have done it, but at least it showed some awareness of the importance of people.

'I don't know how I feel about retiring,' Meg says more to herself than in response to Sam. 'I thought I would want to. I've been dreaming, longing for this day for a while. But now it's here I've come to realize that I like it here. I'm good at what I do, I know how everything works here, and I feel respected. Does that sound odd?' she said, noticing Sam. 'Now I'm retired, who am I?' Sam smiles in a puzzled, but sympathetic, way. Suddenly, she notices Simon Chance standing at the podium.

'Hello … hello everyone—if I could have your attention for only a few minutes.' A couple of people sigh, but in a friendly way. 'Today,' begins Chance, 'we are celebrating two major events: our long-serving and esteemed colleague Meg's retirement, and the first anniversary of the Second Chance Consortium buying Junction Hotel. Now, we have been through a lot, all of us together, over the last year, and I wanted just to say a few words about what we have achieved, as well as how important Meg has been to this.

'When I walked into Junction Hotel for the first time just over a year ago I thought that we were buying just another hotel. How wrong I was.' Some of the audience laugh. 'You are unique, and I mean that in a good way. We have been though a challenging journey over the last year and I am sure that we have all learned a lot. I thought I would share with you today a few things I have learned.

'Things have been tough, and some tough decisions have been made. I know that they have not always been popular, but I think time will prove them to be correct.

'However, I have learned never to judge things by appearances. While this hotel might look ordinary, there are some extraordinary and talented people here. I have learned that what works well in other places will not necessarily work well here. I really hope that we can all grow together. Junction Hotel is a special place.

'Finally, I want to say a few words about Meg. As many of you will know, Meg began her working life here as a cleaner and has worked her way up to the top of her profession. It is this attitude of hard work, customer care, and dedication to her staff that has made her the model professional and I, for one, will be sad to see her go. Although we have not always seen eye to eye on everything, I know that she is Junction Hotel through and through, and you can never doubt her dedication to the cause.

'So from all of us to you I would like to give you this … ' At this point Chance hands over an enormous leaving card, a big bunch of flowers, a cheque, and, finally, a mug with a picture of Junction Hotel on the front ' … for your world cruise, so you can never forget us.' 'And the mugs that work here!' Effingham pipes up, to much laughter.

> Then Meg begins to speak. She says how proud she has been to work at Junction Hotel and how much it has meant to spend so much of her time there. She is leaving with a heavy heart and thanks them for the great support she has received. 'Lots of things have changed over the last 40 years,' she says. 'Who would have thought that we would now have all this technology and bookings coming from all over the world.' Then, with a subtle passing shot directed at Chance, Meg ends by saying 'Yet some things never change—the basics, listening to people, and good service—remember, keep the Junction Hotel spirit alive'. With that, Mortimer sits down to her second round of rapturous applause of the day.

This chapter has sought to do two key things. First, it is important, when studying OB, to understand that it is not a series of isolated topics, but an interconnected discipline. To gain a strong understanding, it is vital to explore how the topics connect together. This will give you a deeper appreciation of the subject, as well as the potential of a better grade.

Second, we have reintroduced some of the key underlying themes that have run throughout the book. The purpose of doing this is to invite you to use them as a starting-point to develop your own analysis and thinking about the topics that you are exploring. By asking these more fundamental questions you can get into debating the deep-seated assumptions of organizational behaviour and with it potentially gain a higher grade.

A final note: in our experience, having taught organizational behaviour to thousands of students, the issues that we have covered in this book are best understood when connected to actual practice. We have had many students approach us after a placement year or at graduation saying that the issues we have covered here have only really made sense to them after seeing them in practice. They have been grateful for the insights that they have gained, which have helped them understand themselves and others better, and enabled them to cope with the complexities of organizational life.

References

Alvesson, M., and Willmott, H. 1992. *Making sense of management*. Sage: London.

Alvesson, M., and Willmott, H. 1996. *Making sense of management: A critical introduction*. SAGE: London.

Cederström, C., and Fleming, P. 2012. *Dead man working*. John Hunt Publishing.

Fleming, P., and Sturdy, A. 2011. 'Being yourself' in the electronic sweatshop: New forms of normative control. *Human Relations* 64 (2): 177–200.

Fournier, V., and Grey, C. 2000. At the critical moment: Conditions and prospects for critical management studies. *Human Relations* 53(1): 7–32.

King, D., and Land, C. 2018. The democratic rejection of democracy: Performa-

tive failure and the limits of critical performativity in an organizational change project. *Human Relations* 71 (11) 1535–57:

Lukes, S. 2005. *Power: A radical view*. Palgrave Macmillan: Basingstoke.

Morgan, G. 2006. *Images of organization*. Sage Publications: Thousand Oaks, CA.

Peters, T.J., and Waterman, R.H., Jr. 1982. *In search of excellence: Lessons from America's best run companies*. Harper Row: London.

Willmott, H. 1993. Strength is ignorance; slavery is freedom: Managing culture in modern organizations. *Journal of Management Studies* 30 (4): 515–52.

GLOSSARY

16 personality factor A personality test which measures personality on a set of 16 scales of opposing character traits.

Acquisition The purchase of another company or business.

Aesthetic labour Usually found in customer- or client-facing service work where, in exchange for a wage, the worker is expected to manage their appearance and comportment in a manner directed by the organization.

Agency The capacity individuals have to act independently of social structures and make free choices.

Algorithms Software tools that apply rules and procedures to data.

Alienation In critical writings on capitalism, the estrangement of people from a number of human qualities, noted particularly by writers such as Marx and Braverman as a consequence of rational work design.

Analyse Widely associated with deeper intellectual thinking, it is the process of breaking things down into their constituent parts, investigating the underlying cause or basic principles.

Anti-globalization movement A collective term for protestors and critics of the power and effects of multinational corporations, which they see as making the world less fair and more homogenized.

A priori Independent of experience.

Artificial intelligence Computer systems that can perform tasks that would otherwise require human intelligence.

Assembly line An automated conveyor that moves a product in front of workers who perform a small, repetitive task to each product that passes before them.

Assessment centre A recruitment strategy where different selection techniques are blended in a selection process.

Authentic leadership An approach that emphasizes leadership through use of personal experiences, emotions, needs, and beliefs.

Autocratic A command and control leadership style.

Automation The process whereby more and more human work is carried out by machines or by computer algorithms.

Background In describing perception, that which is not noticeable and does not command attention (as opposed to foreground).

Backstage A theatrical metaphor to represent areas of the organization where workers are out of view of customers and clients.

Bad apples A phrase that dismisses an occurrence as just down to a few bad people or organizations, while claiming that others should not be judged as the same.

Banking education Freire's critique of learning and teaching styles which see learners as being like bank accounts in which amounts of knowledge are to be 'deposited'.

Behavioural psychology/behaviourism An area of psychology which suggests that learning can be managed through the use of rewards and punishments.

Behavioural theory A psychological perspective which seeks to understand and change the behaviour of individuals.

Big data The vast amounts of data held by organizations, including information about their processes, their customers or clients, and their employees.

Big five personality scale A personality test which measures personality according to a set of five traits: openness, conscientiousness, extraversion, agreeableness, and neuroticism.

Bing A term used during the Hawthorne studies meaning flicking the ear or arm of a person who is working too hard.

Bolshevik An insult indicating that a person is a Russian communist; in other words, that they are troublemakers who want revolution.

Bureaucracy From the French *bureau*, meaning office; bureaucracy covers official, formal elements of rational organizational design, such as the hierarchical organization structure, the rules and procedures, and the official paperwork, which exert impersonal control over the organization.

Bureaucratic Describing the process of bureaucracy, sometimes used in a derogatory sense.

Bureaucratic personality A tendency to follow rules to the letter rather than seeing the wider picture and making more common-sense judgements.

Business ethics A form of ethics applied to business. It is the study and evaluation of decision making within businesses through various moral concepts and judgements.

Butterfly effect The suggestion in chaos theory that a small action can have unpredictable knock-on effects of a greater magnitude.

Buzzword A word or phrase that is a fad for a period of time.

Call centre An organization or department set up to handle a large volume of telephone calls, often managed efficiently using rationalized techniques.

Camaraderie A sense of togetherness and bonding.

Capital Investment in a business to set up the means of production, often used as a term to refer to business owners or capitalists who make that investment.

Capitalism The dominant economic system, which is based on private ownership of the means of production of goods and services for the purposes of making profit.

Capitalist wage–labour relationship The relationship between capitalists, who pay wages, and labour, who work in return for those wages.

Ceremony A public act, often planned and formal, which celebrates a particular event, achievement, or anniversary, largely planned by senior management or as part of an organization's established calendar. Ceremonies often have symbolic meaning that emphasizes important aspects of the organization's culture.

Change The process by which an organization makes changes in practices, processes, culture etc., whether in a planned or emergent fashion.

Change agent A manager, consultant, or other person who instigates and manages change.

Change management An effort or initiative undertaken to alter a particular aspect of the organization.

Channels of communication Ways in which a message is expressed, e.g. in spoken or written words.

Chaos theory A branch of science which sees natural systems as both ordered and, at the same time, unpredictable.

Classical conditioning A type of conditioning of behaviour where a reward or punishment accompanies and reinforces every instance of the behaviour to be conditioned.

Classical Management School A set of theories of management which draws upon rational methods of managing and organizing. Having developed from the early 1900s, it encompasses a number of theorists and practitioners who advocated 'one best way' of management. Examples of management styles and techniques which the school draws upon include Fayol and Taylor.

Cliques Exclusive groups.

Coercion Being forced in some way into performing a behaviour.

Collective action Any form of resistance against management taken by a group of workers.

Collisionable hours A measure introduced by Zappos to assess the effectiveness of workspaces; those that encourage the most 'collisions' or interactions between people are seen as the most effective.

Colonialism Invasion and conquering of land, taking of natural resources, and enslavement of people, in Africa, the Americas, and Asia from the 1500s to the 1900s, by European countries such as England, Spain, Belgium, Portugal, France, and the Netherlands.

Command and control A top-down leadership style that emphasizes the importance of the leader who tells others what to do.

Communication A process whereby information is transferred from a sender (or senders) to a receiver (or receivers).

Communication technology Technology that facilitates communication between people and the sharing of information.

Communities of coping Mutual support among co-workers to cope with stress and other negative factors of emotional labour.

Communities of practice Social groupings based around a common occupational practice and set of knowledge, who develop and share that knowledge among themselves.

Complexity theory The application of chaos theory to social systems, such as organizations, suggesting that small changes can have unpredictable and potentially limitless consequences.

Comprehension The ability to understand something.

Conditioning A change in behaviour brought about using stimulus–response techniques typical of behavioural psychology.

Confirmation bias A form of selective perception where people only tend to take note of information that confirms their already held perceptions.

Conformity Everyone in the group thinking and acting in the same way.

Consumption The purchase and use by customers and clients of goods and services that have been created by an organization.

Content theories Theories of motivation which suggest that the content of work should be designed so as best to meet the needs which motivate workers.

Context In describing perception, the situation surrounding a communication that influences how its meaning is perceived.

Contingency leadership See Situational leadership.

Contingency theory Suggests that the best structure for an organization is determined by factors such as environmental uncertainty, the organization's size, and the technology that the organization uses.

Control group Used in scientific research, a control group does not receive any intervention and therefore is seen as representing the population as a whole. The control group is used as a standard of comparison to the research group, who do receive intervention.

Core workforce In a flexible-firm model, the workers who are a permanent part of the organization's workforce.

Corporate social responsibility A contested term with different interpretations but generally taken to be the social and environmental responsibility that corporations have towards their stakeholders.

Cost The amount in wages and materials that it costs to produce a good or provide a service.

Craft knowledge Knowledge of a particular skill, often the result of a long period of training or apprenticeship.

Critical (as in 'critical management studies') A critical perspective, among other things, draws on Marxist theory and seeks to challenge the assumptions of mainstream management theory by stressing the impact that it has on employees and society.

Critical analysis To question the underlying assumptions of a perspective. In the study of organizational behaviour, this may have particular emphasis on how power and inequality occur.

Cross-cultural management Managing a workforce from different national and cultural backgrounds.

Cultural change From the perspective that sees culture as a possession, this refers to change driven by management or consultants with the intention of making the organization more productive.

Cultural homogenization A tendency for culture to become the same globally.

Cultural typology A classification of the types of organizational culture.

Customer-facing work See Interactive service work.

Cyber-physical system A system where software, people, and objects are linked together in one control mechanism.

Data Facts or statistics collected together to be examined or analysed, often using computer software.

Database A computerized store of structured, organized data.

Dataveillance Surveillance brought about by examining electronic data which is held about individuals.

Decoding Converting a received message into the meaning perceived by the recipient.

Deep acting Emotional labour where the worker internalizes and believes in the performance in which they are engaged; compare with surface acting.

Deep learning Learning that tries to achieve a deeper understanding of, and engagement with, the material being learned; compare with surface learning.

Dehumanization Work that reduces people to part of a machine-like process, ignoring their human attrib-

utes. Widely associated with rational work design that was criticized by Harry Braverman.

Delegation Passing a job, task, or order down to lower levels of a hierarchy.

Democratic A leadership style which encourages the involvement of the group, but the leader ultimately makes the decisions.

Description In academic writing, a piece of writing that describes a theory or case study with little attempt at providing analysis. Often considered more superficial and therefore, in student coursework, results in lower grades.

Deskilling The obsolescence of workplace skills caused by rational work design or the introduction of new technology.

Deutero learning Bateson's conception of a higher level of learning whereby people are aware of how they 'learn to learn'.

Digital divide A divide between people who have access to computer hardware and network infrastructures, such as the internet, and those who do not.

Dimensions of culture See Hofstede's dimensions of culture.

Direct control Face-to-face control of workers by a manager or owner.

Discretion The ability of an individual to act according to their own independent judgement, rather than being told exactly what to do.

Discrimination Where a person is treated negatively and unfairly because of their membership of a particular social group, e.g. because of race or gender.

Disenchantment For Max Weber this was a loss of 'magical elements' in society, and suggests some of the dehumanizing elements of bureaucracy.

Disneyization Term coined by Bryman which describes characteristics of the Disney theme parks that can be seen in other service and leisure organizations.

Distributive leadership An approach which emphasizes that leadership can occur throughout the organization and can be practised by a wide variety of organizational members.

Division of labour Breaking down a job into more simple, individual tasks.

Double-edged sword of bureaucracy Refers to the fact that while bureaucracy allows efficient control to be exerted, it may come at a price: the dehumanization of workers.

Double-loop learning Learning in organizations which goes beyond achieving a goal to question assumptions behind the goal being set, and that questions assumptions, values, and strategies more widely in the organization.

Downsizing Reducing the size of the workforce.

Dress code Standards of dress and appearance prescribed by an organization to its workers.

663

Dysfunctions of bureaucracy Unintended consequences of bureaucracy which lead to it not functioning in the efficient manner for which it is designed.

Economies of scale Cost reduction that comes from producing a product in large amounts.

Efficiency The minimization of cost, doing the same for less input of time and money.

Electronic Panopticon The ability organizations have to monitor our lives through the amount of electronic data and records held about us.

Embodied dispositions (habitus) Our natural way of acting and reacting—a deeply held repertoire of instinctive behaviours.

Emergent approach to change An approach to change which sees the organization as being like a river, in constant flow, and suggests that in such an environment change emerges in the course of events rather than being planned in advance.

Emoticon Punctuation marks used in electronic communications, designed to simulate facial expressions.

Emotional intelligence The ability to monitor, understand, and respond appropriately to one's own and others' emotions.

Emotional labour Work where, in exchange for a wage, the worker is expected to manage their emotions so as to put on a particular emotional performance in front of customers or clients, especially in interactive service work.

Emotion management Any management of personal emotional displays inside or outside of a working relationship.

Empowering A process by which workers are given greater power and autonomy. Critics suggest this approach also places a greater burden on workers.

Encoding Converting the intended meaning of a communication into a form that can be sent as a message.

Environment The world outside of an organization which can have an impact upon that organization.

Environmental leadership A self-sustaining group where employees find gratification through the group and task.

Equity theory A process theory of motivation which suggests that people are either motivated or demotivated depending on how they are rewarded in the workplace compared with others.

Equivocality Situations where meanings are ambiguous and open to interpretation.

Ergonomics The design of workplace environments and tools to best fit the movements of the human body.

Ethical capitalism A business approach which seeks to integrate corporate social responsibility as central to the purpose and activity of an organization.

Ethical egoism The belief that people acting in their own best interests is the best way to get a good society.

Evidence In academic writing, support for claims made.

Expectancy theory A process theory of motivation which suggests that people will be motivated into actions and behaviours that they can link with them achieving goals and rewards that they desire.

Experience In discussing consumer behaviour, describes what the consumer seeks when consumption is of the organization itself rather than any product or service that it provides.

Experiential learning Learning which comes from experiences and reflecting on those experiences.

Explanation In academic writing, the ability to explain a theory or perspective.

Explicit knowledge Knowledge that is expressed to other people as a set of words, facts, diagrams, or instructions.

Exporting Selling and distributing a good to another country.

Extinction Where a conditioned behaviour dies out because the reward or punishment is no longer provided.

Extraversion A tendency to focus and gain energy externally rather than from within the self.

Extrinsic motivation Motivation that comes from outside the worker, usually on the basis of reward (e.g. wages) and punishment (e.g. the danger of being sacked).

Extrinsic reward A reward that a person receives which is provided by somebody else.

False consciousness A Marxist term—false beliefs held by the proletariat (workers) who do not know their true position in society as the revolutionary force to overthrow capitalism. Instead, they see the current structure of society as unchangeable and largely fair.

Feedback Reaction or response to a message.

Fixed mindset In goal orientation theory, the belief that people's qualities (e.g. intelligence, talent) are innate and fixed; compare with Growth mindset.

First Industrial Revolution Beginning in the 1760s, this saw the introduction of mechanization and large factories, with labour moving in huge numbers from agriculture to factory work.

Fixed reinforcement A reward or punishment provided at fixed time intervals or fixed numbers of instances of a behaviour to be reinforced.

Flexible-firm model Describes a firm with a permanent, core workforce and a peripheral workforce of people who can be hired on a temporary basis.

Followership In leadership theory: (a) the importance of looking at followers and (b) the ability to follow a leader.

Followers Those who are led; from the post-heroic leadership perspective, followers have importance not only as people who get things done, but also in shaping the actions of leaders.

Followership theory Stresses the importance of followers in theory and practice.

Force-field analysis A technique whereby triggers for change and sources of resistance to change are plotted on a diagram in order to identify areas to focus on in a change-management programme.

Fordism The use of a moving assembly line to mass-produce goods.

Foreground In describing perception, that which is noticeable and holds the attention (as opposed to background).

Foreign direct investment Setting up a production or office facility in another country.

Formal communication Official communication within an organization, following authorized pathways.

Formal rationality Technically efficient means of achieving particular ends without thinking of the human or ethical consequences.

Founder The person who established the organization.

Four humours The four elements that Hippocrates suggested made up the human body and which also divided into four personality types.

Fourth Industrial Revolution The effects of the internet, big data, automation, and artificial intelligence in transforming every arena of life, including the world of business.

Franchising Granting the right to another company to operate an outlet or branch of a particular organization, subject to adhering to standards and conditions of the franchising company.

Free-riding See Shirking.

Front-line work See Interactive service work.

Frontstage A theatrical metaphor to represent areas of the organization where workers are in contact with customers and clients.

Functional differentiation See Horizontal differentiation.

Gaia hypothesis A theory popular in environmental movements where the whole world is seen as an interconnected system.

Gestalt psychology An area of psychology which suggests that we perceive things as forms, patterns, and connections rather than as a set of discrete individual items.

Gig economy Work arrangements whereby workers undertake short-term jobs as directed by digital platforms.

Glass cage Gabriel's metaphor to represent the visibility of workers in service-sector organizations, both from the surveillance of rational organizational control and the visibility of being 'on show' in front of customers and clients.

Glass ceiling An invisible barrier that minority groups and particularly women cannot pass through to get to senior positions in the organization.

Glass escalator Occurs when men enter female-dominated professions and glide past female workers to more senior positions.

Global culture A homogeneous, worldwide culture that emerges as a result of globalization and the activities of global organizations.

Globalization Defined in many different ways, globalization is where activities take place on an increasingly global scale.

Global village A metaphor to describe a perception of the globe shrinking in size as a result of the speed and global reach of transport and communications technologies.

Glocalization Adapting global practices and products to local conditions.

Goal setting theory An approach that argues that motivation is influenced by the difficulty and specificity of reaching your goals and the feedback you receive as you progress.

Gossip Rumours and information communicated through informal means.

Great man theory A theory that certain individuals are born great and have an innate ability to lead organizations and societies.

Group In team theory, a collection of people with a sense of shared identity and something in common but not with a shared purpose.

Group dynamics The processes involved in interaction between group members, with particular emphasis on the tensions, conflicts, and adjustments that occur.

Group norms The unwritten rules that shape behaviour within a group.

Groupthink A psychological phenomenon which limits the range of alternatives being considered because there is an overwhelming desire for consensus within a group.

Growth mindset In goal orientation theory, the belief that even a person's most basic qualities (e.g. intelligence) can be changed and developed through hard work and dedication; compare with Fixed mindset.

Habitus See Embodied dispositions.

Halo/horns effect The tendency for people to continually reaffirm their initial impressions of a person, whether good or bad.

Haptic feedback Feedback that is conveyed through the sense of touch, e.g. vibrations produced by a smartwatch or fitness tracker.

Hawthorne effect The fact that the very act of observation changes behaviour.

Hawthorne studies A series of studies which ran from 1924 into the late 1930s. Widely credited with discovering the human side of the organization.

Heroic leadership In leadership theory, the suggestion that great leaders have personality traits or innate characteristics that give them a natural ability to lead others.

Heuristic device Used to help simplify a theory and make it more understandable.

665

Hierarchy The levels and ranks of an organization. Any one level reports to the level immediately above and commands the level immediately below.

Hierarchy of needs Maslow's theory which suggests that individuals have a set of needs in hierarchical order, whereby people are motivated by the most immediate unsatisfied need.

Hofstede's dimensions of culture Four numerical scales on which national management cultures can be located.

Horizontal differentiation (functional differentiation) The process whereby different parts of the hierarchy are grouped according to criteria, such as the function performed, the geographical area served, or the product or service provided.

Horizontal loading Increasing the scope of a job by adding elements of work of a similar nature and at the same level of hierarchical responsibility.

Human cloud A term for parts of the gig economy, characterized as a meshing together of data and algorithms (across computer networks) with physical objects and humans (across a geographical area) so that digital technology coordinates the dispersed activities of workers.

Human relations A movement emerging out of organizational development that studies the behaviour of people in groups.

Human resource management (HRM) The part of an organization which concentrates on policies and procedures relevant to the recruitment and management of people within the organization (sometimes known as personnel management).

Human touch Describes human capabilities that robots and artificial intelligence do not have, e.g. creativity and discretion, or tasks that they cannot carry out and for which human intervention is needed, e.g. perception and manipulation.

Hybrid consumption Different types of consumption activity, which might otherwise take place in separate organizations, appearing together in one organization.

Hygiene factors For Herzberg, characteristics of a job which cannot bring about increases in the job satisfaction and motivation of workers, but which can cause demotivation if they are not addressed sufficiently.

Hyper-reality An artificial reality which is better than anything that could be experienced in the reality that it aims to reproduce.

Hypothesis A proposition that needs to be tested.

ICT Information and communication technologies.

Ideographic approach An approach which sees personality as complex, unique to each individual, and dynamic.

Impersonal control Control of workers that is not done face to face, for example through delegation or through rules and procedures.

Impersonal fairness The idea that standardized bureaucratic procedures treat people equally and avoid the personal prejudices and preferences that individual managers might have.

Implosion Where a large amount of an organization's activity takes place through computer systems and is stored as computer code.

Impression management Attempts by people, including in the workplace, to manage stimuli, such as dress and digital presence, so as to encourage others to have favourable perceptions of them.

Industrial action Any action taken by workers in a dispute between capital and labour.

Industrial revolutions Periods in history when hugely influential changes took place in the conduct of business, with knock-on effects throughout society; see entries under First / Second / Third / Fourth industrial revolution.

Inertia A tendency for an organization as a whole to resist change or lack the impetus for change.

Influence The capacity to impact others, directly or indirectly.

Informal communication Communication in an organization not following official and formal guidelines.

Informal culture (unofficial culture) Culture that is often not known or supported by management but that many of the employees share. It can be in opposition to official, management-led culture.

Informated organization Where a large amount of an organization's activity and knowledge is stored as computer code in a database.

Information and communication technologies A set of contemporary electronic technologies which facilitate communication between people and the sharing of information.

Inputs In equity theory, efforts and contributions made by an individual to their work.

Intangible Something that you cannot touch.

Intangible global space In the context of globalization, the realm in which global connectedness is established without movement over actual land, through intangible means such as media transmissions and data in computer networks.

Intensification of consciousness Alongside the rise of the global village, an increased awareness of events and people worldwide.

Interactive service work (customer-facing work, front-line work) Work in the service and leisure industries where the worker interacts with the customer or client, either face to face or by telephone.

Interdisciplinary team (multifunctioning team) A team of people that is comprised of people coming from different disciplines. This approach can produce a wider perspective and knowledge but can also produce greater conflict.

Interpersonal perception The way in which one individual perceives the personality of another.

Interpersonal relationships The way group members relate to each other.

In-tray exercise In employee recruitment, this refers to an exercise in which a job candidate is asked to carry out tasks similar to those they would perform on the job so that their skills and ability can be assessed.

Intrinsic motivation Motivation that comes from within the worker, e.g. deriving from the satisfaction of performing well, helping others, or working with a team.

Intrinsic reward A reward that a person senses for themselves, rather than it being provided by someone else.

Introversion A tendency to focus and gain energy more from within the self rather than externally.

Iron cage of bureaucracy/rationality Max Weber's observation of the increased presence of bureaucracy in society and its potential to trap people in its routines and procedures.

Job description A document which outlines the formal duties and activities that the holder of a particular office will be expected to perform, and their place within the overall organizational structure.

Job enlargement Where more tasks are added to increase the challenge and variety of the job.

Job enrichment Where the quality of work is increased through the provision of increased responsibility, autonomy, and variety of tasks.

Job rotation Where workers alternate between different tasks of a similar nature.

Job simplification Where a job is broken down into simple tasks, as with Taylorism or Fordism.

Joint venture Cooperation between two or more companies on a particular project.

Just-in-time management A form of management that tries to promote efficiency by reducing the amount of stocks that an organization holds, with components delivered as and when needed.

Keirsey's temperament sorter A personality-testing instrument which relates personality types to suggested occupational roles.

Knowledge and learning An aspect of organizational behaviour which emphasizes the importance of information, understanding, and practical skills for organizational success. In particular it examines the capacity of the organization to share this knowledge in effective ways.

Knowledge clusters Geographical areas where a number of knowledge-intensive organizations in a particular industry are congregated in close proximity.

Knowledge-intensive firms Organizations whose main business involves the development and innovation of knowledge.

Knowledge workers Workers employed for their specific knowledge and their ability to use this knowledge to innovate, and develop new ideas and products.

Kolb's learning cycle A model of experiential learning which suggests that people learn through different stages of experience and reflection, and that people have particular learning style preferences for different parts of that cycle.

Labour Work done in return for a wage; the term is also used to refer to waged workers collectively.

Labour process How work is designed and controlled by management.

Laissez-faire A leadership style which leaves all decisions to the group.

Leaderful Where everyone has the capacity to be a leader or take a lead through doing activities.

Leadership The process of leading or influencing the behaviour of others. In the broadest definition, it can be carried out by anyone in the organization.

Leadership as a practice In leadership theory, a perspective that sees leadership as a social process rather than as being about traits or behaviours.

Lean management A contemporary form of Taylorist rational organization that attempts to eliminate waste, or anything that does not add value, from organizational processes.

Learning organization An organization which is set up so as to facilitate continual learning at individual and organizational levels.

Learning styles The different ways in which different individuals approach learning.

Learning styles questionnaire Based on Honey and Mumford's development of Kolb's learning cycle, a questionnaire which ascertains people's preferred learning styles.

Libertarian A perspective that stresses individual freedom above all other concerns.

Licensing Granting the right to another company to produce a particular branded good.

Liquid modernity Bauman's characterization of modern-day society as dynamic, changeable, and flexible.

Lottery question A question which asks whether people would give up work if they acquired enough money to live on without having to work, e.g. by winning the lottery.

Mainstream The dominant or accepted view that emphasizes managers' right to manage and the central objective of organizations being to make profits for shareholders.

Management The everyday practices of running the organization in a smooth fashion.

Mass consumption Large-scale purchasing of a product by consumers within society.

Mass production The production of a large volume of a standardized product, often making use of an assembly line.

Matrix structure An organizational structure that combines a traditional functional hierarchy with separately managed project teams that draw people from across different functional departments.

McDonaldization (of society) The principles of efficiency, calculability, predictability, and control by which fast-food restaurants are managed and organized, as applied by Ritzer to other contemporary organizations.

McJobs Deskilled jobs found particularly in service industries, such as the fast-food restaurant.

Means of production Tools, premises, and other property used to manufacture goods.

Media Plural of Medium.

Media richness theory Examines the ability of different communications media to communicate rich, personal meanings rather than lean, impersonal information.

Medium (plural: media) A specific form of technology or technologies which convey and carry information.

Mehrabian's 55-38-7 ratio Findings from a study by Mehrabian that indicated the importance of body language in spoken communication: 55 per cent of communication is through body language, 38 per cent from tone of voice, and just 7 per cent from the actual words.

Merchandising The image or brand of one company or organization appearing on other products.

Merger Two companies joining together to become one single entity.

Message An item of communication sent from a sender to a recipient.

Metaphor A figure of speech whereby we try to understand something by suggesting a resemblance to the characteristics of something else.

Michigan studies Early leadership studies which stressed the benefit of being employee-orientated rather than task-orientated to improve output.

Mindset (perceptual set) A framework which each individual develops which then influences their future selective perception and perceptual organization; expresses the idea that people are predisposed to perceive certain stimuli in certain ways.

Miscommunication Where some of the meaning of a communication is distorted.

Mission statement The stated aim of an organization—often with the intention of inspiring employees and differentiating them from others.

Mock bureaucracy A situation where policies and rules exist, but are ignored.

Monitoring Ongoing observation, e.g. periodically checking the quality of an employee's performance.

Motivating factors For Herzberg, characteristics of a job which can bring about increases in the job satisfaction and motivation of workers.

Motivation The will and desire that a person has to engage in a particular behaviour or perform a particular task.

Multifunctioning team See Interdisciplinary team.

Multinational corporation An enterprise operating in more than one country but managed from one (home) country.

Multiple intelligences Gardner's theory that there are different types of intelligence that people possess in different combinations.

Myers–Briggs Type Indicator A personality-testing instrument based on the personality types described by Jung.

Naïve approach to change An approach to change which sees the organization in simplistic terms, as if it were a set of building blocks which can be rearranged easily.

Nature versus nurture The debate about whether our personalities are something natural, i.e. that we are born with, or are nurtured and develop over time.

Neo-Fordism A form of rational organization which combines Fordist efficiency and control with the ability of computer technology to introduce flexibility into the work process.

Networks The sharing of data through linked computer systems or through the internet.

Neuroticism Emotional instability.

No-frills A model of organizational cost reduction which offers a basic product, charging customers for anything extra to this basic offering.

Noise Anything which distorts the transfer of a message from source to recipient so that the intended and perceived meanings differ.

Nomothetic An approach which views personality as a set of measurable traits or types.

Office A defined role within an organization.

Office politics Behaviour and interactions that involve competing for status, power, or influence in a workplace; participation in office politics may be seen as game-playing or manipulation, but can also be seen as an essential part of organizational life.

Official A person who fills a particular role in an organization. When working in that role, a person is said to be working in an official capacity.

Ohio State studies Conducted at a similar time to the Michigan studies and also suggested that leaders were either people-orientated or task-orientated.

One best way Rational management techniques that propose there is one most efficient way to perform any task.

Open source and online collaboration A form of knowledge sharing and collaboration where computer code is made publicly available and developed collaboratively.

Operant conditioning A conditioning of behaviour which recognizes that rewards and punishments do not need to be continuous, but can be scheduled in a way to still condition behaviour.

Organizational behaviour modification The use of operant conditioning techniques in a workplace setting.

Organizational culture The collective behaviour exhibited by members of an organization, often seen as comprising values, beliefs, practices, history, and traditions.

Organizational justice A concept that stresses the importance of the process, as well as the outcome, for the perceived fairness of a decision.

Organizational knowledge Knowledge which is a collective property of an organization rather than belonging to an individual.

Organizational learning Sharing and transfer of individual knowledge so that it becomes a collective property of the organization.

Organizational structure The roles and positions in an organization, often depicted as horizontal and vertical levels in the form of an organization chart diagram.

Organization chart A diagram of the structure of an organization.

Organization development A wide-ranging set of change management techniques, including techniques which derive from behavioural and Gestalt psychology.

Orientations to work A perspective which suggests that people have a predisposed attitude to work that is influenced by their lives outside work and the meaning that they attach to work.

Outcomes In equity theory, the rewards and results of a person's inputs.

Panopticon A prison design that allows surveillance to take place efficiently over all prisoners, used as a metaphor for surveillance and control in organizations as a whole.

Paperwork Official documentation and record-keeping within an organization.

Path–goal theory Developed by House, this theory argues that the leader's effectiveness is dependent on the motivation, satisfaction, and performance of her subordinates.

Perception The ways in which people actively create meaning from sensory stimuli.

Perceptual bias A generic term for various kinds of mental short-cut, e.g. stereotyping, that people take in order to assess a person or situation; such biases can lead to inaccurate or unfair conclusions.

Perceptual organization The ways in which people group perceptions in their mind into particular forms or patterns.

Perceptual set See Mindset.

Performative labour Paid interactive service work where the worker is engaging in some form of performance, as if on stage. Refers, in particular, to emotional and aesthetic labour.

Peripheral workforce In a flexible-firm model, workers who can be hired on a temporary basis, perhaps to meet increased demand, and then let go when not needed.

Personality A set of characteristics and behaviour displayed by any individual.

Personality test A written test whereby the responses to a set of questions are said to provide a measure of personality.

Personality types Broad personality groupings which are associated with a set of particular traits.

Person specification A formal list of the main requirements for a successful candidate for a particular job.

PEST model A model which depicts an organization's environment in four sectors: political, economic, social, and technological.

Philanthropy Originally meaning 'for the love of humanity', it is now taken as meaning the giving of time or, more commonly, money for good causes.

Physical global space In the context of globalization, the actual land of the globe itself across which people and goods move and are connected, e.g. as in colonisation; compare with intangible global space.

Planned approach to change An approach to change which sees change as planned over a series of long-term steps, paying attention to human and social aspects of change, which are seen as 'hidden aspects' below the surface, as if the organization were an iceberg; closely linked with organization development.

Policies See Rules, policies, and procedures.

Politics A process of game-playing and tactics, often where different individuals jostle with each other to gain personal advantage; see also office politics.

Post-bureaucracy/post-bureaucratic organization (structureless organization) A trend away from rigid, bureaucratic rules and structures in organizations towards more flexible and less hierarchical, rule-driven structures.

Postcolonialism A perspective suggesting that although the colonial era has ended, the global inequalities that it created still remain with us today.

Post-Fordism A break away from Fordism and towards management techniques which use the skill of workers and grant autonomy to workers, emphasizing communication and competencies rather than command and control.

Post-heroic leadership theory A collection of theories that argue that traditional leadership over-emphasizes the importance of leaders and under-emphasizes that of followers.

Post-industrial A move in society and economy away from the dominance of manufacturing, towards a more flexible, service-based economy.

Power The capacity to get things done or to influence others.

Power as productive A perspective that sees power as something that produces new ways of thinking and acting, rather than as a negative force that prevents action.

Power as property A perspective that sees power as something possessed by individuals or groups.

Power as structure A perspective that sees power as being produced by the social structure.

Precarious work Working arrangements that put workers in a weak position regarding their employment contracts and the security of both availability and quality of work in future, e.g. with zero-hours contracts.

Predictive validity The ability of a test to predict a candidate's job performance.

Preferred learning styles Describes the idea that different individuals have different ways of approaching learning and of learning effectively.

Prepotency One characteristic having dominance over others.

Procedures See Rules, policies, and procedures.

Process theories Theories of motivation which suggest that motivation is a result of individual processes of perception, comparison, and calculation.

Processual Always in a process of changing and developing.

Processual approach to change An approach to change which emphasizes the messy and political nature of change.

Production The work done in an organization by the workers within that organization.

Professional knowledge A common body of knowledge relevant to a particular profession or occupation.

Pro-forma A type of paperwork, sometimes called a form. It is a blank template with standard fields for different types of relevant information, which is filled in as a means of capturing information for the records of an organization.

Proximity principle The tendency to perceive objects that are close to each other as being grouped together or connected.

Psychodynamic A description of Freud's approach to personality which sees personality as continually being developed and changed by various influences.

Psychological Arising from the mind or emotions.

Psychological noise Psychological tendencies that cause different people to derive different meanings from the same communication: e.g. interpreting words differently, or attaching greater or less importance to different parts of the message.

Punishment In behaviourism, a negative response that is received for performing a particular behaviour.

Quality circles A group of workers who come together, often under the supervision of a leader, to identify, analyse, and solve organizational problems.

Rationalization Designing work so as to achieve maximum efficiency and reduce costs, often using principles of bureaucracy and scientific management.

Rational–legal authority According to Weber, this is power that is legitimated by rules and procedures

associated with an office rather than by traditional or charismatic means.

Rational organizational design The design of organizational structures and activities in order to achieve the organization's goals in the most technically efficient manner; it suggests an organization which is designed logically and systematically, even scientifically, so as to achieve its aims.

Rational work design The design of work tasks to achieve maximum efficiency and reduce costs.

Recipient In communication theory, the person that receives a message.

Records Information held by the organization relevant for bureaucratic functioning, including information about workers.

Recruitment The process of attracting a pool of candidates for a particular job vacancy.

Red tape An unintended consequence of bureaucracy, where rules and paperwork get in the way of work and activities, rather than helping tasks to be performed efficiently.

Reflective practice A form of professional development and training where workers reflect on actual workplace experiences and events.

Reflexivity Where an individual is connected in some way to a text they are reading about or writing, rather than simply looking at a text to which they are completely unconnected.

Reinforcement In behavioural psychology, the continued encouragement of a behaviour by the provision of a particular reward.

Reputation economy Describes how the reputation and trustworthiness of workers and organizations are determined by online scores and ranking.

Resistance In critical theory, the processes by which marginalized and oppressed groups (such as workers and minorities) resist the aims and requests of more powerful groups, such as management.

Resistance to change Forces which resist a change taking place.

Reward In behaviourism, a positive response that is received for performing a particular behaviour.

Rhizome An underground root system, typified by the way grass grows, consisting of a mass of decentralized, random, tangled connections which some suggest is similar to the nature of computer networks and of organizations that are built around such networks.

Richness In communication theory, the amount and quality of information conveyed by any one message.

Rite A solemn act or procedure to observe an event or occasion.

Rituals Everyday habits that individuals do without thinking, which once had meaning but have gradually become part of the everyday activities of the organization.

Romantic view of leadership Describes a tendency to see leaders as being central to an organization's success, either through force of character or through skill, with passive followers responding to the leader's actions.

Rule of thumb A rough estimate of the time needed to perform a task, based on a worker's expert knowledge of that task.

Rules, policies, and procedures Formal instructions that govern how particular activities in an organization are to be performed.

Schedules of reinforcement A blend of fixed and variable reinforcements designed so as best to reinforce desired behaviours.

Scientific management The use of scientific techniques to design work to be as efficient as possible.

Scientific selection Defining the precise characteristics of the ideal candidate for a job.

Second Industrial Revolution Describes the period beginning in the 1870s when management innovators such as Taylor and Ford developed formal bureaucratic structures and standardized means of production with the aim of rationalizing business organization and production.

Selection The process of selecting the most appropriate candidate from a pool of applicants for a particular vacancy.

Selective perception The tendency to foreground certain perceptions above others.

Self-actualization For Maslow, a realization, or actualization, of an individual's ultimate human and creative potential.

Self-discipline The process by which individuals train and control themselves, usually for the purposes of self-improvement.

Self-managed team A team, often of professionals or highly qualified people, who manage themselves.

Separation of planning and doing Tasks designed by management, with workers having no input other than to perform those tasks.

Servant leadership theory A bottom-up perspective which sees the leader being the most effective where they support followers to enable them to do their jobs.

Service sector Non-manufacturing industries, such as retail, leisure, transport, finance, and media.

Sexually commodified When the sexual attractiveness or desirability of a worker is used as part of the work they perform for customers or clients.

Shirking (free-riding) Describes an individual who does not pull their weight but is carried by other members of the group.

Similarity principle The tendency to perceive things that have outwardly similar characteristics as being similar throughout, grouped together, or connected.

Single-loop learning Learning in organizations which merely adapts to achieving a particular goal.

Situated knowledge Knowledge that exists in a dynamic form in interactions between people in specific organizational contexts.

Situational leadership (contingency leadership) A theory which stresses the importance of adapting the leadership style to meet the situation.

Smart factories Cyber-physical systems that are able to tailor supply closely to individual demand by bringing together digital elements (e.g. algorithms) with physical elements (e.g. robots and raw materials) and data about individual human customers.

Social The human side of the organization, in particular the relations between people at work.

Social facilitation The tendency that individuals have to work harder when being watched by others, particularly on simple tasks.

Social identity theory Drawing from psychological theory, how an individual's identity is derived from being part of a group.

Social loafing The behaviour of people who, when working in groups, do not work as hard because, perhaps unconsciously, they rely on others to do the task.

Social organization A concept that reflects the underlying belief that the social relations between people are a key factor in shaping how people act in organizations.

Social presence theory Examines the degree to which the physical presence of the sender of a message can be felt in a particular communications medium.

Social–radical approach The view that organizations have an effect on the personality of their members.

Social reward A reward that comes from the feeling of being part of a group or team.

Social structure In sociology, the arrangement of institutions within which people interact in a society and the recurring patterns which influence the choices available to people; social life is largely determined by the social structure, which may be difficult to change.

Social theories of motivation Theories of motivation that see motivation as part of the role of work in creating meaning and identity for people within society.

Soldiering Techniques used by workers to create time for themselves during the working day. Soldiering means that workers are not working at the most efficient level possible.

Source In communication theory, the sender or originator of a message.

Span of control The number of workers controlled by a manager at any one particular level in a hierarchy.

Stake A claim or interest.

Stakeholder Someone who has an interest or claim in the activities of the organization.

Standardized Made uniform according to pre-established rules or specifications.

Stereotype Where a characteristic is attributed to a person because of their membership of a particular social group, e.g. because of race or gender.

Stimulus–response The underlying relationship of behaviourism, whereby a particular response, or behaviour, is the result of a particular stimulus.

Strike A form of collective action where workers withdraw their labour.

Structured interview An interview with a set format and standard questions, based around job-specific questions.

Structureless organization See Post-bureaucracy.

Subcontracting Hiring another person or company to perform a particular process or service for an organization.

Subculture A localized culture with its own set of values and behaviours that reflects, but is distinct from, the wider culture.

Substantive rationality Rationality from a human and ethical perspective—if something is formally rational and efficient it does not make it substantively rational when considering its human and ethical consequences.

Surface acting Emotional labour that is performed by workers conscious of the fact that they are engaged in an artificial performance; compare with deep acting.

Surface learning Learning a set of facts in themselves, possibly for the purposes of a test or exam, rather than with any additional depth; compare with deep learning.

Surplus value Profit that capitalists gain over and above the wages they pay to workers.

Surveillance The observation, either overt or covert, of people to gain information about them or to exert order and control over them.

Sustainability The long-term stewardship and maintenance of the environment; also applied to the long-term prospects of a firm or organization.

Synchronicity The degree to which something happens immediately or after a delay.

Systemic approach to change An approach to change which recognizes the organization as an interconnected system whereby change in one area can have consequences and knock-on effects in other areas.

Tacit knowledge Knowledge which is personal, a form of second nature or knowing things 'off by heart', and which is difficult to explain to others.

Task orientation Focusing on tasks rather than on people.

Taylorism The work process designed by Taylor, associated with the division of labour into small tasks, which are then redesigned to be performed as efficiently as possible.

Team A group who meet together with a common purpose and some degree of mutual interdependence.

Teleworking, telecommuting Working away from a physical place of work using online platforms.

T-group (training group) An activity which aims to get a group to understand and change its dynamics and attitudes.

Theming As with a theme park, this is where the image and identity of an organization, and the experience that it provides for consumers, is based around a particular theme.

Therapy group A group who meet together with a trained counsellor or facilitator for therapeutic purposes, where the group members decide what to talk about.

Third Industrial Revolution Describes the rise of digital technology and automation, beginning in the late 1960s, and their effects on work and society.

Three-step model of change Lewin's model whereby a process of change goes through three stages of unfreezing, movement, and freezing.

Time and motion study Rational work design where tasks are measured and timed, and redesigned to maximize efficiency.

Toxic triangle Describes a situation in which three elements—a destructive leader, susceptible followers (who either conform or collude), and a conducive environment (seen as unstable or threatening)—may lead to bad consequences.

Trade unions Membership organizations which collectively represent the interests of a group of workers.

Trained incapacity Where people are so used to their behaviour being controlled by bureaucratic rules and procedures that they become inflexible and unable to think for themselves and show initiative.

Training group See T-group.

Trait A characteristic of the person, often seen as comprising the behaviour, thoughts, and emotions that the person exhibits, considered stable over time.

Trait theories Nomothetic theories of personality which see individual traits rather than broad personality groups as the foundations of personality.

Transactional leader A leader who does deals with employees in order to get the task done. Seen in opposition to transformational leaders, who offer a better vision of the world that employees can buy into.

Transformational leader A leader who is able to transform the organization by offering workers a better vision for the future and engaging them in working towards it; compare with transactional leader.

Triggers for change Factors which push towards a change taking place.

Typologies A system of classification of traits that organizations have in common.

Uncertainty A lack of knowledge about a particular factual issue.

Unconscious From psychology, particularly psychoanalysis, the area of thinking that is not directly available to the conscious mind, and is below the level of personal awareness.

Unofficial culture See Informal culture.

Unstructured interview An interview with no preset formal structure.

Utility The benefit that an individual might gain from an action.

Value engineering A form of cost analysis that compares the cost of an item or process against its perceived value.

Variable reinforcement In behaviour modification, a reward or punishment provided at varying time intervals or varying instances of a behaviour to be reinforced.

VARK model A model and questionnaire which places individuals into one of four preferred learning styles—visual, auditory, reading and writing, or kinesthetic.

Vascular skin reaction A white line on the wrist, created by a blunt instrument, which disappears more quickly when the person is fatigued.

Vertical differentiation The process whereby a hierarchy creates a number of different layers of management within an organization.

Vertical loading Where a job is enriched by adding tasks which would normally be associated with elements of responsibility linked to positions higher in an organizational hierarchy.

Work–life balance A balance between work and career on one hand, and wider aspects of life, such as family and leisure time, on the other.

Work to rule A form of industrial action where workers follow rules, regulations, and instructions precisely—this often results in the speed of work slowing considerably.

Zero-hours contract A contract whereby an employer is not obliged to guarantee any minimum number of working hours and the employee is not obliged to accept any minimum number of working hours.

673

INDEX

677

682